The Beginner's Guide to
COUNSELLING and
PSYCHOTHERAPY

SAGE was founded in 1965 by Sara Miller McCune to support the dissemination of usable knowledge by publishing innovative and high-quality research and teaching content. Today, we publish more than 750 journals, including those of more than 300 learned societies, more than 800 new books per year, and a growing range of library products including archives, data, case studies, reports, conference highlights, and video. SAGE remains majority-owned by our founder, and after Sara's lifetime will become owned by a charitable trust that secures our continued independence.

Los Angeles | London | Washington DC | New Delhi | Singapore

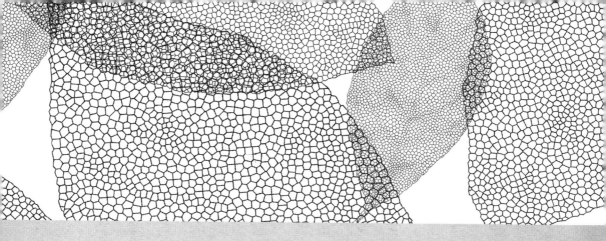

2nd Edition

The Beginner's Guide to COUNSELLING and PSYCHOTHERAPY

Edited by

Stephen Palmer

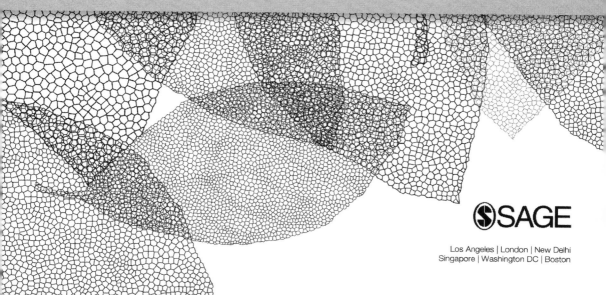

$SAGE

Los Angeles | London | New Delhi
Singapore | Washington DC | Boston

Los Angeles | London | New Delhi
Singapore | Washington DC

SAGE Publications Ltd
1 Oliver's Yard
55 City Road
London EC1Y 1SP

SAGE Publications Inc.
2455 Teller Road
Thousand Oaks, California 91320

SAGE Publications India Pvt Ltd
B 1/I 1 Mohan Cooperative Industrial Area
Mathura Road
New Delhi 110 044

SAGE Publications Asia-Pacific Pte Ltd
3 Church Street
#10-04 Samsung Hub
Singapore 049483

Editor: Susannah Trefgarne
Assistant editor: Laura Walmsley
Production editor: Rachel Burrows
Copyeditor: Elaine Leek
Proofreader: Derek Markham
Indexer: David Rudeforth
Marketing manager: Camille Richmond
Cover design: Shaun Mercier
Typeset by: C&M Digitals (P) Ltd, Chennai, India
Printed and bound by CPI Group (UK) Ltd,
Croydon, CR0 4YY

First published 1999 as *Introduction to Counselling and Psychotherapy: The Essential Guide*

Reprinted 2002, 2004, 2006, 2008, 2010, 2011, 2012, and 2013
This edition published 2015

Library of Congress Control Number: 2014954255

British Library Cataloguing in Publication data

A catalogue record for this book is available from the British Library

ISBN 978-0-85702-234-9
ISBN 978-0-85702-235-6 (pbk)

To Maggie and also the future generations:

Kate, Kevin, Tom and Arina

Emma, Leonora, Rebecca, Laura, Imogen, Joshua,
Samuel, Harry, Aniket and Tejal

Contents

Lists of Figures
and Tables

LIST OF FIGURES

LIST OF TABLES

About the Editor

Stephen Palmer, PhD is the Founder Director of the Centre for Stress Management and Centre for Coaching, London. Since 2001, he has been the UK's first Visiting Professor of Work Based Learning and Stress Management at the Institute for Work Based Learning, Middlesex University. He was formerly Honorary Visiting Professor of Psychology during the 2000s at City University London. He is Consultant Director of the New Zealand Centre for Cognitive Behaviour Therapy.

Stephen has authored more than 225 articles and 40 books on a range of topics including counselling, psychotherapy, stress management, positive and coaching psychology, suicide prevention, death and bereavement. He is also Editor of several journals and former Managing Editor of *Counselling*.

He is Honorary President of the International Stress Management Association (UK) and the International Society for Coaching Psychology. He is also Honorary Vice President of both the Institute of Health Promotion and Education, and Society for Dialectical Behaviour Therapy.

Stephen is a Chartered Psychologist and HCPC Registered Health and Counselling Psychologist. He holds the European Certificate in Psychology (Clinical & Health) and the European Certificate of Counsellor Accreditation. He is a UKCP registered psychotherapist and Fellow of the Association for Rational Emotive Behaviour Therapy. He has Professional Counselling and Psychotherapy Diplomate status with the International Academy of Behavioral Medicine, Counseling and Psychotherapy.

In 2000, Stephen received the Annual Counselling Psychology Award from the British Psychological Society, Division of Counselling Psychology, for his 'Outstanding professional and scientific contribution to counselling psychology in Britain'. In 2008, he received a Distinguished Award for his outstanding and continued contribution to coaching psychology from the British Psychological Society Special Group in Coaching Psychology. He appears occasionally on radio and television discussing counselling, stress management and wellbeing.

His interests include jazz, art and coastal walking.

List of Contributors

Gerhard Baumer studied psychology and trained as an Adlerian psychotherapist in Berlin. He has been working in private practice for 33 years and writes articles, gives lectures and runs workshops regularly in Germany and England. He is an international Adlerian trainer, has worked for the international summer school ICASSI as a lecturer, board member and co-chairman, and has co-authored chapters in Dryden (ed.), *Handbook of Individual Therapy* (Sage, 2002) and *Dryden's Handbook of Individual Therapy* (Sage, 2007), as well as the first edition of this book.

Anja Bjorøy, MHS, MFSP works as a family therapist, couples therapist and mediator, and is associated with the University of Diakonhjemmet as a teacher and supervisor in the Masters programme of Family Therapy. Her work is informed by social constructionist ideas. She holds a Masters in the Theoretical Foundation of Health Sciences, and a Masters in Family Therapy and Systemic Practice at the University of Oslo. FO, Norway has granted her an authorization as a clinical approved psychotherapist.

Frank W. Bond is Director of the Institute of Management Studies at Goldsmiths, University of London. He trained as both a clinical and as an occupational psychologist, and his research and practice incorporates theories, methods and practices from both disciplines. Professor Bond has published widely in the area of Acceptance and Commitment Therapy (ACT), particularly as it relates to health and productivity at work. He has worked with ACT in a wide range of organizations, including UK government, the banking sector, advertising and broadcasting.

Robert Bor is Lead Consultant Clinical Psychologist at the Royal Free Hospital, London. Professor Bor is a Chartered Clinical, Counselling and Health Psychologist registered with the HCPC as well as a UKCP Registered Family Therapist, having specialized in family therapy at the Tavistock Clinic, London. He is extensively involved in the training of psychologists and psychotherapists. He has published 30 books and more than 150 academic papers. Rob is co-director of a clinical and corporate psychology consultancy, Dynamic Change Consultants (www.dccclinical.com). He is also a Churchill Fellow and a Fellow of the British Psychological Society and Royal Aeronautical Society.

Mick Cooper is a Professor of Counselling Psychology at the University of Roehampton and a practising counselling psychologist. Mick is author and editor of a wide range of texts on person–centred, existential and relational approaches to therapy, including *Pluralistic Counselling and Psychotherapy* (Sage, 2011, with John McLeod), and *Essential Research Findings in Counselling and Psychotherapy: The Facts are Friendly* (Sage, 2008).

Berni Curwen is accredited by the British Association for Behavioural and Cognitive Psychotherapies and by EMDR Europe. She co-authored *Brief Cognitive Behaviour Therapy* (Sage) and has written a number of book chapters. Berni originally trained as a psychiatric nurse, has worked in the private sector, and is currently employed within the NHS as a Cognitive Behaviour Psychotherapist where she has regularly led CBT groups and supervises trainee cognitive behavioural psychotherapists.

Christine Dunkley, DClinP is a Consultant Psychological Therapist and senior trainer in the British Isles Dialectical Behaviour Therapy Training Team. She is retired from the NHS after 30 years of clinical work and now supervises treatment teams across the UK and Ireland in the delivery of DBT. She is co-author of *Teaching Clients to Use Mindfulness Skills* (Dunkley and Stanton, Routledge, 2014) and the 'Core components of DBT' DVD series with Michaela Swales. She is the first chair of the Society for DBT (www.SfDBT.org) and is an honorary lecturer for Bangor University on the postgraduate certificate in DBT.

Graham Dyson, PhD, DClinPsy is an HPC Registered Clinical Psychologist currently working in independent practice in the South Durham area. He also works as a Senior Lecturer in the Doctorate in Clinical Psychology at Teesside University where he is responsible for recruitment and personal professional development. Prior to working independently, he worked as a clinical psychologist in the NHS for six years, primarily with adults in a low security setting. He completed his interpersonal therapy training in 2005 and since then he has used the IPT model within clinical work, teaching, research, training and supervision.

Carina Eriksen is a Chartered and HCPC Registered Counselling Psychologist with an extensive London-based private practice for young people, adults, couples and families. Dr Eriksen is an accredited member of the British Association for Behavioural and Cognitive Psychotherapies and a Dynamic Change Consultant. She has managed a team of psychologists, CBT therapists and psychotherapists in the NHS for several years and she used to be an external supervisor for The Priory. She has extensive experience consulting in clinical and organizational settings in the UK and Europe. Carina is an author and a co-author of several books and her work has been published in prestigious journals.

Ken Evans is Visiting Professor of Psychotherapy at USEE. Dr Evans approaches psychotherapy from a relational–developmental perspective and is currently interested in exploring the interface between technical skills and the therapist's use of self in the therapeutic relationship. He has written several books, book chapters and articles on psychotherapy practice, supervision and research. Ken is co-director of the European Centre for Psychotherapeutic Studies www.eurocps.eu and a visiting trainer at several training institutes across Europe.

Colin Feltham is Emeritus Professor of Critical Counselling Studies, Sheffield Hallam University, and External Associate Professor of Humanistic Psychology, University of Southern Denmark. His many publications include the *Sage Handbook of Counselling and Psychotherapy*, edited with Ian Horton (Sage, 3rd edn 2012) and *Counselling and Counselling Psychology: A Critical Examination* (PCCS, 2013).

Fay Fransella was Founder and Director of the Centre for Personal Construct Psychology at the University of Hertfordshire, a Fellow of the British Psychological Society and Visiting Professor in Personal Construct Psychology at the University of Hertfordshire. Sadly, Fay passed away in early 2011.

Maria C. Gilbert is a UKCP registered Integrative Psychotherapist, a Chartered Psychologist (BPS), a Registered Clinical Psychologist (HCPC), an APECS Accredited Executive Coach, a BACP Senior accredited supervisor, and a visiting Professor at Middlesex University. She is Faculty Head of Applied Psychology, Psychotherapy and Counselling at Metanoia Institute in West London where she runs an MSc in Integrative Psychotherapy. She has a small private practice where she works as a supervisor, a psychotherapist and a coach.

Paul Gilbert OBE is Professor of Clinical Psychology at the University of Derby and Consultant Clinical Psychologist at the Derbyshire Health Care Foundation Trust. He has researched evolutionary approaches to psychopathology for over 35 years with a special focus on shame and the treatment of shame-based difficulties – for which compassion focused therapy was developed. In 2003 he was president of the British Association for Behavioural and Cognitive Psychotherapies and was involved in writing the first NICE guidelines for depression. He has written/edited 20 books and more than 150 papers. In 2006 he established the Compassionate Mind Foundation charity with the mission statement: To promote wellbeing through the scientific understanding and application of compassion (www.compassionatemind.co.uk). He was awarded an OBE in March 2011.

Juliet Grayson is a UKCP registered NLPtCA accredited and COSRT Accredited Therapist and Supervisor, and certified Pesso Boyden System Psychomotor Therapist. Her focus is on relationships, sexual problems and personal development using Pesso Boyden Systems Psychomotor. In 2014 she published a chapter 'Back to the Root: Healing Potential Offenders' Childhood Trauma with Pesso Boyden System Psychomotor' for the book *Sexual Diversity and Sexual Offending: Research, Assessment and Clinical Treatment in Psychosexual Therapy* edited by Glyn Hudson Allez. She is the co-founder of Stop Sexual Offending, www.stopso.org.uk, which is a network of therapists who will work sexual offenders.

Terry Hanley is a Senior Lecturer in Counselling Psychology at the University of Manchester. He is a Chartered Psychologist and HCPC Registered Counselling Psychologist with a background of working therapeutically with young people and young adults. He is the current Editor of the BPS's *Counselling Psychology Review* and is lead author of *Introducing Counselling and Psychotherapy Research* (Sage, 2013) and lead Editor of *Adolescent Counselling Psychology* (Routledge, 2012). Terry's research has primarily focused upon the development of accessible services for young people and training counsellors and psychotherapists in research skills.

Jean Hardy, PhD worked for 25 years in universities teaching sociology and political philosophy. She discovered psychosynthesis in the early 1980s, writing *A Psychology* *with a Soul* (Woodgrange, 1996) out of curiosity about the ideas underlying transpersonal psychology. Now retired, she taught on the Psychosynthesis and Education Trust MA in London and is former editor of *Green Spirit*.

Catherine (Kate) Hayes, MBACP(acc) is Assistant Professor in Counselling at the University of Nottingham. She lives in Norfolk and works as a therapist, trainer and supervisor. She contributed to a chapter for *Implausible Professions* (eds House and Totton, PCCS, 2nd edn 2011) and regularly contributes articles to the membership journal of the British Association for the Person-Centred Approach (www.bapca.org.uk).

Chris Irons is a Clinical Psychologist working in the NHS with adults with severe and enduring mental health problems. He is a board member of the Compassionate Mind Foundation, a charitable organization set up to 'promote wellbeing through the scientific understanding and application of compassion'. He has been working for more than 10 years in researching, teaching and training in compassion focused therapy (CFT).

Stephen Kellett completed his core training in Clinical Psychology at the University of Sheffield (1986–90) after working in the corporate sector as an Organizational Psychologist. He worked in Secondary Care in Barnsley in adult mental health on qualifying and progressed to a Lead Consultant Clinical Psychologist. He completed cognitive analytic therapy practitioner training (2000–02) and is currently completing CAT psychotherapy training. Dr Kellett is currently Consultant Clinical Psychologist with Sheffield Health and Social Care NHS Foundation Trust.

Ian B. Kerr graduated in medicine from Edinburgh University and has worked in the NHS for several decades. After several years spent in oncology research he trained as an analytic (Jungian) psychologist, psychodynamic therapist and cognitive analytic therapist and supervisor. He currently works as a Consultant Psychiatrist in Psychotherapy and leads a tertiary psychotherapy service. His clinical and research interests include further development of integrative models of therapy and work with more 'severe and complex' and 'hard to help' patients, largely based around the cognitive analytic therapy model. He has published numerous papers and book chapters on these topics.

Joda Lloyd is a lecturer and researcher in occupational psychology at Goldsmiths' Institute of Management Studies (IMS). She teaches in the areas of organizational behaviour and workplace coaching and counselling, whilst her research focuses on investigating acceptance and commitment therapy (ACT), and its proposed mechanism of change, psychological flexibility, in the workplace. Dr Lloyd regularly presents on her research in both UK and international conferences, and she is involved in a number of special interest groups and societies concerned with the promotion and dissemination of ACT focused research and practice.

Stephen Madigan, PhD is the Director of the Vancouver School for Narrative Therapy (www.therapeuticconversations.com). The American Psychological Association has released his book *Narrative Therapy* (2011), along with a six-part video series of his therapy work. The American Family Therapy Academy honoured Stephen with their Distinguished award for Innovative Practice in Couple and Family Therapy.

John McLeod is Emeritus Professor of Counselling at the University of Abertay, Dundee. He is author of books and articles on many aspects of counselling and psychotherapy theory, practice and research.

Roy Moodley, PhD is associate professor of counselling psychology at the Ontario Institute for Studies in Education, University of Toronto. He is Director of the Centre for Diversity in Counselling and Psychotherapy. His research interests include critical multicultural counselling/psychotherapy, race and culture in psychotherapy, traditional healing, culture and resilience, mixed-race relationships and gender and identity.

Lesley Murdin is a psychoanalytic psychotherapist practising in Cambridge. She taught English for many years in the UK and the USA and taught courses for the Open University. She has been Chair of a UKCP Section and of its Ethics Committee. She has been Director of WPF Therapy and has taught and supervised there and for other training organisations for many years. She has chaired her professional body, the Foundation for Psychotherapy and Counselling, and currently sits on their Governing Board. She has published numerous books and papers on psychodynamic and psychoanalytic psychotherapy.

Michael Neenan is an Associate Director of the Centre for Stress Management and Centre for Coaching, Blackheath, London. He is an accredited (with the British Association for Behavioural and Cognitive Psychotherapies) cognitive behavioural therapist. He has written and edited more than 20 books, including *Developing Resilience: A Cognitive Behavioural Approach* (Routledge, 2009).

Richard Nelson-Jones has many years' experience as a counselling psychology trainer and psychotherapist in Britain and Australia. His books have helped train thousands of counsellors and helpers worldwide. He is a Fellow of the British and Australian Psychological Societies and of the British Association for Counselling and Psychotherapy.

David Nylund, LCSW, PhD is a professor of Social Work at California State University, Sacramento, the Clinical Director of the Gender Health Center and a clinical supervisor at La Familia Counseling Center. Dr Nylund is also on the faculty of the Vancouver School for Narrative Therapy. David is the author of several books, articles and chapters on narrative therapy, cultural studies and queer theory.

Margaret Oakes is a Counselling Psychologist with experience of providing psychological interventions in primary care and NHS specialist services. She is also a pilot, flying short haul and medium haul routes in Europe, Africa and Asia. Margaret is actively involved in teaching, including part of the Aviation Psychology modules in the MSc in Air Transport Management programme at City University. Dr Oakes has a particular interest in anxiety disorders, post-traumatic stress disorder and the psychological impact of cancer. She is a consultant with Dynamic Change Consultants. Margaret is co-author of several books and has published her research in peer reviewed journals.

Alanna O'Broin is a Chartered Psychologist and HCPC Registered Practitioner Psychologist. After a career in the financial sector in fund management, she trained as a Counselling Psychologist, working in the NHS in primary care for several years. Dr O'Broin works with adults in her private practice and has lectured on the postgraduate counselling psychology course at City University London. Her professional interests include the therapeutic relationship and its boundary with the coaching relationship.

Bill O'Connell is Director of Training at Focus on Solutions. He was formerly the Programme Leader for the Masters in Solution-Focused Therapy at Birmingham University. His background is in social work, youth work, lecturing and counselling. He is the author of *Solution-Focused Therapy* (Sage, 3rd edn 2012) and *Solution-Focused Stress Counselling* (Sage, 2001) and co-author of *Solution-Focused Coaching in Practice* (with Stephen Palmer and Helen Williams, Routledge, 2012) and co-editor (with Stephen Palmer) of *The Handbook of Solution-Focused Therapy* (Sage, 2003).

Donald J. Robertson is a cognitive behavioural psychotherapist in private practice. He specializes in evidence-based, cognitive behavioural approaches to clinical hypnosis. His writings include *The Practice of Cognitive-Behavioural Hypnotherapy: A Manual for Evidence-Based Clinical Hypnosis* (Karnac Books, 2013) and *The Discovery of Hypnosis: The Complete Writings of James Braid* (National Council for Hypnotherapy, 2009).

Elizabeth Robinson completed her core professional training as a psychiatric nurse in 1986. She received her IPT training and supervision in 1997 from Professor John Markowitz and Kathleen Clougherty, both of whom were trained by Gerald Klerman, the originator of IPT. She was the principal IPT research therapist for two clinical studies; the latter, a brain imaging study of IPT in treatment-resistant depression was for her PhD at Durham University. She works part-time in private clinical practice and as an IPT trainer and supervisor as part of the government initiative Improving Access to Psychological Therapies.

John Rowan is a Fellow of the BPS, the BACP and the UKCP. He has been working as a therapist since 1980 and has presented workshops in 25 countries. He has published some 20 books. His most recent work has been in the field of the dialogical self, which is described in his book *Personification* (Routledge, 2010). He lives in Chingford.

Peter Ruddell is accredited by the British Association for Behavioural and Cognitive Psychotherapies and the Association for Rational Emotive Behaviour Therapy, of which he was a senior board member for many years. He co-authored *Brief Cognitive*

Behaviour Therapy (Sage, 2001) and has contributed chapters to a number of books. He has worked in the voluntary and private sectors and is currently clinical director of the Centre for Stress Management.

Julia Segal is a Fellow of BACP. She trained with Relate and for the past 30 years, in the NHS and privately, has been counselling people with neurological conditions and members of their families, using the ideas of Melanie Klein to understand and illuminate everyday experience. She has also always been interested in the effects on professionals of working with people who have neurological conditions, and has run many workshops for professionals in different settings. She has written extensively on the effects of illness on relationships. Julia is best known for her books, which include *Phantasy in Everyday Life* (Penguin, 1985; Karnac, 1995), *Melanie Klein* (Key Figures in Counselling and Psychotherapy Series, Sage, 1992) and *Helping Children with Ill or Disabled Parents* (Jessica Kingsley, 1996). She has a blog http://thetroublewithillness. wordpress.com as well as a website: www.mscounselling.com.

Ian Stewart is Co-Director of The Berne Institute, Nottingham. He is a Teaching and Supervising Transactional Analyst, UKCP Registered Psychotherapist and Master Practitioner in Neuro-Linguistic Programming (NLP). Ian is the author of three books on TA published by Sage, *TA Counselling in Action* (4th edn 2013), *Eric Berne* (Key Figures in Counselling and Psychotherapy Series, 1992) and *Developing TA Counselling* (1996), and co-author of *TA Today* (Lifespace, 2nd edn 2012) and *Personality Adaptations* (Lifespace, 2002). He has presented TA trainings nationally and internationally.

Jean Stokes, MA is a Professional Member of the Association of Jungian Analysts (AJA) and the International Association of Analytical Psychologists; she is a Training Analyst and Supervisor for AJA and other training bodies. She is a Psychoanalytic Psychotherapy member of FPC/WPF and a member of the British Association for Psychoanalytic and Psychodynamic Supervision. She has written on Jungian supervision, teaches on the AJA training and has a private practice in South-West London.

Shafik Sunderani, PhD is a psychotherapy and research associate in the Centre for Diversity in Counselling and Psychotherapy. His research interests include: understanding psychotherapy processes with oppressed, minority and marginalized groups, therapist self-disclosure, counter-transference dynamics and discovering ways to de-stabilize the power imbalance between therapists and clients using two-person relational approaches.

Kasia Szymanska is a Chartered Psychologist and Associate Fellow of the British Psychological Society. She is registered with the HCPC and accredited as a cognitive behavioural psychotherapist by the British Association for Cognitive and Behavioural Psychotherapies. She is also an accredited coaching psychologist (ISCP). Currently she has a private practice and is an Associate Director of the Centre for Stress Management and a Director of the International Academy for Professional Development.

Laura Anne Winter is a Chartered Psychologist and HCPC Registered Counselling Psychologist. She currently works as a Lecturer on the Doctorate in Counselling Psychology at the University of Manchester and in practice for Manchester Mental Health and Social Care Trust, where she is based within a Complex Primary Care Service. Dr Winter's research interests centre on issues of social justice within psychology. For example, she has explored the social justice interest and commitment of counselling psychologists, and is currently involved in the supervision of a number of research projects that focus on documenting the experiences of marginalized or oppressed members of society.

Emmy van Deurzen is a philosopher, a counselling psychologist and an existential psychotherapist, who has worked in the mental health field since 1972. She is the founder and Principal of the New School of Psychotherapy and Counselling in London, has published 13 books and has been translated into 16 languages. Amongst her best-known books are *Existential Counselling and Psychotherapy in Practice* (Sage, 3rd edn 2012), *Everyday Mysteries* (Routledge, 2nd edn 2010) and *Psychotherapy and the Quest for Happiness* (Sage, 2009).

Jenny Warner was a Speech and Language Therapy Manager in the NHS and an Adlerian therapist, family counsellor, supervisor and international trainer. She is now retired. She has written chapters on Adlerian therapy in *Individual Therapy: A Handbook* (ed. Dryden, Open University Press, 1990), *Handbook of Individual Therapy* (ed. Dryden, Sage, 1996) and *Handbook of Counselling and Psychotherapy* (eds Feltham and Horton, Sage, 2000), and has co-authored chapters in *Handbook of Individual Therapy* (ed. Dryden, 2002, 2007) and *The Sage Handbook of Counselling and Psychotherapy* (eds Feltham and Horton, Sage, 2nd edn 2006, 3rd edn 2012).

Diana Whitmore, MAEd is Chief Executive and a founding Director of Teens and Toddlers UK. She is co-chair of the Trustee Board of the Psychosynthesis and Education Trust, trained in Psychosynthesis with Dr Roberto Assagioli and is one of the UK's leading trainers of transpersonal counselling and psychotherapy and coaching. Diana has been a member of the trustee board of the Findhorn Foundation for the past nineteen years. Diana is author of *Psychosynthesis Counselling in Action*, Fourth Edition and *Psychosynthesis in Education: A Guide to the Joy of Learning*.

Mark Widdowson is a teaching and supervising transactional analyst and a UKCP registered psychotherapist based in Manchester. He is a lecturer in counselling and psychotherapy at the University of Salford. His clinical research has primarily focused on the process and outcome of transactional analysis (TA) psychotherapy for the treatment of depression. He is the author of *Transactional Analysis: 100 Key Points and Techniques* (Routledge, 2009).

Acknowledgements

I thank all the contributors and their clients involved with this book. This venture was a large task, which needed everyone's ongoing cooperation. The support and encouragement received from the publishers, in particular Laura Walmsley, Kate Wharton, Rachel Burrows and Susannah Trefgarne, at Sage, was invaluable. My thanks also to the copyeditor, Elaine Leek.

Foreword

Cary Cooper

The first edition of this book, *Introduction to Counselling and Psychotherapy*, was a landmark tome for the field, highlighting the current theory and practice in the fields of counselling and psychotherapy. The second edition has updated this guide to take into account some of the novel and innovative practices that have emerged since the first edition. With one in four people in most countries suffering from the common mental disorders of depression, anxiety and stress, the need for advanced theory and effective practice is essential to attack the 21st Century equivalent of the Black Plague: mental ill health. Professor Palmer has brought together the leading scholars and practitioners in the field of counselling and psychotherapy to provide a guide that is unparalleled in the existing literature. If you want to know about these fields, this is the state–of–the–art beginner's guide, a compendium of knowledge and effective practice that can't be found anywhere else. For both sufferers and practitioners alike this book is a 'must' in understanding what is available, how effective the interventions are and all the issues surrounding the leading cause of morbidity in the developed and developing world.

Professor Sir Cary Cooper
Distinguished Professor of Organizational Psychology and
Health at Lancaster University, Chair of the Academy of
Social Sciences and President of RELATE

Preface

Stephen Palmer

This book is a guide to 26 different approaches to counselling and psychotherapy. It is written for beginner counsellors, counselling psychologists and psychotherapists in training or those more experienced who wish to have one text that covers the majority of the main counselling and psychotherapy approaches practised. This second edition includes additional chapters on 'The Therapeutic Relationship', 'Diversity in Counselling and Psychotherapy' and 'Professional Issues in Counselling and Psychotherapy'. The book has also been written for the layperson or casual reader who would like to increase their understanding of the different forms of therapy.

Stephen Palmer

Introduction

Stephen Palmer

Why an introductory book focusing on different counselling and psychotherapy approaches? Over the years I have trained many counsellors, psychotherapists and psychologists in a range of therapeutic approaches. So often, the questions 'What is cognitive behaviour therapy?' or 'What exactly is multimodal therapy?' are asked by prospective trainees before they attend a course at the training centre at which I work. On other occasions trainees have admitted that they attended their first training course elsewhere without even realizing that many different approaches of counselling and psychotherapy existed. For beginner counsellors, counselling psychologists and psychotherapists entering into this profession it can appear similar to walking into unknown and possibly hostile terrain. If they refer to a counselling or psychotherapy textbook then prior knowledge of the subject may be expected. Considering the number of approaches to counselling and psychotherapy available, how many counsellors and psychotherapists have trained in an approach that either clashes with their personality or is unsuited to the client group with which they wish to work?

Let us now consider those who are thinking about entering into therapy. Where can they obtain information or guidance about the different approaches to counselling and psychotherapy that does not require prior knowledge? How easy is it for them to compare and contrast the different therapies available and read case studies illustrating how each theory is applied to the practice of the particular approach? What help can they receive in choosing an appropriate approach that would suit their temperaments and be relevant to the particular presenting problem(s)?

In the light of some of the difficulties often encountered by beginner counsellors and psychotherapists (as well as their potential clients) this book provides information about the theory and practice of 26 different approaches to counselling and psychotherapy. It will help potential trainees and clients to enter training or counselling with informed consent. The chapters reflect what is currently practised in many therapy rooms. Therefore where earlier forms of psychotherapy have been included the contents have a pinch of postmodernism. I have not included the most recent forms of therapy on body work, which are less associated with the field of counselling. In addition, when various approaches are better known by the term 'therapy', this is reflected in the chapter titles, for example, 'Acceptance and Commitment Therapy'.

Feedback from some readers of the first edition of the book suggested we should include a couple of extra chapters on topics that were very relevant for beginner counsellors and psychotherapists whilst they were reading the approaches chapters. These chapters are 'The Therapeutic Relationship', 'Diversity in Counselling and Psychotherapy' and 'Professional Issues in Counselling and Psychotherapy'.

In Chapter 1 Colin Feltham and I introduce the subject of counselling and psychotherapy and provide an overview to the therapeutic approaches covered in this book. For beginner counsellors and psychotherapists this is probably a good place to start reading this book. For convenience, we divided the different approaches into psychodynamic/psychoanalytic, cognitive behavioural, humanistic–existential, integrative and eclectic, and constructivist approaches. These are the main groupings that are normally applied within the field of counselling and psychotherapy.

In Chapter 2, Alanna O'Broin reflects on the therapeutic relationship. She highlights the developments in our knowledge of the therapeutic relationship and then outlines a pan-theoretic model of the therapeutic alliance and looks at ways of working with the therapeutic alliance in counselling and psychotherapy.

Chapters 3–28 cover the different therapeutic approaches, which, for the reader's ease, have been listed in each section in alphabetical order. In these chapters, to help the reader compare and contrast each approach the contributors were asked to maintain an identical format as below:

Introduction
Development of the therapy
Theory and basic concepts
Practice
Which clients benefit most?
Case study
References
Suggested reading
Discussion issues

However, within each section the contributors were given some flexibility to include factors that were relevant to their particular approach. All chapters include suggested reading material and discussion issues, the latter to stimulate further reflection or deliberation. Some of the discussion issues are also suitable as essay titles.

In Chapter 29, Roy Moodley and Shafik Sunderani focus on the issue of diversity in counselling and psychotherapy. They start the chapter with the historical journey that multicultural counselling has undertaken since the 1960s. They also consider how multiculturalism has been limited by the 'strait-jacket' approach of focusing only on race, culture and ethnicity to clinical work in the current era; and then they highlight the benefits of changing to diversity, which has been more inclusive of all aspects of difference, in terms of gender, sexual orientation, religion and disability.

In Chapter 30, Carina Eriksen, Robert Bor and Margaret Oakes consider professional issues in counselling and psychotherapy. This is potentially a large area to cover in one chapter. However, the authors look at safe practice when working with suicidal clients; the ethical issues that counsellors and psychotherapists may need to consider for ensuring good practice; and how therapists can ensure that they continue to develop both on a professional and personal level. They also cover styles of supervision before proceeding to give helpful tips on how to gain the most from supervision. They then give an outline of continual professional development and finally discuss ethical and legal issues and advertising.

In Chapter 31, Terry Hanley and Laura Anne Winter consider research in counselling and psychotherapy. They provide an introduction to a number of issues counsellors and psychotherapists in these fields may encounter when engaging with research, including core methodological approaches and ethical issues. They ask an important question: 'Has research demonstrated the effectiveness of counselling and psychotherapy?'

A select glossary of key terms and concepts used in this book has been provided. Appendix 1 lists professional counselling and psychotherapy bodies from around the world, highlighting that useful resources can often be found on their websites, such as free newsletters, articles and guides. Appendix 2 comprises an extended list of therapies to highlight the wide range of approaches practised although not necessarily easily available. Appendix 3 offers a checklist that may be given to potential clients uncertain about what to ask the counsellor when attending their first counselling session. The Afterword includes my contact details.

Every attempt has been made to convey ideas in readily understandable language, but readers may find that certain approaches are less immediately accessible than others. This is probably because they rest on rather complex concepts or chains of ideas not easily conveyed in brief chapters. It simply *is* the case that some approaches are theoretically more complex than others. In such cases, interested readers are advised to consult the glossary where necessary and also to follow up on recommended further reading. It should, moreover, be acknowledged that individual readers may find more of an affinity with some approaches than with others, so that certain chapters seem easier to absorb.

Although it is usual practice to read books starting at the beginning and reading through to the end, this book has been written to allow readers to dip into any chapter that gets their attention or is necessary for study if they are attending a training course.

1

An Introduction to Counselling and Psychotherapy

Colin Feltham and Stephen Palmer

In recent years both counselling and psychotherapy have been demonstrated on television with real clients and discussed on radio programmes. There are numerous YouTube clips illustrating therapy too. So it is very likely most people today probably have at least some notion of what counselling is, since the term is now used so widely. However, misunderstandings and disagreements still abound about what the differences are between advice giving, counselling, psychotherapy, coaching, mentoring and similar terms. Although we cannot go into it all here, it is true to say that a whole host of activities, professions and relationships, from befriending, co-counselling and mutual aid groups, to clinical psychology, counselling psychology, coaching psychology, psychiatry and social work, in some ways resemble and overlap with each other. In this chapter we will focus on understandings of counselling skills, counselling and psychotherapy, before going on to look succinctly at different approaches.

Throughout this book, when various approaches are better known by the term 'therapy', this is reflected in the chapter titles, for example, 'Acceptance and Commitment Therapy'.

COUNSELLING SKILLS

Terms such as counselling skills, communication skills, interpersonal or relationship skills are often but not always used interchangeably. It is sometimes thought that there are certain communication and relationship-building skills that all or most approaches have in common, and these tend to be skills used intentionally in conversation towards certain helpful ends. Counselling skills may be said to differ from everyday, casual conversation in the following ways.

- While much ordinary conversation is characterized by rather casual, perhaps somewhat inattentive listening, a key counselling skill is active listening, which involves the conscious discipline of setting aside one's own preoccupations in order to concentrate as fully as possible on what the other person is expressing. This may involve a high level of awareness of one's own prejudices and idiosyncrasies.
- While ordinary conversation may contain a great deal of interaction, anecdotes, sharing thoughts and ideas and changing the subject aimlessly, another key counselling skill involves the discipline of responding mainly to the other person, in a purposeful, non-judgemental and often rather serious way, which tends to mean that such conversation usually has a somewhat one-way character.
- While ordinary conversation is not usually constrained by any agreements about confidentiality, counselling skills are usually backed up by either an implicit or explicit understanding about confidentiality.
- While ordinary conversation is often thought to be 'natural' and to have no particular rules governing it, counselling skills may often feel or be experienced as somewhat unnatural. For example, the person using counselling skills may strive to understand very accurately and demonstrate this striving by sometimes repeating parts of the other's statements in order to clarify or deepen understanding.
- Finally, while much ordinary conversation wanders across many subjects with no necessary goal, counselling skills are generally associated with some sort of goal, be it helping with decision making, offering an opportunity to discharge emotions, offering alternative interpretations or suggesting strategies for making desired changes.

Although there is some disagreement about the extent to which counselling skills may be possessed naturally by many people, it is widely (although not universally) believed that the skills have to be identified, understood, learned and practised repeatedly if one is to be able to be a consistently good listener and effective helper. Also, it is important to remember that while skills of this kind may be learned by many professionals, sometimes for their own ends (for example, salespeople intending to win customers over), the use of counselling skills is properly associated with therapeutic, helping or healing ends and not with self-centred agendas.

Counselling skills may be used in all sorts of situations in the classroom, at a hospital bedside, in training settings, or at bus stops or parties! In other words, they may be used within professional contexts, in voluntary work, or simply in everyday social and domestic settings, when someone is trying to listen in a disciplined manner, to be as helpful, constructive or interested as possible. Fairly typically, students on counselling skills courses may be nurses, teachers, ministers of religion, residential social workers and similar professionals, as well as those engaged in voluntary work. Typical too on counselling skills courses is some sort of model (three or five stages of the helping process) drawn from the ideas of Gerard Egan (Emeritus Professor of Psychology and Organizational Studies), Richard Nelson-Jones (Counselling Psychologist), Sue Culley (Counsellor) and others, usually advocating systematic practice in basic and advanced empathy, paraphrasing, summarizing, open questioning, challenging and so on.

COUNSELLING

Counselling differs in its formality from interactions where counselling skills are used. Counselling is generally characterized by an explicit agreement between a counsellor and client to meet in a certain, private setting, at agreed times and under disciplined conditions of confidentiality, with ethical parameters, protected time and specified aims. In the past decade the setting has become more flexible, with the advent of internet-based therapy websites, and Voice-Over-IP providers such as Skype and VSee.

Usually (although not always) the counsellor will have had a certain level of training (beyond the level of a certificate in counselling skills, typically a diploma or above), will belong to a professional body with a published code of ethics and will receive confidential supervision for her or his counselling. In some countries state licensure exists, such as in the USA, which is independent of the professional bodies. (See Appendix 1 for a list of professional bodies.)

It is widely accepted that counselling may be a suitable form of help for a variety of personal problems or concerns, the most common being depression, anxiety, stress, bereavement, relationship difficulties, life crises and traumas, addictions, self-defeating behaviour and thwarted ambitions. It can help with issues of loss, confusion and other negative conditions or it may also be used more proactively and educationally to learn, for example, how to relax, be more assertive, deal with stress and lead a more fulfilling life.

It is not essential to know where counselling comes from etymologically, historically and so on, but it probably does help to consider a few facts. The term itself does of course stem from the verb 'to counsel', which has always meant to advise, so it is not surprising that some people still have this misconception about counselling. Although some forms of counselling contain some advice-giving components, counselling is mostly dedicated to enhancing or restoring clients' own self-understanding, decision-making resources, risk taking and personal growth. Telling people what to do is therefore usually eschewed as a short-term and often counterproductive remedy.

Historically, a great deal of counselling in Britain has been associated with the non-directive, client-centred approach of the psychologist and psychotherapist Carl Rogers, and indeed we have to thank Rogers as one of the most active promoters of counselling in the USA. Many early British counsellors, too, took their ideas and training from Rogers' approach which, as we shall see later in this book, rests heavily and optimistically on belief in the innate resourcefulness and goodness of human beings. But it is important to know that hundreds of different theoretical approaches to counselling now exist (see Appendix 2), many of which do not share Rogers' views, and some of which may be almost diametrically opposed to Rogers. In some countries, such as England and Wales, there has been an increasing demand by the National Health Service (NHS) for counsellors to practise brief cognitive behavioural therapy in order to limit therapeutic costs. Counselling can be seen as a very broad and potentially confusing field of learning itself.

It may help when you come to consider differing approaches to counselling and psychotherapy to remember that each is necessarily an imperfect product of a certain time and place, which in its own way strives to make sense of distress and to promote methods of effective help. While each approach emphasizes certain aspects of human functioning and therapeutic skills, it has been argued that most depend on common factors such as a healing (second chance) relationship, a good fit between client and counsellor, the readiness of clients to be helped, the belief of clients and counsellors in the efficacy of counselling, and the plausibility of espoused theories.

desired result   *adopt / embrace*

PSYCHOTHERAPY

Do not despair or blame yourself if you are confused by the differences between counselling and psychotherapy; the alleged differences are indeed confusing and even many of the most prominent practitioners disagree. Psychotherapy originally referred to a less intense form of psychoanalysis and is still understood by some professionals as being, properly speaking, psychoanalytic psychotherapy only. However, the client-centred or person–centred approach is referred to as both counselling and psycho-therapy, usually without distinction. Various forms of brief psychotherapy challenge the simplistic claim that psychotherapy is long term and counselling is brief. It is probably advisable to ask anyone who uses the term psychotherapy exactly how they are using it, and with what justification!

Most psychotherapy, like counselling, is fundamentally talking-based therapy, rest-ing on psychological contact, theories and techniques. It is ultimately difficult to distinguish between counselling and psychotherapy, and indeed other similar practices. None the less, it is important to accept that some practitioners (mainly those trained as psychotherapists) strongly believe in significant differences. Since clients or potential clients sometimes ask about such matters, it is important in the long run to become informed about them. We now outline what we think are the basic differences as claimed by many psychotherapists.

- Psychotherapy (and its psychoanalytic variants in particular) involves lengthy train-ing (three to four years and sometimes more) which usually includes ongoing man-datory personal therapy for all trainees, exposing them to the subtle, unconscious layers of conflicts and defences they inevitably have. Working through one's own unconscious conflicts lessens them, makes it unlikely that clients' and therapists' issues will become confused or that clients will be intentionally or unintentionally exploited or abused, and is the best way of experientially understanding the theory and enhancing the practice of psychotherapy. In some countries' counselling train-ing, personal/training therapy has recently become mandatory, with counselling psychologists and counsellors having to complete at least 40 hours as partial fulfilment of requirements for chartered and accredited status respectively.
- Psychotherapy addresses the deep, unconscious, long-standing personality and behaviour problems and patterns of clients (frequently referred to as patients), rather than focusing on and superficially resolving only their presenting symptoms. Psycho-therapy is about radical, far-reaching personality change which is likely to be much more robust than the symptomatic and temporary changes effected by counselling.
- Psychotherapy, originally closely associated with the medical profession, takes very seriously clients' **psychopathology**, or entrenched psychological distress pat-terns, usually thought to derive from very early relationships in childhood and/or from partly innate drives. Psychotherapy holds out hope of making real differences

to the lives of some very disturbed or damaged people who could not benefit from once-weekly, symptom-oriented or crisis-related counselling.
• Psychotherapy requires a substantial time commitment, sometimes demanding that patients attend several times a week for several years. Counselling, by contrast, is often very short term and usually once-weekly.

It is important to state that such a brief summary risks caricaturing both psychotherapy and counselling. Also, it is true to say that many practitioners do not adopt antagonistic positions such as these, instead agreeing that valuable work is carried on under different names or that different kinds of work are being usefully carried on by two (or more) different professional groups. By examining the literature of the relevant professional bodies and related forums for your country or region (see Appendix 1) you may become acquainted with such issues in greater depth if you so choose.

APPROACHES TO COUNSELLING AND PSYCHOTHERAPY

There follows a condensed overview of the main approaches to counselling and psychotherapy to be found in this book. The purpose of this admittedly whirlwind tour is to encourage readers to:

• get an overall sense of the field, some of its complexity, its historical and theoretical breadth
• begin thinking about the key differences between approaches why they differ, how the differences are of interest and use, and how they are perhaps not so useful
• begin to consider what the main, common effective ingredients of the approaches may be
• ask themselves why they may be especially attracted to some approaches more than to others, and on what grounds.

Given that this is a highly complex and controversial field, you are cautioned that we, like all practitioners, are likely to have our own biases and limitations in understanding. The positive value of a book such as this is that it condenses and represents multiple theories and practices in a manageable format. If you intend to look more deeply into the intricacies of particular approaches and the debates between counsellors, it is usually advisable to refer both to traditional literature (original sources) and to the latest editions of specialist texts by those representing their own **theoretical orientation**. We have arranged this overview according to the convention of psychodynamic/psychoanalytic, cognitive behavioural, humanistic–existential traditions, integrative and **eclectic**, and lastly the constructivist approaches. This reflects the order in which the therapeutic approaches are arranged in the sections of the book.

PSYCHODYNAMIC AND PSYCHOANALYTIC APPROACHES

Psychoanalysis was the creation of the physician Sigmund Freud at the end of the nineteenth century. Many of Freud's early adherents split from him for theoretical and personality reasons, and many psychoanalytic approaches have evolved from Freud's in recent decades. The terms psychoanalytic, analytic, dynamic, psychodynamic and depth psychological may be said to share a stake in belief in the existence and power of the unconscious dimension of the mind, with its complex conflicts, symbolisms and defence mechanisms; in the importance of early childhood development and its long-standing effects; and in the replay of unconscious forces in the therapeutic relationship in various kinds of transference phenomena. Critics suggest that these approaches may be elitist, expensive, ineffective and based on implausible theories. However, we would prefer readers to keep an open mind and this book allows the reader to find out more about each approach or school of therapy.

Adlerian

Alfred Adler, a physician, had also been a colleague of Freud before launching his own 'individual psychology' around 1912. Adler disputed Freud's emphasis on psychosexual development and instead stressed the importance of a holistic view, incorporating the social and educational dimensions. Adler examined issues of power in families, particularly in sibling relationships, faulty private logic leading to mistaken life goals, and many other phenomena. Sometimes criticized for being too akin to common sense (and therefore arguably not psychoanalytic), Adlerian therapy or counselling has also been claimed by some (for example Albert Ellis) as influential in the development of cognitive behavioural therapy. *CBT*

Freudian

Sigmund Freud is probably regarded by a majority of counsellors as the single most significant founding figure in the development of counselling and psychotherapy. Although some now argue that there is no truly current Freudian therapy (because other variants have incorporated and bettered Freud), we must credit Freud with a particular view of a complex unconscious system made up of innate drives as well as early developmental vulnerabilities. Freud's concepts of ego, id and superego, his identification of defence mechanisms, insistence on the unconscious significance of dreams, jokes and slips of the tongue, on the importance of working through transference material in therapy, and other contributions have had an enormous influence on counselling and on popular culture.

Jungian

At one time very close to Freud, the psychiatrist Carl Jung established his own 'analytical psychology', or Jungian analysis (although he was not happy with the latter term), from the early part of the twentieth century. Jung disagreed with Freud's stress on childhood as the seat of all later ills, gave due weight to adulthood and old age and the complexity of the psyche, and focused on a lifelong process of individuation. Jung was influenced by mythology, anthropology, theology, astrology, alchemy and other disciplines, advocated a collective as well as an individual unconscious, and introduced many non-Freudian techniques. Modern Jungian therapy has its own schools of developmental, archetypal and classical therapy and is sometimes considered a transpersonal (spiritually oriented) approach.

Kleinian

Melanie Klein, psychoanalyst, represents a second or possibly third wave of psychoanalytic development, dating from around the 1920s and 1930s. Klein was more interested than Sigmund Freud in infant observation, in inferences about the long-standing influence of early relationships ('object relations') and in formulating developmental stages aligned with vulnerable early relationships with primary caregivers. She also developed methods of child psychotherapy and theory, and practice relating to psychoses. Klein, who developed much of her work in Britain, was affiliated with the object relations school whose therapeutic work is characterized by a belief in the inevitable replay of powerful, damaged early states as unconsciously driven reactions towards the therapist.

COGNITIVE BEHAVIOURAL APPROACHES

Historically, behaviour therapy pre-dates the cognitive therapies and these may be seen as quite distinct from each other. However, in the last few years a kind of merger has been tacitly acknowledged. Behaviour therapy, stemming from psychological science in the 1920s and clinical psychology in the 1950s (in the UK), is based on an attempt to produce scientific therapy by observing problematic behaviour accurately, generating testable theories and robust and effective remedies. Broadly speaking, it is about eliminating or reducing distressing behaviour and is not concerned with alleged causes or global personality changes. With the cognitive dimension comes the recognition of certain mediating thought processes between behaviour and distress. The cognitive behavioural approaches seek to assess and treat identified symptoms and concerns in an efficient, largely here-and-now, verifiable manner, using precise assessment techniques, and a range of in-session and homework-based tasks. A key strategy is to restructure and modify unhelpful thoughts and beliefs. However, a new generation (sometimes known as 'third wave') of cognitive behaviour therapies have been added to the family. These include acceptance and commitment therapy or ACT, compassion focused therapy (CFT) and dialectical behaviour therapy (DBT). These new approaches focus less on restructuring beliefs and more on encouraging the clients not to be judgemental about their cognitions and feelings – just to accept them as beliefs and not facts. This has been an interesting development and has seen mindfulness training increasingly used as an intervention within these new approaches.

Acceptance and commitment therapy

Acceptance and commitment therapy (ACT) is part of the 'third wave' of cognitive behavioural therapies. In conversation and in the literature it is usually shortened to 'ACT', pronounced as a single word 'act'. ACT was developed by Steven C. Hayes and associates during the 1980s. It is informed by relational frame theory, which is a theory of language and cognition. ACT is described as a 'contextual' cognitive behaviour therapy (CBT) as it attempts to alter the psychological context of a client's internal experience. So rather than challenging unhelpful beliefs, as occurs in CBT, ACT takes a mindful approach to them instead so that the client can find them less distressing. In addition to the application of mindfulness to be present in the moment, the 'Defusion' technique clearly illustrates this process. It involves clients repeating painful phrases or words until they become just sounds, not attached to distressing overwhelming memories.

Behaviour therapy

Stemming from a number of countries and pioneers, behaviour therapy set out to promote a scientific theory of behaviour, behavioural problems and their remedies, without recourse to gratuitous and unprovable concepts. We learn unhelpful behaviours (by using faulty ways of dealing with stress, by always responding with panic to certain situations, for example) and proceed to reinforce our unhelpful behaviour. Behaviour therapists identify precise situational factors associated with problem behaviours and teach coping and social skills, systematic desensitization (gradual exposure to what we fear, while learning to relax) and response prevention (learning not to keep checking electrical appliances, for example, as in obsessive–compulsive disorder). It is said to be especially successful with phobias, obsessive–compulsive problems and other well-specified conditions.

Cognitive behavioural therapy

Aaron Beck, psychiatrist and psychotherapist, developed cognitive therapy from the 1950s, in an attempt to improve upon psychoanalytic methods. Noting that we frequently appear to have automatic thoughts about our circumstances and that we make many incorrect inferences about our situation that may both create and worsen negative moods, Beck successfully applied his findings initially to depression. In more recent years there has been a gradual integration of cognitive and behaviour therapies and it has become known as cognitive behavioural therapy (CBT). The approach is based on collaboratively helping clients to understand how their own cognitions (thinking) affect their moods and behaviour, and how certain common lifelong belief patterns can be overthrown methodically. CBT is becoming widely available in many countries due to the research highlighting its effectiveness with a wide range of disorder.

Compassion focused therapy

Compassion focused therapy (CFT) is an integrated and multimodal approach that is informed by a number of key areas: evolutionary, neuroscience, social, Buddhist and developmental psychology. The multimodal aspect is reflected by the interventions, which include Socratic questioning, behavioural experiments, guided imagery, chair work, mindfulness, method acting and expressive writing. Over 25 years ago a psychologist, Paul Gilbert, noted that some clients with complex mental health problems could understand the logic of the questions he asked them in order to examine their unhelpful thinking but the CBT style of questioning did not change how they viewed themselves. Gilbert started to encourage clients to develop an inner warm voice, but some clients who were experiencing shame and who were highly self-critical encountered great difficulty in this exercise. In the past 25 years, Gilbert and his associates have developed CFT to assist clients with these type of problems.

compusion Forward

Dialectical behaviour therapy

Dialectical behaviour therapy (DBT) is a mindfulness–based cognitive behavioural approach. Unlike other forms of CBT, DBT is delivered by a team of therapists rather than an individual counsellor or therapist. DBT was developed by Marsha Linehan in the 1980s. She was studying suicidal self-harming women, some of whom also had a diagnosis of borderline personality disorder. Many of them were distressed by the usual cognitive and behavioural interventions as they perceived the therapist as not understanding the extent of their challenges. This is unhelpful for the therapeutic relationship and can lead to discord, especially if the therapist continues to focus on the goals of their therapeutic approach. Influenced by Zen philosophy, Linehan introduced mindfulness as a method to focus on acceptance. Linehan believed that the therapist needed to be able to acknowledge the dialectical tension between the acceptance and change positions, hence the name 'dialectical behaviour therapy'.

Hypnotherapy

Forms of hypnosis have existed for centuries and Freud experimented with and later discarded hypnotic techniques. Hypnotherapy has sometimes attracted misplaced interest, being caricatured as an almost magical process conducted by mysterious, master practitioners, and associated sometimes with unscrupulous, exploitative and superficially trained practitioners. It is adaptable for use with other approaches, such as CBT and REBT, is often successful for pain control (for example in dentistry) and some habit disorders (for example smoking), and is often preferred by clients seeking rapid results or who have not found predominantly talking approaches helpful. In this book the chapter on hypnosis has shown how it is used within a cognitive behav-ioural framework and so it has been placed in that section.

Rational emotive behaviour therapy

Albert Ellis, a clinical psychologist, created rational emotive behaviour therapy (REBT), originally called rational therapy, then rational emotive therapy, from the 1950s as an attempt to provide a more efficient approach than the psychoanalytic methods in which he had been trained. REBT is an active–directive, here–and–now, cognitively affiliated therapy (that is, based primarily on thinking), drawing from stoical philosophy and arguing that we are not upset directly by events in our lives but by the irrational beliefs we hold about ourselves and about life. REBT aims to help overcome situational problems (for example exam anxiety) and self–rating problems (for example low self–esteem) among others, using a range of educational, emotive, imaginal, confrontational and other techniques.

HUMANISTIC-EXISTENTIAL APPROACHES

What the humanistic approaches share broadly speaking is an optimistic belief in the self–determination of the person. Thus, the emphasis is more on the present and future than on the past, more on trusting feelings and their expression than on limited rational thinking and traditional science, more on looking hopefully at holistic poten-tial than at psychopathology and symptoms for behavioural change, more on shared human growth than on professional expertise, more on radical social change than on adapting to a sick society. Many of the humanistic schools emerged from or found their natural home in California in the 1960s and 1970s. 'Humanistic' is not used in its atheistic sense but in contrast to alienating, scientistic, medically and expert-oriented approaches. Critics suggest that the humanistic approaches are romantic, self–indulgent, not necessarily concerned with ordinary people's everyday pressing worries and are often hostile to attempts at scientific verification.

Existential therapy

A number of therapists who became disillusioned with analytic approaches, or regarded them as insufficient, drew inspiration from ancient and modern philoso-phers. Instead of dwelling on individuals' psychopathology, existentialists argue that the human condition confronts us all with challenges of life and death, freedom, meaning, values, choice and commitment. Counselling is an intensely specific, rela-tively atheoretical and technique-free process guiding clients to identify their own responsibility for life values and choices.

Gestalt therapy

Fritz Perls, originally a neuropsychiatrist, with his wife, Laura, and others devised Gestalt therapy (*Gestalt* is German for 'whole' and suggests looking at all aspects of being and behaviour), partly as a reaction against psychoanalysis and intellectualizing systems, placing much more emphasis on non–verbal and bodily language, here–and–now behaviour and potential, and the client's conscious responsibility for his or her actions, decisions, thoughts, feelings and awareness. Perls was influenced by, among other things, Zen Buddhism, existentialism and psychodrama. Modern Gestalt uses a range of powerful techniques such as chair work and is not necessarily the confrontational approach it is often caricatured as.

Person-centred therapy

Carl Rogers, rejecting the traditions of psychoanalytic and behavioural approaches and the powerful profession of psychiatry that claimed to have the answers, developed his non-directive (later called client-centred, and now person-centred) therapy from around the 1940s on the basis of experience and research suggesting that therapeutic conditions such as unconditional positive regard, empathy and congruence were the key to successful personal growth. This optimistic philosophy and practice, championing the view that human beings are essentially and positively self-actualizing, has informed much training in the UK and Europe especially.

Primal integration

The 1970s spawned many heavily feelings-based therapies, one of the most sensational being the psychologist Arthur Janov's primal therapy (a variety of which, incidentally, is now espoused by Alice Miller). Primal integration, related to this, dwells on the uncovering and expression of deep feelings, often suppressed for decades. These feelings may relate to painful birth (or pre-birth) experiences, childhood or later abuse (physical, sexual or emotional) or deprivation, but they may also relate to joyful and spiritual experiences and can result in profound psychological and bodily changes.

Psychosynthesis

Originally a psychoanalyst, Roberto Assagioli started formulating psychosynthesis in the early part of the twentieth century, drawing on various religious traditions, yoga, humanistic psychology and adding many of his own ideas and techniques (for example mental imagery, inner dialogue, ideal model). Psychosynthesis is a transpersonal approach that seeks to include but go beyond a focus on personal problems stemming from the past, and everyday problems, into questions about the purpose of life, the superconscious, higher self and collective unconscious.

Transactional analysis (TA)

Eric Berne, psychiatrist and psychoanalyst, departed from the psychoanalytic tradition by focusing on observable interpersonal interaction as well as private, inner, unconscious states. In Berne's model, personality can be manifested in any of three distinctive patterns of thinking, feeling and behaviour, known as ego-states. In the

Adult ego–state, the person is 'in the here and now'. In Parent, she is copying her parent-figures; and in Child she is replaying her own childhood. People can be helped consciously to recognize how and why they move between states, and can use this knowledge to move proactively out of lifelong repetitive dysfunctional patterns.

INTEGRATIVE AND ECLECTIC APPROACHES

Eclecticism in counselling and psychotherapy could be viewed as an 'anything goes' approach to therapy whereby therapists might take a 'pick-and-mix approach' to choosing which techniques to use with their clients. This approach probably was more popular with some therapists in the 1970s and 1980s. It is easy to be critical of practitioners who are essentially practising intuition-based therapy by using techniques not based on research evidence but on what they feel is right in the situation. A variety of eclectic approaches were developed by practitioners, including those with a more empirical approach. For example, psychologist Arnold Lazarus developed multimodal therapy, which is described as technically eclectic as it uses techniques taken from many different psychological approaches and then applies the techniques systematically based on data taken from client qualities, the therapist's clinical skills and specific techniques, underpinned by established theories such as social learning theory.

Lazarus argued that it is difficult to integrate certain therapeutic approaches, whereas the systematic application of techniques taken from approaches was easier. The integration of behaviour and cognitive therapy approaches and techniques is fairly straightforward. We have also seen the development of other integrative therapies such as interpersonal psychotherapy (IPT) and cognitive analytic therapy (CAT), both of which can point to research highlighting their effectiveness. In this section we also include Lifeskills counselling, developed by Richard Nelson-Jones, which integrates a wide range of skills and techniques. In this century we have also seen the development of pluralistic therapy, whereby therapists apply the most useful features of other models within a pluralistic framework. The developers of the approach, Mike Cooper and John McLeod, assert that it differs from other integrative models in the extent to which it takes account of client preferences and resources.

Cognitive analytic therapy

Cognitive analytic therapy (CAT) is commonly presented as an integrative approach because it is in fact an integration of elements of psychoanalytic (particularly object relations) therapy, personal construct psychology, and cognitive and behavioural approaches. It is one of the few British-grown approaches, devised by Anthony Ryle (originally a doctor), in the 1980s to fit NHS needs for realistically short-term treatment for a relatively wide variety of problems, including eating disorders, borderline personality disorders and suicide attempts. Many diagrams and paperwork exercises are used.

Interpersonal psychotherapy

Interpersonal psychotherapy (IPT) is a manualized time-limited therapy that was originally developed for the treatment of depression. It helps the client to understand the nature of depression and to identify social and interpersonal factors such as relationships with significant others, which may have triggered the onset or maintenance of problems. IPT has now been applied to a range of mental health problems, including eating disorders and social anxiety, and has adapted to delivery by telephone.

Lifeskills counselling

Associated with Richard Nelson-Jones and others, this essentially psychoeducational approach focuses on identifying and coaching people in the acquisition, refinement and maintenance of skills they need to learn to overcome problems in everyday living and to establish more successful coping styles. Most problematic areas of functioning, for example those including intimate relationships and job seeking, can be broken down into units amenable to concrete improvement and can be addressed successfully by such an approach.

Multimodal therapy

Arnold Lazarus, originally a prominent behaviour therapist, sought greater breadth and techniques tailored to individual clients and devised this systematically eclectic form of therapy based on identifying the primary modalities in which people function, acquire and correct their problems: behaviour, affect, sensation, imagery, cognition, interpersonal and drugs/biological and lifestyle factors (**BASIC I.D.**). Assessment allows counsellors to apply the techniques (borrowed from any other approach) most likely to be helpful in each case, which may include assertiveness training, anxiety management, visualization and so on. Because the approach focuses on mainly cognitive and behavioural therapeutic techniques it is sometimes viewed as a cognitive behavioural approach.

Pluralistic counselling and psychotherapy

Pluralistic therapy, as developed by Mike Cooper and John McLeod in this century, attempts to provide a framework for counselling and psychotherapy that does not get stuck with what could be perceived as the rigid application of the theory and practice of any particular therapeutic school or approach. However, the therapists will apply the most useful features of other models. The therapist accepts that there may be many factors that contribute to the client's presenting problem(s) and works collaboratively with the client to find out what is most helpful for that person at that particular point in time.

CONSTRUCTIVIST APPROACHES TO COUNSELLING AND PSYCHOTHERAPY

Constructivism can be considered as the study and theory of knowledge which is centred on the active engagement of the person in construing their own reality. From the therapeutic perspective, constructivist approaches focus on exploring the internal constructions of reality of the clients rather than reality. The approaches may use storytelling as a technique and attempt to avoid psychopathologizing clients.

Narrative therapy

Theorists such as Jerome Bruner had suggested that storytelling was an important method people use to communicate and understand their experiences and their world. Taking this notion one step further, Michael White and David Epston applied narrative informed discussions to their work with families and they became key developers of the approach during the 1980s, although the term narrative therapy did not appear until 1989. Narrative therapy is now used with individuals and couples too, and more recently has been adapted to the field of coaching.

Neuro-linguistic programming

Developed by John Grinder, Assistant Professor of Linguistics, and Richard Bandler, psychologist, from the 1970s, neuro-linguistic programming (NLP) draws on certain Gestalt, hypnotherapeutic, cybernetic and other ideas and techniques and is concerned not only with counselling but with accelerated learning and management development. We can re-programme our minds by means of reframing, visualization and substituting constructive for self-defeating beliefs and inner dialogue. NLP is replete with techniques and strategies, including some that aim to produce rapid and complete cure of phobias, for example.

Personal construct counselling and psychotherapy

Personal construct practitioners (more likely to be psychologists than counsellors or psychotherapists) may disagree with the view that theirs is a cognitive behavioural approach. The psychologist George Kelly formulated personal construct therapy

(PCT) in the 1950s as a theory of personality and therapy, also known as constructive alternativism, which demonstrates among other things that we usually (and inaccurately and unhelpfully) construe our experiences in extreme polar opposites, with which we become stuck (for example if I am not brilliant I must be stupid). PCT is a complex approach, utilizing specialist concepts and, sometimes, tabulated exercises. It has been very influential in the development of the so-called 'narrative-constructivist' approaches and of cognitive analytic therapy.

Solution-focused therapy

Also known simply as brief therapy, originated by Steve de Shazer and other American strategic family therapists from the 1970s (and influenced by Gregory Bateson, Jay Haley and Milton Erickson), the solution-focused approach challenges several cherished assumptions and proposes new methods. Instead of searching for putative causes of problems in clients' pasts, instances of effective coping are sought, clients' imaginations are enlisted by using techniques that encourage them to visualize themselves producing solutions, and in effect questioning their own tendency to psychopathologize themselves.

CONCLUSIONS

By now you should have begun to get an impression of the breadth, complexity, fascination and problems of the field of counselling and psychotherapy. As a field that is now more than 100 years old, that is represented by numerous and competing traditions, theories and techniques as well as by several similar professions, and that is continuously being developed, no individual can hope to ever 'know it all', nor does anyone need to know it all or to feel demoralized by any relative ignorance. Researchers are busily attempting to identify exactly what is most effective in the field, and some forecasters attempt to pinpoint trends, such as the apparent decline of certain approaches and the growth and success of others. Currently, cognitive behavioural approaches have become popular within health services whilst mindfulness training appears to have become part of the zeitgeist with regular articles in the press about its benefits.

Critics from outside and inside counselling and psychotherapy note some clients' claims of abuse, exploitation and ineffectiveness. We believe it is important that if you wish to learn more about this field, that you find questions and frameworks to guide your learning and to help you become selective in a manner that is as free from prejudice as possible and as committed as possible to the shared understanding and pursuit of better mental health and wellbeing.

SUGGESTED READING

Dryden, W. and Reeves, A. (eds) (2014) *The Handbook of Individual Therapy*, 6th edn. London: Sage. This handbook covers a wide range of different approaches in depth and includes historical context and development, theoretical assumptions, and also strengths and limitations.

Feltham, C. and Horton, I. (eds) (2012) *The Sage Handbook of Counselling and Psychotherapy*, 3rd edn. London: Sage. This is a definitive handbook on the theory, research, skills and practice of counselling and psychotherapy.

McLeod, J. (2013) *An Introduction to Research in Counselling and Psychotherapy*. London: Sage. This book introduces the basic principles of research theory and practice. When learning about different approaches to counselling and psychotherapy it is also useful to consider the issues relating to research.

Nelson-Jones, R. (2013) *Introduction to Counselling Skills: Text and Activities*, 4th edn. London: Sage. This book provides an easy-to-follow three-stage model and covers counselling skills, putting skills into practice, working effectively with diversity, ethical issues and dilemmas.

Palmer, S. and Woolfe, R. (2000) *Integrative and Eclectic Counselling and Psychotherapy*. London: Sage. Following an exploration of the origins of integrative and eclectic processes, 10 integrative and eclectic approaches are explained in depth. This is one of the last textbooks to focus solely on integrative and eclectic therapeutic practice.

DISCUSSION ISSUES

You may apply these questions both to what you have read in this chapter and to the chapters following.

1. How important is it to decide on the real differences between counselling and psychotherapy (and similar professions), and what will guide your decision?
2. To what extent do the summarized approaches seem to belong reasonably cohesively to the groups to which they are allocated, as opposed to seeming like unrelated endeavours? Why does this matter?
3. Which of the approaches seem to rely most on the relationship between client and counsellor/psychotherapist, which on the expertise, theory and techniques of the practitioner?
4. Which of the approaches do you personally find most compelling, and why? How would you go about finding objective evidence that any approach is superior to another?

2

The Therapeutic Relationship

Alanna O'Broin

As social beings with our own ideas of what relationships are, we will have our own perspective on what the therapeutic relationship is. Meanwhile the commonly held view in the research literature is that the therapeutic relationship is a term that defines 'the feelings and attitudes that therapist and client have toward one another, and the manner in which these are expressed'.[1,2] Beyond this broad, consensual definition, disagreements and multiple perspectives exist on what constitutes the therapeutic relationship (also commonly termed the **alliance**, the *therapeutic alliance* and the **working alliance**). Each of the chapters in this book includes its own perspective on the therapeutic relationship, either through the lens of a particular theoretical approach, or through the lens of research, professional, or diversity issues. Regardless of the degree, level, and kind of therapeutic relationship emphasized in each approach, common to most if not all forms of counselling and psychotherapy is the minimum requirement for a bond (or connection) and collaboration between therapist and client as a necessity for effective work to take place. In this chapter I will focus on briefly highlighting developments in our knowledge of the therapeutic relationship before outlining a pan-theoretic model of the therapeutic alliance and looking at ways of working with the alliance in counselling and psychotherapy with clients.

DEVELOPMENT OF THE THERAPEUTIC RELATIONSHIP IN CLINICAL AND RESEARCH DOMAINS

Early in the twentieth century, Freud's psychoanalytic theory was the first influential focus on the therapeutic relationship, asserting that therapeutic relationships were transference-based (see Chapter 4). His idea was that positive transference kept the client actively engaged in therapy and co-operating or allied with the therapist when the client's negative or resistant transference was activated. Later psychodynamic writers extended the idea of positive aspects of the therapeutic relationship.

Zetsel introduced the term 'therapeutic alliance' in 1956,[3] and Greenson the terms 'real relationship' and 'working alliance' in 1967,[4] the latter concept emphasizing the client's ability to work purposively in the therapy.

By the 1970s, a number of developments outside the scope of the psychodynamic approach had introduced the possibility that the alliance may be common in all models of counselling and psychotherapy. First was Rogers' person–centred therapy, based on the concept of the *actualizing tendency*, or the innate ability of all humans to grow and develop positively and constructively given the right conditions of empathy, congruence and unconditional positive regard (see Chapter 16). These conditions, considered essential to and sufficient for change in person–centred therapy, and arguably essential to all forms of positive and healing relationships, formed a conceptualization of the therapeutic relationship that differed from, yet overlapped with, the alliance. Second, despite vigorous attempts to prove otherwise between the 1950s and to this date, psychotherapy research has consistently found that therapy based on different theoretical models produces roughly equivalent client outcomes. The predominant interpretation of this finding is that common factors (such as the alliance) underlie different counselling and psychotherapy treatments and are largely responsible for effective therapy outcomes. Third, in pursuing the role of common factors, the alliance subsequently became the most researched topic in psychotherapy. It has consistently over decades demonstrated a modest yet robust association with therapy outcome across theoretical approaches (including those often considered more technique-focused, such as cognitive behavioural therapy), and across research designs, researcher allegiance and time of assessment during the course of therapy.[5] Fourth, the growing interest since the 1930s in integrating different psychotherapy theories and methods for their effectiveness rather than restricting their use within a strict 'school' of therapy became more prevalent. The alliance was an obvious candidate for use within such integrative frameworks.

Whilst most research on the therapeutic relationship focused on and repeated the finding of an association between alliance and therapy outcomes, a surge of research interest was also generated in seeking to reveal the variables that account directly *and indirectly* for common factor effects. The most recent task force researching evidence-based therapy relationships or what 'works' in the therapy relationship concluded that several elements of the therapeutic relationship were 'demonstrably effective' in terms of their contribution to therapy outcome as it is currently researched. These elements included the alliance in individual, youth, family and group therapy; empathy; collecting client feedback; and adapting to the client (in terms of client resistance level, preferences, culture, religion and spirituality). Further relationship elements of goal consensus, collaboration, positive regard and adapting to the client (stages of change, and coping style) were found to be 'probably effective'.[6] For a more detailed and broader discussion of counselling and psychotherapy research see Chapter 31.

Clinical theorists such as Luborsky and Bordin had also developed broader conceptualizations of the alliance common to all helping relationships, transplanting it outside its psychodynamic roots. Bordin's pan–theoretical **working alliance** model,[7,8] has become the most prominent and widely used alliance theory, both clinically and in research.

Multiple perspectives on the therapeutic relationship

It is helpful to bear in mind factors underlying the multiple perspectives on the therapeutic relationship, which arise largely from unanswered questions remaining despite decades of prodigious research and comment (yet limited clinical theory) on the therapeutic relationship. These differences include varying use and definition of the terms therapeutic relationship, therapeutic alliance and working alliance by those of different theoretical approach or approaches, divergent descriptions of the alliance process, and diffuse measurement of overlapping, yet incomplete constructs of the full scope of the therapeutic relationship. Client and therapist views on their therapeutic alliance also differ, the client's view often proving a better predictor of therapy outcome than the therapist's.

As yet, measurement of different alliances for treatments from different theoretical approaches remains relatively unexplored. The further question of whether the relationship or techniques are pre-eminent in determining counselling and psychotherapy outcome has divided opinion. However, this issue is increasingly perceived more realistically as a 'both/and' rather than 'either/or' consideration as practitioners and researchers alike recognise the inextricable link between the two, and seek to capture these admittedly more complex interacting variables in research studies. The detail of these differences lies outside the scope of this introductory chapter, however interested readers are directed to suggested reading texts[9,10,11] for more detailed coverage.

THEORY AND BASIC CONCEPTS

Counsellors, counselling psychologists and psychotherapists will hold their own perspective on the therapeutic relationship. However, Bordin's working alliance model[7,8] and later extensions of his work[12,13,14,15] offer a broad, overarching and pan-theoretic framework within which particular theoretical approaches can be placed, and will now be the focus.

Alliance theory

Alliance theory views therapy as collaborative work by both client and therapist towards a goal. The goal may be a specific outcome or outcomes, or may represent a broader sense of positive change (the latter for instance in the therapist's provision of core conditions in person-centred therapy in seeking client wellbeing and growth). Change will occur in proportion to the extent that the dyad work together as expected, and the stronger the alliance, the better the predicted outcome of therapy. Active collaboration is therefore the lynchpin on which the alliance is based, requiring negotiation between client and therapist on how the therapy will takes place and to what end.

Theoretical profiles of the alliance

Each theoretical approach holds a set of expectations and requirements for how client and therapist will work together; each theory of therapy (e.g. personal construct, transactional analysis) stipulates the work expected of therapist and client in effecting change. As long as the dyad work to these expectations through negotiating and carrying out the therapy work, alliance theory predicts that change will occur.

Bordin's alliance theory operationalized the negotiation process into three components: mutual agreement on goals of therapy; collaboration on the activities or tasks required by therapist and client to achieve the goals; underpinned by establishment of a suitable bond. Although described separately below, they are inter-connected.[13]

Bonds

Whilst rapport and friendliness may be characteristics present in the therapeutic relationship, as they often are in personal relationships, the bond in the working alliance has a purpose, which is to facilitate and support the therapy work. Within different theoretical approaches, and with individual clients, this means that the optimal bond will differ in terms of the degree, level and kind of bond required to facilitate engagement and treatment.[13] The therapist's provision of the core conditions, for instance, may be seen as sufficient in person-centred therapy for change to occur, whilst in cognitive behavioural therapy such conditions may be viewed as necessary, but not sufficient in and of themselves, also requiring work on techniques in the change process. The client's general ability to trust and relate with others, and their belief in the therapist as a credible agent of change may be further considerations in establishing and maintaining an alliance with them, as will the fit of interpersonal styles between client and therapist, and their tendency to think, feel and behave towards the other person in a way that is affected by their previous interaction with a significant other. The implication of this variation in the optimal bond in working with individual clients is that the therapist needs to be flexible and able to tailor their interpersonal style to suit the needs of the client, not only with each individual client but also possibly throughout the duration of the therapy programme. Initially, engaging the client may require complementing the client's interpersonal style to develop a strong enough alliance to withstand any strains or **ruptures** introducing challenges in the alliance.

Goals

An integral part of building an alliance involves negotiating and working closely with the client in identifying their most meaningful change goal. In the initial stage, this process involves achieving a mutually understood and agreed-on change goal, which is made explicit. In those theoretical approaches which are not goal-focused (e.g. existential, person-centred), the change or outcome goal may be the therapist's and/or client's way of being (for instance the therapist cultivating the core conditions), or a more general goal (such as opening up possibilities in existential counselling and psychotherapy).

Tasks

Tasks are the specific activities that the dyad will engage in to facilitate change in working towards change goals. The kind of activities engaged in vary depending on the theoretical approach concerned, and may be broad (such as loosening the client's construing in personal construct psychotherapy) (see Chapter 27) or more specific, such as using the major target problem procedures diagram for promoting self-observation in cognitive analytic counselling and psychotherapy (see Chapter 20).

In working on the alliance, the client needs to understand both the *purpose* and *content* of the tasks, as well as recognizing the intrinsic value of carrying the task or tasks out, and having the personal or other resources necessary to do so. If the client does not fully understand or is not able to carry out the task the therapist needs to work with the client in either modifying the task so that the client is able to perform it or helping the client equip themselves with the skills needed to conduct the task. Finally the client needs to understand what the therapist's tasks are, their purpose, and how they relate to their own tasks. In each case a lack of understanding or ability to conduct the tasks poses a threat to the alliance. Ensuring that the client fully understands and agrees with their tasks will more easily enable both participants to effectively carry out their respective tasks, however the skill with which the therapist carries out their tasks will also impact on the client outcome.[13]

In conceptualizing the Working Alliance model in this way, it can form an overarching, or integrative framework[14,15] for the therapeutic process that includes working with the strains and ruptures of the alliance,[12] and is supported by the findings on elements of the therapeutic relationship in evidence-based literature.[6] Not all theorists, researchers and practitioners agree that 'elements' of the therapeutic relationship can be isolated and measured separately in this way; that elements such as alliance and collecting client feedback operate at the same level as each other; that relationship elements can be measured separately from the techniques of therapy; or that the contributions of therapist and client to these 'elements' can be disentangled. However, relationship elements can provide an understanding of current scientific knowledge which therapists can then choose to apply in the context of their work with the individual client. In this way, elements can be conceptualized as sitting between the theoretical approach and its specific techniques.

PRACTICE

All forms of therapy aim to establish and maintain a good working relationship. In alliance theory, a good alliance is achieved when the client and therapist are working collaboratively and well towards the goals of therapy. This is achieved with different clients, therapists and theoretical approaches, in different ways. For instance, variety in the alliance may exist or be required due to several factors, including:

- what the client brings as the focus of the therapy
- client individual differences
- changes in the client's needs during the therapy
- the therapist's use of a particular theoretical approach (suggesting the creation of a particular kind of therapeutic relationship)
- the therapist's personality and style
- the therapist's individual emphasis on, and use of, the interpersonal dynamics and communication in the therapy process.

Change process

In alliance theory, three key elements are identified as having a bearing on change:

- the strength of the alliance
- power of therapeutic tasks
- dynamics of strain in the alliance.

If the client and therapist are able to negotiate and collaborate in the expected work of the therapy, then the alliance is predicted to be strong. The stronger the alliance, then the better the predicted therapy outcome. Effectively, the capacity to achieve change is seen in large measure as a reflection of the strength of the alliance. Alliance theory assumes that engaging in therapeutic tasks impacts the person seeking change; and that there are particular beliefs about the particular tasks, for instance in different theoretical perspectives. The tasks are closely related to the change goals. The interaction of tasks with any unhelpful behaviours bringing the client to therapy may create strains in the alliance. Successful settlement of these strains or ruptures in the alliance can often be a key to positive change.

A negotiated alliance

A significant contribution made by alliance theory is in its emphasis on negotiation, and the client's active contribution to this negotiation. Drawing from Greenson, Bordin's theory also reflects Rogers' and others' emphasis on the client as an active force in the change process. The therapist may be the major source of selection of therapeutic tasks, however the client needs to understand and agree with the relevance of these activities to the change process and ultimate goal.

Later extensions to the concept of negotiation in alliance theory[12] focused on explicitly responding to the client's disagreement or reservations about the therapy rationale or treatment (see also Dryden, 2008a).[14] Reflecting the finding in the literature of the link between resolution of ruptures and good outcome, there needs to be openness by client and therapist about the contribution each partner makes to the particular strain or rupture. The therapist candidly acknowledging and exploring, rather than avoiding or ignoring withdrawal or confrontation ruptures, is beneficial. In the event that the therapist is able to manage the strain or rupture satisfactorily, rupture resolution may provide opportunities for positive change in therapy.

Strategies

In an overarching or integrative framework of alliance, an evaluative approach places alliance one conceptual level higher than elements or techniques. Hence the focus is on the question of whether the elements (e.g. collecting client feedback, empathy) are facilitating the active collaboration of the client and therapist.

As discussed above, the findings of the task force on what 'works' in the therapy relationship identified several elements as 'demonstrably effective' in terms of therapy outcome. Elements can add to understanding and knowledge of the therapeutic relationship, and the therapist can choose to apply these elements in their work with individual clients where appropriate. Practitioner points and strategies on elements of empathy, collecting client feedback and adapting to the client are discussed below; for further detail on these and 'probably effective' elements, see Norcross and Wampold, 2011.[6]

Empathy

Empathy, akin to the alliance, has a positive association with client outcome across theoretical approaches in counselling and psychotherapy; has no single universal definition; and has been measured in different ways. Given its predictive relationship with therapy outcome, therapists should endeavour to understand their client and their client's perspective, and demonstrate this understanding to the client in-the-moment and in terms of the client's change goals. Therapist understanding can be demonstrated through **empathic affirmation**, **empathic evocation**, **empathic exploration**, **empathic understanding** responses. Therapist understanding attends to what is and is not said, and is always subject to the client's verification and correction.

Collecting client feedback

The research supports the conclusion that using feedback systems in clinical practice improves client outcome, although there are a relatively small number of studies in the literature measuring their effectiveness. Feedback systems questionnaires measure the therapeutic alliance, and mental health functioning of clients (outcome measures), and their use can supplement rather than replace the therapist's clinical judgement. As feedback systems rely on accurate self-recording, therapists need awareness of the possibility of clients understating or overstating their problems in feedback questionnaires. Some questionnaires can detect clients at risk of worsening in therapy, and use of electronic versions of questionnaires at commencement of sessions can provide instant feedback to the therapist. Whilst it may be helpful for feedback to be provided to both client and therapist for some clients, this is not universally so.

Adapting to the client

Therapists have long recognized that therapy needs to be tailored to the client, and the commonest form was to tailor the treatment to the client's problem area (e.g. panic disorder). Whilst this form of matching treatment to problem area is useful with certain disorders, it is not universally effective, and the person of the client is ignored. Increasing evidence shows that frequently it is effective to tailor the therapy to the person in their particular situation. Four client characteristics have been shown to be demonstrably effective in adapting therapy: reactance/resistance to change; client preferences; culture; and religion/spirituality.

Reactance/resistance to change

Even when they fundamentally believe that engaging in therapy will be useful, clients can be ambivalent about, and resistant to change. Clients may be described as *resistant* when they do not comply with therapy procedures (such as expressing dissatisfaction or anger towards the therapist). From another perspective, *reactance* denotes a therapy environment in which factors, including that of the therapist, may contribute to client non-compliance. Therapists can assess the level of client resistance or reactance, and match their directiveness accordingly. To defuse the in-the-moment consequences if expressions of dissatisfaction are raised, therapists can acknowledge the client's concerns, and discuss and renegotiate the therapeutic contract regarding goals and roles of the dyad within the alliance, including reconsidering the methods they are using in the therapy.

Client preferences

Incorporating client preferences is a central tenet in the strategy of collaborating with the client, and a key component of evidence-based practice. In contrast to client *expectations*, which are what the client believes will, or should happen in therapy, client *preferences* reflect what the client would choose the therapy to be like. Client preferences can be described as *role preferences* (the client's preference for the activities and behaviours of themselves and their therapist during therapy, such as preferring individual rather than group therapy); *therapist preferences* (preferred characteristics in their therapist, for instance a therapist of the same gender); and *treatment preferences* (preference for the type of treatment, for example preferring a cognitive behavioural approach, rather than medication).

Culture

Although in a broad sense all mental health treatments could be argued to be informed by cultural contexts, *cultural adaptation* involves considering the client's language, culture and context when adapting the evidence-based therapy being used by the therapist to be congruous with the client's cultural meanings and values. Research supports the tendency of the client to benefit from the therapist's attempts to make such cultural adaptations, where possible by conducting therapy in the client's preferred language. The therapist should therefore seek to make these adjustments when working with their clients.

Religion/spirituality

For those clients seeking religious/spiritually oriented therapy, such therapies are a valid treatment option, and are a treatment of choice for those clients valuing spiritual outcomes highly. Therapists should ask clients about their religious/spiritual beliefs at assessment, and incorporate religious/spiritual oriented therapy following the needs and preferences of the client, particularly with those clients who are highly religious or spiritual.

Session format

There is no set format for sessions when working with the alliance or therapeutic relationship. However, for most theoretical approaches there may be a particular emphasis in the initial stage for engaging the client in a good therapeutic relationship. Some approaches may focus on the therapeutic relationship between client and therapist as the work of the therapy, either at one or some points, or throughout the programme of therapy. The quality of alliance early in the therapy programme is a predictor of outcome, however there is less clarity on association of the alliance with outcome at the mid- or end-point of therapy. It is important to focus on the in-the-moment experience of any strain or rupture in the alliance, and address these difficulties or the client may withdraw or even discontinue their therapy.

WHICH CLIENTS BENEFIT MOST?

In theory all clients benefit from the establishment of a strong alliance, and this alliance will help to underpin the therapy work. The alliance is not static, however; it evolves and fluctuates in strength and quality as the therapy continues, and as progress, challenges or strains occur. Implications arising are that the therapist needs to adapt to the client and that the alliance may require renegotiation over time.

CASE STUDY
The Client

Mia was a 29-year-old single woman. She had been made redundant two years previously from her job as a legal secretary, after which it had taken her several months to secure another job, with lower status and pay. She was coming to therapy due to panic attacks experienced during the past two months. Her panic attacks were sometimes triggered by an imminent social occasion such as a gathering of friends at a bar or restaurant, and sometimes spontaneous. They focused on her fear of dizziness or breathlessness causing a panic attack during which she feared she would faint or collapse on the floor and others would judge her as weak, pathetic, or inferior. Mia's partner, with whom she found it difficult to be assertive, had expressed irritation at her avoidance of some social occasions. Mia's relationship with her mother, whom she described as anxious, was good, and she said her father was domineering and critical of her and her elder sister.

The Therapy

The course of therapy

Following assessment of her difficulties and situation, Mia and the therapist agreed that CBT was the theoretical approach of choice, and a course of 10 sessions of CBT was contracted. Two change goals were mutually agreed on: eliminating her panic attacks, and eliminating avoidance of social occasions.

In the first treatment session, the therapist mapped out Mia's panic circle of a recent panic attack to demonstrate the possible catastrophic misinterpretations of her bodily sensations (interpreting dizziness or breathlessness as a sign that she was about to have a panic attack and collapse or faint rather than as a sign or anxiety or of a physical sensation, such as hunger). The therapist then socialized Mia to the CBT approach and model, as well as identifying her misinterpretations of dizziness/breathlessness (I am going to have a panic attack and faint or collapse); her beliefs (I'm weak; They will think I'm weak/pathetic; I'm not good enough) and safety behaviours (taking deep breaths, avoiding feared situations). Mia completed a panic diary listing misinterpretations for homework.

Session 2 used the panic episode recorded in Mia's diary to map out her panic circle again, using verbal and behavioural reattribution techniques to focus on her key beliefs. Homework consisted of maintaining Mia's panic diary and conducting a behavioural experiment to drop using deep breaths at the onset of dizziness or breathlessness. During the middle part of therapy in sessions 3–6, Mia and the therapist continued the techniques used in session 2, also introducing behavioural experiments using exposure, developing use of techniques as required. Mia's frequency of panic attacks had reduced by session 6 and she was beginning to return to some of her less feared social situations, although was still avoidant of particularly difficult social situations.

The final part of therapy in sessions 7–10 continued to challenge remaining beliefs, worked on remaining avoidance and safety behaviours, and introduced work on relapse prevention. At the conclusion of her final review session, Mia's panic attacks had ceased and she had been able to return to all but one of her most feared social situations. Mia considered that she had learned strategies for handling her panic-provoking situations, and her therapy ended at the 10-session point.

How the client and therapist worked together in the alliance

In gathering background information as part of the assessment session, the therapist was warm and empathic and made observations relevant to

(Continued)

(Continued)

the alliance. First, from Mia's language and responses the therapist noticed that her understanding of counselling and psychotherapy seemed to be as an advice-giving process in which she would be a passive recipient. Second, the therapist became aware of herself fulfilling the role of 'friendly-dominant' therapist to Mia's 'friendly-submissive' client in terms of their respective interpersonal styles. Third, the use of humour by Mia, and her own response suggested a way of increasing rapport by use of appropriate humour. The therapist therefore used every opportunity in the assessment session to negotiate with, and encourage, Mia's collaboration and by including Mia's views and preferences in the suggested treatment approach and plan for recommending traditional CBT, which Mia clearly accepted with enthusiasm.

In the first treatment session the therapist used the topic of Mia's change goals as the vehicle for a negotiated discussion, at the same time managing the tension of emphasizing the collaborative nature of CBT and the therapy process, whilst encouraging Mia to contribute her own views and opinions about her therapy and goals. Their discussion resulted in adjustment on the part of both Mia and her therapist. The therapist had verbalized the view that Mia's panic was part of a broader self-esteem issue, possibly suggesting longer-term goals. Mia, however, strongly wished to remain focused on achieving more modest change goals of eliminating her panic attacks and avoidance of social occasions, which were the final change goals mutually agreed as a result of their discussion.

As the therapy progressed, the therapist continued to emphasize and encourage Mia's active collaboration: during agenda setting; by using Socratic dialogue in a collaborative way (encouraging Mia to be active in modifying her behaviour and cognition); inviting her to actively suggest homework tasks; asking Mia to summarize her main points of learning, and overall reaction to the session at the end of each session, which could then feed in to the agenda of the next session.

When socializing Mia to the CBT approach and model, and then throughout the therapy programme, the therapist was at pains to negotiate, and then explicitly discuss with Mia the mutually agreed tasks (or activities) they would each be carrying out, the reasons for and value in carrying them out, and how their respective tasks impacted on each other, in seeking to achieve her change goals.

Mia readily engaged in verbal reattribution (thought challenging); however, she showed some reservations about engaging in panic induction behavioural techniques (inducing in session sensations similar to the dizziness and breathlessness experienced by Mia in anticipation of, or in the event of a panic attack); and was fearful and reluctant to participate in behavioural experiments to expose her to avoided social situations. The therapist was equally aware of the particular benefit of behavioural experiments in working with panic disorder. This impasse reached a point in session 6 where a strain had occurred in the alliance between Mia and the therapist, which seemed to be holding back further progress, and threatened Mia's withdrawal from full participation in the therapy.

The therapist suggested a discussion with Mia to 'step outside' and reflect on their alliance and the issue of Mia's fear of the behavioural experiments and the therapist's belief that these techniques would be helpful. Mia agreed. The discussion focused on how they experienced their working together and how they might better understand together and deal with this issue. Mia's thoughts and feelings about the difficulty were explicitly elicited, and the therapist outlined her own understanding and feelings to emphasize their co-creation of the current difficulty. Mia seemed relieved that they were addressing this point, admitting that she was fearful about 'failing' the behavioural tasks, and was unclear of the full extent of what would be asked of her. The therapist realized from this feedback that she needed to be clearer on operationalizing the behavioural tasks with Mia; working with Mia on breaking them down to more manageable tasks; introducing coping strategies to enable Mia to enter the behavioural experiments; and working empathically on eliciting Mia's trust and engagement in overcoming her feelings of vulnerability about the tasks. The outcome was that Mia did engage with the tasks and was largely able to overcome the avoidance through use of the whole spectrum of techniques employed in their work; although there remained a social situation which she was unable to enter, she was continuing to work on this. They both voiced recognition of a greater feeling of working together on Mia's difficulties as a result of their discussion, and the alliance appeared to have been strengthened following the strain it had experienced.

REFERENCES

[1] Gelso, C. J. and Carter, J. (1985) 'The relationship in counseling and psychotherapy: components, consequences, and theoretical antecedents', *Counseling Psychology, 13*, 155–243.

[2] Gelso, C. J. and Carter, J. (1994) 'Components of the psychotherapy relationship: their interaction and unfolding during treatment', *Journal of Counseling Psychology, 41*, 296–306.

[3] Zetsel, E. R. (1956) 'Current concepts of transference', *International Journal of Psychoanalysis, 37*, 369–75.

[4] Greenson, R. R. (1967) *The Technique and Practice of Psychoanalysis*, Vol. 1. New York: International Universities Press.

[5] Flückiger, C., Del Re, A. C., Wampold, B. E., Symonds, D. and Horvath, A. O. (2011) 'How central is the alliance in psychotherapy? A multilevel longitudinal meta-analysis', *Journal of Counseling Psychology, 59(1)*, 10–17.

[6] Norcross, J. C. and Wampold, B. E. (2011) 'Evidence-based therapy relationships: research conclusions and clinical practices', *Psychotherapy, 48(1)*, 98–102.

[7] Bordin, E. S. (1979) 'The generalizability of the psychoanalytic concept of the working alliance', *Psychotherapy: Theory, Research & Practice, 16*, 252–60.

[8] Bordin, E. S. (1994) 'Theory and research on the therapeutic working alliance: new directions', in A. O. Horvath and L. S. Greenberg (eds), *The Working Alliance: Theory, Research and Practice*. New York: Wiley. pp. 13–37.

[9] Haugh, S. and Paul, S. (eds) (2008) *The Therapeutic Relationship: Perspectives and Themes*. Ross-on-Wye: PCCS Books.

[10] Muran, J. C. and Barber, J. P. (2010) *The Therapeutic Alliance: An Evidence-Based Guide to Practice*. New York: Guilford Press.

[11] Norcross, J. C. (2011) *Psychotherapy Relationships that Work: Evidence-Based Responsiveness*, 2nd edn. New York: Oxford University Press.

[12] Muran, J. C., Safran, J. D. and Eubanks-Carter, C. (2010) 'Developing therapist abilities to negotiate alliance ruptures', in J. C. Muran and J. P. Barber (eds), *The Therapeutic Alliance: An Evidence-Based Guide to Practice*. New York: Guilford Press.

[13] Hatcher, R. L. (2010) 'Alliance theory and measurement', in J. C. Muran and J. P. Barber (eds), *The Therapeutic Alliance: An Evidence-Based Guide to Practice*. New York: Guilford Press.

[14] Dryden, W. (2008a) 'The therapeutic alliance as an integrating framework', in W. Dryden and A. Reeves (eds), *Key Issues for Counselling in Action*, 2nd edn. London: Sage.

[15] Dryden, W. (2008b) 'Tailoring your counselling approach to different clients', in W. Dryden and A. Reeves (eds), *Key Issues for Counselling in Action*, 2nd edn. London: Sage.

SUGGESTED READING

Dryden, W. and Reeves, A. (eds) (2008) *Key Issues for Counselling in Action*, 2nd edn. London: Sage. This is an excellent book for counselling, counselling psychology and psychotherapy practitioners, which takes a broad and integrated approach to the process of counselling and therapy. It uses the therapeutic alliance as a framework within which many relevant issues and strategies for practitioners are covered, including those for forming and enhancing, as well as dealing with disruptions to, the therapeutic alliance.

Haugh, S. and Paul, S. (eds) (2008) *The Therapeutic Relationship: Perspectives and Themes*. Ross-on-Wye: PCCS Books. This book takes a thoughtful look at the therapeutic relationship through research, the main therapy traditions and through other relevant and cross-theoretical aspects and issues.

Muran, J. C. and Barber, J. P. (2010) *The Therapeutic Alliance: An Evidence-Based Guide to Practice*. New York: Guilford Press. Eminent experts across the field review the evidence for, and provide their perspectives on, the therapeutic alliance. Their discussions on how to foster, develop, maintain and renegotiate therapeutic relationships provide valuable insights for practitioners, trainees and trainers.

Norcross, J. C. (2011) *Psychotherapy Relationships that Work: Evidence-Based Responsiveness*, 2nd edn. New York: Oxford University Press. Provides a review of the effective 'elements' of the therapeutic relationship (or what works, and what works in adapting to the client) found by the latest American Psychological Association task force investigating evidence-based practices in psychotherapy. Each 'element' is the subject of a chapter that addresses the relevant research, clinical examples, contribution of the client and limitations of the research, and offers points for therapeutic practice, primarily from the perspective of the therapist's contribution.

DISCUSSION ISSUES

1. Can the therapeutic relationship be fully conceptualized within a particular theoretical approach? How much is your perspective on the therapeutic relationship influenced by your own personal relationships?
2. Alliance theory is essentially a theory of therapy as purposive work. Discuss.
3. What are the implications for the client and therapist respectively of a fully negotiated alliance?
4. To what extent is tailoring the therapy to the client helpful? How might the therapist know when adapting to the client is helpful or unhelpful?

PART 1

Psychodynamic Approaches

3

Adlerian Counselling and Psychotherapy

Jenny Warner and Gerhard Baumer

Adlerian therapy is a cognitive approach, which means that clients are encouraged to look at and understand, and possibly change, the ideas and beliefs that they hold about themselves, the world and how they will behave in that world. In addition, Adlerian therapists set assignments with their clients that challenge existing ideas and beliefs and which represent changes in their habitual pattern of behaviour. The Adlerian approach has an optimistic view that people have created their own per–sonalities and therefore can choose to change. Clients are encouraged to value their strengths and to acknowledge that they are equal members of society who can make a worthwhile contribution.

DEVELOPMENT OF THE THERAPY

Alfred Adler, who was a medical doctor, developed a new school of psychology called Individual Psychology in 1911 in Vienna. He had previously been part of Sigmund Freud's Psychoanalytical Society but broke away from Freud when the two men's approaches became too divergent. Adler wanted to show his holistic approach to personality – the word *individual* really means indivisible. As a physician, Adler became interested in patients who were suffering from physical ailments that did not have a physical cause; we call these functional disorders or hysterical conditions. Adler himself was a brilliant, insightful practitioner who did not formalize his therapy approach but talked about patients in his lectures to show how they demonstrated his theory of personality and his philosophy of society. After the First World War he changed his focus from working with neurotic patients to working with people who could change society; he considered that teachers who were able to influence children should be the focus of his attention and he held open teacher–child coun–selling sessions. Adler reluctantly left Vienna in 1934 and settled in America, as did many of his followers. Some Adlerians went to Europe and practised and taught

Individual Psychology to medical and educational professionals, and several institutes and Adlerian societies were set up. During the Second World War Adlerian activity ceased in Europe, but it later revived and Adlerian approaches are now practised in many Western and Eastern European countries, in Japan, Scandinavia, Australia, USA and many other countries. Nowadays the term Individual Psychology is little used and the approach is called Adlerian. The Adlerian Society (of the UK) and Institute for Individual Psychology (ASIIP) website has details of counselling training courses in Buckinghamshire, Cambridge and Wales.

THEORY AND BASIC CONCEPTS

Holistic

Adler's view was that people's actions, thoughts and feelings had to be seen as one consistent whole. People choose to be the sort of people they are through trial and error as children and consistently remain those sorts of people throughout their lives. Adler called this consistency their style of life, pattern of life or *lifestyle*; people form views of themselves and of the world and the people in it and how they will behave in that world. The ideas and beliefs in the lifestyle are generalizations: for example, I always have to be better than others or I always have to be liked by everyone. Adler was not so concerned with what people inherited from their parents as with what they did with their genetic inheritance and how they responded in their own unique way to their environment. He considered individuals were each responsible for the sort of people they were.

Social

Adler suggested that, as people were social in nature, their behaviour had to be interpreted in a social context. He was therefore interested in how they behaved in the first group to which they belonged – their family of origin – and how they behaved in their school groups as children and their work groups as adults; and how they behaved within their friendship groups and within intimate relationships. The human baby is born in an inferior position, quite helpless and dependent on others for survival; this dependence lasts well into teenage years in Western society. Wise parenting will enable children to grow to feel that they are social equals in their families; social equals have equal rights, equal respect and share equal responsibilities. Children who belong as equals expect their views to be taken into account whenever decisions are being made that affect the whole family; an example would be family holidays or moving house. They expect to be spoken to with respect and treated with respect. They are willing to take their share of chores and responsibilities to enable family life to run smoothly. The parents will have the same expectations of the children. The parents will not pamper the child; that is, they will not do anything for the child that the child can do for him or herself. Pampering is the most disabling form of parenting and perpetuates the child's initial feelings of inferiority. Spoiled children who are used to getting their own way from doting parents find school and adult life rather hostile; fellow pupils and teachers and work colleagues are not willing to give in to them. Children who are made to feel special and superior to others will also find school and adult life difficult. Peer groups may not want to give that person special status and will be irritated by their attention-seeking behaviour. Children who act in a superior way will find themselves isolated and their peers will feel put down by them.

Teleological

This word comes from the Greek word *teleo*, meaning goal. Adler thought that all behaviour had a purpose. In order to understand someone's behaviour we must know what goal they are unconsciously seeking by behaving in this way. What is the purpose, for example, of always being late? People will give all sorts of excuses but the Adlerian psychologist will want to know that person's goal. Are they putting other people's affection for them to the test wanting to know whether people will still like them even if they are always late? Or are they late to show people how busy they are? The underpinning belief is that people will only know how busy I am if I am consistently late for all my appointments. Or perhaps they need to show that they will always do what they want to do; that they are in control and no one can make them be on time. Lateness could serve some other purpose. The goals are unconscious so the person will be unaware of the goal of his or her chronic lateness and the underlying belief that supports the behaviour. Adlerians call the beliefs that underpin people's goals of behaviour *private logic*; this is because the belief makes sense to the person and is logical to them, but in fact to everyone else it is neither logical nor common sense. Not everyone would consider it necessary to be late for all appointments in order to show people how busy they were.

Psychological disturbance

As described already, some children are ill-prepared for the demands of life. The pampered child might find learning at school difficult, making decisions impossible and gaining independence unattainable. The pampered child will have been used to parents doing things for him and guiding and protecting him; the consequence of this is that as the child grows older he will become less and less confident about his ability to face challenges and make decisions. He will not have had the learning experience of making independent decisions and living through the consequences of those decisions; he will not have experienced learning through his mistakes, and discovering that mistakes are okay. It could happen that a child such as this starts to make decisions as a teenager when his parents can no longer exert total control over him and these decisions are unwise; this merely confirms the parents' and the child's belief that the child needs help and is incapable of being wise. There are many pampered adults who rely on others stronger than themselves to make their decisions for them; they may not have done well at school and may not be able to get a job. They will feel alienated from society and could be led into crime, develop chronic illness, avoid social relationships and, most testing of all, be unable to maintain an intimate relationship. They have a sense that they are not realizing their potential but they have not had the experience of doing things for themselves and have a great fear of the unknown which keeps them just where they are. Spoilt children will find that the world does not give them what they want; this makes them resentful as they were always made to feel very special and powerful by their families and unbelievably the world just treats them as one of the crowd. They find ways to feel powerful and, if they are really angry, to get even. Crime is one activity that these people find satisfying; they might see something they want, so they take it; this makes them feel powerful. They might also want to feel that they are getting their own back on a society that has let them down and has not acknowledged how special they are. They may have difficulties making relationships with others because they want to be in a position of power. They will expect that the temper tantrums they had as children which terrorized their doting parents into giving into them should work with their friends; as a result friends could drift away and intimate partners leave them. They would then experience a sense of loss of their special place, and they might take alcohol or drugs excessively in order to avoid feeling the pain of their loss. These people feel inferior because they have never experienced social equality; they only know about competition and acting as superior to, or feeling inferior to others. Adler described a person's sense of equality as *gemeinschaftsgefuhl*, which does not translate easily into English. It means that a person feels he or she has an equal place in society and a sense of belonging to the community. Adler preferred the translation of '*social interest*'. Each child is born with the potential to develop social interest and with the appropriate upbringing this will develop. Those children who grew up to feel inferior may need therapy to become aware of the beliefs and ideas they have about themselves which are causing them discouragement. They need to understand their lifestyle and their private logic and the mistaken goals and hidden purposes of their behaviour. They then have the opportunity to change their beliefs and their behaviour. Adler considered that each person has chosen to be the person that he or she is; we are the authors of our own creations of ourselves. This approach is very optimistic because it gives people the opportunity to change themselves if they wish. However, change is not easy for an adult; we are all expert at being our old selves and will be clumsy beginners at being a different version of ourselves.

PRACTICE

The goals of the Adlerian approach are:

- to uncover with clients their mistaken goals and underlying ideas so that they understand their own unique lifestyle
- to encourage clients to acknowledge that they are social equals.

This is achieved in four phases of therapy:

- establishing a relationship
- gathering information in order to understand the client
- giving insight
- encouraging reorientation.

Establishing a relationship

The first phase is to establish a relationship of social equals in which the partners have equal respect, equal rights and equal responsibilities. Most clients have never experienced such a relationship before and the relationship with their therapist may be their first democratic relationship. The therapist acts as a good parent, accepting the client unconditionally, developing with the client an understanding of who she is and encouraging the client by pointing out her strengths and abilities, and believing that the client can make changes if she wishes. The client needs to feel safe to explore her innermost thoughts and express deep feelings with the therapist. The therapist will also expect respectful behaviour from the client so that agreements about appointments and payments are kept. The client and therapist will need to be sure that they share common goals for the therapy. The therapist must not play games with the client, for example by getting into power games and fighting with the client, or by being controlled or pleased by the client.

Gathering information

The second phase, of understanding the person, will start as soon as the client enters the room. Adler was reported to be expert at gathering information about the client by observing the way the client entered the room and how he sat down and how he spoke and behaved in the sessions. Direct questions are asked by the therapist, not only about why the person has come for therapy but also about himself generally; a great deal can be learned about a client by what he tells and does not tell, as well as by the content of his answers. The therapist will be interested in the client's participation in the workplace, his friends and social life and if he has an intimate relationship and how it is going on. The therapist will also want to know about the person's family of origin; it was in this family that the client developed his lifestyle, containing his thoughts, goals and feelings. The therapist will ask him to describe his siblings and parents when he was a child. He chose to be a particular child in his family through trial and error. His siblings were also making choices about the sort of children they would be. The therapist and the client will be beginning to develop hypotheses about the personality that the child developed. Was this client an eldest child who was threatened by a younger brother or sister who had decided to strive to be better than his or her siblings and in the process lost no time in putting the other siblings down? Or was this client a pampered youngest child who had two parents and older siblings doing things for him and over-protecting him?

It is now necessary for the therapist to gather information from another source. The client will be asked to give a few early memories: Adler discovered that people remember things that reinforce the beliefs and ideas in their private logic; the memories are symbolic representations of these ideas and beliefs. The memory may be of an insignificant occurrence in the client's childhood and yet out of all the things that have happened to him, he produces that memory; that memory is produced because it has particular significance to him and symbolizes a belief maybe about himself or about the world or about how he should behave in his perceived world. Dreams are also used for interpretation as they too contain symbolic representations of a person's private logic. Together the therapist and the client interpret the early memories and dreams.

Giving insight

The third phase is giving insight. The therapist will have formed some hypotheses about the client's view of himself, his view of the world and his unconscious decisions about how to move through life. These guesses need to be checked out with the client. The client can agree or disagree. Very often the therapist will know that she has guessed correctly when the client shows recognition either verbally or through a non-verbal response, such as a smile. The client needs to own the insight and the therapist would not impose her suggestions, as this is a working partnership. The feelings, beliefs and ideas are recognized by the client, who also has an understanding as to how he came to have these, so that there is no mystery. The client may recognize how his private logic has restricted him and may want to change his ideas and goals; the therapist may have to challenge the client's goals and ideas so that the client can align his goals with common sense and not with his private logic. The therapist will help the client see how his presenting problems fit in with his lifestyle: for example, if you are a person who believes that life is danger-ous then you will be very frightened of new and demanding situations and may have presented with a problem of feeling stuck. If you are a person who likes to be better than everyone else then it is likely you will end up lonely and without real friends.

Encouraging reorientation

The reorientation phase then starts and this is where the client has the hardest work. The therapist will be there, guiding and encouraging as the client finds a way to change. The therapist will encourage the client by pointing out the client's strengths and by believing that the client will find a way to move on. Progress can be sporadic and the therapist is there to point out when the mistaken ideas are still holding the client back. Attainable assignments are set with the client; these challenge the private logic and break through blocks that the client may have had in his life. They are new behaviours for the client and the therapist will be able to hear how the client experi-enced a new behaviour and will congratulate the client on achieving such a change. There is no set format for a session. Adlerian therapy respects the individual and so clients can lead the session at the beginning if they wish, bringing to the session what they want to talk about. The therapist may refer to previous sessions if there are issues that are common; in fact there usually are recurrent themes running through all the sessions because they are looking at the consistent lifestyle. The therapist may end the session in order to finish on time and to set assignments if appropriate.

WHICH CLIENTS BENEFIT MOST?

The Adlerian approach uses verbal descriptions from the client, and therapist and client explore interpretations with the therapist wanting recognition from the client to confirm that they are on the right track. This requires from the client a certain level of language ability. I (J.W.) once described the Adlerian approach to a member of the public at a conference, and when I had finished she said, 'Oh, so you do it with words' – other stalls were using crystals, colours or were looking into people's eyes, etc. Adlerians do not always use words; psychodrama, art therapy and non-verbal exercises are also used. However, the client needs to talk about and understand what they discover about themselves during their art or drama. When the Adlerian family counsellor works with children she meets the whole family and may need to speak to the children only to check their goals; the rest of the work is done with the parents or carers. This can also be done with the families and carers of adults who do not understand language. The Adlerian approach is based on a distinct philosophy of human life – that people want to belong as equals and a society of equals allows each person to develop to their full potential. If a person agrees with this goal for society and for its members, then they will be able to work with an Adlerian therapist. Clients who are able to accept responsibility for their behaviour and who are willing to take risks and make changes will benefit from the approach.

CASE STUDY
The Client

Mary was 28 when she was referred by a psychiatrist with depression and suicidal tendencies.

Mary told me that she felt very low and exhausted and had a sense of emptiness. She worried a lot, her negative thoughts going round in vicious circles; one of these thoughts was of committing suicide. She had vague guilt feelings. She had lost her appetite, slept badly and had no interest in sex. She added that she was no longer able to concentrate and found it difficult to follow the lessons at the adult education centre where she had just started doing some A levels. In class Mary believed she had nothing to contribute and when she was asked a question she would blush and stammer or just remain silent. She felt stupid and inferior to the other students so she avoided contact with them and as a result felt very lonely. She had thought about leaving the course.

(Continued)

(Continued)

I wanted to find out more about her situation now. I looked at her strengths: what things made her an attractive, useful or at least tolerable person? After some hours of exploration it was obvious she liked to please people; she also looked after people and felt responsible. I acknowledged these strengths. For Adlerians, **encouragement** is quite important; I used it to stabilize her low self-esteem and to start her thinking that she could make a useful contribution. Looking at Mary's positive side gave me an idea of her potential growth areas. During a long period of therapy this would give both of us positive goals to work towards and would constantly reaffirm to Mary that she had value as a person.

During further sessions I learned that she had been in a relationship with a man for five years. When they first met he used to be very active and sociable, studying Social Science and working in a night-club. Over the past few years he had given up his studies, played strange music with strange friends, consumed alcohol and cannabis, and earned money at a nearby pub helping in the kitchen. Mary was very unhappy about the way he was living his life and about their situation, and felt they no longer had much in common. She had trained as a pharmacy assistant and worked part-time in a pharmacy; she complained about the poor wages and the amount of work she had to do because of staff shortages, but she could not leave her job because she did not want to disappoint her boss.

Here is her **family constellation**: Mary was brought up on a working farm that her mother had inherited. Mother was described as quiet and very caring. Father was seen as authoritarian; he got cross easily, shouted and punished the children; he was moody and unpredictable. Mary tried to avoid him. He liked spending money on his own pleasures and bought big cars, bred horses and dogs, was a member of the local hunt and threw parties for its members. After some years the farm was run down financially and it was sold, with her father carrying on as tenant for a while.

Understanding the client

Mary had four siblings: a sister five years older, a brother 18 months older, a sister two years younger and a brother 10 years younger. Her older sister, Susan, was a bully, stood up to her father, and dominated the younger siblings. Mary saw her as very selfish. This was Susan's reaction to being dethroned; she had been an only child for three-and-a-half years and had lost her special place. Susan left home when she was 18, married and was rarely seen at home from then on. The older brother was described as very sensitive and as children he and Mary were very close. As a teenager he committed suicide. His death was still an unresolved problem for Mary when she came for therapy.

Mary used to like looking after her younger sister, Lizzie. Lizzie had been the youngest for eight years and was very sociable. The baby brother, Nick, was very pampered by his father and had become dependent on him. Mary was very angry with her father and tried to influence him but she did not succeed. It appeared from the family constellation that Mary had chosen to be the good child, the responsible one.

I asked Mary for three early recollections in order to learn more about her lifestyle. This was the first memory given: 'I was about five years old and I was sitting on the back of a pony and was very proud. All of a sudden there was a loud noise; the pony startled and I fell off. My sister laughed at me. I felt very ashamed and incompetent.'

The second memory was thus: 'I was about eight years old. The family was all in the living room. All of a sudden my older sister stood up, walked over to my father, who had nodded off behind his newspaper, and demanded her pocket money. He refused, she insisted and there was a terrible row. I was sitting next to Mother, clinging on to her arm in despair. My sister left the room, slamming the door after my father had tried to kick her. I think my sister was a trouble-maker and I hated her for that. It was a spoilt Sunday afternoon.'

The third memory was: 'I was about eight years old and I was helping Mother in the kitchen. It was a really bright day and I looked out of the window and saw my brothers and sisters playing out there. I felt very excluded and sad; I felt envious and thought life is unfair.' And she added: 'I always helped Mother. Helping in the kitchen was my job. It was a safe place. I used to dream a lot while I was doing my chores.'

We have seen that in Mary's family constellation she chose to be the good child and from these early recollections we can also see her belief system giving more information about her view of herself, what she expects from others and how she moves through life. The first early recollection shows the whole tragedy. When I am active and try to have fun something might happen that will spoil it. The message is: life is dangerous, expect the unexpected to happen and do not trust people. The second memory confirms this view of people and events and shows Mary inactive and frightened. It also shows how powerful men are and may indicate that Mary sees herself (or women) as a victim. The third memory shows Mary withdrawing from real life and living in a fantasy world. It is important for her to feel safe and she lacks courage to join in. The price she has to pay is sadness. She sees her life as a burden and her frustration and anger are a consequence of this. She is not talking in that early recollection; Mary has not learned how to express herself.

The Therapy

During the first phase of therapy we worked a lot on practical problems that she was experiencing at the time – how to make contact with other people and how to react in certain situations. We discussed her self-image, her expectations and how she behaved in her lessons. She developed a more realistic view of her situation and was more connected with reality. She got rid of the anger she had been keeping in for years. I was empathetic, supportive and encouraging whenever possible. She felt better and three times during the first year she stopped coming. Each time she came back, depressed again. It was not easy for her to trust but we had some serious discussions about the fact that she still had a lot to do in therapy, so she finally agreed to make a full commitment. After our relationship became stable I offered her a place in a group in addition

(Continued)

(Continued)

to one-to-one therapy. This was quite a challenge for her. Her social interest or feeling of belonging was limited and it was not easy for her to talk with others about herself. At first she was very quiet, then she gave others good advice. She had to learn that it is not always appropriate to give advice, at least not before people have reached a certain level of awareness. She slowly gained insight and learned how to share her experiences with others. She became more sociable. She was also more active and her self-confidence grew. We were now able to work on her past, her childhood and her family experiences; this was painful for her.

At the end of the second year we went through a difficult phase. She was able to cope with her mother's death but it was too much that her father started to spend the children's inheritance. He even sold most of their antique furniture. At the same time she learned that her boyfriend was in love with somebody else, and the friendship with her best friend became unstable. Mary had a very serious setback. I acted in the next group meeting, expressed my fears and asked her to promise not to commit suicide for the next six months. It took the whole evening for her to agree. I knew she would not let anybody down once she had given her word. We could now go on to solve her problems. She was really angry with me; she felt I had forced her and that caused a strong father transference where she reacted to me as though I was her father. It took more than six months for her to be able to accept my intervention. Mary made progress again. She did well in her exams and made some new friends. She left her partner and found a new boyfriend. She saw that her mother merely had limitations and was not a victim. She discovered aspects of herself which reminded her of her father. It became obvious that she was seeking power and she also needed to improve her tolerance. In the fourth year of therapy she became more and more confident. Her social life improved and her mood became stable. At the same time she decided to study agriculture and education. We both agreed at that point that we could finish the therapy. The last thing I heard was that she had started teaching at an agricultural college and that she was living a busy and fulfilled life.

SUGGESTED READING

Adler, A. (2009) *Understanding Human Nature,* trans. Colin Brett. Oxford: Oneworld Publications. This book is based on a series of lectures that Adler gave at the People's Institute in Vienna. The aim of the book is to enable people to understand themselves and each other better. This is a new translation from the original, by Colin Brett.

Adler, A. (2009) *What Life Could Mean to You,* trans. Colin Brett. Oxford: Oneworld Publications. Once again, Colin Brett, in translating Adler's original text, has produced what is probably the most readable book available on Adler's theory and practice.

Mosak, H. H. and Maniacci, M. P. (1999) *A Primer of Adlerian Psychology*. Philadelphia: Brunner/Mazel. This book is written by two very experienced Adlerians and covers the basic tenets of Adlerian psychology.

Oberst, U. E. and Stewart, A. E. (2003) *Adlerian Psychotherapy: An Advanced Approach to Individual Psychology*. Hove: Brunner–Routledge. This is a fine overview of Adlerian therapy and counselling, including an advanced version of the theory which relates to contemporary family life.

DISCUSSION ISSUES

1. Many contemporary psychological and psychotherapeutic approaches have adopted Adler's ideas without acknowledgement. Describe three examples and discuss.
2. The Adlerian counsellor will want to explore the client's childhood with the client. Why?
3. All experience is subjective. How does this idea affect the way Adlerian practitioners think about people and work with them?
4. Early memories provide a window onto the personality. Discuss with an example.

4

Psychodynamic (Freudian) Counselling and Psychotherapy

Lesley Murdin

INTRODUCTION

Freudian psychodynamic therapy is the practice of coming to understand what goes on in your mind beyond the edge of your consciousness. Sometimes you think or say something and wonder 'what came over me?' What came over you was an unconscious wish that bore little or no relation to what you consciously want to do. Unconscious wishes become understandable in relation to two key themes. The infant has desires that can be described as sexual and they coalesce in the Oedipus complex, which describes through the myth the child's emotional connections, anxieties and desires with each of the parents or significant others.

A psychodynamic therapist seeks to understand the effect of these early relations on the adult in the present and therefore for the future.

This does not mean that the present or the conscious intention is ignored. This therapy is mainly concerned with the present and seeks to find ways of making the past a help not a hindrance. The name implies the dynamic nature of the psyche in which conflict between wishes and demands causes suffering. Conflicts are brought into the open because they are repeated and repetitions are emphasised in a paradoxical process of leaving the past behind.

DEVELOPMENT OF THE THERAPY

Psychodynamic therapy was given a coherent body of theory by Sigmund Freud (1856–1939). Freud was trained as a doctor and his theory takes account of the needs and demands of the body although he developed a 'talking therapy'. Freud saw himself as a scientist and his ideas were derived from observation. He was ready to change his view if observation led to a different conclusion. The value of talking emerged with Josef Breuer, whose patient lost her symptoms by remembering difficulties with her father. Freud and Breuer published an account of her therapy[1] and so founded the modern discipline.

Freud analysed his own thoughts and dreams and this self-analysis formed the basis of his theory. He discovered longings that underlie oedipal relationships and although he was not able to show how this works for the woman, he established a theory that feminists could modify.

Freud's ideas have led to contemporary models. The earliest divergences were from his own colleagues, Carl Jung and Alfred Adler. Important for Freud was his arrival in England and his reception in the United States, which made him one of the most influential thinkers of the twentieth century. His works have been translated into most languages but the translation into English by James and Alix Strachey enabled English speakers to know and understand the theory. Later, Carl Rogers and others not calling themselves psychodynamic, followed. Most recently the French school led by Jacques Lacan proposed a review of the theory of desire.

THEORY AND BASIC CONCEPTS

Following Freud, psychodynamic theory recognises that more goes on in the mind than the individual can think consciously. Freud used the image of a horse and a rider. The conscious mind is carried along by the horse whose thoughts are unknown, only guessed or assumed. What Freud saw in each individual was a struggle about who was to be in charge: horse or rider. If an individual is willing to explore his own mind he may be able to guide the horse, whereas the person who goes on with all his power in the horse beneath him may be taken in any direction at any speed.

Questioning defences

This unconscious material is not inaccessible. It is actively repressed for a purpose. That purpose is defence. Since we live in a society in which we have to coexist with our fellows of both sexes, we repress some of our desires. Psychodynamic therapy proposes that repression is common but does not always increase contentment. When repression is rigid and only painful symptoms show above the parapet, the sufferer is likely to seek help. Anxiety and depression are very common results of repression. Freud pointed out that anxiety may be a sign that something important is being repressed but is not easily kept quiet. If whatever is being repressed can be put into words, the anxiety is lessened and can eventually disappear. This relates to another way in which Freud thought of this process. He defined three areas of the mind, called the ego (I), the superego (the over-I or authority in the mind) and the id (it), which is the part that we do not know.

The psychodynamic therapist uses dreams, slips of the tongue and wandering of the mind when no particular thinking is required. From this material, we might get the idea that most people have suffered some form of abuse from their parents. Freud himself came to a different conclusion which caused great shock to his contemporaries.

He believed that hidden deep within us we still carry that wish of the small child to possess his or her parent of the opposite sex. This is so unacceptable that we all bury this wish and go through many twists and turns in an effort to hide it both from ourselves and from others. So does this matter if it is so hidden from our conscious minds? The psychodynamic therapist thinks that it does.

The Oedipus myth

The main way in which this matters is best understood from a story. This is the myth of Oedipus, in which the baby is left to die on a hillside because a fortune teller said that he would one day kill his father and marry his mother. He is brought up, not knowing his origins, by a shepherd's family, and as a young man he meets his father at a crossroads where they argue and Oedipus kills his father, not knowing who he is. Later, Oedipus solves the riddle of the Sphinx and as a reward is offered the hand of the widowed queen, who is actually his mother. He thus unknowingly fulfils the prophecy. Not knowing is an important part of the story. Many people suffer from a feeling of guilt or inadequacy that seems to have insufficient basis in reality to account for it. This sense of guilt may in some cases relate to the crimes that have only got as far as wishes, rather than being brought to reality.

Guilt

Killing a parent is a crime that is unlikely to be enacted, but people may suffer guilt for the wish to carry it out. Other reasons may arise for these wishes beyond the desire to have one parent all to yourself. Parents can be difficult and dominating, and eventually they will grow old and may well be troublesome for that reason. Here again, the wish to get rid of him or her may be found somewhere in the midst of care and concern that is also genuine. Guilt and self-punishment may be excessive and can be helped when it can be put into words.

Siblings

Oedipus had no brothers and sisters, but writers like Juliet Mitchell have found that oedipal feelings arise in relation to older and younger brothers and sisters and rivalry like that with the parent may become virulent, even violent.

Depression

Depression is another major modern phenomenon that Freud addressed. The cause of depression may be physiological but it may also be psychological, expressing a reaction to loss. The sufferer is managing the effects of losing not only a person but sometimes a stage of life, such as a happy childhood or a satisfying job. It is more difficult if the experiences have been unhappy so that what is lost is only imagined, but the loss is all the greater. Freud pointed out[2] that depression leads to self-hatred and hopelessness. He pointed out that the hatred is appropriate to someone else, not the sufferer, and this is where anger needs to be tracked down. It is very often hidden because it is a dangerous and damaging emotion that cannot be allowed expression in the social life of the family or the workplace.

Sexual abuse

Another area of suffering is the experience of sexual abuse. Certainly in the late nineteenth century there was repression and hypocrisy over sexuality. All societies need to find ways of curbing the free expression of lust and the control of the powerful over the most vulnerable. The twenty-first century has shown that we suffer from the failure to curb sexual feelings even about young children and little girls and boys. Laws and social stigma both seek to restrain these impulses in our animal nature and make us into civilised beings. Psychodynamic theory shows how we suffer as a result of forcing ourselves to follow the rules of society. Freud tells the story of a little boy who was terrified of horses. Freud tracked this fear to his belief that his father would punish him for enjoying time in his mother's bed each morning. There was no sexual abuse in this case unless you would consider his mother's somewhat permissive attitude to the little boy's affection to count as abuse.

Human development

Psychodynamic thinking is helpful in understanding human nature from its beginnings in the new baby. The baby is primarily interested in feeding and in a few areas of physical pain or comfort. The mouth and lips are the main area of pleasure in the first weeks and months and this pleasure in feeding mixed with the pleasure of closeness to the mother never entirely fades in the adult, as smoking and all forms of sucking and biting, eating and drinking still show. For the infant the focus moves to the bowels and the need to learn to control excretion. Because most main carers put a great deal of emphasis on the child learning to use the toilet, the adult retains the significance of holding on and letting go, of making a mess or being rigidly clean. The individual can meet problems in seeking to control himself or his environment. The origins of otherwise inexplicable preoccupations that might bother the adult can be understood. Once understood, these thoughts can be managed.

The third stage of development is the genital stage in which the child of five or so begins to be interested in his own genitals and those of his sister. Freud was primarily able to give an account of the boy's sexual history and found the girl much more of a mystery. The boy is proud of his penis and enters into contests over its size and capacity. The sight of his sister or any girl is liable to make him anxious. It is possible to be without a penis and this is the origin of the castration fear that Freud saw as the foundation of conscience. If I anger my father he will punish me by taking away my penis. This fear is borne out to some extent by observation but it presented a problem in relation to girls. What keeps their impulses in check if they have already lost the penis? Freud left the 'dark continent' of the woman's sexuality to the later feminists such as Karen Horney.

Freud regarded dreams as very important in understanding the parts of the self that were hidden. He saw the dynamic psyche as being often in conflict because we are faced with opposites that seem unreconcilable. For example, the patient may say 'I want to see my daughter but I know she needs to be left alone to make her own life'. Therapists help people to live with conflict and the problematic of life, not saying that these conflicts could ever be removed.

PRACTICE

Goals of the psychodynamic approach

Patterns

The goals of this approach remain those set out by Freud and elaborated by his successors. Most practitioners try to make the unconscious conscious. That means that beneath the everyday thinking about what is happening or has just happened and the worries and preoccupations that people can tell us if they choose to do so, lie patterns of thinking and feeling that have developed into more or less rigid responses. These rigid patterns have developed into sources of pain, confusion, relationship difficulties and blockages. Working out what might be the old pattern that is being reactivated by present events is a large part of the work.

Freud also famously said that the aim of discovering old patterns would be to turn neurotic misery into ordinary human unhappiness: 'much will be gained if we succeed in transforming your hysterical misery into common unhappiness. With a mental life that has been restored to health, you will be better armed against that unhappiness'.[1]

By neurotic misery we might mean the sense of something wrong that need not be if one could only understand it better. The sorts of problems that might be in this category would be depression, anxiety and phobia. These sources of misery leave the sufferer feeling that they are not themselves. They have lost the ordinary person that they used once to be. This is why a person who is depressed feels worse on a beautiful sunny morning: I ought to be happy but I am not. Freud understood that all of us will be unhappy sometimes and unable to enjoy a beautiful morning sometimes, but we know that it is not permanent.

Changes in thinking

Both of these goals illustrate the overriding aim of psychodynamic work, which is to arrive at a position from which we can think about our mental state. You might wonder about the value of thinking when people are often distressed by obsessive rumination about their anxieties. What is desirable is a very specific kind of thinking in which a person can reflect on her own mental state. This requires being able to stand outside it a little. In other words, it becomes possible to recognise that a state of mind is temporary, has causes as well as effects and can be changed. The possibility of change is a great step forward and shows that a person is able to use imagination and perhaps forgiveness directed to herself. This leads to stating another goal, which is to accept guilt for the destructive behaviour that we have all engaged in at times without making one's self into an arch criminal. This is part of the process of allowing one's self to be just ordinary, not particularly bad and not particularly good. That is not to say that there cannot be aims to be good or better but that acceptance of the way one has been up to now is a possible beginning whereas excessive blame is a dead end.

Ordinariness

This is therefore one of the goals of this approach. We all had an area of development in which we moved from making ourselves the centre of the universe to allowing someone else to play a part. The baby begins by thinking that everything in the world is part of herself. This is known as primary **narcissism**. She has to move into a state in which she accepts that someone else controls the source of food and comfort and she is subject to others in these crucial ways. As the child gets older she acquires more power and independence but the early injuries to self-respect can leave wounds that lead to anger and resentment against those who have power in the present. Therapy can help people to understand what is left over from the early struggles and to disentangle it from their current attitudes to others and to their own power.

Rivalry

Rivalry with the parent of the same sex is a particular problem for men and their fathers and may underlie stories of failure where a man is frightened that his father cannot allow him to succeed without being undermined disastrously. Sometimes this might be the case but more often in therapy the father's weakness can be seen to be only in the hopes and fears of the son. Mothers and daughters can struggle with the same contest often over jealousy of youth and beauty. The Oedipus story shows us that people will get entangled with their parents or siblings while they move on from seeing them as the centre of the universe to finding a partner with whom to commit and maybe have children of their own.

External reality

The psychodynamic therapist is interested in both the internal state of mind of the client and also the external context. Freud saw these two strands as both loving and working.[3] One major area of psychodynamic work would be the social context in which people live. D. W. Winnicott is a writer who made very clear that he understood that we all live in a social context. He understood that the ability to attach to others will depend to some extent on the ways in which the mother and father treated the child when she was first ready to love and be loved. The depressed mother and the mother who is unable to see her child's needs as separate from her own, will leave a person with problems that can persist through life and be handed on to the next generation unless they are resolved.

Free association

In order to discover what is hidden from the person, the therapist encourages what is known as 'free association'. By this is meant only that the person should try to say as much as possible of what is in his mind and should notice what he wishes to censor and if possible speak about it. Most people find this very difficult and the impossibility of speaking freely of what is in the mind makes clear straight away the extent of inhibition that most social contexts require. This introduces the person very quickly to the concept of defence. Few therapists would use this kind of technical language but would be helping the client to see that the way in which he reacts to the freedom to speak shows just how little freedom he allows himself.

Since people are told that they need to try to say what is in the mind, the therapist can examine the reasons for silence or a narrative that is always a factual account or a recital of the same woes time after time. The therapist will try to help the person to find what is being avoided.

Dreams

The assessment session is usually considered important to the psychodynamic therapist. One of the reasons is that it is an opportunity to discover which aspects of the past come to mind and are important to the patient. It also allows the therapist to mention dreams, which are a way in which something of the unconscious reveals itself. There are many different ways of approaching dreams. Psychodynamic therapists wait to hear what the dreamer thinks of her dream but will also look for its connection to the past and to the present. Freud taught us to look for a wish in a dream. Does anyone in the dream seem to connect with the therapist and make the dream sound like a comment on the work?

Transference

When a person hopes to change relationships to others, we can see that the relationship that is formed with the therapist will be the material that forms the main part of the work. Therapists hope to be the screen onto which difficulties from the past can be projected. Therapists are both protagonists in the relationship and observers, feeding back to the person some of what is observed about the ways in which others are feared, avoided or attacked. Since she will be confronted by something that is happening or has just happened in the room, this kind of feedback can be powerful.

Counter-transference

The therapist will recognise that sometimes the response does not seem to fit with what she has found to be the reality of her impact on most people. She can check this with her clinical supervisor and if she is sure that the response is leading her to be angry or cold or foolish beyond her normal reality, she can begin to think what this is telling her about the client.

Typical session

There is no set format in this approach. The therapist waits for the client to begin because she does not wish to impose her agenda and stop the free association. She may make some comments to show that she understands or needs help to understand what is being said. Occasionally she will make an **interpretation** in which she tries to elucidate the unconscious wish behind what the client knows. Most interpretations will be based on an attempt to understand the transference that is taking place.

WHICH CLIENTS BENEFIT MOST?

The sorts of problems that can be addressed cover the whole range of mental and emotional difficulties. Because these therapists work with the kind of relationship that the client sets up with them, the special benefit of this approach is found by those who have relationship problems either personal or at work. Some people just feel that life could be better and could offer more. They need to find a new value for themselves and their lives. Sometimes clients find a new approach to values or to spirituality. Because the therapist will work with the relationship in the room, clients will arrive at a better understudying of themselves and therefore of their impact on others. This is demanding and means that those people who are interested in how the mind works will be prepared to consider what they find themselves saying, thinking and feeling. Someone who is hoping only that other people will change is unlikely to find this method helpful.

People suffering from psychosis, in which the client has an entirely different sense of external reality and perhaps hears voices that seem to be real and external, not just part of his own mind, need medication and psychiatric help and will not usually benefit from a psychodynamic approach. Clients need to be interested in the way their mind works. This is the single most important requirement. Someone who is able to and willing to try to put into words what they are thinking and feeling will find this method fascinating and valuable.

CASE STUDY

The Client

George is a good-looking man of 39 who sought therapy because he had just been made redundant from his job as a research assistant because his project had lost its funding. He was very emphatic in the assessment session that he hated women and could not bear to be with a therapist who found this a problem.

(Continued)

(Continued)

His female therapist was quite shocked by the implication that she might be shocked and was more determined to take him on because of this challenge to her tolerance. He described his childhood as 'part of my problem', then added 'well, I suppose you would think so as you are bound to think that the past is important aren't you?' The therapist was not used to what she felt was a degree of attack in the assessment session, when most people are wishing to make themselves seem desirable. She stored this away to see what it might be telling her and asked him to tell her more about this part of the problem. He said that he was 10 when his sister was born and that the first 10 years of his life were a terrible story. He said that his mother had a job as a secretary, which she hated. She was not able to do anything the way she wanted to and she took this out on her family at home, bullying George's father into silence and submission. During a later session he wept when talking about his father. 'I didn't help him; I let her do whatever she liked. I hate her.'

The Therapy

The therapy began with a great deal of material about the way in which the redundancy had been enforced in a remarkably cruel and uncaring way. To begin with the therapist just listened, with the occasional empathic response to show that she understood how painful it all was for George. She began to think about the connection between the boss, Michael, who had carried out most of the process at work, and the way in which George's mother had treated her family. She seemed to have felt that she was not valued at her work and she did not seem to value her little boy either. In fact she often said that if she hadn't rushed home to collect him from the child minder, she would have been able to do much more to reorganise the office and make it work well. She complained about the time that he needed from her to feed him, and also his father – she complained endlessly to both of them. The therapist noted that George came to his session at six o'clock in the evening because he had said that he would like to be able to take on a new job in the day time. It was not very convenient for the therapist but she was willing to do it and go home afterwards to make dinner. George began to worry about it and once or twice at the end of the session he said, 'Now you can have your evening.' The therapist saw the operation of a transference pattern here and said, 'It sounds as though you are worrying that I will not want to see you and will think you are a nuisance, as your mother seemed to do.' He seemed startled by this and said, 'Oh no, it's completely different. You are nothing like my mother.' He then was silent and left a few minutes later. In the next session he came in and sat in silence not looking at her. After a little while the therapist asked him whether he was feeling unhappy about what she had said at the end of the previous session. He twisted his hands together and then said, 'You should know what is true but if you are right and you are like my mother, I can't speak to you any more.' The therapist was pleased that he had said this because she was able to say, 'I think I just said that it might seem to you at that moment that I was like your mother. The important thing is that I am not your mother and we can make this experience be different.'

This was a turning point because, after it, George seemed to be able to understand that he might be encountering aspects of his mother in his present circumstances. He began to see that the people who had made him redundant were responding to external circumstances of their own but were not persecuting him personally. This change in his attitude led him to be less accusing when speaking to new interviewers.

On the other hand, George did not suddenly become happy. He had revived the memory of his very unhappy early years and was able only gradually to find other figures who had welcomed him. He had a good but distant relationship with his sister but was able to talk to her about her experience, which had been different from his but was also very difficult. She had carried their mother's hopes and aspirations and was told that she must be a doctor. She had no interest or enjoyment in scientific subjects and made her way in an arts teaching job. Most importantly the therapist was able to help George to rehabilitate his father. At first he had merely declined to talk about him much but the therapist kept in her mind the sense in which she would be not only like the mother but also like the father. She listened to George's material, particularly to the times when he seemed to despair that she would ever be able to help. There she saw a trace of the helpless father who could do nothing to protect him from the narcissistic self-centred complaints of his mother. He could see that both these transferences were important but that the therapist was more than either of these things. Gradually he was able to begin to think that maybe his parents were more than this. One day he brought an idea that his mother's father had wanted good things for her. She was an only child and she had interpreted whatever he wanted as a demand. Because of this she felt inadequate in being just a secretary and constantly tried to raise it in her own mind into something of greater status. As he talked about his mother he began to consider that maybe she could be forgiven for some of the pressure that she put on herself and on her own children. He could then see that he felt that losing his job was going to be a disaster from the point of view of how she might see him. 'I haven't told her yet,' he admitted, six weeks after the event. 'That shows me how much I dread disappointing her.' All of that seemed to lead to a more affectionate stream of feeling about both his parents.

At about this time he had a dream, which he reported to his therapist: 'I was in a big hall where there were lots of groups of people that I probably knew but what I could see was a baby in one of those high-sided cots that little babies sleep in. The baby was crying and no one was taking any notice. After what seemed a long time a woman came from one of the groups. I don't know who she was but she took the baby out of the cot and it stopped crying. I was so glad, the noise was terrible.' The therapist spent some time asking him to tell her what he thought of the dream and who the people were. He said that he hated to hear the baby crying and it wasn't just that it was an awful noise. He was actually sorry for the loneliness of the infant but had not thought this was a dignified thought to tell his therapist. He looked at her wryly and said, 'You wouldn't have thought that would you? It's my mother again.' 'Well, maybe it is. But someone picks the baby up and makes him feel better. Isn't that your mother too? And I think it may be perhaps what you hope we are doing here as

(Continued)

(Continued)

well?' He looked immensely relieved but said nothing and left at the end of the session without further comment. From then on he was able to speak of his mother with anger but not with the poisonous hatred that he had expressed before. At about this time he began to date a young woman whom he had met before and now wanted to know better. He found a job that was not as senior or well paid as the one he had lost but he said wryly, 'I think I have to start again in more ways than one.' The therapist was pleased because he seemed to have the option of a new beginning but no longer had to leave all the past behind.

REFERENCES

[1] Freud, S. (1895) *Studies in Hysteria*, translated and edited by James Strachey. Pelican Freud 3. London: Pelican Books.
[2] Freud, S. (1917) *Mourning and Melancholia*. Standard Edition 14. London: Hogarth Press.
[3] Freud, S. (1929) *Civilisation and Its Discontents*. Standard Edition 21. London: Hogarth Press.

SUGGESTED READING

Bettelheim, B. (1991) *Freud and Man's Soul*. Harmondsworth: Penguin Books. This text shows the more human as well as the spiritual side of Freud's thinking.

Jacobs, M. (2005) *The Presenting Past*. London: McGraw Hill International. A useful text on human development, showing how the past stays with us.

Murdin, L. (2010) *Understanding Transference*. London: Palgrave. This book looks at the meaning and use of transference in the practice of analytic work.

Sandler, J., Holder, A., Dare, C. and Dreher, U. (2005) *Freud's Models of the Mind*. London: Karnac. This is a good standard work on the main ideas of the Freudian approach.

DISCUSSION ISSUES

1. Why should we accept the concept of the unconscious?
2. What stops a person from changing?
3. Why might we need to know about a person's past losses?
4. Empathy is enough. Is it?

5

Psychodynamic (Jungian) Counselling and Psychotherapy

Jean Stokes

Jungian therapy is a psychodynamic therapy. It places value on the lifelong struggle towards awareness of how our inner and outer worlds relate and on personal growth and development throughout life. The focus is on fostering relatedness both to Self and others. The aim is for the client to become both psychologically stronger and more aware of what is creative and destructive in themselves and their lives. This represents an inner journey of self-discovery and personal meaning, sometimes arduous but profoundly rewarding, and unique to each person. The client is then in a position to pursue psychological growth independently and in their own individual way.

DEVELOPMENT OF THE THERAPY

Carl Gustav Jung (1875–1961) was a Swiss psychiatrist who worked in Zurich with psychotic patients. He also brought to his work a keen interest in myth, philosophy and religion. He became interested in the ideas of the neurologist and psychoanalyst Sigmund Freud, whose ideas about the unconscious he found initially sympathetic to his own. In fact, from 1907 until 1913 he was the key member of Freud's psychoanalytic circle. However, by 1912 he was finding Freud's view of psychological energy as rooted in the sexual instincts too limited and concrete. For Jung it was something more neutral, closer to a life energy, and so capable of taking many forms: biological, psychological, spiritual and moral. Jung's differing views were unacceptable to Freud and the famous rift between them occurred.

Where Freud had worked with neurotics needing to recover the ability to 'love and work' Jung worked out his theory firstly from his experience with psychotics. His own experience of near breakdown also had a creative outcome for his theories and work, which he then saw also applied to other kinds of troubled people. Jung saw many people in mid-life desperately seeking personal meaning despite outwardly successful lives, and in this way widened the group of people who could benefit from psychotherapy, previously limited to the younger adult. To distinguish his ideas from Freud's, Jung used the term *analytical psychology* for his work.

In his clinical work he stressed that both therapist and patient are affected by the work they do together. He regarded the therapist's emotional response to the patient as invaluable information. Recognizing, however, the emotional demands and responsibility this inevitably placed on the therapist, Jung pioneered the necessity for all would-be therapists to themselves have an analysis as part of their training. His ideas were attractive to people from all walks of life, resulting in the formation of Analytical Psychology Clubs from which grew today's Jungian professional societies. This included in the 1940s the British Jungian movement, with Michael Fordham at its centre. As a child psychiatrist, Fordham related Jung's ideas to working with children. He further developed Jung's ideas by connecting them with those of the object relations school of psychoanalysis, especially the work of Klein.

THEORY AND CONCEPTS

Jung used the word *psyche* (from the Greek, meaning 'mind, spirit, soul') to describe people's inner world, their subjective experiences and attitudes. Some of these we are fully aware of and able to articulate. These are our **conscious** *attitudes*. However, we also have attitudes of which we remain unaware, or are unwilling or unable to acknowledge to ourselves, let alone to others. These are **unconscious** *attitudes*. They tend to reveal themselves in our behaviour, for example, we 'forget' the birthday of someone we cannot admit we dislike. Jung called these unconscious attitudes, which were rooted in our personal history of family and society, *the personal unconscious.*

The personal unconscious contains those attitudes that were not seen as acceptable by those around us in early life and so were pushed out of consciousness. For example, a child with parents who frowned when he got angry will learn to deny these feelings, first to his parents and, if there is no other outlet, eventually to himself. The personal unconscious also contains those aspects of ourselves we have simply not yet developed, such as our adventurous side. These less acceptable or unknown aspects of ourselves Jung described as the *shadow* of the personality.

What we have pushed out of consciousness or not yet become conscious of we tend to attribute to others. This is called **projection**, and it means that we rely on the other person to carry the projection for us, that is, to be what we think they are. We criticize or unduly admire others for what we are not getting to grips with, for example our sexuality, success, ability to make money, etc. Scapegoating in families and groups is the result of *projection of the shadow* at work. The problem in attributing (projecting) either negative or positive qualities on to others is that we are depleting our own personality by remaining unconscious of these aspects of ourselves. This will limit our potential to develop psychologically. Seen in this light, if through relationships with others we can 'own' what is in our shadow and so *withdraw the projections,* then we have a chance to enrich the personality by becoming more conscious and less at risk of the shadow contents taking us over, for example, the sudden judgemental attack on someone who has done something we ourselves secretly do or want to do.

Jung saw consciousness and unconsciousness as the two primary opposites of our inner or psychological life. Psychological development and health mean bringing conscious and unconscious attitudes as far into balance as possible. He called this *holding the tension between the opposites,* suggesting that this is a balance we are constantly having to redress as new experiences in both our inner and outer worlds challenge the status quo. This is the basis of human development. At each stage of life from infancy through to old age we are faced with new tasks in all areas: physically, mentally, psychologically, morally and spiritually. How we negotiate the tasks of one stage will affect for good or ill how we face and negotiate the next stage. The mid-life crisis is a case in point: the person who behaves like an adolescent is making a statement both about fear of the second half of life and about something unfulfilled in the adolescent task of leaving the child behind. The drive to redress this imbalance comes from what Jung calls the Self. *The Self is the central core of the personality, which perpetuates psychological development throughout life.* It is the Self which strives to balance our need to live in society with the need to feel personally alive in a unique way. This process, which is ongoing, Jung called the **individuation** *process.*

Jung viewed the psyche as *self-regulating,* like the body. The unconscious attitudes will make their presence felt through symptoms, such as depression, when the clash with conscious attitudes becomes too great and holding the tension between the opposites therefore becomes too stressful. This is often the point of crisis at which someone will seek help. Therefore the unconscious has a *compensatory function* in relation to the conscious mind. It is exactly this self-healing capacity that can be harnessed in therapy where the client learns to see symptoms as indicators of psychic stress as well as problems in themselves.

As part of the individuation process we all struggle to hold the same opposites. We all try to separate from and to merge with others, to address good and bad in ourselves and others, to love and to hate, to face the unknown in our lives and in ourselves. We struggle to commit and to be alone, to relate to parents, friends, lovers, siblings, partners and children. We struggle with the need to find a balance between being outward-looking (extroverted) and inward-looking (introverted), to be a member of a group and yet unique. Jung saw the same themes and figures expressed **symbolically** in myth and religion, fairy-tales and the arts, and across different cultures. He saw that they resonated psychologically for people down the ages, and posited the existence of a *collective unconscious* containing the residue of human psychological evolution.

To these universal figures and experiences, images of which he observed often appeared in people's dreams, Jung gave the name **archetypes**. Examples of *archetypal images* are: the forces of good and evil, the union of masculine and feminine, the witch mother/tyrannical father, the nourishing earth mother, the Wise Old Man and Woman, the Puer or Peter Pan figure. Other archetypal images are the heroic fight with a monster, the journey into the unknown (present even in *Winnie the Pooh,* and a powerful metaphor for the experience of counselling and therapy), and 'the dark night of the soul'. We come across modern versions today in films, on the television, in politics, children's stories, novels and even cartoons.

An archetype is a human predisposition. It is an innate psychological readiness to relate to people: to a mother, to a father, to parents as a couple, to siblings and friends, to partners, to one's children. It is also a readiness for key human experiences such as birth, separating from the parents, the emergence of sexuality, marriage or partnering, becoming a parent, the loss of innocence, awareness of mortality and death. Each involves initiation, sacrifice and gain. It is a sort of DNA for psychological development, the basis for individual human experience. Every child is born but each child's experience of this rite of passage into the world will be individual and unique, depending on the child themselves and the actual physical and technical circumstances of birth, the mother's state of health and mind, and family and social attitudes. Even at this early stage the balance of inner and outer, of positive and negative will colour the child's conscious and unconscious attitudes.

The conscious part of our personality Jung called the Ego. The Ego develops as a result of relating, through human interactions first with the parents and then with others. Through these crucial interactions the child's innate, *archetypal expectations* or *projections* of 'Father' and of 'Mother' meet with experience of an actual relationship with a mummy and a daddy and are modified. (Children's books with their witches and fairy godmothers, giants and princes, reveal just how archetypal and unmediated by experience a young child's inner world tends to be.) A network of experiences and fantasies forms around these early significant relationships and these *associations* become the basis for expectations/projections about future interactions and relationships.

Growth occurs as at each stage of life from infancy onwards we struggle with challenges to these archetypal expectations. For adult life to have a secure basis and change to be tolerated and even welcomed there need to be good enough conditions for the inevitable losses and gains of each stage to be tolerated. This means that if the child is neither inappropriately hastened on nor held back by circumstances or unconscious family influences then all will go well. The child will become an adult with realistic expectations of Self and others. Where things go wrong the adult is likely to have an inflated sense of Self to compensate for feelings of unworthiness and insecurity, or tend to be anxious and controlling of others to avoid what they feel to be the inevitable disappointment of relationships.

When the network of associations to these early important relationships is largely negative, for example a mother's depression clouds joy in her child, or a father is overly critical, then a **complex** is formed with the problem relationship at its core. This is a kind of 'psychological magnet', a heightened sensitivity to any subsequent situation perceived as similar. The protective strategies (*defences*) the child developed at the time to cope with the original distress and anxiety come into action again in the adult. 'Then' becomes 'now' the client with the depressed mother is unconsciously attracted to close relationships with depressed people in which he feels he must be bright and cheerful to survive. He has a negative mother complex. He remains unconscious of the fact that as an adult he could behave differently and constantly repeats the experience. The complex has him in its grip and he sees all-important relationships through the lens of this complex.

The mature adult also needs to have a flexible *persona,* the role we take on in different social contexts, together with the accompanying behaviour, dress, language, manner, etc. Problems occur when either the range of roles is too limited or, more commonly, someone becomes *identified with their persona* (for example, the teacher who 'teaches' whoever she/he is with) and where loss or change of role results in feeling a profound loss of Self.

Jung also noted that partnerships begin with projections. Falling in love involves projecting the image of the archetypally ideal partner on to an otherwise ordinary man or woman whose 'warts and all' humanity is temporarily obscured. When this goes on too long individuals become limited and the relationship is stifled because partners collude in carrying each other's projections, for example, one person projects his nurturing side on to his partner who allows him to carry his/her assertion in the world. Tied by their mutual projections they each remain only half a person. Psychological maturity for both the individuals and their partnership depends on withdrawal of these projections from each other so as to learn from the partner and develop these qualities and capacities in themselves. In this way the Self can also use partnership as a route to individuation.

PRACTICE

The goals of the approach

Jungian therapy sets out to bring about inner change of a long-term nature. It aims to facilitate the client in making conscious those projections, complexes, unconscious attitudes and protective strategies (*defences*) which, as long as they have been unconscious, have held up development and therefore the process of individuation. By helping the client to put into words previously unconscious ideas (*fantasies*) about him or herself and others, the therapist aims to enable the client to develop his own capacities for understanding his feelings, thoughts and relationships. Through a process of experiencing and reflecting, the client is gradually helped to come to terms with what he is and is not, and realize what he still can be: to move from an inflated inadequacy to accept being ordinary and yet unique.

The counsellor aims to provide a setting both physical and psychological in which the client can begin to build sufficient trust to allow the often painful reliving of complexes and accompanying fantasies to take place. Continuity over time is therefore important. Consequently, Jungians usually work within an open-ended or long-term contract, of at least a year and often longer. The ending is planned for at a point when the client feels able to take over the work on his own inner process.

The general format of sessions

These take place at regular intervals weekly, or more frequently in the case of psychotherapy. They last for 50 minutes each. This boundary of time and of confidentiality is firmly maintained by the counsellor, who does not usually interact with the client in other capacities as this interferes with the counselling relationship and the potential for necessary projections to emerge. Client and counsellor sit in similar comfortable chairs positioned so that the client can both look and be looked at or not, as he wishes. A couch is also available for the psychotherapy client wishing to get more in touch with the inner world.

As this is one of the 'talking therapies', the client is encouraged to say whatever comes to mind. There is no set agenda or focus. In fact the client is actively encouraged to go with whatever spontaneous images, feelings and thoughts come up, and to relate dreams and fantasies as they occur. Silence can mean just as much as talking. For this reason the counsellor will probably not interrupt a silence unless she feels the client is struggling. The client is also encouraged to voice feelings about the way he experiences sessions and the relationship with the counsellor as well as exploring life and relationships outside the sessions. The counsellor offers her understanding of the meaning of what is being said and experienced both in and out of the session, and encourages the client to reflect and offer further associated memories, feelings and fantasies. If the client chooses, he can also use poetry, painting, music, etc., to explore his inner world, his experiences and his relationships.

Often the first session with a client will contain in a condensed form the central complex(es), such as negative father complex, Oedipal or exclusion complex. Sometimes an early dream indicates the central issues that the client is unconsciously concerned with, by showing in dramatized form via the dream figures the state of the person's relationship to themselves and others. (In the dream the I is the conscious personality, the Ego, while the dream itself is a spontaneous product of the Self.) For instance, a woman very enmeshed in the relationship with her mother dreams that she walks past a mother and child playing on a beach. She knows in the dream that the child is her. She leaves them and walks on to join friends. This dream had a powerful effect on the dreamer and was something she often came back to in sessions, where the main work was around separating psychologically from the mother.

Throughout the sessions the Jungian counsellor will be listening for whether the client's expectations of themselves and of relationships are of actual people or archetypal figures. Does their description of their partner suggest a god or goddess or a real person? Have they come to see their parents as human beings or do they still seem more like a witch and a tyrant? Or perhaps mother is the archetypal ideal woman or father the perfect man? These standards that they strive to live by and against which they constantly feel they fail, how realistic are they? And this same-sex friend of whose snobbery they are so critical, does this person represent their shadow?

Jungian counselling often starts with helping the client to come to terms with their shadow, that rejected undiscovered part of themselves. As she gets to know the client the counsellor will become aware of both negative and positive projections, and those attitudes that the client has unconsciously absorbed, without question, from significant others. In addition, because the relationship between client and therapist is crucial, the Jungian counsellor will be noting how the client responds to her, and monitoring her own responses to the client himself and his story. The importance of this is that there will be triggers in the therapeutic relationship for the client to relate to her as he has related to significant others in his past and as he relates to others in the present. He will not only consciously tell the counsellor where his difficulties are, in so far as he can, but he will also *show* her by the way he experiences and treats her. He will enact the unconscious attitudes in the session. In the counselling setting this form of projection is called *transference*. Through the transference the Self brings the core complex straight into the counselling process.

To facilitate the emergence of transference projections the Jungian counsellor will not reveal a great deal about herself beyond what is professionally essential or obvious from where she works or who she is. This is in order not to deprive the client of the opportunity to experience feelings towards her which he may otherwise feel he needs to hide, as he has done in the past.

As the counselling situation is not equal in the sense that one person is seeking help from another, a common archetypal projection on to the counsellor is of one or other of the parents. If the client has an authority complex because he experienced his father as a harsh, critical, god-like figure or his mother as a cold and withholding 'stone mother', then at different times he will perceive the counsellor as critical or cold, and struggle for a while with a negative transference.

The counsellor's task is to help the client put into words (*make conscious*) his perception of himself and others, and to assist him in taking back the projections that inhibit real relationship and individuation. She does this by pointing out how she observes and experiences him, perceiving his relationships through the lens of the complexes that grip him, and endeavours to help him link these up with other experiences past and present, for example, 'From the closed-up look on your face and the way you go silent when I say something, I think you feel I've taken over just as you did when you talked with your older brother.' This work of understanding and connecting by the therapist is called *interpreting*. The therapist will also encourage the client to reflect on when, and with whom, such feelings and thoughts have been around before. Then the client will be able to make his own connection or interpretation of his experience. Gradually he will begin to develop his own capacity to think about and understand his feelings, fantasies, thoughts and bodily sensations, and so be less dominated by his complexes.

Earlier we mentioned the importance that Jung placed on the therapist's own emotional response to the client. This is known as the **counter-transference** and refers to the feelings aroused in the counsellor by the client, what he says and the way he is in the sessions. The counsellor feels what the client is feeling unconsciously, or she may feel with him as others do in his presence. The counter-transference is a vital source of information about the client's unconscious inner world, about how he relates and about how others relate to him. It is a more primitive, unconscious form of communication between people on a par with that between mother and child, which Jung called 'participation mystique'. The Jungian counsellor needs to monitor this important emotional response during the session and make conscious what the client seems not yet to know or be able to put into words himself. The counter-transference may take the form of an image, an intuitive perception, a thought or a feeling. Or the counsellor may experience a bodily sensation when with the client; one counsellor described feeling very puffed up and then suddenly very small with a client who swung between feeling an inflated sense of Self and feelings of great inadequacy.

As reflects the nature of the complex, the 'work' client and counsellor do together has a spiral quality. The 'psychological magnet' of the complex and the compensatory nature of the unconscious means that in an unconscious effort to understand what seems incomprehensible, the client repeatedly finds himself in situations and relationships where the same painful feelings and defences are triggered. As the counsellor helps to make him conscious of this *compulsion to repeat* and the fantasy behind it, the client is helped to explore its meaning. He unravels the network of associated experiences and feelings that has built up around a particular formative experience. The grip that the complex had on him gradually lessens as it cannot stand the light of consciousness.

However, this much-longed-for change is also feared and resisted. Change means risk and giving up the familiar 'devil I know'. So to help establish and maintain a working rapport the counsellor also helps the client to think about the anxiety, which means he both wants to change, and to protect himself against change. The counsellor observes what protective strategies (defences) the client relies on, when he resorts to them and what may be the reason, for example changing the subject when a painful point is reached, or denying anger when anxious of the effect expressing it would have. Then by being encouraged to get in touch with the fantasy behind the need to protect himself (for instance, fear that the counsellor, like his father, would withdraw if he got angry), the client can begin to give up those protective strategies that get in the way of life, intimacy and further development. The Ego is stronger, there is less anxiety and change is really on the way.

WHICH CLIENTS BENEFIT MOST?

Many clients who find their way to a Jungian therapist complain of lack of meaning in their lives, of the feeling that 'there must be something more to life than this'. Others are seeking to renew or find a sense of inner purpose lost or greatly changed through life experiences such as a relationship crisis, death of a loved one, or a major change of circumstances such as redundancy. Some may come because they feel an inner purpose has never been established and they have no sense of their identity, or of self-worth. Because relationship is at the heart of Jungian therapy clients with difficulties in making relationships can be helped over time. Clients with difficulties in early life, such as repeated losses or parents themselves struggling to be emotionally mature, or where early circumstances have meant they have had to grow up too soon (sick parents, abusive experiences, childhood illness or handicap), find the long-term nature of Jungian therapy valuable. It helps the Self to unfold and the Ego to strengthen through a gradual approach to increased consciousness. Creative people, who fear the analytic stance will by definition damage their creative capacities, often respond well to a Jungian approach as their art, music, writings, etc. can become part of the work and be viewed as an expression of the Self.

Jungian therapy is less suitable for the person who has a problem-solving attitude to difficulties, as they are likely to find it slow and frustrating. Nor is it for the person who seeks cure, rather than insight into themselves and growth. Some very extroverted people may struggle with the emphasis on the inner world but this can shift if they are able to persevere. Clients with seriously disabling behavioural problems such as addictions, incapacitating panic attacks, or eating disorders, which are severe enough to prevent the person from leading anything like a normal life, would only be able to benefit from any form of psychodynamic counselling once the symptom was sufficiently under control to enable the person to attend regularly and to tolerate some degree of psychic pain.

CASE STUDY

The Client

Paul was in his mid-twenties, a professional single man working in finance. Despite aptitude, he hated the work, and rebelled against the 'business man' persona in his appearance and dress. His real interests lay with people, and with writing and composing songs and music for the group he played in.

Presenting problem

Paul sought help because 'There are parts of myself that I don't understand', and 'relationships with women go wrong'. He felt he didn't know how others saw him or how he saw himself. He could no longer sort this out on his own.

In fact both actually and symbolically there were unknown parts of himself, for Paul had been adopted as an infant. He had always known this and it had been a successful adoption. However, he knew nothing about his birth parents and when he looked at his adoptive parents and adopted sibling Paul did not see himself mirrored back. The 'dual mother' motif portrayed in many myths and fairy-tales, and children's fantasies about really being the child of much more exciting parents, was right there for Paul in his actual experience. He had a negative mother complex with anxieties about rejection, and a negative father complex to do with belonging.

Paul's problems had come to the fore during adolescence, the turbulent period of identity crisis. He was rejecting his own Celtic culture, imagining his birth father was English. He felt unrelated to his own masculinity and aggression, which he projected out on to his adoptive father and male relatives as 'all machismo'. He had good male friends, but was more aware of their deficiencies in the feeling and sensitivity area than their strengths, suggesting an over-developed relationship to the inner feminine. With women he formed archetypally intense short-lived relationships which echoed his unresolved relationship to his birth mother.

The Therapy

From the outset Paul's early experience of relationship reflected in the process. He was referred shortly before the therapist went on her summer break, so just as bonding began to take place, separation followed. His high anxiety and undifferentiated feeling meant he was likely to unconsciously perceive this separation through the lens of the complex as abandonment and rejection. Without bringing this to consciousness the chances were that the relationship would not survive the break. So the therapist interpreted the connection between this potential attachment and immediate separation and that with his birth mother. Paul was able to see the similarity, as well as the differences that his therapist pointed out (namely that their separation was temporary, they would meet again soon, etc.) and hold on to it, which augured well for his capacity to use the therapy. It also brought immediately into the open the negative mother complex in the form of a potential negative transference towards the therapist/mother.

(Continued)

(Continued)

However, unlike with his birth mother, these feelings could be expressed prior to the separation. The working rapport thus established survived the break.

Very shortly afterwards, Paul's shadow, his undeveloped capacity to handle aggressive feelings in himself or others, came abruptly into the process, when one night he was hit in the face by a man and was concussed. His passivity in response symbolized his inability to assert himself appropriately, while his tendency to be 'hit in the face' by his own unconscious feelings remained a useful image in the work once the traumatic event itself had been processed.

Paul's songs were very important in his psychic process. Through them he articulated raw feelings of rage and despair about separation and rejection in images archetypal in their power of sirens who lured men on to the rocks, of black holes and neglectful women. At one level these referred to the painful on–off nature of his relationship with his girlfriend, but they were equally applicable to the raw pain of that first separation. Paul's therapist treated them as spontaneous unconscious material like dreams, and so a product of the Self which was guiding his work on himself.

The rejection and abandonment complex inevitably continued to surface in the transference. Paul would leave sessions feeling he had been thrown out and left to cope with his own feelings, and he would report back that he hadn't known what he was doing in his car when he left the session. Genuinely concerned about this potentially dangerous dissociated behaviour, the therapist patiently interpreted the negative transference feelings towards her as the mother who each session abandoned Paul to his fate. She engaged his Ego in thinking with her about the risk of such behaviour.

Paul became more able to voice rather than act out negative feelings and so to manage his anxiety better himself. As he began to see that life lived more consciously was actually less painful, he developed more of a capacity to wait. The plan of searching for his birth mother went on hold, as he realized that seeking out his external identity was not enough on its own. Instead, he paid more attention to how he experienced his existing relationships, with his adoptive parents and with the girlfriend who attracted so much of the archetypal good mother projection. For a long time the mother complex was split between therapist and girlfriend. The therapist was experienced as sometimes the abandoning mother and sometimes the adoptive mother who offered, as he came to realize, continuing care and availability. The adoptive triangle of birth mother and adoptive mother and Paul also appeared in the transference. In the counter-transference the therapist was aware, as she imagined his birth mother had been, of the neediness of her patient, of guilt at the ends of sessions. She felt the intolerable pain that, like his adoptive mother, she could only nurse him through but not assuage, and she had to withstand the angry attacks for not being there all the time, and his disappointment that she was only a poor substitute for the perfect mother he felt he had lost.

As the rejection complex emerged in his projections on to his therapist and others, and as these were explored in the work, Paul realized that to protect himself he either disengaged from relationships before rejection could happen or he failed to see it coming. He noticed that when anxieties about rejection began to surface again, it was a sign that he was under psychic stress.

After about 18 months Paul felt that to seek out his birth mother would no longer be a quest for the archetypal ideal mother but to know his origins, her story and discover who he looked like. His relationship with his adoptive parents had matured into one in which he could feel supported by both as his actual parents, having faced the fear that they too might reject him if he went ahead with the search for his birth mother. In the sessions Paul and his therapist worked hard on his anxieties about the momentous meeting with his birth mother and how best to be in control without being controlling. Further strengthening of his Ego thus took place.

Gradually Paul showed in various ways that he did now know who he was. He made a good friendship with his birth mother and had more realistic expectations of relationships with women. More at ease with his masculinity and able to identify with his Celtic background, he also found his own style at work. He sought out and met his Irish birth father, and processed the feelings this evoked with the minimum of help from his therapist and a greater ability to find support in friends and family. He made conscious his wish to settle down and to become a father himself in time, and re-developed a relationship that had blossomed too early in his therapy and gone on hold.

After two years he had a dream that he and his therapist both felt presaged his readiness to end therapy: *We are in the hall that leads to your consulting room, near the front door. You are showing me a map and helping me plan a journey.* His associations to this were that the hall was between the inner and the outer world and that it represented a stage of transition. Both Paul and his therapist recognized how important it was that he should be the one to leave her, and also that the ending of the therapy should be one that allowed for gradual letting go. This experience of ending would in itself be a key part of Paul's therapy and one that only long-term work could have offered him. So, over several months, the therapy wound down by increasing the gaps between sessions, allowing Paul the opportunity to explore feelings about ending and new beginnings. He left with a New Year and potential long-term relationship on the threshold, knowing that his therapist's door remained open to him should he want to knock, but with both feeling he would not need to do so.

SUGGESTED READING

Cavalli, A., Hawkins, L. and Stevns, M. (2013) *Transformation: Jung's Legacy and Clinical Work Today.* London: Karnac Books. This edited book looks at the legacy of C. G. Jung. Distinguished post-Jungian thinkers from Britain, Europe and the USA reassess Jung's work.

Kalsched, D. (2013) *Trauma and the Soul: A Psycho-Spiritual Approach to Human Development and Its Interruption.* Hove: Routledge. Kalsched describes work with trauma survivors. The book includes extended clinical vignettes with therapeutic dialogue and dreams.

(Continued)

(Continued)

Kast, V. (1992) *The Dynamics of Symbols: Fundamentals of Jungian Psychotherapy.* New York: Fromm Psychology. A more extended account of how a Jungian therapist works and thinks about the psychological development of clients, with particular emphasis on the relationship between conscious and unconscious complex and archetypes, and the way they appear in dreams, drawings and fairy-tales as part of the therapeutic process. Very accessible and brought alive with examples and case material.

Storr, A. (1995) *Jung.* London: Fontana Press. A short account of Jung's life and work and the relationship between the two.

DISCUSSION ISSUES

1. The notion that unconscious thinking and action is compensatory to conscious action and thinking is an important one in Jungian therapy. Choose a life issue such as relationship, job, friendship, and discuss how a client might reveal conscious and unconscious attitudes that are in conflict with one another. How might the counsellor help the client towards a more integrated attitude?
2. Consider the idea that projection is both limiting and a means of growth. How can experiencing a transference on to a therapist help a client to grow? You might like to refer to the case study as a starting point.
3. The case study could be said to exemplify the Ishmael complex (Ishmael was Abraham's illegitimate son who, with his mother, was cast out of the tribe into the wilderness). Many myths, legends and fairy-tales, ancient and modern, portray complexes and the task of unravelling them. Choose a favourite story and discuss the meanings it holds for you and others.
4. Compare and contrast the information about the aims and practice of Jungian therapy with another psychodynamic approach or a humanistic or cognitive one. What differences and similarities do you observe?

6

Psychodynamic (Kleinian) Counselling and Psychotherapy

Julia Segal

INTRODUCTION

The Kleinian approach to **psychodynamic** psychotherapy depends on the capacity of therapists to make contact with their clients' **inner world**, including the hidden anxieties that disrupt their clients' lives. Therapists' sympathetic but realistic understanding of frightening and frightened elements of clients' minds and personalities can enable clients to reassess, reclaim and modify previously rejected aspects of themselves. At the same time clients are able to reassess memories and experiences of other people in their lives, both past and present. With the help of the therapist, the client's inner world is rebuilt on firmer foundations. This has lasting and significant consequences for future relationships, both with the self and with others.

Some of these concepts may seem strange: Kleinians are sometimes noted for their difficult and odd ideas. However, many people find that once they get used to them, the ideas are both comprehensible and useful. Children seem to have less difficulty understanding them than some adults.

Many forms of counselling and psychotherapy have developed in opposition to the ideas of Freud. Kleinian therapists of all kinds, however, are more likely to emphasize the debt owed to the psychoanalytical inheritance. Melanie Klein[1,2] herself was a psychoanalyst: although she disagreed with Freud over some important issues, fundamentally she saw his method and understanding as the foundation on which she based all her work. Similarly, Kleinian counsellors and psychotherapists see Klein's method and understanding as providing the foundation on which they base their work. Their emphasis on the value of carrying over into the counselling relationship much that has been learnt in the more intensive setting of psychoanalysis gives their work a distinctive aspect.

Kleinian therapists, for example, are very strict about their own time-keeping; they are unlikely to discuss any aspect of their own lives with clients; they are likely to keep their rooms, setting and own appearance as unchanging as possible. All of these things, they believe, have significance to clients which clients may not immediately recognize, but which affect the work which can be done. They also pay attention to the unspoken anxieties of the client and do not rely simply on what the client says directly.

DEVELOPMENT OF THE THERAPY

Melanie Klein began work in Vienna with Sandor Ferenczi and moved to Berlin where she had the support of Karl Abraham. In 1926 she moved to Britain, where she remained until her death in 1962. In Vienna she already found that Freud's ideas about the interpretation of dreams[3] gave her insight into her own son's fantasies and play. Detecting some anxieties, she talked to him about them and his response was immediate. One day, for example, he told her he was 'not afraid any more of the things that have been explained to him even when he thinks of them'.[4] Although Klein discouraged others from analysing their own children, this could stand for the essence of the Kleinian method. By enabling the person to understand frightening thoughts and feelings, the fear is reduced *without the need to avoid thinking.*

Klein paid meticulous attention to the words and actions of her patients, and was rewarded with remarkable insight into the ways the mind works. Her followers learned to understand some of the fears behind psychotic states of mind as well as more 'normal' ones, and developed important insight into the feelings and reactions of therapists themselves. They became convinced of the importance of careful observation as a means of understanding the client's reaction to the therapist; and thereby of getting in touch with anxieties forming the most significant basis for a client's relationships with others.

Klein herself believed that analysis five times a week was the only way to allow the deepest anxieties to emerge and to enable fundamental changes. However, many insights obtained originally in five-times-a-week psychoanalysis can be used by therapists and counsellors offering sessions once, twice or three times a week. Even small reductions in anxiety obtainable in a one-off session can sometimes have significant effects on the lives of clients.

THEORY AND BASIC CONCEPTS

Klein's ideas about the way our minds work were revolutionary. Her observations led her to believe that children were very much aware of the world, dynamically interacting with it and actively making sense of it from a very early age. She developed a concept of *unconscious phantasy,*[5] by which she meant something more than the fantasies that children and adults weave to entertain themselves. Unconscious phantasies are the mental representations of the child's first experiences. For example, Klein thought that a child might experience being angry as an unconscious phantasy in which the child was fighting someone. A baby feeling loving towards its mother experiences love in some concrete way, for example, as a **phantasy** of giving her something wonderful. She found that children experience their mothers in phantasy in age-appropriate ways: to begin with as something with the vastness, power and swell of the ocean; later something closer to a living, warm, containing and loving room; a comfortable piece of furniture. Only gradually do they become aware of their mother's relationship with other people and her ability to go and to return. To begin with, her absence may be felt concretely, as darkness is felt as more than the absence of light.

Such phantasies, created very early on out of primitive experiences and attempts to make sense of them, leave their mark in the ways we later relate to our living spaces; or to the ocean, the moon and the sky as poets have always described. Our earliest phantasies involved us doing things to, and things being done to us by, those closest to us; these most basic phantasies have two important consequences. Because they are dynamic, they depend on outside events as well as internal ones. For example, if a baby in phantasy fights with a monsterbreast coming at it (when its stomach hurts and it doesn't want to feed, for example): the phantasy goes on, the breast monster (probably) goes away. What happens next is important. The pain may also go and the breast return and be experienced as a wanted, loving good object that can fill the beginnings of a hole. Alternatively, the pain may not go away. The baby may feel the loving breast is lost forever. From the baby's point of view the fight with the breast monster had an outcome. Phantasies develop in relation to events; and they may not always be entirely under the baby's control.

Secondly, such phantasies form the basis for the child's and then the adult's understanding of the world. A child whose phantasies regularly include a sense of control over a basically good world will understand events and people in a different way from a child whose phantasies always involved a sense of dissatisfaction, frustration and impotent helplessness. Expectations aroused by early experiences will be carried over into later ones. So, for example, a baby who has experienced the world as a good place is likely to develop into an adult who expects to give and to get good things from life. Equally, someone who lost a parent at the age of 10 may in some deep sense 'expect' to lose their partner after 10 years; or when their own first child is 10. They may behave in a way that is determined by this fear and may actually bring it about.

It is important to note that the baby's experience of the world depends only partially on those around them. Melanie Klein observed that the child's experience seemed to depend not only on what was actually provided, but also on the child's ability to make use of it. Some children are more tolerant and forgiving, others more demanding. Although some of this can be understood as a reaction to the parenting the child receives, Klein thought there were other factors at work as well. In particular she thought the child's tolerance of pain and its constitution were important elements of experience. Bad experiences may be made worse by cruel or neglectful parenting, and good parenting may mitigate them; but good experiences may also count for more for some children than for others.[6]

As babies grow into children and then adults, the ways they relate to the world continue to be influenced by early phantasies, modified to a greater or lesser degree by later ones. For example, when we are small we do not know how much effect our angry or loving phantasies have in the outside world. If we became very angry with our mother and she then went away or went into hospital, we may be afraid it was our phantasied attacks which caused it, and that our phantasies of making her better were useless. We may grow up afraid of attacking people in phantasy; afraid our anger can cause injury.

There are many ways we can behave if we fear our own anger too much. We may, for example, try always to be very nice to people in the hope that they will be nice to us. This may work for strangers, but it may be obvious to close family that this niceness at times covers up fury; and they may react angrily themselves. When they are angry we know *we* are not angry but *they* are; and this may in a way be satisfying.

A new lover, our own children, or a therapist may all have the capacity to challenge our fear of our own anger, and may gradually enable us to recognize and use it appropriately. However, in less happy circumstances, we may choose a lover who will act to confirm our belief that our anger is dangerous; or we may be unable to be overtly angry with our children. We are likely to be afraid of being angry with our therapist but if we are lucky, he or she will recognize this, point it out and help us to examine and lose our fear.

Klein drew attention to the ways in which we try to get rid of our own uncomfortable states of mind, and how damaging this can be. Work done since has increased our understanding of such processes, and of the role of therapy in modifying them. In phantasy we can cut out bits of our minds, thrust them into others, or have bits of others thrust into us; we then claim that all of these are 'not me'. 'It is my child/spouse/mother who is angry/sad/dependent/frustrated, not me.' Therapy can help us to see where we have done this, and to reclaim disowned aspects of ourselves.[1]

Painful emotions of grief and mourning are involved when we bring together parts of our minds that previously we kept separate. In order not to admit we have lost someone, for example, we may maintain a phantasy that we are them; or that they inhabit our body. We may feel we act in ways that are 'them' not 'us' at times; and perhaps feel out of control of parts of our body or mind. Recognizing that a lost person 'lives' inside us metaphorically though not concretely can only happen after grief and mourning, in which feelings of loss are experienced.[7] In phantasy we have to recognize what of 'them' is really us; what is them that we can make ours; and what of them we have truly lost. Kleinians see mourning as a powerful process in which the person may make new discoveries about themselves and the world; a process of growth. However, they also recognize how painful it is. The presence of an understanding person makes the pain of mourning easier to bear and less likely to be cut off from perception in a damaging way.

Klein found that even small children can have powerful feelings of hatred towards both their parents, as well as very strong desires to keep them alive and well.[8] These conflicts are both a spur to development and, sometimes, a cause for difficulty. Some awareness of having attacked the person they love, for example, can make a child want to make things better; this can be a motive force for creative work of all kinds, in childhood and adulthood. However, too much guilt about damage done to the mother in infancy, for example, can be paralysing; or can motivate attacks on the self and on others.

Adults can find it reassuring as well as surprising to recognize in therapy some aspect of their emotional life which they have always considered bad and have tried to hide all through their life. Jealousy, hatred or envy are emotions that are commonly denied and may be uncovered in this way. Although these are emotions people dislike having, there is a sense of security in no longer having to maintain a lie about oneself. There is also some security in the discovery of the extent and limits of the badness: one woman was astonished that it was possible to consider just how much she hated her mother, for the thought had always seemed so bad she had to 'stuff it down a well' and obliterate it from her mind. She was shocked when the counsellor asked how bad it was; did she want her mother actually dead? Or perhaps a million miles away? Oh no, she said, she just wanted her to come round rather less often every week. Once it was spoken, she realized it was not such a terrible thought after all.

PRACTICE

In the work of Kleinians, understanding the fears or anxieties connected with relating to others is seen as the main force for change. Such understanding is achieved through the relationship between client and therapist. By providing a safe setting in terms of the physical and emotional surroundings, the therapist enables the client to allow feelings and thoughts into consciousness which previously were unrecognized or rejected. By observing and reporting on links the client appears to be making without recognizing them, the therapist uncovers connections the client has been unaware of making but which may have been highly significant in determining actions and beliefs.

The therapist also models a more tolerant and sympathetic way of understanding less desired aspects of the self, thus enabling clients to be less harsh on themselves. This helps to reduce clients' anxieties and tension. Clients have to work less hard to maintain illusions about themselves and others. With this relaxation comes a new tolerance of the self and others which improves clients' relations with themselves and with the rest of the world.

The goal of psychodynamic psychotherapy or counselling is to open up areas of the mind and emotional responses to conscious awareness. In this way it differs from those therapies (including many drugs) that work to close down aspects of the mind. The therapist works on the assumption that reality is safer than pretence; that knowing is ultimately more bearable than not knowing; that much can be tolerated within a good relationship with a therapist that could not be tolerated alone, and that the expansion of consciousness and strength which such therapy can offer will bring benefits to the client and to those around.

People are sometimes afraid that psychodynamic counselling and psychotherapy may open up 'cans of worms'; but with careful attention from a skilled therapist, the 'worms' melt away or transform into quite different objects under the clear light of day. Therapy may bring out things that were previously 'swept under the carpet' and the client may want to push everything back under the carpet as they leave, but the bump in the floor will be smaller and less liable to trip people up.

How the theory is applied

The therapist's beliefs about the importance of the client's relationship with the therapist govern much of the way in which therapy is offered. For example, the therapist is aware that very primitive phantasies can be stirred by feelings of dependence and consequent fears of change and of abandonment, and will pay considerable attention to making arrangements for sessions clear and predictable, and avoiding as far as possible changes to the room, to the timing of sessions and even to the general appearance of the therapist. The therapist looks for ways in which the client reacts to breaks in therapy, such as at Christmas, Easter and the summer. These reactions can tell the therapist and ultimately the client how the client responds to being left to their own devices. Old conflicts connected with being left by parents, perhaps through illness or death, may emerge at such times; if these issues are not taken up and understood sufficiently, clients often miss sessions just before or just after a break.

The therapist also uses the theory to help understand what is going on for the client and to try to show the client his understanding. For example, a client who appears very self-confident but makes the counsellor feel quite useless might be using a mechanism Kleinians call **projective identification**[9] to 'get rid of' feelings she cannot bear into the counsellor. The counsellor will wonder first if he is really being useless; he will then use his recognition of this process to wonder (aloud or in his own head) whether the client too feels quite useless inside, but cannot bear the feeling. Suggesting this tentatively to the client may give some indication of whether the client is prepared to work in this way with the counsellor; where one client would experience a relief in being understood, another client may furiously reject the suggestion.

Change process and therapeutic relationship

In the here–and–now relationship with the therapist, the client's past and present difficulties will be reflected. Focusing on this relationship can bring into the room in a lively way issues that have been neglected for years. For example, a woman who does not stand up to her husband is likely not to stand up to the therapist: the therapist may be able to discover and understand some of the roots of the hesitancy in the relation with himself, and thus ultimately transform the relation with the husband. (If the therapist does not ensure the client understands why he is working in this way, some clients become annoyed at the apparent over-valuing of the relation with the therapist at the expense of consideration of 'real–life' relationships. Because of this, in short-term work some Kleinian counsellors restrict the use of overt **transference** interpretations. They may, for example, use their understanding of the client–counsellor relationship to illuminate the client's relationship with her husband, but talk to the client of it mainly in terms of the relationship with the husband, using material from the relationship with the therapist only to make it more convincing.)

Kleinian therapists focus on their clients' anxieties, the worries that seem to underlie the ways they think and behave. For example, a client was talking nonstop and not allowing the counsellor time to think or answer. Using the client's appearance – which included very thick make-up – and something of the content of what she was saying as clues, the counsellor took advantage of a moment's break to wonder gently if the client was afraid that she had to put up a real barrier of words between herself and the counsellor in order to prevent the counsellor getting in and seeing that underneath the bravado and the fun she was afraid she was 'really' a terrible person. The client took a deep breath and stopped talking. When she began again it was with a completely different tone and she began to tell the counsellor how her mother had often told her she had killed her twin brother, who had died in infancy.

Questions will seldom receive direct answers from a Kleinian therapist or counsellor. How they react will depend on the context. Counsellors may explain that they find it more helpful to try to understand what a question is about, rather than to answer it. If a client asks if the counsellor has children, for example, an answer either way may block the client's willingness to reveal their own feelings about children and parenthood. Exploring the significance of the question for the client without answering it may be far more revealing. (For further discussion of this see Segal, 1993.)[10]

Partly because there is an expectation that their clients (unlike many counselling clients) will already have some idea that they need psychotherapeutic help, psychodynamic psychotherapists are less likely to explain. Rather than enter into a discussion about the theory and practice of psychotherapy, the therapist may simply interpret a client's questions in terms of their perception of the client's anxieties. This itself may become a focus of discussion. The way the client responds may show both therapist and client a lot about the client's way of dealing with a world that does not do just what they expect it do. Although the client may be annoyed (at the therapist taking charge of the conduct of the therapy, and not simply behaving like a social acquaintance) they may also experience relief. A social relationship brings with it responsibilities as well as rewards; the relationship with the counsellor works under different rules and the counsellor holds responsibility for these. This can liberate a client, particularly if they have always felt responsible for looking after others, for example.

Format of a typical session

A psychodynamic counselling or psychotherapy session is likely to start with the counsellor or psychotherapist greeting the patient in a serious but warm manner, saying very little, if anything. The counsellor will listen carefully to any 'small talk' and will respond courteously, but will be trying to understand what it betrays about the client's state of mind. The counsellor will probably not join in discussing, say, the weather or the journey. The first thing she says will probably be addressed as closely as possible to the client's anxieties as understood by the counsellor at that moment. What the client has said will be understood as conveying something to the counsellor about his state of mind, his hopes and anxieties at that moment about coming to counselling.

The session will continue with the client talking about whatever occurs to him. The counsellor will respond, listening and commenting on what seems to be important for the client.

The counsellor will be constantly on the look-out for what is going on in the relationship, and the ways the client is talking as well as what they are saying. For example, a client who claimed to be very keen on counselling greeted everything the counsellor said with 'no …'. Eventually the counsellor pointed this out, whereupon the client said 'no I don't' and they both laughed. The client was then able to use this intervention in a way she had been quite unable to use anything the counsellor had said before; together they could begin to explore what it was that made her so scared to allow anyone else to have an idea and give it to her. In this case it led to exploration of a very painful childhood memory, when she had been unable to say 'no' effectively to an uncle who abused her regularly. The 'no' not only constantly asserted her ability to keep people out of her body and her mind; together with her seductive enthusiasm for counselling it also created in the counsellor something of the feeling of being misused and perversely ill-treated.

The counsellor or psychotherapist may say at least one thing about the relationship between the client and herself in the session. In particular, she will be alert for any negative reactions that betray any sense of unease or discomfort towards the counsellor or therapist. For example, she may pick up the way a client seems to be trying to please; or the way he has not mentioned anything about a coming holiday, though there is reason to believe he is afraid of being left to his own devices at this time. If a client is talking about troubles with his partner, the counsellor may pick up some way in which the relationship with the counsellor may be related to the particular issue that seems to be troubling the client on that day. Idealization of the therapist will probably be understood by the therapist as a defence against persecutory beliefs or phantasies; a client who is always pleased or happy with what the therapist says may have quite terrifying secret beliefs about how dangerous it is to question what is going on, or to admit to any dissatisfaction. In looking for ways the client feels about counselling the counsellor will not be simply listening for the client to say 'I was unhappy with what you said last week …', which very few clients are capable of admitting directly. More subtle hints may have to be taken, and there must be a careful and sensitive process of checking out whether the counsellor's understanding is correct.

It is comments about what is going on in the room, between client and therapist, if sensitively timed and directed, that Kleinians think are likely to bring about the most change.[11] If used insensitively, however, they can simply give the client the feeling that the therapist is feeling left out and wants to be noticed; or that issues that really matter to the client are being ignored. For this reason, the therapist is likely to acknowledge seriously the overt issue that is being discussed as well as any possible underlying transference issue. The client's immediate response, as well as material brought up later, will help the therapist to work out whether their intervention made sense to the client and was useful, or whether it needed modifying or rejecting outright.

The session will include careful attention to any imminent changes of date or time caused by therapist or client; there will be some attempt to elucidate any meaning such changes might have for the client. These are important, since unspoken reactions can be 'acted out' by sessions being cut short or missed, or the therapy being brought to an abrupt end.

WHICH CLIENTS BENEFIT MOST?

There is now empirical evidence available for the effectiveness of psychodynamic therapy. Jonathan Shedler's (2010) paper,[12] for example, quotes five meta-analyses which found that 'the benefits of psychodynamic therapy not only endure but increase with time'.

Psychodynamic psychotherapists and counsellors work with people with a wide range of difficulties, including quite severe mental disturbances (such as borderline personality disorder; depression; eating disorders) as well as people with neurological problems, including cognitive or speech problems. They also work with people who do not feel there is much wrong with themselves, but who are facing difficult circumstances or simply want to understand themselves better in order to function better in their profession. Any client who presents him- or herself for psychodynamic therapy would be assessed for their interest in working with the particular therapist, at that particular time and in that particular setting.

Those clients who benefit most are probably those who have the most interest in understanding themselves, for whatever reason. There is also evidence that more frequent sessions and longer-term therapies bring more benefits than short-term or infrequent sessions, although briefer therapies can be effective and sufficient for a client's purpose.

It may be helpful to remember that, in the long term, it is not only the client who is likely to benefit from the reduction in anxiety a successful therapy brings, but also the client's family and other people who come into contact with him or her.

CASE STUDY

The Client

Ann arrived in a state of despair. She wept as she told the counsellor how unfair she felt her family were towards her. In her twenties she had worked in films and earned a lot of money; she had always given her sister and her mother expensive presents and had kept regular contact with them. But when she had had a child by a married man, shortly after being diagnosed with arthritis, they had completely failed to support her. She felt absolutely at the end of her tether. Her mother hated her; her sister hated her; her neighbours were no support at all, and her friends all had their own problems. By the age of 46 she felt she really ought not to need support like this, but she just could not cope. Her

(Continued)

(Continued)

arthritis made every action painful and she had very little money, but nobody was prepared to help her. The only good thing in her life was her son, who was all a son could be to her.

She had tried various kinds of therapy earlier in her life. After a suicide attempt in her thirties, she said, one therapist had told her she disgusted him. This was all she remembered.

The Therapy

The counsellor herself felt somewhat overwhelmed by Ann's predicament and the way she presented herself, and she was afraid Ann would expect her to be disgusted, as her previous therapist had been. She acknowledged to Ann how unsupported Ann felt, and how she must be afraid that she, the counsellor, would turn against her too. Ann's response to this was to relax visibly and become more thoughtful.

In many of her sessions Ann talked almost non-stop. It was as if she was completely overloaded. The counsellor pointed out that Ann seemed to feel she had to do all of the work herself. This led to Ann talking about the way she had never felt supported. Her father had died when she was 10; her older sister had left home and she had felt she had to support her mother. The counsellor linked this with Ann's sense of being unsupported now, in particular because her son was now nearly 10 too. Though Ann was surprised that there could be a link, she talked for the first time of her father and how she had felt about him. She talked of his sudden death; how nobody had ever told her anything about it, and how she never thought about him as she was growing up. She did remember feeling very lonely as a teenager.

When she was a young woman, men had wanted to marry her, but she had left each of them, two after relationships of six years or so. The counsellor wondered with her if this was because she was afraid they would leave her, like her father had. Ann was not sure about this; they would all have made good husbands; she was still not sure what had been wrong about the relationships. She 'didn't know'.

The counsellor helped Ann to focus on the way she used 'I don't know' to stop trains of thought in the session. The thoughts often seemed to run 'So-and-so is not very nice to me, it must be my fault, oh I don't know.' The counsellor pointed out that Ann seemed unable to think about whether it was her fault or not; she wondered if Ann had had similar thoughts about her father's death, thoughts that she had stopped before discovering it really was not her fault that her father had died. Ann did not respond by talking further about her father, but she did begin to allow her thoughts about other people to develop further. Gradually the counsellor helped Ann to talk in more detail about the many people in her life who were really *not* very nice to her. This seemed to be a new process for Ann, who felt somehow that nice people should not think such thoughts.

The counsellor helped Ann to see that she could actually make clear judgements about the behaviour of certain members of her family, about her employer and about her friends. She could discriminate between those who were 'nice to her' and those who were not. She remembered with tears how much she had supported her much older sister through a bad marriage, and how the sister had then turned against her, accusing her unjustifiably of being in love with her husband. She remembered with a shock how her sister's first husband had in fact made a pass at her, and how disgusted she had been. She also remembered her envy of her sister for being older and prettier, and the times she had not been nice to her, but she was able to evaluate this differently. She no longer felt that all her sister's ill-treatment of her was justified. She could now recognize that her sister and brother-in-law were not supportive people; they never helped her mother but constantly borrowed money from her which they did not repay.

This clearer view enabled Ann to stop asking them for help and affection, which she had finally realized she was not going to get. Her relations with her mother improved too, partly because she stopped constantly trying to get her mother to condemn her sister; she accepted that her mother too did not want to see how mean and selfish her sister was.

During the counselling Ann remembered more about her previous therapy; she remembered that the therapist had actually been very supportive at times, though she was still hurt by his comment. She now wondered if he had been trying to say something different from what she had thought. Her new ability to think things through had enabled her to regain some memories of a good relationship; it was no longer lost in the memory of the bad ending.

When Ann decided she was able to stop counselling, she still did not have a partner but she was feeling much more self-confident. She could recognize that she was bringing her son up well and had a good relationship with him; she was also encouraging him to see his father regularly. She had completely changed her social circle, so that she was no longer seeing people who had been cruel to her, and had made a stronger friendship with some kinder friends. Her mother was no longer unkind to her; and she had found a new job where she was much happier. She was grateful to the counsellor for helping her to feel more secure and less in a state of constant panic, though she was also disappointed she had not managed to find a husband.

The counsellor was pleased that Ann's life had changed so much for the better, but she was also left feeling that there were important issues that had not been fully addressed. Counselling had to stop after two years: this was not long enough for some of Ann's most painful feelings about her father to emerge and be **worked through**. The counsellor was aware that some of Ann's relationships showed signs of reflecting an ambivalent attachment to and identification with her father, and would have liked to be able to address this further. However, although Ann could now allow herself to think a little more clearly about other people, there still seemed to be an embargo on further thoughts about her father, just as there had been when, as a teenager, she 'never thought about him'. The counsellor was afraid this had meant that she had not properly separated from him in her unconscious phantasy, and that this was preventing her from attaching herself to a new partner. However, Ann had talked through some of her feelings about separating from the counsellor and the counsellor was hopeful that Ann would be able to take some of the work further on her own.

[I am grateful for permission to use this case. I have altered several details to disguise identities.]

REFERENCES

[1] Segal, J. C. (1992) *Melanie Klein*. London: Sage.

[2] Website for Melanie Klein Trust: www.melanie-klein-trust.org.uk.

[3] Freud, S. (1901) *On Dreams*, in vol. 5 of the *Standard Edition of the Complete Psychological Works of Sigmund Freud*, ed. J. Strachey. London: Hogarth Press and Institute of Psychoanalysis.

[4] Klein, M. (1921) *The Development of a Child*, in vol. 1 of *The Writings of Melanie Klein* (1975). London: Hogarth Press and the Institute of Psychoanalysis. p. 42.

[5] Segal, J. C. (1985) *Phantasy in Everyday Life*. London: Pelican Books. (Reprinted London: Karnac Books, 1995; and New Jersey: Aronson, 1996.)

[6] Klein, M. (1957) *Envy and Gratitude*, in vol. 3 of *The Writings of Melanie Klein* (1975). London: Hogarth Press and the Institute of Psychoanalysis.

[7] Klein, M. (1940) *Mourning and Its Relation to Manic-Depressive States*, in vol. 1 of *The Writings of Melanie Klein* (1975). London: Hogarth Press and the Institute of Psychoanalysis.

[8] Klein, M. (1937) *Love, Guilt and Reparation*, in vol. 1 of *The Writings of Melanie Klein* (1975). London: Hogarth Press and the Institute of Psychoanalysis.

[9] Segal, H. (1981) 'Countertransference', ch. 6 in *The Work of Hanna Segal: A Kleinian Approach to Clinical Practice*. New York and London: Jason Aronson. (Reprinted London: Free Association Books (1986) with a new title: *Delusion and Artistic Creativity and Other Psychoanalytic Essays.*)

[10] Segal, J. C. (1993) 'Against self-disclosure', in W. Dryden (ed.), *Questions and Answers in Counselling in Action*. London: Sage.

[11] Malan, D. H. (1963) *A Study of Brief Psychotherapy*. (Reprinted) New York and London: Plenum, 1975.

[12] Shedler, Jonathan (2010) 'The efficacy of psychodynamic psychotherapy', *American Psychologist*, February–March, pp. 98–109.

SUGGESTED READING

Segal, H. and Abel-Hirsch, N. (2007) *Yesterday, Today and Tomorrow*. Routledge, Hove, UK and New York: Routledge. (The title paper of this book can be downloaded from the website of the Melanie Klein Trust. www.melanie-klein-trust.org.uk/downloads.) This book, the last papers of Hanna Segal, includes a mixture of clinical and political papers, interviews and theory. Some are written for psychoanalysts and may be hard for the beginner to understand, but many are accessible and apply psychoanalytical ideas to important political issues.

Segal, J. C. (1985) *Phantasy in Everyday Life: A Psychoanalytical Approach to Understanding Ourselves*. London: Pelican Books. (Reprinted London: Karnac Books, 1995; and New Jersey: Aronson, 1996.) Written for the lay public, this book developed from a series of adult education classes in Manchester. It uses psychoanalytical ideas to illuminate relationships in marriage, work and everyday life.

Segal, J. C. (2002) 'Phantasy', in Ivan Ward (ed.), *On a Darkling Plain: Journeys into the Unconscious*. London/USA: Icon Books/Totem Books. www.iconbooks.co.uk. This small book is a distillation of Segal's understanding of the Kleinian concept of unconscious phantasy. It includes a description of an analysis from the point of view of the patient.

Waddell, M. (1998) *Inside Lives: Psychoanalysis and the Growth of Personality*. London: Duckworth. A book written for the lay public; very readable, which takes the reader through the different stages of life, offering psychoanalytical insights into the way personality develops.

DISCUSSION ISSUES

1. Should a counsellor share their own experiences with a client? Why do psychodynamic counsellors oppose this?
2. What goes on in the process of mourning?
3. What are the differences and similarities between psychodynamic psychotherapy and mindfulness training?
4. What does it mean to say that an impulse or a phantasy is unconscious?

PART 2

Cognitive Behavioural Approaches

7

Acceptance and Commitment Therapy

Joda Lloyd and Frank W. Bond

INTRODUCTION

Acceptance and commitment therapy (ACT) is best described as a **contextual cognitive behaviour therapy** (CBT). Contextual CBTs are a recent addition to the cognitive behavioural tradition and are distinct from earlier approaches (e.g. Beck's cognitive therapy) in both their proposed mechanisms of change and core therapeutic techniques. Whilst earlier forms of CBT focus on changing the content, form or the frequency of people's difficult or challenging internal experiences (e.g. thoughts, feelings, physiological sensations, images and memories), contextual CBTs seek to alter the psychological context, or perspective, in which people approach these experiences. Thus, rather than focusing on challenging and disputing problematic thoughts and feelings, contextual CBTs encourage people to approach those internal events from a mindful and open perspective. In so doing, these unwanted events are less likely to overwhelm them and determine their actions.

DEVELOPMENT OF THE THERAPY

Steven C. Hayes and his colleagues began formulating ACT during the mid-1980s. It is directly based upon a theory of language and cognition called **relational frame theory** (RFT), which itself is an extension of the work of B. F. Skinner. Unlike applied behaviour analysis, which was based upon Skinner's work, RFT, and hence, ACT, highlights the potential importance of internal events in influencing mental health and behavioural effectiveness. In this way, it is similar to the CBTs of Ellis and Beck in the 1960s and 70s in emphasising the importance of the relationship amongst thoughts, feelings, and actions. RFT, however, suggests that thoughts cannot reliably be changed or made to occur less frequently; rather, it maintains that the detrimental function of thoughts and feelings on mental health and behavioural effectiveness can be altered, such that they no longer have such negative effects. The goal of ACT, therefore, is to alter the function of these internal events, as opposed to attempting to challenge and change them, as is the aim in Beck and Ellis's CBTs. This is accomplished through enhancing **psychological flexibility**, or people's ability to fully contact the present moment and pursue their meaningful life directions even when experiencing difficult or challenging internal experiences.

Consistent with this RFT/ACT approach to mental health and behavioural effectiveness, research is increasingly showing that enhancing psychological flexibility serves as the mechanism by which ACT produces its benefits.[1,2,3] We now discuss this concept of psychological flexibility, which describes ACT's model of mental health and behavioural effectiveness.

THEORY AND BASIC CONCEPTS

Psychological flexibility: the ACT model of mental health and behavioural effectiveness

ACT posits that mental health and behavioural effectiveness are compromised when people's responses to their difficult or challenging internal experiences reduce their contact with the present moment and prevent them from behaving in ways that are consistent with their meaningful life directions. For example, when carrying out a task at work people may experience engagement, enjoyment and a sense of reward; however, they may also experience worry, nervousness and a degree of apprehension. Whilst the former experiences may be perceived as positive, pleasant and something to be welcomed, the latter may be perceived as difficult, challenging and something to be avoided. If people focus excessively on, attempt to avoid, overanalyse, or otherwise interact unhelpfully with, those latter experiences they may begin to feel overwhelmed and distracted. In turn, this may make it difficult for them to focus on the present moment and work effectively on their task. Eventually this may lead them to lose sight of their meaningful life directions, as well as to an increased risk of emotional and/or behavioural difficulty. In the following section, we will examine these (1) unhelpful responses to internal experiences, when they function (2) to remove people from the present moment, and (3) thwart their ability to pursue their meaningful life directions; in so doing, we hope to explicate how they work together to produce ACT's core process of psychological flexibility.

Unhelpful responses to internal experiences

From an ACT perspective, people's unhelpful responses to their internal experiences derive from two core psychological processes: *experiential avoidance* and *cognitive fusion*.[4] Experiential avoidance, or simply avoidance, involves people's attempts to change, control or avoid their internal experiences, even when doing so may lead to psychological and/or behavioural harm.[5] For instance, when suffering from depression people may experience sadness, anger, guilt, shame, or tiredness. Since these are unpleasant, people may engage in practices to avoid, get rid of, or escape from, these experiences. One common avoidance strategy is *thought suppression*; this involves the use of internal, or thinking–related, strategies to suppress or avoid internal events that are experienced as aversive, or that lead to other aversive experiences. Paradoxically, whilst avoidance may lead to some short-term relief (at least some of the time), when employed on a long-term basis it may have damaging effects. For instance, in the short term, thought suppression may reduce the frequency of aversive thoughts; however, in the long term, thought suppression has been found to lead to a substantial increase in the frequency of the avoided thoughts.[6]

When people feel the need to change, control or avoid their thoughts, it is likely that they are also fused with those cognitive events. Cognitive fusion describes a psychological process in which people are entangled in, dominated by, or enveloped in their internal experiences; a process in which a thought, feeling or memory of an event (past or future) seems 'immediately present and highly likely'; where 'the fearsomeness of the world has been discovered, not constructed'.[4] For instance, when suffering from depression people may be consumed by thoughts that they are inadequate, useless and helpless. Rather than standing back from these thoughts and feelings and seeing them for what they are (i.e. mere products of the mind), people may get caught up in them, believe them, become blinded by them and let them determine their actions.

Removal from the present moment

According to ACT, people's unhelpful responses to their internal experiences, in turn, may function to remove them from the present moment; this is characterised by *inflexible attention* and *attachment to the conceptualised self*.[4] Inflexible attention involves a reduced ability to allocate one's attention in a voluntary and flexible fashion. That is, rather than thinking, feeling and sensing 'in the moment', people get carried off into a remembered past or imagined future. Avoidance may reinforce this process since the more energy people expend being avoidant, the less they have for paying attention to current inner experiences, as well as what is happening in the world around them. Equally, the more energy people expend being fused, the less they have for being psychologically present. When fused, people tend to dwell on painful memories, ruminate about past events, or worry about a future that has not yet happened.

Attachment to the conceptualised self is where people become fused with, entangled in, or dominated by their self-descriptors. To explain, from a young age we are taught to describe and categorise ourselves according to what we like or dislike, the roles we play and the relationships we have. Whilst these descriptors can be useful for helping us to understand who we are and what we value, if held too rigidly, they can dictate our behaviours and limit our choices. For example, if one holds rigidly to the perception of himself or herself as an outspoken person, then more restrained ways of behaving are unlikely to be considered or chosen even when they may be more appropriate in a given moment. As with inflexible attention, attachment to the conceptualised self is characterised by a lack of psychological presence and attention to the here–and–now, as well as a source of psychological suffering.

Thwarted pursuit of meaningful life directions

ACT posits that unhelpful responses to internal experiences and removal from the present moment, eventually, may function to thwart people's pursuit of their meaningful life directions; this is characterised by a *lack of values clarity or contact*, and/or *engagement in unworkable action*.[4] Starting with the former, as actions become driven by avoidance and fusion, and governed by inflexible attention and attachment to the conceptualised self, people may lose touch with, neglect, or forget their values. For example, people suffering from social phobia may attempt to control, change or suppress internal events that provoke anxiety (e.g. thinking about socialising with friends). Whilst their efforts may lead to a reduction in anxiety (at least temporarily), they will also reduce their awareness of their own thinking and therefore make it difficult for them to contact their valued life directions (e.g. building intimate relationships). Furthermore, they may be fused with self-limiting beliefs (e.g. 'If I go out socialising I won't be able to cope'). These beliefs may loom so large, and over time become so embedded in their conceptualised self (e.g. 'I'm not somebody who has close friendships'), that people cannot see beyond them and contact with values may be lost.

In addition, as actions become driven by avoidance and fusion, and governed by inflexible attention and attachment to the conceptualised self, people may increasingly engage in unworkable action that thwarts their pursuit of their values. For example, whilst people suffering from social phobia may be aware of their valued life directions (e.g. having a meaningful social life), the immediate relief afforded by avoidance strategies may dominate over more reasoned and purposive values-based actions. Also, they may be fused with self-limiting beliefs (e.g. 'If I go out socialising I won't be able to cope') making them inattentive to their external environment and the opportunities it affords them to approach their valued life directions. In such a situation, impulsive, reactive and automatic patterns of avoidant action seem likely to dominate over more considered purposive ones.

Psychological flexibility: the core ACT processes

We will now consider how ACT attempts to promote greater psychological flexibility and, hence, better mental health and behavioural effectiveness. Broadly, ACT attempts to promote psychological flexibility using *acceptance and mindfulness processes* in combination with *values-consistent commitment and behaviour change processes*. Acceptance and mindfulness processes help people to fully contact the present moment and approach internal experiences from a curious and open perspective. Commitment and behaviour change processes help people to fully contact the present moment, clarify and take steps towards their meaningful life directions. These two broad processes emerge from six constituent psychological processes: (1) *acceptance*, (2) *defusion*, (3) *present moment awareness*, (4) *self-as-context*, (5) *values*, and (6) *committed action*. Processes 1–4 produce acceptance and mindfulness processes, whilst processes 3–6 produce commitment and behaviour change processes.

In a recent conceptualisation of the ACT model, the six processes have been further grouped into three process pairs: acceptance/defusion, present moment awareness/self-as-context, and values/committed action.[4] These process pairs represent flexible response styles and are referred to as *open, centred* and *engaged* respectively.[4] We will use the three response styles to organise our discussion of the six ACT processes and illustrate how these can counteract the inflexible patterns of behaviour described in the previous section.

Acceptance/defusion: the open response style

Together, acceptance and defusion support an open response style which helps people to better manage their unhelpful responses to internal events (i.e. avoidance and fusion). Acceptance allows people to engage with difficult and challenging internal experiences without attempting to change, control, suppress or avoid these experiences. It encourages people to approach all aspects of their experience in a mindful, curious and non-judgemental manner, and without struggle and defence. Defusion allows people to step back, separate or disentangle from their internal experiences, and view them as ongoing mental activities that do not need to be believed, analysed, or scrutinised. It involves altering people's relationship with their internal experiences even if the form or frequency of those experiences doesn't change or changes only slowly.

Present moment awareness/self-as-context: the centred response style

Together, present moment awareness and self-as-context support a centred response style which helps people to make contact with the present moment. Present moment awareness helps people to allocate their attention in a flexible fashion and connect with whatever experience they are having in that moment. Self-as-context allows people to engage with their personal descriptors and conceptualised self without feeling wholly defined (and dictated) by it. This involves establishing a perspective from which people can be in contact with the content of what they are thinking, feeling or experiencing, but nevertheless psychologically distinct from it.

Interestingly, the centred response style has been conceived of as a lynchpin between the processes of acceptance and defusion, on the one hand, and values and committed action, on the other.[4] Centredness (i.e. being a conscious person in the present moment) facilitates the use of acceptance and defusion when these are needed to overcome barriers to engaging in values-based action. Equally, centredness facilitates a commitment to taking values-based action when this is needed to justify engaging in the challenging processes of acceptance and defusion.

Values/committed action: the engaged response style

Together, identifying one's values and taking committed action towards them represent an engaged response style that helps people to pursue their meaningful life directions. Values describe what people want their lives to stand for and help guide them on a moment-to-moment basis (e.g. being a good father). These are different from goals (which emerge from values) that will end once attainment is reached (e.g. attend your son's football match [the goal] in aid of being a good father [the value]). Committed action involves setting concrete goals and helps move people towards their values. Whilst values are more of a compass-bearing, pointing in a direction that will never be reached (e.g. one can always keep heading west), committed action involves short-, medium- and long-term goals that can be achieved along that course (e.g. travelling to Wales from London on the journey west).

PRACTICE

In this section we will describe therapeutic techniques that facilitate the three response styles just discussed. These include mindfulness and behavioural activation techniques and nonconventional language use (e.g. metaphor and paradox). Importantly, the three response styles (and six therapeutic processes) are all interdependent and must be working in alignment if psychological flexibility is to develop.[4] To this end, ACT techniques tend to enhance multiple processes simultaneously. Nevertheless, in the current review we have discussed techniques only in relation to their focal processes, for the purposes of clarity and simplicity.

Using acceptance and defusion to promote an open response style

An example of a therapeutic technique for increasing acceptance is the *Tin Can Monster Exercise*. In this exercise, the client is first asked to think of a particularly troubling thought, feeling or memory. The client is then guided through imagining that experience as a tin can monster, which can be disassembled into its component parts that are easier to deal with one at a time. The therapist helps the client get in touch with a mindful and non-judgemental 'observer' perspective, and then uses this perspective to explore the different aspects of the problem (e.g. physical sensations, thoughts, feelings, etc). The focus of the exercise is on staying with the uncomfortable, unwanted experiences while letting go of any struggle with them.

A popular therapeutic technique for promoting defusion is the *Milk Milk Milk Exercise*, in which clients are first asked to say the word 'milk' once and to imagine and report on the properties that come to mind (e.g. creamy, white, cold, etc). They are then asked to repeat the word out loud rapidly for a minute or so. After the rapid repetition, clients are asked to report on what they notice about the meaning of the word, which tends to dissolve into the background amongst the phonetic sounds of the word. This exercise seeks to illustrate that, in certain contexts, the literal meanings of words (and our self-descriptors and self-stories) can be weakened, and that they can be seen as ultimately just words and sounds.

Using present moment awareness and self-as-context to promote a centred response style

A technique that is frequently used to promote present moment awareness is the *Leaves on a Stream Exercise*. In this exercise, clients are asked to focus on their breathing and body; they are then guided to imagine themselves sitting next to a stream with leaves floating down it, and to practise placing their thoughts on these leaves. If a client notices that they are getting distracted by, or absorbed in a thought to the point where they are no longer observing or noticing it, they are asked to note that experience and gently return to placing thoughts on leaves. The goal of this exercise is to help clients to practise attending to the fact that our mind endlessly provides us with a stream of thoughts that we can choose to let float down our mental stream, without needing to become absorbed or immersed in them.

A therapeutic technique for promoting self-as-context is the *Chess Board Metaphor*. In this metaphor, the self is likened to a chessboard, and the client's internal experiences are likened to the chess pieces. The therapist then attempts to establish a sense of self distinct from one's internal experiences through elaborating on the metaphor; it may be noted that the pieces play their game whilst the board stays constant, and that the pieces, whilst threatening to each other, do not threaten the board. This exercise is used to help people to see themselves as the arena, or context, in which experiences take place, and, therefore, distinct from, and unthreatened by, the content of these experiences.

Using values and committed action to promote an engaged response style

An example of a technique used to help people define their values is the *What Do You Want Your Life to Stand For? Exercise*. In this exercise, clients are guided into a mindful state and are then asked to imagine that they have died but through a bizarre twist of fate have ended up attending their own funeral in spirit form. They are asked to imagine the eulogies offered and for what they would want people to remember them. The therapist then explores what emerges as most important and any dissonance between the client's values and current actions. After this, the client will often note down their identified values on a record sheet for future reference. This exercise aims to help the client identify their values, explore their current actions, and highlight the importance of values-based living.

An example of a technique to help people to build patterns of committed actions is the *Goals, Actions, Barriers Exercise*. In this exercise, the client is first asked to use their previously identified values to generate specific goals. They are then asked to specify actions that can be taken to achieve those goals, and identify any barriers that may waylay them. The client is then encouraged to enact certain acts in the form of homework and report back on their experiences in the subsequent session. The goal of this exercise is to generate an action plan that the client can take into the real world in order to practise taking committed actions. It is also to identify both internal (e.g. fear) and external (e.g. lack of resources) barriers that may emerge in the process of moving towards one's values.

WHICH CLIENTS BENEFIT MOST?

ACT takes a *transdiagnostic* approach to psychological disturbance. That is, rather than classifying psychological disorders according to the standard clinical taxonomies (e.g. syndromes described in the *Diagnostic and Statistical Manual of Mental Disorders – DSM*), ACT suggests that all disorders (or poor life functioning) can largely be explained by the impact of people's difficult or challenging internal experiences on their ability to contact the present moment and pursue their meaningful life directions; that is, psychological flexibility. Consistent with this stance, ACT has been found to be useful across a variety of syndromes described in the DSM and even some life-limiting actions not included in the DSM, for example poor work performance and stigma.[1]

Since ACT is a broadly focused CBT, the clinical goals are largely the same across all target populations; that is, cultivation of the six core processes. How these concepts are taught (e.g. which exercises are used and/or when), and how they are mapped on to each client, follows a thorough functional assessment of each individual. The common goal remains, though: to undermine the impact of difficult or challenging internal experiences, promote contact with the present moment and facilitate pursuit of meaningful life directions, in order to enhance psychological flexibility.

CASE STUDY

The Client

David was a 28-year-old single Caucasian man who lived alone in Birmingham. He worked as a customer service advisor for his local council and had been at the organisation for five years. He was referred to counselling by his GP because he was experiencing work-related stress and anxiety and had increasingly been absenting himself from work. The symptoms began after David's organisation announced a large-scale restructuring that would lead to changes in his role requirements and responsibilities. In addition to intense feelings of worry and insecurity, David had developed insomnia and gastrointestinal problems. He explained that he often felt overwhelmed at the thought of going to work and so would just call in sick.

The Therapy

Session 1: David explained his recent experiences whilst the therapist listened and sought clarification where necessary. David described feelings of worry regarding his organisation's restructuring, fears of 'falling apart' at work and concerns that his recent behaviour would lead to him becoming 'a washout'. It was clear that David valued his relationships with his co-workers and the customer groups he served. Before his recent difficulties, he had approached his line-manager about doing a coaching course to improve his skills in supporting others. At the end of the discussion, the therapist explained the ACT approach to David and agreed on some initial treatment goals. They were for David to learn skills to better handle his unhelpful thoughts and feelings and to get back to managing his workload effectively. In summary, session 1 elicited David's history, established a rapport and set the goals for the counselling.

Session 2: The therapist began by ascertaining how David had been trying to cope with his difficulties. David described a number of internal and external avoidance behaviours, such as 'trying to not think about it' and taking sick days. The therapist then used techniques to help David connect with the problems that may arise from avoiding internal experiences. One such technique was the *Polygraph Metaphor*; in this metaphor David was asked to imagine a scenario in which he was hooked up to a polygraph machine and instructed to stop feeling anxious under the threat of receiving an electric shock if he failed. The therapist drew parallels between this impossible task and the way in which David's efforts to avoid difficult thoughts and feelings may also be likely to fail. David noted that whilst many of his strategies made him feel better in that moment, the difficult thoughts and feelings usually resurfaced. The therapist also examined the ways in which these strategies may prevent David from pursuing his values. David shared a recent experience in which he had missed an opportunity to become a staff representative on a working group for health and wellbeing because he had felt too overwhelmed to apply. At this point he was very emotional and yet willing to state that his responses to his internal experiences had prevented him from doing something meaningful. The therapist then engaged David in the aforementioned *What Do You Want Your Life to Stand For? Exercise* to help him clarify his valued life directions. It emerged that David wanted to be thought of as someone who excelled at work and someone that colleagues could rely on. In summary, session 2 began to promote an open response style by helping David to become aware of his unhelpful attempts to control his inner experiences. It also began to promote an engaged response style by uncovering David's broader life values. These two styles were promoted in unison when discussions focused on the quality of life consequences of David's avoidance strategies.

Sessions 3 and 4: Between sessions 2 and 3, the therapist had asked David to try to notice his efforts to avoid or control unhelpful thoughts and feelings and what happened to his values when he did. After reflecting on his experiences, the therapist suggested that together they could explore a different way of coping. One technique that was used during this time was the *Take Your Keys with You Metaphor*. This involved asking David to imagine that his keys represented his worry, stress or anxiety, and exploring how holding onto the keys did not prevent him from going where he needed to go. David noted that he had always perceived his anxiety as impeding his actions, and how 'taking it with him' was a novel perspective. Another technique that was used was the aforementioned *Leaves on a Stream Exercise*. This exercise helped David to sustain attention to, and awareness of, the ongoing and changing thoughts and feelings he was having, without becoming absorbed or immersed in them. In summary, sessions 3 and 4 continued to promote an open response style by helping David to carry his difficult

(Continued)

(Continued)

internal experiences without defence and without being deterred by them. It also began to weave this into a centred response style by helping David to notice times where he was becoming engrossed in his unhelpful thoughts and feelings, and how it is possible to step back into the present moment when this happens.

Sessions 5 and 6: Between sessions 4 and 5, the therapist had asked David to practise some exercises that cultivated a mindful and open perspective. After reflecting on his experiences, the therapist suggested that whilst mindfulness was helpful in its own right, it could also be a means of gaining further self-understanding. One technique that was used during this time was the aforementioned *Chess Board Metaphor*. This exercise helped David to gain a better awareness of his own self descriptors (e.g. being 'a washout') and how these may be limiting his movement towards his values. It also helped him connect with a sense of self distinct from, and therefore not governed by, these descriptors. Another technique that was used was the *Passengers on the Bus Exercise*. In this exercise David was asked to imagine himself as the driver of a bus moving towards a valued destination. The passengers represented his unhelpful thoughts and feelings that were attempting to interfere with the journey through shouting, jeering, instructing, etc. The exercise helped David to realise that he could commit to values-based actions even when his internal experiences presented barriers. In summary, sessions 5 and 6 continued to weave together the open and centred response styles by helping David to be open enough to explore his negative self-evaluations and connect with a sense of self distinct from these. Further, the open response style was used to facilitate an engaged response style by helping David be open to his unhelpful thoughts and feelings but not deterred from his values-based action.

REFERENCES

[1] Hayes, S. C., Luoma, J. B., Bond, F. W., Masuda, A. and Lillis, J. (2006) 'Acceptance and commitment theory: model, processes and outcomes', *Behaviour Research and Therapy, 44*, 1–25.

[2] Flaxman, P. E. and Bond, F. W. (2010) 'A randomised worksite comparison of acceptance commitment therapy and stress inoculation training', *Behaviour Research and Therapy, 48*, 816–20.

[3] Lloyd, J., Bond, F. W. and Flaxman, P. E. (2013) 'The value of psychological flexibility: examining psychological mechanisms underpinning a cognitive behavioural therapy intervention for burnout', *Work & Stress, 27(2)*, 181–99.

[4] Hayes, S. C., Strosahl, K. D. and Wilson, K. G. (2012) *Acceptance and Commitment Therapy: The Process and Practice of Mindful Change*, 2nd edn. New York: Guilford Press.

[5] Hayes, S. C., Wilson, K. W., Gifford, E. V., Follette, V. M. and Strosahl, K. (1996) 'Experiential avoidance and behavioural disorders: a functional dimensional approach to diagnosis and treatment', *Journal of Consulting and Clinical Psychology, 64(6)*, 1152–68.

[6] Beevers, C. G., Wenzlaff, R. M., Hayes, A. M. and Scott, W. D. (1999) 'Depression and the ironic effects of thought suppression: therapeutic strategies for improving mental control', *Clinical Psychology: Science and Practice, 6*, 133–48.

SUGGESTED READING

Flaxman, P. E., Blackledge, J. T. and Bond, F. W. (2011) *Acceptance and Commitment Therapy.* The CBT Distinctive Features Series. Hove: Routledge. A short text that summarises the key features of ACT and explains how it differs from earlier forms of CBT.

Harris, R. (2009) *ACT Made Simple: An Easy-To-Read Primer on Acceptance and Commitment Therapy.* Oakland, CA: New Harbinger. An accessible introductory text that offers basic explanations of the six ACT processes and guidance on how to begin using them in practice.

Hayes, S. C., Strosahl, K. D. and Wilson, K. G. (2012) *Acceptance and Commitment Therapy: The Process and Practice of Mindful Change*, 2nd edn. New York: Guilford Press. The second edition of the main ACT text.

Luoma, J. B., Hayes, S. C. and Walser, R. D. (2007) *Learning ACT: An Acceptance and Commitment Therapy Skills-Training Manual for Therapists.* Oakland, CA: New Harbinger and Reno, NV: Context Press. A practically focused text offering a step-by-step guide to mastering ACT and integrating it into your practice.

DISCUSSION ISSUES

1. In what ways do contextual CBTs differ from earlier forms of CBT?
2. How would you explain the ACT approach to a client at the beginning of therapy?
3. How might an open response style help to promote centred and engaged response styles?
4. Using ACT's core propositions how would you approach a client suffering from social phobia?

8

Behaviour Therapy

Berni Curwen, Peter Ruddell and Stephen Palmer

Behaviour therapy is aimed at changing observable and measurable human behaviour. These changes are chosen by the therapist and the client together. As this approach is aimed at behaviour change, some problems, such as phobias, are better suited to behaviour therapy than others. The therapist is psychoeducational and **directive**, giving the client clear guidelines about what to do in order to bring about such changes. This direction is guided by the therapist's detailed assessment. The assessment considers three main areas: the factors immediately preceding the problem, the problem behaviour itself and the consequences of the behaviour for the client (as well as those people around him or her).

There has been a gradual decline in the teaching of behaviour therapy on therapeutic training courses since the 1990s in favour of cognitive behaviour therapy (CBT), although many therapists still use the **exposure therapy** technique for dealing with phobias and **response prevention** for obsessive–compulsive disorder. More recently there has been a revival in some of the techniques, such as behavioural activation, due to their efficacy in tackling depression.

DEVELOPMENT OF THE THERAPY

In the early 1900s, Ivan Pavlov, a physiologist, demonstrated classical conditioning.[1] A dog will salivate when it is shown food. As this happens naturally and automatically it is called an *unconditioned response*. The unconditioned response is triggered by something, in this case food. This trigger is known as the *unconditioned stimulus*. If showing the food to the dog is paired with ringing a bell at about the same time, the dog will eventually salivate at the sound of the bell alone. As the bell, not the food, now triggers the dog salivating, the ringing of the bell is now known as the *conditioned stimulus*. This new response of salivating to the sound of the bell alone is known as a *conditioned response*. If the conditioned stimulus (bell) is presented too many times without the

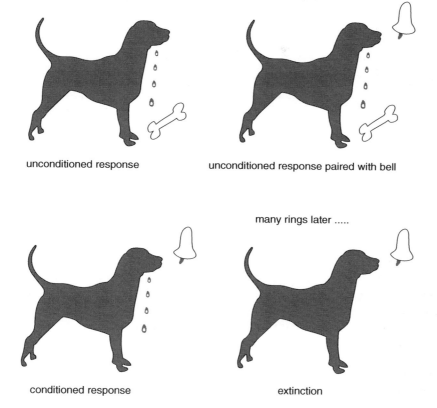

unconditioned response

unconditioned response paired with bell

many rings later .....

conditioned response

extinction

FIGURE 8.1 *Classical conditioning*

unconditioned stimulus (food), the conditioned response (salivation) will fail to occur when the bell is rung. This process is known as *extinction* (see Figure 8.1).

John Watson, a psychologist, and his associates, in 1920, proposed that phobias were just this process.[2] A conditioned emotional response (fear) had been paired with a previously neutral stimulus, such as a spider. Joseph Wölpe, in 1958, outlined a practical treatment procedure, called systematic desensitization, where relaxation training is paired with the conditioned stimulus. The confrontation of the feared stimulus, in this example, a spider, is a central part of behaviour therapy, known as *exposure treatment*. There are a variety of ways in which this exposure may be carried out and these will be described more fully later.

Prior to the development of classical conditioning, Edward Thorndike, a psychologist, had demonstrated that behaviour was mainly determined by its consequences;[3] if a particular behaviour is rewarded by a favourable outcome, it tends to be reinforced and repeated. This reward learning became known as operant conditioning or instrumental conditioning. For example, if a cat is in a box and accidentally touches a lever which opens a door allowing the cat to escape (the reward), the action of touching the lever becomes reinforced: the lever-touching behaviour is therefore mainly determined by the consequence of escape. This work was formalized in one of the most influential works in American psychology, *Animal Intelligence*, 1911.

Behaviour therapy was first developed in a consistent form by Burrhus F. Skinner, a psychologist, in the 1950s. Skinner proposed that all behaviour, whether helpful or unhelpful, was brought about by operant conditioning and that changing behaviour merely required the appropriate operant conditioning. Another key psychologist in behaviour therapy was Arnold Lazarus, who popularized it in the late 1950s and who emphasized the role of thought in behaviour. Two psychologists, Hans Eysenck and Jack Rachman, and two psychiatrists, Isaac Marks and Michael Gelder, were important figures for developing and applying behavioural therapy.

THEORY AND BASIC CONCEPTS

Behaviour therapy covers a range of concepts. At one end, the focus is entirely upon behaviour; thoughts (cognitions) are not denied but are considered to be peripheral to therapeutic work. At the other end, thoughts are considered to be a central and mediating factor of behaviour, and are taken fully into account in bringing about behaviour change. The range of approaches merges into CBT, which is covered elsewhere in this book. We shall therefore focus entirely on the behavioural end of the range.

Therapists from many different orientations now generally accept that thoughts (cognitions), feelings (emotions) and actions (behaviour) all go hand in hand. A change to one will usually lead to change in the other two. For example, if a person moves from feelings of depression to feelings of happiness, she will tend to think about herself, the world and the future more optimistically and to adopt behaviour that she had previously neglected. Behaviour therapists focus their work on bringing about changed behaviour. By non-avoidance of irrational fears, anxiety is reduced and increased behavioural activity lifts mood thereby reducing depression.

You may wish to remind yourself at this point of the terms *classical* and *operant conditioning, and exposure treatment* introduced on pp. 99, as these are basic elements of behaviour therapy.

Behaviour therapy takes the view that all behaviour, whether helpful or unhelpful, normal or abnormal, is learned through classical or operant conditioning. Symptoms are seen as unwanted behaviours. For example, a person bitten by a dog may become fearful of dogs: through classical conditioning, he may associate the conditioned response of fear with the previously neutral stimulus of dog. Oliver Twist's thieving behaviour was rewarded and reinforced by his peers through the process of operant conditioning.

Once psychological disturbance has been acquired, it is perpetuated either through failure to learn new behaviour or through avoiding feared objects/situations that results in a conditioned response failing to be extinguished. For example, the dog phobic avoids the feared stimulus, dog. The conditioned emotional response, fear, fails to be extinguished as exposure to the dog without adverse consequences has not taken place. Therapy is seen as changing such behaviour through new learning, or unlearning old behaviour through exposure treatment. This is where the skill of the behaviour therapist is essential.

First, it is very frightening to confront your fear. If the therapist simply asks a client with a phobia of dogs to go and stroke dogs, or a client with agoraphobia to enter a busy supermarket, the clients will be unlikely to do so and will consider the therapist's suggestion as unhelpful or too challenging. Therefore the therapist employs a range of strategies and techniques which are designed to bring the client into contact with the feared situation in a planned fashion that is acceptable to the client. These will be described later.

Second, the person with symptoms in need of help will often be unaware of all the occasions when the problem behaviour is present. For example, a person with social anxiety may be aware that they experience anxiety with groups of people but not be aware of the specific features of social situations which trouble them, such as making eye contact, being the focus of others' attention, or making requests. As we shall see in the next section, the therapist conducts a detailed assessment called a **behavioural analysis**.

Third, unless a new adaptive behaviour is practised frequently, over a sufficient period of time, therapy will usually fail. Often, clients do not persist in their new behaviours for long enough. The therapist therefore takes appropriate steps to build a therapeutic relationship through which the client's motivation is encouraged and maintained in the face of difficulties. Motivation is aided by negotiating clear goals with the client and providing a detailed explanation of how this may be accomplished. This will include discussing with the client the way in which the proposed programme differs from the client's own (failed) attempts at overcoming the problem. The client is encouraged to adopt the role of a 'scientist', in which role tasks are carried out. These tasks are viewed as behavioural experiments where the client gains valuable insight into their problem. Where a client is unable to perform a task, this will not be viewed as a failure, but as important new information about her problem. This approach is helpful in maintaining motivation.

PRACTICE

The general goals of behaviour therapy are to bring about desired and realistic changes in behaviour through a planned and consistent approach. Specific goals will be negotiated with the individual client and a treatment programme tailored to fit the goals. For the reasons outlined above, the approach focuses directly on behaviour and not on non-conscious processes; compare this with psychodynamic therapy. Instead, behaviour therapy assumes that changed emotions and thoughts will follow on automatically from changed behaviour. When anxiety and fears are involved, the aim is not to rid the person completely of these (an aim which is unlikely to succeed in any case), but to bring them to a point where they are in perspective and manageable rather than incapacitating.

The main tools of behaviour therapy are exposure therapy, behavioural activation, response prevention, skills training and **self-control training** which are consistent with the principles of classical and operant conditioning respectively, described earlier.

Assessment

A person with her particular problems will usually have been assessed and referred on for behaviour therapy if appropriate. If the person and her problems are suitable for behaviour therapy, a full *behavioural assessment* of the problem would be carried out. This is also known as a *behavioural analysis*. The therapist takes a problem–oriented and directive approach, asking the client direct questions about the nature of the problem. Typical questions would be as follows:

- Can you tell me about your problem?
- When did it begin?
- Can you give me a recent example?
- Returning to your example, can you tell me what was going on immediately before it happened?
- Is it constant or fluctuating?
- When is it at its worst?
- When is it least of a problem?
- Do any factors help it?
- Does anything make it worse?
- Why have you come for help *now*?
- In what way(s), if any, does it stop you getting on with your life?
- Is there anything the problem leads you to avoid?
- In what way(s) would your life be different if you no longer had the problem?

These types of questions would be used with a range of problems, such as phobias, anxiety, sexual dysfunctions, passive or aggressive behaviour, obsessive–compulsive behaviour, and so on. The questions would not be asked mechanically and are not in a specific order. They are designed to discover the full extent of the problem and to find out what behaviours are present before, during and after the problem. This would include seeking information about behaviours, both helpful and unhelpful, which the client currently uses to cope with the situation. An example of helpful behaviour may be the person who talks about her fears with her spouse. Unhelpful behaviour might be the person who dulls her anxieties by drinking alcohol or taking illicit drugs. Often, much of the information being sought would be volunteered in response to relatively few questions: for example, the question, 'Can you tell me about your problem?' might well lead a client to give a detailed description about when it began, a recent example, the context in which it occurred, etc.

Once the problem has been described generally using this approach, further information then needs to be gained which is specific to a particular type of problem. For example, a person experiencing difficulty in taking part in social situations (social phobia) might be asked whether this applies to going into shops, bars, restaurants, work, meeting people she does not know, starting friendships, making eye contact. More enquiries would be made about other specific situations. If you imagine about 40 such situations, a person might experience no discomfort in some of these situations, great discomfort or avoidance for other situations and moderate discomfort in yet other situations. A more scientific way of assessing and evaluating the scope of the problem is to use a questionnaire. The situations would be listed individually and the client would be asked to rate the discomfort she experiences in the situation on, say, a five-point scale where 1 is no discomfort, 2 is a little discomfort, 3 is moderate discomfort, 4 is great discomfort and 5 maximum discomfort/**avoidance**. There are questionnaires for a range of clinical problems such as obsessive–compulsive disorder and post-traumatic stress disorder.

Apart from finding out about the scope and detail of the problem, this type of questionnaire has other advantages. First, it helps the client to appreciate the problem in context, and to understand better where it begins and ends and in which particular situations it occurs. Second, it helps the therapy by showing which areas need most work, which need least and where best to begin; some areas will need no work at all. Third, the rating of each item enables the client and the therapist to gauge the degree of change taking place in therapy. This is particularly helpful when setbacks occur, as they often do, for they act as reminders of the progress that has been made by the client. Fourth, the individual items of the questionnaire can be used to design tasks for the client to carry out between sessions. We will describe some of these tasks later, but it is important to emphasize that tasks carried out by the client between sessions form the bedrock of behaviour therapy.

The process of therapy

Once the target problem has been fully assessed, therapeutic work can begin. This will include some form of exposure therapy and may or may not include self-control or skills training. These terms are explained later. Progress in therapy is achieved by clearly explaining to the client what is involved in therapy, how the process works, what is expected of the client and the part the client will play in her own progress. Any pitfalls the client anticipates will be openly discussed and solutions generated. Such an open exchange can only take place if a good therapeutic relationship, initiated by the therapist, has been developed between client and therapist early on. Client drop-out from therapy is highest at the start of therapy, and if a good working relationship is not quickly established, the chances of drop-out are heightened. The therapist develops this relationship by being empathetic and shows respect and support throughout the therapeutic process.

Exposure therapy

We previously gave an example of exposure therapy[4] in which a person afraid of dogs was exposed to them. The principle of exposure is always the same. By continued exposure to the feared object or situation, anxiety will initially rise, but eventually will habituate and fade to a tolerable level. This requires consistent and continued practice. Longer periods of exposure leads to better and quicker results. You may have thought that this is no different from the call to 'pull yourself together'. The difference is that exposure is carried out in a structured and manageable fashion, always with the client's understanding and consent but also with a clear rationale being given. How long the exposure needs to be, so as to be effective, and how quickly the client should face her worst fears, depend upon the client, the amount of discomfort she can tolerate, the nature of the focal problem and how long it has been established. The exposure programme is individually tailored to fit the client, but outlined below are some broad forms this may take.

To describe exposure techniques, we will use as an example a person with spider phobia (arachnophobia). The range of the problem may be slight anxiety if imagining a money spider but extreme fear and panic if suddenly handed a large hairy spider. The most rapid form of exposure is **flooding**. This is where the person is exposed to the worst feared situation for a prolonged period, remaining with it until her fear subsides. In this example, this would mean handling the large hairy spider. Many people would not be willing to do this, and one of the other approaches described below would be used. However, some clients are willing to face their worst fear in this way.

Another flooding technique, using the worst feared situation, but in imagination only, is called **implosion**. All types of exposure can be carried out either in reality (*in vivo*), or in imagination (*in fantasy*).

Where a client is not willing to confront the most feared situation, either in reality or in imagination, or where there are medical reasons for not doing so (such as a person with asthma or heart disease), a more gradual form of exposure is required. Such an approach is graded exposure. Here, the client lists all the situations, from the least (money spider) to the most (large hairy spider) anxiety-provoking, in ascending order of difficulty. The therapist then helps the client to expose herself systematically to the range of anxiety-provoking situations on the list, starting with a manageable item and gradually working up to the most difficult.

The client may be able to enter the feared situation alone (self-exposure), or accompanied by the therapist (therapist-aided exposure). Sometimes, family members or friends are called upon to act as co-therapists or aides. Clients and family members may also read useful self-help books that explain behaviour therapy.[5]

Exposure is often made difficult because the client engages in *avoidance*. As behaviour is mainly determined by its consequences, a particular behaviour if rewarded by a favourable outcome tends to be reinforced and repeated. If a person with dog phobia runs away from a dog (avoidance), he will experience a lowering of anxiety at the time. This leads to the avoidance being *reinforced* and strengthens the phobia. *Avoidance is therefore a key area to be worked on in therapy.*

A specific form of avoidance is ritualistic behaviour. For example, a client with *obsessive–compulsive disorder* may wash compulsively after contact with dirt (real or imagined). She will be encouraged to refrain from carrying out the rituals so that she is exposed to the fear-evoking cue (dirt on hands). The client will be encouraged to find something else to occupy herself initially until the urge to perform the washing ritual lessens. This is known as *response prevention*.[4]

Skills training

Much human behaviour is learned. Many people learn a wide range of skills in many different areas but may lack skills in other areas. Part of the behaviour therapist's work is therefore involved with *skills training*. This is carried out step by step. Common areas in which the therapist engages are assertion skills training, social skills training and sexual skills training. A range of techniques is used for all types of skills training. In **modelling** the therapist demonstrates appropriate behaviour, component by component, and encourages the client to follow the example, giving feedback and praise for good performance. For example, assertion skills training might include verbal and non-verbal behaviour such as eye contact, facial expression and posture. *Role play*, in which the client and therapist enact problem scenarios, is also commonly used and may take place within a group setting. For example, the client might role-play changing goods in a shop, asking a favour of a friend or refusing a request. In these cases, the therapist models the behaviour at an appropriate level for the client.

Self-control training

Self-control training is aimed at helping the client to control their own behaviour and feelings. Often a problem behaviour is immediately preceded by events that trigger the problem behaviour. But these triggers or cues may be unrecognized by the client. He will often be asked to keep a daily record of the problem behaviour and the circumstances in which it happens. This form of self-monitoring is used widely in behaviour therapy. For example, a problem drinker would record what he drinks, when he drinks it and associations between drinking and either stressful events or unwanted emotions. From self-monitoring, the client may be able to identify specific cues that trigger the drinking behaviour and encouraged to exercise self-control when these occur. The client is encouraged to reward himself in some way for doing so. This is called self-reinforcement.

Behavioural activation

Behavioural activation is based on operant learning theory and is a behavioural approach to dealing with clinical depression.[4] It brings together a number of different behavioural techniques and strategies. The client is encouraged to monitor their activities (*activity monitoring*), schedule relevant activities (*activity scheduling*), target avoidance behaviour for change (e.g. start to socialize instead of withdrawing from social interactions), and include rewards after the completion of agreed tasks (*contingency management*). Often skills training will need to be included in a therapy programme. It is worth noting that cognitive processes such as rumination are seen as maladaptive or unhelpful 'coping' strategies and are a form of avoidance, which are discussed in therapy.

Format of a typical session

The main assessment session is different from ongoing sessions as it is designed to find out a great deal of information about the client and his problem.

Subsequent sessions will to some extent be determined by the nature of the client's particular problem but will follow a general plan. The therapist will welcome the client and negotiate an agenda for the session. If any questionnaires need to be completed, these will often follow next. Assignments outside of therapy sessions are central to behaviour therapy and this homework is reviewed and discussed in some detail. Further and ongoing treatment aims will be considered, with any in-session work such as role play, exposure therapy and so on, being focused on a target problem for the session. Homework will be negotiated for further therapeutic work needing to be carried out before the next session. The session will then be reviewed with the client. Feedback is encouraged and the client given due praise for work done and progress made.

WHICH CLIENTS BENEFIT MOST?

Behaviour therapy has been applied to a wide range of people with a variety of problems.[6] It may take an experienced therapist to recognize certain behaviours to be problematic. People who are able (with help if necessary) to decide upon clear behavioural goals are most likely to benefit from behaviour therapy provided they are willing to cooperate and to do homework assignments outside of sessions. Motivation, or the ability to be motivated by the therapist, is also an important factor. People with some major physical or mental complications that would make the exposure and skills training work too difficult, even with therapist assistance, are least likely to benefit. Others least likely to benefit are those who take in excess of two units of alcohol or 10 milligrams of diazepam (medication prescribed for anxiety), or similar, daily. If they are willing and able to reduce this to a suitable level beforehand, with help if necessary, they may be suitable.

We will now outline the types of problems most suitable for behaviour therapy.[7] Most phobias, such as spider, height or blood phobia, agoraphobias or social phobias, are suitable. Obsessive–compulsive disorders, especially where pronounced habits are involved, have been successfully treated. It is also beneficial for a range of sexual problems such as premature ejaculation, painful intercourse in women (vaginismus) and masochism. Habit disorders, such as stammering and bed-wetting, are well suited to behaviour therapy. People with social skills problems respond well to training.

CASE STUDY
The Client

Penny was referred for therapy by her General Practitioner. She is 32 years old and lives with her only son, aged six, in a ground-floor maisonette. She has never been married, and separated from her last partner shortly after the birth of their child. She works part-time as a laboratory assistant in a local university.

The referral letter from the General Practitioner stated that Penny had a five-year history of anxiety. She had been prescribed tranquillizers on a number of occasions but was not currently taking any. On assessment, she was found to be experiencing social anxiety where she feared a wide range of social situations and avoided many of these. She said that in these situations she became very shaky, experienced palpitations and a tight feeling in her chest, breathlessness, sweating and tingling of her fingers. Her concentration was severely affected at these times. Assessment did not show her to be suffering from panic disorder. These symptoms had progressively worsened over a five-year period and Penny was visibly distressed at this in the session. She had developed a pattern of drinking alcohol to control her anxiety in social situations. This problem had intensified in the last two years and she was now consuming alcohol prior to attending work, and had also started to show signs of depression, although this was not pronounced. She said this was since her new line manager had been in post and was more attentive of her work and required her to take part in staff meetings. She said that she was on the verge of not being able to go to work because of the problem and this is why she came for help now.

The Therapy

The first session explored Penny's problems as outlined above. She was asked to complete a *social situations questionnaire* to establish which aspects of the problem caused her most concern. This enabled goals for treatment to be negotiated. From these goals, tasks would gradually be identified throughout the course of therapy. One such task, which it was important for Penny to achieve, was to reduce her consumption of alcohol to a maximum of one to two units daily. This is important in behaviour therapy, because alcohol cancels out the benefits of exposure therapy and has other negative effects, such as being a depressant. The principles of behaviour therapy were fully explained to Penny and the difficulties regarding alcohol were included. She seemed to be very diligent in her employment and maintained her sense of humour despite her difficulties. The therapist made a note of these as being positive attributes in the therapeutic process.

From the assessment and the social situations questionnaire, the following goals for therapy were negotiated:

- to mix with people in groups, both in social settings and at work
- to attend and actively participate in staff meetings
- to go into restaurants, pubs, cafes and discos
- to start and maintain conversations with people she does not know very well
- to start a friendship with someone of the opposite sex
- to give own opinions which conflict with those of others
- to talk about self and feelings in conversation with others.

With these goals as the focus for therapy, tasks would be set at each session to achieve them. The main work would be *exposure therapy* to a range of social situations. The therapist thought that some *assertion training* might be necessary later on in therapy.

(Continued)

(Continued)

The tasks set at the end of the first session were:

- to read the sections on social phobia and bodily changes during anxiety in *Living with Fear*[4]
- to practise relaxation skills daily, using the audio recording provided
- to contact her friend, Ann, and to go to a chosen pasta restaurant, and remain there until her anxiety reduces
- to monitor her anxiety in staff meetings and social situations on a 0–5 scale.

Progress was reviewed at the start of each session, and at the second session, the client had successfully carried out all of the tasks except for relaxation training. Praise was given for her diligent work in the other areas. Penny said that she was surprised at enjoying herself in the restaurant, although feeling anxious initially. She had completely stopped taking alcohol in the mornings and had committed herself to be alcohol-free for the sessions. She felt very pleased with herself for doing this. Tasks continued to be set for subsequent sessions consistent with the goals outlined above. Practice is very important in behaviour therapy.

By the sixth session Penny had firmly grasped that in order to make progress, it was essential for her to face up to her fears. She recognized that avoiding them was easier at the time, but led to long-term difficulties. Facing her fears was only possible in practice by a structured programme of self-exposure. She persevered with self-exposure in many social situations that she had previously avoided, until her level of anxiety in each was much lower and acceptable to her. These social situations were all in relation to the goals stated above. Penny had done some work towards achieving all of her goals except for the last two:

- to give own opinions which conflict with those of others
- to talk about self and feelings in conversation with others.

She had worked hard up to this stage. It would still be important for her to continue with self-exposure towards the goals already partly achieved until the process became 'natural' to her.

However, Penny did encounter a setback which prompted her to deal with the goals she had not yet worked upon. She said that she had been unfairly criticized by her boss at work. Although angry, she felt unable to tell him that she found his criticism unjust. This led to her feeling 'low' and drinking up to 10 units daily. Within the session, Penny was encouraged to role-play an assertive response towards her boss's unfair criticism and employed her humour to good effect in this! Her task at the end of this session was to speak to her boss assertively on this matter and to share her feelings about it with her friend Ann. In the following session, she said she had been surprised at her performance with her boss, and the positive comments she had received from colleagues!

She continued to make good progress in therapy and found exposure to the feared situations caused her some discomfort but she was able to endure this. She said that the benefits of taking part in these social activities far outweighed the discomfort.

In a follow-up session three months after counselling had ended, Penny continued to maintain her progress. She completed some self-evaluation questionnaires which showed her anxiety to be minimal in most of the social situations identified. Although she still found it difficult to give her own opinions when they conflicted with those of others, she had taken positive action by enrolling in an assertiveness class at her local adult education centre. She no longer had symptoms of depression and she now only drank socially and not to excess. Her humour was no longer suppressed by her feelings of social anxiety.

REFERENCES

[1] Pavlov, L. P. (1927) *Conditioned Reflexes.* London: Oxford University Press.

[2] Watson, J. B. and Rayner, R. (1920) 'Conditioned emotional reactions', *Journal of Experimental Psychology, 3,* 1–14.

[3] Thorndike, E. L. (1911) *Animal Intelligence.* New York: Macmillan.

[4] Foa, E. B., Yadin, E. and Lichner, T. K. (2012) *Exposure and Response (Ritual) Prevention for Obsessive Compulsive Disorder: Therapist Guide (Treatments That Work),* 2nd edn. New York: Oxford University Press.

[5] Marks, I. M. (1978) *Living with Fear.* New York: McGraw Hill.

[6] O'Carroll, P. J. (2014) 'Behavioural activation', in W. Dryden and A. Reeves (eds), *The Handbook of Individual Therapy,* 6th edn. London: Sage.

[7] Jena, S. P. K. (2008) *Behaviour Therapy: Techniques, Research and Applications.* New Delhi: Sage.

SUGGESTED READING

Foa, E. B., Yadin, E. and Lichner, T. K. (2012) *Exposure and Response (Ritual) Prevention for Obsessive Compulsive Disorder: Therapist Guide (Treatments That Work),* 2nd edn. New York: Oxford University Press. A useful therapist guide describing how to use exposure and response prevention techniques to tackle OCD.

Jena, S. P. K. (2008) *Behaviour Therapy: Techniques, Research and Applications.* New Delhi: Sage. This book provides an up-to-date guide to the theory and practice of behaviour therapy.

Marks, I. M. (1978) *Living with Fear.* New York: McGraw Hill. This popular self-help book is very easy to read and gives a wide range of information that is still relevant today. It combines a deep knowledge of the subject with some interesting anecdotes.

Richards, D. and McDonald, B. (1990) *Behavioural Psychotherapy.* London: Heineman Nursing. This book is subtitled 'A Handbook for Nurses'. It is a clear and practical guide to behavioural psychotherapy and will be useful reading for a range of practitioners other than nurses.

DISCUSSION ISSUES

1. To what extent is it necessary to focus on clients' thoughts in bringing about client change in therapy?
2. Behaviour therapy considers symptoms and behaviour but leaves underlying psychological problems unresolved. Discuss.
3. Do thoughts determine behaviour and feelings or does changed behaviour bring about changes in clients' feelings and thoughts?
4. Exposure therapy is no more than telling a person to 'pull themselves together'. Discuss.

9

Cognitive Behavioural Therapy

Kasia Szymanska and Stephen Palmer

Cognitive behavioural therapy (CBT) is an approach that combines the use of cognitive and behavioural techniques to help clients modify their moods and behaviour by examining and changing their unhelpful thinking. Cognitive theory postulates that thoughts and beliefs about events or situations (imagined or real) largely determine emotional and behavioural responses and not the event *per se*. Cognitive theory is based on informational processing theory which highlights how in adverse situations when a person becomes more distressed their thinking becomes more inflexible, rigid and absolutist.[1] The person may process and distort incoming information by focusing on the negative and then overgeneralize based on insufficient data.

The therapist acts like a trainer or coach, explaining cognitive theory and teaching clients techniques and strategies they can use to overcome their problems. It is used in the treatment of a wide range of psychological problems such as stress, anxiety and depression in a variety of settings. These include hospitals, doctors' surgeries and within the corporate training field, specifically in the arena of stress management and coaching.

DEVELOPMENT OF THE THERAPY

Historically, CBT has roots in both the cognitive and behavioural approaches. The former can be traced back to the work of the philosopher Epictetus, who, in the first century AD, suggested that people 'are not disturbed by things but by the view they take of them'. Later influences include psychiatrist Alfred Adler, who in his book entitled *What Life Should Mean to You*[2] wrote, 'Meanings are not determined by situations, but we determine ourselves by the meaning we give to situations' (p. 14). Also in the 1950s, George Kelly, the originator of personal construct therapy, argued that individuals are scientists who develop ideas and then test them out by acting on them.[3] His work paved the way for the development of cognitive therapy. Subsequently the work of psychologists such as Albert Ellis,[4] the founder of rational emotive behaviour therapy, and Donald Miechenbaum[5] emphasized the importance of cognitive processes. In the 1960s cognitive therapy became established through the work of psychiatrist Aaron Beck who was dissatisfied with the lack of scientific basis for psychoanalytic theories. The journal *Cognitive Therapy and Research* was first established in 1977 and one of Beck's best-known books in this field, *Cognitive Therapy for Depression*[6] was published by Beck and his colleagues in 1979.

While the behavioural component's more recent roots lie in the work of John Broadus Watson,[7] a behavioural psychologist who is known as the 'father' of the behavioural approach, and the work of the Russian physiologist Ivan Petrovich Pavlov who, on the basis of his animal research, derived the principle of classical conditioning. In the 1950s Skinner developed the principle of operant conditioning.

Since the 1990s the combination of cognitive and behaviour therapy (i.e. CBT) underpinned by cognitive theory has flourished around the world. More recently, a new generation of cognitive behaviour therapies have been added to the family; these include: acceptance and commitment therapy (ACT); mindfulness-based cognitive therapy (MBCT); compassion focused therapy; and dialectical behaviour therapy (DBT).

THEORY AND BASIC CONCEPTS

Basic assumptions

The basic premise of cognitive theory is that how an individual perceives or appraises an adverse situation largely determines how he or she emotionally feels. For example, if you perceive a task such as driving on motorways as threatening then you are likely to feel anxious. In addition to your thoughts, you may also hold in your mind's eye an image of your car crashing on the motorway, which can also exacerbate anxiety. In CBT, perceptions, thoughts, attitudes, rules, beliefs and images are known as cognitions. Negative unhelpful cognitions can greatly contribute to troublesome emotions such as anxiety, anger, depression, guilt, jealousy, envy and shame. A person may also experience physiological responses; for example, with anxiety they notice palpitations, sweaty hands and butterflies in the stomach. With anxiety, they may respond behaviourally by avoiding driving on motorways, eventually becoming phobic of driving on motorways. As a **safety behaviou**r they may actively encourage their partner to do all the driving, which over time undermines their own confidence even further. The relationship between these modalities is illustrated in Figure 9.1 and the diagram is often used to educate clients about the links.

In CBT an ABC model can be used to explain the relationship between events, beliefs and emotional responses. 'A' represents an activating event or adversity, 'B' represents beliefs about the event, and 'C' the consequences. The example below illustrates the application of the ABC to a specific problem, fear of flying.

A Activating event
David is on a plane which is flying through severe turbulence.

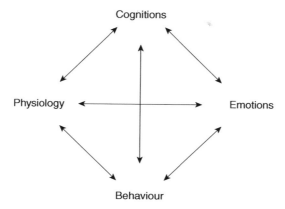

FIGURE 9.1   *The relationship between the modalities*

A Activating event

David is on a plane which is flying through severe turbulence.

B Beliefs about the situation

- This plane is going to crash
- I'll never see my family again
- This is it
- I can't bear this

C Consequences

Emotional response

- Anxiety/panic

Behavioural response

- Seeks reassurance from the air steward
- Tries to read his newspaper as a distraction
- Drinks alcohol to 'calm' nerves

Physiological response

- Racing heart, shaking, sweating

Diagrammatic illustration of the presenting problem using the ABC can serve to strengthen a client's conceptual understanding of the link between thinking and their responses to events. In the above example, David's anxiety at C is not due to the turbulence but rather to his *appraisal* of the turbulence at B. Often in the initial appraisal of real or imagined events these cognitions seem literally to just pop up and in CBT literature they are referred to as **automatic thoughts**. If they are unhelpful they are often termed negative automatic thoughts or NATs. They can occur very quickly and may appear to be both plausible and realistic to the person. They can also be present in the form of images or pictures. In the previous example a typical image a client may have would be imagining the plane crashing.

Becoming aware of automatic thoughts can be a difficult task as clients are not usually accustomed to focusing on the content of their thoughts. Therefore, clients may need assistance in identifying their unhelpful or dysfunctional thoughts, particularly during the beginning stages of therapy. One method is for the client to keep a record of situations in which they feel upset and to note down the accompanying upsetting thoughts and troublesome emotions. An example of a record/diary is shown in Table 9.1.

Having identified the NATs and understood their interaction with emotions and behavioural/physiological responses, clients are then encouraged to identify **thinking errors** (also known as 'cognitive distortions' because they lead to a distortion of reality).[1] Often NATs are also thinking errors, as in the record above. Commonly used categories of thinking errors are listed below:

- all-or-nothing thinking – evaluating experiences using extremes such as 'excellent' or 'awful', e.g. 'If I don't get this job, I'll never work again.'
- mind reading/jumping to conclusions – assuming a negative response without the relevant information, e.g. 'As he didn't say "good morning" to me, that means he is annoyed with me.'
- personalization – blaming yourself for an event, e.g. 'It's totally my fault that our relationship ended.'
- over-generalization – drawing sweeping negative conclusions on the basis of one or more events, e.g. 'Because my report had a mistake in it, my appraisal will be terrible and I won't get my pay rise.'
- fortune-telling – assuming you know what the future holds, e.g. 'Now I've had one panic attack, I'm always going to have them.'
- emotional reasoning – confusing feelings with facts, e.g. 'I feel so anxious about driving on motorways, therefore it must be dangerous.'
- labelling – using unhelpful labels or global ratings to describe yourself or others, e.g. 'I'm so stupid' or 'They are totally useless grandparents.'
- magnification – blowing things out of proportion, e.g. 'Forgetting to phone my client today was probably the worst possible thing I've done.'
- demands – being overly demanding of yourself and others, using words such as 'must', and 'should', e.g. 'I should be the perfect partner.'

TABLE 9.1 *Example record*

Date	Situation (Activating event)	Negative automatic thoughts (NATs) (Beliefs)	Feelings (Consequences)
1st Nov.	Have just broken up with my boyfriend	I'm never going to meet anyone again, I'll be alone forever. (Fortune-telling)	Depression
		I'm a useless girlfriend (Labelling)	Depression

Informational processing theory postulates that as a person becomes more distressed their thinking is likely to become extreme and inflexible. Hence it becomes easier for the client to recognize thinking errors in stressful situations. For example, a client who has just had a poor performance review and is feeling depressed, may have the following thoughts: 'I know I'm going to be made redundant' (fortune-telling) and/or 'I'm a total failure' (labelling). A client suffering from post-traumatic stress who was involved in a car accident may think: 'cars are very dangerous' (jumping to conclusions) and/or 'it was all my fault' (personalization). While everyone has unhelpful thoughts from time to time, individuals with emotional problems such as depression or anxiety, tend to experience them more frequently.

Thinking errors and NATs are considered to be surface thoughts. There are two other deeper levels of cognitions which greatly influence a person's approach to life. **Intermediate beliefs** consist of underlying assumptions that are normally articulated as 'if … then' or 'unless … then' statements (e.g. 'If I make a mistake then I'll be a failure'). Intermediate beliefs include rules (e.g. 'I must not make mistakes'). Below the intermediate beliefs are **core beliefs**, which are usually developed in childhood and are often deep-seated and rigid.[1] They can include beliefs such as 'I'm worthless' or 'I'm total a failure'. If the person successfully manages to apply their rules which they have developed then they may prevent their negative core belief from being activated. Intermediate and core beliefs can also be positive. For example, 'If I perform well then I'll be a success' and 'I'm a success'.

Over time we start to process and view the world through our own personal lenses, which can be positive, neutral and negative. Similar core beliefs become embedded within what is known as a schema, such as 'unlovability' or 'helplessness'. Clark and Beck[8] described schemas as 'relatively enduring internal structures of stored generic or prototypical features of stimuli, ideas, or experiences that are used to organize new information in a meaningful way thereby determining how phenomena are perceived and conceptualized' (p. 79). In the same hierarchical manner, a collection of similar schemas can form a mode.

How psychological problems are acquired

A number of factors contribute to the acquisition of psychological problems. They include:

- challenging life events such as relationship problems (e.g. bullying), bereavement, redundancy and physical illness
- social factors such as poor housing, stress at work and loneliness
- developing poor coping strategies (e.g. increased alcohol consumption to alleviate the symptoms of stress).

In response to a range of negative, neutral and positive experiences in childhood and adolescence, young people start to develop intermediate and core beliefs in order to help them understand and cope with situations. A young person with a critical parent may start to develop the core belief, 'I'm stupid'. To counter this idea they learn to study hard and over-prepare for exams, thereby not activating their core belief as long as they perform well. However, a sibling in the same family may instead learn to procrastinate and if they don't pass their exams, they can just put it down to not working hard thereby not activating a core belief such as 'I'm stupid'.

In the example used at the start of this section, it is possible that as a child David was told by his anxious parents to be careful, avoid risks and be on his guard, and so developed the core belief 'The world is a dangerous place', and this general schema together with his intermediate beliefs/assumptions were activated as a result of his negative automatic thoughts about the severe turbulence the plane was experiencing.

How psychological problems are perpetuated

Psychological problems are perpetuated by the maintenance of NATs, thinking errors, intermediate beliefs and core beliefs, often by avoidance of situations that may trigger them. For example, a person who became highly anxious while giving a lecture at work may have held the following beliefs: 'Everyone will have noticed my hands were shaking, how embarrassing' (jumping to conclusions) and 'My boss will probably sack me' (fortune-telling). Underlying these surface thoughts they may hold the intermediate beliefs such as: 'If I perform badly then I'll be seen as a failure' (an assumption); 'I should always perform well' (a rule); and 'I'm a failure' (core belief). If the person continues to hold onto the assumption and core belief then he or she may avoid giving future presentations (avoidance behaviour) in order not to experience the embarrassment again. Or the person may continue to speak publically and develop safety behaviours instead, such as holding their hands behind their back in the previous example. Thus psychologically based problems are perpetuated.

How an individual moves from psychological disturbance to psychological health

The move to psychological health involves the systematic application to the problem(s) of specific cognitive and behavioural techniques by both the therapist and client. In certain cases where the emotional disturbance is very strong (for example, suicidal ideation as part of depression) this may be coupled with medication, as prescribed by the client's doctor or psychiatrist. In addition, a decrease in the influence of external, non-psychological pressures can contribute to increased wellbeing (for example, a new job with better pay and flexibility). It is important to note, however, that the reduction of external pressures alone is unlikely to result in good psychological health. The person who is anxious about giving presentations may receive temporary relief from the symptoms of anxiety on leaving the job, but if in the future he or she is asked to give any presentations the symptoms may return. Therefore technique-application with the aim of helping the client to cope with problems in a constructive manner and modify their thinking is viewed as central to the acquisition of psychological health.

PRACTICE

CBT is an educative and problem–orientated approach, the goals of which are:

- to ameliorate and resolve difficulties or problems
- to help the client acquire constructive coping strategies
- to help the client modify thinking errors and/or schema
- to help the client become their own 'personal therapist'.

Since the therapy is goal–orientated, at the start both client and counsellor discuss what the client would like to achieve by the end of the counselling (**goal–setting**). The client's goals are usually written down and examined to see whether they are realistic and achievable within the time limit available. For example, if a client came to see a cognitive behavioural therapist for a phobia about travelling on trains, it would be unrealistic for the counsellor and client to predict that by the end of the first session the client would be 'cured'. Therapists work in the 'here and now', helping clients become aware of their unhelpful beliefs and then modify these beliefs using cognitive and behavioural strategies. The aim is that clients should use these strategies to deal with any future problems, without therapeutic support, and thus become their own personal therapist.

Case conceptualization

Assessment of the client's problems, also known as case conceptualization or formulation, is an important component of CBT. Over the first and often second sessions, the therapist, with the information the client has provided and using appropriate questioning, can gain an in–depth picture of the client's problems from a cognitive and behavioural perspective. This tentative formulation can then guide both the client and therapist in understanding how they arose, how they are perpetuated and which techniques would need to be used by the client to overcome his or her problems.[1] Some of the main features of the case conceptualization include:

- a detailed description of the client's problem(s), specifically in relation to the modalities of cognitions, behaviour, emotions and physiology
- an understanding of the problems in terms of development and course, that is, whether the problem(s) developed suddenly or slowly, and whether they get better at certain times and worse at others
- identification of any factors that exacerbate the problem – for example, clients who experience anxiety when speaking publically to people they don't know – may make the problem worse by drinking alcohol to gain courage before speaking to others
- compiling of a problem list by the therapist and client, for those clients with more than one problem
- discussing and setting achievable and realistic goals
- if appropriate, request that the client fill out questionnaires to supplement the therapist's knowledge of the client's problem(s).

Session structure

A key characteristic of CBT are the structured sessions, a typical format for which is outlined below:

1. Review client's current psychological state (how does the client feel emotionally?).
2. Negotiate the agenda for the session (what is it that the therapist and client would like to focus on in this session?).
3. Review homework assignments, carried out since the last session (for example, did the client complete the recommended reading?). If a client does not do the negotiated homework assignment, this issue is discussed, focusing on what can be learnt.
4. Work on specific session targets, which have been agreed on when negotiating the agenda (for example, how to cope with being alone at weekends).
5. New homework assignments are negotiated that relate to the session's agenda (for example, the client with a phobia of travelling on crowded trains may be asked to undertake a behavioural experiment and travel on a half-full train for a specified period, noting down their thoughts and rating their emotions on a 0 to 10 scale where 10 is high anxiety; in subsequent therapy sessions they may travel on a train and use cognitive anxiety management techniques instead).
6. The therapist obtains feedback from the client as to how they found the session (that is, did they understand everything that was discussed in the session, did the therapist say anything unduly upsetting, and are they clear about the homework?).

In addition to structured sessions, other characteristics of CBT include:

- A collaborative or team approach to therapy. The therapist and client work together to tackle the client's problems. The client is encouraged to ask questions when appropriate, the emphasis being on an open, transparent relationship.
- The therapist and client work towards goals which are specific, measured, achievable, realistic and time-limited (known as **SMART goals**).
- Sessions last 50 minutes or an hour. (This may be reduced dependent upon the needs of the clients.)
- Therapy is normally short-term (between six and 20 sessions), although long-term therapy is often more appropriate with clients who have more difficult problems.
- NATs and thinking errors are usually the focus of the beginning part of the therapy, whereas the middle and ending parts tend to focus on modifying intermediate beliefs and core beliefs/schema. (Core beliefs or schema may not be explored in brief therapy.)

Techniques and strategies

Cognitive behavioural therapists use a wide range of cognitive and behavioural techniques, a selection of which are outlined below.[1] Cognitive techniques are used to help clients identify, evaluate, modify and restructure NATs, intermediate and core beliefs, while behavioural techniques serve to help clients to elicit beliefs and test out the validity of new helpful beliefs. It is important to remember that these techniques are not applied on a random basis. The information gathered during the initial assessment enables the therapist to make a tentative case formulation, thereby informing technique selection.

Cognitive techniques

Questioning

Direct questioning, also known as Socratic questioning, is used to help clients become aware of their negative thoughts/images and to modify unhelpful beliefs. To identify negative thoughts, clients are asked to think of situations in which they experienced strong negative emotions such as anxiety or depression and then ask themselves what was going through their minds at that moment. Having identified negative beliefs, the next step is to examine the validity of them by using Socratic questions, which include:[8,9]

> Where is this way of thinking getting you?
> Is there any evidence for this belief?
> Are there any alternative ways of looking at the situation?
> What is the effect of thinking this way?
> What are the advantages and disadvantages of thinking this way?
> Are you jumping to conclusions?
> Is this an example of mind-reading or fortune-telling by you?
> Are you taking things personally which have little or nothing to do with you?

Automatic thought forms

These forms (also known as Daily Thought Records) are usually divided into four sections: (a) the situation or activating event; (b) negative automatic thoughts (NATs); (c) emotional and behavioural consequences; and (d) alternative helpful explanations or thoughts. Clients use these forms to record their NATs, feelings and actions regarding events they are upset about and the subsequent self-helping responses that they have developed to deal with the situation. They can also rate the strength of the emotions on a 0 to 10 scale and the believability of the NATs and alternative helpful thoughts.

Advantages and disadvantages

The therapist and client can work together on listing the advantages and disadvantages of holding the NATs, thinking errors, intermediate and core beliefs. Normally there are more disadvantages than advantages. Realistic, helpful beliefs can then be developed and the same process repeated and applied to them.

Distraction

Distraction exercises may help clients to stop thinking negatively, allowing them to tolerate situations for longer periods. Examples include: counting back from 100 in threes; reading an interesting book; remembering a pleasant image in detail, for example a day from your last holiday, what you were doing, the conversation, the colours, any smells etc.

Double standard method

Often people are much harsher on themselves than on friends or colleagues, so clients are asked to treat themselves more compassionately as they would a friend in the same situation.

Looking for other explanations

In some situations people often draw incorrect conclusions where other more rational explanations may be possible. If a client holds the belief 'When I got home tonight my husband didn't say hello, therefore he must be angry with me', she is asked to consider alternative explanations – for example was her husband annoyed with her in the morning; if not, is it possible that he was preoccupied in thinking about work?

Dealing with emotional reasoning

Clients are encouraged not to confuse feelings with facts; for example, if a person *feels* out of control, is there evidence that they *are* out of control?

Testing out the validity of their automatic thoughts

After having examined their beliefs and developed more helpful ones, clients are asked to test out their new beliefs by using behavioural experiments. For example, to test out the new belief 'I can stand travelling on buses for 15 minutes', the behavioural exercise would be to take a bus journey for 15 minutes.

Coping imagery

The client shares with the therapist their fears about an event or situation they are anxious about. They then discuss how to troubleshoot each concern, for example 'If I am asked a difficult question when giving the presentation, I can calmly say that I will find out the answer and get back to them.' Once a list of strategies has been developed, the client imagines in their mind's eye giving the presentation and dealing with the feared difficulties as they arise. Coping imagery can be practised daily before the feared event to build up self-efficacy and confidence.

Eliciting underlying assumptions and core beliefs

The process for identifying underlying assumptions and core beliefs is known as the downward arrow and it focuses on the personal meaning of events:

> *Client:* I know the customer hated the presentation because I didn't get the contract.
>
> *Therapist:* Let's suppose that's true, what does that mean to you?

Client:	That I'm useless at giving presentations.
Therapist:	And if that was the case, what does that mean to you?
Client:	If I can't do my job well, then I'm a failure.

In the above example, the hypothesized underlying assumption is 'If I can't do my job well, then I'm a failure' and the core belief is 'I'm a failure'. This is shared with the client and if they are in agreement with it, the therapist and client then tentatively develop alternative more helpful and realistic assumptions and core beliefs, such as 'If I can't do my job well, then I can still accept myself as fallible'.

Modifying core beliefs

A three-step process is adopted by Greenberger and Padesky,[10] which involves:

1. Writing down the belief, then underneath listing experiences that indicate that this belief is not 100 per cent true.
2. Writing down a new, more realistic belief and then underneath it recording experiences that support this belief.
3. Rating confidence in the new belief on a regular basis.

Behavioural techniques

Behavioural experiments

These experiments can be used to uncover NATs in specific situations and also to test out the validity of new more helpful beliefs. For example, initially a client who was phobic about travelling on the tube stood on the train platform and soon realized that he was anxious about his prediction 'I will collapse and be a nuisance to others on the tube if the train stopped between stations'. Later in therapy he was asked by his therapist to board the tube train for a short journey and to use a coping belief they had developed in the session: 'I can cope if I collapse on a train. I won't unduly upset other people'. A different example of a behavioural experiment using a form is illustrated below in Table 9.2.

TABLE 9.2 *Behavioural experiment form*

Unhelpful thoughts targeted	Realistic response	Behavioural assignment	Outcome
Every time I send a document I have to keep checking that I have sent the documents to the correct recipient(s)	I can check once only, this will save me time	For the next 5 days only check each document once every time	Felt anxious doing this task during days 1 and 2 but I then felt better and less worried

Graded exposure

This is a behaviour therapy technique that is still used within CBT for specific pho-bias, although the trend is now to focus on behavioural experiments instead. It can be used to help clients face their fears, step by step, starting with the least anxiety-provoking step. For example, if the goal of a client who is scared of spiders is to hold one in their hand, the first step could be to read a magazine with photographs of spiders in it, the second to sit in the same room with a spider in a jar, and so on, until the client is able to hold the spider in their hand without feeling anxious.

Relaxation

There are a number of different techniques available which can be used to help clients control their physiological responses to stress, such as a racing heart, headaches and knots in the stomach. Relaxation is a form of cognitive distraction that helps to relax the mind and body. In recent years it has become less popular as an intervention.

Scheduling activities

Often clients who are depressed, who lack motivation and who hold the belief 'I can't be bothered to do anything' may benefit from planning their activities on an hourly and daily basis. This enables them to be active and to recognize that by doing things they can become more motivated and less depressed. (Research has found that Behavioural Activation is effective in tackling depression.)

WHICH CLIENTS BENEFIT MOST?

CBT is practised in various settings and applied to a number of different client problems, such as anxiety; phobias; depression; eating disorders; obsessive–compulsive disorder; psychosomatic problems; sexual dysfunctions; chronic fatigue; schizophrenia; post-traumatic stress disorder; substance abuse problems; and personality disorders. Over recent years, the number of therapists using CBT has grown and the demand for it continues to increase. Being research-based and short-term, CBT is widely used within medical settings where the need for a cost-effective treatment is vital. The techniques are also used in the growing industries of stress-management training and coaching.[1]

This approach may not benefit clients who want to explore their past in great depth, as the emphasis is largely on the here-and-now, or clients who are not motivated to make changes in their lives. Acceptance of the cognitive model and willingness to undertake **homework assignments** are crucial factors when con-sidering suitability for CBT.

CASE STUDY

The Client

David is a 42-year-old deputy director of a large geological company, who came for therapy after having experienced severe anxiety on a number of airline flights over the previous two years. His anxiety was triggered after a flight which involved severe turbulence. Since then he found himself starting to worry about any flight a few days before he was due to fly out. On arriving at the airport he follows a set pattern. He checks in and then heads straight for the bar to have a drink to 'calm his nerves'. He then continues to drink on the flight, arriving at his destination tired and at times quite drunk. On several occasions the stewards on the plane refused to serve him more alcohol because he appeared very drunk, causing him severe embarrassment. In addition, the previous month he had arrived intoxicated for a meeting in Germany. The meeting had to be cancelled as a result and on his return to the UK his director had warned him that his job was in jeopardy unless he 'sorted out' his drinking. This triggered his request for help.

David is married with two young children and his wife is supportive of his endeavour to seek counselling.

The Therapy

Session 1

This session involved the assessment of the client's problems, taking into account David's background. David had no history of anxiety and his anxiety was confined to the few days before the flight and during it. He noticed that five days before the flight he would start to feel restless and have trouble sleeping, and he would be 'extra nice' to his wife and children in case his worst fear happened, the plane crashed and he would never see them again. David was an intelligent client who recognized that his fear was irrational but when on the plane he 'felt certain that he was going to die'.

In this assessment session the therapist explained to David the rationale behind cognitive therapy and the importance of structured sessions (in particular homework assignments), and together the therapist and David identified his goal, namely to reduce his level of anxiety while flying and to stop drinking while on the flight. The therapist explained to David that using alcohol to reduce his anxiety was unhelpful as it was a depressant and only prevented him from getting used to flying. Finally, the therapist and David agreed to meet for six weekly sessions of 50 minutes. The therapist and David negotiated the first homework assignment – to buy a book on overcoming the fear of flying which focused on the use of cognitive behavioural techniques. The therapist and client developed a tentative case conceptualization which outlined David's problem and indicated which interventions might be beneficial to help him overcome his irrational fear of flying.

Session 2

At the start of the session the agenda was negotiated and the therapist asked David about the homework assignment (this process was repeated at the start

(Continued)

(Continued)

of every session). He had purchased the book and had started to read it. He was comforted by learning that he was not the only person who suffered from a fear of flying. The focus of this session was to identify David's NATs which contributed to his anxiety.

To help this process the therapist asked David to describe the last flight he was on. As he talked about the flight David began to feel anxious. He experienced knots in his stomach, tension in his shoulders and his heart began to race. He identified a number of associated NATs:

'This pilot doesn't know what he is doing.'
'This plane is going to crash.'
'My heart is going to stop.'
'I can't bear it.'

The therapist then asked David to link his NATs to thinking errors; for example, 'This plane is going to crash' involves fortune-telling. Finally, the therapist demonstrated how to fill out the automatic thought form, inserting the negative beliefs described above. For homework David decided to continue with the reading, and the therapist suggested adding NATs about the flight to the automatic thought form.

Sessions 3 and 4

The focus of these sessions was on examining David's NATs and modifying them with more realistic and helpful beliefs. An example of the dialogue pertaining to his last flight went as follows:

Therapist:	[*refers to automatic thought form*] You have written here, 'this plane is going to crash'.
David:	Yes, that's right. On the plane I know it's going to crash.
Therapist:	David, how many times have you had this thought while flying?
David:	In total at least 100 times.
Therapist:	And what has happened?
David:	Nothing.
Therapist:	What does that suggest to you?
David:	That it's only a thought and thoughts don't equal facts.
Therapist:	That's right and in your book what does it say about the chance of crashing?
David:	That to be sure to be in a major disaster you need to fly every day for 26,000 years. [He had previously learnt this statistic from reading about flying.]
Therapist:	So based on this fact what is the likelihood of your next flight crashing?
David:	I think I've got more chance of winning the lottery [*laughing*].

The therapist and David worked on examining his NATs and writing down alternative realistic thoughts, such as 'My heart is not going to stop because

I feel anxious, that is not possible' on the automatic thought form. For homework David was asked to continue reading his book and to read through the session notes, focusing on the alternative thoughts.

Sessions 5 and 6

In these two sessions the therapist and David went over the more helpful and realistic thoughts that David had been writing down both in sessions and as part of his homework. The therapist encouraged David to note down some of the more 'powerful' thoughts in the form of statements on to a small card which he could read on a regular basis to remind himself of the realistic, more helpful thoughts; for example, 'I've got more chances of winning the lottery than the plane crashing.'

Coping imagery was also introduced. The client was asked to picture himself coping on the flight using the techniques previously mentioned. For homework he was asked to keep practising using the coping imagery daily. The therapist and client also negotiated a date for a follow-up session which was scheduled for after David's next flight. During the follow-up session David reported that his anxiety had greatly reduced, and that in particular he found using the coping statements and imagery very helpful. However, if he had remained very anxious whilst flying, the therapist may have negotiated additional therapy sessions to focus on David's intermediate and core beliefs.

REFERENCES

[1] Szymanska, K. and Palmer, S. (2012) *Understanding CBT: Develop Your Own Toolkit to Reduce Stress and Increase Well-being.* London: Kogan Page.

[2] Adler, A. (1958) *What Life Should Mean to You* (ed. A. Porter). New York: Capricorn. (Originally published, 1931.)

[3] Kelly, G. (1955) *The Psychology of Personal Constructs*, vols 1 and 2. New York: Norton.

[4] Ellis, A. (1962) *Reason and Emotion in Psychotherapy.* New York: Lyle Stuart.

[5] Miechenbaum, D. (1997) *Cognitive Behaviour Modification: An Integrative Approach.* New York: Plenum Press.

[6] Beck, A.T., Rush, A. J., Shaw, B. F. and Emery, G. (1979) *Cognitive Therapy of Depression.* New York: Guilford Press.

[7] Watson, J. B. and Rayner, R. (1920) 'Conditioned emotional reactions', *Journal of Experimental Psychology, 3*, 1–4.

[8] Clark, D. A. and Beck, A.T. (1999) *Scientific Foundations of Cognitive Theory and Therapy of Depression.* New York: Wiley.

[9] Palmer, S. and Dryden, W. (1995) *Counselling for Stress Problems.* London: Sage.

[10] Greenberger, D. and Padesky, C. (1995) *Clinicians' Guide to Mind Over Mood.* New York: Guilford Press.

SUGGESTED READING

Beck, J. (2011) *Cognitive Behavior Therapy: Basics and Beyond*, 2nd edn. New York: Guilford Press. This book covers the fundamentals of CBT including how to engage patients, developing case conceptualizations, plan treatment and structuring sessions. Seven reproducible clinical tools can also be downloaded from a website.

Neenan, M. and Dryden, W. (2011) *Cognitive Behavioural Therapy in a Nutshell*. London: Sage. This excellent short book covers the CBT model and the core techniques used during the therapeutic process to elicit and examine negative automatic thoughts, uncover and explore underlying assumptions, rules and core beliefs (schemas), and maintain gains from therapy.

Szymanska, K. and Palmer, S. (2012) *Understanding CBT: Develop Your Own Toolkit to Reduce Stress and Increase Well-being*. London: Kogan Page. This book is aimed at individuals and counsellors interested in using CBT-based strategies to tackle different psychological problems in order to achieve a better work–life balance.

Westbrook, D., Kennerley, H. and Kirk, J. (2007) *An Introduction to Cognitive Behaviour Therapy: Skills and Applications Managing Anxiety: A Training Manual*. London: Sage. This book covers the basics of CBT, it provides information on techniques and their applications to mental health problems.

DISCUSSION ISSUES

1. What part do automatic thoughts play in the perpetuation of clients' psychological problems?
2. How would you explain the rationale behind cognitive behaviour therapy to a client?
3. In what ways does cognitive therapy differ from other therapies?
4. What homework tasks would you negotiate with a client who is suffering from stress due to work pressures?

10

Compassion Focused Therapy

Paul Gilbert and Chris Irons

INTRODUCTION

Compassion focused therapy (CFT) is an integrated therapy that utilises a range of standard processes and interventions including Socratic questioning, guided discovery, inference training, behavioural experiments, exposure, guided imagery, chair work, mindfulness, method acting, identity focusing and expressive writing. The key to CFT, however, is to ensure that the client is capable of engaging affiliative rather than hostile emotion to the self (see below) and cultivates compassionate motivation as the process of change. So an analogy is that if you wanted to help somebody climb Mount Everest the first thing to do would be to help them get fit and understand safety procedures when climbing. Compassionate mind training is partly around helping people develop the inner courage and support systems to be able to engage with painful material – helping them become 'mentally fit' to do the work.

DEVELOPMENT OF THE THERAPY

CFT began over 25 years ago when one of us (P. G.) noted that people with chronic and complex mental health problems would say: 'I can see logically from the evidence that I'm not a failure, but I still *feel* like I am,' or 'I know that it wasn't my fault for being sexually abused as a child, but I still *feel* like I'm bad and to blame.' When P. G. explored the emotional tone people used when thinking of their alternative thoughts, this was often laced with disappointment, hostility, contempt or dismissal.

So CFT interventions began simply: to practise creating supportive and helpful emotional textures/tones alternative thoughts, new coping behaviours and exposure experiences; *to create an inner warm voice*, as if one was talking to a friend, and really try to *feel* the impact of that kind voice. It turned out that many shame and self-critical patients struggled to do this. Many were resistant, whilst for some, feelings of kindness felt 'uncomfortable and unnatural'.[1] For others, it started a grief process of (for example) recognising how unloved they have felt for a long time.[2,3] So CFT involves understanding the blocks, fears and resistances to both compassionate motivation and affiliative feelings in the change process.

THEORY AND BASIC CONCEPTS

CFT is rooted in an evolutionary model of the mind, with a number of key psycho-educational points.[4] Our minds are the products of evolution and contain within them a range of motives (e.g. for sex, status and attachment) and emotional dispositions (anger, anxiety, disgust, joy, sadness) shaped over hundreds of millions of years. We share these with many other animals. But about 2 million years ago pre-humans began to evolve complex cognitive systems too – we got smart. Our newer capacities for thinking, imagining, ruminating, anticipating, self-monitoring, self-awareness interact with our older motives and emotions, and can become caught up in unhelpful and non-rational 'loops'. We share with our clients the example of a zebra escaping a lion. Once the stimulus of the lion is no longer in the sensory, auditory or olfactory field there is nothing to maintain threat and so the zebra will become calm and return to grazing. However, humans can literally *bring the stimulus inside the head* through a process of imagination and anticipating – imagining what could have happened if they'd been caught, what it would be like to be eaten alive, what might happen if they encounter a lion tomorrow or even two, and what about the children out playing!

We use these examples so that people can understand that the human brain is prone to complex loops and irrationalities through no fault of our own. It is a tragedy, because this is why we end up with the horrific atrocities that humans bring about, because once the new brain competencies get caught up in old motives (say, for vengeance), it can be pretty nasty.

A second theme is a social constructionist aspect. Our sense of 'self' is also constructed through social circumstances. We often share with our clients the example of imagining what type of person we (the therapist) would have become if we had been kidnapped as a three-day-old baby into a violent drug gang. We explore what characteristics we might have (e.g. for aggression, violence or lack of care), and how *that version of us* would be very different from the one in front of the client today. We use this to facilitate a recognition that much of our sense of ourselves – including what goes on in our minds – was designed for us but not by us, and therefore is *not our fault*. The version of the client is only one of many potential versions. So CFT focuses a lot of shifting from shaming/blaming to responsibility taking and training in helping clients recognise they can choose and cultivate different versions of themselves, especially the compassionate version of themselves, and the advantages of doing so.

A third theme is to understand the 'functional nature of emotions' and how they interact. Evolutionary functional analysis suggests that we have at least three (functional) *types* of major emotion regulation systems.[5,6] These are:

- *Threat and self-protection focused system* – this evolved to alert and direct attention to detect and respond to threats. This system has a menu of threat-based emotions such as anger, anxiety and disgust, and a menu of defensive behaviours such as fight, flight, submission and freeze. It is now known that this is our most dominant affect-processing system and gives rise to *the negativity bias*: that is, it is easier for us to pay attention to negative stimuli, to remember aversive events and be influenced in our decision-making by aversive events, rather than positive ones.[7]
- *Drive, seeking and acquisition focused system* – designed to notice and pay attention to advantageous resources, and experience drive and pleasure in pursuing and securing them. If something very good happens to us, like we win a fortune on the lottery, or we are getting married in a week or two to someone we love, the chances are we can have intrusive fantasies and feelings with elevated states of excitement that might make it difficult to sleep. So this positive system is activating.
- *Contentment, soothing and affiliative focused system* – enables states of quiescence and peacefulness when individuals are no longer threat focused or focused on seeking out or consuming resources. This allows the body to 'rest and digest' and also have open attention. Over evolutionary time, this system of calming was adapted for some of the functions of affiliative and attachment behaviour; especially a parent's ability to calm distress in an infant.

These three interacting systems are depicted in Figure 10.1.

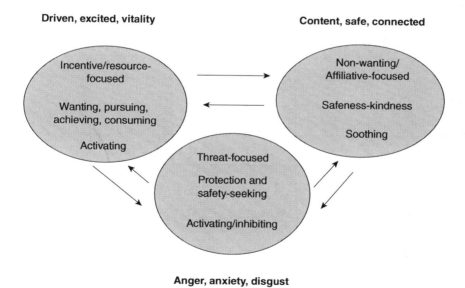

FIGURE 10.1   Three types of affect regulation system. (From P. Gilbert (2009) *The Compassionate Mind*. With kind permission from Constable & Robinson)

Attachment theory and affiliation

Affiliative behaviour is linked to feelings of friendliness, helpfulness, concern and prosocial interest. There are activating aspects of affiliative behaviour, as when we are excited at seeing friends and enjoying things together, we feel valued in the minds of others. Affiliative relationships can also be a source of threat, such as in an argument or when something bad happens to a friend. Central to CFT is a recognition that affiliative relationships are also often central to the ability to feel safe, have calming qualities, feel soothed when distressed and encouraged when facing difficult things. This is called affiliative soothing.[4] Attachment theory developed by the British psychiatrist John Bowlby[8] plays a key role in this aspect of the CFT approach.[9]

Attachment theory proposes three basic functions of attachment:

1. An urge for *proximity seeking* whereby infant and parent monitor the closeness (availability and accessibility) of each other and respond to unwanted 'distance' with threat and reparative behaviours.
2. The provision of a *secure base* where infants are protected, fed, cared for and are able to live in a safe context. This provides the context for developing courage to go out and explore, learning about social relationships and the nature of our emotions.
3. A *safe haven* which provides a soothing regulating function such that when distressed the infant has access to a calming, soothing object. Over time these are internalised.

CFT was built on the recognition that the evolution of caring behaviour has major regulatory and developmental functions. Indeed, caring affects how the brain matures and even gene expression. So working with the systems that are involved in the affiliative regulation of emotion is essential in therapy.[3,10] As we noted above, affiliative emotion can be difficult for some clients, especially when they try to direct them to themselves.

The nature of compassion

CFT routes compassion in the evolved motivational systems for caring and affiliation, and uses standard definitions of compassion such as it being 'a sensitivity to the suffering of self and others, with a commitment to try to alleviate or prevent it'. Compassion can also focus on promoting wellbeing. Here are *two different psychologies* that underpin caring and compassion:

1. The cultivation of abilities for turning *towards* suffering; noticing, paying attention, and engaging *with* suffering (in contrast to not noticing, denial, avoidance, dissociation etc.). These include capacities for motivation and willingness to engage, distress awareness, sympathy, distress tolerance, empathy, acceptance and non-judgement.[4,11,12]
2. Developing the wisdom of how to alleviate and prevent suffering. This requires investment of time in acquiring skills and practices that will aid our ability to deal with suffering and advance wellbeing. These skills can include: learning to pay attention to what is helpful, being able to take different perspectives and reason in helpful ways, generating helpful behaviours, which at times can involve courage, using breath control, voice regulation and body postures, and the use of compassion imagery.

PRACTICE

The goals of CFT reflect the definition of compassion: to help clients to become more sensitive to their own and others' suffering, and to develop the motivation and skills to alleviate this suffering and prevent it from returning. This is facilitated by:

1. The development of a therapeutic relationship that facilitates the process of engaging with suffering and the development of skills to alleviate this.
2. Developing non-blaming compassionate insights into the nature of human suffering, built upon sharing of key psychoeducation on the core principles and theory of CFT.
3. Developing the capacity for attentional stability and the ability to experience and develop compassionate attributes (for example, attention training, mindfulness, breathing and imagery practice).
4. Developing the flow of (i) feeling compassion for others, (ii) being open to the compassion from others, and (iii) developing self-compassion – using behavioural, emotive, imagery, body and 'acting' practices.
5. Putting compassion to work – interventions that once clients have access to a sense of their 'compassionate self' they can use to approach and work with whatever difficulties they are experiencing in life (for example, working with different memories and emotions, chair work, letter writing).

Therapeutic relationship

Compassion focused therapists seek to create a safe and secure therapeutic relationship, that can both contain and enable the client to move towards and learn how to alleviate their distress. CF therapists are mindful of the balance of both their clients and their own 'three systems', and pay attention to difficulties that may emerge from these in the interpersonal dynamic (e.g. through the processes of transference and counter-transference). They strive to create a flexible compassionate stance, fostering a sense of collaboration and 'we-ness' in working together to understand and work with clients' distress.

Compassionate insights

As noted above, we share ideas that the human brain is very tricky and not that well put together; it is prone to maladaptive and unhelpful loops and highly socially influenced. We did not choose our genes, nor the social circumstances that have choreographed and shaped our brains and our sense of self. Both these principles begin to dig into the foundations of personalisation and a sense of shame, and puts responsibility on a different basis. We find that when people reduce shame-based blaming they are much more ready for taking responsibility in a helpful way. Indeed, when people begin to understand how and why so much of what goes on inside our heads is *not our fault* they can be very moved, even tearful. As one client said, 'I've always thought there was something basically bad about me because of the kind things that go on in my mind.' Having clear insight that this was not her fault, and that the human brain is quite capable of generating such content, was a great relief to her but also inspired her to start to choose the version of herself she wanted to cultivate.

Developing compassion capacities

Attention training and mindfulness

We can begin to take responsibility when we learn to pay attention to how our minds work and what arises within them. Attention can be understood to be like a spotlight, 'lighting up' whatever it focuses upon. So if we pay attention to a happy memory, or sad memory, different types of bodily sensations and feelings emerge. Helping clients to understand the power of attention ('attention plays the body') is an important insight that we build upon by engaging in a variety of attention and mindfulness practices to cultivate greater attentional awareness and stability. Many clients find this helpful as a way of noticing and stepping outside of the 'loops in the mind' discussed above.

Soothing breathing rhythm

The practising and cultivating of certain types of breathing – usually that are slower and deeper than 'normal' – may have a variety of health benefits, especially on the parasympathetic soothing system[13] and contribute to creating a helpful physiological base to engage in other therapeutic interventions (e.g. imagery or engaging in threat emotions.[12] CFT helps clients to develop a sense of slowing down in the body, with groundedness and stability that may bring a sense of alert stillness (this is quite different from the more floppy-muscle type relaxation). An example here might be the gymnast who stops and composes themselves, before attempting the final set of tumbles in their routine.

Imagery

Imagery can powerfully affect our physiology and specific brain systems. For example, think of the power of sexual fantasy while lying in bed! So we can use these aspects of our new brain to stimulate specific systems in the brain that will promote compassion and affiliative processes. An example here would be 'safe place' imagery in which the client creates images in their mind of a place in which they may feel a sense of safeness, peacefulness or tranquillity. But it is also a place for joyfulness.

Compassion-based imagery and relating

Here, clients are taught a variety of compassionate imagery exercises that are tied into the concept idea of *compassion as flow:*

- compassion from *others* to *self*
- compassion from *self* to *others*
- compassion from *self* to *self*.

Developing an ideal compassionate other

Clients are encouraged to think about their ideal qualities of compassion as being personified or objectified in some way as in an image. This image does not have to be human, but once qualities of this image are formed and associated with certain qualities of compassion, wisdom, strength, caring-commitment the therapist helps the client to practise generating this image when needed as a way of engaging their distress/threat systems. Clients are encouraged to consider: 'what would your compassionate image think and feel about this?' and 'what could your compassionate image suggest might be helpful for you given this situation?'. Developing 'compassionate other' imagery can be a helpful step in facilitating the experience of compassion flowing inwards.

Developing an ideal compassionate self

Here, we use a variety of skills linked to imagery, empathy and acting techniques to help clients develop a sense of their compassionate self. Clients are helped to consider the type of mind (motivation, intention, ways of thinking, feeling and behaving), facial expression, voice tone, body posture and so forth, that their compassionate self would have, and then to 'practise' (through imagination but also 'in the moment' with the therapist and, initially, safe others) these qualities so they become more accessible. The compassionate self may be focused in two key directions:

- Compassion flowing out (Compassion to others)

  Here, the qualities of the compassionate self are directed towards a person or animal that the client cares for, with a focus on the hope and desire for them to be able to tolerate distress, be happy and flourish. From the compassionate self, we can help the client to imagine how they would want to be with this person they care for, how they would speak, act and respond. It is also important to explore the joyfulness if this could be true that there is an inherent pleasure in helping others.

- Compassion flowing in (Self-compassion)

  Here, the client is helped to bring their imagery of their compassionate self to mind. The qualities of this compassionate self are then directed towards the self. This might be via creating an image of the self towards which, looking through the eyes of the compassionate self, the client then can direct empathy, understanding, care and warmth. Clients are encouraged that from this part of themselves, they can imagine themselves to be happy and flourishing, or having the strength to tolerate whatever difficulties are arising at the moment.

Putting compassion to work – developing compassionate skills

As clients develop a sense of their 'compassionate self/mind' we can then bring this into a variety of situations that the client needs to engage with from life events to internal conflicts

Working with different emotion-based 'selves'

CFT highlights the fact that a lot of people's complex difficulties are linked to conflicts between emotions and motives, both currently and in the past. For example, some people can be afraid of the angry self while others can be fearful of their sadness. So one emotion can block another. We use a variety of techniques to give voice to different emotions as if they were separate parts of self, and then explore thoughts, actions and memories of each of them and the conflicts between them. Focusing on one's compassionate self can be used to work, accept and understand our different parts of self (e.g. the thoughts, actions and memories of angry self, anxious self or sad self).

Chair work

As with other therapies, chair work can be used in a variety of ways to explore different relationships between parts of the self, memories and past or current relationships and also to practise responding in specific ways – which in CFT involves compassionate thinking and responding.[3]

Compassionate letter writing

CFT utilises expressive writing. Clients are encouraged to write letters to themselves about certain difficulties or struggles they are having, but crucially, to write these letters from the compassionate part of themselves. These letters often include a specific type of focus, including on empathy and understanding for one's struggle/distress ('not your fault', and an understanding how the difficulty arose and how it may be understandable given knowledge of key fears in life), consideration of what might be helpful to cope with the difficulty (e.g. ways of paying attention, thinking or behaving). Clients are encouraged to hold in mind the two psychologies of compassion – willingness to be sensitive to suffering but also the motivation and wisdom to discover and practise what might be helpful.

WHICH CLIENTS BENEFIT MOST?

There is increasing evidence for the value of various forms of compassion focused interventions.[14] As discussed above, CFT was developed to help people with high levels of shame and self-criticism. In the first CFT outcome study Gilbert and Procter[15] found that following a 12-week group for day hospital clients with a variety of chronic, complex mental health problems, there was a significant reduction in self-criticism, anxiety and depression, and an increase in self-reassurance.

Three studies have looked at CFT in populations of people experiencing psychosis. In a small case series study (n = 3) of voices hearers, Mayhew and Gilbert[16] found reductions in levels of interpersonal sensitivity, depression, anxiety and paranoia scores. There was a reduction in the hostility of voices, and an increase in the degree to which voices were experienced as reassuring. In a group-based CFT approach for people with diag-noses of schizophrenia and bipolar disorder in a maximum security hospital, Laithwaite et al.[17] found significant pre to post reductions in negative social comparisons, shame and depression symptoms, and changes in the Positive and Negative Syndrome Scale (PANSS). In a randomised controlled trial for recovery from psychosis, Braehler et al.[18] found CFT to be highly acceptable, without adverse events, and had low attrition rates. Relative to the 'treatment as usual' CFT increased compassion and was significantly asso-ciated with reductions in depression and perceived social marginalisation.

Lucre and Corten[19] found a 16-week CFT group for people with personality disorder produced significant reductions in negative social comparison, shame, self-hatred and depression symptoms, and a significant increase in self-reassurance, wellbe-ing, and social functioning. These benefits were maintained at a one-year follow up. Gale et al.[20] found significant improvements on a variety of eating-based measures, particularly for those with a diagnosis of bulimia, after completing a group that inte-grated CFT into a traditional CBT for eating disorders treatment programme.

As CFT is a relatively young psychotherapy, further research needs to be con-ducted looking more specifically into who benefits most from the approach, and whether there are certain people, or certain difficulties, that are less amenable to change from this approach.

CASE STUDY

The Client

Sandra was a 39-year-old white British woman whose current depression was of four months' duration. She was referred to one of us (C. I.) by her psychiatrist. She struggled to get any pleasure in life, and described feeling de-motivated, lacking energy and feeling 'beaten down' by life and her 'head'. She was cur-rently signed off from work due to her depression. She was married with two young children. She described herself as a highly self-critical person in many areas of her life (e.g. her performance at work, being a bad friend/wife/mother).

Sandra recalled early experiences with her father as positive, but that he was often away for long periods of time with work. Her relationship with her mother was difficult; at times her mother was caring and available, but could often and unpredictably 'flip' into angry outbursts with her. At these times her mother was very critical of Sandra, pointing out 'flaws' and shout-ing 'why can't you just be good and get things right'. She described feeling anxious around her mother, and often having a sense that her mother was 'disappointed in her'.

Although she had lots of friends at primary school, she described feel-ing increasingly isolated and insecure during adolescence after moving to a large secondary school. Here, Sandra engaged in a lot of social compari-son on different domains, for example, her intelligence, academic or sport-ing achievements, and attractiveness and popularity. She described having the sense that she didn't 'measure up'. Although she achieved good exam

(Continued)

(Continued)

results at school, college and university, she rarely derived any pleasure from these, and instead, felt that she needed to strive to 'achieve more and prove myself to everyone'.

As we discussed these experiences, we began to make notes together on a form like the one shown in Table 10.1, which eventually led to our formulation of her difficulties. This formulation attempted to link together how some of her early experiences had left her with a number of key external (about what others thought and felt about her, or what they might do to her) and internal (arising inside herself) fears and threats. We then explored the ways in which Sandra had tried to protect herself from these fears (column three 'safety strategies'), which had at least in part been helpful at stages, but how these had led to some unpleasant unintended consequences.

TABLE 10.1   *Sandra's threat-based CFT formulation*

Key background experiences	Key fears/threats	Safety/protective strategies	Unintended consequences
Mother caring at times but unpredictable, angry and critical	**External:** • Being shamed/ put down by others • 'Others will reject me'	**External:** • Hypervigilant – always observe others and try to 'stop criticism/ conflicts before they happen' • Try to please others	**External:** • Felt exhausted always being on alert. Feeling pathetic and weak as others always walk all over me • Ashamed and fearful of hidden anger
Father loving but often unavailable through work travel			
Difficult experiences at school – sense of being 'lesser than' other girls and of being bullied/ostracised	**Internal:** • Feeling worthless, inadequate and inferior • Feeling alone • Expressing own needs and feelings	**Internal:** • Strive harder to achieve and impress Suppress own feelings and needs • Go into hiding	**Internal:** • Tired and exhausted at striving to please • Feel overwhelmed, lost and out of control of my life. Rarely feel genuinely loved or wanted

The Therapy

Following formulation, C. I. took Sandra through some key psychoeducation points. This included discussion of the 'loops in her mind' based on fear of others, self-criticism and rumination. We explored the emotional regulation 'three systems' model and Sandra was able to note that her systems were 'out of balance', particularly in terms of having a very powerful threat system, but (currently) under-active drive and soothing systems. She saw that for much of her life, she managed her threat system by engaging her drive system (striving, trying to achieve things and 'people please'), and how this actually created a lot of exhaustion and distress for her. She noticed that she had the idea that 'if I criticise myself, then no one else can surprise me by doing the same'. Sandra also noted that, for as long as she could remember, she felt little sense of safeness, security or contentment (soothing system). We therefore agreed that it might be important for us to try to develop this system, so that it could 'do it's job' and help to regulate threat and drive system.

Although Sandra found attention training and soothing breathing practice difficult at first, through encouragement she began to feel more at ease, and began to be more aware (mindful) of the loops in her mind (e.g. 'I'll never make anything of life'). Over a number of weeks, she described feeling more able to step outside these loops, partly by focusing on her soothing breathing rhythm, and a sense of slowing down in the body and groundedness. As we began to practice compassion-based imagery, Sandra found it relatively easy to imagine both her **ideal compassionate self**, and an **ideal compassionate other**. Moreover, she became skilled at directing these towards other people and, in time, herself. She began to see that a basic desire to feel loved, accepted and belong was a key driver for many of her safety behaviours and strategies.

As with many other people, Sandra could generate (logically) helpful alternative thoughts but she did not 'believe' them for herself. It is always important to anticipate and explore the fears, blocks and resistances to compassion. For Sandra (as is not uncommon) these were linked to unprocessed anger towards her mother, the fear that anger made her a bad person, and with a sense of betrayal and that to be compassionate one should not have these feelings (In fact compassion helps us to be honest about them and experience them.) As compassion grew she connected her anger and striving to a deep sense of having felt alone a lot of her life and a yearning to feel loved and accepted. We used her developing sense of strength, wisdom and caring commitment – tied to her compassionate self – to help her tolerate her fear of anger and the shame that emerged around that. Once she was able to tolerate this anger through engaging her compassionate self, Sandra became quite tearful and sad. She grieved for what she had been through as a child, and what she felt she had missed.

Although there were some setbacks at times, Sandra made good progress in therapy. She no longer met diagnostic criteria for depression and engaged with a variety of activities that she had struggled with. She returned to work, and had a less judging and critical stance with herself and her performance. Crucially, she began to notice a sense of yearning for greater connection, and although this scared her as it was a foreign feeling, she used her compassionate self to engage more closely and with greater warmth with her husband and her children. At times Sandra still had what she referred to as 'bad days', but saw these as a reminder of the importance in engaging her compassionate self as a way of understanding what had contributed to this, but crucially, what would be helpful in coping and trying to alleviate where possible the difficulties of those days.

REFERENCES

[1] Pauley, G. and McPherson, S. (2010) 'The experience and meaning of compassion and self-compassion for individuals with depression or anxiety', *Psychology and Psychotherapy: Theory, Research and Practice, 83*, 129–43.

[2] Gilbert, P. (2010) *Compassion Focused Therapy.* The CBT Distinctive Features Series. London: Routledge.

[3] Gilbert, P. and Irons, C. (2005) 'Focused therapies and compassionate mind training: shame and self-attacking', in P. Gilbert (ed.), *Compassion: Conceptualisations, Research and Use in Psychotherapy.* London: Routledge. pp. 263–325.

[4] Gilbert, P. (2009) *The Compassionate Mind: A New Approach to the Challenges of Life.* London: Constable & Robinson.

[5] Depue, R. A. and Morrone-Strupinsky, J. V. (2005) 'A neurobehavioral model of affiliative bonding', *Behavioral and Brain Sciences, 28*, 313–95.

[6] LeDoux, J. (1998) *The Emotional Brain.* London: Weidenfeld & Nicolson.

[7] Baumeister, R. F., Bratslavsky, E., Finkenauer, C. and Vohs, K. D. (2001) 'Bad is stronger than good', *Review of General Psychology, 5*, 323–70.

[8] Bowlby, J. (1969) *Attachment. Attachment and Loss,* Vol. 1. London: Hogarth Press.

[9] Mikulincer, M. and Shaver, P. R. (2007) *Attachment in Adulthood: Structure, Dynamics, and Change.* New York: Guilford Press.

[10] Gilbert, P. (2013) 'Attachment theory and compassion focused therapy for depression', in A. H. Danquah and K. Berry (eds), *Attachment Theory in Adult Mental Health: A Guide to Clinical Practice.* London: Routledge. pp. 35–47.

[11] Gilbert, P. (2014) 'The origins and nature of compassion focused therapy', *British Journal of Clinical Psychology, 53*, 6–41.

[12] Gilbert, P. and Choden (2013) *Mindful Compassion.* London: Constable & Robinson.

[13] Brown, R. P and Gerbarg, P. L. (2012) *The Healing Power of the Breath.* London: Shambhala.

[14] Hoffmann, S. G., Grossman, P. and Hinton, D. E. (2011) 'Loving-kindness and compassion meditation: potential for psychological intervention', *Clinical Psychology Review, 13*, 1126–32.

[15] Gilbert, P. and Procter, S. (2006) 'Compassionate mind training for people with high shame and self-criticism: a pilot study of a group therapy approach', *Clinical Psychology and Psychotherapy, 13*, 353–79.

[16] Mayhew, S. and Gilbert, P. (2008) 'Compassionate mind training with people who hear malevolent voices: a case series report', *Clinical Psychology and Psychotherapy, 15*, 113–38.

[17] Laithwaite, H., Gumley, A., O'Hanlon, M., Collins, P., Doyle, P., Abraham, L. and Porter, S. (2009) 'Recovery after psychosis (RAP): a compassion focused programme for individuals residing in high-security settings', *Behavioural and Cognitive Psychotherapy, 37*, 511–26.

[18] Braehler, C., Gumley, A., Harper, J., Wallace, S., Norrie, J. and Gilbert, P. (2013) 'Exploring change processes in compassion focused therapy in psychosis: results of a feasibility randomized controlled trial', *British Journal of Clinical Psychology, 52*, 199–214.

[19] Lucre, K. M. and Corten, N. (2012) 'An exploration of group compassion–focused therapy for personality disorder', *Psychology and Psychotherapy:Theory, Research and Practice, 86*, 387–400.

[20] Gale, C., Gilbert, P., Read, N. and Goss, K. (2014) 'An evaluation of the impact of introducing compassion focused therapy to a standard treatment programme for people with eating disorders', *Clinical Psychology and Psychotherapy, 21*, 1–12.

[21] Gilbert, P., McEwan, K., Matos, M. & Rivis, A. (2011). Fears of compassion: development of three self–report measures. *Psychology and Psychotherapy, 84*, 239–55.

SUGGESTED READING

Gilbert, P. (2005) *Compassion: Conceptualisations, Research and Use in Psycho-therapy*. London: Routledge. An edited book with chapters outlining some core principles of CFT, but more broadly, the use of compassion in psychotherapy and its relationship with attachment theory, prosocial behaviour, forgiveness and cruelty.

Gilbert, P. (2009) *The Compassionate Mind: A New Approach to the Challenges of Life*. London: Constable & Robinson. A detailed overview of many of the theoretical ideas of CFT, along with a variety of exercises to practice. A useful guide for both therapists and the general public.

Gilbert, P. (2010) *Compassion Focused Therapy*. The CBT Distinctive Features Series. London: Routledge. A step-by-step guide to the different features of CFT, in small, easy-to-read chapters. A helpful guide for therapists to use as they are developing their CFT knowledge and skills.

Gilbert, P. and Choden (2013) *Mindful Compassion*. London: Constable & Robinson. Co-authored by Buddhist expert Choden, this is a very accessible book that interweaves core aspects of CFT with mindfulness practices.

DISCUSSION ISSUES

1. Critically discuss the definition of compassion, and the qualities and skills used in CFT to develop it.
2. Many clients find the experience of compassion – and affiliative emotion generally – threatening. Some of the fears and blocks to compassion were discussed by Gilbert et al.[21] What might be some of the common fears that people describe in:

   i. Being compassionate to other people?
   ii. Experiencing compassion from others?
   iii. Directing compassion to ourselves (self-compassion)?

3. Consider what skills and attributes you need to be a compassionate therapist. How might they change depending on the presenting problems and interpersonal styles of different clients you work with?
4. Critically discuss the use of evolutionary psychology ideas in psychotherapy.

11

Dialectical Behaviour Therapy

Christine Dunkley and Stephen Palmer

INTRODUCTION

Dialectical behaviour therapy (DBT) is a **mindfulness**-based cognitive behavioural therapy. It is often described as 'CBT with a capital B' as it is so strongly behavioural. It is slightly unusual in the cognitive therapies, being delivered by a team of therapists rather than an individual practitioner working alone. All therapists delivering DBT must belong to a consultation team and the weekly consultation meeting is built in to the structure of the therapy. This ensures that the principles of the treatment are applied to the therapist as well as the client. DBT is primarily used to treat suicidal and self-harming behavioural problems associated with borderline personality disorder, although subsequent adaptations have been developed to treat substance misuse, eating problems, suicidal adolescents, treatment-resistant depression and over-controlled personality disorders. Despite being a behavioural treatment the overarching goal in DBT is to deliver the client a 'life worth living', only treating the problem behaviours because they block the client from achieving this goal.

DEVELOPMENT OF THE THERAPY

The developer of DBT, Marsha Linehan, began in the 1980s to study suicidal self-harming women. She noted that a number of women in her target population also had a diagnosis of **borderline personality disorder** (BPD). She found that applying standard change-focused CBT to this cohort increased the clients' distress, as they perceived the therapist did not understand the extent of their difficulties. Dropping the change agenda and moving to a position of acceptance also caused problems – as then clients saw the therapist as simply abandoning them to their fate. Linehan realised that for maximum progress the therapist needed to be able to acknowledge the **dialectical** tension between these two positions of acceptance and change, moving freely between them as the need arose. She went on to highlight further dialectical tensions arising in therapy with this hard-to-treat population, and to incorporate a dialectical philosophy into treatment itself, hence the name 'dialectical behaviour therapy'.

After two randomised controlled trials (RCTs) on female patients with a diagnosis of BPD,[1,2] the original treatment manuals[3,4] were published. More recently the therapy has been extended to other hard-to-treat behavioural problems, as listed in the Introduction. DBT teams are currently implementing the therapy in a variety of clinical settings: community outpatient, inpatient, secure hospitals and prisons.

THEORY AND CONCEPTS

The 'D' in DBT stands for 'dialectical', and if two words could be applied to make sense of this term they are 'It depends'. The ancient Greeks assumed dialectical philosophy as a method of debate, holding that any argument or position (the thesis) would have an opposing argument (the antithesis) and that there would be validity in both sides. The task in the debate would be to synthesise these two opposing truths – finding the way of combining polar ideas effectively to create a new argument or position. This synthesis would then become a thesis and so would have an antithesis of its own. In this way the world unfolds moment by moment – no position is ever fixed, the next moment comes along and what held true a moment ago may no longer be valid. This concept of fluidity and constant change is particularly helpful to counteract the black-and-white thinking that is a feature of most disorders treated with DBT.

An example of a dialectical tension might be that the client wishes to be admitted to hospital. The client's position that hospital is safe is valid, as is the therapist's position that the client cannot recover by retreating to hospital as a way of resolving distress. The synthesis may be if the therapist can increase the availability of support in the community the client may agree to stay at home or have a shorter admission. But this is not a permanent solution; it resolves the current tension, but then new tensions will arise due to the increased support level which will ultimately have to be resolved. But slowly the client moves to a more skilled level of functioning.

Being dialectical does not mean being indecisive or passive. The dialectician can take positions wholeheartedly. For example, when the client wonders 'Should I stand up for myself and be assertive?' it really does depend on the current circumstances; if the shopkeeper refused to give you a refund for faulty goods – don't just walk away. But if your violent partner threatens you in a drunken rage, now is not the time to stand your ground. The therapy values both being assertive and being under-assertive when the conditions call for it. So DBT teaches principles rather than rules, and encourages both client and therapist to take multiple factors into account. The idea is to strive to reconcile polarised positions by looking for the validity in both sides.

Major dialectical tensions recognised by the therapy are those between acceptance and change, nurturing and demanding, reverence and irreverence. The therapist is wary of always taking the same side, for example always being nurturing. The role of the consultation team is to ensure that the therapists and clients vary their positions according to what is effective in any given moment. This dialectical philosophy permeates every aspect of the therapy. The DBT therapists looks for the 'both/and' position, rather than 'either/or', and always asks 'what if both sides are correct?'.

In true dialectical fashion DBT resolves the 'nature versus nurture' debate by suggesting that BPD arises as a result of a transaction between a biological vulnerability and an invalidating environment. The biological vulnerability consists of an acute sensitivity to emotionally evocative stimuli. The typical emotional response of a client with BPD is to flare up more quickly than average, reach a more intense emotional experience than most people and take a longer time to return to a baseline emotional state. This can lead sufferers to engage in extreme problematic behaviour, often in an attempt to downregulate the painful emotion.

The invalidating environment is one that does not teach the client to regulate emotion or communicate pain effectively, but ignores pain communication (as in the case of abuse), implies the client is not trying hard enough or that problems are easily solved. In response to this invalidation, the client's distress and problem behaviours escalate, until often the environment capitulates, thus intermittently reinforcing harmful actions. In simple terms one thing leads to another over time, with the behaviour slowly escalating by degrees from minor behavioural problems to incidents requiring large-scale intervention. There is no single key factor, either biological or environmental, that is the trigger event.

The mechanisms maintaining the disorder are therefore two-fold – a lack of skill by the individual in being able to regulate emotion in an effective harm-free way, plus an environment that punishes skilled behaviour and at least intermittently rewards unskilled behaviour.

Given that DBT holds there is no absolute truth, and that any situation or set of circumstances can be distilled into component and often opposing factors that make up the whole, then it makes complete sense that this would be a mindfulness-based therapy. No situation can be fully predicted ahead of time, and no past events hold complete control over the current scenario. Whilst the client's current behaviour may be influenced by memories, associations or habits that began historically, behaviour is thoroughly analysed to discern the factors that brought it about in the immediate context in which it occurred. Thus DBT favours explanations of behaviour that are rooted in the present moment.

Linehan has incorporated some of the Zen philosophy of acceptance into the therapy itself, and both clients and therapists are encouraged to engage in mindful practice. Therapists assist clients to problem-solve where this is possible, and to apply acceptance strategies where these are called for. The emphasis is on being the most skilful or effective in any given situation, so the basic approach to any unwanted situation for the client is to do one of four things:

1. Change the situation (solve the problem).
2. Change your response to the situation (mostly through **emotion regulation** or interpersonal effectiveness strategies).
3. Accept your response to the situation (often using **distress tolerance** or mindfulness strategies).
4. Stay miserable (DBT maintains that this is also one of the client's choices).

An apparent paradox in DBT is the relentless pursuit of problem solving with non-attachment to outcome; if solutions turn out to be ineffective the DBT therapist turns to the next best idea and strategies can either be change- or acceptance-based. Where solutions fail, this is seen as helpful information in honing, refining or changing course. Consistency is not expected either between therapists or with the same therapist and the same client over time. There is freedom to disagree with each other or with oneself in order to achieve the most rounded picture of the current scenario, and the best way forward.

Another concept in DBT is that the principles of behaviourism apply to the therapist as much as to the client. The therapist is shaped up to behave in particular ways by a system of internal and external reinforcers and punishers in just the same way as the client. Therefore in DBT therapists apply the treatment to themselves and each other. At the weekly consultation meeting therapists practise mindfulness, and perform chain and solution analyses on their own therapy interfering behaviours.

PRACTICE

Goals of dialectical behaviour therapy

The overarching goal in DBT is to help clients achieve 'a life worth living' based on the idea that people who have that do not think about killing or harming themselves. For most clients the problematic behaviours that brought them into therapy – suicidality, self-harming, eating disorders, drug or alcohol misuse, behaviours maintaining depression or anxiety – get in the way of them achieving a life worth living, so eliminating these behaviours from the client's response repertoire becomes the secondary goal of treatment. It should never be forgotten that the only reason to rid the client of these problems is to reach that life worth living.

Structure of the therapy

As mentioned previously, DBT is delivered as a programme, usually with a minimum of four therapists working as a treatment team. Each programme has five components:

1. A weekly consultation team meeting in which the therapists get together. The function of this component is to keep the therapists to the model, and to get more than one position.
2. A weekly skills training group, usually staffed by two skills trainers. The function is to create a learning environment in which the task is just to ensure the client acquires the skill of the week. They learn the name of the skill, when it is used, how it is used and have a chance to practise in the group via role play or discussion. Then they have homework to practise the skill during the week. Homework feedback is taken the following week.
3. Weekly individual therapy for each client. In this component the therapist selects a target behaviour from a diary card that the client fills out daily. This is the component in which the individual therapist gets to coach the client in how to use the skills in his or her unique circumstances.

4. Telephone coaching. The function of this component is to help the client to generalise the skill from the therapy room into their natural environment.
5. Structuring the environment. These are additional interventions that are
   designed to encourage the environment to support skilled behaviour – so
   they may include ad hoc education sessions for family or staff members in
   behavioural principles.

Table 11.1 gives a snapshot of a typical week in a DBT programme for one client.

Skills training modules

The skills that are taught in the skills group are aimed at tackling the areas in which
clients have the most difficulty:

1. Core mindfulness – to help clients learn how to turn their attention away from
   emotionally evocative triggers, and to focus on whatever they need to do to be
   effective in the moment.
2. Emotion regulation – to help clients understand the anatomy of an emotion and
   learn how to regulate each one naturally without resorting to harmful or problematic behaviour.
3. Interpersonal effectiveness – to help clients learn how to say no to demands
   when necessary, and to make requests appropriately.
4. Distress tolerance – to help clients accept and get through situations that must
   be endured, without making things worse.

TABLE 11.1   *Sample DBT programme*

Day	Client attends appointments	Client completes diary card and practises skills	Client has access to out-of-hours skills coaching	Therapists all go to weekly consult meeting
Mon	10:00 am – 12:30 pm skills training group with 9 clients and 2 skills trainers	Daily	As required	
Tues		Daily	As required	
Wed		Daily	As required	
Thur	2:00–3:00 pm individual therapy with client's own primary therapist	Daily	As required	
Fri		Daily	As required	9:00–11:00 am all 6 therapists delivering DBT meet together
Sat		Daily	As required	
Sun		Daily	As required	

5. Middle path (adolescent adaptation) – to help clients and their families learn the skill of seeing both sides and finding the most effective synthesis.
6. Radical openness (over-control adaptation) – to help clients be more emotionally expressive, more open to novel stimuli and to accept feedback from the environment.

Targeting in individual therapy

The therapist will meet with the client for four sessions of pre-treatment before the client enters the treatment proper. During this time they will first identify the 'life worth living' goal of the client (examples might be to find a partner, to get my kids out of care, to get to university). They also notice how the self-harming suicidal behaviour is an impediment to this goal. For example, you can't find a partner if you're dead, or get your children out of care if you're in Accident and Emergency every week. Then they make a list of the behaviours that the therapy is aiming to treat for this client. The principle is that the therapist is going to start on the most serious behaviour that the client has in their response repertoire, and work down systematically to the least serious, checking each week via the diary card to see what is the highest problem behaviour on the hierarchy that has occurred since the client and therapist last met. This systematic approach to problem behaviours, starting with the worst and working down slowly, is one of the key features by which DBT deals successfully with very complex multi-diagnostic cases.

The headings used by DBT therapists to rank target behaviours are:

1. Life-threatening behaviour – suicidal, homicidal or imminently life-threatening behaviour, non-suicidal self-injury, and urges to engage in any of these. Urges are included here because if urges are not addressed it is possible that the behaviour has just been suppressed.
2. Therapy-interfering behaviour – anything that interferes with the client getting therapy (e.g. missed sessions) or anything that reduces the therapist's motivation to treat, e.g. threatening the therapist, repeatedly saying 'I don't know'.
3. Quality-of-life interfering behaviour – these are severe destabilising conditions or other diagnoses that might be treated as a referral to a public body (e.g. severe depressed episode, restricted eating, or school refusal).

To be a target behaviour the incident must be one that can be pin-pointed in time. The therapist must be able to say, 'At what time did this happen?' This is because once the top target incident has been selected each week from the diary card, the therapist will proceed to conduct a behavioural chain-and-solution analysis on this incident. The function of the chain is solely to identify what the client might be able to do differently if the exact same incident occurred again. Although it may seem odd to look in such detail at what occurred in the previous week, by using an actual incident the therapist is working from data and not from speculation. This is a key point. If the client is asked a vague question, such as 'What happens when you self-harm?', they will give their best guess or interpretation. If, however, the therapist looks in detail at one specific incident, the process often flushes out details that are a surprise to both parties. The therapist constantly refers back to the factual data.

Over a course of treatment, patterns may occur, but the DBT therapist is aware that pattern recognition or insight is *not* the mechanism of change. An analogy might be that if your car keeps breaking down you might have noticed a pattern, and can tell the mechanic – 'It *always* happens just after I have turned left.' This is helpful, but this insight is not the solution. The problem is solved when the mechanic takes you to a specific left turn, and gets you to drive round at 2 miles per hour while he peers under the bonnet, looks in the window and generally watches you do it. Then he says, 'I see what's wrong, we need to tighten this cable. Now do it again with that alteration and let's see if it's fixed.' The therapist is always looking for solutions to employ, and will ask the client to rehearse doing things a different way, utilising skills that have been learned in group alongside other strategies. This behavioural rehearsal is vital to the change process.

In conducting the chain and solution analysis the therapist uses behavioural principles to see what factors are reinforcing the problem behaviour, and what factors are punishing the skilled behaviour. By manipulating the contingencies and using exposure strategies, the therapist works on increasing the likelihood that a skilful response will occur over that of a harmful or problem behaviour.

WHICH CLIENTS BENEFIT MOST?

Undoubtedly DBT works best for clients who have behavioural problems as it is an approach that targets behaviours to be reduced or increased (for example treating a person who has an eating disorder might involve increasing the behaviour of eating a set amount of food at mealtimes). Because of the systematic approach, DBT is very helpful for clients who have multiple diagnoses, and the main RCTs have focused on borderline personality disorder. The therapy has a number of components and in a standard outpatient therapy setting the recommended treatment duration is one year. The skills training modules taken over one session per week take 6 months to complete, and it is advised that patients go through the entire cycle twice. For this reason DBT is most cost-effective when applied to more serious behavioural problems where clients are utilising a lot of resources, such as crisis admissions to hospital and emergency services.

DBT has developed an evidence base with a number of different problems, as listed below, with the key authors associated with each specialty:

DBT for suicidal adolescents (Miller; Rathus)
DBT-S for substance misuse (van den Bosch; Verheul)
DBT for binge eating disorders (Safer; Telch)
RO-DBT (RO = radical openness) for disorders of over-control (Lynch)
DBT for forensic populations (McCann; Trupin)

CASE STUDY

The Client

Sophie is a 24-year-old single woman who is being treated in an outpatient DBT centre. She was sexually abused in childhood by an uncle. She has a diagnosis of borderline personality disorder and engages in frequent cutting of her arms with sharp implements. She wants to be in treatment so that she can return to her university course.

The Therapy

Sophie has been in therapy for three months. In group she has completed four mindfulness sessions and the whole of the emotion regulation module. Her target hierarchy is illustrated below:

Life-threatening behaviour

1. Overdosing on paracetamol
2. Cutting my arms with a razor
3. Urges to do any of the above

Therapy-interfering behaviour

4. Missing group

Quality-of-life interfering behaviour

5. Drinking over 5 units of alcohol on any one day

This extract from an individual session includes notes on the reason for the therapist's responses.

Each week the individual therapist, Anna, asks to see the diary card where Sophie records skills use and her target behaviours, and they conduct a chain analysis, part of which is reproduced here:

Anna: I see you had no overdoses this week, and no suicidal urges or actions, that's great. **(Reviews the diary card)**

Sophie: Yes, I don't think of killing myself as much now.

Anna: Brilliant. But I see you did cut your arm twice, on Tuesday and Friday, so we'll look at one of those incidents. Which was worst? **(Selects target behaviour according to seriousness)**

Sophie: Both the same. [*Sophie shows Anna her arm.*]

Anna: Ok, we want to make sure this doesn't stop you getting back to uni. I'm sure I can help, we just need to work out what was the function of cutting, and see how we can achieve the same thing without you harming yourself. Which episode would be most helpful to chain? **(Links the chain to the client's goal, allies herself with the patient against the target behaviour)**

Sophie: Tuesday, probably.

Anna: Yes, you've been doing really well till then. What time and where did you cut yourself? **(Pinpoints the incident in time and place to ensure she draws on factual data)**

Sophie: 2:00pm, in the bathroom.

Anna: With what?

(Continued)

(Continued)

Sophie:	A razor from the cabinet ...
Anna:	Can we get rid of those? **(Goes straight into problem solving a key link – separating the client from the means of harm)**
Sophie:	There was only that one.
Anna:	OK, until you've stopped having urges to cut, we need to keep razors out of the house. What was going on the few minutes before you cut yourself? **(Draws out more links in the chain of events)**
Sophie:	I'd had a text from Mum saying my sister has got in to Cardiff Uni.
Anna:	Ah, I guess that was hard. **(Offers validation)**
Sophie:	First I was really pleased, then I thought, she's not throwing away her chances like me, I'm such a loser.
Anna:	So those were the thoughts, what was the emotion? **(Labels 'thoughts' as a link in the chain, looks for an emotion link)**
Sophie:	Umm ... probably shame, my face was hot, and I didn't want anyone to see me. I was thinking; I'm such a loser. I just wanted it to stop.
Anna:	What exactly? The thought 'I'm such a loser' or the emotion of shame? **(Asks 'what' questions not 'why', so as not to elicit interpretations. Seeks out the controlling variables of the behaviour)**
Sophie:	The emotion mostly, I thought it wouldn't go away unless I did something to get rid of it.
Anna:	And what happened when you cut yourself? Did the shame go down? **(Hypothesises that the function of cutting might be to reduce shame)**
Sophie:	Yes, it made things seem a bit surreal, I kind of numbed out.
Anna:	OK, if you were trying to reduce the emotion, let's start there. **(Starts problem solving based on the client's stated goal to down-regulate the emotion)** Do you remember how to do that from your emotion regulation module in skills group? What's the first step? **(Encourages the client to remember the teaching from group)**
Sophie:	Name the emotion?
Anna:	Yes, just naming it engages the cortex of your brain and will start to have a dampening effect on your amygdala. Just saying out loud, 'I'm feeling the emotion of shame'. Imagine yourself back there on Tuesday, and what you were feeling, and try it out now. **(Does some psycho-education, tries to elicit new behaviour from the client)**
Sophie:	[*Looks down*] I'm feeling the emotion of shame.
Anna:	Now we want to ask, is this emotion justified? **(Reminds the client of the next step in emotion regulation)**
Sophie:	Well, yes; I have wasted opportunities.
Anna:	OK, so how much shame on a 0 to 10 scale do you think would be appropriate? **(Does not attempt to argue with the client, gives the client responsibility for setting the level)**

Sophie:	10.
Anna:	The same as having killed someone? **(Keeps a light tone but tests out the client's conclusion using an irreverent response)**
Sophie:	[*Laughs*] 8 then.
Anna:	Or run off with an elderly neighbour's life savings? **(Another irreverent response)**
Sophie:	OK, maybe 4 or 5. But I've done things I'm not proud of.
Anna:	Right, so on one hand we want to get rid of shame, and on the other hand it can be a useful emotion to remind us of our values – sounds like we want to lower the amount of shame to a more appropriate level. Do you remember from skills group how to get an emotion down if the level of it is too high for the circumstances? **(Points out a dialectic – on the one hand this, on the other hand that – looks for the truth in both sides)**
Sophie:	Act opposite to the action urge?
Anna:	Yes, act opposite to shame urges in every way. Let's start with your temperature – you were hotting up so we needed to find a way of cooling down. **(Coaches how to reduce physiological arousal)**
Sophie:	Splash my face with water?
Anna:	Great. What about your posture? **(Attends to physiology before cognitions)**

[*Sophie demonstrates hanging her head and hiding behind her hair.*]

Anna:	Let's change your posture and then make a factual statement that fits with our '4 out of 10' aim, maybe you could use words like 'regret' or 'disappointment' which are less evocative of shame. Remember to keep your voice tone appropriate to the level you're aiming for. **(Elicits more behavioural change in the therapy room, wants to see the client do it differently. Includes some exposure to the cue that set off the emotion)**
Sophie:	[*Raises her head but looks away and mumbles*] I regret not making the most of my chances …
Anna:	Try it again but this time look at me and speak clearly, as though you mean it. **(Gives corrective feedback and asks the client to repeat the behavioural rehearsal)**

[*Sophie complies*]

Anna:	How did that feel? Is the level of shame higher or lower than on Tuesday? **(Checks on the relevance by linking back to the data point)**
Sophie:	Definitely lower. I feel more guilty than ashamed now.
Anna:	And if you'd been able to do this on Tuesday, do you think you'd have been more likely or less likely to cut yourself? **(Constantly checks solutions against the target behaviour)**
Sophie:	Less likely, but I still would've thought about doing it.
Anna:	Then we need to add something else in. We've lowered the emotion by acting opposite, what about the guilt? If you think this is warranted,

(Continued)

(Continued)

> how can you make a repair? **(Evaluates the solutions. Believes the client's appraisal that these are not sufficient to avert the target behaviour and looks for more strategies to add in)**
>
> *Sophie:* What do you mean?
> *Anna:* If you think some guilt is justified because of wasting resources we need to commit to something that makes good use of resources, sort of listen to what the emotion is telling you. **(Highlights how to use the emotion to inform actions, models not being afraid of feeling guilt)**
> *Sophie:* Er … I don't know.
>
> *[Anna waits]*
>
> *Sophie:* I could start to build my photography portfolio again.
> *Anna:* *[Nods]* Let's go over it again. If on Tuesday you'd reduced your temperature, changed your posture, held your head up, said 'I'm pleased for my sister but regret not making the most of my chances' in a firm clear voice, had kept away from the bathroom or any razors, and had resolved to pick up your portfolio again, would you have been more likely or less likely to want to cut yourself? **(Goes back to the original data point and evaluates the solutions again)**
> *Sophie:* Less likely, but it's remembering to do it …
> *Anna:* You're right, we need to work on how to set up reminders – also don't forget if you get an urge to harm yourself you can text me and I'll call you back. I'm 100 per cent on your side in trying to get rid of these painful behaviours and get you back to uni, and if you practise and it goes well, will you text me? **(Adds reminder to use telephone coaching and asks for commitment)**

Each week as Sophie comes back Anna works on the top target behaviour that occurred that week. If the same behaviour crops up multiple times and the solutions don't work, they identify the point at which there was a problem either implementing the skill or finding it wasn't sufficient for the task. Then they either make a change or add a new skill in. Sophie gradually learns that every problem is one to be solved and with help from Anna, Jodi and Matt the target behaviours slowly reduce.

Sophie completes each module of skills training twice; second time around she is called a 'Senior' in skills group and is expected to help new people to implement the skills by offering encouragement and ideas on how to get more effective. Anna cycles into the skills training group as a trainer, as do all the therapists on the consultation team – so that every therapist gets a chance to keep their skills up and to meet all the clients in the programme.

At the end of the skills training modules Sophie is given a graduation certificate and invited to join a monthly peer-led support group. She no longer self-harms and has applied for a place to do photography and graphics at a regional university. If she finds herself having urges to self-harm (which rarely happens) she starts to complete the diary cards again, and to do her own chain and solution analyses.

REFERENCES

[1] Linehan, M. M., Armstrong, H. E., Suarez, A., Allmon, D. and Heard, H. L. (1991) 'Cognitive-behavioral treatment of chronically parasuicidal borderline patients', *Archives of General Psychiatry, 48*, 1060–4.

[2] Linehan, M. M., Heard, H. L. and Armstrong, H. E. (1993) 'Naturalistic follow-up of a behavioral treatment for chronically parasuicidal borderline patients', *Archives of General Psychiatry, 50*, 971–4.

[3] Linehan, M. M. (1993a) *Cognitive Behavioral Therapy for Borderline Personality Disorder.* New York: Guilford Press.

[4] Linehan, M. M. (1993b) *Skills Training Manual for Treating Borderline Personality Disorder.* New York: Guilford Press.

SUGGESTED READING

Dimeff, L. A. and Koerner, K. E. (2007) *Dialectical Behavior Therapy in Clinical Practice: Applications Across Disorders and Settings.* New York: Guilford Press. An edited book with chapters by specialists who have adapted DBT for specific clinical populations or settings and have researched the findings. Chapters on, for example, DBT with eating problems, substance misuse, older adults, adolescents and in forensic environments.

Dunkley, C. and Stanton, M. (2013) *Teaching Clients to Use Mindfulness Skills: A Practical Guide.* Hove: Routledge. A simple introduction for therapists to the way mindfulness is taught in DBT as a skill rather than a meditative practice.

Pryor, K. (1999) *Don't Shoot the Dog.* New York: Bantam. An excellent introduction to behavioural principles written in an entertaining way by an animal behaviourist who shows how reinforcers and punishers can be applied to people in everyday situations.

Swales, M. A. and Heard, H. L. (2008) *Dialectical Behaviour Therapy: Distinctive Features.* Hove: Routledge. An easy reader listing the main features of DBT and how it differs from CBT. A short and very accessible overview of the treatment.

DISCUSSION ISSUES

1. How does dialectical behaviour therapy differ from general cognitive behavioural therapy?
2. The main active therapeutic ingredient in dialectical behaviour therapy is just mindfulness? Discuss.
3. What is the nature of the therapeutic relationship in dialectical behaviour therapy?
4. What is a 'dialectical philosophy' and how can it help suicidal clients?

12

Hypnotherapy

Donald J. Robertson

INTRODUCTION

Hypnotherapy is the use of hypnosis as the main strategy of psychological therapy. The expression 'clinical hypnosis' is often used to refer to the treatment of clinically-severe problems, such as social anxiety disorder, in combination with some other form of psychotherapy. However, hypnotherapy is also widely used to treat less severe (subclinical) problems such as ordinary public-speaking anxiety or fingernail-biting.

It is sometimes suggested that hypnotism does not constitute a fully fledged 'therapy' in its own right, but rather a cluster of techniques, with minimal theoretical framework. It can be used alone but is normally combined with some other form of psychotherapy. Indeed, there are many different cognitive behavioural, humanistic and psychodynamic approaches to hypnotherapy. However, in modern literature on the subject, clinical **hypnosis** is most commonly integrated with some form of cognitive or behavioural therapy (CBT).[1] Moreover, the original Victorian approach to hypnotherapy did employ a simple theoretical model that is broadly consistent with modern CBT.[2] So this chapter will primarily focus on the integrative approach known as **cognitive behavioural hypnotherapy** (CBH), or sometimes just 'cognitive hypnotherapy' for short.

DEVELOPMENT OF THE THERAPY

Hypnotherapy has a longer history than any other modern form of psychological therapy. It is commonly confused with Mesmerism but they are essentially two different things. Around 1774, Franz Mesmer (1734–1815) developed a therapeutic technique based on the idea that an invisible force called 'animal magnetism' could be channelled from an 'operator' to his patient, through dramatic hand gestures, etc. Hypnotherapy was introduced in 1841 by the Scottish surgeon James Braid (1795–1860). Braid was a scientific sceptic who based his theory of 'neuro-hypnotism' on the philosophical psychology known as 'Scottish Common-Sense Realism'.[2] He wanted to explain the apparent effects of Mesmerism, but completely rejected its theory of 'animal magnetism' as pseudoscientific.

By the nineteenth century, the controversial practice of Mesmerism had become widespread in Europe and America. However, shortly after Braid's death, hypnotism began to supersede Mesmerism in popularity. In France, during the 1880s, Ambroise-Auguste Liébeault and Hippolyte Bernheim founded the influential Nancy school of hypnotism. A major disagreement took place between them and the famous neurologist Jean-Martin Charcot's Salpêtrière hospital in Paris over the nature of hypnotism. Charcot believed hypnosis was an unusual neurological condition, consisting of distinct stages. However, Bernheim won the argument and his claim that hypnotism works mainly through a form of **suggestion** shaped the development of hypnotherapy throughout the twentieth century.

Sigmund Freud travelled both to the Salpêtrière and later Nancy to study hypnotism, in the late 1880s, and his earliest psychological publications were on hypnotherapy. Freud and his colleague Joseph Breuer were responsible for popularising the technique of age regression and emotional 'catharsis' during hypnosis. Although Freud soon abandoned this approach to develop psychoanalysis, hypnotic regression remained popular with many hypnotists who were influenced by his work. However, with the subsequent development of humanistic and cognitive behavioural therapies, in the 1950s and 1960s, hypnotists gradually started to abandon psychodynamic theory and practices. This meant returning to an approach closer, in some ways, to the original Victorian 'suggestion' hypnotism of Braid and Bernheim, combined with a more diverse mixture of concepts and techniques from different modern psychotherapies. Most modern hypnotherapy is therefore highly 'technically eclectic' and something of a creative melting-pot of therapeutic strategies.

THEORY AND BASIC CONCEPTS

Braid called his original approach 'neuro-hypnotism', or 'hypnotism' for short, and coined the terms 'self-hypnotism' and 'hypnotic therapeutics'. The words 'hypnosis', 'self-hypnosis', and 'hypnotherapy' were introduced later, probably by followers of the Nancy school, who were also the first to use the English word 'psychotherapy' – at a time when hypnotherapy was essentially the first and *only* form of psychotherapy. Modern authors, unlike Braid, use the word 'hypnotism' to refer solely to the theory or procedures. 'Hypnosis' can refer either to the procedure or the state of mind induced in the hypnotic subject: We use *hypnotism* to induce *hypnosis*. As we've seen, the modern field of hypnotherapy is highly eclectic. However, it can be broadly divided into three overlapping traditions:

1. Neo-Ericksonian hypnotherapy, which is based on the work of Milton Erickson (1901–1980) and also includes many hypnotists employing neuro-linguistic programming (NLP).

2. Psychodynamic hypnotherapy, which mainly consists of age regression and catharsis, and largely originated with Freud and Breuer.
3. Cognitive behavioural hypnotherapy (CBH), which gradually evolved out of scientific research conducted on traditional hypnotherapy, and became increasingly popular from the 1980s onward.

Few people now would practise hypnotherapy in the 'traditional' Victorian style, which relied almost solely on direct verbal suggestion. However, in some ways, CBH, as we will see, involves what we might call a partial 'Return to Braid', or to traditional principles of hypnotism in preference to Ericksonian or psychodynamic concepts. CBH also places greater emphasis than previous approaches on the *cognitive* aspects of therapy, which it explains in terms of ordinary psychological processes.[3]

Braid originally believed that hypnosis was a special neurological state he described as 'nervous sleep', which could be induced by tiring the eyes. However, he gradually revised this view in light of his clinical experience and many experiments. He made the acquaintance of an eminent academic and scientist, William Carpenter, who was professor of physiology at the University of London, and had proposed what he called the '**ideo-motor reflex**' theory of suggestion. ('Motor' here refers to the muscles of voluntary movement, or skeletal muscles.) Carpenter argued that many ordinary psychological phenomena could be explained as the reflex–like effect of the imagination upon the body, independent of the conscious will. For example, when we listen to a ghost story, we may tremble with fear, even though it is just words, because our imagination has the power to evoke such bodily reactions in an automatic manner. Carpenter, Braid and other men of science used this theory to debunk Victorian spiritualists and complementary therapists. For example, they showed that 'table-turning' séances, where a ghostly spirit supposedly causes a card table to tilt or flip over, could actually be explained by muscular movements in the hands and arms of the people seated around the table, movements so miniscule they were unconscious of making them. Ironically, therefore, hypnotherapy actually evolved out of scientific *scepticism*. The traditional theory of hypnotism would therefore argue that many complementary therapies popular today work simply by suggestion, or what we now call the 'placebo effect'. Hypnotherapy itself, by contrast, is the only *non-deceptive* placebo, because subjects are explicitly told beforehand that it works mainly through imagination and suggestion, and their informed consent is obtained to the procedure on the basis of this understanding.

Braid was quick to adopt Carpenter's theory as an explanation of hypnotism. He replaced Carpenter's 'ideo–motor' with the broader expression 'ideo–dynamic', meaning the 'power of the mind over the body'. This was to accommodate his observation that the imagination could also affect responses such as the secretion of saliva or changes in heart rate, and that suggestion could *inhibit* as well as evoke various bodily responses. Braid also coined the general term 'psycho–physiology' to describe the study of the mind's interaction with the body, as in the field we now call 'psycho-somatic medicine'. The terminology is important because many hypnotherapists today must dispel confusion caused by the name 'hypnosis' and its connotation of sleep – *hypnos* means sleep in Greek. Although Braid coined the term, he later complained that it misled his patients into believing they should be unconscious or asleep during the procedure. Braid said only about 10 per cent of his patients felt as if they were asleep, the remainder reported being perfectly conscious during hypnosis – and modern research consistently supports this observation.

Braid therefore proposed changing the name from 'hypnotism' to 'mono–ideo–dynamics' – which doesn't trip off the tongue quite as well! However, it is important to notice that he sought to replace the notion that hypnosis is a sleep–like state with the, more accurate, depiction of it as a state of focused *conscious* attention. Braid said hypnotism involved concentration on a 'dominant expectant idea', a thought or mental image accompanied by the belief that it will evoke a corresponding bodily response. The prefix 'mono' was used because in hypnotism the effect of suggestion is supposedly intensified by adopting a single–point of focused attention, upon the suggested result alone. For example, a hypnotist might suggest to a patient that her body is relaxing much more deeply than normal. That response will typically occur, more or less as suggested, so long as the subject concentrates on the idea of sleepiness or relaxation, is willing to relax, and expects to do so. Indeed, modern researchers have consistently found that attitudes and expectations are crucial in determining how people respond to hypnotic suggestion. Contrary to the widespread misconception that hypnotists talk in a monotone, from the outset Braid and others emphasised that hypnotic suggestions must normally be *evocative*, like rhetoric or oratory. The way they're phrased, and the tone of voice used, are crucial in determining the hypnotic subject's response.

Braid therefore moved progressively further away from the 'magical' model of the Mesmerists and toward the less-dramatic 'common sense' conclusion that hypnosis is merely an extension of *ordinary* psychological processes, such as concentration, imagination and expectation. He never actually used the word 'trance' to describe ordinary hypnosis. Indeed, the longest-running argument in the field of hypnotism has been over the existence of a *special* 'hypnotic state', also described as an 'altered', 'abnormal' or 'trance' state. This theoretical controversy is known as the 'state versus nonstate debate'. State theorists have argued that hypnosis consists of a special neurological or psychological state, induced by the hypnotist or through self-hypnosis. By contrast, nonstate theorists argued that this was basically a myth, and that hypnotism could be sufficiently explained in terms of *ordinary* psychological processes. These processes typically include identification with a role, expectation and other positive attitudes, focused attention and the use of evocative mental imagery techniques, etc. Put crudely, state theorists tend to view hypnotism mainly as the art of inducing an altered state of consciousness, or 'hypnotic trance', whereas nonstate theorists view it more as the art of suggestion. Nonstate theorists are also known as 'sceptical', 'socio–cognitive' or 'cognitive behavioural' theorists. Although there's still some debate in this area, the two positions have come much closer together, largely because state theorists have progressively abandoned the assumption that hypnosis is a special or abnormal psychological state, arguably watering-down their assumption until it bears little resemblance to what most people would think of as 'hypnotic trance'. Although the cognitive behavioural (nonstate) theory of hypnosis and cognitive behavioural therapy (CBT) are two different things, they naturally tend to complement each other, as we will see later.

Braid's original hypnotism didn't have a very sophisticated therapeutic theory, but he did clearly state that 'hysteria' was caused by a morbid form of hypnotism.

This supposedly occurred when individuals focused their attention, for whatever reason, on unhealthy 'fixed ideas'. Hypnotism was therefore used to explain both the *cause* and *cure* of hysteria. ('Hysteria' is an obsolete psychiatric term that would roughly correspond to a variety of different emotional and psycho-somatic disorders in modern terminology.) Victorian hypnotists believed it was necessary to diagnose these fixed ideas and counteract them using a combination of direct hypnotic suggestion and rational persuasion. Psychoanalysis eclipsed this model, at the start of the twentieth century, replacing it with a completely different approach. However, when Aaron T. Beck published his first book on cognitive therapy, *Cognitive Therapy of the Emotional Disorders* (1976), he noted that the new 'cognitive' model of emotion had more in common with Victorian hypnotism than with Freud's intervening approach. From the late 1970s onward, therefore, hypnotists increasingly integrated both the theory and practice of CBT.

Beck's hypothesis that emotional disturbance is caused by 'automatic negative thoughts', or underlying schematic beliefs, is sometimes expressed, in the literature on hypnosis, by saying that problems are due primarily to negative *autosuggestions* or rather negative *self-hypnosis* (NSH). For example, cognitive processes such as morbid worry or rumination can be viewed as forms of negative self-hypnosis, involving prolonged focused attention on unhealthy thoughts and images. So, in practice, CBH may begin, like CBT, by asking clients to self-monitor their thoughts, actions and feelings, as a homework assignment, in order to observe the relationship between them. This heightens the client's awareness of the role of negative self-hypnosis in their problem. It also allows the therapist and client to collaborate on a conceptualisation of the problem, in terms of negative autosuggestion, and to develop and implement a hypnosis–based treatment plan together.

PRACTICE

The goals of CBH are typically to reduce symptoms and to prevent future vulnerability and relapse, primarily by counteracting the effects of negative self-hypnosis, or mental absorption in negative thoughts and beliefs. Change can be understood in terms of the gradual effect of hypnotic suggestion in modifying underlying beliefs (schemas), as in the cognitive therapy of Beck. Indeed, suggestions *are* cognitions. It is the meaning of the words that subjects respond to rather than just their sound, although the hypnotist's tone of voice and attitude may help make his suggestions more effective. Hypnotherapy is therefore part 'cognitive' and part 'imagination' therapy. More specifically, CBH typically uses focused attention, imagination and evocative ideas to help clients modify their relevant core beliefs, change their behaviour and alleviate their symptoms.

Basic techniques and strategies

Hypnotherapy employs a large armamentarium of techniques and strategies. When combined with another approach, particularly CBT, it becomes probably the most technically eclectic therapy of all. However, for simplicity, this chapter will focus on a typical sub-set of basic interventions.

The induction and deepening of hypnosis, and the use of verbal suggestion techniques, is fundamental to any form of hypnotherapy. There are many different methods of hypnotic induction but the most common techniques are variants of Braid's original 'eye-fixation' technique. This method is also by far the most commonly used in scientific research studies on hypnosis. It requires subjects to raise their gaze to stare at a point on the ceiling or an object held within a few feet, while the hypnotist suggests that their eyes are growing heavy and sleepy, and are beginning to close. This is typically followed by general suggestions of relaxation, and often a 'counting deepener', which involves counting backward with additional suggestions that hypnosis and relaxation are progressively increasing. As we have seen, hypnosis is generally understood to consist of a heightened state of suggestibility. It is not, therefore, inherently a state of either mental or physical relaxation. *not relaxing* Indeed, most of Braid's subjects tensed their whole body while *increasing* their heart rate and blood pressure, during hypnosis. No modern researchers equate hypnosis with relaxation. However, most modern hypnotists do *suggest* relaxation to clients, for the following reasons:

1. It is one of the easiest suggestions to respond to, making it a logical starting point for socialisation to hypnotherapy.
2. Relaxation is useful for managing symptoms, such as anxiety, pain and insomnia.
3. Clients expect to be told to relax, and are comfortable with this approach.

Hypnotherapy has also tended to make extensive use of mental imagery techniques. In fact, CBH often employs a simple ABC strategy that requires clients to mentally rehearse anticipated situations, of a challenging nature, while practising changes in their feelings, actions and thoughts (or 'affect', 'behaviour' and 'cognition' = ABC). For instance, a client who wishes to overcome anxiety and manage pain during childbirth might be guided through the process of mentally rehearsing the experience during sessions, and asked to repeat this each night for homework by listening to a self-hypnosis recording.

- **A**ffective changes can be rehearsed by actively accepting feelings, and riding them out, or by relaxing them away during hypnosis.
- **B**ehavioural changes can be rehearsed using mental 'coping' imagery in hypnosis, in order to increase skill and confidence and allow creative problem solving.
- **C**ognitive changes can be rehearsed, by repeating rational coping statements, or alternative ways of thinking, in the form of autosuggestions, in order to gradually modify underlying beliefs and attitudes in hypnosis.

Relaxation, visualisation and autosuggestion are, of course, very familiar tools in traditional hypnotherapy. Today they tend to be employed in ways that are integrated more carefully with therapeutic strategies derived from other schools of thought, such as CBT.

Typical treatment format

Traditionally, hypnotherapists have tended to carry out treatment over a brief period of time, typically averaging around 5–6 sessions. Although some hypnotherapists offer single-session treatment, this is often not regarded as very credible, except in exceptional cases or for simple habit-breaking, etc. On the other hand, hypnotherapy is seldom employed as the main treatment strategy for more than about 10 sessions unless it involves regression or other psychodynamic methods, and this is becoming rare nowadays. Of course, hypnosis may form part of a longer treatment plan when combined with other modalities of psychotherapy.

Perhaps because of the brevity of hypnotherapy treatments, less attention has been paid than in other forms of psychotherapy to the initial processes of assessment, conceptualisation and socialisation, and to the ending of therapy. Nevertheless a conscientious therapist will plan a treatment that roughly divides across three stages: beginning, middle and end.

1. **Assessment**, during which the problem is conceptualised, treatment is planned and the client is prepared for hypnosis and for other therapy procedures to be used. Training in self-hypnosis often begins at this stage.
2. **Treatment proper**, during which the treatment plan is followed during the session and in terms of homework assigned to the client, in particular coping skills are learned and underlying beliefs are re-evaluated, using hypnosis as the main catalyst of change.
3. **Relapse prevention and termination**, the final stage, during which clients are prepared to leave therapy and maintain their improvement over the longer-term, without the therapist, often spreading their improvement across a wider range of situations, and continuing their use of self-hypnosis and autosuggestion techniques post treatment.

CBH therefore begins with at least one assessment sessions, in which the client is interviewed in a manner similar to other cognitive behavioural approaches. Hypnotherapists must also assess clients for issues that would suggest hypnotism or related techniques may be inappropriate ('contra-indicated'). There is considerable disagreement over the risks of treatment. However, most therapists would consider it inappropriate to hypnotise someone who suffers from psychosis or who is currently suicidal or otherwise at risk of harming themselves, mainly because such clients can react in unpredictable ways to unusual psychological experiences. Also, the brevity of most hypnotherapy does not provide much scope for detailed assessment and management of risk in cases of severe psychological disturbance. However, there is no real support for the belief that hypnosis *per se* is dangerous.

Clients will often be orientated (socialised) to hypnotherapy by training them in techniques of self-hypnosis and autosuggestion prior to being hypnotised by the therapist (hetero-hypnosis). For example, they may be taught first simply how to make their own eyelids feel heavy by using autosuggestion and imagination. This process, known as 'hypnotic skills training', allows the hypnotist to correct common misconceptions about hypnosis, which are known to be a major obstacle to treatment. It also allows the hypnotist to informally assess the client's responsiveness to hypnotism and relevant skills, such as their ability to relax and visualise images. The therapeutic relationship is clearly important in any form of hypnotism, particularly CBH. A favourable relationship, or 'rapport', with the hypnotist must typically exist for suggestion to be effective. However, as in CBT, it tends to receive less attention than in the literature of other modalities of therapy, which assume this to be the primary catalyst of change. Once the working relationship is established and the client has been orientated to hypnotherapy, by learning basic skills, the process of teaching them self-hypnosis proper usually begins. Many modern hypnotists will say 'All hypnosis is self-hypnosis'. As Braid claimed from the outset, it is primarily the client who puts herself into hypnosis, and the hypnotist is merely a guide, providing cues in the form of suggestions and instructions. It is therefore logical to train clients in *self-hypnosis* before the therapist attempts to hypnotise them in the conventional manner.

Clients will normally be hypnotised more formally by the therapist in the first session following assessment, having already been introduced to the basic concepts and techniques via training in self-hypnosis. As sessions proceed, clients' skill and confidence as hypnotic subjects will tend to improve. Less time and effort is normally required to hypnotise them and it is often possible, by the third or fourth session, to induce hypnosis simply by saying: 'Please close your eyes, put yourself into hypnosis, and nod your head when you're ready to continue …' In other respects, the middle section of CBH treatment is similar to certain forms of CBT, which emphasise training in coping skills. Clients are taught one or more coping skills and sessions are spent rehearsing these in hypnosis, with hypnotic suggestions used throughout to build confidence and evoke the desired thoughts, feelings and actions. Clients rehearse changes in imagination and then test out their ability to cope with challenges between sessions.

As CBH proceeds, the therapist, in a sense, 'progressively puts himself out of a job', by empowering the client to take more responsibility for her own treatment. Clients should be making more skilled and confident use of self-hypnosis, and other strategies. Treatment normally concludes with at least one session where the primary focus is upon prevention of relapse, by helping to make improvements more lasting and applicable to a wider range of situations in life, often through the continued use of self-hypnosis or related techniques outside of therapy.

Typical session format

Hypnotherapy sessions are similar to those in other psychotherapies, except that more time is normally spent with the client's eyes closed, while the client engages in guided mental processes. This typically takes at least 15–20 minutes, sometimes much longer, and forms the central part of most sessions. As in other cognitive behavioural approaches, CBH practitioners will normally begin by setting a rough agenda for the session, in collaboration with the client. The client's homework, especially use of self-hypnosis, will be reviewed, along with an update on their problem, and sometimes daily self-monitoring records, symptom measures, or other documents will be reviewed. Typically the therapist will discuss the client's progress, the conceptualisation of their problem and next steps in the treatment plan. Most hypnotherapists will then engage in therapy techniques prior to hypnosis, which may be identical to those employed in other psychotherapies. For example, clients may be taught relaxation techniques, mental imagery, or the disputation of dysfunctional beliefs.

The client will then be hypnotised and similar interventions employed, usually with eyes closed and focused attention. In CBH, this often involves the rehearsal of challenging anticipated situations, which the client will face between sessions, over the following week. For example, a client with a phobia for birds may be asked to repeatedly visualise walking through a local park, exposing herself in hypnosis, i.e. in her imagination, to the feared situation. In hypnotherapy, this will often involve exposure or rehearsal of coping skills, similar to other cognitive behavioural therapies, but will also be accompanied by direct and indirect suggestions regarding symptoms and the client's responses to them. Sessions normally conclude with further training in self-help strategies, such as self-hypnosis, autosuggestion, or the use of hypnotic triggers, to be employed as homework. After debriefing and ending the session, clients will normally be expected to monitor their progress while continuing to engage in daily use of the agreed strategies. Although many of these techniques obviously resemble those found in modern CBT, hypnotherapy is over a century older, and hypnotists often employed these techniques first, although usually in a more primitive form.

WHICH CLIENTS BENEFIT MOST?

Statistical research on hypnosis, as far back as the Victorian era, offers evidence that children aged around 6–12 are typically slightly more responsive than adults. It has also long been known that hypnotic susceptibility follows a roughly bell-shaped distribution. That is, most people respond moderately well to hypnotic suggestions, while a minority of people are either highly responsive or respond poorly. Only around 5 per cent of people in experiments on hypnosis show no response at all to suggestions given as tests. It is therefore generally believed that *everyone* can potentially be hypnotised. The main obstacles are simply common misconceptions and fears about the procedure, such as the belief that it involves being 'controlled' by someone else, or being unconscious or asleep, etc. These misconceptions often go back to the popular confusion of hypnotism with Mesmerism and have been deliberately perpetuated by some stage hypnotists for dramatic effect or, more recently, by misinformation on the Internet.

Throughout its history, hypnotherapy has been thought to be of benefit especially in the treatment of pain, anxiety, insomnia and 'psycho-somatic' or stress-related conditions, such as tension headaches or irritable bowel syndrome (IBS). Modern research on hypnotherapy has tended to broadly support these claims, particularly in relation to managing pain and anxiety.[4] There is some evidence to suggest hypnotherapy may be effective for mild habits or addictions, particularly quitting cigarettes. By contrast, there is a lack of good evidence to show that hypnotherapy, by itself, is effective in treating severe mental health problems such as psychosis or more serious addictions, including alcoholism. Both in research studies and in daily practice, hypnotherapy is used for a far wider range of problems, and with a wider range of different populations, than most other forms of psychological therapy. That is mainly because it is a particularly brief and flexible strategy.

CASE STUDY

As with all approaches to therapy, it is important to maintain a high level of confidentiality. This case study ('Helen') is therefore a composite picture based on several clients who presented with similar issues.

The Client

Helen was aged 35 and lived in London, where she worked in the offices of a publishing company. Her reason for seeking help was that she suffered from a fear of flying. She was going to be married in four weeks' time and planned to honeymoon abroad, which meant getting on a plane, something she dreaded. Helen showed no evidence of full-blown panic attacks or of other mental health problems. However, her phobia for flying was so severe that even talking about it made her highly anxious, and could cause her to burst into tears. Her husband-to-be was supportive but she felt that she owed it to herself to overcome her problem and had made a commitment to attempt travelling by plane, despite her anxiety.

It was important to her to overcome the problem because she felt it restricted her ability to engage in normal activities. She had only flown once before and this had been a highly unpleasant experience, mainly because her intense anxiety about the return flight had 'ruined the holiday', as she put it. Their honeymoon flight was booked and so she had set herself a tight schedule for overcoming the problem. This was compounding her current anxiety, because she also feared that she would be unable to make the trip and that this would let down her husband and family. She had no previous experience of therapy but was drawn to hypnotherapy specifically because she practised Buddhist meditation. She found this generally helpful and saw hypnotherapy as a kindred method.

The Therapy

The first session focused on assessment, developing an initial conceptualisation of her problem and treatment plan, and socialisation to hypnotherapy. This involved preliminary training in self-hypnosis. The limited time available and her lack of opportunity for real-world exposure to being on a plane created some obstacles for the therapy. However, it was agreed that a brief course of hypnotherapy seemed appropriate, as her goal was primarily to manage anxiety. Although no formal hypnotism was carried out during the initial session, Helen was taught how to use eye-fixation and counting as a basic self-hypnosis and relaxation method. She was also given a 20 minute audio (MP3) recording containing a 'hypnotic desensitisation' script. This guided her through physical and mental relaxation more systematically, followed by repeated exposure, in her imagination, to the feared event. We developed a simple hierarchy of events, which began with Helen simply visualising the approach to the airport car park. She rated the intensity of her anxiety at 50 per cent during even this scene but reported that she found it manageable enough to work on. In the

(Continued)

(Continued)

past, desensitisation procedures exposed clients to very minimal levels of anxiety but in hypnotherapy exposure often begins at moderate level of anxiety because the procedure also employs coping skills and hypnotic suggestions.

Helen kept a written record of daily sessions using the recording. When she attended her first session she was able to report that her anxiety during this scene had already reduced to 0–10 per cent, which she considered a significant improvement. This proved to her that she had found a workable method of coping. However, she still experienced high anxiety when picturing the flight itself. We therefore undertook a more systematic approach to desensitisation over the following weeks, exposing her to progressively more anxiety-provoking scenes. Exposure in imagination works surprisingly well in most cases, especially when hypnotic suggestions are given for benefits to 'generalise' to the real world. Nevertheless, it is important to supplement this with other forms of exposure where possible as this can help improvements become more robust and prevent relapse.

Helen was not in a position to take another flight or physically visit the airport in the weeks prior to her wedding. However, we agreed that an alternative test would be for her to watch videos of planes, including scenes of passengers in turmoil and distress, something that initially caused her great anxiety and which she said she struggled to imagine being able to watch for more than a few minutes. It is easy nowadays for therapists to find video clips online, which can be played full-screen and repeated on a loop for prolonged exposure. Helen spent most of her third session doing this, and continued it at home between sessions. She was hypnotised briefly beforehand and hypnotic suggestions continued after she opened her eyes to watch the videos. The emphasis was gradually shifted onto using relaxation as a way of remaining in the situation rather than as a means of eliminating unwanted feelings. Likewise, the content of hypnotic suggestions shifted from relaxation on to her motivation for exposure and ability to accept her feelings while relaxing 'into them', accepting them and waiting for them to abate naturally. As she learned to progressively let go of her struggle against the anxiety in this way, she found it naturally reduced more quickly anyway, because her inner battle with her feelings had actually been making the problem worse. This allowed her to make the flight with negligible discomfort and she reported that she also found herself much more able to manage anxiety in general, particularly in relation to her wedding ceremony.

REFERENCES

[1] Lynn, S. J. and Kirsch, I. (2006) *Essentials of Clinical Hypnosis: An Evidence-Based Approach.* Washington, DC: APA.
[2] Braid, J. (2009) *The Discovery of Hypnosis: The Complete Writings of James Braid, the Father of Hypnotherapy.* Maidenhead: National Council for Hypnotherapy.
[3] Robertson, D. (2012) *The Practice of Cognitive-Behavioural Hypnotherapy: A Manual for Evidence-Based Clinical Hypnosis.* London: Karnac.

[4] British Psychological Society (2001) The Nature of Hypnosis. Report prepared by a Working Party at the request of the Professional Affairs Board of the British Psychological Society. Leicester: BPS.

SUGGESTED READING

Alladin, A. (2008) *Cognitive Hypnotherapy: An Integrated Approach to the Treatment of Emotional Disorders*. Chichester: Wiley. A detailed introduction to cognitive hypnotherapy and its application to a selection of common problems. Alladin has carried out important research showing that cognitive hypnotherapy was superior to standard CBT on some measures, in the treatment of clinical depression.

Dowd, T. E. (2000) *Cognitive Hypnotherapy*. New Jersey: Jason Aronson Inc. A slightly older book but nevertheless worth reading as it comes from an experienced cognitive therapist who specialises in clinical hypnosis. The foreword was written by Aaron T. Beck himself, the founder of cognitive therapy.

Lynn, S. J. and Kirsch, I. (2006) *Essentials of Clinical Hypnosis: An Evidence-Based Approach*. Washington, DC: APA. Another excellent introduction from two of the leading scientific researchers in the field of hypnosis. Written from a cognitive behavioural perspective on theory and practice, with chapters dedicated to a selection of common problems.

Robertson, D. (2012) *The Practice of Cognitive-Behavioural Hypnotherapy: A Manual for Evidence-Based Clinical Hypnosis*. London: Karnac. This text provides a detailed and comprehensive overview of the cognitive behavioural approach to hypnotherapy.

DISCUSSION ISSUES

1. What is hypnosis? Is it a *special* neurological or psychological state, which fundamentally differs from normal psychological functioning? Alternatively, is it just a special way of using *ordinary* cognitive abilities, such as concentration, imagination and expectation?
2. How dangerous is hypnosis? Can you imagine any risks associated with the use of hypnotherapy? How real are those risks? Could anything be done to prevent or minimise them?
3. What is the difference between hypnotherapy and other psychological therapies, such as CBT? What is special or unique about hypnotism? To what extent should hypnosis be combined with other forms of psychotherapy? Does hypnosis add anything important or introduce any problems?
4. What clients and problems would hypnotherapy be most suited for? In what circumstances might hypnotherapy be inappropriate? When might it be the best option in terms of treatment?

13

Rational Emotive Behaviour Therapy

Michael Neenan

Rational emotive behaviour therapy (REBT) is a system of psychotherapy that proposes that rigid and extreme thinking (**irrational beliefs**) lies at the heart of emotional disturbance. Rigid thinking allows no other views to be considered (e.g. 'I must never fall below my high standards') while extreme thinking provides a very unbalanced assessments of self, others and events (e.g. 'because if I do fall below them, this will mean I'm an abysmal failure'). Flexible and non-extreme thinking (**rational beliefs**) is the foundation of emotional health, e.g. 'My high standards are very important to me but I realize I will probably fall below them sometimes. If I do, this is something to regret, learn from but not to condemn myself for.' REBT's emphasis on the way thinking powerfully influences emotion places it within the cognitive behavioural tradition, of which it is a founding member.

DEVELOPMENT OF REBT

REBT was founded in 1955 by Albert Ellis (1913–2007), an American clinical psychologist. He originally practised as a psychoanalyst but came to disagree profoundly with its viewpoint that present emotional problems have their roots in early childhood experiences.[1] In seeking to develop a different therapeutic approach, he found inspiration from Epictetus (AD 55–135), a Stoic philosopher, who provided the cornerstone of REBT: 'People are disturbed not by events, but by the views which they take of them.' Emotional disturbance such as anger, anxiety or depression is mainly a product of how individuals evaluate events in their lives (e.g. 'I shouldn't have lost my job. I'm nothing without one'). Ellis was more interested in how individuals maintain their problems through their belief systems rather than how these problems were acquired or developed, such as a 40-year-old woman who still sees herself as unlikeable because of parental neglect when she was a child. REBT would show her that it is her *current* thinking about past events ('I can't be worth much if they treated me that badly') which requires therapeutic attention.

In order to highlight the use of reason in tackling upsetting thinking, Ellis initially called REBT 'rational therapy'. However, this name created the false impression that exploring clients' emotions was of little importance to Ellis. To counter this view, he changed the name in 1961 to rational–emotive therapy (RET). This twin focus on thoughts and feelings in the process of change still did not sufficiently reflect the actual practice of Ellis's approach as it seemed to overlook the role of behaviour in this process. Therefore in 1993 RET became rational emotive behaviour therapy (REBT). It took Ellis nearly 40 years to state clearly what he had been practising from the outset: that clients have to think, feel and act against their irrational beliefs in order to change them. REBT had come full circle.

THEORY AND BASIC CONCEPTS

ABCDE model of emotional disturbance and change

REBT offers a simple model (simple means straightforward, not simplistic) to show how irrational beliefs largely determine our disturbed reactions to events and how these beliefs are challenged and changed:

A   activating event – e.g. being rejected by your partner.
B   irrational beliefs – 'He shouldn't have done this to me. I'm worthless without him.'
C   emotional and behavioural consequences – depression and withdrawal.
D   disputing irrational beliefs – 'I would greatly prefer to still have his love *but* there's no reason why I *must* still have it. Without it, I can learn to live alone, accept myself and move on. No label such as worthless can ever define me or my life.'
E   new and effective rational outlook accompanied by emotional and behavioural changes – sadness and a return to socializing and dating.

REBT asserts that irrational beliefs comprise rigid musts, shoulds, have to's, got to's, oughts. These beliefs act as demands we make upon ourselves, others and the world (e.g. 'My life should be easy and free from problems'). Flowing from these rigid demands are three extreme conclusions:

1. Awfulizing – nothing could be worse and nothing good can ever come from any-thing so bad.
2. Low frustration tolerance – the inability to endure discomfort or frustration in life.
3. Evaluations of worth – giving yourself or others a global, negative rating, such as useless or inferior.

These rigid and extreme beliefs are called irrational because they are illogical, unre-alistic and unhelpful. They generate emotional disturbance that interferes with goal achievement; you are not usually a good problem solver when you are upset. REBT deals with both emotional and practical problem solving, e.g. dealing with your anxiety about being assertive and teaching you how to be assertive.[2] Ellis believed that all humans have a strong biological or innate tendency to think irrationally. This assertion is based upon the seemingly limitless ability of humans to disturb them-selves about virtually anything. While the effects of adverse conditions (e.g. poor housing, high crime area, alcoholic parent) upon human functioning are not mini-mized, nevertheless they are deemed as an insufficient explanation for any resulting emotional disturbance.

In order to tackle emotional disturbance, REBT suggests developing a belief system based on flexible preferences, wishes, wants and desires, e.g. 'I want an easy and problem free life, but there's no reason why I *should* have what I want.' These beliefs are called rational because they are seen as logical, realistic and helpful. They aid goal-attainment and reduce our level of emotional upset when facing difficult situations. Flowing from these flexible preferences and wishes are three non-extreme conclusions:

1. Anti-awfulizing – negative events could always be worse and valuable lessons can be learnt from coping with them.
2. High frustration tolerance – discomfort and frustration are worth bearing in order to attain your goals.
3. Acceptance of self and others – humans are seen as fallible (imperfect) and in a state of continuous change; therefore it is both futile and inaccurate to pin a label on a person as if this captures their essence. Aspects of the person can be accu-rately rated, e.g. 'I'm unpunctual in attending meetings, which I want to correct.'

REBT suggests that we have a second, biologically-based tendency to think about our thinking, that is, to reflect rationally upon our irrational ideas and thereby coun-teract or minimize the potentially harmful effects of our distorted thinking. By devel-oping a rational outlook, individuals can greatly moderate their disturbed feelings as well as increase their striving for self-actualization (realizing one's potential).

Two types of disturbance

REBT argues that two types of emotional disturbance underlie most, if not all, neu-rotic problems, i.e. these are problems (such as shame) that do not involve loss of contact with reality or are not caused by physical disease. The first type is called ego disturbance and relates to unmet demands made upon self, others and/or the world, e.g. 'She should have said yes when I asked her out and she's made me feel as if I'm no good.' The second type is called discomfort disturbance and relates to unmet demands on self, others and/or the world about life conditions, e.g. 'I shouldn't have to work this hard to reach my goal. I'm giving up!'

Ego and discomfort disturbance are separate categories but frequently overlap in emotional disturbance, e.g. you condemn yourself as weak (ego) for continually complaining about the pressures of coping with a hectic home and work schedule (discomfort).

Understanding emotional states

REBT suggests that emotional reactions to unpleasant life events can be divided into unhealthy and healthy negative emotions as follows:

Unhealthy negative emotions	Healthy negative emotions
Anxiety	Concern
Depression	Sadness
Guilt	Remorse
Shame	Regret
Hurt	Disappointment
Anger	Annoyance

Underlying unhealthy negative emotions are rigid demands and extreme conclusions, e.g. 'I did a bad thing, which I absolutely shouldn't have done, and therefore I'm a bad person', which leads to guilt. Underlying healthy negative emotions are flexible preferences and their non-extreme conclusions, e.g. 'I did a bad thing which I'm sorry for and will do my best to make amends for but what I won't do is call myself a bad person on the basis of a particular action', which leads to remorse – your conscience still pricks, but not so painfully.

The above list of negative emotions is not meant to dictate to clients how they should feel about events in their lives, but to generate discussion about which ones may be more adaptive when trying to cope with adversity. Positive emotions are not included as you are unlikely to feel happy when facing unpleasant situations but they may appear later when you have resolved the problem.

Self-esteem versus self-acceptance

Many counselling approaches want to raise clients' **self-esteem** so that they can 'feel good about themselves'. REBT believes this approach has serious drawbacks. What rises also falls. Self-esteem is based on certain requirements being present in your life, such as good looks, ideal weight, job, having friends, dream house, respect of your colleagues, in order to feel self-respect – that you have worth as a person. Although these things are very desirable to have, the individual's self-respect is built upon them. If she loses some or all of these things it is highly likely that she will condemn herself (e.g. 'I'm a failure') as the foundations of her self-respect begin to crumble. Therefore, self-esteem usually works temporarily and carries the potential for emotional disturbance when things go wrong in one's life.

To guard against such developments, REBT advocates unconditional **self-acceptance**, whereby individuals refuse to measure or value themselves no matter what is happening in their lives – you have worth just because you exist. Individuals are neither raised up nor cast down, like shares on the stock market, depending on their fluctuating fortunes in life, e.g. 'I lost my job and the respect of my colleagues and we'll have to move to a smaller house. Too damn bad! What I haven't lost is my self-acceptance because it was never on the line in the first place.' Unconditional self-acceptance (USA) is the basis of psychological stability throughout your life. However, USA is something one should strive for but will usually fall short of; greater self-acceptance (GSA) is probably the more realistic aim for fallible human beings.

The role of insight

As discussed earlier, REBT's view of the acquisition of emotional distress is largely biologically based with significant reinforcement from environmental conditions. The perpetuation of such disturbance is more complex but can be summarized in three major REBT insights:

1. Emotional disturbance is largely determined by irrational beliefs – we feel the way we think.
2. We remain disturbed in the present because we continually brainwash ourselves with these beliefs, i.e. we accept them uncritically.
3. The only enduring way to overcome our disturbance is through persistent hard work and practice to think, feel and act forcefully against our irrational beliefs.

PRACTICE

Goals of REBT

REBT helps individuals to overcome their problems in order for them to lead happier, healthier and more fulfilling lives. This is achieved through individuals thinking more rationally and as a consequence feeling less disturbed and acting in goal-directed ways. REBT therapists aim to make themselves redundant by teaching clients how to become their own self-therapists for present and future problem solving.

Elegant and inelegant solutions

The preferred strategy of change in REBT is for clients to stop thinking in rigid and extreme ways. This will achieve what Ellis called a 'profound philosophical change' and he viewed this as the elegant solution to emotional problem solving. Not all, or even most, clients will wish to embark on such an ambitious course and therefore these clients pursue the inelegant solution or non-philosophical change. This kind of change does not focus on uprooting rigid and extreme thinking; instead, solutions are:

1. Behaviourally based – e.g. teaching relaxation skills so you don't freeze during an interview rather than challenging and changing your shame-based belief that it would be awful for that to happen.

2. Inferentially based – only your assumptions are examined, e.g. your claims to be friendless are proved false instead of the therapist encouraging you to assume the worst (you have no friends) and learn to accept yourself even if no one else is interested in you at the current time.
3. Changing activating events – e.g. moving away from a table filled with cakes and pastries instead of standing there and tolerating the acute discomfort of resisting temptation in order to acquire higher frustration tolerance as part of sticking to your diet.

While these inelegant goals may make sense to the client, REBT argues that the underlying irrational beliefs are still intact and likely to be reactivated under similar circumstances in the future.

Socializing clients into REBT

This means teaching clients what is expected of them so that they can participate effectively in REBT. Clients are shown two forms of responsibility: (1) **emotional responsibility** – their emotional disturbance is largely self-induced even though they may blame others for it; (2) **task responsibility** – in order to overcome this disturbance they need to carry out a number of goal-related tasks.

To help clients absorb these responsibilities, REBT teaches clients to view their problems through the ABC model: separating their presenting problems into their A (events or situations), B (beliefs) and C (emotions and behaviours) components. This therapist-as-teacher approach includes moving clients away from A–C thinking ('Public speaking makes me feel anxious') to B–C thinking ('How do I make myself anxious about public speaking?'). Using B–C language helps to reinforce emotional responsibility and boosts motivation to carry out tasks ('What do I need to do to feel concerned rather than anxious about public speaking?').

The relationship between therapist and client

REBT regards the core conditions of empathy, respect and genuineness as highly desirable, but neither necessary (some clients want a business-like approach) nor sufficient to promote optimum client change – this is achieved by clients carrying out homework tasks to internalize a rational outlook in the situations that trigger (but do not cause) their emotional problems.

Assessment

This is a process that seeks to understand the client's presenting problems. REBT therapists seek clear and specific information (where possible) from clients in the first session in order to place their problems within the ABC framework. This teaches clients a concrete way of understanding and tackling their difficulties. For example, a client says he feels 'uptight' about public speaking (A). What unhealthy negative emotion does 'uptight' refer to? By encouraging the client to describe in some detail his uncomfortable sensations, the therapist helps him to reveal that the disturbed emotion is anxiety (C).

However, at this early stage in therapy, neither therapist nor client is aware of what the latter is most anxious about with regard to public speaking. What a client is most upset about in relation to his presenting problem is called the critical A. One way to pinpoint the critical A is through a process known as inference chaining, whereby the client's personally significant inferences are linked together through a series of 'Let's assume … then what?' questions.

Client:	I'm anxious that I might give a poor presentation.
Therapist:	Let's assume that you do. Then what?
Client:	My colleagues might look down on me.
Therapist:	Let's assume they do, then what?
Client:	They'll think I'm incompetent.
Therapist:	And if they do think that?
Client:	They'll be right – I would be incompetent.
Therapist:	So are you most anxious about being exposed as incompetent if you give a poor presentation?
Client:	That's it. (*The client confirms that the critical A has been located*)

The next step is to help the client find his demand (a must, should, have to or got to statement) about the critical A, such as, 'I must give a great presentation in order to avoid being exposed as incompetent' (B), which largely determines his anxiety at C. This irrational belief is composed of a rigid demand (must) and an extreme conclusion (incompetent). A wide range of techniques is used throughout the course of therapy to dispute (D), this irrational belief (the client probably has other irrational beliefs that also need to be addressed). From this disputing process, clients learn how to develop a new and effective rational outlook (E). It is important to point out that disputing is really an examination of the client's beliefs and certainly not in–your–face confrontation as the client is likely to feel he's in the witness box being prosecuted by the therapist, so proceed carefully with the disputing process.

MULTIMODAL DISPUTING TECHNIQUES

Cognitive

These techniques help clients to think about their thinking in more constructive ways. They are taught to examine the evidence for and against their irrational beliefs by using three major criteria:

1. **Logic.** Just because you very much want to give a great presentation, how does it logically follow that therefore you must give one? Does it seem sensible to demand this?
2. **Reality testing.** Where is the evidence that the world obeys your demands? If it did, then you would be guaranteed to give great presentations all of the time without experiencing any anxiety. Is this actually the case?
3. **Helpfulness.** How helpful is it holding on to this belief? Where is it going to get you if you keep on demanding that you must give a great presentation or help you when you fall below this standard?

Behavioural techniques

These are negotiated with the client on the basis of being challenging, but not over-whelming: tasks that are sufficiently stimulating to promote therapeutic change but not so daunting as to prevent clients from carrying them out, e.g. the client agrees to give two presentations a month to his colleagues, not one a week as the therapist (overeagerly) suggested. While carrying out the presentations he mentally challenges the demand that 'I must give a great presentation' while endorsing his strong (flexible) preference for giving one.

Emotive techniques

These involve fully engaging clients' emotions while they forcefully dispute their irrational beliefs. Among these techniques are shame-attacking exercises whereby cli-ents act in a 'shameful' way in real life in order to attract public ridicule or disapproval, e.g. standing outside a railway station and asking passers-by for directions to the station, and at the same time vigorously striving for self-acceptance with rational statements such as 'Just because I'm acting foolishly doesn't make me a fool'. Clients can learn from these exercises not to label themselves on the basis of their behaviour or others' reactions to it, and the world doesn't come to an end if you act foolishly. The client tells his audience he feels anxious when he gives presentations and there are no shock waves from them.

Imagery techniques

The principal technique is rational emotive imagery, whereby the client is encouraged to feel anxious by imagining giving an incompetent presentation to her colleagues and then, without altering any details of this mental picture, to change her emotion to one of concern. This emotional shift is achieved by the client replacing her irrational belief with a rational one. Of course, part of her goal-striving includes a determination to learn from her mistakes and give better presentations and maybe one day, great presen-tations, without her worth being dependent on whatever the outcome is.

The process of therapeutic change

This involves a number of steps:

1. Taking emotional and task responsibility for problem solving.
2. Accepting irrational beliefs as central in perpetuating problems.
3. Identifying realistic goals and understanding that changing irrational beliefs to rational ones is the best way to achieve these goals.
4. Carrying out homework tasks in order to strengthen rational beliefs and weaken irrational ones.
5. Progress requires persistence and tolerating discomfort.
6. When goals are achieved, a relapse management plan is devised in order to cope with any post-therapy setbacks.

The ABCDE model provides the framework in which this process of therapeutic change occurs.

Format of a typical session

This would involve setting an agenda. The agenda would include reviewing the client's homework tasks from the previous week; agreeing the topics to be discussed in the present session; negotiating further homework tasks that directly arise from the work done in the session; and eliciting client feedback about the session. REBT views agenda setting as the most efficient way of structuring the time spent with the client.

WHICH CLIENTS BENEFIT MOST?

REBT has been shown to help, among others, the following groups: adults with anxiety, anger, guilt, shame and/or depression; severely disturbed adults who seem to be stubbornly resistant to change (e.g. clients who display long–term anti–social behaviour); those who are suicidally depressed; individuals who are chronic substance abusers; adolescents who may be withdrawn and exhibiting behavioural problems such as excessive temper tantrums; and children as young as 7 or 8 years with, for example, difficulties making friends at school.

Failures with clients in REBT usually occur because they do not accept (a) emotional responsibility as they blame other factors (e.g. a partner or job) for causing their problems and therefore demand that these factors change before they can; and/or (b) task responsibility as they avoid the persistent hard work required of them to make progress.

CASE STUDY

The Client

Paul (not his real name) was a 40-year-old married man with one daughter. He worked as a college lecturer. He sought therapy for the guilt and anger he was experiencing with regard to an affair he had 18 months previously and his wife's behaviour towards him for it. A provisional course of six sessions of REBT was agreed upon.

The Therapy

Beginning therapy

After gathering more background information on Paul and his problems, the process of socializing him into therapy began, including establishing his goals for change. Paul's goals were to stop feeling guilty and angry (negative goals – what you don't want); but what alternative emotions were going to replace them? This would be discussed later but the present focus was on understanding his guilt and anger within the ABC framework. The therapist asked for a specific and current example of when he felt guilty (rowing with his wife) in order to uncover his critical A – what he felt most guilty about:

Therapist:	What is guilt-provoking in your mind when you row with your wife?
Paul:	She always throws the affair in my face and I always tell her that our relationship was on the rocks and I thought we were going to break up, so I had the affair.
Therapist:	Given that explanation, why do you still feel guilty?
Paul:	She won't let me forget it.
Therapist:	Are you still hanging on to it?
Paul:	It still troubles me what I did.
Therapist:	Can you put your finger on it?
Paul:	I really hurt her by betraying her. She was faithful to me but I wasn't to her. I feel this sense of being a bad person despite what I said about the relationship being on the rocks.
Therapist:	So are you most guilty about hurting her through your betrayal and you're a bad person for doing it?
Paul:	Exactly. *(The client confirms that the critical A has been found)*
Therapist:	And when does your anger occur?
Paul:	When I'm rowing with her.
Therapist:	Do you know what you're most angry about?
Paul:	Yes, but I don't say it to her – 'Stop needling me about the affair and making me feel more guilty you spiteful bitch!'
Therapist:	Which of these two emotions do you want to work on first?
Paul:	Guilt is the big one.

(Continued)

(Continued)

The therapist taught Paul the differences between rigid and extreme beliefs and flexible and non-extreme beliefs and how they lead to unhealthy and healthy negative emotions respectively. The theme in guilt is violating your moral code, what you should or should not have done, and Paul saw how he was constructing his irrational beliefs out of this moral lapse:

Paul:	I'm demanding that I shouldn't have betrayed my wife and hurt her, but as I did I'm a bad person.
Therapist:	And if you want to move from guilt to remorse, what needs to change?
Paul:	My rigid and extreme beliefs.

Having established the ABC components of his presenting problem, Paul was next shown how to dispute (D) this belief using the criteria of logic, reality testing and usefulness. Paul found the usefulness disputes the most convincing and the ones most likely to help him change (which is frequently the case with many clients):

Paul:	If I keep on thinking I'm a bad person, I'll feel bad, my wife can push the guilt button whenever she wants and I'll keep on getting angry when she needles me about the affair.
Therapist:	So who's responsible for your guilt?
Paul:	I would have said my wife, and often accused her of making me feel guilty, but after you showing me the ABC model I can see where it really comes from [*tapping his head*].
Therapist:	So based on our discussions today, what could be a homework task?
Paul:	To read that REBT self-help book on guilt you mentioned to reinforce the points we've been discussing.

Paul was shown that he was largely responsible for his own emotional disturbance, not events or other people, and therefore he could achieve emotional change; he did not have to wait for his wife to forgive him. A homework task was agreed.

The course of therapy

In the following sessions other homework tasks included noting on a card, which he carried with him, the benefits of surrendering his guilt and moving to remorse; carrying out daily imagery exercises whereby he changed his guilt to remorse while rowing with wife and, still using imagery, turned anger into annoyance by accepting that she could needle him if she chose to but he didn't have to respond to it, and stopped calling her in his mind a 'stupid bitch'. His new rational belief, based on remorse, was: 'I may have done a bad thing by having the affair even though I genuinely thought our relationship was over, but I refuse any longer to condemn myself as a bad person on the basis of it.' A remorseful person accepts that he did a bad thing but crucially does not condemn himself as a bad person because of it and seeks, but does not beg, forgiveness from others. Whether or not he receives this forgiveness, he can forgive himself within the context of compassionate self-acceptance as a fallible (imperfect) human being who, while striving to stay on the straight and narrow, is not always successful. The affair was an incident in his life, not the story of his life or the essence of his character.

At first, Paul found that his new rational belief lacked conviction because he was still feeling guilty when his wife brought up the affair, but he kept on reminding himself that the rational belief was the accurate belief and this is what he wanted to believe at a deeper level. The breakthrough came during another row:

> **Paul:** I forget what we were arguing about and, of course, the affair came up but I didn't bite this time. I told her I was fed-up with the issue and explained my new perspective on it. The guilt was gone and so might I be if she couldn't also put it to rest. The guilt button doesn't respond any more. She's been rather wary ever since and the rows have diminished.
>
> **Therapist:** What next then?
>
> **Paul:** Now this burden of guilt is lifted, I'll give it six months or so to see if things improve. I tell my wife that I love her and want the marriage to survive, so we'll see.

In the last session – therapy consisted of five sessions in total – the therapist asked Paul if there were any key ideas or techniques that he particularly valued:

> **Paul:** The revelation for me was that I could change how I feel, both the guilt and anger – it was in my control. The solution was sitting here [*tapping his head*] but I didn't know it was there until you showed me.
>
> **Therapist:** Something else to remember. There's an important difference between getting better and staying better: you've been getting better in therapy by internalizing a rational outlook to deal with your emotional problems, but staying better means keeping and strengthening this outlook to deal with whatever comes your way in life.
>
> **Paul:** Sounds like a heavy responsibility when you put it like that, but I know what you mean. I'll do my best not to forget it.

Therapy ended with a business-like saying of goodbyes and a follow-up appointment was made for three months' time to monitor Paul's progress, i.e. was he staying better?

REFERENCES

[1] Ellis, A. and MacLaren, C. (1998) *Rational Emotive Behaviour Therapy: A Therapist's Guide.* Atascadero, CA: Impact.

[2] Dryden, W. and Neenan, M. (2015) *Rational Emotive Behaviour Therapy: 100 Key Points and Techniques.* Hove: Routledge.

SUGGESTED READING

Ellis, A. and Ellis, D. J. (2011) *Rational Emotive Behavior Therapy.* Washington, DC: APA. Posthumously published overview of REBT by its founder and the grandfather of the CBT movement.

Hauck, P. (1988) *How to Be Your Own Best Friend.* London: Sheldon. Explains how to get the best out of life by avoiding self-neglect, i.e. not letting people walk all over you or always putting others first.

Neenan, M. and Dryden, W. (2011) *Rational Emotive Behaviour Therapy in a Nutshell*, 2nd edn. London: Sage. A clear, concise and comprehensive account of REBT.

Neenan, M. and Dryden, W. (2014) *Life Coaching: A Cognitive Behavioural Approach*, 2nd edn. Hove: Routledge. Shows how REBT principles and techniques can be used to increase personal effectiveness.

DISCUSSION ISSUES

1. REBT views our beliefs about events rather than the events themselves as the main cause of our emotional reactions. Does REBT go too far in suggesting that no event can totally determine our emotional response to it?
2. Why does REBT view striving for self-acceptance rather than raising self-esteem as likely to be the more enduring form of psychological stability?
3. REBT's focus is on identifying, challenging and changing people's irrational beliefs. Does this mean that people's feelings are of little importance in therapy?
4. REBT's emphasis on how people's problems are being maintained rather than how they were acquired or developed can appear to minimize the importance of past events. Is it always essential to look back in order to understand the present?

PART 3
Humanistic-Existential Approaches

14

Existential Therapy

Emmy van Deurzen

INTRODUCTION

Existential therapy is a philosophical approach. It aims to help people get more clarity and perspective on their difficulties. It zooms in on the detail of a person's predicament, following their feelings to connect to their deepest point of pain in order to understand what it is that matters most to them. Existential therapy highlights the contradictions and **paradoxes** in a person's experience and places these issues in the wider context of the inevitable challenges of human existence. It facilitates a better grasp of life, greater **engagement** with the world and a sense of inner authority, passion and liberation. It does this by inviting the person to ask her own questions, considering her troubles from many different angles and by teaching her to think for herself in tackling each problem. Such thoughtfulness is arrived at by carefully following emotions, intuitions and the felt sense of what the person values in life.

Philosophical clarity comes from understanding our own struggles with life against the background of the rules and tasks of human existence. The therapeutic encounter is based in calm presence and open dialogue. The therapist engages with the client in a conversation that is searching, often challenging and playful where possible. The therapist never imposes or prescribes, but opens up new possibilities, encouraging the client to discover her own ability to explore and make sense of life. The objective is always to tackle apparent contradictions, confusions, fears and anxieties, starting from personal hurt, doubt, despair or curiosity. The aim is that of achieving real depth of understanding and with it a renewed sense of purpose and direction. Existential therapy helps people to uncover hidden meaning and recover lost freedom and possibility. The objective is for a person to become more at ease in life and more capable of finding her own wisdom in dealing with life's inevitable challenges.

DEVELOPMENT OF THE THERAPY

Existential therapy has a long pedigree, going back to ancient Greek philosophers who helped people to live better lives by interrogating their difficulties and misconceptions.[1] When Socrates dialogued with the young men of Athens, calling himself a philosopher or lover of wisdom, he helped them distinguish between the illusions and errors of judgement that made them go astray and the realities and clarity of understanding that could point them in the right way. Later philosophers, such as Aristotle, the Epicureans and the Stoics, developed entire schools of philosophical therapy, which evolved and refined talking interventions.

Philosophy lost touch with this objective till the nineteenth century, when philosophers like Kierkegaard and Nietzsche reconnected with this idea. Their work inspired many existential therapists, as did the work of twentieth-century philosophers like Heidegger and Sartre. But it was the nineteenth-century methodology of phenomenology, founded by Brentano and Husserl and literally meaning the science of appearances, that provided the method of observation and description so invaluable to therapists and psychologists. Several psychiatrists, including Jaspers and Binswanger, applied these ideas directly to psychotherapy at the start of the twentieth century.[2] Heidegger's phenomenology led to Medard Boss's analysis of human existence or *Daseinsanalysis* and Sartre's ideas inspired R. D. Laing's work and that of many other therapists. Viktor Frankl created a method named '*Logotherapy*' or 'meaning therapy' to help people discover meaning in experiences of suffering, as he did when confined in concentration camps during the Second World War. For the past decades the method has evolved rapidly, especially in Europe,[3] through the writing of authors like Deurzen[2] and Spinelli[4] and in the United States through humanistic–existential therapists like Yalom[5] and Schneider.[6] The creation of training schools for existential therapists like the New School of Psychotherapy and Counselling in London and the creation of the Society for Existential Analysis have further consolidated existential therapy as a method of choice for those who favour independence of thought.[7]

THEORY AND BASIC CONCEPTS

The worldview of existential therapy is that human beings are meaning- and purpose-seeking. It is our consciousness that allows us to rise above our troubles. We are not just organisms primarily moved by instincts, determined by our genes and programmed by cognitive concepts. While all these aspects of being human need to be taken into account, the emphasis of the therapy itself is always on the human capacity for overcoming problems and transcending suffering or trauma. Existential therapists assume that people are generally strongly motivated by a deep desire to live a worthwhile and purposeful life in which their actions not only make sense but are freely undertaken and aimed at consequences that are beneficial, productive and fruitful. But existential philosophy is not humanistic, i.e. it does not foreground or idealize human beings, nor does it place them above and beyond other forms of life. It recognizes that the universe of which human beings are only a very small part is a complex place, where we are subject to many diverse forces and givens that we can only influence in minor ways. This includes the realities of space and time, of birth and death, of gravity and movement, of ageing and weakness, of adversity and conflict, love and hate, labour, failure and guilt, all of which we have to learn to reckon with and take in our stride along the way. The forces of nature, the laws of society, the rules of psychology and the principles we want to live by need to be carefully considered, before we start to make choices in life. It helps to understand something of the apparent contradictions, tensions and paradoxes that seem to abound, if we want to get better at making order out of chaos, or learn to live in tune with the universal harmony.

Existential therapy is a wonderful opportunity for a person to learn the value of their capacity for sensation, perception, memory, emotion, imagination, thought, experience and understanding. Therapy is the start of an experimental and adventurous exploration of human living. When people come to therapy they are usually feeling confused, lost, overwhelmed, hurt, despondent or lonely. Existential therapists engage with their state of mind and propose a joint exploration of the things that need to be done for the person to free himself and open his mind and his life. Existential philosophers recognize that objectives like perfection, blissful happiness, ideal love or celebrity lifestyles are not realistic and invariably lead to further grief. It is, however, always possible and desirable to help a person discover and develop their capacity for perfectibility and for productive, loving and diligent living. Existential therapy celebrates the enterprising spirit of each person who wishes to take stock of life before opting to take a new path at the crossroads of their daily existence.

Existential thinkers do not see depression and anxiety as negatives or symptoms of mental illness that have to be cured. Rather they view these as necessary experiences in the process of becoming a complete, sensing–thinking–feeling–intuitive human being. Anxiety is inevitable, as it is the rising of our energy in the face of a new challenge. We cannot live without exposing ourselves to anxiety and we have to be prepared to use the energy of anxiety and take action. When you feel your heart beating with apprehension about the dangers in the world you know that life is asking something of you and that you need to find an effective way to respond to this challenge. We can all learn to heed these signs and benefit from this renewal of our energy. Anxiety primes our capacity for action unless we try to suppress it, remaining frozen in forced passivity, so that the energy of our anxiety starts looping in on itself and turns to panic, which is anxiety without purposeful action. Anxiety when employed effectively leads us towards engagement with the world and helps us to focus on the goals we set ourselves. This creates both movement towards feeling high and the tightness and tiredness of the stress that this naturally implies.

Conversely depression is the feeling of coming down from something we had hoped for, worked towards or valued and it is associated with the loss of that value. When our energy dips away from effortful work towards our chosen objectives we feel low, which comes from a sense of disappointment, disaffection or distress. But when we learn to let go and relent, it may begin to feel like a kind of relief and release instead. It is also a preparation for a renewed bout of anxiety and energy as we lift our eyes and spirit towards a new goal, after a rest.

All human living is cyclical and rises and falls. We cannot stay on the heights or with the peaks of achievement or happiness all the time, as we would totally exhaust ourselves. What goes up must come down and so the relaxation of loss and depression are equally necessary and can be experienced as not only restful but also as helping us to penetrate into the roots of our lives, where we can reconsider what we value and what really matters. We will then be better equipped next time to take the ride of our anxiety–fuelled energy towards a brand new, or slightly reshaped and newly understood, objective.

When people live fearfully they are afraid of their emotions and of the actions and experiences in the world that evoke them. **Angst**, or existential anxiety, is a good indication that we are awakening to life. When we begin to see the wisdom of our own sensations, emotions, thoughts and intuitions we can learn to follow the flow of their natural course up and down with the rhythm of life. The human capacity for conscious understanding makes all the difference and gives us courage. We can make sense of all this intensity and all this confusing and complex experience that might otherwise either leave us perplexed or desirous to switch off and hide away from the world in a cocooned existence. Of course most of us will try all these methods sooner or later and unless we have the clarity of sight to understand what we are doing and where we are going wrong or what targets we may want to reach and how we might improve the way we are living, we might be put off our own lives and feel sick of living and desperate, to a greater or lesser degree. In the extreme we may even want to fall ill, die or escape from the world by committing suicide. Existential therapists are very much at ease with such strategies and such existential crises. They know that people often have to come to a halt and experience dark nights of the soul, in fear and trembling, before they are able and willing to start thinking more carefully about their life. Such suffering matures a person, in the same way in which losses can break our hearts and open them up like soil clots torn asunder in winter, ready for new growth in spring. Where we feel hurt and upset and bereft and broken we become human and capable of aspiring to goodness and kindness and wholesome productive efforts to live a better life. In our distress we come to ourselves for the first time and we learn that we can be aware of ourselves and of the world in a constructive manner to make life work better.

We need to make mistakes to learn and while we may sometimes regret the past or the person we are, reflecting on this tells us what we do want to aim for. If the world seems unfair or harsh, we can learn how to contribute to a more fair society or family life. Existential therapists help people to evaluate reality and to learn from life.

PRACTICE

Existential therapists are trained, not just by studying philosophical theories but also by living intensely themselves to discover how to make use of ideas in practice. Training also teaches the insights and dialogical methods to engage effectively and productively with all the upsets, problems, disappointments, suffering, despair and defeats that people will bring to their therapist. To be an existential therapist is to be fully present with the other, open to both the person's distress and her purpose and values. Existential therapists make themselves fully available to engage with the issues and aim to help the client come to grips with them and really understand what it is she is struggling with and how she may struggle more effectively.

The first port of call is to learn to be co-present with the other in order to encounter the other with clarity and openness and candour. Then we aim to listen with kindness and firm attention as clients unfold their stories undisturbed. Existential therapists work with dialogue, in a friendly and open exchange where warmth and a companionable searching for truth is the established modus operandi. An existential therapy will usually include some of the following elements of theory and method.

Time

Existential therapists trace a person's evolution through life, from past through to the present and into the future. Philosophers are aware that all dimensions of time are important and need to be taken into account. A person will often also want to consider what their view of eternity or timelessness is. This exploration will bring out the values and beliefs of the person. Both past and future come together in the present and are altered by being reconsidered and reconfigured. A person is dynamically transforming at all times. As soon as she begins to become more aware of this, she can more effectively steer the changes in the direction she wishes to take. The story of a person's life needs to be woven together in such a way that she feels ownership over it again and recovers her authority to take charge of it.

Worldview

Existential therapy is mindful of the way in which each person has come to see and interpret the world. This personal outlook is made explicit and engaged with. The person is helped to see how his worldview alters and colours the world. The therapy takes shape when it becomes more obvious how the person's lens on the world might be sharpened or softened and how his knowledge and comprehension can be extended. This work often starts by helping people spot the unspoken assumptions that they operate with.

Fourfold world

The work is aided by the mental map of the challenges of human existence that we all have to contend with on the different dimensions of our lives. The **fourfold world** is composed of:

1. Our bodily existence in a *physical* environment, where we learn to manipulate objects, get to know and develop our own bodies and interact with the bodies of others, as well as with the wider natural world and even the global background of the cosmos.

2. Our interpersonal existence with other people in a *social* world, where we have to build a sense of ego, in relation to the expectations of society, but where we also learn to love and be loved, to stand up for ourselves and to respect other people.
3. Our *personal* existence where we come to feel at the centre of ourselves and get to know our own character and personality, our strengths and our weaknesses and learn to hone our talents and accept our limitations.
4. Our ideological or *spiritual* existence in relation to the values, beliefs and ideals that we form for our own existence, guiding our choices and our evaluation of what we do, feel and think. Here we contend with the rights and wrongs of life and the challenges of good and evil.

Paradox

At each of these levels and dimensions of existence we learn to grapple with the contradictions, conflicts and dilemmas thrown up by life. We can expect on-going tensions at all levels and need to learn how to take these in our stride. The more we learn to trust that we can solve any problems that daily life throws at us, the more life will seem like an adventure, where challenges make the journey more interesting. Some philosophical contemplation will often reveal that the avoidance of these problems inexorably creates bigger problems, whereas each time we face a challenge, the advantage is on our side. So, for instance we discover that to love another person requires us to allow our doubts and disagreements and even our feelings of disillusion or hatred for them rather than deny these negative feelings. As long as we avoid the idea of death, we will fear illness and do anything we can to avoid it, but make ourselves unwell in the process. When we face up to what it is like to live in relative poverty, we learn to appreciate material comforts in a new way. Allowing ourselves to explore the extremes of life makes us more flexible and able to see what is real.

Dialectic progression

What existential therapy often shows is how such contradictions and opposite polarities lead to dialectical progression. This means that we learn to walk forwards by balancing our weight from one leg to the other. Progress is made by being light on our feet and allowing opposites to create a forward movement. The main thing is to know which direction we want to go in and to learn to make sense of apparent contradictions and surpass these, while retaining the lessons learnt on each side of the equation.

Emotional compass

Our emotions are essential in the process of recognizing what is good and bad for us, what we value and fear. They show us the way towards the things that are best and they also show us how to make the most of the times when we deal with the loss of value. The **emotional compass** (Figure 14.1) shows how each feeling points in a

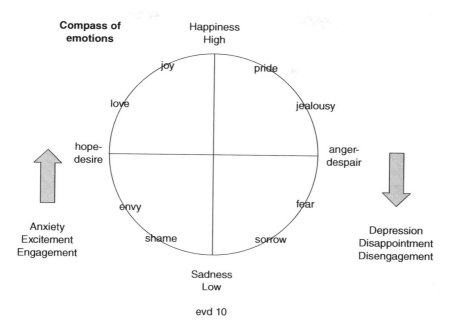

Compass of emotions

Happiness
High

joy

pride

love

jealousy

hope-desire

anger-despair

Anxiety
Excitement
Engagement

envy

shame

fear

sorrow

Depression
Disappointment
Disengagement

Sadness
Low

evd 10

FIGURE 14.1   *Compass of emotions*

particular direction, towards or away from a value, towards or away from our feeling high or low. Feelings are really about values and meanings. Feelings show us the way, but our reflection helps us refine the values that are worth working towards.

Values and purpose

It is when we understand our values and have a chance to think them through that we can notice not only what we desire, but also what is important to us and what we are good at and have special talent for. It is important to learn to make a realistic assessment of who we are and what we are capable of and can contribute to the world. People feel a great deal more satisfaction if they have purpose and meaning and a readiness to take right action towards things that are not only good for themselves but also for other people.

Engagement and meaningful living

This is how existential therapists aim to encourage clients to reengage with life in a more effective and more satisfying way: they help them become more self-reflective and more aware of the advantages of their own consciousness and ability to make the most of their lives. They help them put their lives into context and perspective so that they can be more connected, and meaning emerges.

Freedom and responsibility

There is always a strong moral aspect to the work. People, rather than becoming self-ish in their pursuit of freedom and purpose, learn to think for themselves, weighing the choices and options available to them, daring to be different and self-motivating. But there is no real freedom without answerability. Existential therapists are always aware of the impact each person has on the world and they challenge clients to be responsible towards themselves and those around them, checking the effect and consequences of their actions.

Truth

The change process comes about when clients learn the skills of attunement and understanding that help them become aware and more observant of their own feelings. This applies also to thoughts, sensations, intuitions and actions. People learn to review their experiences as well as their ideas and also to check their impact on the world around them. The touchstone of progress in therapy is always the truth about what is actually the case in reality. Clients will soon discover that truth is by far the best test for progress in life. And while it is always aimed for in therapy, in truthful modesty both therapist and client will recognize that we rarely know the whole truth about any matter. We have to keep asking questions.

Format of session

Sessions are open-ended and conversational in nature, usually lasting 50 minutes. The therapist brings knowledge and wisdom about life and a spirit of open-minded discovery. The atmosphere of a session is always serious though friendly and warm-hearted and humorous when possible. Therapists seek to encourage and empower and learn to stand back in favour of the client's own lights whenever possible. Creativity is encouraged.

WHICH CLIENTS BENEFIT MOST?

Existential therapy is particularly indicated for anyone who is going through a life crisis or who has suffered a loss. It is also very effective with people who are going through a normal life change or transformation, i.e. teenagers, young adults, those wondering about having children, people in midlife crisis, those considering retirement or people coming to terms with old age or the challenges of illness and death. People who have migrated to a different country or region and who feel estranged from their environment also benefit enormously from existential therapy as it allows them to consider their position in the world and get some perspective on their situation. Those who feel a sense of social alienation, either by being lonely or not fitting into their reference group for specific reasons, for instance because their life story is different to that of most other people around them, may also find this way of considering their problems helpful. But the existential approach has a long history of working well with much more challenging mental health issues too. It is almost essential to come from an existential angle when approaching someone who is suicidal or who feels desperate about life. The isolation, anxiety and withdrawal of people with autism can also be understood very well with a more philosophical approach, which does not pin the person down as suffering from a particular pathology but helps them deal with life from the position they find themselves in.

Schizophrenia, as described by existential therapist R. D. Laing,[8] can be tackled from the perspective of a person's alienation from their family and from themselves. Existential work will always emphasize a search for meaning within the realistic parameters of a particular person's life situation.

Existential therapy should not be considered the first port of call when someone is not very interested in reflection or self-reflection or wishes to be treated from a more medical or positivist perspective. When medication and symptom resolution are desired existential therapy is not the best method. However, existential aspects of a person's troubles may usefully be highlighted alongside other issues and some existential explorations alongside other methods, say CBT or a more person–centred or problem–solving-based way of working may go a long way in helping a person find a new way of viewing their life situation.

CASE STUDY

The Client

Lizzie is a nurse in her mid-twenties, who finds herself in a terrible quandary, as she feels unable to carry on with her hospital duties after the death of her mother in the same hospital. She has always been very close to her mother and has lived with her for her entire life up to the moment of hospitalization. As soon as her mother went into hospital, Lizzie felt paralysed and panicked at the idea that some of her colleagues would be looking after her. Though she visited her mother on the ward regularly, she felt unable to continue working there and had to take sick leave. By the time she comes for therapy she has been off sick for eight months and she is very worried, as her sick pay has been reduced. The personnel department has required her to have a medical assessment and the doctor she has seen has referred her on for therapy for what he terms a diagnosis of complex grief.

Lizzie is somewhat reluctant and sceptical but at the same time expresses her sense of relief at finally being able to talk about something that she 'cannot make head or tail of but which has totally grown over her head'. These are

(Continued)

(Continued)

striking expressions, especially as a little later in the session she speaks of her mother's illness as having 'messed with her head'. When the emphasis on the word 'head' is mentioned, she immediately states that she believes that 'Mom's done her head in'. When asked whether she means that it is Mom's death that has done her head in, she hesitates and says 'I suppose'. When I point out that she does not seem sure about this, she falls silent. I say: 'Is it Mom's death that's the problem, or Mom herself?' She now shamefully admits that she feels relieved that Mom is gone and she no longer has to look after her. 'She was a bit of a handful, you know. I could not really do what I wanted while I lived with her,' she says with a red face and in a rather frightened and defensive tone. 'You sound like you feel guilty to feel relieved,' I observe mildly. She nods ponderously, moving her head up and down very slowly and very affirmatively, three or four times. She tells me she can't go to work because everyone there now claims to like her mother so much and to have made such a great connection with her before she died. She really does not want to be there and be reminded of Mom. She also wants to savour the experience of being alone at home and having the place to herself. She needs to keep doing this until her head has cleared, she says. She sighs deeply. She has hardly seen anyone since her mother's death. For there is so much to think about and so much buzzing around in her head that she cannot afford to share it with anyone. While others think she has collapsed into grief and mourning and can't manage without her mother, she is actually just feeling like she is taking time to settle herself.

I say, 'You seem to know what is right for you. You are doing something very important for yourself. It sounds a bit like giving birth to yourself.' She stares at me for a short while before tears start trickling down her face. She has tried so hard to explain to herself what was happening and here it is. She is stunned by the realization it has taken her precisely *nine months* to get to this point. She has never felt as if she could really be herself, truly be alive and now that Mom has died, this is her moment. She needs to catch up with herself and find out what is in her own head. She had to be alone to do that. She has put her colleagues off visiting her when they offer and she has no other friends and no siblings. But now, perhaps, she is ready to accept this was all part of her needing to give birth to herself. She suddenly feels so much better. And yet, it is only our first session.

The Therapy

The full story emerges slowly and is elaborated on over the next weeks as we discuss her situation carefully. Her father left her mother when Lizzie was two years old and she has never seen him since, though he has sent her birthday cards and presents every year. She had a boyfriend, Richard, for a couple of years when she was 18 and 19, but had to end the relationship eventually when Richard wanted them to move in together. She never had sex with him and was afraid to lose her virginity. Mom was always very dismissive about sexuality and warned her not to make the same mistake as she had made. Lizzie is shocked when she discovers how hurtful and controlling Mom's remarks often were. Mom always made it clear that Lizzie owed her total loyalty, having been such an imposition on her. Lizzie felt she needed to sacrifice her relationship to Richard, since her mother needed her more than Richard did. It takes several months of therapy before she can see the link between her mother's demands and her feeling unclear about what is in her own head.

At first she says she has no regrets as Richard is now happily married to one of her colleagues. She has lost touch with them. I say nothing and wait, patiently, glancing at her occasionally and observing her inner struggle. There is silence between us. Then, in a sudden burst of anger, she remarks that they did not even bother to come to her mother's funeral. She sounds very upset about this and she becomes tearful speaking about it with vehemence. As I point out how strongly she actually seems to feel about losing Richard, she sobs bitter tears and blows her nose repeatedly. She agrees that in spite of her quickly given forgiveness, she actually still feels terribly slighted by Richard, who seemed to get over her very rapidly. It was as if she had not mattered to him at all. She weeps more gently now. She feels raw at the thought that he never fought to keep her. He never even tried to make her leave Mom. He just married someone else instead. Now one of her values shows up clearly: love is the most important thing on earth, she declares. But she accepts my gentle challenge when I point out that she seems to define love as doing things for other people. Is that the kind of love she wants? She has done loving things for Mom, but has deeply resented them. Perhaps Richard did a loving thing for her, wrongly assuming she wanted to stay with Mom and not insisting she come with him instead. She did the loving thing for Richard, forgiving him for marrying someone else. But in all of that what happened to the truth of the matter? She sighs deeply, rubbing her eyes and blowing her nose. She so longed for someone to know how she truly felt inside. 'Is that what love is then,' I challenge very gently, 'mind reading?' She shakes her head. She is beginning to realize that there has been no communication, no explanation, no search for truth, no real meeting of minds. This is how she lost herself: she did not even know what she thought or felt any longer. She tried so hard to think and feel what she thought she ought to think and feel, for Richard, or her mother. And now she weeps for the loss of herself.

In the next sessions Lizzie will slowly work out how her mother's death has broken the taboo. She will briefly consider how her mother's death opens the possibility of talking with Richard about their past relationship, but she soon realizes this is not really what she wants. She just wants to get to know her own mind. Lizzie needs to learn to listen to herself and not to jump into decisions that are based on a morality that alienates her from herself. She practises getting to know her feelings and intuitions and leave aside all the judgements for the moment. She finds it much easier that way to stay true to herself. She begins to see that she has been divided against herself and has tried to impose thoughts and feelings on herself way too much. Now she feels it is actually possible to get her own head sorted out. This brings great relief and hope.

(Continued)

(Continued)

We work hard towards clarity, which means examining all she senses, feels, thinks, dreams, longs and hopes for and consider it in relation to what is true and how things actually work. Lizzie's first little chuckle to herself comes when she says she is very good at muddling herself. Now that she is beginning to place trust in her own 'head', she reckons everything else will be easy.

As Lizzie engages with the therapy more deeply she soon begins to feel a sense of safety in expressing her contradictory emotions. What we quickly recognize, together, is that she is afraid of her own feelings of wanting things for herself and becomes paralysed each time she begins to feel something deep inside of her pushing her towards desire, longing and self-affirmation. At those moments she freezes and withdraws. This happens also in the sessions. It is as if her mother has placed a taboo on her that she has fully accepted as the foundation of her existence. She is not allowed to feel any selfish feelings. Even now that her mother is gone, she feels she has to uphold this general principle. It is a principle underpinned by a strong sense of religion as well and we talk much about her beliefs. She feels it is too late to change her way of being now and that her mother is probably still watching her from somewhere up in heaven, expecting her to be good and caring instead of selfish. When asked to define what it means to be selfish, she describes it as having feelings of longing and yearning for something of her own. She hiccups with held-in tears and tries to swallow them. I speak for her. 'Something of your own, like being loved by Richard, or by someone else?' Oh yes, loving and being loved are her heart's desire and so it frightened her very much. Loving Richard was the prototype of such selfish longings. She rejects the idea that it is about sexuality. It is more about having someone to call your own. Secretly she wants to be able to love and be loved, but she feels she has wasted her opportunity by sacrificing Richard to care for her mother. She admits to having misgivings about this now. Did she make a mistake? Should she have chosen for Richard instead of for her mother?

It will take many weeks of going over all these past choices and reasons for Lizzie to start making sense of herself. Even now it still 'messes with her head' to let herself think what might have been, she says. She feels a buzz in her brain and a sensation of the brain becoming blocked and frozen as soon as she imagines the possibility of having gone off from home to live with Richard. It takes a long time for her to see that she is constantly working from the presumption that there had to be an either/or choice and a total commitment one way or the other. Was it not possible for her to be with Richard and also still look after her mother, sufficiently to do right by her, but not so much as to do wrong by herself and Richard? Her brain is very full with this tempting idea for a bit, but she can't get her head around it, she says. She looks slightly excited and tells me she feels quite 'heady' when she leaves.

The next week it becomes clear that Lizzie is afraid that she will lose her identity and her very worth if she starts acknowledging her own feelings, let alone act on them. She can't quite work out whether it is allowed to try to find solutions and combine different needs and demands to come to a conclusion that suits many people and different values. So, we begin to have philosophical discussions about morality and trace the assumptions about life and human beings that are holding her back and are 'doing her head in'.

Changes made

The work with Lizzie becomes relatively straightforward once she engages with this exploration of her values and worldview. It becomes easier for her to understand why she was muddled and what it was that stopped her from moving on. She can still feel the guilt at feeling such liberation at her mother's death, but she can also allow herself to feel the liberation fully. As soon as she does this, she feels the grief for Mom as well. And she can now let both feelings remain alongside each other without feeling compelled to cut herself off. There are many fears that need to be tackled. Was she a bad girl? Was she mentally ill? Had she failed? Was she unlovable or unloving?

Answering all these questions honestly and openly, helps Lizzie find new ground under her feet. The real breakthrough comes when she finally finds compassion for her own suffering and confusion in the past. She learns to pinpoint her feelings and to translate them into values and meanings. One thing she knows from the guilt she is still feeling about staying home so long is that it matters to her to be productive and work in the world. We agree that is a sound principle for life. Another thing she learns from her raw grief over Richard is that she would value being in a relationship in a real way. For all these years she has been her mother's good servant and has done what she felt she had to, rather than what she wanted to or what was right. Now she can affirm her own wish to take charge of her life.

Much of my work simply consists in encouraging Lizzie to speak her mind and to express every feeling, worry, fear, anxiety, hope and disappointment she has experienced in her life. Sometimes I have to add a bit of educational material, such as saying 'If you don't allow yourself to think what you need to think about, your brain seizes up, for you are giving it contradictory instructions', or 'There is no harm in wanting your freedom and if your mother had been able to let you be free she would have taken delight in finding you are able to be moral at the same time as free to feel. Perhaps Mom needed badly to find some freedom for herself as well.' While Lizzie is occasionally a little shocked by such plain speaking, she learns to laugh at irreverent statements and shows a delicious sense of humour of her own in talking about the way she has been her own jailer. It is good when she stops blaming things on Mom and Richard and takes charge of her own decisions, both in the past and the present. She becomes very clear about her own value system: she does want to be a good person, who cares for others, but not at the expense of herself any more. She is keen to start experimenting and decides to go back to work. Virtue is no longer about cyphering herself away, it is about being fair to all concerned – to others as much as to herself. Her head is clear and she can think through any challenges rather effectively, with a little bit of help from therapy, but under her own steam, nevertheless.

(Continued)

(Continued)

Discussion

The client

Lizzie, over the 16 months of therapy, learnt to value her own existence in a new way. She began to want so many things that there was no time for regrets and withdrawal any more. She recognized that she had been paralysed by her desire to serve and be good on the one hand and her suppressed desire to live and to be free to love and be loved on the other. Lizzie discovered that she had very strong morals and intuitions about wrong and right. She learnt it was better to think about morality than to assume she already knew. This was not about abandoning morality but rather about getting morality more right, so she could find her own moral compass.

She let go of her obsession with Richard as soon as she heard that Richard's wife (a colleague of hers) was miserable in the marriage. She did not envy her. She said it would have been like jumping from the frying pan into the fire to marry Richard. He would have exploited her even more, as he was now doing with her friend. It was harder for her to evaluate her relationship to her mother. She could never say that Mom had exploited her goodwill, but she did realize that Mom had been caught in the same trap as herself: hiding away and trying to be good by not spending much time with others. That was enough and it allowed her to remember some of the good things she and Mom had shared. She became able to speak about her mother's limitations as well as about her loving and caring nature. She knew she was very much like Mom and wanted to learn from her mistakes. She was determined to learn to keep her brain free to think for itself. To this effect she decided to take a course in mental health nursing, which her employers decided to support her in doing by giving her day release from her job whilst placing her in another depart-ment of the hospital. As soon as Lizzie began her training, her mood lightened and some new strength was released in her with the realization that she was actively changing her life for the better. She began to dress in a more relaxed and contemporary manner and started to make new, much closer friends.

The therapy

Initially the work was about creating a strong enough relationship with Lizzie for her to trust that she could speak her mind and would not be judged or berated. This was essential to break the stalemate in her mind, which paralysed her. Also, all my interventions were enabling and had the objective of releasing her tension about herself. This was done by reassurance as well as by challenging some of her false assumptions and beliefs. It was also done by showing her how life works and using evidence from her own descriptions to help her acquire a picture of the way she was stopping and freezing herself in an untenable position.

Then the work moved to a phase of philosophical explorations of egoism versus altruism and of the examination of moral values and virtues versus sins. At this point it was important not to make any value judgements about Lizzie's belief system, even though it was still very tight and fearful at that time.

Lizzie was shown how she could gradually begin to question her assumptions and make a little bit of room for doubt or alternative views. At this point I had to translate her experiences into language that was clear and reassuring and helped her get a map of the world that she could use to find her way in it. This was all about helping her claim the freedom to be herself and find her own direction. Approving of the ways in which she had tried to do this (by falling ill, by not nursing her mother in the hospital and by shunning her friends for a while) rather than showing all these actions and attitudes to be pathological was a sure fire way to help her relax into understanding and being compassionate with herself. What mattered more than anything was to show her that she had been more expert about what had been wrong in her life than she dared to admit at first. She soon felt that her 'head opened up' and at that point it was essential to give her back the authority to think for herself. She discovered with a bit of encouragement that her intuitions and feelings were spot on and would help her to find the right track. Encouraging Lizzie to feel good about herself and the opportunities now available to her enabled her to see the new paths ahead of her, and she could not wait to take them.

REFERENCES

[1] Deurzen, E. van (2009) *Psychotherapy and the Quest for Happiness.* London: Sage.
[2] Deurzen, E. van (2010) *Everyday Mysteries: Handbook of Existential Therapy.* London: Routledge.
[3] Deurzen, E. van and Adams, M. (2011) *Skills in Existential Counselling and Psychotherapy.* London: Sage.
[4] Spinelli, E. (2015) *Practising Existential Therapy*, 2nd edn. London: Sage.
[5] Yalom, I. (1980) *Existential Psychotherapy.* New York: Basic Books.
[6] Schneider, K. J. and Krug, O. T. (2009) *Existential-Humanistic Therapy.* Washington, DC: APA.
[7] Cooper, M. (2003) *Existential Therapies.* London: Sage.
[8] Laing, R. D. (1965) *The Divided Self.* London: Penguin.

SUGGESTED READING

Adams, M. (2013) *Existential Counselling in a Nutshell.* London: Sage. A very brief and clear introduction to existential counselling and psychotherapy for complete beginners.

Cooper, M. (2012) *The Existential Counselling Primer.* Ross-on-Wye: PCCS Books. Another concise and simple introductory book to check out whether existential counselling and psychotherapy is for you.

(Continued)

(Continued)

Deurzen, E. van (2012) *Existential Counselling and Psychotherapy in Practice*, revised 3rd edn. London: Sage. A straightforward introduction to existential counselling and psychotherapy for those who want to start using some existential ideas and methods in their work.

Spinelli, E. (2015) *Practising Existential Therapy*, 2nd edn. London: Sage. Practical introduction to existential therapy based around a relational, three-phase model of practice.

DISCUSSION ISSUES

1. Is happiness the true objective of existential therapy?
2. What is the role of time in existential therapy?
3. How might an understanding of the idea of paradox improve human existence?
4. What does it mean to say that the practice of existential therapy is philosophical?

15

Gestalt Therapy

Ken Evans and Maria Gilbert

Gestalt psychotherapy is an approach to counselling and psychotherapy located within the humanistic and existential tradition drawing also from phenomenology and field theory. Humanistic psychology stresses the importance of a person's own inborn capacity for growth and change. Existentialism stresses the responsibility people have for their own lives and their choices. Phenomenology gives precedence to the subjective experience of the individual as their 'truth'. Field theory moves beyond the simplistic Newtonian linear concept of 'cause and effect' to admit all parts of a person's field as worthy of study. Thus Gestalt psychotherapy takes account of what happens in the client's world outside of therapy in the broader cultural, economic, socio–political and ecological systems that are seen as interconnected, interdependent and significantly influencing a person's sense of well-being. Gestalt therapy requires both the therapist and the client to focus on their immediate perceptual and sensory experience. What is directly perceived and experienced in the here–and–now is considered most significant in therapy and in life.

Frederick (Fritz) Perls, the most charismatic of the founders of Gestalt therapy, was originally trained as a psychoanalyst, so that Gestalt therapy is sometimes viewed as a school of psychoanalysis, albeit a very radical offspring.

DEVELOPMENT OF THE THERAPY

Gestalt therapy has evolved over the past 70 years and it is now possible to distinguish between *classical* Gestalt developed by Perls[1] and *contemporary dialogical* (relational) Gestalt. In recent years the 'I–Thou' dialogue of Martin Buber,[2] where the other is met as a human being (rather than an object to be manipulated, 'I–It') has been increasingly assimilated into Gestalt theory and clinical practice.[2]

In contemporary dialogical Gestalt the focus is on contact, that is, an awareness not only of our self, but also our relationships with others and the world and the quality of these relationships. Consequently there is a greater emphasis on the unfolding nature of the therapeutic relationship in current Gestalt theory. What is happening *between* the client and the therapist is frequently the material of therapy. Client and therapist both share their own experience in the course of a session. Differences in how they perceive the process between them may lead to further dialogue.[3] We want to emphasize the importance of not polarizing the two broad schools within Gestalt psychotherapy because they are not mutually exclusive.

In the first edition of this book we focused on the classical Gestalt model, while in this edition we will give precedence to contemporary dialogical Gestalt psychotherapy.

THEORY AND BASIC CONCEPTS

From a Gestalt perspective, human beings are thought to resist change because in the course of childhood **creative adjustments** are made in response to particular circumstances in our families and surroundings, which subsequently become our habitual ways of being in the world. Some rigid and habitual patterns of behaviour may even have been life-preserving in our family of origin but now in adulthood can impede **organismic self-regulation** (the ability to take in what is nurturing from the environment and reject what is toxic).

Blocks to awareness

Introjection

Leading on from the above, classical Gestalt understood the process of internalizing the beliefs and attitudes of significant others as forming the basis for the principal block to **awareness**, that is, **introjection**. Some introjected beliefs may prove helpful to a person; but many beliefs, held rigidly and without careful consideration, block a person's awareness. Introjects manifest as the 'musts', 'shoulds' and 'oughts' of everyday life. These undermine free choice: for example, 'I must not question authority.' Introjection is maintained by secondary blocks to awareness, chief among these being projection, retroflection and confluence.

Projection, retroflection and confluence

Projection is where a person attributes to others thoughts, feelings and attitudes that are denied in themselves. To continue the example above, we may say of others: 'You know best,' defending an introjected belief that 'I do not'.

Retroflection involves turning back on oneself certain thoughts, feelings and behaviours that would be more appropriately expressed to others. In the above example, 'I am so stupid', said angrily to oneself, leads to feelings of low self-esteem and self-deprecation.

In *confluence*, we blur the boundary between self and other. For example, we may stay in a relationship with a partner who can feel important only at the cost of putting oneself down, because this feels familiar and 'true' to us. In confluence, a person merges with the other and does not acknowledge their own needs.

In recent years, Gestalt therapy has come to appreciate that the above blocks to awareness, while significantly impacting our 'way of being in the world,' are preceded by our earliest attachment patterns formed in relationship with our primary caretakers. Working with early and preverbal experiences requires a greater emphasis on the healing potential of the therapeutic relationship than is possible solely via the classical approach, which is exemplified in the following core belief of the classical approach to **self-responsibility**.

> Being responsible for oneself is at the core of [classical] Gestalt therapy. Clients are assisted to move from a position of dependence on others, including the therapist, to a state of being self-supporting. They are encouraged to do many things independently. Initially they see their feelings, emotions and problems as somehow outside themselves: they use phrases such as 'he makes me feel so stupid'. They assume no responsibility for what they are, and it seems to them that there is nothing they can do about their situation other than accept it.[4]

Several influential sources have encouraged a major critique of the Western cultural notion of self-responsibility. These sources include developmental psychology, attachment theory, inter-subjectivity theory, relational psychoanalysis and recent discoveries from neuroscience. Thus while the capacity for autonomy is necessary and useful we would nevertheless maintain that maturity further requires a capacity to go beyond self-reliance to be able and willing to ask for help. Rather than being automatically seen as weakness or dependency, which is likely a culturally influenced introject, paradoxically we see the capacity to seek support as empowering. In our clinical practice we frequently meet male and female clients whose creative adjustment includes the 'John Wayne syndrome', a macho hero forever destined to ride off alone into the sunset. Such clients are typical of the post-war generations of children who grew up without the support of the extended family and experienced little 'healthy dependency'. Frequently such clients grew up too quickly and present in therapy with an unrecognized and unexpressed pre-verbal longing for intimacy and contact. They are frightened of being seen, but even more frightened of not being seen.

Theory of change

Both classical and contemporary Gestalt therapy adhere to the paradoxical nature of change which maintains that change occurs when a person becomes who they are, not when they try to become who they are not. Change does not take place through self coercion or by the demands of another person such as a partner or the therapist. Change takes place if a person takes the time and effort to become who they are. Through acknowledging what is, you may then become who you want to be. So, paradoxically, by accepting and staying with a person's present experience, the Gestalt therapist may help create the atmosphere in which change is possible.[5]

PRACTICE

Contact – the goal of Gestalt therapy

Acknowledging *what is* and *who we are* requires identifying what we like and what we may dislike about ourselves, so that change invariably requires we learn to increasingly tolerate stepping beyond our 'discomfort zone' and risk questioning our habitual perceptions of our self, others and our consequential behaviour(s). Here, the Gestalt therapist can be experienced as a non–judging other whose consistent attitude of support and acceptance might eventually be internalized by the client, who grows to be more accepting of themselves. However, 'true' contact also requires the appreciation of difference so that alongside offering support the Gestalt therapist will seek to balance support with challenge. As the therapeutic relationship deepens and strengthens the Gestalt therapist will self-disclose, with discrimination, their authentic experience of the client and thus model authenticity. The client will gradually learn to trust the honesty and authenticity of the therapist and thereby increasingly allow themselves to be more present also. From a Gestalt perspective it is in and through our relational connections we come to know ourselves.

In the current view of dialogical Gestalt psychotherapy there are three interconnected foci of attention for the therapist in the pursuit of the goal of contact. First, the therapist listens empathically to the client (inclusion); secondly, the therapist listens and attends to his or her own authentic presence; and thirdly, the therapist surrenders to what might emerge in the relational space between therapist and client.

Dialogical Gestalt therapy draws inspiration from the writings of the Jewish philosopher and educator Martin Buber, the most significant influence in dialogical Gestalt therapy, who wrote about the I–Thou relationship. In this relationship, each person is accepting of, and open to, the other. The I–Thou relationship aspires to be free from judgement, demand, objectification, or even anticipation. Persons respond creatively to each other as human beings, in the moment, eschewing instrumental and habitual ways of interaction found in the I–It relationship, which seeks to objectify the other.

Four defining features of dialogical Gestalt therapy can be identified: presence, inclusion, intersubjectivity and reflexivity.

Presence

The therapist's presence requires they be bodily and emotionally engaged, receptive and transparent.[6] Presence involves the capacity for 'being there' with the whole of ourselves — bodily sensations, emotions, thoughts and fantasies — in order to respond fully to the client. Zinker and Nevis distinguish between presence and charisma thus, 'charisma calls to itself, whereas presence calls to the other'.[7]

In addition, presence involves receptiveness to the other, being ready to respond to whatever emerges in the therapeutic relationship and being prepared to tolerate and cope with not-knowing, uncertainty and ambiguity.[8] To develop a capacity for surprise and unpredictability. There is a real willingness to listen, and understand with humility.

Transparency refers to the way the Gestalt therapist endeavours to be honest, authentic and open. Transparency may include some selectively and judiciously applied self-disclosure where the therapist shares his experience of the process between himself and the other in the here-and-now of the therapy session. As we shall discuss later such self-disclosure (arising within and a reflection upon the relational encounter between therapist and client and rarely about the therapist's life outside therapy) can be highly effective in bringing unconscious dynamics into awareness where they can then be addressed. When deciding whether or not to self-disclose the Gestalt therapist will need to primarily consider whether or not a self-disclosure would be likely to further the goal of contact.

Inclusion

While presence supports us to be as fully available to the other as possible, we also need to have a sense of where the other is and to include the other without losing oneself or the other, or losing oneself in the other. Inclusion refers to a developing process where a person is able to stay in his or her own world of experience, empathize with the world of the other and hold a meta-perspective on this relational mutuality. Inclusion and presence are two sides of the same coin as each requires the other in a contactful relationship. With presence, Gestalt therapists are focused on themselves; with inclusion, the focus is on the client.

Holding both, the challenge is how to be inside the relationship practising inclusion and simultaneously, sufficiently outside the relationship, maintaining a grounded presence and not becoming lost (confluent) in the client's process. This capacity of holding both grows and develops with experience.

In Gestalt therapy the process of including the client and confirming the person's existence is also seen to provide the client with a reparative experience of a positive relationship in the present. The client gains an experience of being seen and acknowledged, which may have been largely absent in their prior experience. The dialogical Gestalt therapist also allows himself be affected by the experience. Here, the therapist may well change as he feels a range of emotions in response to the client and is impacted by the experience of the other. From a Gestalt perspective the counter-transference is all the therapist's emotional reaction to the client, not to the client's pathology!

Together, presence and inclusion lie at the heart of the concept of co-creation in relationship, making possible a sense of mutual influence, of both persons changing in response to the other. To be present without inclusion is to be 'out of contact', cut off or alienated from the client. To be immersed in the client but lose one's sense of being present is to be overly merged with the client and also 'out of contact'. In either case there can be no contact, no real meeting or engagement since one is either isolated from the client or fused together with the client. Practising inclusion, while remaining present, may be the most challenging skill for the dialogical Gestalt therapist.

Intersubjectivity

While therapist and client are separate, the concept of intersubjectivity highlights their entangling, i.e. how past and current aspects of the self of the client can be elicited and interact with those of the therapist in the present, and vice versa! With the growing acknowledgement of the significance of the therapeutic relationship as the primary vehicle for change, Gestalt therapy has begun to address the challenging phenomenon of unconscious processes made manifest in and through the dynamic of the transference.

We can all identify experiences in our lives when we have felt a greater or lesser degree of negativity toward another person, whether or not they are familiar and close to us or a complete stranger, that was disproportionate to the current circumstances or event. In such an experience we may be 'seeing' (transferring) someone other than the actual person in front of us. What triggers the transference may be a facial characteristic of the other, their tone of voice, perceived superior attitude, etc., all reminiscent of a different person from the past but now evoking feelings toward the stranger or other person in the present.

Each person in a therapeutic relationship touches and impacts on the other in ways that inevitably affect how the therapy unfolds. Client and therapist meet on two levels, the conscious level and the unconscious level. In the movie blockbuster *Titanic* the ocean liner is filmed as running directly into the enormous wall of the iceberg. Actually, the far larger mass of an iceberg is under the sea and invisible, so that *Titanic* would have hit the iceberg a long way from its visible wall. Similarly, the unconscious is invisible until we run into it!

When this occurs there is no simple set of techniques laid down to explore the unconscious and no manual setting out the steps to 'treatment'. Indeed, unconscious processes emerging *between* therapist and client are often characterized by ambiguity, uncertainty and unpredictability. So alongside the practice of inclusion is something of a surrender, a yielding, to what might be emerging between two people and a recognition of mutual intersubjective interconnection.

Dialogical Gestalt therapists assume both therapist and client bring to the encounter the sum total of who they are in all their complexity and with their own individual histories and ways of organizing their experience and their unconscious processes. Both are then faced with the challenge of meeting the other in all his/ her complexity.

Reflexivity

Given the complexity of this intersubjective space, reflexivity is essential, i.e. a self-aware thoughtfulness about the therapy dynamics and process in order to discover *with the client* the meaning behind the transference and how it is impacting on the quality of contact.

Being present in these engaged, receptive, transparent ways, supports the possibility of mutuality of contact in the 'between', where neither person controls the other. They stand – both together and apart – in their vulnerability and difference. Clearly, in this sense therapy is not simply about techniques but is rather, as Zinker and Nevis[7] describe it, a way of being with, without doing to. In practice, this engaged, receptive presence can sometimes be hard to maintain.

Dialogical Gestalt therapists are ethically required to commit to bringing themselves fully into the clinical room and to deal directly with relational impasses that may occur between themselves and the client. This calls for the ongoing monitoring of their presence (or absence of presence) in relation to the unfolding process. At some point a decision needs to be made about what is helpful to share in the interests of deepening the exploration and understanding of the process. This depends more on the willingness of the therapist to critically reflect on his own counter-transference and what can be learned from this, combined with a careful and respectful attention to the needs of the client. The case study that follows will illustrate reflexivity in practice and demonstrate how the therapist explores their own and the client's process thoughtfully while being critically aware of there being broader dynamics and processes in the relational field. The therapist's subjectivity and intersubjectivity will be fore-grounded through reflexivity so as to begin the process of separating out what belongs to the therapist and what belongs to the client.

WHICH CLIENTS BENEFIT MOST?

Gestalt therapy is potentially suitable for a wide range of client groups in the private, public and voluntary sectors, depending on the experience, level of training and knowledge of the therapist. Gestalt therapy, like most in-depth therapies, helps clients to re-assess their way of being in the world, developing their self-awareness and their capacity for contact in relationship. To be able to manage the process, clients need to have sufficient ego-strength so as not to experience personality fragmentation. Even so, the process of therapy can at times be destabilizing and provoke strong feelings and challenge long-standing beliefs. There is inevitably pain involved in such a process and it is important to inform the client that therapy can be both exciting and exacting.

CASE STUDY

The Client

In this case study a key episode has been selected from a period of once-weekly therapy with a client we shall call Malcolm, that ran for four years, and in order to demonstrate how the aforementioned theory, specifically inclusion, presence, inter-subjectivity and reflexivity, may be applied in practice. The key episode occurred about one year into the therapy.

Malcolm is a senior English teacher in a large comprehensive school. He came to therapy because he said he struggled to establish and maintain intimate relationships. He had what he described as two or three serious relationships but each one ended after about 18 months.

The Therapy

In this session Malcolm reported an emergency hospital admission in the past week of a long-standing friend. Malcolm spoke with his fairly characteristic flat tone of voice, incongruent with his alleged attachment to his friend, who was in postoperative intensive care following a heart attack. Malcolm said the friend was one of the few people in his life with whom he had kept in touch since his university days.

After a short while Malcolm suddenly became silent and looked thoughtful and anxious. Eventually, in barely a whisper he recalled a dream he had had following news of his friend's heart attack wherein he was trapped inside a building that was about to be demolished. Despite repeated banging of the exit door and screams for help, no help came and he felt as if he did not exist and was about to die. Malcolm then looked puzzled and 'spaced out'. Ken made several empathic attempts to elicit more of Malcolm's experience but he remained seemingly locked in a world of his own such that Ken could appreciate how difficult it must be for anyone to be allowed emotionally close to him.

Ken drew Malcolm's attention to his emotional withdrawal, which had been a consistent theme of therapy to date. Malcolm's dream seemed to acknowledge he was 'stuck in his head' again and struggled unsuccessfully to express himself. However, he did appear a little anxious, as if his normal coping strategy (creative adjustment) of retroflecting his emotions was not entirely working.

Ken checked his own experience and felt perplexed and frustrated. Unable to elicit any further dialogue from Malcolm, Ken turned his attention inward to himself: How might I be missing Malcolm? How might others have missed him in the past?

Ken then became aware he was not feeling anything in response to Malcolm's dream. His emotional response, what we may think of as his counter-transference, was not congruent with the content of the dream and neither was Malcolm's. Ken was not allowing himself to be impacted by the dream at an emotional level. Why not? What might Malcolm be wanting Ken to avoid or what might Ken be avoiding?

We believe counter-transference is never a simple one-way phenomenon but almost invariably a reciprocal process, where therapist and client alike are co-creating the field. Bearing this in mind, and tolerating a sense of 'not knowing', Ken risked sharing with Malcolm that he was going to take some time to recall what he (Malcolm) had told him about his dream and try to actively imagine the dream was his (Ken's) own dream because while he heard his (Malcolm's) words, strangely he could not hear the music behind them. Malcolm continued to look anxious but less puzzled and more attentive. As Ken began to re-tell the dream reported by Malcolm he did so in the first person present tense as if it were his own dream. This is a long-standing technique to dream exploration from classical Gestalt that gives a sense of immediacy to the dream teller and usually leads to an awareness or insight. Soon after entering the dream, Ken very quickly touched upon a recent powerful memory of a hospital admission of his own and his profound experience of isolation and abandonment. While containing his feelings, Ken nevertheless allowed himself to acknowledge them to himself and feel them at a level that was strong but not overwhelming. He felt present now and began to consider how and what of his own experience might he disclose to Malcolm in order to model the process of emotional literacy. Had Ken repressed his feelings he would have paralleled Malcolm's process of retroflection and likely repeated Malcolm's habitual patterns of behaviour. However, verbal self-disclosure proved unnecessary. Malcolm had sensed or intuited Ken's presence and Malcolm's body language had profoundly altered. He no longer looked withdrawn but was instead tearful. For the first time in almost a year of therapy, Malcolm's immediate emotional and intellectual experiences were congruent.

Through tuning in to (practising inclusion) Malcolm's experience, Ken paradoxically entered more deeply into his own presence. Then by being able to tolerate his own deeper sense of presence, he in turn supported and modelled this capacity for Malcolm.

Malcolm acknowledged his sadness and cried.

Malcolm: These tears feel good, Ken, how come?
Ken: I suggest you just stay with the feelings, Malcolm, and don't try to analyse them just now. It's OK to feel what you feel.
Malcolm: Not in my family it wasn't ... no I'm not going there, I want to feel this .... I want to feel me ... God, its good. I really like him, you know ... Alan, my friend.
Ken: Have you told him?
Malcolm: [Crying deeply] Never ... isn't that just stupid? I have never really told him in 25 fucking years. I'm sure he knows ... but ... is it OK to tell him?
Ken: You sound scared and a little angry when you say that.
Malcolm: I am ... I'm frightened to tell him how much he means to me ... he might not like me then ...

The remainder of the session Malcolm stayed present with his heart and his head and at the end said:

(Continued)

(Continued)

Malcolm: Thank you, Ken, for wanting to understand me and staying with me, it means a lot. I don't think I have shown myself like that to anyone. Am I OK with you?

Ken: Do you mean, am I OK with you?

Malcom: [*smiles*] Yeah.

Ken: Yeah.

This turned out to be a key episode in Malcolm's therapy. In subsequent weeks he went on to share his fear of loneliness and abandonment and to connect this not only to his friend's ill health but also to his childhood experiences at home as an only child with emotionally distant parents and including a time at the age of five when he had been hospitalized for two weeks. With a look of incredulity he said he could not remember his mother or father visiting him. He believed they probably didn't.

Significantly, as he continued to share more of his emotional experiences in therapy his feelings of loneliness diminished, then intensified and then diminished again, repeatedly over several months. Malcolm became more fully alive. He did not always enjoy the experience but he relished 'catching up with lost years of feelings' and began to like himself more and more.

Sadly his friend, Alan, died of a second heart attack some months later but Malcolm spent some rich time with Alan and his immediate family before his death. Malcolm shared his love with Alan and is now the unofficial adopted uncle to Alan's two teenage children.

Ken's initial lack of empathy threatened to seriously curtail the quality of contact between himself and Malcolm and parallel Malcolm's emotional inhibition, and might also have repeated Malcolm's earlier experience of abandonment as a child. Was this incongruence in Ken triggered by Malcolm or by Ken? We understand this to be an example of projective identification. In our clinical experience projective identification requires that an experience, event, situation or remark touches some significant history in both client and therapist. By whom it is triggered is less relevant than processing its meaning. Reflexive thinking on the part of the therapist is supported and enhanced if such reflection is motivated by curiosity. If the therapist is burdened by judgement (a professional introject such as: 'I am a therapist and therefore I should not feel this way'), then it is unlikely the therapist will allow their experience into awareness, own it and use it in the service of the client. In this case Ken's commitment to deepening his attunement toward Malcolm enabled him to be more present with himself. In turn his deeper sense of his own presence renewed and deepened his empathic understanding (inclusion) toward Malcolm. Significantly, Ken's deepened sense of presence and inclusion was intuited by Malcolm even before Ken spoke to confirm it. This is sometimes referred to as a phenomenon emerging from the 'relational unconscious' which has been described as the unrecognized bond that wraps each relationship, infusing the expression and constriction of each partner's subjectivity and individual unconscious within that particular relationship. Malcolm came to realize that to a significant degree his experience of his therapist's desire to understand him, both prior to this key episode and afterwards, was in stark contrast to his experience as a lonely child at home and gave him permission. 'I want to lean into you for a while, Ken.'

The therapist's willingness to be more fully present in the therapeutic relationship modelled the process for Malcolm. As Zinker and Nevis maintain,[7] presence is the ground against which the figure of another self or selves can flourish, and stand out fully. The presence of the therapist calls forth, and gives permission, for the presence of the client to come forth, and then there can be a mutually reciprocal experience of contact where each impacts further upon the other.

All contemporary relational approaches to psychotherapy share with dialogical Gestalt this attention to the therapist's own process as a valuable resource to deepen the focus on the client. Such work needs to be undertaken with curiosity and not judgement, since judgement triggers shame while curiosity supports a deeper level of reflexive practice. Any 'mistakes' are viewed with curiosity and as a path to growth and learning.

REFERENCES

[1] Perls, F., Hefferline, R. F. and Goodman, P. (1951) *Gestalt Therapy.* New York: Julian Press.

[2] Buber, M. (1923/2004) *I and Thou* (trans. W. Kaufman). London: Continuum.

[3] Hycner, R. (1991) *Between Person and Person.* New York: The Gestalt Journal Press.

[4] O'Leary, E. (1992) *Gestalt Therapy: Theory, Practice and Research.* London: Chapman and Hall.

[5] Beisser, A. (1970) 'The paradoxical theory of change', in J. Fagan and I. Shepherd (eds), *Gestalt Therapy Now.* Palo Alto, CA: Science and Behavior Books.

[6] Finlay, L. and Evans, K. (2009) *Relational Centred Research for Psychotherapists.* Chichester: Wiley–Blackwell.

[7] Zinker, J. and March Nevis, S. (1994) 'The aesthetics of Gestalt couples therapy', in G. Wheeler and S. Backman (eds), *On Intimate Ground: A Gestalt Approach to Working with Couples.* Cleveland, OH: Gestalt Institute of Cleveland Publication.

[8] Evans, K. and Gilbert, M. (2005) *An Introduction to Integrative Psychotherapy.* Basingstoke: Palgrave Macmillan.

SUGGESTED READING

Francesetti, G., Gecele, M. and Roubal, J. (eds) (2013) *Gestalt Therapy in Clinical Practice: from Psychopathology to the Aesthetics of Contact.* Milan: Franco Angeli. Edited by three psychiatrists who are also practising Gestalt therapists, the book brings together more than 25 authors relating Gestalt theory to practice across a wide variety of presenting problems. Translated also in Russian, French, Italian, German and Romanian.

(Continued)

(Continued)

Gerson, S. (2004) 'The relational unconscious: a core element of intersubjectivity, thirdness and clinical process', *Psychoanalytic Quarterly, LXXIII*. A must-read for anyone interested in exploring the challenge of working with unconscious processes in the psychotherapy relationship.

Wheeler, G. and McConville, M. (2002) *The Heart of Development: Gestalt Approaches to Working with Children, Adolescents and Their Worlds*. Hillsdale, NJ: Analytic Press/Gestalt Press. A fine introduction to the application of Gestalt therapy in work with children and young people.

Yontef, G. M. (1993) *Awareness, Dialogue and Process*. New York: The Gestalt Journal Press. Yontef is probably the most influential theorist in contemporary Gestalt therapy.

DISCUSSION ISSUES

1. Presence, inclusion and reflexive thinking are the foundations of contemporary relational Gestalt therapy.
2. The therapeutic relationship is the major vehicle for change in contemporary Gestalt therapy.
3. There is no such thing as the past. There is history, what happened last month, last year, 50 or 100 years ago, but the past is always present in the ground influencing both client and therapist and the direction of the work.
4. The Gestalt therapist maintains an attitude of curiosity and exploration; rather than judgement or interpretation, in order to support the client to find their own meaning.

16

Person-Centred Therapy

Kate Hayes

The foundation of person–centred therapy is built on an understanding that people thrive when they are trusted, people have potential for creative ways of expression and are naturally social. Person-centred therapy was identified as a new approach to psychotherapy in 1940 by Carl Ransom Rogers. It was considered new and revolutionary as it believes the human being has potential for growth and change despite emotional distress. Originally it was called client–centred therapy, a term still used today.

Rogers identified, by listening to his patients, whom he chose to call clients, that the client knew what hurt and what direction he or she needed to move in.[1] In the 1940s this concept was counter–cultural and the client was, for the first time, perceived as the active agent of change in the therapeutic relationship.[2]

Rogers identified the positive view of a person's capacity to overcome difficulty and, furthermore, an approach to being in the world that held beneficial implications for developing a peaceful community and society.[3] The person–centred approach is a positive psychological approach to therapeutic change.[4,5,6]

Many approaches to therapy align themselves to the person–centred approach (see Figure 16.1). These include focusing-oriented therapy, emotion-focused therapy, experiential person–centred therapy and counselling for depression.[7]

All aspects of the approach are best understood after engaging in a person–centred or client–centred therapy diploma training. Psychologists, nurses, general practitioners and psychiatrists have all been known to train in the approach. It is possible to train at diploma, degree and postgraduate level, and many go in to research and gain doctorates and professorships.

In this chapter I discuss the development of the therapy, the key concepts and what could be considered ways a therapist will respond to a client. There is also a case study involving my client Peter, who has generously agreed to me sharing his experience of therapy for this chapter.

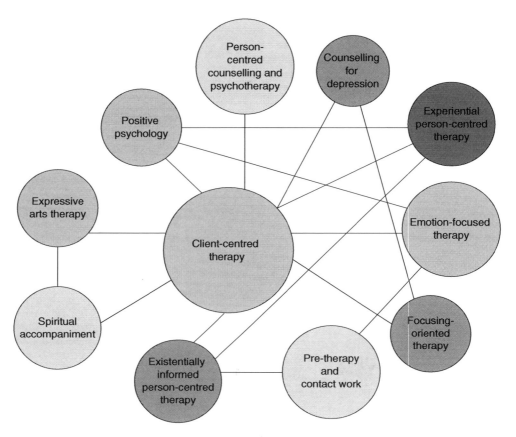

FIGURE 16.1   *Person-centred therapy*

DEVELOPMENT OF THE THERAPY

Carl Rogers democratised counselling and psychotherapy by using recordings and films in order to fully understand what enabled a client to move forward.[8] Arguably, person–centred theory was developed by clients. Rogers bucked the trend of making the therapist an expert. This exploration of therapy led to key principles, also described as 'The Necessary and Sufficient Attitudes of Therapeutic Personality Change' (in recent years this has come to be known as **'core conditions'**).[9] (I say more about this later).

Rogers realised that with these conditions the client would discover their own answers, answers that the therapist might never imagine. Rather than the therapist *doing* something to the client, the therapist pays attention to their own way of *being* in the relationship (see Figure 16.2).

The latest development for the person–centred approach is Counselling for Depression (CfD).[10] CfD is the first NHS-approved approach to person–centred and experiential therapy and is validated by NICE (National Institute for Health and Care Excellence). It is available freely in the NHS and is a significant development in the twenty–first century, placing the person–centred approach on an equal footing with cognitive behavioural therapy.

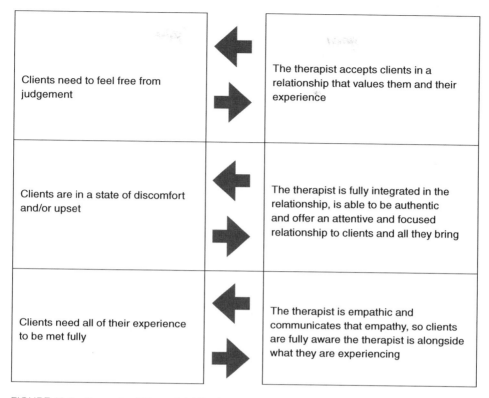

FIGURE 16.2   *Example of Therapist Attitude*

THEORY AND BASIC CONCEPTS

Carl Rogers grew up on a farm and developed a fascination for science.[2] As a young man he observed how, despite dreadful conditions, many plants and creatures attempted to grow and fulfil their development. He pondered that, in the same way, individuals who, for example, are met with judgement and criticism all their growing lives, seek growth to fulfilment.[8] This observation, and much research, led him to develop a key aspect of the theory behind person–centred therapy.

The actualising tendency

The concept of the **actualising tendency** is unique to person–centred work. It identifies the client as the agent of change; the client knows what hurts. Rogers, through his work, initially with young people and later with adults, identified the client is best able to determine a way ahead when met in a relationship that is free of threat.

Empathy

In order to create a relationship free from threat the therapist has intent to understand the world of the client. This is most commonly understood by the term **empathy**. The therapist is not identifying with the client but is checking and ensuring their grasp of the client's experience, and thereby the client feels met and understood, Alongside empathy, other conditions were identified, including unconditional positive regard (acceptance) and congruence (being authentic). These were named The Necessary and Sufficient Attitudes of Therapeutic Personality Change; there are six conditions in total.

The conditions

The six conditions are:

1. Two persons are in psychological contact.
2. The first, whom we shall term the client, is in a state of incongruence, being vulnerable or anxious.
3. The second person, whom we shall term the therapist, is congruent or integrated in the relationship.
4. The therapist experiences unconditional positive regard for the client.
5. The therapist experiences an empathic understanding of the client's internal frame of reference and endeavours to communicate this experience to the client.
6. The communication to the client of the therapist's empathic understanding and unconditional positive regard is to a minimal degree achieved.[11]

Many therapists and counselling courses mistakenly decide these conditions act as a base line from which the therapist determines various techniques.

It may be helpful to consider a dialogue with another person, who is clearly upset and struggling with life, where you do not offer suggestions or advice. By doing this you will discover how very difficult it is to remain alongside a client and remain in their world, allowing the client to connect further in to their own experiencing.

By enabling the client to feel respected and valued in the relationship, the client is secure that they will not be summed up, analysed or pathologised. This means the client is free to explore the most difficult or potentially hidden aspects of themselves, safe in the knowledge that their therapist is not going to declare that somehow the person is beyond help.

Terry

At this point I'd like to introduce you to Terry. I will be using Terry's experience of growing up and his subsequent decision to seek therapy to explore aspects of theory.

Terry grew up in a judgemental atmosphere. He never got anything right in the eyes of his father and quickly discovered if he kept quiet he would not be a subject of criticism. By not receiving criticism, Terry felt accepted.

Conditions of worth

In person–centred theory Terry's belief that he needed to be quiet, is described as a **condition of worth**. It is how Terry can feel free from threat and accepted by others. This 'condition of worth' is, 'I am acceptable as long as I am quiet'. It results in him developing a **self-concept**, and makes his life feel more bearable. He has a self-concept that involves him being a quiet person who does not cause any difficulty to anyone else because he is quiet. He believes he is naturally quiet and this is likely to have been re-enforced by those around him. Family members could describe him as a 'thinker' or as 'shy' and that he is a 'good boy' because of this. He received a reinforcement of his condition of worth and by not causing any 'trouble' by expressing himself, he is perceived as being good.

It is easy to see that Terry's condition of worth and his resulting self-concept will come under threat as he seeks out relationships and wishes to develop a life of his own.

Person–centred theory considers individuals hold potential that is inherently seeking growth – this growth may be in directions that promote happiness and wellbeing. Equally, the growth may develop in areas that are not necessarily socially acceptable and a sense of self-worth is experienced by participating in activities that exploit him or others, thereby also developing a degree of self-hatred or self-disgust. These feelings will be hard to own or acknowledge, so may be out of the client's awareness and become recognised as facts about life and how to survive it.

What is also considered to be a uniting aspect of being human is the wish to be accepted by others. Social, cultural and emotional environments will have a significant part in the direction of growth. It may be that parts of the self-concept grow in constructive and life-enhancing ways whilst other parts exist in ways that cause upset either to the self or to others, depending on what is considered to be acceptable and what enables the person to feel acceptance. The conflict between an idea of a real sense, an ought self and an ideal self, can cause much emotional distress.[12]

Self-acceptance

A key concept in person–centred thinking considered to be essential to psychological health is **self-acceptance**. The chance of a person growing in a way that is self-accepting in conditions where they are constantly criticised is quite low. Terry has found a way of avoiding criticism by being quiet. He believes he needs to be quiet in order to experience acceptance from others. By believing he causes others to judge him, he starts to believe he is at fault. This is, in person-centred theory, an example of how a person develops low self-esteem.

On encountering situations where Terry needs to speak out it is likely he will experience a high degree of anxiety. His self-concept is under threat as his condition of worth is being put into a conflict. It is in these circumstances Terry may go to see his doctor as he realises having strong feelings of anxiety that may involve panic attacks is preventing him from progressing. Terry may be using drugs or alcohol or food in order to cope and could be described as feeling depressed as a result of this.

Unconditional positive regard

This attitude is one where the therapist not only withholds judgement of the client but positively accepts all of the client's experiencing. Each aspect of the client's expression is valued equally. There is no discrimination from the therapist towards a client's difficult experiencing and the client's positive experiencing. This enables the client to experience the therapist as a person who will hear all that is shared and thereby the client can begin to accept aspects of themselves that perhaps before they had never imagined was possible. You will see this illustrated later on in the case study.

PRACTICE

Therapist goals

Unlike many other therapies, the goals of the person–centred approach are focused on the therapist. There are no pre–determined goals for the client from the therapist's point of view.

It is the therapist that is offering the conditions to the client and so in this respect these are the goals any therapist has in mind. Rogers described an 'if'–'then' approach to the client's process of change.[13] As a therapist I ensure I am fully in touch with how I am responding to the client from moment to moment in the session. In order to achieve this I reflect on this process throughout my client work and in supervision with a person–centred supervisor.

Therapist reflection

Uniquely to this approach any questions that arise in therapy are about the therapist's own attitudes.[14] For instance, can the therapist stay with the client as their story unfolds? Can the therapist accept all the client is sharing, and can the therapist communicate their understanding of the client's experience in a way that the client knows they are accepted and understood?

In the person–centred approach initial meetings with the client will enable both the client and the therapist to identify what the client feels is most relevant for them in regards to attending therapy. However, the client may change this direction at any point – and do so informally; they would not need to state explicitly to the therapist their wish to change focus, the therapist would follow the client throughout their exploration and meet authentically any aspect they chose to share. Aspects of therapist training are expanded on by Mearns and Thorne.[5]

Here is a brief example involving Terry.

Client: I really dislike myself. I feel pathetic when I clam up in meetings. I often know what I want to say but I just get too shaky to speak.

Therapist: You really dislike how you feel in meetings and really dislike yourself for feeling like that, even though there is something inside you wish to say, you feel pathetic because you can't speak?

The therapist is communicating to the client that she has understood exactly what the client has said and is reflecting the client's meaning – which in the theory is called *core meaning*.

Client: Yes – that's right. I feel so weak-willed.

The client confirms this is correct and expresses more about how he feels. Part of the client's *self-concept* is that he is weak-willed.

Therapist: If only I had the will to say something.

The therapist is aware that the client is referring to how he clams up and has listened very carefully, rather than focus on why the client feels weak-willed, the therapist is staying in the client's *frame of reference* – the therapist does not move the client into different territory by asking a question such as 'how long have you felt weak?', which would be driven by the therapist's interest rather than following what the client has offered. The therapist's response is empathic and captures the client's core meaning. The client has an ideal self-concept which involves him not being weak-willed, which presently feels unobtainable.

Client: Yes! I know what I wish to say may be helpful.

The therapist's brief response has meant the client can still continue his train of thought and is able to express he knows he has something of worth to say. The client is aware that he has value – his *actualising tendency* is apparent and is in conflict with the self-concept that he is weak-willed.

Therapist: You have something to offer but somehow you just can't get the words out.

Again the therapist stays with the client; the therapist resists asking what the client may say. She reiterates that the client knows he has something to offer

(Continued)

(Continued)

but cannot express it. The therapist is supporting the client's actualising tendency in this positive affirmation that the client has something of value to offer but is not judging the client. The therapist is staying with the acceptance that presently the client cannot express his worth.

>   *Client:*   I was always told to shut up as a child.

The client has recalled a memory as a result of the therapist carefully reflecting what has been said. The client has identified a *condition of worth*. In order to be accepted, he had to shut up.

>   *Therapist:*   That remains with you now.

The therapist recognises the importance of the delicate moment; the client is remembering something – the therapist does not ask for more detail but states that she is aware the client is in touch with this memory as he is speaking.

>   *Client:*   I only just remembered that.

The client is aware of the importance of the memory. He is aware of this condition of worth, possibly for the first time.

>   *Therapist:*   You can remember that.

The therapist still does not ask questions as the client is clearly retrieving the memory and the therapist is aware that the power of the client in this moment needs to be valued and not interfered with by any statement the therapist could offer.

>   *Client:*   Yes. God, if only my father had been kind to me. I wouldn't treat a child the way he did.

The client is fully in touch with the memory and accesses strong feelings as a result of it. There is also evidence of self-compassion – the client would not treat a child like that.

>   *Therapist:*   You feel he didn't help you to find your voice.

Here the therapist, having listened very carefully, is offering an empathic response based on what the client has shared – the client found this memory whilst struggling with why he clams up in meetings and the therapist offers back this awareness in her empathic response.

>   *Client:*   That's it; every time I go into a meeting I am being silenced by my father. How dare he still do that to me!

The client accesses a strong emotion at this point. This is a significant moment as he is also able to have insight into how he has carried that difficult feeling through to his present life. He is able to see his ought self (I should shut up) is a *condition of worth* and his ideal self (I wish I could speak) can become his real self (I can speak in meetings without fear of being told to shut up by my father).

As you can read above, the client is being 'tracked' or 'followed' closely by the therapist. The therapist is capturing the client's 'core meaning' and is expressing empathy. As a result, the client accesses a deeper awareness of himself and is able to realise the influence he is still living under. In a relatively brief exchange the client's sense of feeling 'weak-willed' is able to move from a position of self-blame to a position of anger at how he was treated.

Rogers identified seven stages of therapeutic change.[16]

Stage 1 The client is defensive.

Stage 2 The client is able to start talking about external experiences and other people.

Stage 3 The client begins to reflect on their experience and builds a relationship with the therapist.

Stage 4 The client is able to engage with their emotional awareness and express and acknowledge their emotions.

Stage 5 The client is able to reflect and own all aspects of their experiencing.

Stage 6 The client is able to be flexible in their thinking, is able to be spontaneous and is not threatened by difference from outside forces and this is likely when therapy comes to an end.

Stage 7 The client is actualised in their experience.

These seven stages are observations of how a process can evolve – they are not fixed or predictable. A person may well move in a different way through an experience of relationship. If there is a therapeutic encounter where the conditions are present the likelihood of movement from a state of incongruence to congruence is higher than if the conditions are absent.

WHICH CLIENTS BENEFIT MOST?

One of the core aspects of the person-centred approach has always been that it does not diagnose or pathologise individuals. Initially the therapist and the client

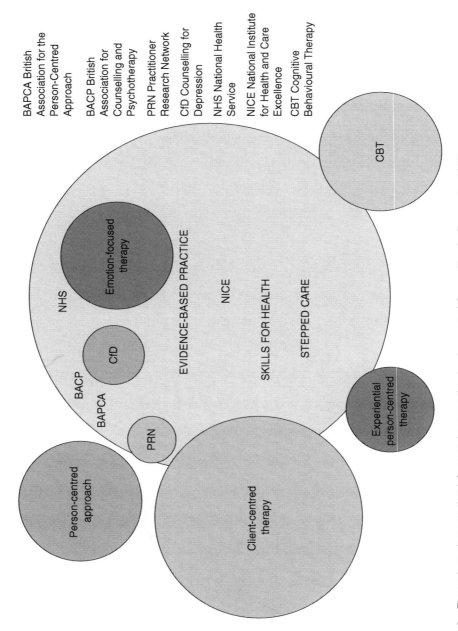

BAPCA British
Association for the
Person-Centred
Approach

BACP British
Association for
Counselling and
Psychotherapy

PRN Practitioner
Research Network

CfD Counselling for
Depression

NHS National Health
Service

NICE National Institute
for Health and Care
Excellence

CBT Cognitive
Behavioural Therapy

CBT

Emotion-focused
therapy

NHS

EVIDENCE-BASED PRACTICE

NICE

SKILLS FOR HEALTH

STEPPED CARE

CfD

BACP

BAPCA

PRN

Experiential
person-centred
therapy

Person-centred
approach

Client-centred
therapy

FIGURE 16.3   *The various elements that inform and support the development of Counselling for Depression (CfD)*

would determine together if they wish to work together, and this would be reviewed throughout the contact. If it becomes evident the client is not experiencing anything of worth by attending therapy, the therapist would support the client to identify a different approach to therapy or would offer to work with them specifically focusing on something new so far. If it emerges that the therapist cannot work ethically with the client, for example, the therapist feels they are not competent to offer the conditions to the client, the therapist needs to ensure the client is referred on elsewhere. Mostly, when issues arise in therapy that are challenging to the therapist's ability to offer the conditions the therapist will explore this with their person–centred supervisor and explore any blocks that may be present. If this cannot be resolved, the therapist will refer the client elsewhere. The conditions are the bedrock of the approach and it is the therapist who is involved in offering them to the client. It is the therapist who needs to ensure they can be authentic in the relationship.

Research[16] shows that the person–centred approach is equal to CBT in regards to working with clients experiencing anxiety and depression and, as mentioned above, is now offered in the NHS under the name of 'Counselling for Depression'[10] (see Figure 16.3).

Clients experiencing trauma benefit from a person–centred approach.[17] People often considered to be the most hard to reach, such as long–term psychiatric patients, benefit from the person–centred approach.[7] Many people use the approach for personal development and one of the prominent writers and thinkers of the approach in the UK, Professor Brian Thorne, developed this aspect of personal development and created a diploma in 'Spiritual Accompaniment'[18] for individuals who are seeking a new dimension to their life based on the theoretical concepts of Carl Rogers.

CASE STUDY

The Client

Peter, a man in his fifties, agreed for me to write this account of his experience of accessing counselling. Peter was referred to counselling as a result of having problems with anxiety and panic attacks. I had been told that Peter had mobility difficulties. He had seen a CBT therapist and had attended a group a few years before.

The Therapy

Establishing a relationship

Session 1

Peter had the use of one arm – the arm he needed in order to use a stick. One leg had very limited mobility. I considered how difficult it must be to navigate this uneven and complicated world of steps and swing doors and

(Continued)

(Continued)

uncomfortable chairs. The chair in the room had no arms, making it difficult for him to stand up out of it. I made a note that next week I would find a chair with arms

Peter spoke for 20 minutes. There was much he had to say about his life since an accident 33 years before. He lived with guilt and sadness and fear. Peter's eyes filled with tears as he retold various aspects of his life. He spoke about prejudice he had encountered as a disabled man. He was able to express his anger and frustration. I did not interrupt him, acknowledging what he was saying, clarifying some of the things he said, as Peter's speech had also been affected by the accident. I did not wish to misunderstand him.

Given the freedom to speak, he allowed a dreadful story to emerge. When he went back to work at the chicken factory after the accident many of the staff had now changed and he was with people who did not know him. One day a man whom he barely knew picked Peter up and put him in to a freezer with the chicken carcasses, saying 'that's how much use you are'. He sobbed at the memory. He'd held on to it for the best part of 30 years. The tears flowed freely and towards the end of the appointment he explained that no one had ever listened to him for so long before. I acknowledged what a painful memory it had been for him to share and expressed my gratitude that he had shared this story with me. By doing this I had accepted Peter unconditionally and respected him. I authentically responded to what he said.

The conditions

Session 2

The next week Peter brought in the police accident report. He really struggled with guilt and that he had been held responsible. He had always been a good and careful driver. There had been an accident, he had survived it but had no recollection whatsoever of the experience. I reflected that he found it very hard to believe he had made an error in his driving, but at the same time he felt responsible. I accepted the feelings he had of responsibility and his inability to view the experience as an 'accident'.

He went on to share what help he had had before, and how hopeless he felt as he had not progressed. He had decided to 'do something 'about his fear and anxiety four years before, and the therapist he had seen told him he needed to revisit the accident. This had not been successful and he had remained stuck with an intrusive image that he had been directed to focus on. He was told he needed to persevere with his reluctance to be a passenger in a car. This pressure made him more anxious, guiltier and caused him dreadful stress with his wife. He felt he needed to 'do' something and that by not getting it right he was even more to blame for his emotional distress. In response to this need to do something, I asked if he wanted to be talked through a relaxation – he said he did. I guided him through a brief relaxation, aware that given he was stuck with a previously implanted image I did not wish to add to his feeling of not getting things right or failing. After he opened his eyes he explained he felt less tense. In the person-centred approach therapists do not offer techniques unless directed by the client. In this instance Peter was keen to try anything and I offered him the chance to try a method of relaxation that was not focused on an image but involved tensing and relaxing parts of his body and breathing slowly and deeply. If I had had no experience of this I would not have been able to offer this but could have discussed the possibility of sourcing a relaxation CD or guide.

In this relaxed state we discussed what he wanted from the sessions. He said he needed to get over his fear of travel as his family were really fed up with him.

As the session came to an end he said this felt very different to anything he had experienced before – that being listened to felt so important and he felt more relaxed. By offering this remark to me I knew Peter was experiencing the conditions from me, that my responses were affirming that I was listening to him and that his experience was being met by me.

Unconditional positive regard

Session 3

It was clear Peter was frustrated: 'My wife is wondering what good this is doing'. He was still unable to relax about travelling. I reflected that there was an expectation for him to 'get better' and there was pressure on him to do something. He agreed and was able to connect in to his sense of trying, always trying. I responded what an effort that seemed to be, how hard he keeps trying. He was able to connect in to a wish that maybe he could stop trying. His face lit up. 'Yes. That's right. I wish I could be left alone.' We explored this further and he realised that the pressure he was under was adding to the stress. He had been trying for 33 years and now it was time to not try. He was amazed that this could be the case. To have acknowledgement of all the effort he had been making and that perhaps enough was enough felt very liberating. I had not judged Peter or made suggestions about what to do. I had fully accepted his struggle and this showed him my unconditional positive regard for all he was experiencing.

For me this was a crucial moment in the therapy as I was aware I was also experiencing the despair that somehow there was something we needed to do in order to help him overcome the anxiety. Fortunately, in the moment, I was able to empathise with the experience of 'having to do' and this released Peter in to recognising how he would love to stop trying. It was a very powerful experience for him and for me as he had been struggling to achieve this for so long and if I had been defensive I may have missed that moment.

Seven stages of change

Session 4

Peter described his agitation again and revealed that in fact he was hardly ever with me in 'the room'; he was always 30 minutes ahead thinking about the drive home and how he would manage the junction and the traffic. He decided to try to be in the room for the rest of the session – and managed to engage with being in the here and now. At this stage of the therapy Peter was moving through the seven stages of change. He had been able to talk about his emotions, he was able to

(Continued)

(Continued)

empathise with others around him and he had expressed trust in the relationship. In this session he connected in to the importance of being in the here and now – in the present – and had recognised how rare it was that he achieved that.

Therapist congruence

Session 5

Peter seemed much happier but also spoke about his 'deep worry'. He spoke about a poem he had written. He had been affected by a relative's experience in the First World War and had shared his poem with a previous therapist. The therapist had said, 'Oh, you don't want to be thinking about that sort of thing.' Peter felt his poem had been discarded and undermined. The fact he risked telling me about his poetry at all was courageous. We looked at the courage he had shown and the family he had grown despite all the trauma and upset he had been through. I responded with how aware I was of how much he had achieved despite the appalling tragedy of his accident. Peter looked surprised. He had never viewed himself as having achieved anything before. I had been congruent by expressing directly to him what I perceived as a result of being in contact with him over these five weeks.

Actualising tendency

As the sessions continued Peter brought in more poems. I read them to him. He was able to connect to deep emotion and self-compassion as he listened back to his struggles and fears.

We talked about the possibility of publishing one of his poems. He had started writing poetry when he was in hospital. He had been unable to speak at all so someone had brought in a typewriter and he started expressing some of his thoughts as he recovered in the hospital bed. I contacted a colleague who published an e-magazine for friends of MIND and he was very happy to publish the poem.

One day, to his amazement, Peter had made a decision to go and visit a relative with his wife, a journey he had not made for a very long time. He felt that as there was not pressure on him he could make a decision to go. He asked me why I thought that, when he woke up at night, rather than worrying about everything he felt a deep sense of peace. We explored why that might be and he decided it was because he had been heard properly and that he no longer felt any pressure to get better.

Here it is clear that Peter's actualising tendency had been in process right from the start of his trauma. He had discovered that writing was very important and even at a time when it was most difficult, he had persevered. The fact he connected to the value of this in therapy is of great significance. It enabled him to discover self-worth that he had not considered or recognised before.

We agreed to finish therapy within the given number of sessions available through the NHS. Subsequently, Peter has continued writing. He has problems in his day-to-day life, but he continues to contribute poems to an e-magazine and is in touch with other poets.

CONCLUSION

The person–centred approach is a discipline that requires the therapist to pay great attention to how they respond to the client. It views each session as a unique experience, led by the client.

This approach inherently accepts that the client will find their unique way ahead if the conditions are present. Any person who is interested in the person–centred approach has to be prepared to be surprised, to be proven wrong about any precon- ceived ideas, to challenge their own prejudices and assumptions and to be open to learn as a result of each encounter.

ACKNOWLEDGEMENTS

The author wishes to thank Professor Stephen Joseph for his guidance whilst devel- oping this chapter, Dr David Murphy for his ceaseless encouragement, and Paul Wilkins and Pete Sanders for suggesting she wrote it.

REFERENCES

[1] Rogers, C. R. (1961) *On Becoming a Person*. London: Constable.
[2] Kirschenbaum, H. (2007) *The Life and Work of Carl Rogers*. Ross-on-Wye: PCCS Books.
[3] Rogers, C. R. (1978) *On Personal Power*. London: Constable.
[4] Joseph, S. and Worsley, R. (2005) *Person-Centred Psychopathology*. Ross-on-Wye: PCCS Books.
[5] Joseph, S. and Worsley, R. (2007) *Person-Centred Practice*. Ross-on-Wye: PCCS Books.
[6] Joseph, S. and Murphy, D. (2012) 'Person–centered approach, positive psychology and relational helping: building bridges', *Journal of Humanistic Psychology, 53(1)*, 26–51.
[7] Sanders, P. (2013) *The Tribes of the Person-Centred Nation*, 2nd edn. Ross-on-Wye: PCCS Books.
[8] Rogers, C. R. (1951) *Client-Centered Therapy*. Boston, MA: Houghton Mifflin.
[9] Rogers, C. R. (1957) 'The necessary and sufficient conditions of therapeutic personality change', *Journal of Consulting Psychology, 21(2)*, 95–103.
[10] Sanders, P. and Hill, A. (2014) *Counselling for Depression*. London: Sage.
[11] Rogers, C. R. (1957) 'The necessary and sufficient conditions of therapeutic personality change', *Journal of Consulting Psychology, 21(2)*, 95–103, esp. 95–6.
[12] Watson, N., Bryan, B. C. and Thrash, T. M. (2014) 'Change in self–discrepancy, anxiety, and depression in individual therapy', *Psychotherapy, 51(4)*, 525–34.
[13] Rogers, C. R. (1959) 'A theory of therapy, personality, and interpersonal relation- ships as developed in the client-centered framework', in S. Koch (ed.), *Psychology: A*

Study. of a Science, vol. 3: *Formulations of the Person and the Social Context*. New York: McGraw Hill. pp. 184–256.

[14] Elliott, R. and Westwell, G. (2012) Person–Centred & Experiential Psychotherapy Scale-10 (v. 1.2, 12/12/12). Reproduced in P. Sanders and A. Hill, *Counselling for Depression*. London: Sage. pp. 186–91.

[15] Mearns, D. and Thorne, B. (2013) *Person-Centred Counselling in Action*, 4th edn. London: Sage.

[16] Elliott, R. and Hill, A. (2014) 'Evidence-based practice and person–centred and experiential therapies', in P. Sanders and A. Hill, *Counselling for Depression*. London: Sage. pp. 5–20.

[17] Murphy, D. and Joseph, S. (2013) *Trauma and the Therapeutic Relationship*. Basingstoke: Palgrave Macmillan.

[18] Thorne, B. (2012) *Counselling and Spiritual Accompaniment*. Oxford: Wiley–Blackwell.

SUGGESTED READING

Mearns, D. and Thorne, B. (2013) *Person-Centred Counselling in Action*, 4th edn. London: Sage. This is a classic text in counselling literature and essential for all students of the approach.

Rogers, C. R. (1951) *Client-Centered Therapy*. Boston, MA: Houghton Mifflin. This is a core text and establishes the depth of research and breadth of thinking shared by Carl Rogers.

Rogers, C. R. (1961) *On Becoming a Person*. London: Constable. In this text Rogers writes personally and offers insight into the depth of sincerity and transparency he sought and offered.

Sanders, P. (2013) *The Tribes of the Person-Centred Nation*, 2nd edn. Ross-on-Wye: PCCS Books. This is an excellent contemporary introduction to the person-centred approach.

DISCUSSION POINTS

1. Does the person-centred approach match your values?
2. Do you consider experiencing distress is a disease like cancer is a disease?
3. Is it possible to grow emotionally as a result of distress?
4. If you train as a therapist is it necessary for you to receive counselling?

17

Primal Integration

John Rowan

INTRODUCTION

The word 'primal' means 'of the beginning' or 'of the origins'. The word 'integration' means 'making into one' or 'completing the whole'. Primal integration is an approach that takes seriously the possibility of dealing with personal problems in a fundamental way by going back to their origins. In this, of course, it is not unique; many different therapies say the same thing. But primal integration has an open-ended notion of how far back those origins might be. Some forms of therapy will only consider childhood. Others will also consider infancy. Primal integration also takes into account the process of birth, and the fetal life which preceded that.

There is a knowing inside each of us about what we need to do to become more whole and actualize our potential. This knowing is part of the power within us all, the spark of self that we need to acknowledge and nurture. There are various ways of getting in touch with this source of inner strength; some are spontaneous and some are guided. In primal integration we learn to trust the process and eventually to trust our own inner wisdom to guide us on our journey. Those of us who have been through this process have often experienced very special moments of revelation and transformation. This is a form of therapy which is about liberation rather than adjustment to the established norms of society.

Primal integration is based on a natural phenomenon that has been recognized and used for a long time. It is a creative letting go of conscious control of the body and emotions which opens up the unconscious to awareness. This allows both insights and healing to emerge. The body wants to heal, to release the tensions and pains it is holding inside. If this is done well, a real transformation can take place. Hence it is a form of therapy that is particularly good for people who have done some therapy before, and recognize the importance of this process of letting go of control. People who have done no therapy before tend to be too scared of the truth-telling effects of this process, but people who have some experience of therapy are more likely to recognize the necessity of facing and dealing with the truth, no matter how unpleasant it may be.

DEVELOPMENT OF THE THERAPY

Development of the therapy goes back to the early 1970s, when a number of people got together in the USA to form the International Primal Association. The founders included experienced therapists such as Bill Swartley, Tom Verny, Michael Broder and others. At the same time, Frank Lake, a pioneering psychiatrist in Britain, was making the same sort of discoveries. In 1966 he published a book called *Clinical Theology*, which included a number of very striking case histories – so much so, that they would probably not be allowed into print today, with the increasing timidity of publishers.

In the late 1970s Bill Swartley led training groups in England, and since then a number of people have been practising in this country. My own work has been written up in a chapter in the book I co-edited with Windy Dryden mentioned in 'Suggested reading' later on p. 203. One of the main developments has been the group work, which takes place at the Open Centre in London, under the very able guidance of Richard Mowbray and Juliana Brown (members of the Independent Practitioners Network), with assistance from Betty Hughes and others. All these were trained by Bill Swartley. They have written about their work in a book edited by David Jones.[1] At the same time, some very interesting work has been going on at the Amethyst Centre near Dublin, under the direction of practitioners Alison Hunter and Shirley Ward. They have made some very interesting contributions to the theory and practice of the work. Shirley Ward's collected papers were published by the Centre in 1992. In 1993 there appeared, again from the Amethyst Centre, *The Fractal Dimension of Healing Conception*, a paper and video presentation prepared for the 6th International Congress of the Pre and Perinatal Psychology Association of North America in Washington. This is a very important organization, which produces a quarterly peer-reviewed journal. In America there is active development of the practice in the International Primal Association (IPA), who hold yearly conferences and put on a number of other activities.

Another pioneer in Britain was William Emerson, also a member of the IPA, who spent a good deal of time in Europe. He had been trained as a clinician, and worked for some time in hospitals, but got more and more involved with **regression** and integration therapy. He also started calling his work primal integration, and was a quite separate source of influence in Europe. He pioneered the idea of actually working in a primal way with children, and produced a pamphlet on infant and child birth re-facilitation, and a video film of his work with them.

THEORY AND BASIC CONCEPTS

The theory says that the most difficult personal problems which need the attention of a therapist have their origins in early **trauma**, before the age of five years old, and will not be fundamentally resolved unless and until that origin is reached and dealt with. Some people do not believe that babies can remember their own birth, but there is good research and writing about these matters by people such as David Chamberlain,[2] a highly respected psychologist. The importance of early trauma is a very well established theory in psychotherapy, and is held by many people other than primal integration practitioners. Sigmund Freud, the originator of psychoanalysis, and Carl Jung, the great psychiatrist who followed him, certainly held to the theory, and so do such varied people as the body therapists and the hypnotherapists.

What tends to happen is that some very early event causes panic. This panic gives rise to a form of defence. This defence works sufficiently well at the time, and the person gets by for the moment. When the next emergency arises, panic is again dealt with by the same defence that worked before. But this defence then becomes part of the character structure of the person, and they are stuck with it. It gets to be too good. It protects all too effectively, cutting the person off from their real experience.

Because primal integration emphasizes early trauma, people sometimes think it will put all one's problems down to just one trauma, happening once in one's life. But of course traumas are seldom as dramatic as this. The commonest causes of mental distress are simply the common experiences of childhood – all the ways in which our child needs are unmet or frustrated. This is not necessarily a single trauma, in the sense of a one-off event; that is much too simplistic a view. Rather we would say, with the psychoanalyst Michael Balint,[3] that the trauma may come from a situation of some duration, where the same painful lack of 'fit' between needs and supplies is continued.

The goal of primal integration is to contact and release the real self. This is the part that was defended, and therefore is now surrounded by all the defences that were erected over the years. But it has remained intact behind all the layers of defence, and can be contacted in therapy, with rich results. It is interesting to see, in book after book and paper after paper, how people do not really change in any substantial way unless they go through some kind of therapeutic work at this deep level.

Historically, this approach is close to early Freud, the early work of psychoanalyst Wilhelm Reich (who placed great importance on the body being directly involved in therapy) and Arthur Janov (author of *The Primal Scream*). But all of these adopted a medical model of mental illness, which primal integration rejects. As the late Thomas Szasz, the great critic of formal psychotherapy, pointed out long ago, neurosis is only a metaphorical sickness, not a disease in the true sense of the word. Rather, primal integration stands with those who are less concerned with cure than with growth.

As soon as one gets down into the early roots of mental distress, deep and strong feelings come up, because the emotions of early life are less inhibited, less qualified and less differentiated than they later become. In other words, they are cruder and clearer. And so the whole question of the importance of **catharsis** in psychotherapy arises here. Catharsis means the expression of strong emotions. It was Reich and Fritz Perls (the originator of Gestalt therapy), not Janov, who discovered the techniques for deep emotional release that are used to produce primals. As many people now know, a primal is a deep emotional experience in which one gets in touch with the pain and terror of one's earliest bad experiences.

The Reichian-oriented therapist Charles Kelley used the term 'an intensive' years before Janov to describe experiences identical to primals.

It makes sense to say that catharsis has two related but separate components: one is cognitive (the thinking function) and relatively intellectual – the recall of forgotten material; the second is emotional and physical – the discharge of feel-ings in deep sobbing, strong laughter or angry yelling. But in the kind of work we are interested in here, it seems better to be more specific, and to say that catharsis is the vigorous expression of feelings about experiences that had been previously unavailable to consciousness. This lays more emphasis upon the necessity for the emergence of unconscious material.

What Bill Swartley, Frank Lake, Stanislav Grof (the great writer on the birth experience) and others did was to bring together the idea of catharsis and the emphasis on getting down to the origins of disturbance with another very important question – the **transpersonal** and the whole area of spirituality. This means that primal integration can deal with the major part of the whole psychospiritual spectrum mapped out by author Ken Wilber in his many books.[4] What Wilber is saying is that we are all on a psychospiritual journey, whether we like it or not, and whether we know it or not. We are moving from the pre-personal (infancy and childhood) through the per-sonal (adult life, language and logic) towards the transpersonal (which goes beyond conventional thinking and everyday taken-for-granted beliefs). I have written about this at greater length in my book *The Transpersonal: Spirituality in Psychotherapy and Counselling*.[5] I believe primal integration is the only therapy that can handle this whole spectrum, except possibly for the holonomic (law of the whole) approach described by Grof,[6] which is so close as to be almost the same thing.

Much of the thinking behind object relations (the very popular branch of psychoanalysis associated with the names of Donald Winnicott, Michael Balint, Harry Guntrip and others in Britain) is compatible with what we find in primal integration. This is because these theoreticians also hold the idea of a real self behind all the defences.

In my belief, primal integration is the fullest form of psychotherapy, because it covers all the four functions of which Jung spoke. It deals with the sensing func-tion through body work and breathing. It approaches the feeling function through emotional contact and release. It handles the thinking function by means of analysis and insight. And it deals with the intuiting function through guided fantasy, art work, dream work and so forth. In terms of the theory of Ken Wilber, it covers the pre-personal (early experience and child development), the personal (adult life in the here and now) and the transpersonal (spiritual experience and visions of the future). So it runs the whole gamut of human experience.

PRACTICE

The practice is based on the theory of Stanislav Grof,[6] which says that our experi-ence is organized into COEX systems. A COEX is a system of condensed experience whereby a certain pattern of physical sensations, emotional feelings, thoughtful ideas and spiritual impressions are held firmly together in the mind. This pattern comes from an experience we have had in the past. This experience, memorable and per-haps traumatic, sticks with us as a whole, not as a series of parts. When we come into a similar situation, it brings back the whole of that feeling in an exaggerated form, turning a whisper into a shout. This means that we are always meeting the same situation with the same reactions, the same defences.

So in therapy we may start with a recent experience of distress, such as being upset and angry with an authority figure. As the client is encouraged to express feelings of anger, etc., they may find the feelings really taking over. There is usually the sense of giving oneself permission to go with it. During that process, there may be a flash or vision from the past. In this case, it could be a parent figure and perhaps a memory scene. Then, if the client feels safe, he/she may re-experience a traumatic event and release the feelings from the past. A connection is made between that scene and the present. This generally releases the energy of the current situation and the client is able to function better. The more we can release our pent-up emotions, the more we can open to love and our own power within.

Now it is obvious that a procedure like this takes time, and it is really best to go all the way with a particular COEX in one session, rather than trying to take up the tail of one session at the head of the next, which usually doesn't work. This means that the primal integration therapist tends to prefer long sessions, which also enable the client to take a break or breather if need be during the session. I personally conduct some one-hour sessions, but I also have some one-and-a-half-hour, hour, and two-hour sessions; some people working in this area have used up to 10-hour sessions. The process is basically self-directed, so that each person will open up and progress at their own pace. This maintains safety and also provides support for those who are not ready or willing to go into the deeper parts of their psyche.

It is important to say, however, that all of this is primal integration, not primal trauma integration. It is not the intention to hive off traumas (bad and unforgettable experiences), and deal only with those. Whatever we do by way of therapy is part of an attempt to do justice to the whole of life, not just part of it. As Juliana Brown and Richard Mowbray[7] have said well, it is about 'continually bringing a deeper way of living into being, and a deeper way of being into living'.

The work of Frank Lake, which is extremely important, is now being carried on by the Bridge Foundation, which is at present running training courses in primal integration.

Important research in primal integration was done by Ninoska Marina,[8] who found that it was particularly effective in dealing with such problems as relating to people, relating to oneself, having more energy and enjoying sex. The researcher found that people tended to discover 'a sense of self different to what it had been in the pre-therapy period'. This is a radical change, and not everyone is ready for this. So primal integration is a form of depth psychology, and needs to be taken in that light as something to tackle when we feel ready. In this process people open themselves up to deeper feelings, and thus become more vulnerable. So a high degree of trust has to be built up between client and therapist. But in reality, trust is not a feeling, it is a decision. Nobody can ever prove, in any final or decisive way, that they are worthy of this trust, so the client just has to take the decision at some time, and it may as well be sooner as later.

If we believe, as Michael Broder (one of the earliest theorists of primal integration) suggests, that the primal process consists of five phases – Commitment; Abreaction (catharsis); Insight (involving the restructuring of thoughts and feelings); Counter-action (fresh behaviour in the world); and Pro-action (making real changes) – then it must be the case that the later phases are just as important as the earlier ones. In other words, working through is just as significant as breaking through. The glamorous part, and the controversial part, of our work is the 'primal', the cathartic breakthrough; but in reality the process of integration is necessary and equally exciting in its quieter way. For example, it is a great thing for a man to get to the cathartic point of forgiving his mother; it is another thing for him to start treating women decently in daily life, as a result of this.

One of the things that happens in primal work is that the deeper people go in recession and regression, the more likely they are to have spiritual experiences too. Shirley Ward of the Amethyst Centre in Ireland believes this is because the psychic centres open up. In other words, people get in touch with the higher unconscious, what the great Italian theorist Roberto Assagioli called the superconscious. However, in this area there is one very common error we have to guard against. Grof points out that blissful womb states, which primal clients sometimes get into, are very similar to peak experiences and to the cosmic unity that mystics speak of as contact with the Divine. This has led some people, like David Wasdell (of the Unit for Research into Changing Institutions), for example, into saying that all mystical experiences are nothing but reminiscences of the ideal or idealized womb. This is an example of reductionism, that is, of always trying to reduce what is complex to what is simpler. The whole point is that we repress not only dark or painful material in the lower unconscious, but also embarrassingly good material in the higher unconscious. John Firman and Ann Gila[9] of the psychosynthesis school founded by Assagioli have written an important theoretical work on this subject.

WHICH CLIENTS BENEFIT MOST?

The ideal client is someone who has been in other forms of therapy that have introduced them to the basic ideas of working on themselves and exploring things at an unconscious level. Primal integration is really very effective with such basic problems as depression and anxiety. These are the most common presenting issues for therapists of all persuasions today. It is also suitable for more immediate matters, such as panic disorders, grief, rage, sexual abuse, rape, incest and the like. It can deal much better than most other approaches with pre-verbal traumas, issues around birth and pre-birth experiences, abandonment, rejection and other problems that are much more serious and troubling. These are some of the hardest issues for clients to work with, express, feel and release.

Because of its concern with the whole person in the social context, primal integration is also able to pay attention to such things as sexism and racism. Sometimes people's problems come from outside, not from inside. Any adequate therapy must be able to handle this fact. We have to be able to listen with the fourth ear of political awareness as well as with the third ear of emotional awareness.

In reality, every problem has two components: the one has to do with the real situation as it exists in the everyday world, the consensus reality in which we all live. The other has to do with our own private reactions and responses to the world, which may be based on old tapes from the past, still playing in the present. In therapy we can handle the second of these two, and deal with whatever may be unrealistic or detrimental about that. Then when we have done that, the real situation will still remain, but we shall have greater strength and ability to deal with it in the best way possible, because we shall not be fighting against ourselves.

CASE STUDY
The Client

This is the case of Heidi, a 40-year-old school teacher. She came to me complaining of having such severe depression that she had had to give up work. Her doctor had given her a certificate and some tablets. She was crying a great deal, and also had a lot of anger with her sexual partner, with whom she was also breaking up with at the same time.

At first all I had to do was to let her cry. She needed nurturing and mothering, and I just listened to her and at times held her in my arms. What came out was that she had been taking on more and more duties at work – it seemed that she was a very good and well-liked teacher, who found it hard to say no when interesting projects came up. She had ignored her own needs and thought only of doing a good job and making people happy.

At the same time she had for some years been having a sexual relationship with a man, which had been a great strain. He had another woman, and when choices had to be made it seemed that the other woman took priority. At various times he had talked about leaving the other woman, but Heidi had now come to the conclusion that he was never going to do so, and that this was an unsatisfactory relationship for her, even though she could not help still being attracted to him. She had spent a lot of time trying to work out a three-way relationship. They had all wanted to be 'alternative', and she had not, as it were, wished them bad weather; she often thought they had agreed to something, but then had felt betrayed by some action of theirs. She had desperately wanted to do justice to both people, but as of now she had run out of energy for it. So she was deeply disappointed about that, too. Every time she thought about making a final break with him she would look round her house and see all the things he had helped to make – he had been of such practical help to her. There were a whole lot more very complex feelings, too, which came out later.

It seemed that the combination of these two strains had just become too much for her. It was made worse by the fact that both her lover and the other woman were teachers in the same school, so that she had to see him quite frequently and her, a bit less often, in the normal course of the day.

The Therapy

Heidi became extremely sensitive to any suggestion that she might go back to work. Her self-esteem had sunk to a very low ebb. The school policy was to

(Continued)

(Continued)

give generous sick leave to senior teachers, so this was an ideal opportunity to do some deep work on herself. We started off with two-hour sessions once a week, and after two months moved to one-hour sessions twice a week, and after another month to one hour once a week; this latter lasted for a month. The rationale for this was that at first there was a great deal of distress, and the two-hour sessions were very good for dealing with this, giving time for the client to come up from the very deep levels she was getting into. Later there was less distress, and so we could proceed in a more considered and chosen fashion, deciding what needed to be done and doing it as expeditiously as possible. Later again it was more a question of just tidying up the remaining loose ends and working through any new problems quite quickly.

After the first few meetings, the energy seemed to settle mainly around her father. He had died before she was born, at the end of the Second World War, but her mother had not known this for sure until she was two years old. During that time her mother had been distressed, anxious and impatient, and seemed to have passed on to her in some way the feeling 'Is he or isn't he?' (This was very similar to the feeling she had about her lover – is he or isn't he with me?) Her grandfather had stepped in and allowed the two of them to stay with him until Heidi's mother remarried, when Heidi was six years old. This grandfather was sensitive, intelligent, worldly-wise but in some ways innocent, and very devoted to the two of them. He taught Heidi many things and spoiled her, telling her she was wonderful and very clever.

But her father, though absent, had been more important for her. She had idealized him as a child, and thought of him as a hero. She had to live up to his expectations and do him credit. She did do well at school, and passed all her examinations with flying colours, first at school and then at the university. In her present job she had always had the feeling of doing well, and had been given special projects and extra responsibility.

It was then we discovered one of the points we often come across in therapy – it is the things we like that stop us developing, much more than the things we dislike. As we went deeper and deeper into Heidi's memories about her father, we found that she had taken on board as an absolute injunction that she must live up to his expectations. Even when she fought against this, and did things she knew he would not have approved of, she had to do them perfectly, so as to be able to face him. It would be too much to do something of her own and then find that she had to face his disappointment. So her job had become a challenge to him – a challenge she could never meet, because he could always raise the standard in a way that left her powerless.

It was clear at this point that her father had turned into an internal persecutor. She had turned him into an implacable and impossible figure, very close to what Freud called the superego, Perls called the top dog, Jung called the father complex, and so on. As she became more and more aware of this, so her emotions started to become deeper and more engaged, I encouraged her to stay with these feelings and really experience them, rather in the manner that Mahrer calls 'carrying forward the potentials for experiencing'.[10] The emotions became more and more primal in their intensity. Suddenly when she was talking directly to her father on the other cushion, a wave of primal rage came over her, and she said 'I don't have to please you any more!' I encouraged her to repeat this phrase with more and more intensity, until she went into a powerful catharsis, and then collapsed. I covered her up and watched over her until she recovered enough to leave.

In the following session a great weight seemed to have fallen off her shoulders. She came in smiling, and said 'I didn't really believe in all that therapy stuff, but now you've convinced me.' She was able to talk about visiting her parents abroad for a holiday, getting a new job, having a friend over to visit and going on a psychosynthesis weekend.

She found it much easier now to express her anger towards her ex-lover, with whom she had now definitely parted. Although she was still attracted to him, and found the whole issue a painful one, the degree of pain was now much more bearable. Getting clear in one area made it much easier to get clear in the other.

It is important not to lay too much stress on this one incident, of course. There were at least four other factors that had made this breakthrough possible: the previous course of the therapy, which prepared the way for this act and made it seem natural; a change in medication, which meant that she was less drowsy, more alert than before; some autogenic training (involving full relaxation), which made her better able to be present in the here and now; and a stay with a friend who had looked after her with a lot of care. Heidi began to talk about going back to work, but still genuinely could not face the twin threat of the work and the lover. So the therapy turned more on to the problems around him, which turned out to be very complex. But in the end, Heidi was able to breathe more easily and take back nearly all of her illusions and projections on to him.

This case was very suitable to illustrate this chapter, even though it does not bring out the full holonomic process; because it was quite short and concentrated, the main lines are not lost in a mass of detail. We have the initial presenting problem – quite a complex mixture of work and private life; we have the gradual focusing upon one issue, always going by the client's energy and directions; we have the resolution of that issue in a cathartic experience; we have the working out of the complex relationship with a lover; and we have the progressive working out of the practical matters which then emerged.

Factors in the success of the case

A number of factors helped to make this case a success. First Heidi had a good friend, Victoria, who spent a lot of time with her, simply listening to her and comforting her and telling her she was OK. We find that the support network of a person can be quite crucial in allowing the client to get the most out of their therapy. In fact, Swartley often said that the 'second-chance family', which is often found in intensive primal integration groups, could be a highly significant

(Continued)

(Continued)

element in the process of therapy. The fact that Victoria could provide just such a second-chance family, allowing Heidi to regress almost to a baby stage and then grow up, was in my opinion of inestimable benefit.

Second, the fact that Heidi had very good employers, who were willing to support her for three months while she worked out her problems, and who were then prepared to lose her without any criticism, was also of great value. She did not take this for granted, but appreciated it very much as a gift.

Third, the fact that the man she had been with did not pester her or burden her or make life difficult was very helpful. There were certainly occasions when he did suggest coming round or going out with her again, but not in a way that put great pressure on her.

Fourth, her mother and stepfather held open house and were very supportive when she wanted to take a holiday with them. The fact that they lived in another country probably helped to make the holiday she took even more refreshing and different for her.

It is very important to recognize these factors and the part they played. Therapists sometimes write as if therapy sessions were the whole of life, or at least most of it, and of course this is never so. The everyday life of the client can be immensely influential in helping or hindering the kind of work a client needs to do in therapy. And it is everyday life which lasts when therapy is over.

REFERENCES

[1] Jones, D. (ed.) (1994) *Innovative Therapy: A Handbook*. Buckingham: Open University Press.

[2] Chamberlain, D. (1998) *The Mind of Your Newborn Baby*. Berkeley, CA: North Atlantic Books.

[3] Balint, M. (1968) *The Basic Fault*. London: Tavistock.

[4] Wilber, K. (1996) *The Atman Project*, 2nd edn. Wheaton: Quest.

[5] Rowan, J. (1993) *The Transpersonal Spirituality in Psychotherapy and Counselling*. London: Routledge.

[6] Grof, S. (1992) *The Holotropic Mind*. San Francisco, CA: Harper.

[7] Brown, J. and Mowbray, R. (1994) 'Primal integration', in D. Jones (ed.), *Innovative Therapy: A Handbook*. Buckingham: Open University Press.

[8] Marina, N. (1982) 'Restructuring of cognitive–affective structure: a central point of change after psychotherapy', unpublished doctoral thesis, Brunei University.

[9] Firman, J. and Gila, A. (1997) *The Primal Wound*. Albany, NY: State University of New York Press.

[10] Mahrer, A. R. (1986) *Therapeutic Experiencing: The Process of Change*. New York: W. W. Norton.

SUGGESTED READING

Blum, T. (ed.) (1993) *Prenatal Perception, Learning and Bonding.* Berlin: Leonardo Publishers. Fifteen articles by different writers, including an excellent chapter by David Chamberlain on 'Prenatal intelligence'. Quite academic and professional.

Chamberlain, D. (1998) *The Mind of Your Newborn Baby.* Berkeley, CA: North Atlantic Books. A very full and professional book, with many research references.

Noble, E. (1993) *Primal Connections: How Our Experiences from Conception to Birth Influence Our Emotions, Behavior and Health.* New York: Simon & Schuster. A personal book using much material from Elizabeth Noble's work with the late Graham Farrant, a pioneer of working with primal material. Makes many fascinating points.

Rowan, J. (1988) 'Primal integration', in J. Rowan and W. Dryden (eds), *Innovative Therapy in Britain.* Milton Keynes: Open University Press. A fairly full account of primal work in action, paying attention to both the theory and the practice.

DISCUSSION ISSUES

1. Is there conscious experience in the womb?
2. Is there such a thing as the trauma of birth?
3. Can anyone remember their own birth?
4. Can therapy in the present undo the experiences of childhood?

18

Psychosynthesis

Jean Hardy and Diana Whitmore

Psychosynthesis is a psychology that addresses not only human problems but also our potential. While few ever reach their potential, in the searching we can learn to live our lives more fully. Psychosynthesis therefore has an optimistic view of the human race, but it is not a new approach. It is based on thousands of years of consideration of what people are truly like, both in the West and in the East.

Psychosynthesis is a spiritual, or **transpersonal** psychotherapy. It has been called 'a psychology with a soul'. A core principle is that we share an inner wisdom and a transcendent nature that is common to all peoples, but is often unrecognized in the modern world, particularly in our rushed and materialistic societies. It is the function of the psychosynthesis therapist to respect the spirit within and to know that any person can find the answers to his or her own problems from within, with non-invasive guidance. Therapy is therefore gentle and creative, using art, guided imagery and visualization, autobiography and reflection.

DEVELOPMENT OF THE THERAPY

The roots of psychosynthesis are deep in the past. Roberto Assagioli, its founder, lived from 1888 to 1974. He was an Italian psychiatrist, born in Florence, that most Renaissance of cities, and he was deeply influenced by the transpersonal awareness of its historical background, its arts and writing – including Dante's *The Divine Comedy*, which is a major inspiration for his therapeutic work. His family became involved with theosophy around the turn of the nineteenth to twentieth centuries, and he too was influenced by Eastern as well as Western thought in his understanding of the nature of the person. He was Jewish and it is possible to see the wisdom of the Kabbalah in his psychosynthesis model.

Assagioli met both Freud and Jung at the early International Conferences of psychotherapy at the beginning of the twentieth century. Sympathetic with the Jungian approach, he believed there is a coherence between the spirit of the universe and all living creatures, including humans: that we all are our true selves when we are born within that spirit – though of course we often lose touch with our truth, the higher self, in many ways. His basic vision of the nature of the person contains a possibility of each of us finding our own potential, becoming the unique truth we are meant to be. And within this, there is a bigger vision for the human race, our relationship with the earth and her creatures as an intrinsic part of the living universe.

Because of this width of vision and inspiration, increasingly graduates of the psychosynthesis training become therapists not only on a one-to-one basis. Some work in organizations where the skills acquired are relevant to group process, group conflicts, community living: the skills then include mentoring as well as therapy. Others create individual businesses relevant to compassionate services to do with health or welfare – for instance there is a funeral business whose compassionate approach is deeply based in the psychosynthesis training of the owners: and 'Teens and Toddlers' have worked for many years with young children and young adults in Central London. Books and dissertations increasingly study the wider social and natural world as well as the human psyche.

THEORY AND BASIC CONCEPTS

Psychosynthesis has a well-worked out theory about human nature, about who we are. This is represented by what is called the 'egg-shaped diagram', thus:

1. The lower unconscious
2. The middle unconscious
3. The higher unconscious
4. The field of consciousness
5. The 'I'
6. The higher self or soul
7. The collective unconscious

In this representation (see Figure 18.1), 4 is the field of our consciousness, in other words, the way we experience our daily lives. It is all the things we are immediately aware of. For many people this field of consciousness seems to be the whole of life. But, as most depth psychologists in this century believe, human beings live in a depth of unconsciousness too, that which influences our lives but of which we are most often unaware. The rest of the diagram is about unconscious forces: 2 is the middle, 1 the lower, 3 the higher and 7 the collective unconscious.

We can reach the middle unconscious in ourselves relatively easily. It comprises dreams, memories of past times and the deeper processes within us that are more accessible and of which we may be partially aware. It is where the line between the everyday world and the inner world is least well defined. The lower unconscious is the area first investigated by Freud: deep past material, childhood experience, trauma that has been covered up. It is here that we meet our many defensive strategies, perhaps ways of being cut off, or perhaps depressions, that we have used most of our lives to keep painful or disturbing material in some kind of control.

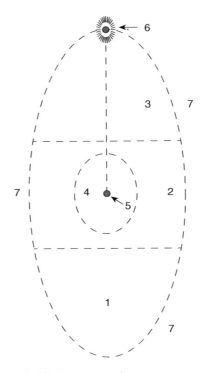

FIGURE 18.1   *Assagioli's model of the human psyche*

However, we are often as unaware of our great potential as we are of our deep problems. Psychosynthesis has a picture of the higher unconscious of which we can catch glimpses from time to time – of joy, of unity with the whole of life, of love, of beauty – that overwhelm us and place our lives in a much wider perspective. These glimpses, like those of all unconscious material, can either be ignored and suppressed, or accepted and embraced. Through psychosynthesis therapy we can begin to recognize and then relate to all that we truly are, often uncovered from within those forces that affect our behaviour and actions of which we are largely unaware.

Both Jung and Assagioli also postulated a collective unconscious, that which we share in as members of our culture and race, of our gender, of nationality and as members of the whole human race. The view is that we carry these memories as much collectively as we do individually. In the twentieth century, for instance, most people in the West would carry with them at an unconscious level much knowing about the two world wars beyond what actual information they had about these wars. Now, in this century, we might feel that our unconscious influences are ecological – a sense that we are collectively part of the amazing story of the whole universe and all the plants and animals within it. With the growing recognition of the interdependence of all life, few of us remain shut off from the experiences of the world we are a part of. The permeable lines in the diagram indicate there is movement within and between all the parts of who we are.

The diagram, however, is about more than this. The T (5 in the diagram) is that part of ourselves which is the observer, which has always been present. When we feel 'together', centred, we are aware of the T but we can easily lose that awareness when swayed, disturbed and disorientated, which may be much of the time. In learning to become more centred we can more easily access the last part of the picture, 6, the higher self, or soul, which is all we may be not only as an individual, but also as a full part of the living web of life. Together, 5 and 6 are the process of living an aware, fully alive life, seeing life as a journey that makes sense. The higher self represents our fully alive being, that we can often glimpse through the higher unconscious, but which is fully aware. It is when we live out life most fully in the way we feel we are all meant to. As Marianne Williamson writes, 'we were all meant to shine as children do'.[1]

One part of Assagioli's picture of the person is not on the diagram. It is the concept that we all consist of many **subpersonalities**. The clown, the frightened child, the critic, the witch, the king, the mystic and the hermit are all possible components of one person. We each have our own array of them. These subpersonalities or characteristics are formulated by our life experiences and the strategies we employ to cope in times of trouble.

Though the diagram is necessarily static, the process in which we are involved is not so. Problems may erupt from any part of ourselves; subpersonalities get out of hand and take over, depressions and isolations emerge from the past, life crises potentially bring new awareness, or a feeling may arise of dissatisfaction because life seems less than it could be. Our lives, if they are to be satisfactory, cannot stay still. The psychosynthesis journey is a movement towards ever-greater awareness, learning to recognize the whole orchestra that we are, even the quiet triangles stuck away at the back and the out-of-rhythm drums. Learning also to recognize the conductor, who is the T, by which we manage that orchestra and therefore play more in tune, is an important part of that journey. We may even change the music through a realization of the higher self.

The task of the psychosynthesis therapist is to help his or her client get in touch with their own wisdom, at whatever stage of this journey they are. This is a lifetime process. The work does not impose any particular belief system on a client. A therapist will work with the beliefs that any person already holds or is reaching towards. Always the movement is towards the inclusion of the elements in the person that have been ignored and that are now causing problems. Always the work is towards more wholeness.

PRACTICE

Goals of psychosynthesis

Assagioli recognized two levels of psychosynthesis therapy which are necessary and indeed core to an individual's psychological health and spiritual wellbeing: *personal* psychosynthesis, which aims to foster the development of a well-integrated personality, capable of actualizing itself through the individual's life; and *transpersonal* psychosynthesis, which offers the possibility of realizing one's deepest, most essential self and its purpose in life.

The goals of psychosynthesis work could be summed up as the redemption of suffering and the evocation of potential in the client. It seeks to evoke our strengths and latent potential, to foster integration between our inner and outer worlds, to enable us to increasingly create our life as one that is rich with meaning and purpose, to enhance the quality of life and finally to enable us to find our own inner authority and wisdom.

Psychosynthesis does not hold a 'normative' view of **psychospiritual** health nor of what the client's process of therapy *should be* like. Instead, supreme importance is placed upon the individual's experience of inner freedom and upon gaining mastery over his or her own universe. A goal is to help clients enlarge their possibilities and choices in life.

The therapeutic relationship

Psychosynthesis holds that the human relationship is both core and essential to psychospiritual health and wellbeing. This principle forms the context and centrepiece of psychosynthesis therapy, with the relationship between client and therapist being foremost as well as sacred. Current research has shown that the quality of the human relationship has an important influence in determining the outcome of therapeutic work. Without a *bifocal vision*, one that sees both the light and the shadow in clients, and without a context that perceives the client as essentially much more than his or her problems, challenges and weaknesses the therapeutic relationship would be limited and incomplete.

The heart of psychosynthesis work is based on an 'I–Thou relationship', in which the therapist fosters the strengths and potentialities of the client. The psychosynthesis therapist seeks to perceive the client as ultimately a self, a being, who has a purpose in life and has challenges and obstacles to meet in order to fulfil that purpose. The psychosynthesis therapist will relate to the client in a less mysterious and detached manner than classical analysis, and will seek to build a relational context that is holistic and healing.

Transference

The concepts of transference and counter-transference, the centrepiece of conventional analytic forms of therapy, are also an essential part of the psychosynthesis therapeutic relationship, but not the whole picture. Traditionally, transference is seen to be a 'playing out', with the therapist, of one's early relationships with parents or significant others. The client projects on to the therapist characteristics that he or she has in the past attributed to parents, and relates to the therapist with similar attitudes, behaviour patterns and emotional responses. Although Assagioli agreed with this Freudian definition and included it in psychosynthesis therapy, he stressed some essential differences in the importance placed on it and the strategy for working with it.

Assagioli *reframed* the concept of transference as a healthy thrust in the individual to complete a Gestalt, finish **unfinished business** regarding our intimate relationships (of which parents are our first models) and to heal childhood trauma. This thrust is a part of the individual's continuing search for unity, to belong and be included in the universe. It is a response to the separation, alienation and isolation that many have experienced in childhood and represents an unconscious desire to heal the past. The therapeutic relationship offers a laboratory of sorts for us to work through these issues and learn to be intimate with another human being. If we learn to do this in the safe arena of therapy, we are learning skills for also doing so in life. The therapist helps the client evolve towards a more meaningful resolution of the transference by finding healthier, less dysfunctional ways of relating.

How does the therapist do this? In psychosynthesis therapy the goal is to dissolve the transference 'as it emerges' in the relationship. In the safety and contained environment of the therapeutic relationship, we will naturally and spontaneously experience ourselves regressing to more childlike states. We temporarily become dependent upon this person who accepts us unconditionally, mirrors to us that we are valuable and worthwhile, and supports us in dealing with childhood conflict and trauma. There is nothing pathological in this. The therapist will be watchful of the client regressing and relating to him or her in a more childlike manner, which signals the existence of transference.

With many clients, as the personal relationship becomes stronger, the transference will gradually lose its power and will resolve itself developmentally as we endure a process of maturation from child to adolescent to adult. It is often a matter of just letting it take its course. This is in accordance with the view of Perls, who believed that the client will relate to the therapist as he or she related to parents, and depending on how well the therapist is able to hold and respond to this challenge, the client may go through a process of development.[2]

At any point along this journey, the psychosynthesis therapist may address and work with the transference with the client. This may occur through *intrapsychic* techniques, that is through consciously addressing the client's childhood and parental relationships, or *interpersonal* with attention being paid to the patterns of relating that are currently revealing themselves between client and therapist. Intrapsychic work with transference involves the client getting to know his or her own inner child. After all, it is this inner child who is transferring and who is seeking to become whole. The therapist's goal is for the client to know this wounded inner child intimately and eventually to provide, from her own inner resources, the wise parenting that every child deserves but seldom has. This builds the client's capacity for self-nurturing as well as independence and has a great impact on the transference.

Working interpersonally with the transference involves bringing the quality, the reality, the behaviour patterns that are being re-enacted in the therapeutic relationship into the foreground, so at least the therapist must be aware of it, respond to it, but ideally the client too needs to become conscious of the perhaps childish, obsolete and dysfunctional way he or she is responding. With awareness comes the opportunity for change. It is the therapist's task to create the environment in which the client can learn more mature and healthy ways of relating.

Counter-transference

Therapists are not immune from the relationship with the client evoking their past childhood patterns of relating and responding. Therapists must look within themselves for their own affective responses to clients. Transference cannot be addressed without looking at the counter-transference. Two people are involved in this relationship and both must learn to come to healthy intimacy. In addition, therapists will be unable to serve the client truly if their vision and perception of the client is obscured by their own psychological material.

The therapist must use discrimination and self-knowledge to monitor his or her responses and ways of relating to the client. For instance, if the client feels judged, the therapist must examine whether this might actually be happening through the counter-transference. How will the therapist respond to the moment in every therapeutic relationship when the client needs to assert his or her own **identity** and not conform or cooperate with the therapist's interventions? Will the therapist merely respond in the *same old ways* that the client experienced in the past and collude with the transference?

Some, but not necessarily all, of the counter-transference may stem from an earlier part of the therapist's life. However, it may also be an authentic human response to the client and not be judged as inappropriate. The therapist may also be sensing and feeling some of the affect that the client is unable to access in his or herself (projective identification). The therapist needs to become aware of 'blind spots' and historically repetitive behaviour patterns in his or her way of relating to the client.

The transpersonal context of psychosynthesis therapy trains the therapist to develop the ability to perceive the client as an inviolable being with immense potential. If this perception is lost, it is imperative for the therapist to ascertain and confront that in him- or herself which is inhibiting the process.

The process of change

As previously mentioned, in psychosynthesis we do not follow normative definitions of what healthy human functioning *should* be like. There are no ultimate truths, no recipes to follow, but rather, the client is held as a unique unfolding self, aspiring for meaning and purpose. Furthermore, the client's challenges, problems and presenting issues are seen as intimately connected with this journey and not merely the result of inadequacy, childhood conditioning or wounding.

Psychosynthesis acknowledges that all human states and experiences are valid in their own right, valuable moments that have something to offer and which contain the opportunity for growth or learning. Life is a journey and not a destination. Consequently, whatever the existential moment contains for the client is worth accepting, embracing and hopefully learning from. The process of change for an individual is not predictable.

What is guaranteed is that the process of change will include moments of darkness and despair to be faced; moments of joy and beauty to be embraced; there is an unknown to be allowed with no guarantees of security; disintegration may be necessary before integration. There will be times when we cooperate with this life process and our therapy will be creative and fruitful. On the other hand there will be times when we resist, rebel and try to suppress this very human condition. The process of change requires the full acknowledgement of the human condition and acceptance of the journey.

Basic strategies

The psychosynthesis therapist's first highly valued strategy for working with a client is to both encourage and allow the client to 'lead the way'. Consequently there is no set format which a psychosynthesis session would typically follow. Initially the therapist wants to learn what the client's history is, what difficult issues and challenges are being faced and, equally importantly, the way the client envisions the therapy going, what their goals are and what outcome they aspire to. This strategy (if it can be called one) evokes the client's own motivation for change and empowers him or her to commit to a forward direction. Then when the going gets rough, as it inevitably does as we face our own humanity, this motivation can be drawn upon.

Another strategy of the therapist for working through tenacious and difficult life issues is to address them on three complementary levels: the past, the present and the future. Our psychological history often contains the apparent roots of a problem or life issue. Therapeutic work may require us to delve into the experiences from our childhood that contributed to or sometimes created the problem in the first place. However, the client is experiencing these concerns in the present existential moment, which is often the starting place. How the client experiences the problem, when, where and with whom, needs to be consciously addressed. Both levels of work are common to most forms of therapeutic work.

Psychosynthesis therapy adds a third level of inquiry, that of the future. By future we mean the creative potential contained within the problem, the possibility for the resolution of this issue to help the client evolve further on their life journey. In fact, we hypothesize that something 'new' is trying to be born for this client through the problem – there is a creative possibility immanent within the difficulty.

For example, the client's presenting issue may be that she is afraid to take risks in her life. The therapist's strategy will be to offer the client the opportunity to address the three levels mentioned above. First there might be an exploration of how the client experiences being unable to take risks presently, in what areas of her life she has the opportunity to do so and how she experiences emotionally and mentally her fear and resistance to doing so. This process may evoke memories from childhood where the client was unsuccessful with risk-taking and probably got hurt while trying to do so. Certain past relationships, such as with an authoritarian punishing figure, may have contributed to her inhibition. But equally importantly, the therapist may seek what qualities and strengths the client will cultivate through learning to take risks. How will it serve her to deal with this? What steps forward in her life will it enable her to take? What is the progressive context here in which the client can experience herself and make choices?

Basic techniques

The psychosynthesis approach is primarily pragmatic and existential. Although the overall goals and perspective may be similar among psychosynthesis practitioners, the methods they use may vary considerably. These will include relaxation, concentration, catharsis, critical analysis, psychological journal, subpersonality work, Gestalt dialogue, body movement, ideal models, symbolic art work and free drawing, mental imagery and the use of symbols, meditation, creative expression, inner dialogue and self-identification.

As the therapeutic relationship is central to psychosynthesis therapy it consequently uses the human interaction and traditional active dialogue as a ground for the work. Assagioli recommended first starting with a technique he called critical analysis. Critical analysis is a dialogue method that can be used to expand the client's self-knowledge, assess blocks and obstacles as well as creative potentials, and initiate an exploration of the unconscious in order to discover the 'history' of the client's issues. Psychological journal-keeping is another technique to achieve the same purpose and encourages the client to reflect subjectively. Early on, many psychosynthesis practitioners will invite the client to write an autobiography. This stimulates the unconscious and evokes awareness and understanding.

Active dialogue, psychological journal-keeping and autobiographical work can go a long way towards understanding psychological problems. Self-knowledge and awareness in itself can be healing and transformative. However, for many psychological issues the cognitive aspect needs to be complemented with *experiential* techniques designed to evoke and explore deeper levels of the unconscious.

Experiential work has the value of engaging the client on different levels when addressing an issue: the physical, the emotional, the imaginative and the mental. A psychosynthesis therapist might use a variety of practical experiential techniques. Among those most commonly used are the following.

Mental imagery work

Images and symbols are the language of the unconscious. The imagination follows no rules of reality. Mental imagery work provides the client with a means of getting in touch with deeper levels of his or her unconscious in order to expand awareness and move towards change. The client's deep inner reality may be revealed in symbolic form through the use of imagery and visualization. For example, the client can evoke an imaginative image for her fear as well as recall a past experience where she felt that fear. The process can even be taken further with the use of the imagination to allow the symbols to change and transform or by evoking an image of what needs to happen in order to heal the fear. The therapist may also invite the client to empower her images with speech and movement. We can get to know a part of ourselves, say the 'frightened child', by getting an image for it and imaginatively dialoguing with that image. This type of experiential work facilitates the process of change.

Mental imagery and visualization can also be used to 'reprogramme' the uncon-scious, that is, to recondition the psyche with images that are developmental and positive. The client can be offered selective images that set in motion chosen psy-chological processes such as a flower blossoming or a tree with its roots firmly in the ground, which evoke the corresponding affective state.

Disidentification and self-identification

This is an experiential technique that is central to psychosynthesis therapy. It is based on the principle that firstly it is essential that we allow ourselves to experience 'what is' for us, be that feelings of fear, anger, resentment. We all live much of our lives unconsciously identified with emotional states. These states then give us a sense of identity. If we are feeling insecure, we imagine that we *are* an insecure person, or when an unacceptable emotion like anger surfaces, we cling to our preferred identi-fication as a good 'nice' person, rejecting the anger. A basic tenet of psychosynthesis is that we are dominated by everything with which our self is identified. In a sense we are enslaved by a limited consciousness and we lose accessibility to the rest of our personality. This means that we lose the richness and resources of the rest of our being.

The disidentification technique allows us to recognize, own and accept these iden-tifications and then to experience that we are more than them. It allows us to detach ourselves consciously from various aspects of our personality. This leads to a deeper sense of personal identity, the 'I', and equips us with both self-awareness and choice. It enhances our inner freedom and capacity to regulate our lives and their expression.

As stated by Diana Whitmore,[3] this technique can be used in two ways. The ther-apist can encourage the client to learn the skill of being able to *disidentify* from limiting identities, beliefs, attitudes, behaviours, emotions or roles. For example, a client with a distorted self-image can become aware of the limiting impact this has on her life and *choose* to identify with her gifts and talents. Having the psychological skill to disidentify, the client can expand her perspective and create a more stable sense of identity. After disidentifying comes the possibility of choosing to identify with one's more stable sense of identity, which is the first step towards experience of our deeper self.

WHICH CLIENTS BENEFIT MOST?

Psychosynthesis can be practised as a form of brief therapy or as a long-term depth psychotherapy. It adapts itself to the needs and goals of the client which are often determined in the initial interview and the process of assessment and diagnosis. The potential client's own self-assessment and vision of what they would like from the work is an essential component in determining whether psychosynthesis therapy is appropriate for that individual.

Counselling and psychotherapy is today increasingly losing its 'stigma' of being primarily indicated for those individuals who are unwell and unable to function in their life and in society. With the stress of our modern life, with the breakdown of the nuclear family, with the social problems we face, more and more people are recognizing the need to turn inward, understand and deeply know themselves better. It is undeniable that many today experience life as lacking in meaning and purpose and are consequently depressed or feel isolated and alienated. Psychosynthesis work has proven itself to be highly effective with these issues and this type of existential reality. Many who seek psychosynthesis are inspired to address and enhance the *quality of their lives*.

As a transpersonal psychology or a psychospiritual psychology, psychosynthesis is especially useful for those who wish to reconnect with their own spirituality, their sense of fulfilment, and to explore their purpose in life. They seek a fuller experience of who they essentially are and where they are going with life. They long for their life to embody more richly their potential and capacity for goodness, for joy, for beauty and for creativity. They also most likely recognize that there are obstacles to this, that they have been unsuccessful in changing on their own and know that they would benefit from some support and mirroring. Basically, in Maslow's terms, they are seeking **self-realization**.[4,5]

Potential clients for psychosynthesis need to possess a reasonable motivation to understand themselves, their problems and life challenges. They must be interested in reflecting on life experience for the purpose of making use of the insights gained. A willingness to turn inward and explore one's inner world is important. A reasonable level of openness to engage in the intrapersonal and interpersonal demands of therapy is essential. Although perhaps not yet conscious, a wish or desire to take some degree of responsibility for one's life circumstances is recommended. Although all of the above can be *grown into* through the course of therapy, the *potential* for these characteristics will greatly contribute to a successful outcome.

That is not to say that there may not be quite rigid defence systems to be overcome in the process, or dysfunctional behaviours to be addressed. Psychosynthesis therapy has long worked with individuals who experience strong life issues and problems that affect and inhibit their capacity to function in their daily life and in their community. Long-term psychosynthesis psychotherapy is most likely necessary when there has been severe trauma or abuse, or with addiction issues. This is also true with potential clients with a family history of mental illness. A general guideline is that the degree of disturbance impacts on the length of therapy required.

CASE STUDY

The Client

Susan was a 45-year-old woman who had been married for 20 years, had two children and a successful career. Although Susan's adult life had been incredibly busy, incessantly active with juggling a husband, home, career and family, she had been primarily well and happy until her fortieth birthday. Around that time life had started to feel flat, rather empty and meaningless. Susan found that the things that used to give her such a great sense of achievement – creating a nice home for her family, her activities as a helper (in her free time) at her children's school, her social life with her husband and colleagues – no longer did anything for her.

Before this Susan had never known boredom. She had never felt that her busyness was futile and in vain. She had never before questioned what she was doing and why she was doing it. Gradually she experienced a growing sense of greyness, emptiness and despair. She watched herself in her normal realm of activities and found them sorely lacking, but lacking in what, she did not know. She constantly said to herself: 'What's it all for?' 'I have everything I need to be happy, but I'm not.' 'There must be more to life than this!'

For a couple of years Susan thought she needed a change. The family moved into a house needing major renovations, which kept her busy for a while. But gradually the despair began to creep back. She went to her GP who also thought she needed a change and told her to take a holiday. This too proved fruitless. She decided to change her job and go to work for a firm that was more challenging and demanding of her skills and creativity. But it was to no avail. The feelings of meaninglessness and greyness did not leave her.

At a certain point Susan became suicidal and sunk into a deep depression. Her GP prescribed tranquillizers, which only made her feel worse. Susan felt that she was dying, indeed she was experiencing a kind of psychological death, which she was interpreting as an impulse to take her own life physically. During Susan's period of despair, a friend told her about a psychosynthesis therapist. Although resistant, and feeling she must be really sick and bad to have to see a psychotherapist, Susan rang the therapist and arranged her first session.

She arrived at the initial interview trembling with fear and trepidation but was immediately relieved to find the therapist to be quite a normal person. She began by saying that she feared she was having a breakdown, that too many people needed her, that she had lost her love for her husband and children, and that she often wanted to die but would not allow herself to entertain the thought except in her darkest moments.

The therapist was struck by what an attractive person Susan was. To look at her you would never guess that this woman was seething with despair and despondency. She presented herself as articulate, bright and in control. Her outer appearance and demeanour did not match the words with which she was describing her inner world of dark, dull, grey emptiness. One way that we can define psychospiritual health is that when our outer world is congruent with our inner world we experience wellbeing. This was anything but the case with Susan.

Susan began to speak a little about her childhood. The therapist needed to gather information and know Susan better before she could make an initial assessment of her needs and what the course of therapy could offer her. Susan had come from a working-class family with an alcoholic father. Her mother had more or less raised the children single-handedly and Susan, being the eldest, had carried much responsibility for the psychological care of both her mother and her two brothers.

(Continued)

(Continued)

When she was little, Susan's natural tendency had been to be a bit dreamy, with a rich imaginative life. However, this could not be allowed because of the chaos and the demands that her mother, albeit unconsciously, put on Susan to be the strong and capable one. She learned how to make others in her family smile, to distract them from their dysfunction, and she took charge, helping with the housework, babysitting her brothers, keeping everyone away from her father when he was drinking and, most of all, protecting her mother.

As a child, Susan vowed that *her* life would be different. As she matured, quite unconsciously she set about creating the perfect life for herself. She worked hard, achieved much and created a world for herself that was ordered and safe. She married at 25 and set about establishing first her career and then her family. Those viewing her life from the outside would never guess the inner turmoil that was motivating her actions and controlling her behaviour and direction in life.

So she had done it! She had created the seemingly perfect and normal existence for herself, which is how she imagined most people lived. To have that safe reality come crashing into nothingness was unbearably painful for Susan. Her therapist immediately warmed to Susan and felt compassion for her plight. Her story echoed a universal one that all human beings have a need for a life that makes sense, is rich with meaning and contains moments of connectedness and unity. Susan in her present desperate state was devoid of all of that.

The Therapy

There were two major strands in Susan's experience that needed unravelling. The first was her childhood experiences of taking care of others and having to be the *up-together*, strong one, and the second her extreme depression and despair. The initial step was to make sense of Susan's childhood. The therapist helped her to define the many voices inside her that she recognized as coming from childhood. There was the 'pleaser' who knew how to make people happy and always give them exactly what they needed. There was also the 'critic', who constantly judged her and told her if she was doing things right or *well enough*. Upon discovering this critic (subpersonality in psychosynthesis terms), Susan burst into tears and with the therapist's encouragement cried throughout most of the session. She seemed to believe that this critic spoke the truth about her – she was never quite good enough. There were others, but the discovery of the critic was enough for the moment.

The therapist explained to Susan the principle of subpersonalities, that each of us may have many different parts inside, which are sometimes in conflict. Long lost was Susan's 'dreamer', the one in her who loved to be creative and poetic. With this knowledge, Susan was immediately relieved and felt that some of her depression made sense to her now.

For several sessions the therapist worked mainly with Susan's presenting issues, establishing trust between them and using Gestalt dialogue to help Susan separate and identify the inner voices that were contained within her despair and depression. She found this new sense of clarity and self-awareness immensely relieving and already her depression was beginning to alter.

There was a period in the therapy when Susan began to feel aggressive towards the therapist. She had never before allowed herself to be dependent upon anyone. She liked to be in control and here was this individual who seemed to know more about her than she herself did. She found herself resisting the therapist's interventions, this being something of a rebellion, which Susan had never even contemplated in her childhood. She half expected to be punished for not being her usual compliant self and was not unaware of the unconditional positive regard her therapist seemed to give her. Although she knew she was being rather stroppy, she continued to feel respected and valued by the therapist. She had the sense that her therapist perceived her as *more than* her stroppy rebellion. This inclusion of a wider, more expansive view of Susan allowed her to feel safe enough to really explore these long-lost feelings of aggression and assertion. She found that she quite enjoyed being uncooperative and strong in herself. This enabled her to regain some qualities that she had forgotten.

The next phase of the therapy saw Susan diving head-on into her sense of despair and meaningless. The work she had done before this had enabled her to loosen the hold her depression had on her but there was still the emptiness, the grey lack of anything that made her heart sing. In one session the therapist invited Susan to go back in her imagination to times in her past when she had felt *meaning* and a sense of life being *worthwhile*. To her surprise she was flooded with memories of moments in her life that had been stunningly meaningful the birth of her first child, a sense of unity with her husband while on a walk in the woods, an experience with gardening when she had sensed the *fundamental alrightness* of the universe and her life. These memories had long been forgotten (or suppressed). She recalled her mother's hard-working life and how poignant it was that she cared so much for her family.

Susan began to ask herself the big questions about life: What am I here for? What is my place in the world? Without undue emphasis on finding the right answers to Susan's questioning, the therapist took her questions seriously and helped her to explore them both with mental imagery looking at what the purpose of her life might be and with active dialogue focusing on her search for different and higher values. Underneath her despair, Susan actually had a longing for something she could only define as *spiritual*. She began to awaken to new potentialities within herself, such as her creativity and her impulse to be with others on a deeper level.

She found that her social contacts and life changed quite dramatically. When with friends she no longer made small talk but was keen to know the other on a deeper level. She had a series of experiences where she knew that life was fundamentally good and that human beings had a depth that was accessible in intimate moments.

This journey was not without its setbacks, moments of doubt wondering whether she was conveniently making it all up in order to feel better. She began to 'reality test' her growing new awareness through her contacts with others. She found that some people could respond to her desire to relate on a deeper

(Continued)

(Continued)

level and others were threatened by it. Her husband at first doubted that the therapy was actually helping Susan to come to terms with reality. But he gradually saw that in spite of the ups and downs, there was a renewed sense of vitality in Susan. Little by little she was coming 'home' to herself.

Susan's life did not necessarily 'look' much different externally from before. She did change her career to one that she felt offered more opportunity for connection to others and fulfilled her desire to contribute. However, Susan mainly learned that she needed time *just to be*, that much of her incessant *doing* in her life had led her away from something deep and essential in herself. She was more able to allow chaos and embrace the unknown. Her tight control of herself and others (to ensure that they were all right) loosened and with it came real meaning in her life.

Although psychosynthesis may be employed with a wide variety of presenting problems, we chose this client's therapy as an example of psychosynthesis in action because these kinds of existential issues are becoming increasingly common in today's world. Though we live in the information and communication age, it seems that more and more people are feeling alienated, isolated and hollow, as deeper human needs and feelings are subsumed to material and technological wizardry and quick fixes. We believe that the re-owning of our spiritual nature that is fostered by psychosynthesis offers real hope and help for humanity. If so, psychosynthesis, along with the other transpersonal therapies, will have an expanding healing role for the future.

REFERENCES

[1] Williamson, M. (1996) *A Return to Love*. London: Thorsons.
[2] Perls, F. (1970) 'Tour lectures', in J. Fagen and I. Shepherd (eds), *Gestalt Therapy Now*. New York: Harper & Row.
[3] Whitmore, D. (1991) *Psychosynthesis Counselling in Action*. London: Sage.
[4] Maslow, A. H. (1968) *Towards a Psychology of Being*. New York: Van Nostrand.
[5] Maslow, A. H. (1978) *The Farther Reaches of Human Nature*. Harmondsworth: Penguin.

SUGGESTED READING

Assagioli, R. (1965) *Psychosynthesis*. London: Aquarian Press. The original textbook on psychosynthesis.

Hardy, J. (1996) *A Psychology with a Soul*. London: Woodgrange Press. A book that covers the historical roots of psychosynthesis and the major influences on Assagioli's thinking from Plato to the *Divine Comedy* to Western mysticism.

Marshall, J., Coleman, G. and Reason, P. (eds) (2011) *Leadership for Sustainability*. Sheffield: Greenleaf Publishing. Helen Sieroda has an insightful chapter, 'Like a river flows: how do we call forth "a world worthy of human aspirations"?'.

Whitmore, D. (2013) *Psychosynthesis Counselling in Action*, 4th edn. London: Sage. A practical book for those interested in the basics of psychosynthesis counselling and what could be expected from the therapy. This latest edition includes new content on positive psychology and the therapeutic relationship.

DISCUSSION ISSUES

1. How far do you believe that people are more than their personalities, in other words, do you believe that each of us also has a deeper and more essential self?

2. Do you think that inside we are actually many people? Do we have different parts of ourselves, that can sometimes clash? What are three of your own subpersonalities?

3. In what sense are our lives a journey? Can you trace any themes, consistent patterns or learnings in your own life, or in the life of someone you know very well?

4. Have you experienced moments of 'peak experience', glimpses of a deeper purpose or meaning to life that have been especially important to you and have informed your life? What does this tell you about human nature?

19

Transactional Analysis

Ian Stewart and Mark Widdowson

INTRODUCTION

Transactional analysis (TA) is a model for understanding human personality, communication and relationships. TA got its name because it was originally developed as a way of analysing the patterns of communication – *transactions* – that people use when they are relating in pairs and groups, and this is still an important emphasis within the approach.

A central supposition of TA is that – with practice and appropriate training – you can reliably judge someone's internal experience from their external behaviour. In particular, you can judge by the person's *observable behaviour* whether she is 'in the here and now', or replaying part of her childhood, or unawarely copying the behaviours, thoughts and feelings of one of her own parent-figures.

TA therapy* is most often classed among the *humanistic* approaches to personal change, because of its emphasis on personal responsibility, equal relationship between client and therapist, and the intrinsic worth of the person. However, TA also shares some characteristics with the *behavioural* approaches, notably in its use of clear contract-making; and TA's central theoretical ideas were drawn directly from the tradition of *psychodynamic* thought, in ways we shall explain below.

DEVELOPMENT OF THE THEORY

With a history dating back to the 1950s, TA is among the older-established of today's therapies. Like many other therapeutic approaches, it derives essentially from the work of one person – in TA's case, the psychiatrist Eric Berne (1910–1970).

---

*Throughout this chapter we shall use the word 'therapy' to mean 'psychotherapy or counselling', and 'therapist' to mean 'psychotherapist or counsellor'.

Berne was originally trained as a Freudian psychoanalyst, and the roots of TA lie in the psychodynamic tradition. Among Berne's early mentors were two analysts who had themselves developed their own theories starting from Sigmund Freud's ideas, namely Paul Federn and Erik Erikson. It was from Federn that Berne first learned the concept of **ego–states**, which he built into his own theory (see below). Erikson saw human development as comprising a sequence that occupied the person's entire lifetime, and this also Berne incorporated in his own theory, as the idea of **life-script**.

Berne was a talented and prolific writer. His book *Transactional Analysis in Psychotherapy*,[1] published in 1961, is still an indispensable professional source for the theoretical ideas of TA. In 1964 came the publication of Berne's *Games People Play*. Intended for a professional audience, the book unexpectedly became a best–seller, catapulting both Berne and TA to international media fame. From then until the mid–1970s, TA enjoyed the dubious status of a 'pop psychology'. Numerous books and articles appeared, featuring TA in often watered–down, over–simplified or down–right distorted versions. It took TA many years to recover from the harm done by the media image that was widely peddled during that period of mass popularity.

Even during this episode, however, serious professional activity in TA continued unbroken. Since Eric Berne's death in 1970, transactional analysts have continued to refine and expand both the theory and practice of TA. The approach is widely used in psychotherapy and counselling, as well as in a range of other applications such as education, management and communications training.

THEORY AND BASIC CONCEPTS

Philosophical assumptions

At the heart of TA lie certain philosophical assumptions – fundamental belief-statements about people, life and the nature of change. These assumptions are as follows:

- People are OK.
- Everyone has the capacity to think.
- People decide their own destiny, and these decisions can be changed.

People are OK means everyone has intrinsic worth, value and dignity. This is a statement of essence rather than behaviour, and is held to be true irrespective of race, age, gender, religion, or any other personal feature.

Everyone has the capacity to think (except the severely brain-damaged) and therefore it is the responsibility of each of us to decide what we want from life. Each individual will ultimately live with the consequences of what he or she decides.

Decisional model TA holds that when a grown–up person engages in apparently self-defeating behaviours, or repeatedly feels painful feelings, she is in fact following strategies she *decided* upon as a young child. These strategies appeared to the child to be the best way of surviving and getting her needs met. The child was not *made* to feel or behave in particular ways by her parents, or by 'the environment'.

TA assumes that the same is true for the adult person. Other people, or life circumstances, may exert strong pressures on her, but it is always her own decision whether to conform to these pressures. The person is thus held to be personally *responsible* for all her feelings and behaviour.

Since the person himself is responsible for making these childhood *early decisions*, it follows that later in life he can change any of these decisions – that is, **redecide**. If some of his infant decisions are producing uncomfortable results for him in adult life, he can trace the outdated decisions and change them for new and more appropriate ones.

Thus, TA takes an assertive view of the possibility of personal change. The person will achieve change not merely by gaining 'insight' into old patterns of behaviour, but by deciding to change those patterns and taking action to achieve this change.

TA theory

There are certain key ideas that form the foundation of TA theory, and serve to distinguish TA from any other psychological system. They are as follows.

The ego-state model

Central to TA is the *ego-state model*. An ego–state is a set of related behaviours, thoughts and feelings. It is a way in which we manifest a part of our personality at a given time. The TA model portrays three distinct types of ego-state: *Adult*, *Parent* and *Child*.

If someone is behaving, thinking and feeling in response to what is going on around him here and now, using all the resources available to him as a grown–up person, he is said to be in an *Adult* ego-state.

At times, the person may behave, think and feel in ways that are a copy of one of her parents, or of others who were parent-figures for her. When she does so, she is said to be in a *Parent* ego-state.

Sometimes the person may return to ways of behaving, thinking and feeling which he used when he was a child. Then he is said to be in a *Child* ego-state.

In TA theory, the initial capital letters are always used when we want to indicate that we are referring to the ego-states (Parent, Adult, Child). A small letter beginning the word shows we mean a real–life parent, adult or child.

Transactions and strokes

If I am communicating with you, I can choose to address you from either an Adult, Child or Parent ego-state. You can reply in turn from Adult, Child or Parent. This exchange of communications is known as a *transaction*.

The use of the ego-state model to analyse sequences of transactions is referred to as *transactional analysis proper*. The word 'proper' is added to show that we are talking about this branch of TA in particular, rather than TA as a whole.

When you and I transact, I signal recognition of you and you return that recognition. In TA language, any act of recognition is called a *stroke*. Everyone needs an adequate supply of strokes to maintain their physical and psychological wellbeing.

Life-script

TA asserts that each of us, in childhood, writes a life-story for himself or herself. This story has a beginning, a middle and an end. We write the basic plot in our infant years, before we are old enough to talk more than a few words. Later on in childhood we add more detail to the story, and we may revise it at different stages in life. This life-story provides us with a way of making meaning, and is constructed around implicit conclusions relating to ourselves, other people and the world around us.

As grown-ups, we are usually no longer aware of the life-story we have written for ourselves. Yet all of us, from time to time, are likely to 'dip back into' that childhood story and begin living it out, still without being aware we are doing so.

This unaware life-story is known in TA as the *life-script* (often shortened simply to *script*).[2] The concept of life-script ranks with the ego-state model as a central building-block of TA.

As we have already said, TA assumes that the young child *decides upon* her life-script. That is, she 'writes her own story'. She does this as the best means she can find – with an infant's powers of thinking and experience – for surviving and getting needs met in a world that can often seem threatening.

Though the parents cannot force a particular script upon the child, they are naturally likely to exert a strong influence upon that child's early decisions. In particular, parents give their children *script messages* – instructions about how to be or not be, what to do or not do. Especially significant in most people's scripts are negative messages called *injunctions*. These take the form 'Don't ...', for example Don't Feel, Don't Be Important, Don't Exist, Don't Be You. Injunctions are communicated to the child from the Child ego-state of the parent, and usually have their origins in the parent's own un-met childhood needs.

Script decisions, script beliefs and the script story

When the young child is making her *script decisions*, she weaves these decisions into the 'story' of her script. That narrative helps her to 'make sense of' the world, and so helps in turn to consolidate her script decisions. As she grows to adulthood, if she does not have occasion to change her script story, those same early decisions will become the grown-up person's *script beliefs*.

For example, suppose that a young child received from her parents the injunction 'Don't Be Close'. This script message may perhaps have been conveyed by the parents' modelling – they may never have shown physical or emotional closeness to each other in the little girl's presence. Or the injunction may have been conveyed directly to the child by her mother or father, by frequent rejection of the child's attempts to get close to them. If the child takes this injunction on board, she will make the *script decision* 'I'm not supposed to get close to others'.

If this person grows to adulthood without the opportunity to change her script, then this same *early decision* is likely to persist as one of her *script beliefs* (although she will hold the belief outside of her conscious awareness). And, just as in her childhood, she will continue to 'make sense of the world' in the light of this belief. She may have written a script story whose main theme is 'I'm on my own in the world'.

How problems originate

The existence of the life-script, in itself, is *not* inherently 'a problem'. After all, we already know that the young child's original purpose in constructing her life-script is 'to survive and get her needs met'.

Problems begin, however, when the grown-up person tries to deal with a here-and-now situation by stepping back into her childhood 'script story', instead of employing the present resources and understandings she has available to her as an adult. When someone does this, they are said to be *in script*.

People go into script most often when they are under stress, particularly when the problem situation *resembles* an occasion from their childhood in which they tried to deal with some kind of difficulty and failed to do so. The resemblance will be outside of their conscious awareness.

The person who is *in script* will be responding to his *script beliefs* instead of to here-and-now reality. He will be employing the strategies he used as a child as the best means he could find to deal with a problem. These strategies failed back then, and they will almost always fail again in the present.

How problems are resolved

In principle, TA's account of how to resolve personal problems is straightforward. The client, aided by the therapist, needs to *move out of script*. Instead of replaying their script narrative, they need to respond to the demands of the here-and-now situation; instead of acting out their script beliefs, they need to act, think and feel in response to current reality.

In practice, there are two important hurdles that need to be surmounted if the client is to make these changes successfully. First: the person's life-script will have been outside of their awareness. One of the therapist's tasks, therefore, is to help them become consciously aware of their script story and script beliefs.

Second: ever since childhood, the life-script has offered the client a familiar framework for 'making sense of the world'. What is more, the script was originally written with the Child intent of 'surviving and getting needs met.' Therefore when the prospect arises of moving out of part of the script, the client in Child is likely to be unwilling – indeed, often terrified – to let go of these lifelong objectives.

In the case-study section of this chapter, you will see in detail how a TA therapist helps the client to 'clear these hurdles' and move to personal change. First, however, in the coming section, we shall review the basic principles of TA therapeutic practice.

PRACTICE

The goals of personal change in TA

Berne urged that the proper goal of TA treatment is not 'insight', nor 'progress', but *cure*. While most of today's transactional analysts agree with Berne that cure is their goal, they have differing views about what constitutes cure. Some simply equate cure with completion of the treatment contract between client and therapist.

Autonomy

As a more explicit way of framing 'cure', Berne suggested that the goal of personal change should be **autonomy**. Being autonomous implies the ability to solve problems using the person's full adult resources to think, feel and behave in response to here-and-now reality. The components of autonomy are *awareness, spontaneity* and the *capacity for intimacy*. By *awareness*, we mean the ability to experience things – to 'hear the birds and smell the flowers' – with here-and-now immediacy, rather than in the way we were taught to do by others. *Spontaneity* means the ability to move freely and by choice between Adult, Parent and Child ego-states. *Intimacy* with others, in its TA sense, means the open and appropriate expression of wants, feelings and needs as they arise.

Contractual method

The TA therapist assumes that he and his client will take *joint responsibility* for achieving whatever change the client wants to make.

This follows from TA's philosophical assumption that therapist and client relate on equal terms. It is not the therapist's task to do things *to* the client. Nor can the client expect that the therapist will do everything *for* her. Thus, TA therapy is a collaborative process.

Since both parties take an equal share in the process of change, it is important that both know clearly how the task will be shared. Therefore they agree a **contract**. Eric Berne[3] defined this as: 'an explicit bilateral commitment to a well-defined course of action'.

The term *overall contract* is used to describe the client's main longer–term contract. This will often be for an important script change. Client and therapist are likely to address the overall contract over a number of sessions or for the full duration of therapy. A *session contract*, as its name implies, is a shorter–term contract taken for a single session, or even for part of the time within one session.

It is widely agreed in TA that the contract should include an outcome that is *observable:* that is, that both client and therapist should be able to judge – by what they can see, hear or physically feel – that the contract goal has been achieved.

Treatment direction

The TA therapist does not assume that the 'therapeutic relationship', of itself, will nec–essarily bring about desired changes. Instead, she develops an analysis of the client's problem, and agrees a contract for the changes he will make. She then intervenes actively in a planned and structured manner to help him achieve these changes. This process of planned intervention is summed up in the phrase *treatment direction.*

There is a continual three–way interplay between contract, diagnosis and treat–ment direction. For example, you may revise your diagnosis of the client because you have got to know him better or because he has already changed in the course of treatment. The changed diagnosis may call for a re-negotiation of the contract; and the new diagnosis and new contract will then require you to re-think your choice of interventions.

Client protection

TA lays great emphasis on ensuring *protection* for the client. In practical terms this includes setting up a physically safe environment, guaranteeing confidentiality and using an effective system for medical and psychiatric referral.

Equally important is the psychological aspect of protection. The process of script change can sometimes be frightening for the client's Child, as he steps out of lifelong patterns that he experiences as having ensured his security or even survival. In that circumstance, the therapist may actively move to provide the Child with a protective presence until the script change is securely established.

Practical techniques

TA therapists use a wide range of techniques to help their clients update their *script beliefs* and achieve personal change. You will find guidance to these tech–niques in the 'Suggestions for Further Reading' at the end of the chapter. Here we shall describe two of the most often used, both of which feature in the case study below.

Clearing contamination

In TA theory, **contamination** means a situation in which someone mistakes some of the content of the Parent or Child ego-states for Adult reality. It is as though the Parent or the Child (or sometimes both) 'intrude' into the person's reality testing. The content of a contamination will always correspond to one of the person's script beliefs.

To help the client clear a contamination means asking him to 'stand back' and appraise the functioning of his Adult. The therapy therefore usually takes the form of an Adult–Adult, question-and-answer conversation between client and therapist.

Resolving internal dialogue

TA theory holds that an *internal dialogue* can go on between different parts of the person's ego-state structure. Sometimes the content of this dialogue serves to further a script belief.

When this is so, the therapist may ask the client to externalize the dialogue through a technique called *two-chair work*.[4] Shifting between chairs, the client 'becomes' the part of the ego-state structure on each side of the dialogue. The objective is to bring to awareness whatever is conflictual or negative about the dialogue, and to *resolve* it to the satisfaction of both sides.

WHICH CLIENTS BENEFIT MOST?

TA is notable for the breadth of its application. It has been used successfully to help clients deal with many different types and levels of problem and dysfunction. These range all the way from simple problem situations, through temporary stress reaction, to deeper-seated emotional and relationship difficulties, including depression and anxiety. Used in specialized and protective settings, TA therapy has also had good results in the treatment of some personality disorders.

CASE STUDY

In this case study, we have used *italics* to highlight TA concepts and methods already described in the sections above. The therapy took place over 16 weekly sessions of individual psychotherapy conducted within a private-practice setting. The therapist was Mark Widdowson.

(Continued)

(Continued)

The Client

Ben was in his late thirties, married with two children. He came across as warm and friendly, although slightly hesitant when talking, and confessed that he felt a little apprehensive about coming to therapy. His two main presenting problems were 'feeling down' and 'poor confidence'. On further discussion, I concluded that he was experiencing long-standing mild depression and moderate anxiety. He described what sounded like a relentless self-critical *internal dialogue*, feelings of inferiority, low self-esteem, low mood, a loss of interest in things and social inhibition. My initial diagnosis and case formulation was that Ben had:

- a strong negative and critical *internal dialogue* between his *Parent and Child ego-states*;
- a series of *contaminations* which maintained his poor self-esteem and confidence;
- a set of *script decisions* in which he had accepted at least the 'Don't Be Important' and 'Don't Be Close' *injunctions*;
- a *script belief* that he was 'not good enough'.

The Therapy

The first two sessions were spent exploring Ben's difficulties and their origins in his early life experiences. Although Ben reported that he had a 'fairly typical' childhood, he had been bullied at school and his home life was lacking in affection and praise. This combination of circumstances had led him to develop his *script beliefs* that he was 'not good enough' and was somehow inferior to others. The experiences of bullying in particular had led him to feel somewhat anxious around other people and to expect rejection due to his inadequacy. I noted that Ben rejected and ignored any positive *strokes* I gave to him during these sessions.

In the third session we focused on exploring Ben's negative *internal dialogue*. This was understood as a critical dialogue from his *Parent to Child ego-state* which supported his *script beliefs*. I helped Ben make sense of these in light of his early experiences and encouraged him to express the feelings of fear and shame he had experienced during those events. This placed him face-to-face with his fear of being seen as inadequate. I also invited Ben to experiment with accepting positive *strokes*.

During these first three sessions, we also took time to identify the goals that Ben wanted to achieve in therapy and to agree a workable *contract for change*. Ben's initial want was to break out of his lifetime patterns of low self-esteem and anxiousness. The final *overall contract* was:

- 'I will stop beating myself up and will start to feel good about myself. This will help me to relax and enjoy life. I will know I have achieved this when I feel equal to other people, instead of feeling that I'm not good enough.'

Ben readily agreed to one further sentence that I invited him to add to the contract: 'And when I've got this good feeling of being equal to others, *I will tell you.*' Only through Ben's reporting to me in this way would his achievement of the contract goal become *observable* as far as I was concerned.

At this point, although Ben agreed these were the goals he wanted, he expressed some doubt as to whether he could achieve them. These goals were regularly revisited throughout the therapy to make sure the therapy was 'on track' and also to check if Ben wanted to revise them in any way.

In order to help Ben achieve these goals, my *treatment plan* would be focused on identifying the *contaminations* and *script beliefs* which had been preventing him from feeling good, and helping him to re-evaluate and update these. I also noted that we would probably need to spend time examining his interpersonal relationships to help him overcome his social anxiety.

In sessions four and five Ben described having started to experiment with being a little more emotionally open in his discussions with his wife, who had been supportive of this change in him. I continued exploring his negative *ego-state dialogue* by inviting Ben to engage in a *two-chair conversation* with his critical *Parent ego-state.* During this, he identified that his self-criticism had had a paradoxically protective function: he felt it had protected him from rejection by anticipating it and keeping him out of situations where he risked being criticized by others.

Sessions six and seven focused on Ben's anxiety. Ben had been a real worrier. We identified that he had had a series of *contaminations* which had led him to believe that worrying was necessary to 'prevent things from going wrong'. He had also been afraid to feel joy, believing that happiness would somehow cause bad things to happen, or that it was pointless because it would not last. Here we both saw how Ben's anxiety and depression had been linked to his pessimism and hopelessness. During these sessions, these *contaminations* were re-evaluated and Ben began to realize that worrying did not in fact prevent anything bad from happening – instead, it only prevented him from enjoying life.

In session eight Ben described how over the week he had begun to realize that he had been taking too much responsibility for other people's feelings and trying to 'make everything OK' for everyone around him, at all times. Over the week he had started to relax and not do this quite so often and had been pleasantly surprised to discover that no negative consequences had occurred. This resulted in another experiential challenge to his *life-script*. I picked up this realization and made immediate therapeutic use of it, by asking Ben whether he had been concerned about what I was feeling in sessions. Ben revealed he had been worried that I might be bored. I asked if there had been any indicators that this might be the case, to which Ben said that there had not.

In session nine Ben reflected on his childhood experiences and expressed his sadness over these. In particular, he explored his *injunctions* of 'Don't Be Important, Don't Be You, Don't Feel and Don't Be Close'. I invited Ben to engage in a compassionate, nurturing *dialogue* with his *Child* self. At the end of this, Ben spontaneously expressed that he had come to the conclusion that it was all right for him to feel all of his feelings. I considered this to indicate that Ben had made a **redecision**, and *stroked* him for making this important change.

(Continued)

(Continued)

In the next four sessions we focused on exploring Ben's relationships and on identifying new ways of relating to other people. In particular, he explored analysis of *transactions*, *strokes* and how he could interact with people from a life position of *'I'm OK – You're OK'*. During these sessions, Ben realized that he was increasingly spending time out of his *life-script* and was developing healthier relationships with people around him and was generally enjoying life. During these sessions, I noted that Ben was showing some of the signs of *autonomy* and supported these changes: he had started to increase his *awareness* and be in the 'here-and-now' more often, he was showing greater ability to be *spontaneous* and he was enjoying more *intimacy* in his relationships.

The final sessions were spent on reviewing the therapy process, reinforcing the changes Ben had made, and in identifying 'early warning signals' that might indicate he was slipping back into his script. The use of *two-chair work* to develop his positive, compassionate internal *ego-state dialogue* was repeated twice during these sessions. Ben had realized he was just as good as anyone else, and had stopped feeling inferior. He had not experienced any anxious or depressive symptoms for several weeks.

Throughout the therapy, the case was evaluated using a series of qualitative and quantitative research methods, and the therapy was judged to have been successful. As a further part of the research process, Ben was contacted at several periods over six months. At each of these points, his progress had been maintained and he had continued to remain symptom-free and was enjoying life.

REFERENCES

[1] Berne, E. (1961) *Transactional Analysis in Psychotherapy*. New York: Grove Press.
[2] Steiner, C. (1974) *Scripts People Live: Transactional Analysis of Life Scripts*. New York: Grove Press.
[3] Berne, E. (1966) *Principles of Group Treatment*. New York: Grove Press.
[4] Goulding, M. and Goulding, R. (1979) *Changing Lives Through Redecision Therapy*. New York: Brunner–Mazel.

SUGGESTED READING

Berne, E. (1961) *Transactional Analysis in Psychotherapy*. New York: Grove Press. (Reprint edition: London, Souvenir Press, 1991). This was Berne's first book-length statement of TA principles. It is still the essential source text for some of the central ideas of TA, in particular for Berne's original theory of ego-states.

Stewart, I. (2013) *Transactional Analysis Counselling in Action*, 4th edn. London: Sage. Written for practising and trainee counsellors and therapists, this book gives detailed practical guidance on the use of TA to help people change. The techniques are illustrated in an extended case study.

Stewart, I. and Joines, V. (2012) *TA Today: A New Introduction to Transactional Analysis*, 2nd edn. Melton Mowbray and Chapel Hill: Lifespace. This widely read text explains current TA ideas in straightforward language, starting from basic principles. The teaching material is reinforced by numerous examples and exercises.

Widdowson, M. (2010) *Transactional Analysis: 100 Key Points and Techniques.* London: Routledge. True to its title, this book presents 100 concisely phrased points of guidance on the principles, theory and practice of TA. It is aimed at qualified practitioners and advanced trainees.

DISCUSSION ISSUES

1. How far do you agree with TA's philosophical assumption that 'Everyone is OK'?
2. How, if at all, does your becoming a counsellor or therapist fit into the 'story' that is your life-script?
3. What would you say are (a) the advantages and (b) the potential disadvantages of using *contractual method* as a basic framework for therapy?
4. How far do you agree with Eric Berne's opinion that the goal of successful therapy should be defined as *cure*?

PART 4
Integrative and Eclectic Approaches

20

Cognitive Analytic Therapy

Ian B. Kerr and Stephen Kellett

Cognitive analytic therapy (CAT) is a still evolving and increasingly popular integrative model of psychotherapy and counselling, developed by Anthony Ryle. The model stresses the internalised relational and social factors fundamental to human psychology and to most mental health problems. CAT also focuses on working with problematic relational issues arising within therapy between therapist and client. CAT adopts a proactive, 'doing with', collaborative style characterised by an 'evident compassion' along with an emphasis on clear description of problems and of therapeutic aims. This is achieved through early, jointly constructed, written and diagrammatic **reformulations** which are understood as 'psychological tools'. The approach is characterised by a focus on time limits and on 'ending well'. A major strength of CAT is its ability to engage 'difficult' or 'hard to help' clients and to create a strong therapeutic alliance. CAT has been further developed for use with a range of mental health problems in settings from primary care through to multidisciplinary teams in institutional settings. It is also being used as a consultancy tool for teams and services working with 'difficult' clients making use of extended 'contextual' reformulations.

DEVELOPMENT OF THE THERAPY

CAT arose several decades ago from the efforts by Ryle to integrate the valid and effective elements of the different but often contradictory models that were then prevalent.[1,2,3] These included behaviourism, early cognitive psychology (notably Kelly's personal construct theory) and the various branches of psychoanalysis. It also represented an effort to develop a brief, 'good enough' package for resource-limited

NHS settings. As such, the model arose partly out of and still maintains a strong sense of social awareness and responsibility. CAT has been further transformed by contributions from Vygotsky's activity theory,[1,2,3,5] notions of a dialogical self deriving from Bakhtin,[5] and important developments in infant psychology.[6,7,8] As such, it has by now developed into a mature model in itself of human development and of mental health problems. CAT is also being used to rethink and reconceptualise various clinical problems and 'disorders' (e.g. the 'difficult' patient in various settings, personality disorder, dementia, substance abuse, psychosis), and as an organisational consultancy tool. CAT is acknowledged as a genuinely integrative approach[9,10] and is accruing a body of 'formal' research evidence for its effectiveness.[4]

THEORY AND BASIC CONCEPTS

CAT is founded on a well-defined concept of a self that is fundamentally socially formed and located. CAT understands human psychological development (and so also mental health problems or 'psychopathology') to be rooted in and influenced by the early experience of meaningful human relationships in a particular socio-cultural context.

The way in which this development occurs is being increasingly better understood, especially through the recent work of developmental and infant psychologists. This stresses the actively intersubjective nature of developing infants and their pre-disposition and need for active, playful, collaborative, meaning-making and 'companionship'.[6,7,8] Psychological development occurs in large part through the process of **internalisation** enabled by our capacity for empathy and intersubjectivity. Intersubjectivity refers to the extraordinary ability humans have, even from the first days of life, to 'tune into' others empathically and be influenced by and grow and develop through this. The idea of 'internalisation' is used in a particular sense, following the Russian psychologist Lev Vygotsky, in which this process is understood to be transformative. This means that the psychological structures which enable the process of internalisation are themselves changed by the process. This results in a self that is subjectively and 'objectively' fundamentally different and diverse depending on the formative interpersonal and cultural experiences it has gone through. This process also generates our values and beliefs and the very 'felt sense' of our individual self and our relations to others. CAT also recognises, therefore, the importance of background social and cultural factors (for example social inequality)[11,12] in contributing to mental health problems and also in limiting the outcome of treatment.

CAT understands that it is the experience of whole formative relationships that is internalised. This generates a repertoire of (formative) **reciprocal roles** (RRs). These RRs (see Box) are understood to be complexes of implicit relational memory (i.e. deeply rooted and mostly not conscious) along with associated values, beliefs and emotions. RRs are often clearly associated with specific or general dialogical 'voices' which may be an important focus of therapy. These formative RRs are understood to determine and underlie our sense of self, of self in relation to others, and also the repertoire of responsive or coping patterns we subsequently develop. These are described as **reciprocal role procedures** (RRPs). These may be described as 'traps', 'snags' or 'dilemmas' depending on their patterns. These RRPs are enacted both in relation to other people in the here-and-now (including importantly, of course, the therapist), but also in self-management (in 'self-to-self' role procedures). This may be mediated through a clear internal (e.g. 'critical') dialogic voice. Common reciprocal roles range from, for example, *'properly caring for–properly cared for'* at one extreme to *'neglecting and abusing–neglected and abused'* at the other. Unhelpful or 'maladaptive' RRPs are important therapeutic targets.

CAT is characterised by a proactive, collaborative therapeutic style and by a position of 'evident compassion' which is seen theoretically as important both in engaging clients and generating a firm alliance. This benign relational experience will also gradually in itself be internalised. This position clearly makes assumptions about the kind of person who is able or suited to undertake therapeutic or counselling work. CAT theory stresses the importance of clear, early, joint reformulation of presenting problems and of their developmental background. However, this is seen as a basis for looking forward to working in a 'prospective' manner towards future aims and change for the better. CAT also stresses the need to engage with the client in a way that is accessible and usable by them and at a pace they can deal with. This is described, following Vygotsky, as working in the 'zone of proximal development' (ZPD).

Although CAT offers an overall structure with a sequence of stages and use of psychological tools, it does not prescribe a detailed 'manualised' treatment and overall adopts a 'whole person' approach. Similarly, CAT does not focus principally on symptoms, behaviours or diagnostic labels although these may form part of the overall picture (e.g. in reformulations) and may require attention at some point. This approach does not fit easily with approaches based crudely and solely on diagnostic labels of dubious validity.

CAT aims at change of deep psychological structures and processes through therapy in addition to the nonetheless important roles of support, ventilation and validation. Therapeutic change in CAT is seen in terms of changes and modifications to underlying RRs (and their associated feelings and cognitions) and in our repertoire of often unhelpful RRPs. These would include patterns of relating to others and also to self, as well as various symptoms and behaviours.

An important aspect of change is seen as that brought about through the therapeutic relationship. This is achieved both through work on threats and rupture to the therapy relationship but also through the experience of the relationship itself. In more serious 'borderline' type problems an additional therapeutic aim would be promoting integration of a self that is liable to fracture or split into different self-states and correspondingly to promote self-reflective capacity and insight.

CAT sees 'ending well' in therapy or counselling as an important aim in itself. Ending well would be seen as sharing this experience openly without resorting to old coping patterns (RRPs) and to communicate real feelings. These could include, for example, anger at the therapist for ending. Not ending well risks generating unhelpful dependency and may also result in an unhelpful mutually gratifying and admiring relationship that simply perpetuates previous RRPs and militates against change.

Summary of basic theory and concepts in CAT

The model is based upon a fundamentally relational and social concept of self; this implies that individual mental health problems or 'psychopathology' cannot be considered apart from the social and cultural context from which it arose and within which also it is currently located.

Early relational and social experience is 'internalised' (in the context of individual genetic and temperamental variation) as a repertoire of 'reciprocal roles'.

A reciprocal role is a complex of implicit relational memory (possibly traumatic) that includes emotions, perceptions and cultural values; it is characterised by both childhood-derived and parent/culture-derived poles; a role may also be associated with a clear dialogical 'voice'.

Enactment of a reciprocal role always anticipates, or attempts to elicit, an expected reciprocal reaction from a previous or current other.

Reciprocal roles (RRs) and their recurrent procedural enactments or 'coping patterns' (RRPs) determine both later interpersonal interactions and also, importantly, internal dialogue and self-management.

All mental activity, whether conscious or unconscious, is rooted in and highly determined by our underlying repertoire of reciprocal roles.

More severe and complex damage to the self may occur as a result of chronic developmental trauma/emotional adversity partly as a result of repeated experiences of dissociation. This results in a damaged self prone to 'switch' or 'flip' into different extreme 'self states' with greatly reduced ability to self-reflect and cope adaptively.

PRACTICE

CAT goals and aims of CAT are to achieve fundamental psychological change for clients seen in terms of modification of damaging or unhelpful RRs and RRPs and the acquisition of new more adaptive, flexible and compassionate ones.

Style of therapy and therapeutic position

The CAT approach is proactive and collaborative and characterised by a position of 'evident compassion'. However, CAT would not shirk from trying to understand or challenge 'difficult', self-destructive, or even antisocial patterns of behaviour (seen as RRPs). But this would always be undertaken in a non-critical or non-judgemental way and would assume that these patterns for the most part represent the client trying to do, or cope, the best they can given their circumstances. Therapy would also always aim to work within the client's capabilities (or 'ZPD' as described above).

Suitability

CAT adopts a very inclusive attitude to taking clients on and practitioners would normally be prepared to give most people who request help a chance at therapy or counselling. It regards 'motivation' or 'psychological mindedness' as an aim of therapy and a challenge for our approaches rather than as being a prerequisite. The only serious reasons not to consider a client for therapy would be serious and incapacitating substance abuse (or excess medication), acute psychotic disorder or serious current risk of violent behaviours. High intellectual capacity is not required and CAT is being increasingly used with appropriate modifications in learning disability or forensic settings.

Initial assessment for therapy in CAT would normally be directed towards obtaining some general overview of the client's current difficulties and of their background, especially their early formative experiences. If the client is willing then an initial contract of 16–24 sessions would typically be offered, depending on the apparent extent of the difficulties. The ending of therapy would be flagged up and anticipated right from the beginning.

The early sessions in CAT would be somewhat more proactive and directed towards information-gathering and understanding of the key issues. However, already the style of the approach in terms of understanding problems in terms of the model using RRs and RRPs would be starting along with an exploration of how these might already possibly be enacted within the therapy relationship.

After a few sessions the therapist or counsellor would aim to draw together both a written ('narrative') and diagrammatic (map) *reformulation*. The letter written to the client aims to outline in a sympathetic and non-judgemental fashion a tentative understanding of the key issues (RRs and RRPs) and background to them in terms of formative relational experience. It aims to tell a client's story back to them with the aim of validating this and 'bearing witness' to it. The letter would also anticipate how some (e.g. *placatory* or *rebellious*) RRPs might be, or possibly already have been, enacted within therapy. Hearing a reformulation letter read out and the process of looking at a map can be extremely sobering and powerful for clients, often provoking tears or silence, and contributes powerfully to the subsequent therapeutic alliance.

The diagram or map would ideally be jointly constructed in session through initial rough drafts (see Figure 20.1) and would aim to depict background formative relational experiences (RRs) and subsequent general coping patterns (RRPs). The latter may contain unhelpful or 'maladaptive' behaviours (e.g. self harm, striving and over work, self-criticism) and also symptoms (e.g. depression or bingeing). However, symptoms and behaviours (or diagnoses) are also shown as occurring in the context of the bigger 'whole person' picture. The map aims at an overview, or 'top down' description of general patterns and problems which may apply to many situations, including issues arising between client and therapist (i.e. 'transference' and 'counter-transference'). The reformulations act as a kind of 'route map' for the course of therapy which is helpful for both client but also the therapist. They also act as a framework within which many other activities or interventions may be undertaken depending on needs and wishes.

The *middle phase* of therapy is more open and may depend on issues arising both day to day in the life of the client but also in terms of need to work through and process past experiences often of trauma or loss. For more damaged and wary clients it may be that a longer period of time is needed to gain trust and confidence in the therapist and try out new aims.

Ending

CAT stresses the importance of ending well and focus is always kept on this from the very beginning of therapy. Ending well is seen as an important opportunity to celebrate a possibly anxiety-provoking loss of a trusting and confiding relation and to try to move on without going back to old coping patterns. This is formally acknowledged by means of 'good-bye' letters on both sides. Some clients may later need further help in the shape of more individual therapy or some alternative approach such as trauma processing work or an interpersonal group (possibly CAT-based). However, significant positive personal change can occur within even a brief therapy.

Formal monitoring of change

Use of formal rating charts to monitor recognition and change (revision) of key issues (or target RRPs) may be helpful to maintain focus. Likewise keeping of a notebook or diary can be helpful. CAT therapists would normally use some general outcome measure (e.g. CORE-OM) to evaluate progress bearing in mind these are very broad indicators of wellbeing and change. For more complex disorders the specific PSQ (Personality Structure Questionnaire) may be used.[1] A further tool (CCAT – competence CAT) for monitoring adherence to the CAT approach developed by Bennett and Parry[2,3] may be useful in monitoring fidelity to the model.

Supervision

In working with a relationally based model, on-going supervision either in a peer group or in a formal training situation would normally be in place. This provides the necessary opportunity to check out potentially difficult interactions with the client and to seek support, feedback and advice from colleagues.

A typical session

During an established therapy or course of counselling a session would typically start off with a general enquiry about how things have been, how the client wants to use the time on offer today, or possibly an enquiry about the outcome of a previous session if particularly powerful or upsetting issues have been discussed. These could relate to current day-to-day problems or historic issues or issues arising in the therapeutic relationship. The session would aim to be open and responsive rather than follow a prescriptive sequence of practical interventions. However, discussion would intermittently be related back to the previous reformulations. More focused work might also be undertaken on specific issues if indicated, such as problematic or traumatic relationships from the past. Space would always be allowed in CAT for reflection and thoughtfulness although aiming never to allow silence to become persecutory. Towards the end of a session a more general reflection would occur about issues discussed that day and about progress in relation to formal therapeutic 'aims'.

> ## Key features of the cognitive analytic model of practice
>
> Proactive and collaborative ('doing with') style, stressing the active participation of the client or patient.
>
> Aims at non-judgemental description of mental health problems or 'psychopathology'; these are seen as procedural enactments (RRPs) of reciprocal roles (RRs) and associated dialogical voices, and of the possible tendency under stress to dissociate into different 'self states'.
>
> Therapy is aided by the early collaborative construction of written and diagrammatic reformulations (conceived of as psychological tools) by the end of the initial phase of therapy. These serve as 'route maps' for therapy and also as explicit validating narrative and testimony.
>
> Therapy subsequently focuses on revision of maladaptive RRPs and associated perceptions, affects and voices as they are evident in internal self-to-self dialogue and self-management, through enactments in the outside world, and also as manifest in the therapy relationship (as transference and counter-transference).
>
> The focus from the beginning is on a time limit (whether in individual therapy or CAT-informed approaches in other settings); 'ending well' is seen as an important part of therapy (experience of new reciprocal roles).
>
> Social support and rehabilitation is seen as an important although often neglected aspect of counselling and therapy.

WHICH CLIENTS BENEFIT MOST?

CAT as a model is very open to working with a wide range of patients and problems, given those formative relational issues demonstrably underpin the vast majority of mental health problems and given its whole–person approach. Such presentations may cover a range of specific problems and difficulties or formal diagnoses. It appears that a particular strength of the CAT approach, as noted above[1,4] lies in engaging and working with more 'severe and complex', 'hard to help'-type clients and patients, for example those with 'personality'-type disorders or, with appropriate modification, those with learning difficulties. CAT also appears suitable and welcomed by clients with more common mental health problems in primary care or private practice, where CAT may be successfully used as a first–line treatment approach.

CASE STUDY

We present here an example of identity development using CAT.

The Client

Initial referral and screening

Jim (a pseudonym) was referred for CAT due to concerns that his self-care was poor, his life was extremely chaotic, he was depressed and engaging in high levels of substance misuse. The most marked aspect of the client's presentation was the client's lack of a sense of self; he described not knowing who he was, being markedly swayed by others' opinions and drifting through life, lurching from crisis to crisis, with little sense of core purpose.

Sessions 1–3: Background information leading to narrative reformulation

Personal history

Jim was born without complication in a small Scottish mining village into a working-class nuclear family (mother, father and older sister). His father was a miner, heavy drinker and was frequently violent and abusive towards Jim. He described his mother as somewhat of a peripheral figure in his childhood, who similarly lived in fear of her husband's rage. Jim stated that he always believed himself to be different and an outsider and struggled to make relationships at school, where he was bullied. He left school with one 'O' level and took up a life of squatting in London and abusing substances. He had been admitted for physical problems related to alcohol abuse in the past, such as alcohol-related malnutrition. In terms of relationships, Jim noted that he had a tendency to get involved with women (he was heterosexual in orientation), but for them to get exasperated with his substance misuse and impulsivity and eventually the relationship would terminate. The client had a forensic history due to his arrest for assault – he had little recall of this due to being drunk at the time.

The Therapy

Reformulatory sessions

Ryle emphasises the mapping of states with the patient as an active aspect of collaboration and assessment. During the early reformulatory sessions

(1–3) there was an awareness of the following states: (1) an impulsive state, (2) a lost/abandoned state, (3) a rescuing state, (4) a critic state, and finally (5) a cut-off state (no thoughts or feelings). These states and their origins in early experience were fed back in a narrative reformulation letter at session 4. The client's response to the narrative reformulation at session 4 was one of tearful recognition. The sequential diagrammatic reformulation (SDR) was collaboratively constructed over sessions 4–7 and is presented in Figure 20.1. The SDR also named the self-states as summaries of the RRPs from the narrative reformulation. The RRPs and self-states (SS) in the SDR are described below:

SS1 *'Pain'*

| A1 | Abusive/abusing | to | A2 | Powerless |

SS2 *'Robin Hood'*

| B1 | Idealised saver | to | B2 | Rescued |

SS3 *'Lost/alone'*

| C1 | Abandoning | to | C2 | Abandoned |

SS4 *'Critic'*

| D1 | Ripping apart | to | D1 | Put down |

The SDR was a central CAT tool collaboratively developed and shared between therapist and client, which was used to initially describe and then track the rapidly changing experience of self and others in various self-states. The transference relationship was also analysed via the SDR and openly discussed with the patient. The client stated that the SDR provided a previously missing sense of containment, as it clarified and normalised a previously confusing and often contrasting array of symptoms, processes and perceptions.

Recognition sessions

As the SDR was constructed, the client kept a structured diary in which the states were recognised. The client ticked each time they had noticed the state either (1) before it was going to happen, (2) whilst it was happening or (3) after exiting the state.

Revision sessions

Early revision sessions enabled collation of a number of changes that were labelled as either 'internal' or 'external' changes; these were also placed on the SDR. Table 20.1 contains the collaboratively constructed exits.

(Continued)

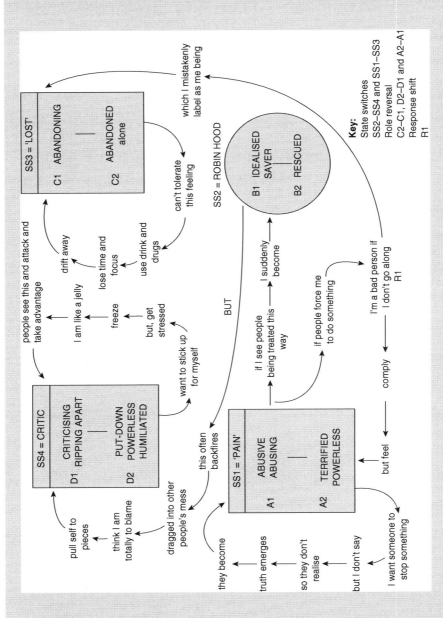

FIGURE 20.1 Sequential diagrammatic reformulation (SDR)

TABLE 20.1 *Early collaboratively agreed exits*

Internal changes	External changes
Saying no to my impulses	OK to say no! Tell people how I feel if they are making me uncomfortable
Recognising my own good work	Don't make alcohol – it's too tempting
Learning from my mistakes – gently!	No drugs
Standing up to my internal critical voice	Connect to interesting people and events
Having and maintaining perspective	Reading
	Connect to my surroundings by noticing stuff (e.g. the colour of leaves on trees)
	Take each day as it comes
	Pacing
	Achievable goals
	Treating and rewarding myself when I have done well

The main content of the revision sessions centred on two aspects of change: (1) reducing substance misuse and (2) attempting to build a more stable sense of self. In relation to substance misuse, the recognition diary keeping had enabled the client to reflect on (for the first time) just how self-destructive and limiting in particular his abuse of alcohol was. The client learnt that the drinking enabled and continued the cut-off state and that the next day was spent in the critical to criticised reciprocal role (as well as feeling physically ill). This temporal ordering of negative state-shifts was a particularly useful insight. The patient decided to terminate all drinking based on the use of the SDR.

The main change method around building a stable sense of self was to articulate and build a value base from which the client could engage in activity consistent with these values. This is a change method from acceptance and commitment therapy (ACT). As part of this initial process the client completed the Valued Living Questionnaire (VLQ), which identified the gap between values that the client aspired to and the gap between those values and the actions the client took in everyday life. This process highlighted that although the client could identify the value (i.e. family being important), he had little idea what this would look like in action. Normal ACT practice shifts from the completion of the VLQ to goal setting. However, as the client had not engaged in the behaviours before, then an intermediate step was taken of defining and operationalising the behavioural content of the value. This process is also advocated by Eifert and Forsyth as a means of staying committed to valued activity. In the current case this involved working collaboratively with the client to define the value (family/father being important) and also then the proposed definition (spending time with his children, doing joint activities and being an effective role model). The table produced by the client as homework between sessions 11 and 12 is reproduced in Table 20.2.

(Continued)

(Continued)

TABLE 20.2   *Value list and associated actions*

Value area	Definition of associated committed actions
Father/family	I should be a consistent part of my children's lives, a good role model and see them as regularly as possible
Friends	To value and keep my friends, but not to own or take over their lives when they are in trouble
Relationship	To share and support each other, to develop together, but to be my own person and not to rescue
Knowledge	To try to develop and grow my knowledge through reading and attending stuff. Don't rule out what feels unfamiliar at first
Community	To be a part of my local community groups – to influence local decisions
Work	To go to work and to try the best I can for my clients without being drawn into rescuing
Self-care	To develop a relationship with myself in which I support and help myself. To mess up and not then throw it all back into my own face

Ending session

The ending of the therapy was planned for in light of the abandoning–abandoned RR and the client was invited to write a goodbye letter (with bespoke headings decided at the penultimate session) and did so. The goodbye letter from the client contained the following themes: (a) more aware of patterns/early life, (b) not drinking, (c) no self-harm and (d) less critical. The letter from the therapist mirrored the content of the client's letter reflecting the alliance during the therapy.

Outcome

The client noted that after abusing substances all his life his decision not to drink alcohol had been life changing. The sobriety enables the patient to connect with and feel the values he had decided for himself, maintain valued activity and crucially feel progress. The client's relationships with people both at work and socially improved and were particularly marked with an increase in assertiveness, a reduction in rescuing and drawing effective self-management boundaries. The client stated that his mood was more stable and he was less prone to depression. The PSQ and the CORE-OM (see Table 20.3) were completed at assessment, termination and 3-month follow-up.

TABLE 20.3   *Psychometric outcomes*

	Assessment score	Termination score	Follow-up score
CORE-OM	27	15	14
PSQ	32	20	15

Scores were analysed using Jacobson's Reliable Change Indicator (RCI). The client made a clinical and reliable change as measured on the CORE-OM and the PSQ between assessment and termination, and analysis showed gains were maintained (non-reliable improvement or deterioration) across the follow-up period for both the CORE-OM and PSQ. At follow-up the client stated that he had used the follow-up period to practise the development of a stable sense of self through consistently connecting with valued activity. The client noted that he had had one episode of binge drinking that had served to reinforce that he could not drink and maintain a positive model of self-care. No other aspects of impulsivity were noted. The client stated that he was coping with life in general in a more effective manner, being more assertive at work and learning a more boundaried interpersonal approach to life.

REFERENCES

[1] Ryle, A. and Kerr, I. B. (2002) *Introducing Cognitive Analytic Therapy: Principles and Practice.* Chichester: John Wiley & Sons.

[2] Kerr, I. B. and Ryle, A. (2005) 'Cognitive analytic therapy', in S. Bloch (ed.), *Introduction to the Psychotherapies.* Oxford: Oxford University Press. pp. 268–86.

[3] Ryle, A., Kellett, S., Hepple, J. and Calvert, R. (2014) 'Cognitive Analytic Therapy at 30', *Advances in Psychiatric Treatment, 20,* 258–68.

[4] Calvert, R. and Kellett, S. (2014) 'Cognitive analytic therapy: a review of the outcome evidence base for treatment', *Psychology and Psychotherapy: Theory, Research and Practice, 87,* 253–77.

[5] Leiman, M. (2004) 'Dialogical sequence analysis', in H. J. M. Hermans and G. Dimaggio (eds), *The Dialogical Self in Psychotherapy.* Brunner–Routledge. pp. 255–70.

[6] Stern, D. N. (2000) *The Interpersonal World of the Infant: A View from Psychoanalysis and Developmental Psychology,* 2nd edn. New York: Basic Books.

[7] Trevarthen, C. and Aitken, K. J. (2001) 'Infant intersubjectivity: research, theory and clinical applications', *Journal of Child Psychology and Psychiatry, 42,* 3–48.

[8] Reddy, V. (2008) *How Infants Know Minds.* Cambridge, MA: Harvard University Press.

[9] Roth, A. and Fonagy, P. (2004) *What Works for Whom? A Critical Review of Psychotherapy Research,* 2nd edn. New York: Guilford Press.

[10] Gabbard, G., Holmes, J. and Beck, J. (eds) (2005) *The Oxford Book of Psychotherapy.* Oxford: Oxford University Press.

[11] James, O. (2007) *Affluenza.* London: Vermilion.

[12] Wilkinson, R. and Pickett, K. (2009) *The Spirit Level: Why More Equal Societies Almost Always Do Better.* London: Allen Lane.

SUGGESTED READING

Gabbard, G., Holmes, J. and Beck, J. (eds) (2005) *The Oxford Book of Psychotherapy*. Oxford: Oxford University Press. This offers a comprehensive comparative overview of differing theoretical traditions and specialist topics in psychotherapy including coverage of the place of CAT.

Ryle, A. and Kerr, I. B. (2002) *Introducing Cognitive Analytic Therapy: Principles and Practice*. Chichester: John Wiley & Sons. This is the current standard introductory text on CAT which gives a more detailed theoretical background to the model and guidance on its clinical application and practice.

Stern, D. N. (2000) *The Interpersonal World of the Infant: A View from Psychoanalysis and Developmental Psychology*, 2nd edn. New York: Basic Books. This is a classic text by a researcher in infant psychology and psychotherapist. It states new and important ideas on the capabilities of the developing infant actually based on observation and experiment.

Wilkinson, R. and Pickett, K. (2009) *The Spirit Level: Why More Equal Societies Almost Always Do Better*. London: Allen Lane. This book has become a classic text that explores the importance of social factors, notably inequality, in determining our collective quality of life including notably mental health. It implicitly raises the issue of how these factors are internalised psychologically and how they might be addressed.

DISCUSSION ISSUES

1. CAT adopts a whole person and transdiagnostic approach that sees symptoms and behaviours as procedures (RRPs) arising from and related to underlying historic formative experiences (RRs). As such it views an exclusive focus on symptoms as potentially unhelpful and possibly reinforcing of formative experiences (e.g. RRs such as 'criticised', 'conditionally loved'), which initially led to the symptomatic RRPs. Discuss.
2. CAT sees the therapeutic relationship and working on its 'ups and downs' (using, for example, the reformulation map) as being a fundamental part of the work of therapy and not just as a vehicle for work. As such it sees the therapy relationship as contributing to fundamental psychological change in itself. Discuss.
3. CAT sees the self and its problems as arising from and shaped by the social and cultural environment in which it developed. It would suggest therefore that social problems should be considered a part of the bigger issue we address as therapist. Discuss.
4. CAT sees time-limitation and ending well as an important aspect of therapy in itself and not simply an imposition of rationing or limitation of something that should ideally be longer. Discuss.

21

Interpersonal Psychotherapy

Elizabeth Robinson and Graham Dyson

INTRODUCTION

Interpersonal psychotherapy (IPT) is a manualised,[1] time-limited, supportive and structured therapy that is used primarily for the treatment of depression, whereby the therapist particularly focuses on the client's interpersonal issues.

IPT focuses on understanding how interpersonal problems can result in a person becoming depressed, as well as how depression can lead to difficulties within relationships. A goal is to foster a greater understanding of the nature of depression and to identify interpersonal factors that may have led to the onset or maintenance of problems. IPT helps the client explore interpersonal difficulties in the here and now to bring about change and improve mood. Problem areas that are explored during the process include: **role transitions** (e.g. moving house, divorce), **complicated bereavement** (suffering a loss without effective mourning), **role disputes** (dissatisfaction or disagreement with others) and **interpersonal sensitivities/deficits** (struggling with forming or maintaining relationships). IPT tries to avoid technical jargon and aims for the therapist and client to work collaboratively to improve the quality of their relationships and increase social support. Relapse prevention and ongoing management form a key component of the therapeutic process.

DEVELOPMENT OF THE THERAPY

The development of IPT was led in the 1970s by a psychiatrist, Gerald Klerman, who was conducting clinical trials of antidepressant medication for people with depression in the USA. He was interested to know if a specific psychotherapy would have the same effect as medication when treating depression. Klerman and colleagues developed and tested IPT in clinical trials of depression.[2,3] Although, IPT was slower to take effect than medication, it was found to be just as effective. Many more studies of IPT have taken place since then and it is now recommended within NICE (National Institute for Health and Care Excellence) guidelines in the UK as a treatment for moderate and severe depression based on the volume of good research evidence. IPT has been adapted for use with other mental health problems, including eating disorders and social anxiety, to good effect. Research has shown equivalent outcomes for IPT and CBT in several studies.[4,5] IPT originally developed as a face-to-face therapy but more recently has also been provided by telephone[6] and in groups.[7]

THEORY AND BASIC CONCEPTS

IPT is a time-limited therapy focusing on the interpersonal aspects of a client's experience of depression. The main aim is to help the individual deal with the interpersonal event or issue, resulting in an associated improvement in their depression. Attention is given to here-and-now events or situations which may lead to and maintain depression for the client. Although the direct focus of IPT is on current relationships and situations, IPT draws upon empirical evidence, including interpersonal[8,9] and **attachment**[10] theories, which suggest that difficulties in these areas during childhood and later development are shown to increase the likelihood of developing mental health difficulties, including depression in later years. The social roots of depression have been widely acknowledged.[11] IPT recognises the value of specifically attending to interpersonal issues and helping a client to develop a sense of influence over their interpersonal world. An insight into past experiences can help clients understand the social context and the current interpersonal consequences on both relationships and functioning. However, the main focus during IPT is on current interpersonal functioning, with specific reference to how this impacts the client's depression. The IPT model uses a medical model to aid understanding, identifying depression as an illness that can be addressed. This is supported by the evidence for physiological change in depression.[12,13] An initial period of psychoeducation helps the client to alleviate guilt and self-blame, as well as challenge the belief that depression is a personal weakness. Sharing the diagnosis, followed by outlining depression as a treatable illness with the emphasis on what can be done to ease symptoms, is an optimistic stance that aims to provide hope of recovery. A measure of depression (e.g. Hamilton Depression Scale)[14] is utilised early on in the process to help clarify symptoms, as well as being used to evaluate change towards the end.

There are four interpersonal focal areas in IPT that contribute to the onset and maintenance of depression.

Complicated bereavement

Bereavements are considered to be one of the most significant life stressors. It is an understandable and natural reaction for an individual to experience intense distress and upset, associated with the loss of a loved one, which is likely to ease off as time progresses. However, there are a smaller number of clients who continue to feel distressed over time and develop depression as a consequence.[15] Ineffective or limited mourning is the interpersonal stressor that maintains depression. Helping a person to begin the mourning process allows them to move forward with their grief and consequently improve their depression.

Role transition

It is very common for an individual to experience frequent changes in personal, social or developmental roles throughout their life, such as divorce or moving house. Often, changes are made without any undue distress and this helps maintain a healthy sense of self and well being. However, some changes in our social or interpersonal world may lead to adjustment difficulties. Changes may be viewed as negative, dissatisfying, unfulfilling or overwhelming and can be perceived as a loss.[16] In some cases this can lead to depression. By helping a client to let go of the previous role and develop the skills and motivation to accept and deal with their changed situation will ultimately lead to improvements in their depression.

Role dispute

It is rare for individuals not to experience conflict and disagreements in relationships. For the most part we look to express differences of opinion and either agree to differ or reach a compromise. However, there are cases when difficulties are not addressed or resolved effectively leading to non-reciprocal role expectations about the relationship.[17,18] For example, there may be differing expectations about how to bring up the children, how to share workload in the office, or who takes responsibility to look after an older relative. The conflicting relationship is perpetuating and maintains a client's depression. IPT helps the client to explore the current difficulties in the disputed relationship, identify differing expectations, highlight communication difficulties and look at alternative approaches to dealing with difficulties that enhance their depression.

Interpersonal deficits/sensitivities

Sometimes individuals may experience difficulties in a number or range of relationships. Patterns of difficulties occur across time and may lead to relationships being viewed as inadequate or unsustaining. As such, individuals tend to withdraw from such relationships or the relationships break down, resulting in increasing feelings of loneliness or isolation.[19] Therefore, a lack of effective and nourishing relationships can lead to the development of depression. Rather than focusing on one specific relationship, as in the case of role disputes, the focus here is on helping the client understand where their difficulties lie in relationships in general. Specifically, it involves helping individuals to look at how to build and maintain their current relationships as well as looking at opportunities to develop new ones.

PRACTICE

The goal of IPT is to improve interpersonal functioning and thereby alleviate the symptoms of depression. IPT is traditionally provided over 16 sessions and has distinct beginning, middle and end phases. The beginning phase comprises the first four sessions. The therapist starts by confirming the diagnosis of depression and work develops from this to place the client in the 'sick role', which helps them to relinquish self-blame and look at what they can do to help with their recovery. There may be an initial period of relinquishing tasks or activities at work or home in order to help with recovery. Accessing help and support from others, as well as encouraging the pursuit of pleasurable activities, form part of this work.

A history is taken assessing details of the client's current experience of depression as well as previous episodes. Interpersonal events or relationships that are linked to the depression are explored. A detailed assessment of current interpersonal relationships and how these may influence their mood (Interpersonal Inventory) is conducted at this point. The Interpersonal Inventory is a key element of the process that informs the rest of the therapy, including the formulation process. The therapist uses an interpersonal formulation to present their understanding of the client's experience of depression, including vulnerability factors and interpersonal areas that may have contributed to and maintained the current depression. The therapist and client both agree on an interpersonal focal area that has meaning to the client and is related to their current experience of depression. This focal area forms the basis of the work of the middle phase sessions.

There are goals and strategies for each of the focal areas used in the middle phase of IPT, which takes place from sessions 5 to 12. Role transition is used as a focus when a client has experienced a change in circumstances, often experienced as a loss that leads to feelings of depression. Here, the aim of work in IPT is to allow the client to mourn the loss of the old role in order to accept and tolerate the new role, perhaps looking at new opportunities as part of their changed circumstances. A role dispute becomes the focus when the client describes dissatisfaction or difficulties in a relationship leading to the onset or maintenance of their depression. The therapist works collaboratively with the client to identify difficulties in the relationship, such as differing expectations or communication issues, and helps the client to explore alternative ways of interpersonal communication or interaction which may help move this relationship forward. Attention is given to complicated bereavement as a focal area after the client has experienced the death of a loved one and has not effectively mourned their loss, resulting in depression. Mourning is facilitated in the sessions as the therapist works with the client exploring their past relationship with their loved one, as well as details of events surrounding and leading up to the death. Much of the work is helping the client recognise, tolerate and deal with the strong affect associated with grief and loss. The client is encouraged to use others in their own interpersonal network to share their thoughts and feelings about the bereavement, facilitating an ongoing mourning process which will help them ease symptoms of depression. Occasionally people experience difficulties in relationships generally; they may feel too shy to get started in relationships, or else they may feel that keeping friendships going is a problem. This can lead to an increased sense of isolation, or general dissatisfaction with the quality of their friendships, which results in depression. The original IPT manual outlined this focal area as interpersonal deficits, highlighting the lack of interpersonal skills the client may have leading to their interpersonal difficulties. Other IPT literature[9,20] refers to this focal area as interpersonal sensitivities; this term may, on some occasions, be more helpful to use with clients. Both terms illustrate the breadth of interpersonal difficulties a client may have. The term 'sensitivities' in practice may be more acceptable to clients, however, this can also be misunderstood and misinterpreted as being 'sensitive'. In reality, clients on occasion may be 'insensitive', blunt, or abrupt with others, for instance, which leads to difficulties in forming and keeping friendships.

Little direct attention is paid to the therapeutic relationship within IPT. Primarily, relationships outside of the sessions become the focus of the therapy. The IPT therapist works with the client to explore their interpersonal resources and how they can optimise them in order to help combat the depression. Initially this may take the form of pursuing pleasurable activities with friends, talking to others about interpersonal difficulties, or general practical help. Later, during middle and end phase work, the therapist explores with the client how they can continue to build up and make use of their interpersonal network in order to maintain any early gains when working with the agreed focus targeting their depression. There is a clear advantage in that the support is geared to what is acceptable and works for the client and this network remains available and accessible when the IPT sessions come to an end. This may be one factor that helps the client stay well once they have recovered.

The end phase of IPT includes the final four sessions. The therapist initially explores how the client feels about ending therapy. There can be a range of feelings noticed by clients at this stage of IPT, including: satisfaction, accomplishment, pleasure, relief, trepidation, anxiety and sadness. With the latter, the therapist acknowledges how sadness can be part of a natural process of endings, and explores with the client whether this is related to the ending process or is likely to be a feature of depression more generally. At the end of IPT the therapist provides a model for healthy endings and shares with the client their own feelings on ending therapy. This can be very helpful to deal with difficult emotions, such as sadness, but in addition allows the therapist to focus on the client's achievements and accomplishments throughout the process. The therapist then invites the client to review and evaluate treatment themselves. This allows an opportunity to identify what specific interpersonal work has been covered that has led to improvements in their depression and interpersonal functioning. Attention is then focused on how this work can continue after the therapy process is finished. Throughout IPT the therapist explores how the client can optimise the use of their interpersonal resources to either continue on their recovery journey or else maintain improvements made. Recognising the possibility of a potential future episode of depression can be important when exploring early warning signs of depression. Employing interpersonal strategies, seeking professional help and reviewing medication can all be recognised as valuable towards maintaining wellbeing in the future.

IPT allows a healthy model for endings and provides the client an opportunity to deal with any concerns and prepare for how they can either continue with progress or maintain their wellbeing.

WHICH CLIENTS BENEFIT MOST?

IPT is a manualised treatment for depression and has been used for individuals with major depression across the lifespan, helping adolescents, adults and older adults.[4,20,21,22] A shorter version (six sessions) of interpersonal counselling[23] has been used for mild depression in primary care settings. Brief IPT, comprising of eight sessions, has been developed in an attempt to offer sessions to groups of clients who may have difficulty attending for 16 sessions, such as women with young families.[24] At present, there is less research data available in support of this approach.

In addition, IPT has been used to treat other problems, such as eating disorders[25,26] and post-natal depression.[27] Anxiety disorders are also showing a favourable response to IPT, including social anxiety disorder.[28] However, the results for IPT with post-traumatic stress disorder are mixed.[29,30] Clients with borderline personality disorder often experience challenging and difficult relationships, and it is perhaps not surprising that a therapy with a distinct interpersonal focus such as IPT could help individuals with personality problems.[31] Also, a modification of interpersonal therapy, combining the approach with social rhythms therapy (**IPSRT**), has been developed, tested and manualised for clients with bipolar disorder, with good results.[32]

IPT offers short-term, targeted treatment plans with measurable outcomes, similar to cognitive behaviour therapy (CBT). The strength of IPT perhaps lies in its lack of jargon and direct relevance in terms of relationships. One study showed that clients and therapists had a preference for IPT over CBT,[33] which could have positive effects on the level of engagement with the process. IPT also involves a relatively short period of training, in comparison with other therapies, given that the method is grounded within the manual. Therefore, it can be seen as an attractive option for healthcare providers aiming to deliver cost-effective healthcare. With a focus on managing loss, conflict resolution, role clarification and interpersonal skill development, IPT enhances strategies for living and therefore can improve functioning and minimise the chance of relapse in the future; studies of recurrent depression support this.[34]

However, IPT requires the person be an active participant in therapy rather than a passive one and it also involves the implementation of alternative strategies of behaviour on the part of the client. It therefore can be difficult to work with clients who are unable or unwilling to put these into effect. IPT has been thought to be limited in its focus on interpersonal issues in the here and now and as such maladaptive ways of thinking or intrapsychic conflicts are not directly addressed. While further evidence is needed on the efficacy of IPT for problems other than depression, the body of research is growing for a range of other mental health problems.

CASE STUDY

The Client

Sarah is a woman in her late fifties who came for help after she had become depressed four months earlier. She was crying a lot and felt sad and empty. She told the therapist that she could not face food and that she felt tense and nauseous when trying to eat. Sarah also reported difficulty sleeping, which included getting off to sleep, staying asleep through the night and waking early. She felt she was 'running on flat batteries' and could not motivate herself to work, attend to her appearance or see friends or family. She felt no pleasure or enjoyment in activities that were previously pleasurable. She did report feeling that life was worthless but this did not translate into any plans to harm herself. Her assessment on the **Hamilton Depression Scale** gave a score of 27, indicating severe depression. Sarah outlined that the onset of her depression occurred after her husband of 35 years had come home from work one day and 'out of the blue' told her he was leaving her for another woman. She felt completely devastated by his decision and could not function well within day-to-day life as a result. IPT was introduced as an option for treatment to help Sarah to deal with her depressed mood. Following identification of the issues surrounding confidentiality, Sarah agreed that IPT sounded like a good option for her and she started weekly sessions.

The Therapy

A time line revealed that this was her first and only episode of depression. She was not taking any antidepressant medication. Her husband's sudden announcement that he was leaving was considered to be the interpersonal trigger that led to the onset of depression.

Completion of an interpersonal inventory with Sarah during the initial phase showed she had a 'bland' relationship with her husband, she felt he was there to provide financial security but she did not get any pleasure from their time together. There had been no emotional warmth or support and he did little in the house to help. Sarah had had no contact with him since he left their marital home. She had two daughters and four grandchildren. While she had had little contact with them before the separation, the contact had increased since her husband's departure. Despite feeling embarrassed and ashamed about this, she enjoyed seeing more of them. She worked at a local factory as a cleaner and enjoyed the company of her fellow workers, but this was limited to time at work as she had not gone to any work social events previously. The therapist felt that there was some scope to increase social contact with her interpersonal network to improve her depressive symptoms. This was explored as part of using the sick role within IPT, accepting depression as a temporary illness

(Continued)

(Continued)

and looking at what steps she could take to help with her recovery. She agreed that she was depressed. The therapist also encouraged her to express her feelings openly, which she had struggled to do within the previous relationship. Although she was struggling with her energy levels, she found some comfort in the social contact when at work. To offer support, her daughters invited her for evening meals, which contributed to a significant improvement in her mood. She was encouraged to start to look at pursuing pleasurable social activities. It was not long before she had started to meet with a friend for a coffee, which gave her confidence and encouraged her to find other ways of engaging.

At the end of the initial phase Sarah and her therapist were in agreement that the depression could best be dealt with by focusing on helping her deal with the role transition and adapt to the recent change in role. Together, Sarah and her therapist explored what life was like when Sarah was married to her husband (reviewing the old role). She outlined many of the things that had been difficult for her; including the fact that he had been critical and controlling. They did not do things together as a couple and he would expect her to manage the home and cook the meals. Her social contact, even with her children and grandchildren, was limited as he did not enjoy this and preferred her to stay at home. Sarah was surprised initially that when she thought about the relationship in detail that there were so many things about which she felt dissatisfied. Sarah had to think hard to come up with any positives in their relationship. She outlined that being in a relationship, having companionship and the securities of a partner were factors that had kept them together.

Next, therapy focused on how events unfolded leading to the separation. The sudden role change for Sarah had led to her feeling devastated initially. The therapist helped her to process her feelings regarding how she felt about her initial relationship (old role) and explored the range of emotions she felt regarding the very sudden change in her life and the loss of her marriage. Focusing on recognising and expressing her affect allowed Sarah to mourn the loss of this relationship and move forward to accept her status as being separated (new role). There were clear opportunities for her in her new role, which were identified. Sarah was seeing her children and grandchildren more regularly, she had joined a local gym and was getting fit, had started to meet with friends from work and also planned a holiday with a friend. Throughout the middle phase Sarah's depression gradually improved, her Hamilton Depression Scale score[14] showed she was mildly depressed at this point in treatment.

During the end phase of the therapy sessions, Sarah acknowledged a clear sense of achievement. She welcomed and enjoyed her new status of being a single woman, as well as her new sense of independence. Evaluating her experience of therapy gave the therapist the opportunity to celebrate Sarah's achievements and reinforce the interpersonal changes she had made which had contributed to her recovery. However, Sarah did reveal some strong feelings of sadness that therapy was ending and this was normalised and explored by the therapist. Sarah was encouraged to look to the future to think about how she could continue to use pleasurable activity, get support from her interpersonal group and recognise any signs of depression to maintain her wellbeing in the longer term.

REFERENCES

[1] Klerman, G. L., Weissman, M., Rounsaville, B. and Chevron, E. (1984) *Interpersonal Psychotherapy for Depression*. New York: Basic Books.

[2] Klerman, G. L., DiMascio, A., Weissman, M. M. and Chevron, E. (1974) 'Treatment of depression by drugs and psychotherapy', *American Journal of Psychiatry, 131,* 186–91.

[3] DiMascio, A., Weissman, M. M., Prusoff, B. A., Neu, C., Zwilling, M. and Klerman, G. L. (1979) 'Differential symptom reduction by drugs and psychotherapy in acute depression', *Archives of General Psychiatry, 36(13),* 1450–6.

[4] Elkin, I., Shea, T., Watkins, J. T., Imber, S. D, Sotsky, S. M., Collins, J. F., Glass, D. R., Pilkonis, P. A., Leber, W. R., Docherty, J. P., Fiester, S. J. and Parloff, M. B. (1989) 'National Institute of Mental Health Treatment of Depression Collaborative Research Programme', *Archives of General Psychiatry, 46,* 971–82.

[5] Wilfley, D. E., Agras, S., Telch, C. F., Rossiter, E. M., Schneider, J. A., Cole, A. G., Sifford, L. A. and Raeburn, S. D. (1993) 'Group cognitive–behavioural therapy and group interpersonal psychotherapy for the nonpurging bulimic individual: a controlled comparison', *Journal of Consulting Clinical Psychiatry, 62(2),* 296–305.

[6] Miller, L. and Weissman, M. (2002) 'Interpersonal psychotherapy delivered over the telephone to recurrent depressives. A pilot study', *Depression & Anxiety, 16(3),* 114–17.

[7] Wilfley, D. E., Mackenzie, K. R., Welch, R. R., Ayres, V. E. A. and Weissman, M. M. (2000) *Interpersonal Psychotherapy for Groups*. New York: Basic Books.

[8] Meyer, A. (1957) *Psychobiology: A Science of Man*. Springfield, IL: Charles C. Thomas.

[9] Stack Sullivan, H. S. (1953) *The Interpersonal Theory of Psychiatry*. New York: Norton.

[10] Bowlby, J. (1969) *Attachment*. New York: Basic Books.

[11] Becker, R. E., Heimber, R. G. and Bellack, A. S. (1987) *Social Skills Training Treatment for Depression*. New York: Pergamon.

[12] Tafet, G. E. (2001) 'Correlation between cortisol level and serotonin uptake in patients with chronic stress and depression', *Cognitive, Affective, & Behavioral Neuroscience, 1(4),* 388–93(6).

[13] Martin, S. D., Martin, E., Rai, S. S., Richardson, M. A. and Royall, R. (2001) 'Brain flow changes in depressed patients treated with interpersonal psychotherapy or Venlafaxine hydrochloride', *Archives of General Psychiatry, 58,* 641–7.

[14] Hamilton, M. (1980) 'Rating depressive patients', *Journal of Clinical Psychiatry, 41,* 21–4.

[15] Zisook, S. and Shuchter, S. R. (1991) 'Depression throughout the first year after the death of a spouse', *American Journal of Psychiatry, 54,* 320–33.

[16] Overholser, J. C. and Adams, D. M. (1977) 'Stressful life events and social support in depressed psychiatric inpatients', in T. W. Miller et al. (eds), *Clinical Disorders and Stressful Life Events*. Madison, CT: International University Press.

[17] Paykel, E. S., Myers, J. K., Dienelt, M. N. et al. (1969) 'Life events and depression – a controlled study', *Archives of General Psychiatry, 21(6),* 753–60.

[18] Perlin, L. I. and Lieberman, M. A. (1977) 'Social sources of emotional distress', in R. Simmons (ed.), *Research in Community and Mental Health*. Greenwich, CT: JAI Press.

[19] Brown, J., Harris, T. and Copeland, J. R. (1977) 'Depression and loss', *British Journal of Psychiatry, 30*, 1–18.

[20] Stuart, S. and Robertson, M. (2012) *Interpersonal Psychotherapy: A Clinician's Guide,* 2nd edn. Boca Raton, FL: CRC Press.

[21] Mufson, L. and Fairbanks, J. (1996) 'Interpersonal psychotherapy for depressed adolescents: a one year naturalistic follow up study', *Journal of American Academics Child and Adolescent Psychiatry, 35(9)*, 1145–55.

[22] Miller, M. D. (2008) 'Using interpersonal psychotherapy (IPT) with older adults today and tomorrow: a review of the literature and new developments', *Current Psychiatry Reports, 10*, 17–22.

[23] Weissman, M. M. and Klerman, G. L. (1993) *New Adaptations of Interpersonal Psychotherapy.* Washington, DC: APA.

[24] Swartz, H. A., Grote, N., Frank, E., Bledsoe, M., Fleming, M. and Shear, M. (2008) 'Brief interpersonal psychotherapy for depressed mothers whose children are receiving psychiatric treatment', *American Journal of Psychiatry, 165(9)*, 1155–62.

[25] Fairburn, C. G., Jones, R. and Peveler, R. C. (1991) 'Three psychological treatments for bulimia nervosa: a comparative trial', *Archives of General Psychiatry, 48*, 463–9.

[26] Wilfley, D. E., Iacovino, J. M. and Van Buren, D. J. (2012) 'Interpersonal psychotherapy for eating disorders', in J. C. Markowitz and M. M. Weissman (eds), *Casebook of Interpersonal Psychotherapy.* New York: Oxford University Press. pp. 125–48.

[27] O'Hara, M. W., Stuart, S., Gorman, L. L. and Wenzel, A. (2000) 'Efficacy of interpersonal psychotherapy for post partum depression', *Archives of General Psychiatry, 57*, 1039–45.

[28] Lipsitz, J. D., Gur, M., Vermes, D., Petkova, E., Cheng, J., Miller, N., Laino, J., Liebowitz, M. R. and Fyer, A. J. (2008) 'A randomized trial of interpersonal therapy versus supportive therapy for social anxiety disorder', *Depression and Anxiety, 25(6)*, 542–53.

[29] Cukor, J., Spitalnick, J., Difede, J., Rizzo, A. and Rothbaumd, B. (2009) 'Emerging treatments for PTSD', *Clinical Psychology Review, 29(8)*, 715–26.

[30] Bleiberg, K. L. and Markowitz, J. C. (2005) 'A pilot study of interpersonal psychotherapy for posttraumatic stress disorder', *American Journal of Psychiatry, 162(1)*, 181–3.

[31] Markowitz, J. C., Bleiberg, K. L., Pessin, H. and Skodol, A. E. (2007) 'Adapting interpersonal psychotherapy for borderline personality disorder', *Journal of Mental Health, 16*, 103–16.

[32] Frank, E. (2005) *Treating Bipolar Disorder: A Clinician's Guide to Interpersonal and Social Rhythm Therapy.* New York: Guilford Press.

[33] Fairburn, C. (1997) 'Interpersonal therapy for bulimia nervosa', in D. Garner and P. Garfinkel (eds), *Handbook of Treatment for Eating Disorders.* New York: Guilford Press.

[34] Frank, E. (1991) 'Interpersonal psychotherapy as a maintenance treatment for patients with recurrent depression', *Psychotherapy, 28(2)*, 259–66.

SUGGESTED READING

Stuart, S. and Robertson, M. (2012) *Interpersonal Psychotherapy: A Clinician's Guide*, 2nd edn. Boca Raton, FL: CRC Press. This book includes clinically-based descriptions with numerous case studies, highlighting key issues in IPT, as well as reproducible diagrams and flow charts for use by therapists and their clients.

Weissman, M. M., Markowitz, J. C. and Klerman, G. L. (2000) *Comprehensive Guide to Interpersonal Psychotherapy*. New York: Basic Books. This guide updated the original manual, published in 1984. It outlines the theory and process of IPT, and includes information on IPT in mood disorders and non-mood disorders, including eating disorders, anxiety disorders and various applications of the model.

Weissman, M. M., Markowitz, J. C. and Klerman, G. L. (2007) *Quick Clinician's Guide to Interpersonal Psychotherapy*. Oxford: Oxford University Press. This was the third update of the original manual. It is aimed at busy clinicians who want to refer to a quick and easy guide to use IPT in practice. It is a practical size and provides easy reading on IPT. It includes the same adaptations as the preceding manual and adds borderline personality disorder. Some additional information is provided on IPT in groups and across cultures.

Weissman, M. M. and Markowitz, J. C. (eds) (2012) *Casebook of Interpersonal Psychotherapy*. Oxford: Oxford University Press. This is the fourth update of the IPT manual. It outlines many case examples of IPT in mood disorders and non-mood disorders, including eating disorders, post-traumatic stress disorder, social anxiety disorder and borderline personality disorder. It also outlines how IPT has been used in diverse populations including adolescents, old age depression, medically ill patients, developing countries and in low income groups. The delivery of IPT in groups, by telephone and in an inpatient setting is presented.

DISCUSSION ISSUES

1. Despite being shown to be as effective as CBT within evidence-based research studies, why has IPT not developed to the same extent as CBT in the UK?
2. What are the potential advantages and disadvantages of encouraging the 'sick role' within IPT?
3. What are the advantages and disadvantages of IPT versus other therapies for depression?
4. What makes IPT readily adaptable for use with mental health problems other than depression?

22

Lifeskills Counselling

Richard Nelson-Jones and Stephen Palmer

Lifeskills counselling, otherwise known as lifeskills therapy, or lifeskills helping, is an educational approach that has as its starting point the problems of living of ordinary people rather than those who have been seriously emotionally deprived or possess a psychiatric disorder. To live effectively and affirm their existence, all people require lifeskills.

Lifeskills counselling's philosophical basis is humanistic–existential – humanistic in terms of the value placed on the individual, in a sense a leap of faith about the improvability of humans; existential in terms of its emphasis on choice and on creating one's existence within the challenges presented by death, suffering, change, meaning, isolation and freedom. On top of this, lifeskills counselling uses insights from 'cognitive behavioural' approaches to counselling, those focusing on altering thoughts and actions, to sharpen the humanistic–existential message and provide clients with the skills they require to be more effective both now and in the future.

DEVELOPMENT OF THE APPROACH

In 1984, the origins of lifeskills counselling appeared in *Personal Responsibility Counselling and Therapy: An Integrative Approach*[1] This book attempted to provide a framework for counselling, **lifeskills** training and self-helping which used personal responsibility as a central concept that integrated or put the different elements of theory and practice together. Right from the beginning, I (R. N.-J.) addressed the struggles and problems of ordinary people and tried to integrate the contributions of leading humanistic, existential, behavioural and cognitive therapists, for instance Carl Rogers, Irvin Yalom, Albert Ellis and Aaron Beck.

In 1988, the second edition of my book *Practical Counselling and Helping Skills*[2] presented the first version of my five-stage model of counselling practice. Then, in 1993, the third edition[3] presented the first full statement of the theory and practice of what was then called lifeskills helping. Here I (R. N.-J.) introduced a simple super-language, called **skills language**, that frees counsellors to draw from different theoretical positions without becoming trapped in their separate languages. In 1997, both the theory and practice of the approach were updated in the book's fourth edition,[4] where the term lifeskills counselling replaced lifeskills helping. My emphasis on developing lifeskills in the wider community is reflected in my education and training books, *Relating Skills: A Practical Guide to Effective Personal Relationships*[5] and *Using your Mind: Creative Thinking Skills for Work and Business Success.*[6]

Lifeskills counselling still represents work in progress. Having moved to Thailand in mid-1997, I (R. N.-J.) explored the application of Eastern philosophy, religion and psychology to Western concerns and issues. I later developed cognitive humanistic therapy, and in 2004 the approach was published in my book *Cognitive Humanistic Therapy: Buddhism, Christianity and Being Fully Human.*[7] In my later book, published in 2007, *Life Coaching Skills: How to Develop Skilled Clients*,[8] I include the CASIE model, which is a new variation of the **DASIE model** described later in this chapter.

THEORY AND BASIC CONCEPTS

Following are some central basic assumptions of lifeskills counselling. Fuller descriptions of lifeskills counselling's theory and basic concepts are provided elsewhere.[4,9]

Skills language

Most commonly, life is regarded in terms of physical or biological life. However, the main concern of lifeskills counselling is with psychological rather than biological life. The primary focus of psychological life is the mind rather than the body and, correspondingly, the primary goal of psychological life is attaining human potential rather than physical health. Human psychological life goes beyond physical existence in that humans have a unique capacity for self-awareness and choice.

Apart from such obviously biological functions as breathing, virtually all human behaviour is viewed in terms of learned lifeskills. The term lifeskills in itself is neither positive nor negative. Lifeskills may be strengths or deficits depending on whether or not they help people both to survive and to maintain and develop potentials. A neutral definition of the term lifeskills is: *lifeskills are sequences of choices that people make in specific skills areas*. A positive definition of the term lifeskills is: *lifeskills are sequences of choices affirming psychological life that people make in specific skills areas*.

Skills language means consistently using skills to describe and analyse people's behaviour. In regard to counselling, skills language means thinking and talking about clients' problems in terms of lifeskills strengths and deficits. In particular, skills language involves identifying the specific **thinking skills** and action skills deficits that maintain clients' problems, and then translating them into counselling goals. Feelings too are important. However, feelings represent people's animal nature and are not skills in themselves. People can influence their feelings for good or ill through their use of thinking and action skills.

The inner and outer games of living

If people are to take charge of their lives, they need to think and act effectively. A simple way to highlight the distinction is to talk about the inner and outer games of living. The inner game refers to what goes on inside you, how you think and feel, or your thinking skills and feelings. The outer game refers to what goes on outside you, how you act, or your action skills. Thinking and feeling tend to be inner processes, whereas actions are out in the open.

Outer game: action skills

Action skills involve observable behaviours. Action skills refer to what you do and how you do it rather than what and how you feel and think. These skills vary by area of application: for instance, relating, studying, or working. There are five main ways that you can send action skills messages:

- *Verbal messages* – messages that you send with words: for example, saying 'I like you' or 'I hate you.'
- *Voice messages* – messages that you send through your voice: for instance, through your volume, articulation, pitch, emphasis and speech rate.
- *Body messages* – messages that you send with your body: for instance, through your gaze, eye contact, facial expression, posture, gestures, physical proximity and clothes and grooming.
- *Touch messages* – a special category of body messages. Messages that you send with your touch: for instance, through what part of the body you use, what part of another's body you touch, how gentle or firm you are, and whether or not you have permission.
- *Action messages* – messages that you send when you are not face to face with others: for example, sending a memo.

Inner game: thinking skills

Though people are influenced by their genetic endowment, learning histories and social and cultural environments, lifeskills counselling assumes that, to a large extent, individuals create their thinking. Each of us possesses the potential to create unskilful as well as skilful thoughts, or a mixture of both.

Below are brief descriptions of 12 thinking skills areas derived from the work of leading psychiatrists and psychologists. The thinking skills are presented in 'you' language both to heighten readers' awareness of their meaning and to make the point that counsellors and clients require the same lifeskills.

- *Understanding the relationships between how you think, feel and act.* You possess insight into how you can influence how you feel, physically react and act, through how you think. You are aware that your feelings and actions in turn influence your thoughts.
- *Owning responsibility for choosing.* You assume personal responsibility for your life. You are aware that you are the author of your existence and that you can choose how you think, act and feel. You are aware of the limitations of existence, such as your death.
- *Getting in touch with your feelings.* You acknowledge the importance of getting in touch with how you feel. You are able to access significant feelings, for instance your wants and wishes, and accurately state them as thoughts.
- *Using coping self-talk.* Instead of talking to yourself negatively before, during and after specific situations, you can make coping self-statements that help you to stay calm and cool, coach you in what to do, and affirm the skills, strengths and support factors you possess.
- *Choosing realistic rules.* Your unrealistic rules make irrational demands on yourself, others and the environment: for instance, 'I must be liked by everyone', 'Others must not make mistakes', and 'Life must be fair'. Instead you can develop realistic rules: for instance, 'I prefer to be liked, but it is unrealistic to expect this from everyone'.
- *Perceiving accurately.* You avoid labelling yourself and others either too negatively or too positively. You distinguish between fact and inference and make your inferences as accurate as possible.
- *Explaining cause accurately.* You explain the causes of events accurately. You avoid assuming too much responsibility by internalizing, 'It's all my fault', or externalizing, 'It's all your fault'.
- *Predicting realistically.* You are realistic about the risks and rewards of future actions. You assess threats and dangers accurately. You avoid distorting relevant evidence with unwarranted optimism or pessimism.
- *Setting realistic goals.* Your short-, medium- and long-term goals reflect your values, are realistic, are specific and have a time frame.
- *Using visualizing skills.* You use visual images in ways that calm you down, assist you in acting competently to attain your goals and help you to resist giving in to bad habits.
- *Realistic decision-making.* You confront rather than avoid decisions and then make up your mind by going through a systematic and realistic decision-making process.
- *Preventing and managing problems.* You anticipate and confront your problems. You assess the thinking and action skills you require to deal with them. You state working goals and plan how to implement them.

In reality, some of the skills overlap. For instance, all of the skills, even visualizing, involve self-talk. To distinguish the skill of coping self-talk I stipulate a definition by stating that it refers to self-statements relevant to coping with specific situations. Inter-relationships between skills can also be viewed on the dimension of depth. Arguably, owning responsibility for choosing is a more fundamental skill which is then exemplified in specific situations by using the skill of explaining cause accurately. Similarly, perceptions may represent underlying rules. Another example is that of explanations of cause underlying predictions. For instance, sales people making cold calls are more likely to be pessimistic if their tendency is to explain the cause of unsuccessful calls as permanent and pervasive rather than as transient and specific.

A deficit can be absence of a skills strength as well as presence of a skills deficit. For example, a person suffering from hypertension might just have the deficit of failing to use relaxing imagery rather than the added deficit of using anxiety-engendering imagery as well. Be careful about inappropriately stating deficits in all-or-nothing terms: for example, for many people insufficient use of relaxing imagery may be more accurate than failure to use any relaxing imagery at all.

Personal responsibility

Focusing on personal responsibility is almost like focusing on one's nose. Though right in front of the face, the concept is not always easy to observe. Lifeskills counselling adopts the existential notion of people as responsible for the authorship of their lives. Another metaphor is that people are responsible for inventing their lives. Authorship or invention requires a continuous process of choosing. Personal responsibility is an inner process in which people work from 'inside to outside'. This process starts with people's thoughts and feelings and leads to their observable actions. Furthermore, especially as people grow older, many if not most of the significant barriers to assuming responsibility are internal rather than external.

PRACTICE

Individual lifeskills counselling, the focus of this chapter, is one of a range of interventions for acquiring, maintaining and developing lifeskills in the wider community. Other interventions include couples and group lifeskills counselling, lifeskills education and training, self-helping, consultancy, and focusing on organizational change.

Goals

Lifeskills counselling goals encompass assisting clients both to manage problems and to alter the underlying problematic skills that sustain problems. Problem–management or problem–solving models are useful, since frequently clients require help to manage or solve immediate problems. However, a big drawback of such models is that they inadequately address the *repetition phenomenon*, the repetitive nature of many clients' problems. Clients require assistance in developing life skills strengths that last into the future and not just in managing or solving specific current problems. In reality, due to practical considerations, often counsellors and clients compromise on the amount of

time and effort they take to address underlying patterns of skills deficits that predis-
pose and position clients for further problems.

The elegant application of lifeskills counselling aims to develop the skilled person.
Below, illustrative lifeskills required by the skilled person are grouped according to the
five Rs of affirming psychological life.

- *Responsiveness.* Responsiveness skills include existential awareness, awareness
  of feelings, awareness of inner motivation, and sensitivity to anxiety and guilt.
- *Realism.* Realism refers to the thinking skills listed earlier, such as coping self-talk
  and visualizing.
- *Relating.* Relating skills include: disclosing, listening, caring, companionship, sexual relating, assertion, managing anger and solving relationship problems.
- *Rewarding activity.* Rewarding activity skills include identifying interests, work
  skills, study skills, leisure skills and looking after physical health skills.
- *Right-and-wrong.* Right-and-wrong skills include social interest that transcends
  one's immediate environment, and ethical living.

DASIE: the five-stage model

The practice of lifeskills counselling is structured around DASIE, a systematic five-
stage model. The model provides a framework or set of guidelines for counsellor
choices. DASIE is a five-stage model not only for managing or solving problems but
also for addressing underlying problematic skills. DASIE's five stages are:

D	*Develop* the relationship and clarify problems
A	*Assess* and **restate** problems in skills terms
S	*State* goals and plan interventions
I	*Intervene* to develop lifeskills
E	*Emphasize* take-away and end

Stage 1 Develop the relationship and clarify problems

Stage 1 starts with pre-helping contact with clients and either ends sometime in the
initial interview or may take longer. It has two main overlapping functions: developing
supportive counselling relationships and working with clients to identify and obtain fuller
descriptions of problems. Supportive counselling relationships go beyond offering empathy, non-possessive warmth and genuineness to more actively fostering client self-support.

Many of the counsellor skills used in stage 1 are the same as those used in
other approaches: for example, reflective responding, summarizing and confronting.
Counsellors collaborate with clients to explore, clarify and understand problems.
Together they act as detectives to 'sniff out' and discover what are clients' real problems and agendas. Then they break them down into their component parts.

Counsellors can use skills language when structuring initial sessions. One possibility is to start the session by giving clients an open-ended permission to tell their

stories. After they respond, the following statement might structure the remainder of the session.

> You've given me some idea of why you've come. Now I'd like to ask some more questions to help us to clarify your problem(s) [specify]. Then, depending on what we find, I will suggest some skills to help you cope better. Once we agree on what skills might help you, then we can look at ways to develop them. Does this way of proceeding sound all right?

Homework in the form of '**take–away**' assignments is a feature of lifeskills counselling. Between-session learning can be enhanced by clients listening at home to audio cassettes of counselling sessions. In addition, counsellors may negotiate other take-away assignments with clients, for instance completing monitoring logs.

Stage 2 Assess and restate problem(s) in skills terms

The object of this stage is to build a bridge between *describing* and *actively working* on problems and their underlying skills deficits. In stage 1, problems were described, amplified and clarified, largely in everyday language. In stage 2, counsellors build upon information collected in stage 1 to generate and investigate propositions or hypotheses about ways clients think and act that contribute to maintaining their difficulties. Stage 2 ends with a restatement of at least either the main or the most pressing problems in skills terms.

The emphasis in counsellors' questions differs in stage 2 from that in stage 1. In stage 1, counsellors ask questions to clarify clients' existing frames of reference. In stage 2, counsellors are likely to question as much from their own as from their clients' frames of reference. While the major focus is on pinpointing skills deficits, attention is also paid to identifying skills strengths and resources.

Counsellors need to develop good skills at restating problems in skills terms and communicating and negotiating these working definitions with clients. Restatements of problems in skills terms are essentially hypotheses, based on careful analysis of available information, about clients' thinking and action skills deficits. As hypotheses they are open to modification in light of further or better information.

I write restatements in skills terms on whiteboards. Visual presentation makes it easier for clients to retain what you say, if necessary suggest alterations, and make written records. I use a simple diagram to present thinking and action skills weaknesses for sustaining each problem. At the top of the diagram there are headings for 'Thinking skills deficits/goals' and 'Action skills deficits/goals'. These headings are divided by a long vertical line down the middle to allow specific deficits to be listed on either side.

Stage 3 State goals and plan interventions

Stage 3 consists of two phases: stating deficits as goals and planning interventions. Assuming counsellors succeed in restating problems in skills terms, stating goals becomes a relatively simple matter. Working goals are the flip–side of restatements: positive statements of skills strengths to replace existing skills deficits. Counsellors can easily change on the whiteboard statements of deficits into statements of goals. Counsellors should ensure that clients understand and agree with goals. Then client and counsellor record this statement as a basis for their future work.

Stating deficits as goals provides the bridge to choosing interventions. Counsellors not only hypothesize about goals, but also about ways to attain them. An important distinction exists between interventions and plans. Interventions are intentional behaviours, on the part of either counsellors or clients, designed to help clients attain problem management and problematic skills goals. Plans are statements of how to combine and sequence interventions to attain goals. Plans may be of varying degrees of structure. Most often I work with open plans that allow clients and myself flexibility to choose which interventions, to attain which goals, when. Clients may be more motivated to work on skills and material relevant at any given time than run through predetermined programmes independent of current considerations. Furthermore, owing to the frequently repetitive nature of clients' skills deficits, work done in one session may be highly relevant to work done on the same or different problems in other sessions.

Stage 4 Intervene to develop lifeskills

Lifeskills counsellors are developmental educators or, in more colloquial terms, user-friendly coaches. To intervene effectively they require good relating skills and good training skills. It is insufficient to know *what* interventions to offer without also being skilled at *how* to offer them. Skilled lifeskills counsellors strike appropriate balances between relationship and task orientations; less skilled helpers err in either direction.

Table 22.1 depicts methods of psychological education or training and methods of learning in lifeskills counselling. Counsellors work much of the time with the three training methods of 'tell', 'show' and 'do'. They require special training skills for each. 'Tell' entails giving clients clear instructions concerning the skills they wish to develop. 'Show' means providing demonstrations of how to implement skills. 'Do' means arranging for clients to perform structured activities and homework tasks.

TABLE 22.1   *Methods of psychological education or training and methods of learning*

Psychological education or training method	Learning method
Facilitate	Learning from self-exploring and from experiencing self more fully
Assess	Learning from monitoring and evaluating
Tell	Learning from hearing
Show	Learning from observing
Do	Learning from doing structured activities and take-away assignments
Consolidate	Learning from developing self-helping skills in all the above modes

Individual sessions in the intervention stage may be viewed in four, often overlapping, phases: preparatory, initial, working and ending. The preparatory phase entails counsellors thinking in advance how best to assist clients. Counsellors ensure that, if appropriate, they have available: session plans, training materials, blank lifeskills counselling take-away sheets, and audio–visual aids, for instance whiteboards and audio cassette-recorders.

The initial phase consists of meeting, greeting and seating, then giving permission to talk. Though a skill not restricted to the initial phase, early on counsellors may wish to negotiate session agendas. For instance, counsellors may go from checking whether the client has any current pressing agendas, to reviewing the past week's homework, to focusing on one or more problematic skills and/or problems in clients' lives. As necessary, agendas may be altered during sessions.

Within a supportive relationship, the working phase focuses on specific thinking skills and action skills interventions designed to help clients manage problems and develop lifeskills strengths. Whenever appropriate, counsellors assist clients to use skills language. Frequently clients are asked to fill out 'takeaway' sheets in which they record skills-focused work done on the whiteboard during sessions.

The ending phase lasts from toward the end of one session to the beginning of the next. This phase focuses on summarizing the major session learnings, negotiating take-away assignments, strengthening commitment to between-session work, and rehearsing and practising skills outside counselling.

Stage 5 Emphasize take-away and end

Most often either counsellors or clients bring up the topic of ending before the final session. This allows both parties to work through the various task and relationship issues connected with ending the contact. A useful option is to fade contact with some clients by seeing them progressively less often. Certain clients may appreciate the opportunity for booster sessions, say one, two, three or even six months later.

Lifeskills counselling seeks to avoid the 'train and hope' approach. Transfer and maintenance of skills is encouraged by such means as developing clients' self-instructional abilities, working with real-life situations during counselling, and using between-session time productively to listen to session cassettes and to rehearse and practise skills. Often counsellors make up short take-away audio digital recordings focused on the use of specific skills in specific situations: for instance, the use of coping self-talk to handle anxiety when waiting to deliver a public speech. Counsellors can encourage clients to make up similar coping self-talk recordings for other situations: for instance, participating in meetings. Thus, not only do clients possess recordings they can use to maintain skills in future, they have also acquired the skills of making new cassettes, if needed.

In addition, counsellors work with clients to anticipate difficulties and setbacks to taking away and maintaining lifeskills (see CASIE below). Then together they develop and rehearse coping strategies for preventing and managing lapses and relapses. Sometimes clients require help identifying people to support their efforts to maintain skills. Counsellors also provide information about further skills-building opportunities.

The CASIE model of self-coaching

Brief counselling is becoming the norm. Unfortunately clients may not learn the knowl-edge required to be able to apply problem-solving skills to issues as they arise in their lives once counselling has finished. I (R. N.-J) developed a simple model that clients can use to self-coach[8]. The model is called CASIE for client self-helping purposes:

C   *Confront* and clarify the area for change
A   *Assess* and restate the area into skills to improve
S   *Select* self-helping interventions
I   *Intervene*
E   *Evaluate* the consequences of self-helping interventions

Clients can be taught the model in the penultimate or final counselling sessions. A take-away sheet can be used to remind the client of the framework.

WHICH CLIENTS BENEFIT MOST?

Lifeskills counselling assumes that clienthood is ubiquitous. Its major emphasis is on the 'screwed-up-ness' of the majority. Illustrative problems for which it is appropriate include those pertaining to study, relationships, work, health and sport. I [R. N.-J.] have successfully used lifeskills counselling with previously long-term, severely depressed redundant executives. Both work and home problems contributed to the severity of such clients' depression. Lifeskills counselling is not just an approach to remedying psychological pain. Counsellors, clients and others wishing to attain superior levels of psychological functioning can adopt the approach and create skilful thoughts in all areas of their lives.

Lifeskills counselling is also appropriate to non-Western cultures. I have run lifeskills counselling workshops in Hong Kong, Malaysia and Thailand. In each country, participants have indicated that, with some cultural adjustments, they can beneficially use the approach.

CASE STUDY

The Client

Louise, age 43, was an accountant made redundant from a very senior posi-tion three years earlier. At the time of entering counselling, Louise worked for a relatively low salary in a position whose status was below where she was two moves ago. In the previous three years Louise had been for numerous interviews for very senior positions. However, she received consistent feedback

(Continued)

(Continued)

that, while selection panels evaluated her technical skills as excellent, they had serious reservations about her people skills and found her too pedantic. Louise was referred to me in my capacity as sessional counselling psychologist for an outplacement consulting firm. She had already been through the firm's standard interview training programme as well as participating in numerous discussions with one of the firm's outplacement advisers.

The Therapy

In the initial session, I started by giving Louise permission to tell her story. As well as using empathic responding, I asked questions that clarified the history of Louise's problem, and her feelings, physical reactions, thoughts and actions in relation to it. All the time I was observing how Louise related to me, looking for clues as to why panels found her so off-putting. She was one of the brightest and most personally overwhelming clients I have ever come across. Stage 1 of the lifeskills counselling model, 'develop the relationship and clarify problems', merged into stage 2, 'assess and restate problems in skills terms', as I asked a series of further questions to confirm or negate hypotheses about how she might be sustaining her problems.

After about 40 minutes, I asked Louise if she would mind my looking at my notes and drawing together threads so that I could put some suggestions on the whiteboard about skills she might address, as the basis for establishing goals for our work together. I told Louise that we could discuss anything about which she was either unclear or unhappy. As appropriate, we could modify, rephrase or erase my suggestions. The groundwork for the restatement in skills terms was laid in the first 40 minutes of the session, so there were no real surprises for Louise. Table 22.2 shows the restatement in skills terms. Note that I have identified and illustrated skills deficits/goals. I use the term deficits/goals to indicate from the start that deficits are goals.

Toward the end of the initial session, I proceeded to stage 3, 'state goals and plan interventions'. I explained to Louise how deficits could be translated into goals.

> Louise, I'd just like to say again that areas shown on the whiteboard as deficits are really skills that we can work to develop. In other words, the deficits are our goals. For example, your thinking skills goals are developing a realistic rule, accurate perceptions and replacing negative with coping self-talk. Your action skills goals are developing good interview skills by focusing on improving your verbal, voice and body messages. I'll now reword each skills deficit on the whiteboard accordingly, but leave the illustrations of the deficits so that we can recall them later. Afterwards, if you agree, we can both write this down on a specially designed assessment of problem(s) form so that we can remember it for future sessions.

Louise and I decided to use an open plan to address her interview skills deficits. In reality her interview skills deficits were just the tip of the iceberg in a well-entrenched, cumbersome, pedantic and off-putting style of professional relating.

Stage 4, 'intervene to develop lifeskills', began in the second session. Throughout this stage, at the start of each session Louise and I would establish an agenda for that session's work. Early sessions focused mainly on building Louise's interview skills. As a take-away assignment Louise made a list of questions she was likely to be asked at interviews. In addition, I wrote up on the whiteboard some points about answering questions. Then Louise and I engaged in a series of cassette-recorded question-and-answer sessions. After each trial we played back the cassettes, looking for specific evidence to confirm or negate her using the skills entailed in the points written on the whiteboard. During her evaluation of the cassettes, Louise became aware of how altering her verbal, voice and body messages could effect interviewers and it became clear that interviews for senior positions had an important relationship as well as knowledge agenda. In the third session, using the whiteboard, I helped Louise to dispute her rule that she must give the perfect answer and then developed with her a statement of a more realistic rule.

TABLE 22.2   *Restatement of Louise's problem in skills terms*

Thinking skills deficits/goals	Action skills deficits/goals
Unrealistic rule	Poor interview skills
• 'I must give the perfect answer'	• verbal: answers too long, perceived as unfocused and lecturing
Perceiving inaccurately	• voice: booming, overpowering
• interviews for senior positions are knowledge exams	• body: stiff posture, eyes glaring, unsmiling knowledge exams (not user-friendly)
• others' reactions to personal style not picked up adequately	
• own strengths insufficiently acknowledged	
Negative self-talk	
• 'I don't know how to improve'	
• 'Things are going to go wrong again'	

Subsequent sessions incorporated the following interventions: more practice in the verbal, voice and body message skills of answering questions; making up a visualized rehearsal cassette starting with some brief mental relaxation skills, followed by appropriate calming, coaching and affirming self-talk for waiting outside interview rooms and then going in and answering the first few questions competently; and identifying and listing Louise's competencies and then cassette-recording them twice, first with my voice and then with Louise's voice.

Stage 5, 'emphasize take-away and end', took place both during as well as at the end of counselling. During counselling, Louise was given a series of take-away assignments both to prepare for sessions and also to consolidate skills targeted in sessions. In addition, Louise was encouraged to practise her skills in her daily professional life, which she did with increasing success. This daily practice was especially important because Louise was not going for interviews.

(Continued)

(Continued)

For both personal and professional reasons, she did not want to leave her present job unless it was for a substantial improvement. Indeed, a second agenda emerged as Louise realized that the skills she was learning for job interviews were similar to skills she required for holding and advancing in jobs. Louise saw me for about 25 sessions over two years. Over the last 18 months sessions were monthly and then bimonthly. As time went by, Louise was getting increasingly good feedback about how well she related in her company, first being promoted to company secretary and then being made a director, with an accompanying salary increase and the provision of a company car. Louise acknowledged that the lifeskills counselling approach had helped her to break down and address obtaining, holding and advancing in a job skills deficits that had, for a considerable period of time, held her back professionally.

REFERENCES

[1] Nelson–Jones, R. (1984) *Personal Responsibility Counselling and Therapy: An Integrative Approach.* London: Harper & Row.

[2] Nelson–Jones, R. (1988) *Practical Counselling and Helping Skills: Helping Clients to Help Themselves,* 2nd edn. London: Cassell.

[3] Nelson–Jones, R. (1993) *Practical Counselling and Helping Skills: How to Use the Lifeskills Helping Model,* 3rd edn. London: Cassell.

[4] Nelson–Jones, R. (1997) *Practical Counselling and Helping Skills: How to Use the Lifeskills Counselling Model,* 4th edn. London: Cassell.

[5] Nelson–Jones, R. (1996) *Relating Skills: A Practical Guide to Effective Personal Relationships.* London: Cassell.

[6] Nelson–Jones, R. (1997) *Using Your Mind: Creative Thinking Skills for Work and Business Success.* London: Cassell.

[7] Nelson–Jones, R. (2004) *Cognitive Humanistic Therapy: Buddhism, Christianity and Being Fully Human.* London: Sage.

[8] Nelson–Jones, R. (2007) *Life Coaching Skills: How to Develop Skilled Clients.* London: Sage.

[9] Nelson–Jones, R. (1995) 'Lifeskills counselling', in R. Nelson–Jones, *The Theory and Practice of Counselling,* 2nd edn. London: Cassell.

SUGGESTED READING

Nelson-Jones, R. (1995) 'Lifeskills counselling', in R. Nelson-Jones, *The Theory and Practice of Counselling,* 2nd edn. London: Cassell. This is a more advanced and thorough textbook presentation, about three times the length of the present chapter, of the theory and practice of lifeskills counselling.

Nelson-Jones, R. (1997) *Practical Counselling and Helping Skills: How to Use the Lifeskills Counselling Model*, 4th edn. London: Cassell. This book is divided into seven parts: part 1 contains four introductory chapters; parts 2–6 contain 15 chapters that systematically present the counsellor skills required for each of the lifeskills counselling model's five stages; and part 7 concludes the book with a chapter on developing your counselling skills.

Nelson-Jones, R. (2004) *Cognitive Humanistic Therapy: Buddhism, Christianity and Being Fully Human*. London: Sage. The book is divided into two overlapping parts: understanding being fully human (mainly theory) and cultivating being fully human (mainly practice). It is a book about how to use therapeutic tools to develop reason and love in the interests of oneself, others and humankind.

Nelson-Jones, R. (2007) *Life Coaching Skills: How to Develop Skilled Clients*. London: Sage. This book provides a practical introduction to the skills needed to be an effective life coach and incorporates a wide range of practical activities for coaches to use to help their clients develop self-coaching skills. It presents a four-stage life coaching model based around the core concepts of relating, understanding, changing and client self-coaching.

DISCUSSION ISSUES

1. Critically discuss the notion of skills language as presented in this chapter.
2. Critically discuss the proposition that people create their thinking.
3. Critically discuss the usefulness of the DASIE five-stage model of counselling practice.
4. What relevance, if any, has the theory and practice of lifeskills counselling for how you counsel and live?

23

Multimodal Therapy

Stephen Palmer

INTRODUCTION

Multimodal counselling and therapy is a **technically eclectic** and systematic approach. The approach is technically eclectic as it uses techniques taken from many different psychological theories and systems, without necessarily being concerned with the validity of the theoretical principles that underpin the different approaches from which it takes its techniques and methods. The techniques and interventions are applied systematically, based on data from client qualities, the therapist's clinical skills and specific techniques.

The approach uses a unique assessment procedure that focuses on seven different aspects or dimensions (known as modalities) of human personality. Not only is a serious attempt made to tailor the therapy to each client's unique requirements, but the therapist also endeavours to match his or her interpersonal style and interaction to the individual needs of each client, thereby maximizing the therapeutic outcome.

DEVELOPMENT OF THE THERAPY

During the 1950s Arnold Lazarus, a psychologist, undertook his formal clinical training in South Africa. The main focus of his training was underpinned by psychodynamic and person-centred theory and methods. In addition, he attended seminars provided by Joseph Wölpe, a psychologist, thereby learning about conditioning therapies based on behaviour therapy. During 1957 he spent several months as an intern at the Marlborough Day Hospital in London, where the orientation was Adlerian (see Chapter 3). He believed that no one system of therapy could provide a complete understanding of either human development or condition. In 1958 he became the first psychologist to use the terms 'behaviour therapist' and 'behaviour therapy' in an academic article.[1]

Lazarus conducted follow-up enquiries into clients who had received behaviour therapy and found that many had relapsed. However, when clients had used both behaviour and cognitive techniques, more durable results were obtained. In the early 1970s he started advocating a broad but systematic range of cognitive behavioural techniques and his follow-up enquiries indicated the importance of breadth if therapeutic gains were to be maintained. This led to the development of multimodal therapy, which places emphasis on seven discrete but interactive dimensions, or modalities, which encompass all aspects of human personality. However, Lazarus has noted that, as a therapy, it does not really exist.

In Britain, as a counselling, health and coaching psychologist, I have developed multimodal therapy and applied it to the field of stress management, counselling and coaching.[2,3]

THEORY AND BASIC CONCEPTS

Modalities

People are essentially biological organisms (neurophysiological/biochemical entities) who behave (act and react), emote (experience emotional responses), sense (respond to olfactory, tactile, gustatory, visual and auditory stimuli), imagine (conjure up sights, sounds and other events in the mind's eye), think (hold beliefs, opinions, attitudes and values), and interact with one another (tolerate, enjoy or endure various interpersonal relationships). These seven aspects or dimensions of human personality are known as modalities. By referring to these seven modalities as Behaviour, Affect, Sensations, Images, Cognitions, Interpersonal and Drugs/biology, the useful acronym and aide-memoire BASIC I.D. arises from the first letter of each.[4] ('Affect' is a psychological word for emotion and 'cognitions' represent all thoughts, attitudes and beliefs.)

From the multimodal perspective these seven modalities may interact with each other, for example an unpleasant image or daydream and a negative thought may trigger a negative emotion such as anxiety or depression. The multimodal approach rests on the assumption that unless the seven modalities are assessed, therapy is likely to overlook significant concerns. Clients are usually troubled by a multitude of specific problems that should be dealt with by a similar multitude of specific interventions or techniques.[5] For example, a client may suffer from a simple fear of spiders, anxiety about giving presentations at work, sleep disturbances, a lack of exercise and a poor diet. Each problem will probably need a specific intervention to help the client improve his or her condition.

Multimodal therapists have found that individuals tend to prefer some of the BASIC I.D. modalities to others. They are referred to as 'imagery reactors' or 'cognitive reactors' or 'sensory reactors' depending upon which modality they favour.

Principle of parity

In multimodal therapy the therapist and client are considered equal in their humanity (the principle of parity). However, the therapist may be more skilled in certain areas in which the client has particular deficits. Therefore it is not automatically assumed that clients know how to deal with their problems and have the requisite skills. The therapist may need to model or teach the client various skills and strategies to help overcome his or her problem(s). It should be understood that having superior skills in certain areas does not make therapists superior human beings!

Thresholds

One key assumption made in multimodal therapy is that people have different thresholds for pain, frustration, stress, external and internal stimuli in the form of sound, light, touch, smell and taste. Psychological interventions can be applied by individuals to help modify these thresholds but often the genetic endowment or predisposition has an overriding influence in the final analysis. For example, a client with a low tolerance to pain may be able to use psychological distraction techniques such as relaxing imagery, but is still likely to need an anaesthetic when receiving minor fillings at the dentist.

Theories underpinning multimodal therapy

Multimodal therapy is underpinned by a number of general theories. Multimodal therapists, however, do not inflexibly adhere to any one theory in a rigid manner.[4] These theories will be briefly discussed below.

People's personalities stem from the interplay between their social learning and conditioning, their physical environment and their genetic endowment. Social learning relates to what is learnt within social contexts, such as how to behave in certain situations (see classical and operant conditioning). Conditioning occurs consciously and sometimes non-consciously when people are rewarded or punished for particular behaviours. For example, a child who exhibits bad table manners may trigger a parent's wrath, and thus becomes conditioned to improve his or her table manners. However, other children may have observed how their parents eat at the table and without consciously thinking (that is, non-consciously) imitate their parents' good table manners. In this case the parents would have acted as good role models. This process is known as modelling. (Learning theory and social learning theory were developed by two well-known psychologists, Burrhus Skinner and Albert Bandura.) People respond to their perceived environment and not the real environment, and many factors can influence their perceptions: attitudes, values, beliefs, selective attention, problem-solving skills and goals. An individual's genetic endowment can greatly affect his or her ability to cope with different thresholds and favoured modalities.

Therefore each client is unique and may need a personalized therapy programme to help him or her overcome his or her problem(s).

According to systems theory, people need other people to give purpose and meaning to their existence. This emphasis on relationships may be the focus of interpersonal difficulties and problems that clients may bring to therapy. For effective therapy to occur, sometimes all the people involved will need to receive group, couples or family therapy to deal with the problem concerned. For example, in sex therapy, if the male partner is impotent, often his partner will need to attend therapy too for therapeutic progress to be made.

Communications theory states that all actions or behaviour imply some kind of message. Communication goes beyond just talking and includes non-verbal messages such as eye contact or posture. These messages make a statement about the two or more people communicating. For example, the same sentence spoken by a manager to their employee with a facial smile or a frown can convey a positive or negative message respectively. Although both parties are communicating with each other it is not necessarily in a productive manner.

The development of problems and how they are maintained

Problems develop and are maintained for a variety of reasons. Social learning, systems, and communication theories discussed in the previous section highlight some of the ways problems can arise and how they are maintained. Of course, underlying all problems is the biological and genetic dimension that goes to help make up a human being. In this section we will review the additional key factors.

Misinformation

Over a period of time people may learn incorrect assumptions and beliefs about life. For example, the beliefs 'I must perform well otherwise I'm a failure', or 'I'm worthless if my partner leaves me', or 'Life should be easy', may be learnt or imbibed by listening to significant others such as peers, siblings, parents or teachers. These beliefs may lead to considerable stress when external life events conflict with them. Couples may also hold on to unhelpful beliefs or myths, such as 'If you feel guilty, confess'.

Due to misinterpreting their doctor's advice many people have misunderstood medical and health-related issues, such as treatment of cancer or heart disease. Unless the health professionals correct these errors then patient compliance to medical procedures may be hindered or even non-existent.

Unlike the case with misinformation, with missing information people have not learnt the necessary skills, knowledge or methods to either understand or undertake particular activities or recognize specific problems. For example, people may not have in their repertoire of behaviour job interview skills, friendship skills, communication skills, or assertiveness skills etc. They may not realize that a pain in their left arm could signify heart disease and that it might be strongly advisable to have a medical check-up.

Defensive reactions

People avoid or defend against discomfort, frustration, pain, or negative emotions such as shame, guilt, depression and anxiety. Although it sounds quite natural to avoid fears or the unbearable pain of loss, people do not learn how to conquer them unless they confront them. For example, if a person has a fear of travelling by airplane he or she could easily avoid this mode of transport. However, there might be certain job expectations that require the person to fly across the Atlantic. If the person wanted to keep the job he or she would need to deal with this problem sooner rather than later. According to learning theory, the main method of overcoming flying phobia is to experience exposure to flying. Although this can be partially undertaken using the person's imagination, the most effective technique is to fly on the airplane. Initially, this might trigger very high levels of anxiety which only gradually subside or to which the person habituates after an hour or two of exposure to flying. This is no different from the advice given to horse-riders who fall off their horse: 'Get straight back on the horse immediately.'

Lack of self-acceptance

People tend to link their behaviour skills deficits directly to their totality as a human being. Depending upon the particular belief the person holds, this tends to lead to anxiety, shame, anger or depression. For example, a person may believe, 'If I fail my exam, I'm a total failure as a human being.' A more realistic and logical way of looking at the situation could be, 'If I fail my exam all it proves is that I've got exam skills deficits. I can still accept myself as a fallible human being.' The unhelpful beliefs may have been imbibed from parents and other significant people in the child's life but they may be reinforced and perpetuated by the person constantly re-indoctrinating him- or herself on a regular basis throughout adulthood. In multimodal therapy the content of self-defeating or unrealistic beliefs is examined and is replaced by more self-helping and realistic beliefs.

From psychological disturbance to psychological health

The key issues discussed in the previous sections and the path to psychological health can be expressed in the form of the BASIC I.D. modalities below:

> *Behaviour:* ceasing unhelpful behaviours; performing wanted behaviours; stopping unnecessary or irrational avoidances; taking effective behaviours to achieve realistic goals.
> *Affect:* admitting, clarifying and accepting feelings; coping or managing unpleasant feelings and enhancing positive feelings; abreaction (that is, living and recounting painful experiences and emotions).
> *Sensation:* tension release; sensory pleasuring; awareness of positive and negative sensations; improving threshold tolerance to pain and other stimuli.

Imagery: developing helpful coping images; improving self-image; getting in touch with one's imagination.

Cognition: greater awareness of cognitions; improving problem-solving skills; modifying self-defeating, rigid beliefs; enhancing flexible and realistic thinking; increasing self-acceptance; modifying beliefs that exacerbate low thresholds to frustration or pain (for example, 'I can't stand it' to 'I don't like it but I'm living proof that I can stand it'); correcting misinformation and providing accurate missing information.

Interpersonal: non-judgemental acceptance of others; model useful interpersonal skills; dispersing unhealthy collusions; improve assertiveness, communication, social and friendship skills.

Drugs/biology: better nutrition and exercise; substance abuse cessation; alcohol consumption in moderation; medication when indicated for physical or mental disorders.

PRACTICE

Goals of multimodal therapy

The goals of multimodal therapy are to help clients to have a happier life and achieve their own realistic goals. Therefore the goals are tailored to each client. A philosophy of long-term hedonism as opposed to short-term hedonism is advocated whereby the client may need to decide how much pleasure they may want in the present compared to the sacrifices they may have to make to attain their desires and wishes. For example, to go to college and obtain a good degree may necessitate working reasonably hard for a period of three years and not attending as many parties as previously.

The relationship between the therapist and client

The relationship is underpinned by core therapeutic conditions suggested by Carl Rogers, a psychologist who developed person–centred counselling. These core conditions are empathy, congruence and unconditional positive regard (see Chapter 16 for explanation). Although a good therapeutic relationship and adequate rapport are usually necessary, multimodal therapists consider they are often insufficient for effective therapy. The therapist–client relationship is considered as the soil that enables the strategies and techniques to take root. The experienced multimodal therapist hopes to offer a lot more by assessing and treating the client's BASIC I.D., endeavouring to 'leave no stone (or modality) unturned'.

Multimodal therapists often see themselves in a coach/trainer–trainee or teacher–student relationship as opposed to a doctor–patient relationship, thereby encouraging self-change rather than dependency. Therefore the usual approach taken is active–directive, where the therapist provides information and suggests possible strategies and interventions to help the client manage or overcome specific problems. However, this would depend upon the issues being discussed and the personality characteristics of the client. Flexible interpersonal styles of the therapist that match client needs can reduce attrition (i.e. premature termination of therapy) and help the therapeutic relationship and alliance. This approach of the therapist is known in multimodal therapy as being an 'authentic chameleon'. For example, if a client states that she wants 'A listening ear to help me get over the loss of my part-ner', then she may consider an active-directive approach as intrusive and possibly offensive. On the other hand, a client who states 'I would value your comments and opinions on my problems', may become very irritated by a therapist who only reflects back the client's sentiments and ideas. Others may want a 'tough, no-non-sense' approach and would find a 'warm, gentle' approach not helpful or conducive to client disclosure.[2] This flexibility in the therapist's interpersonal therapeutic style underpins effective multimodal therapy. Therapists are expected to exhibit different aspects of their own personality to help the therapeutic relationship and clients to reach their goals. The term 'bespoke therapy' has been used to describe the custom-made emphasis of the approach.[6]

The process of change

The process of change may commence even before the first therapy session, as cli-ents are usually sent details about the approach with some explanation of the key techniques, such as relaxation or thinking skills. Occasionally, therefore, the client has already started using simple self-help techniques before the therapy formally com-mences. In Britain, included with the details is a client checklist of issues the client may want to discuss with the therapist at the first meeting[7] (see Appendix 3). This checklist encourages the client to ask the therapist relevant questions about the approach, the therapist's qualifications and training and contractual issues, thereby giving the client more control of the session and therapy.

During the course of therapy, the client's problems are expressed in terms of the seven BASIC I.D. modalities and client change occurs as the major different problems are managed or resolved across the entire BASIC I.D. Initially, sessions are often held weekly. As client gains are made, then the sessions are held with longer intervals in between, such as a fortnight or a month. Termination of therapy usually occurs when clients have dealt with the major problems on their modality profile or feel that they can cope with the remaining problems.

Initial assessment

Assessment helps both the client and therapist to understand the client's presenting problems and their degree of severity. The assessment procedure then leads on to the development of a therapy programme focusing on dealing with each problem. In multimodal therapy, the first or second therapy sessions are used to place the client's problems within the BASIC. I.D. framework (see later). The therapist uses the initial interview to derive relevant information.[2,4]

1. Are there any signs of psychiatric disorder?
2. Is there any evidence of depression, suicidal or homicidal tendencies?
3. What are the persisting complaints and their main precipitating events?
4. What appear to be some important antecedent (i.e. preceding) events?
5. Who or what appears to be maintaining the client's problems?
6. What does the client wish to derive from therapy?
7. Are there clear indicators for adopting a particular therapeutic style?
8. Are there any indicators as to whether it would be in the client's interests to be seen as part of dyad (i.e. two), triad, family unit and/or group?
9. Can a mutually satisfying relationship ensue, or should the client be referred elsewhere?
10. Has the client previous experience of therapy or relevant training? If yes, what was the outcome? Were any difficulties encountered?
11. Why is the client seeking therapy at this time and not last week, last month or last year?
12. What are some of the client's positive attributes and strengths?

In the beginning phase of therapy the multimodal therapist is collecting information and looking for underlying themes and problems. During the first session the client is usually asked to give details about his or her problem(s) near the start of the session, and often within only 20 minutes the client has provided information about a large majority of the 12 determinations. Further questioning will normally fill in any gaps without appearing too intrusive. Then the therapist will usually explain that it is useful to investigate the client's problems in terms of the BASIC I.D. modalities. This can be undertaken fairly easily in the session by using a whiteboard or paper that the client can see. With the therapist's assistance, the client decides which Behaviours he or she would like to stop, introduce or modify. This is written on the whiteboard and then the next BASIC I.D. modality, Affect, is assessed. This process is continued until all of the seven modalities have been assessed. Table 23.1 is a BASIC I.D. chart,[8] more commonly known as a '**modality profile**', which in this example illustrates John's problems (see Case Study below). If appropriate, during the first session the therapist will make a therapeutic intervention such as using a relaxation technique, to help the client cope with his or her immediate problem(s) and inject some hope into the situation.

Depending upon the time left in the session, the therapist and client can either negotiate a therapy programme or postpone this to the following session. If the client reads an article or book about techniques and interventions that are used in multimodal therapy between sessions 1 and 2, then he or she is more likely to be constructively involved in negotiating a comprehensive therapy programme in the next session. The use of books, articles, handouts and audio–visual material is known as bibliotherapy. In addition, the client may be asked to complete a **Multimodal Life History Inventory** (MLHI)[9] at home. This is a 15-page questionnaire which can aid assessment and the development of a therapy programme. It has sections on each modality and includes routine history-taking and expectations regarding therapy. It prevents the therapist asking too many questions during the first session.

In a later session an additional assessment tool is used. To obtain more clinical information and also general goals for therapy, a structural profile is drawn.[4] This

TABLE 23.1   *John's modality profile (or BASIC I.D. chart)*

Behaviour	Eats/walks fast, always in a rush, hostile, competitive: indicative of type A behaviour
	Avoidance of giving presentations
	Accident proneness
Affect	Anxious when giving presentations
	Guilt when work targets not achieved
	Frequent angry outbursts at work
Sensation	Tension in shoulders
	Palpitations. Frequent headaches
	Sleeping difficulties
Imagery	Negative images of not performing well
	Images of losing control
	Poor self-image
Cognition	I must perform well otherwise it will be awful and I couldn't stand it
	I must be in control
	Significant others should recognize my work
	If I fail then I am a total failure
Interpersonal	Passive/aggressive in relationships
	Manipulative tendencies at work
	Always puts self first
	Few supportive friends
Drugs/biology	Feeling inexplicably tired
	Takes aspirins for headaches
	Consumes 10 cups of coffee a day
	Poor nutrition and little exercise

can be derived from the MLHI or by asking clients to rate subjectively, on a scale of 1 to 7 how they perceive themselves in relation to the seven modalities. The therapist can ask a number of different questions that focus on the seven modalities:

Behaviour: How much of a 'doer' are you?
Affect: How emotional are you?
Sensation: How 'tuned in' are you to your bodily sensations?
Imagery: How imaginative are you?
Cognition: How much of a 'thinker' are you?
Interpersonal: How much of a 'social being' are you?
Drugs/biology: To what extent are you health-conscious?

Then in the session the therapist can illustrate these scores graphically by representing them in the form of a bar chart on paper. Figure 23.1[4] illustrates John's structural profile (discussed below in the Case Study). Then clients are asked in what way they would like to change their profiles during the course of therapy. Once again the client is asked to rate subjectively each modality on a score from 1 to 7. Figure 23.2[8] illustrates John's desired structural profile.

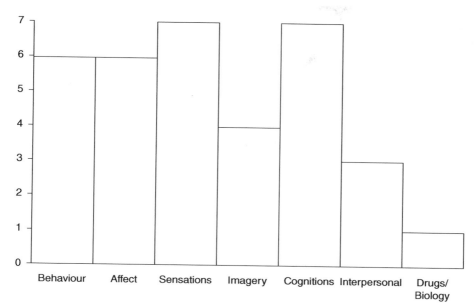

FIGURE 23.1   *John's structural profile*

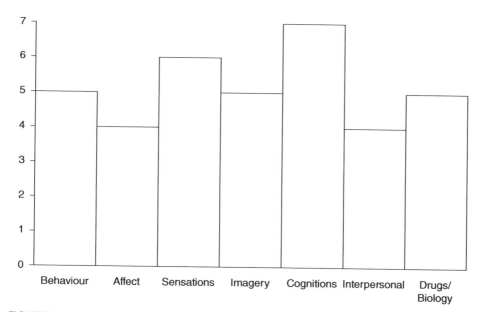

FIGURE 23.2   *John's desired structural profile*

From assessment to an individual counselling programme

Multimodal therapists take researcher Gordon Paul's[10] mandate very seriously: '*What* treatment, by *whom*, is most effective for *this* individual with *that* specific problem and under *which* set of circumstances?' (p. 111). In addition the *relationships of choice* are also considered. After the initial therapy or assessment session, assuming that the therapist believes that he or she can offer the right type of help and approach to the client, they then negotiate a therapy programme.

As multimodal therapy is technically eclectic, it will use techniques and interventions from a variety of different therapies. Table 23.2[8] highlights the main techniques

TABLE 23.2 *Frequently used techniques in multimodal therapy and training*

Modality	Techniques/interventions	Modality	Techniques/interventions
Behaviour	Behaviour activation Behaviour rehearsal Behavioural experiments Empty chair Exposure programme Fixed role therapy Modelling Paradoxical intention Psychodrama Reinforcement programmes Response prevention/cost Risk-taking exercises Self-monitoring and recording Stimulus control Shame attacking	Cognition	Bibliotherapy Challenging faulty inferences Cognitive rehearsal Coping statements Correcting misinformation Disputing irrational beliefs Focusing Positive self-statements Problem-solving training Providing missing information Rational proselytizing Self-acceptance training Thought stopping
Affect	Anger expression/management Anxiety management Feeling identification	Interpersonal	Assertiveness training Communication training Contracting Fixed role therapy Friendship/intimacy training Graded sexual approaches Paradoxical intentions Role play Social skills training
Sensation	Biofeedback Hypnosis Meditation Mindfulness training Relaxation training Sensate focus training Threshold training	Drugs/biology	Alcohol reduction programme Lifestyle changes, e.g. exercise, nutrition, etc. Referral to physicians or other specialists Stop smoking programme Weight reduction and maintenance programme
Imagery	Anti-future-shock imagery Associated imagery Aversive imagery Compassion focused imagery Coping imagery Implosion and imaginal exposure Motivational imagery Positive imagery Rational emotive imagery Resilience enhancing imagery Time projection imagery		

used. Although these are largely based on behaviour therapy, cognitive therapy and rational emotive behaviour therapy, techniques are also taken from other approaches, such as psychodynamic and Gestalt therapy. To avoid repetition, readers are guided to the other relevant chapters in this book to learn about the majority of these techniques. In this section we will focus on techniques and strategies that are used more exclusively in multimodal therapy.

A full modality profile

Once the modality profile consisting of the problem list divided into each modality has been noted down, then the therapist and client negotiate techniques and interventions that can be used to help deal with each problem. Table 23.3[8] is John's full modality profile, which will be discussed later in the Case Study. The modality profile guides the course of therapy, keeping the therapist and client focused on the particular problems and the specific interventions. During the course of therapy, the profile is modified as new relevant information is obtained. It is important for clients to be involved with developing the therapy programme to ensure that they understand the rationale for each intervention recommended and take ownership of their own programme. Often clients will suggest interventions that will be helpful, such as joining an assertiveness, self-hypnosis, exercise, weight management or meditation class. The therapist will always take these ideas seriously as they may well be beneficial.

Second-order BASIC I.D.

Second-order BASIC I.D. is undertaken when the interventions or techniques applied to help a specific problem do not appear to have resolved it. This is a modality profile that solely focuses on the different aspects of a resistant problem, as opposed to the initial assessment, which looks more at the overview or 'big picture'.

Tracking and bridging

Tracking is another procedure regularly used in multimodal therapy in which the 'firing order' of the different modalities is noted for a specific problem. Therapy interventions are linked to the sequence of the firing order of the modalities.

Clients often have a favoured modality which they may use to communicate with the therapist, for example, talking about the sensations, cognitions or images they may experience. They would be known as 'sensory reactors', 'cognitive reactors' or 'imagery reactors' respectively. The highest scores on their structural profiles often reflect the modality reactor. Multimodal therapists deliberately use a **bridging** procedure to initially 'key into' a client's preferred modality, before gently exploring a modality that the client may be intentionally or unintentionally avoiding, such as the affect/emotion modality.

TABLE 23.3 *John's full modality profile (or BASIC I.D. chart)*

Modality	Problem	Proposed therapy programme
Behaviour	Eats/walks fast, always in a rush, hostile, competitive: indicative of type A behaviour	Discuss advantages of slowing down; disadvantages of rushing and being hostile; teach relaxation exercise; dispute self-defeating beliefs
	Avoidance of giving presentations	Behavioural experiment; teach necessary skills; dispute self-defeating beliefs
	Accident proneness	Discuss advantages of slowing down
Affect	Anxious when giving presentations	Anxiety management
	Guilt when work targets not achieved	Dispute self-defeating thinking
	Frequent angry outbursts at work	Anger management; dispute anger-inducing beliefs
Sensation	Tension in shoulders	Self-massage; muscle relaxation exercise
	Palpitations	Anxiety management, e.g. breathing relaxation technique, dispute catastrophic thinking
	Frequent headaches	Relaxation exercise and biofeedback
	Sleeping difficulties	Relaxation or self-hypnosis tape for bedtime use; behavioural retraining; possibly reduce caffeine intake
Imagery	Negative images of not performing well	Coping imagery focusing on giving adequate presentations
	Images of losing control	Coping imagery of dealing with difficult work situations and with presentations; 'step-up' imagery[1]
	Poor self-image	Positive imagery[1, 11]
Cognition	I must perform well otherwise it will be awful and I couldn't stand it	Dispute self-defeating and stress-inducing beliefs; coping statements; cognitive restructuring; ABCDE paradigm[1]; bibliotherapy; coping imagery[1]
	I must be in control	
	Significant others should recognize my work	
	If I fail then I am a total failure	
Interpersonal	Passive/aggressive in relationships	Assertiveness training
	Manipulative tendencies at work	Discuss pros and cons of behaviour
	Always puts self first	Discuss pros and cons of behaviour
	Few supportive friends	Friendship training[1]
Drugs/biology	Feeling inexplicably tired	Improve sleeping and reassess; refer to GP
	Taking aspirins for headaches	Refer to GP; relaxation exercises
	Consumes 10 cups of coffee a day	Discuss benefits of reducing caffeine intake
	Poor nutrition and little exercise	Nutrition and exercise programme

Format of a typical session

The format of sessions is adapted to what would enable the client to reach his or her therapeutic goals. However, it is often useful to employ a recognizable structure. This could include setting an agenda of therapeutic items the client and therapist wish to discuss in the session. The agenda would usually include reviewing the client's homework assignments from the previous session; agreeing topics to be covered in the present session; negotiating further relevant homework assignments; eliciting client feedback about the session and tackling any problems that may have arisen during the session.

WHICH CLIENTS BENEFIT MOST?

Multimodal therapy has been shown to benefit children, adults and older client groups experiencing a wide range of problems. For example, those suffering from anxiety-related disorders such as agoraphobia, panic attacks, phobias, obsessive–compulsive disorders; depression, post-traumatic stress disorder; sexual problems; anorexia nervosa; obesity; enuresis; substance and alcohol abuse; airsickness; schizophrenia. As therapists are expected to adjust their interpersonal style to each client, they may encounter fewer relationship difficulties when compared to other less flexible approaches. This flexible approach should lead to a reduced rate of attrition (i.e. dropout) from therapy.

However, as with other therapies, multimodal therapy has its failures. Some clients are not prepared to face their fears, challenge their unhelpful thinking, use coping imagery, practise relaxation techniques, become assertive with significant others, etc. Others may have psychiatric disorders or other difficulties that prevent them from engaging in therapy at a particular time. Some clients are in the precontemplative stages of change and have not made up their minds to change and take on the responsibility of therapy. However, in these cases the multimodal therapist may initially use Motivational Interviewing skills in an attempt to overcome ambivalence to change. Or the client may choose to return to therapy at a later stage in their lives.

CASE STUDY

The Client

John was a 43-year-old married man with no children. He worked as manager of a branch of a large national food chain. He was referred for therapy by his doctor as suffering from occupational stress. He had been under pressure at work to reach new targets which he believed were unrealistic and unattainable. This led to angry outbursts at work which were causing interpersonal difficulties. For the past couple of months he had experienced sleeping difficulties, palpitations,

(Continued)

(Continued)

tension and headaches. He was concerned that 'my performance at work is suffering and I just seem to be losing control'. His employers were concerned about the profitability of his branch and had become aware of his angry outbursts. They were willing to fund an initial six sessions of therapy.

The Therapy

John was sent an administration letter giving a time for the counselling session, details about the location, a client checklist (see Appendix 3) and a self-help book, *Stress Management: A Quick Guide*.[11]

At the beginning of the first session John was asked if he had any questions about the therapy or about the therapist. He had read the pre-therapy material about the approach and enquired about the therapist's qualifications and training. He understood the benefits of the therapy sessions being audio-recorded: he could listen to the recordings at home and go over any sections he had not fully grasped; the therapist could listen to the sessions with his supervisor in confidence, to ensure that he had not overlooked any important issues and to receive useful guidance. (John liked the idea that three heads were better than two.)

John spent the next 15 minutes explaining his problems while the therapist took a few notes of the key problems. The therapist interjected occasionally to clarify any points he did not understand. The therapist, Stephen, then described the BASIC I.D. assessment procedure:

Stephen: In this approach, to ensure that we have correctly understood the client's problems we usually focus on seven key areas or modalities. I'll use this whiteboard so we can both go through the different issues together. The first area to look at is Behaviour. [*Writes 'Behaviour' at the top left-hand corner of the whiteboard.*] You mentioned that you are 'always in a rush'. [*Writes this in central part of the whiteboard.*] Can you give me some specific examples?

John: I eat and walk fast. My wife always tells me to 'slow down'!

Stephen: You mentioned that you are 'hostile' and 'competitive'.

John: Yes. Mainly at work although I can be outside of work too.

Stephen: [*Writes 'hostile' and 'competitive' on the whiteboard.*] It sounds to me as if you have what is often known as 'Type A' behaviour.

John: You're right. I read an article about it once in a magazine.

Stephen: [*Writes 'Type A behaviour' on the whiteboard.*] You mentioned that you avoid giving presentations at work and you've become accident prone. [*Writes these on the whiteboard.*] Are there any other behavioural problems that you would like to add to this list?

John: No. They are the main ones.

Stephen: OK. The next area we can examine is what is known as Affect or your Emotions. [*Writes 'Affect/emotions' on left-hand side of the whiteboard.*] You mentioned that you are 'anxious when giving presentations' and 'guilty when work targets are not achieved'. [*Writes these on the whiteboard.*] Are there any other emotional problems that you would like to add to this list?

John: No. They are the main ones. Ah! I suppose that we should also mention my angry outbursts at work.
Stephen: OK. [*Writes this on the whiteboard.*]

This process was continued until each modality had been assessed. Table 23.1, presented earlier (see p. 313), is John's modality profile. As John had read the self-help book prior to the therapy session he was in a position to negotiate with his therapist his own therapy programme. Table 23.3 (p. 316) is John's completed modality profile. The techniques and interventions were written on the right-hand side of the whiteboard corresponding to each particular problem. It was explained that the modality profile serves as 'working hypotheses' that can be modified or revised as new information arises. Before the end of the session John was introduced to the MLHI:

Stephen: I have found it very useful if my clients complete this questionnaire at home. [*Shows John the MLHI.*] It saves me taking up a lot of your time asking questions about different aspects of your life. It will not only focus on your anxiety and job performance, but may provide us with information that would help us deal with your other problems too.
John: Sounds like a good idea.
Stephen: You can either bring it to the next session or send it to me beforehand to give me time to read it.
John: I'll pop it in the post.
Stephen: In that case do make sure you mark it private and confidential.

Careful analysis of John's full modality profile indicated that teaching him a suitable relaxation technique would help him deal or cope with a number of different problems. This was brought to his attention and he agreed to listen to a commercially manufactured relaxation tape once a day before his evening meal.

The next session was seven days later. An agenda for the session was set which included looking at how he had got on with the relaxation tape; queries regarding the MLHI; drawing his structural profiles; modifying his self-defeating beliefs; and a new homework assignment. Figures 23.1 and 23.2 were John's structural profiles. It is worth noting that his structural profile (Figure 23.1) had scores of 7 in sensation and cognitive modalities. When high structural profile scores occur in a particular modality, the person is often responsive to techniques used from that modality. John found the sensation and cognitive techniques were very helpful. John was both a 'sensory and cognitive reactor'. It was agreed that session 3 would be a fortnight later.

Over the remaining sessions John found that attempting to slow down, modifying his beliefs, using the relaxation exercises and coping imagery was very beneficial. He reduced his caffeine intake and found that his sleeping improved. The intervals between the last two sessions were increased to four weeks to give him the opportunity to apply the range of techniques he had learnt in therapy.

By the last session John had learnt to slow down, had reduced his feelings of guilt and anxiety, and although he was still prone under extremes of pressure

(Continued)

(Continued)

to become angry, at least it was more controlled. Physically he was feeling much better and more relaxed, with fewer headaches and better sleeping patterns. In addition he had modified his self-defeating beliefs.

The one area that required more hard work was the interpersonal modality. As he was feeling less stressed his interpersonal behaviour was less hostile and aggressive but he still wanted to improve it. John and the therapist agreed that he would attend a follow-up session three months later to review progress and monitor how he was getting on using assertiveness skills.

REFERENCES

[1] Lazarus, A. A. (1958) 'New methods in psychotherapy: a case study', *South African Medical Journal*, 32, 660–4.

[2] Palmer, S. and Dryden, W. (1995) *Counselling for Stress Problems.* London: Sage.

[3] Palmer, S. (2008) 'Multimodal coaching and its application to workplace, life and health coaching', *The Coaching Psychologist*, 4(1), 21–9.

[4] Lazarus, A. A. (1989) *The Practice of Multimodal Therapy: Systematic, Comprehensive, and Effective Psychotherapy*. Baltimore, MD: Johns Hopkins University Press.

[5] Lazarus, A. A. (1991) 'The multimodal approach with adult outpatients', in W. Dryden (ed.), *The Essential Arnold Lazarus*. London: Whurr.

[6] Zilbergeld, B. (1982) 'Bespoke therapy', *Psychology Today, 16*, 85–6.

[7] Palmer, S. and Szymanska, K. (1994) 'A checklist for clients interested in receiving counselling, psychotherapy or hypnosis', *The Rational Emotive Behaviour Therapist, 2(1)*, 25–7.

[8] Palmer, S. (1997) 'Modality assessment', in S. Palmer and G. McMahon (eds), *Client Assessment*. London: Sage.

[9] Lazarus, A. A. and Lazarus, C. N. (1991) *Multimodal Life History Inventory*. Champaign, IL: Research Press.

[10] Paul, G. L. (1967) 'Strategy of outcome research in psychotherapy', *Journal of Consulting Psychology, 331*, 109–18.

[11] Palmer, S. and Strickland, L. (1996) *Stress Management: A Quick Guide*. Dunstable: Folens Publishers.

SUGGESTED READING

Lazarus, A. A. (1989) *The Practice of Multimodal Therapy: Systematic, Comprehensive, and Effective Psychotherapy*. Baltimore, MD: Johns Hopkins University Press. The key revised text on multimodal therapy written by the originator, Arnold Lazarus. It offers a practical, step-by-step guide to every phase of assessment and therapy and includes transcripts of actual sessions. A glossary of 37 therapeutic techniques is included.

Lazarus, A. A. (1997) *Brief but Comprehensive Psychotherapy: The Multimodal Way*. New York: Springer. This book illustrates how multimodal therapy can be brief yet still efficient. Lazarus writes in a lucid style and includes many case examples. The Appendices contain a number of useful questionnaires.

Palmer, S. and Dryden, W. (1995) *Counselling for Stress Problems*. London: Sage. This work provides a comprehensive view of stress counselling and stress management from a multimodal perspective. Techniques and strategies are discussed in depth and are illustrated by numerous case examples with session transcripts.

Palmer, S., Cooper, C. and Thomas, K. (2003) *Creating a Balance: Managing Stress*. London: British Library. This multimodal self-coaching book is suitable for the layperson. This self-help book covers the main methods used in multimodal therapy and coaching and helps the client or reader to negotiate his or her own therapy or coaching programme.

DISCUSSION ISSUES

1. In what ways does multimodal therapy differ from other forms of therapy?
2. Critically discuss the usefulness of the BASIC I.D. assessment procedures.
3. Flexible interpersonal styles of the therapist that match client needs can reduce premature termination of therapy. Discuss.
4. The practice of multimodal therapy places high demands on the therapist. Discuss.

This chapter is dedicated to Arnold Lazarus (27 January 1932 – 1 October 2013).

24

Pluralistic Counselling and Psychotherapy

John McLeod and Mick Cooper

INTRODUCTION

Pluralistic counselling and psychotherapy is an approach to working with clients which recognises that different people make use of therapy in different ways, and for different purposes. At the heart of a pluralistic perspective on therapy is the aim of working collaboratively with the client to find out what is most helpful for that individual at that point in his or her life. Pluralistic values and methods are relevant for all counsellors, psychotherapists, counselling psychologists and other practitioners (e.g. GPs, nurses, teachers, social workers) who make use of counselling skills in their jobs, regardless of the theoretical ideas that they espouse, or the settings within which they work. Pluralistic counselling and psychotherapy is an integrative form of practice, in the sense of drawing on concepts and techniques from established therapeutic traditions, such as psychodynamic, humanistic and cognitive-behavioural. However, a pluralistic framework for practice differs from other integrative models in the extent to which it takes account of client preferences and resources.

DEVELOPMENT OF THE THERAPY

The key ideas of the pluralistic approach to therapy were formulated by Mick Cooper and John McLeod in 2006.[1] They believed that all schools of therapy contained valuable ideas about how to help people to deal with problems in living, and that the arguments and rivalries that existed between different approaches meant that therapy practitioners were in danger of losing sight of what clients actually wanted. Their aim was to develop a way of working with clients that was flexible and tailored to the needs of each client. They also believed that adherence to a single set of ideas about change ran the risk of preventing counsellors, psychotherapists and other helpers from making use of all of their healing capabilities. Over the last decade, many practitioners and researchers have contributed to the further development of the pluralistic approach.

THEORY AND BASIC CONCEPTS

The core idea that underpins theory and practice in this approach is the concept of **pluralism.** This is a philosophical concept which refers to the view that, in respect of important issues relating to human affairs, there is never a single right answer. For example, there exist a huge diversity of ways of thinking about religion and spirituality, the way that society should be organised, or the type of music or art that is most enjoyable or meaningful. From a pluralistic perspective, a fundamental characteristic of being human is the capacity to reflect on situations, and consider different options. Similarly, a fundamental characteristic of human cultures or societies is the existence of debate and dialogue around what is best or true. A pluralistic perspective goes hand in hand with the view that being a person is only possible in the context of a network of relationships. Such networks of relationships sustain on-going conversation about how life should be lived.

Although the concept of pluralism may seem straightforward, its implications are quite challenging. The opposite philosophical position to pluralism is 'monism', which proposes that it is possible and desirable to identify a single right answer to any problem. The world that we live in tends to be dominated by monist thinking, for example in the field of science, or in some religious traditions. It is essential, therefore, for any counsellor or psychotherapist who seeks to work according to pluralistic principles, to consider whether they are genuinely able to respond to clients from a pluralistic stance. A further key implication of the concept of pluralism arises from the realisation that, in reality, people do not believe that all ideas are equally plausible. Based on his or her upbringing and personal experience, each person inevitably has some 'truths' that are central to the way that they make sense of the world. Adopting a pluralistic perspective therefore implies a willingness to be open to acknowledging one's own preferences and beliefs, while at the same time accepting that another person (e.g. a client) may hold quite different preferences and beliefs. In practice, what this means is that the adoption of a pluralistic perspective involves being non-defensively curious about the ideas of other people, and interested in using dialogue to find ways of building bridges between different ways of thinking.

These philosophical ideas may seem quite abstract and remote from the everyday reality of trying to help a client to move on their life. However, they are in fact highly relevant at a practical level, because they act as a reminder that using this approach to therapy is not a matter of implementing certain skills and techniques, but instead depends on the consistent adoption and expression in action of a moral and ethical position of deep respect for the other person, for one's full potential as a helper, and for the capacity of nature and our social world to sustain us.

This basic attitude of curiosity and respect is channelled in three main directions. First, a pluralistic therapist operates from an assumption that a person seeking help has access to personal **strengths** that can be applied to resolving his or her problems or issues. The personal strengths of the client may take many forms, including strategies that they have developed for dealing with similar issues in the past, ideas that help them to make sense of their situation, personal attributes such as humour or perseverance, and so on. Second, it is assumed that there are **cultural resources** available in the social and natural world inhabited by the person that can be helpful to them. For example, a person may be a dog-owner, and use dog-walking as a form of anxiety management and as a way of meeting people. Or the person may find meaning in art, literature or music. He or she may have relationships with other people who are willing to be sources of support, or help the person to learn new skills. The starting point for pluralistic therapy is the notion that a person seeking help has already tried to resolve their problem using strengths and resources, and will continue to engage in these activities alongside whatever happens in therapy. It is also assumed that it is likely that there will be potentially valuable neglected or dormant strengths and resources that the person has used in the past but, for whatever reason, not activated in respect of their current predicament. It must be emphasised that it is rarely helpful to suggest new activities to a person who is seeking help for a psychological or emotional problem. Advice such as 'why don't you tackle your depression by joining a gym and getting more exercise' is probably not going to be helpful for someone who has never been a member of a gym and is currently so socially withdrawn that they can hardly leave their house. A time of personal crisis is probably not the best moment for someone to do something that is new, and possibly scary. The aim, instead, is to create opportunities for the person to review and reflect on what is already there in their lives, or has been meaningful and useful for them in the past.

A third direction in which a pluralistic attitude of respect and curiosity is channelled is toward the therapist himself or herself. Here, it is assumed that people who make the choice and commitment of being counsellors (or any other type of psychotherapeutic practitioner) are individuals with a deep interest in their own emotional life and relationships, the issues and difficulties that people encounter in trying to make their way through life, and the many different ways in which such issues can be managed or resolved. It is assumed that, in principle, such a person will have a lot to offer in a helping role. An important element of the preparation or training to be a pluralistic therapist, therefore, is for the trainee to develop an understanding of what is available on his or her therapeutic 'menu'. A therapist's menu can include skills such as empathic reflection or asking questions, or using theories to make sense of particular issues, or complex interventions such as using relaxation techniques or dream analysis. The advantage of thinking about what a therapist knows, or is capable of doing, in terms of their 'menu' rather than their 'theory' is that it is certain that a theoretical label, such as 'person–centred' or 'psychodynamic', will not do justice to the range of helpful things that the person is able to offer. There is a risk, in describing one's practice in terms of a pre-existing theoretical label, that skills and knowledge that do not fit the theory may be less valued or even ignored. It may not suit everybody to use the metaphor of a 'menu' to describe this aspect of pluralistic therapy. An attraction of the idea of a 'menu' is that it implies nourishing things that are offered to, and chosen by, a client. It also implies the possibility of improvisation: 'Can I have the salad, but with no tomatoes and extra radishes?'

However, there are several other images and metaphors that can equally well be used, such as 'repertoire', 'palette', or 'toolkit'.

A pluralistic perspective does not offer a specific way of understanding how problems in living are acquired and perpetuated, or how the individual may move from distress and stuckness to a state of wellbeing and productive living. Instead, a pluralistic practitioner possesses an understanding and appreciation of the great diversity of theories and ideas, around these matters, that circulate within contemporary society. The aim is to find a way of understanding problems, and their resolution, that makes sense to the client, and that can function as a means of communication between client and therapist. In a lot of cases, what happens is that a client finds meaning in a range of ideas and methods, rather than in one 'big idea'. For example, a client who is depressed may arrive at an understanding of how this problem has evolved in terms of a combination of genetic predisposition, work stress, a painful bereavement and lack of sunlight. In moving on from their depression, the client may be helped by antidepressant medication, talking to their counsellor about the bereavement, developing a fitness regime and church attendance. The openness of a pluralistic way of working tends to lead in the direction of finding pragmatic remedies that can become part of life after therapy, rather than in the search for a breakthrough moment.

PRACTICE

Pluralistic therapy has two main goals. The primary goal is to help the client to accomplish his or her own personal therapeutic goals – to get what they came for. The secondary goal is to offer the person a congenial experience that can buffer them against future troubles, by providing an opportunity for learning about how to take care of himself or herself emotionally, and how to connect with other people through dialogue.

As described in the previous section, pluralistic therapy is based on **collaboration** between client and therapist on identifying relevant client strengths and resources, and therapist skills and knowledge, and then applying these strategies and assets to enable the client to reach their goals. The principle of collaboration permeates all aspects of pluralistic therapy: the information that the client receives before therapy commences, moment–by–moment and session negotiation around the direction of therapy, and deciding on when and how therapy will end. Achieving a collaborative way of working together is not necessarily easy or straightforward. Many, or even most, clients are unsure of how therapy can help them, and may perceive counsellors or other practitioners as 'experts' who will tell them what to do. Some clients may be happy to be told what to do, while others, who have had negative experiences with authority figures in the past, may fight against it. Some clients may have ideas about what they want to happen in therapy, but lack confidence in putting these preferences into words. It can also be hard for some therapists to work collaboratively. For example, a therapist may have a clear idea about what 'needs to happen' to enable the client's problems to be ameliorated. Alternatively, some therapists adopt a rigid non-directive approach in which they are unwilling to tell the client about their ideas about what would be helpful, for fear of overpowering and oppressing the client's own fragile sense of his or her own personal power.

Pluralistic therapists have evolved a number of strategies for dealing with the challenges associated with working collaboratively. These strategies are based on an appreciation of the value of **metacommunication** as a general conversational strategy. Most of the time, in therapy as in other situations, conversation focuses on real-life events or concerns that are of concern to one or other of the participants. For example, a client in therapy may talk about 'feeling panic when my boss asked me a question' or 'worrying about whether I have made the right decision'. Metacommunication refers to moments in the conversation where the therapist (or the client) pauses to reflect on the way in which the topic is being discussed. Examples of therapist metacommunication include statements such as 'you have mentioned several things that are bothering you – which of them would be most useful to look at in more detail right now?' or 'I know we agreed to talk about your worries in relation to this big decision you have to make, but my sense is that it is quite hard for you to talk about this ... is that correct? ... is there some way that I could help you to explore this issue more fully ... would it be helpful if I asked you questions, or if we wrote down the main issues ... or is there some other way we could approach it ... ?'

Making effective use of metacommunicative 'pauses' in the conversation requires sensitivity and good timing. It is probably not helpful to invite reflection on the process of working together at a moment when the client is in full flow and actively making sense of an issue or generating ideas about how to resolve a problem. There are, however, some aspects of therapy where metacommunicative checking-out, exploration and sharing of perspectives is particularly helpful:

- identifying the *goals* of therapy
- clarifying the step-by-step *tasks* that might need to be accomplished in order to reach these goals
- agreeing on the specific techniques, activities or *methods* that might be used to facilitate the completion of certain tasks
- developing a shared *understanding* of the causes of problems, how these problems are perpetuated, and how things might change.

Metacommunication around these questions needs to be on-going. For example, it is helpful to get some idea, at the start, of the client's goals for therapy, in terms of why they are there and what they want to change in their life. As therapy unfolds (even within a single meeting) new goals may emerge, or existing goals may become more clearly specified and defined.

It is essential to be aware of the potential power imbalance that exists in most counselling and psychotherapy encounters. The therapist is someone who understands the process of therapy, has a language for talking about therapy, and is not particularly anxious or threatened at that moment in time. By contrast, the client is someone who has a more limited understanding and therapeutic vocabulary, and is likely to be in the grip of strong emotions and uncomfortable thought process during a session. In the light of these factors, pluralistic therapists make use of a range of tools to facilitate collaborative sharing of ideas about whether and how therapy is being helpful, such as brief questionnaires and report forms that can be used to make it easier for clients to convey their evaluation of therapy. There are several accessible scales that clients can complete to convey their sense of whether things are getting better for them (in terms of achieving their goals, or experiencing reduction is distress and symptoms). There are also other scales that allow clients to report on what they find helpful or unhelpful in the way that their therapist is working with them. These scales are typically completed at the beginning or end of a therapy session. It is helpful to think about them as 'conversational tools'[2] that provide a means of talking about things that would otherwise be hard to discuss. Evidence from research studies that have been carried out into the use of these tools suggests that therapists are not particularly good at picking up whether therapy is being helpful for the client. These feedback tools provide a therapist with information that would not otherwise be available to them.

The use of metacommunication, either as part of the flow of conversation, or in the context of talking about the implications of responses to a questionnaire, can be therapeutically potent in its own right. Metacommunication conveys the message that the therapist cares about the client, is genuinely interested in what the client thinks about things, and believes that the client has strengths and resources that they want to hear about. Receiving such a message, especially when it is demonstrated in action rather than merely being asserted, can be a healing experience for a person who is self-critical and has a low sense of his or her worth. Metacommunication also allows the client to have an experience of positive relationship and meaningful contact and connection with another person. Again, this process can represent an important healing and learning experience for people who have had difficulties in establishing satisfying and supportive relationships with others. Finally, metacommunication invites the client into a position of reflecting on how they deal with an issue, with the implicit message that there are other ways in which that problem might be approached.

Metacommunication directly contributes to achieving client goals in therapy by maximising the chances that the therapist and client will find the most effective way of taking things forward, and reduces the amount of time spent in pursuing ideas and methods that are not helpful for the client. Pluralistic therapy aims to encourage both client and therapist to use their creativity through imagining, and trying out, different ways of making sense of an issue, and different practical activities that can be undertaken in order to bring about change. Establishing a 'culture of feedback' makes it possible to experiment with different change strategies in the knowledge that there is a means of deciding whether that specific method has been useful or otherwise. Metacommunicative conversations also allow therapist and client to learn from strategies that were less than wholly successful, and to generate a pool of alternative strategies.

Pluralistic therapists need to develop a sufficiently rich and varied repertoire/ menu of ways of thinking about problems, and ways of initiating change, to be able to be responsive to the needs and preferences of the clients with whom they work. The repertoire of each therapist will be guided by his or her own interests and capabilities, and by the context within which they work. For example, some therapists find that psychodynamic ideas and techniques are very meaningful for them, while other therapists may be drawn to cognitive behavioural therapy. The work setting or context also influences the knowledge base of a therapist. For example, a counsellor working in a bereavement service may find value in attending training courses that would be of little interest to a sex therapist (and vice-versa). However, any therapist who works in a pluralistic way needs to be able to work with clients around common or universal therapeutic tasks, such as making sense of a problematic experience, changing behaviour that is dysfunctional, resolving painful emotions, or negotiating a life transition. In practice, what this means is that a pluralistic therapist needs to possess a general level of competence in working in an exploratory, meaning-making way with a client, as well as competence in structured behaviour-change activities. A pluralistic therapist does not assume that the client can only accomplish therapeutic tasks within the therapy room. Instead, there is openness to the potential value of a vast range of cultural resources such as self-help reading, spiritual practice and making things.

Pluralistic therapy is a flexible, client-focused approach, and so the format of a typical session will vary according to what seems to be most helpful. Nevertheless, it is usually possible to observe a rhythm or sequence within pluralistic therapy, moving back and forward between metacommunicative reflection, review and planning, and active implementation of an agreed method of exploration or change. Many pluralistic therapists start a session with a discussion of what the client wants to work on, and close a session with an invitation to reflect on how the session went. Depending on the context within which therapy occurs, the application of pluralistic principles may lead to conversations around the structure of therapy (length of sessions, frequency of sessions, who attends, where sessions take place).

WHICH CLIENTS BENEFIT MOST?

Pluralistic therapy is a relatively new approach, and at this point in time it is not possible to indicate, using research evidence, those categories of client for whom it might be more, or less effective. The question of the effectiveness of pluralistic therapy for specific client groups is made more complex by the fact that a pluralistic model implies that good work will depend on the capacity of particular therapists to create the most appropriate menu for whatever types of client they see, and on their ability to use awareness of their own strengths and weaknesses as a basis for specialising in client problems around which they have a special talent. What seems clear is that pluralistic therapy is not a good option for clients who have a definite preference for a particular 'brand-name' therapy. For example, a client who has read a lot about cognitive behavioural therapy and is convinced that this is the answer to their problems may be disappointed with the 'CBT-lite' version that is on offer from a pluralistic practitioner. The question of which clients benefit most is intimately bound up with the way that therapy services are organised. For example, clients with longstanding multiple problems, who are unemployed and socially isolated, are difficult to help with any therapy approach. Successful therapy for such individuals is likely to depend on the length and intensity of the therapy that is available, the possibility of access to different forms of help for different needs, and the level of support available to sustain therapist commitment when progress is slow.

CASE STUDY

The Client

The client, Simon, was 55 years of age and had been referred for counselling by his GP. Formerly a lorry driver, Simon had lost his job in a round of organisational down-sizing, and had been unemployed for three years. He believed that he had little hope of ever working again. Simon was estranged from his ex-wife and adult children, and lived on his own in an apartment in a tower block. Over the most recent 18-month period Simon had visited his local health centre on a regular basis, for a range of minor ailments. At one consultation, with a young locum junior doctor, he had been given the opportunity to talk at length about his situation. As a result of this conversation Simon had been prescribed antidepressants, which he had found quite helpful. At one of his routine medication monitoring consultations, his usual GP had advised him that it was not advisable to stay on antidepressants for an extended period, and that it would be sensible for him to receive some therapy before the point at which medication needed be withdrawn.

The Therapy

The work described in this case took place in a community counselling service that offered low-cost therapy with a limit of 24 sessions. The therapist, George, was a 30-year-old man with a previous career as a retail manager, who was in the second year of a three-year training in pluralistic counselling.

At his first meeting with his counsellor Simon was sceptical about whether George could be of any use to him, because 'you are too young to understand what things are like for a man of my age – it would be like talking to my own son, who is a waste of space'. George acknowledged that this might be a problem, and encouraged Simon to talk about what he wanted from therapy. To assist in this process, he invited Simon to complete a brief therapy preference questionnaire. At the end of the session, he explained that there would be no problem if Simon wished to be passed on to an older counsellor, and suggested that Simon might think about this before their next appointment.

The next week, Simon reported that he had thought about his options, and had decided to stay with George, because 'you obviously have on old head on young shoulders'. In this session, George continued to encourage Simon to talk about the achievements in his life, his present situation, what he hoped to gain from therapy and any ideas he might have about what might be the most helpful way to proceed. George emphasised that he thought that Simon's ideas and life experience were absolutely crucial in terms of allowing them to work together effectively.

At the third session, George asked if it would be acceptable for him to share some of his ideas about what Simon had said up to that point. George used a flipchart page to draw a diagram of the key factors in Simon's life that were contributing to his unhappiness, and the strengths and resources that were available to him to counteract these influences. George was comfortable and confident in using a flipchart diagram in this way, because the process resembled meetings

(Continued)

(Continued)

he had facilitated in his previous career. He encouraged George to make suggestions, ask questions and to be fully involved in what they were doing. The creation of this map and action plan took up the whole session, and at the end Simon reported, in his feedback form, that he had really enjoyed what they had done because it 'took the pressure off him' in terms of having to speak, and because it gave him 'some ideas about how to go forward'.

Arising from this planning session, George and Simon embarked on three main therapeutic tasks. First, Simon acknowledged that when he had seen his life mapped out, it had been obvious to him that he had been hiding himself away and that he needed to get out more, make contact with more people, and find a job or some other way of playing a meaningful role in society. The second task that emerged from this session was the realisation that Simon had experienced phases of depression ever since his father had committed suicide, when he had been 13 years of age. When asked whether this event might have something to do with his present depression, Simon replied that he had never had a chance to talk to anyone, ever, about what had happened: 'it's all locked up in there, it's buried'. The third task, suggested by George, referred to the possibility of re-establishing relationships with his two sons, and playing a part in the lives of his grandchildren.

The next eight sessions of therapy focused on getting out more, and making contact with his sons. Much of this work consisted of using sessions to decide on 'experiments' that would be carried out before the next meeting, such as writing letters to his sons, going for long walks, and doing research on possibilities to do volunteer work for a homelessness charity. Other aspects of work consisted of examining irrational beliefs that Simon used to stop himself from doing things ('no one will want to know me, because I'm useless'). George found some of these sessions to be quite challenging, because of what he described to his supervisor as his 'rudimentary' knowledge of CBT.

George began each session by referring to the flipchart map, and asking Simon which bits he wanted to work on that day. It was not until the twelfth session that Simon said that he was ready to begin to talk about his father. He said that meeting his sons had triggered powerful dreams about fathers and babies. They talked about these dreams in therapy sessions. This was a way of working that was congenial to George, whose own therapist made extensive use of Gestalt therapy dream analysis. Alongside these conversations about absent fathers, Simon continued to use counselling sessions to get support around his efforts to expand his life and make friends with his sons, daughters-in-law and grandchildren.

By the eighteenth session, Simon was ready to talk directly about his experience of his father's death. He and George agreed to book a longer session the following week, to give themselves time to do this 'properly'. The session was hugely painful, triggering waves of anger and despair. George suggested that Simon might write a letter to his father, telling him about the impact that his suicide had made on the life of his adolescent son. Simon went through with this, but did not find it to be particularly helpful.

By this time Simon had started work as a van driver with the homelessness charity. He attended another three times, but admitted that the intensity of the therapy had passed. In terms of the monitoring and feedback forms that were being used, Simon's depression had reduced to a level just above the 'normal' range, and his goals for therapy had been largely accomplished. In his final session with George, Simon talked about how he was now aware of his longing to be in a relationship with a woman, and that he now felt 'almost good enough' about himself to believe that this might be a possibility. In George's end-of-case review session with his supervisor he credited himself with having been instrumental in enabling Simon to 'turn his life around'. But he acknowledged, also, that the 'suicide session' had taken him 'up to and beyond the edge of' where he felt able to go with a client. His supervisor suggested some books by Irvin Yalom, and they talked together at some length about how hard it is to be so close to the terror of death.

REFERENCES

[1] Cooper, M. and McLeod, J. (2007) 'A pluralistic framework for counselling and psychotherapy: implications for research', *Counselling and Psychotherapy Research, 7*, 135–43.
[2] Sundet, R. (2012) 'Therapist perspectives on the use of feedback on process and outcome: patient–focused research in practice', *Canadian Psychology, 53*, 122–30.

SUGGESTED READING

Cooper, M. and McLeod, J. (2011) *Pluralistic Counselling and Psychotherapy.* London: Sage. The main textbook on pluralistic therapy – provides a detailed account of all aspects of the approach.

Duncan, B. L., Miller, S. D., Wampold, B. E. and Hubble, M. A. (eds) (2010) *The Heart and Soul of Change. Delivering What Works in Therapy*, 2nd edn. Washington, DC: APA. This book brings together the ideas and research of key figures in a long tradition of therapy theory and research that has advocated the use of flexible, client-focused methods. The work of Barry Duncan and Scott Miller has been particularly influential in relation to the development of pluralistic therapy.

Levine, B. (2007) *Surviving America's Depression Epidemic: How to Find Morale, Energy, and Community in a World Gone Crazy.* White River Junction, VT: Chelsea Green Publishers. An inspiring and accessible discussion of multiple ways of working therapeutically with people who are depressed.

McLeod, J. and McLeod, J. (2011) *Counselling Skills: A Practical Guide for Counsellors and Helping Professionals*, 2nd edn. Maidenhead: Open University Press. Offers an outline of how a pluralistic approach can be used in front-line, brief counselling undertaken by teachers, nurses, social workers and other helping practitioners.

DISCUSSION ISSUES

1. Think about an occasion when you were able to change an aspect of your behaviour or way of thinking that was causing problems in your life. What was the process of change? Find out how other people you know would answer the same question. How many different types of change process have you been able to identify? What are the implications of what you have learned, for counselling and psychotherapy practice?

2. If you decided that you wanted to attend therapy, at this point in your life, what are your preferences around the characteristics of the therapist, and type of therapeutic process, that would be ideal for you? What would be your least preferred type of therapist and therapy process? Do some research into the therapists and the forms of therapy that are available in your community. How possible would it be for you to access your preferred type of therapy experience, and avoid your non-preferred type?

3. How many different ways can you imagine of eliciting feedback from clients on a session-by-session basis, regarding their feelings about what has been helpful and hindering in the therapy they have been receiving? What are the strengths and weaknesses of each feedback method?

4. What are the distinctive challenges and sources of satisfaction that are associated with being a pluralistic therapist?

PART 5

Constructivist Approaches

25

Narrative Therapy

Anja Bjorøy, Stephen Madigan and David Nylund

Narrative therapy is an ideological *turning away* from prevailing psychological, psychiatric, systemic and all other theoretical and mental health practice views informed by individualism. Instead, narrative therapy practice turns *towards* specific post-structural theories that support a person's identity as discursively created and thereby ever-changing and relational. Narrative therapy practice ideas are situated within the disciplines of cultural anthropology, feminism, post-colonialism, anti-oppression, social justice, literary theory and queer studies (to name just a few of the disciplines). Another primary influence that informs the practice is influenced by the leading voices of French post-structural philosophy (circa 1965 to the present).

From the beginning, a central post-structural tenet of narrative therapy was the idea that we, as persons, are '*multi-storied*'. Simply stated, narrative therapists take up a practice position that within the context of therapy there could be *numerous* interpretations about persons and problems. And, the very interpretations (of persons and problems) the therapist brings forward are mediated through prevailing ideas held by our culture regarding the specifics of who and what these persons and problems are and what they represent (e.g. normal/abnormal, good/bad, worthy/unworthy).

DEVELOPMENT OF THE THERAPY

Australian therapist Michael White and Canadian cum New Zealand immigrant David Epston began their novel therapeutic work in the creation of narrative therapy during the early 1980s but did not coin the term *narrative therapy* until 1989. By the early 1990s their ideas had a relatively small but passionate following throughout North America and Europe. In 2014, narrative therapy finds itself at the theoretical centre of now thousands of therapists' practice – worldwide.

Narrative therapy questions the Western conception of how dominant psychology categorized persons as skin-bounded, unique, more or less integrated within a motivational and cognitive universe, where the client was viewed as a dynamic centre of awareness, emotion, judgement and action. At the heart of White and Epston's practice in narrative therapy is an unswerving commitment to a relational/contextual/ **anti-individualist** therapeutic view of people and relationships. This relational/ contextual/anti-individualist practice was founded on a therapy designed to *counter* psychology's idea of the skin-bound individual humanist self.

THEORY AND BASIC CONCEPTS

Narrative therapy contends that to properly study a 'self', a reader must understand how it is related to his or her own personal concept of self.[a,b] A narrative therapy point of view brings forth a multi-sited and multi-storied idea of the subject. Narrative therapy's approach to the 'self' stretches out beyond the more popular and/or generalized accounts of who persons are (e.g. dominant and/or individualized categories of personhood), and of who the person is stated or categorically labelled to be by the expert of psychological knowledge.

The writings of the French philosopher/historian Michel Foucault prompted narrative therapy to theoretically explore the therapeutic question: is the talk about the problem gaining more influence over the person or is the person's talk gaining more influence over the problem? Their consideration of this somewhat innocent puzzle led them to discover not only the oppressive effects that result from the ways in which problems are usually discussed (personally and professionally), but also, the constitutive and subjugating effects of descriptive knowledge and language itself.

Narrative's therapeutic practice of relationally **externalizing** problem discourse set out to separate the person/client from the problem (and/or the restraints of the problem) that maintained the dominant discourse (problematic stories) about the problem. In a narrative therapeutic practice world, the problem is located outside the person or relationship that had been objectified, identified and specified (as having the problem) and the problem itself is objectified and given a relational name. A standard externalizing question asked would be: 'When did you first realize that anorexia was planning your death?' Problems are viewed within sets of practices that are under the influence of dominant cultural forces and discourses. A young woman's practice of anorexia involves several cultural and discursive practices operating on her body, such as body surveillance, the tyranny of perfection,

---

[a]This discursive self-perception plays a critical role in one's interpretation of meaning. While different post-structural thinkers' views on the self vary, the self under study is said to be constituted by discourse(s).

[b]For example, in a post-structural approach to textual analysis, it is the *reader* of a text that replaces the author as the primary subject of enquiry. This displacement is often referred to as the *destabilizing* or *decentring* of the author (in our case, think of the therapist), though it has its greatest effect on the text itself.

less than worthiness — discourses that she did not create by herself. There are also common practices involved with men's intimate violence against women that often involve negative comparison (if you were more like Jane I wouldn't hit you); inconsistency (I promise to never punch you again); and isolating the victim and so on.

Narrative therapy works to relationally de–mystify problems by resisting psychology's individualist temptation to locate and privatize the problem inside the person's body, thereby acting to totalize/categorize clients within a problem description free of a context of support. This expression of an anti–individualist post-structural commitment affords the narrative therapist an ability to look past the restraints that bind the person's story as fixed and stagnant. Accordingly, narrative explores new conversational pathways through the discursive restraints by exploring discursive exceptions to the problem story known as unique outcomes.

Narrative therapy developed this crucial therapeutic idea further by beginning to more fully understand Foucault's ideas on (1) what dominant cultural and discursive restraints were and how these normalizing ideas acted on how persons came to view themselves; (2) how they operated on persons and how persons responded to and reproduced them; (3) which institutions they originated from, i.e. religion, psychology; and (4) who and what supported them.

As theory meets practice, the prevailing ways of describing clients and problems are viewed as *culture-based constructs* shaped by larger institutional knowledges like religion, media, psychiatry, education, law, science and government. Narrative therapy also realizes that the majority of our psychological practice ideas are not truths but taken–for–granted ideas produced through psychology's institutions and **power/ knowledge** practices, and consequently they are reproduced by the citizenry.

For example, narrative therapy began to question how a large majority of therapists were *locating* what was being called 'ADHD' directly inside young persons' bodies (thereby leaving any contextual factors outside the diagnosis/story being told). They perceived that the hard-and-fast ideas being inscribed upon the young persons' bodies/identities were historical and had been negotiated throughout many different cultural arenas.ᶜ

Historically, narrative therapy has argued that there are always *multiple stories (multiple meanings)* about what and who problems and persons might be. So right from the start, narrative therapy found itself in some rather choppy and unchartered therapeutic waters. This rather alienated experience of therapy was supported within the mandate of the dominant professional, psychological discipline of helping and, there wasn't yet a previous practice map to configure a new consideration of the post-structural, multi-storied, dialogic 'self'.

Finding itself on the 'outs' with psychological, psychiatric and social work thinking (and the institutions that support these fields), narrative therapy found a conspiratorial kinship with the emerging postmodern era and the many challenges being launched

---

ᶜAs far back as the conclusion of the Conference on Stimulant Use in the Treatment of ADHD in San Antonio, December 1996, there were questions as to ADHD's sudden and successful rise. The US Drug Enforcement Administration (DEA) became alarmed by the tremendous increase in the prescribing of stimulants to school-age children for the treatment of attention deficit/hyperactivity disorder (ADD/ADHD). Since 1990 prescriptions for methylphenidate (Ritalin) had increased by 500 per cent, while prescriptions for amphetamine for the same purpose had increased 400 per cent.

against the liberal and Enlightenment frameworks of understanding. These postmodern ideological challenges were at the same time rocking the established schools of philosophy, literary criticism and the human sciences, including anthropology, sociology *and* psychology. At dispute were the many assumed understandings of a unified description of the self, identity and subjectivity.

Narrative therapy found great solace in the challenges being brought forward and, subsequently, the practice of therapy was, through the course of time, strongly influenced by feminism, gay rights/queer theory, and a postcolonial analysis of racism, class and the notion of power and structural inequalities. Up until this point in therapy's history an analysis of power relations had not yet surfaced.

The issues of power relations, structural inequalities and issues of social justice led to narrative therapy questioning who *owned the story telling rights of personhood*. Over a few short years (1982–8), narrative therapy managed to create a uniquely innovative therapy map to incorporate this newly found therapeutic interpretation of a multi-storied, culturally influenced, relational 'self'. The process of therapy involved asking questions regarding how (and through what contexts) the person (and all those lending a discursive hand in the construction of the person and problem identity) came to tell, take up and perform the problem story being told.

For example, the narrative therapy concept of '**re-storying**'[d] assists the person – or groups of persons – who have experienced trauma and abuse to avoid being restrained by another person's finalized account of who they have been, who they presently are and who they might become. Story lines told in a problem-saturated way may omit an analysis of power relations and/or any appreciative alternative version of the person (and their context) where they had been subjected to abuse. The content of this restrained and regressive narrative of persons who have been subjected to trauma and abuse, is often supported by the perpetrator, media accounts, judicial statements, as well as discourse contained with therapeutic, medical and legal texts.

As an alternative, narrative therapy offered a dialogic forum to bring forth untold stories of appreciation and respect regarding how the person responded to and *survived* the abusive context. Narrative therapy conversations were constructed to include an exploration of the person's specific abilities that were employed in order to survive the abusive context (becoming invisible, and having relationships with anger, drugs, remaining silent, running away etc.); appreciated the 'power–over' tactics they suffered under threat of the larger, older and stronger perpetrator; reviewed a context of imbalanced gender relations; and discovered accomplishments people had made in their lives despite the torture they endured. These conversations (known to narrative therapy as **re–authoring conversations**) afforded a dialogic balance to the problem/person description/interpretation, and a reconfigured abusive context that assist people out of the constraints of the predominant problem-saturated stories of passivity, shame and less than worthiness etc.

---

[d]The therapeutic notion of re-storying creates the possibility that change is always possible. Therefore, any totalized description of a person (i.e. as 'chronic') is perceived as a professional description that defines change as *not* possible. Chronic descriptions of life find a difficult fit within the practice of narrative therapy and the concept of re-storying.

PRACTICE

Narrative therapists prefer to speak of practices rather than techniques since it is less mechanistic and objectifying of people. The main practice in narrative therapy is the crafting of questions. The kinds of questions asked in narrative therapy are particular kinds of questions; they are not to gather information but to construct new meanings and experiences.

A narrative therapy interview may begin with externalizing the problem. Through externalizing conversations, narrative therapists put into practice the anti-individualist idea that problems are communally created and located outside persons. Externalization allows space in which people are not seen as pathological; rather, they have relationships with problems. When expressed from a relationally externalizing perspective, people's stories become less informed by blame and are less totalizing.

Once the problem is relationally externalized, the narrative therapist can ask about the *effects* of the problem: 'What impact is the problem having on your view of yourself?' 'What feeds the problem?' 'When does the problem show up?' 'When the problem has the upper hand, what impact does it have on your hopes for your future?' Externalizing questions such as these invite people to consider the relative influence of the problem on their lives and relationships. Externalizing conversations open up space for people to explore areas of their life that have not been dominated by the problem. Persons are then free to explore preferred stories.

Exploring preferred stories

There are a number of corridors to attend to preferred stories. Typically, when mapping the effects of the problem an event, action, or thought spontaneously emerges that contradicts the problem story. An exception to the problem is referred to as a *unique outcome*. Unique outcomes can provide an entry point into new stories. If openings do not develop organically in an externalizing conversation, the narrative therapist can inquire more directly about them. A direct way of searching for openings is to ask about a person's influence on the life of the problem. For example, the therapist can ask questions such as, 'Has there ever been a time when the problem tried to take over, but you were able to resist its influence?' or 'Have you ever been able to give the problem the slip even for a moment?' When questions of this sort follow a careful and thorough enquiry, there are always experiences outside the negative effects of the problem.

Expanding alternative stories

Once an event that has become a candidate as a unique outcomes is identified, it is important for the therapist to ask the person if it is a preferred development or not. For example: 'Is the step you took significant or irrelevant? Why or why not?' Once the unique outcome is established as a preferred and important development, questions are asked to expand the emerging story. A starting point can be what is referred to as a *landscape of action* question. These questions invite the client to situate unique outcomes in a sequence of events that unfold across time according to particular plots. Landscape of action questions can focus on recent or past history of unique outcomes. They imply a grammar of agency. A line of enquiry can include: 'How were you able to take this step given the power of the problem?' 'How have you been advising yourself differently in order to move in this direction?' 'Is there some achievements in your past that can provide a backdrop for this recent development?'

A rich and detailed conversation about the developments in the landscape of action can lead to what narrative therapy refers to as *landscape of consciousness* questions (also referred to as landscape of identity or landscape of meaning). These questions explore the meaning of the preferred developments in the person's life. Conversations about the person's values, knowledges, qualities and skills can then be more fully articulated and performed by asking such questions as: 'What do these recent steps say about what you value and appreciate?' or 'What skills do you think you utilized to move in this direction and away from the path the problem had set out for you?'

After an event is identified, storied and performed, questions are asked that might link it to past events and develop the story of those events so those meanings survive. Questions that might identify and thicken such events include experience questions. These questions invite the person to be an audience to their own story by seeing themselves, in the recent recalling of unique outcomes, through the eyes of others. Lines of enquiry might include: 'Of all the people who have known you over the years, who would be least surprised that you have been able to take this step?' or, 'Of the people who knew you as you were growing up, who would have been most likely to predict that you could achieve this?'

As people's **alternative stories** become more established in the past, they are able to imagine and take steps towards more hopeful futures. Questions can be asked to invite people to speculate about their personal and relational futures now that they have access to a preferred story. For example, 'Where do you think you will go next now that you have embarked upon this new direction?' 'Is this a direction you see yourself taking in the weeks to come?' 'What possibilities do you imagine for your future now that you have retrieved these abilities?'

Therapeutic letters and documents

Narrative therapists rely on therapeutic letters and documents as a way of maintaining preferred stories between therapy conversations. These letters/documents often provide a summary of a therapy conversation with a particular focus on unique outcomes and preferred stories that are developing. Others can announce the preferred developments that are circulated with others. Some can commemorate the alternative story through certificates that position the person as an expert in their own life. Often these letters/ documents are informed by a rite of passage metaphor; an honouring and celebration of the hard work and achievements the person has made in therapy. The intention for all these letters and documents written is to thicken and broaden people's experience of the preferred directions in life and to arrive at new accounts of who they might be.

Response teams

A response team (sometimes referred to as reflecting teams or outsider witness groups) is a group who witnesses a therapy session and, during a break in the session, have a conversation reflecting on the therapeutic conversation while the person and therapist observe. The person is then invited to reflect on the response team's conversation. Response teams create a context where people can tell their preferred stories to a group of outsiders who highlight, appreciate and amplify the stories they witnessed. Response teams can be comprised of therapists and/or people who are invited to join, either because they have insider knowledge about a particular problem or because they are significant in some way to the person being interviewed.

WHICH CLIENTS BENEFIT MOST?

Since narrative therapy does not subscribe to the structuralist idea of a 'fixed' or 'true essence' of a person, the idea of the approach working better with certain people or problems (and not others) is antithetical to the tenets that undergird narrative practices. Persons across cultures commonly make meaning of their experiences that are situated in stories. It is not a question of whether the practices work or do not work but rather what might be the best way to engage with the experiences and meanings of a person that fits with their preferred ways of expression.

Narrative therapists are particularly attuned to issues of social justice, power, privilege and the politics of race, class, gender, sexuality, age, ability and how this creates and influences the way a person comes to view themselves and their identity. A great deal of the training in narrative therapy is to ensure that the therapist does not reproduce dominant discourses that can be marginalizing and 'othering' of persons who seek consultation, especially those from non-dominant cultures. Hence, persons who have been marginalized by the dominant culture (including the mainstream therapy institution) may find a home in narrative therapy because of the privileging of local knowledge and accountability practices on the part of the therapist.

CASE STUDY

The Client

The social work department of an in-patient adult psychiatric ward asked if we would 'see' Peter, a 38-year-old white, heterosexual, married, middle-class man who worked in the local film industry. Peter was described by hospital professionals as 'chronically depressed' and was given very little hope for change. The pessimism was triggered as a result of recent attempts to kill himself while on the ward and having to be physically restrained for pushing a male

(Continued)

(Continued)

orderly. The hospital's plan for health and change involved group and individual cognitive behavioural therapy together with numerous regimes of medication. Despite these attempts, the hospital described to us that 'nothing seemed to be working' and 'change seemed impossible'.

The Therapy

Peter had a total of nine visits with us over the course of four months. After the first six meetings he was able to return home from the hospital. All therapy sessions included a narrative response team. On five of the visits, volunteers of the letter-writing campaign (including family members, long-time friends and his former partner, Caitland, whom the problem had separated him from) were invited into therapy to 'perform' their written work 'live' in front of Peter.

During the first interview, Peter explained that 11 months prior to our talk, his 3-year-old daughter (whose mother was his former partner, Caitland) had died in a tragic drowning accident. He stated that initially he had only felt 'bitter and angry', and 'cut off' from the 'real meaning to life' and he had 'turned down support from anyone that mattered'.

Peter stated that he had responded to his daughter's death by 'barricading myself away from the world' – 'I blamed myself' – and shortly thereafter he separated himself from his marriage 'to be alone'. In a short period of time Peter had virtually removed himself from anyone who cared about him. He was eventually admitted to the ward after a neighbour found him 'in the garage with the motor running'.

The problem, which he referred to as 'an inability to go on', had taken over his daily life. He let us know that he was 'haunted day and night' and 'couldn't remember much of his life' from before the day his daughter, Mara, died. He said that he 'felt hopeless' and could not remember the 'sound of Mara's voice'.

Briefly outlined below are a few initial therapeutic counter-viewing questions from a narrative therapy perspective that we engaged Peter in:

1. Do you think 'giving up on hope' is the way in which your conversations with hopelessness find a way to help you believe that 'giving up' is a good answer – the only answer?
2. How do you think the community looks on a father who has lost his 3-year-old daughter?
3. Do you feel it is fair that everyone keeps telling you that you'll 'get over it'? Why not?
4. Do you believe that these people believe there is a proper time-line for a grieving father?
5. Are there places of past hope that you can remember that are currently blocked out by hopelessness and despair?
6. How is this hope possible?
7. Was the hospital accurate in diagnosing you as chronically depressed or do you think it might be about your experience of hopelessness helping you in not knowing 'how to go on'?

8. Has this deep sorrow you've explained to us been a sorrow that you could share with anyone else?
9. Is there any person or idea that promotes a life of hopelessness within your day-to-day living?
10. Is there anyone in your life, looking in on your life, that you think holds out hope for you – and holds onto your hope for you – until you return to it?
11. Was there ever a time that you disputed your internal conversations of blame and hopelessness?
12. Is the love you hold for Mara in any way helpful to the restoration of hope in your life?

After three sessions, Peter, myself and the team drafted a narrative therapeutic letter to his community of concern. He chose a dozen people to mail the letter out to. The logic behind a narrative therapy community letter-writing campaign is an attempt at finding ways to respond to certain problem identities growing stronger within the structures of the psychiatric institution. Often a tension exists between the person in hospital/institution/child care facility being cut off from hope and forgotten experiences of themselves, and those forgotten relational identities that live outside of their 'sick' identity. This is a tension worthy of therapeutic exploration. Our practice of narrative therapy, in part, hinges on creating counter-balances within the tension by including a community of **re-membering** and loving others who hold the stories of the client, while the client is temporarily restrained by the problem to remember these preferred and alternative memories. These desired stories live outside the professional and cultural inscription that defines the person suffering – and stand on the belief that *change is always possible*.

Letter-writing campaign structure

Letter-writing efforts can take on a variety of shapes and forms, but the most standard campaigns involve the following:

1. The campaign emerges from a narrative interview when alternative accounts of who the person might be are questioned, revived and re-remembered. The person is asked to consider whether there are other people in his/her life who may regard the person differently from how the problem describes them. These different accounts are then spoken of. We might ask the following questions: 'If I were to interview _____ about you, what do you think they might tell me about yourself that the problem would not dare to tell me?' Or 'Do you think your friend's telling of you to me about you would be an accurate telling, even if it contradicted the problem's tellings of you?' Or 'whose description of you do you prefer, and why?'
2. Together, the client and myself (along with the client's family/partner, friend, therapist, insiders, etc., if any of these persons are in attendance) begin a conversation regarding all the possible other descriptions of the client as a person that she/he might be, but has forgotten to remember because of the problem's hold over her/him. We dialogue on who the client might be,

(Continued)

(Continued)

who the client would like to be, and who the client used to be well before the problem took over her/his life.
3. We then begin to make a list of all the persons in the client's life who would be in support of these alternative descriptions. Once the list is complete, we construct a letter of support and invitation.
4. If finances are a problem our office supplies the envelopes and stamps for the ensuing campaign.
5. If privacy is an issue, we use the office as the return address.
6. The preference is for as many of the community of concern letter writers to *attend* the sessions.
7. If the client comes to the next session (with the letters) alone, we will offer to read the letters back to him/her as a textual re-telling.
8. The client is asked to go through the collection of letters as a way of conducting a 're-search' on herself/himself.

The 'general' structure for reading and witnessing the letters in therapy is as follows:

1. All campaign writers are invited to the session (if this is geographically possible) and in turn are asked to read aloud the letter they have penned about the person. In attendance is usually the client, myself, the other writers of their community and sometimes a therapy team that may include insiders.
2. After each writer reads aloud, the client is asked to read the letter back to the writer, so both writer and client can attend to what is being said/written from the different positions of speaking and listening.
3. After each letter is read by the writer and discussed with the client, the community of others in the session (who are sitting and listening) offer a brief reflection of what the letter evoked in their own personal lives.
4. This process continues until all letters are *read, re-read, responded to and reflected upon.*
5. Each response team member (usually but not always made up of professionals) then writes and reads a short letter to the client and his community. They reflect on the counter-view of the client offered up by the person and their community, the hope that was shared and aspects of the letters that moved them personally.
6. Copies are made of each letter and given to every one in attendance.
7. We then follow up the session with a therapeutic letter addressed to everyone who attended the session including the client, the community of concern and reflecting team.

Letter campaign contributors

Our experience has shown that once support persons have received a letter inviting them to contribute to a campaign, they will often feel compelled to write more than once (three and four letters are not uncommon). Contributors often state that they have had the experience of feeling 'left out' of the helping process. Contributors to the campaign have reported feeling 'blamed' and 'guilty' for the role they believe they have played in the problem's dominance over the person's life. They suggest that many of these awkward feelings about themselves have been helped along by various professional discourses and self-help literature.

Peter's therapeutic letter writing campaign read as follows:

Dear friends and family of Peter

My name is Stephen Madigan and I am a Family Therapist working along-side Peter. Since Mara's tragic death Peter has let me know that 'he hasn't known how to face the world'. Up until recently a sense of 'hope-lessness' has pretty much 'taken over his life', to the point that it almost killed him. Another debilitating aspect of this profound loss is that Peter cannot 'remember much of his life' since before Mara's death. Peter also feels in an 'odd way responsible for Mara's death', even though he knows 'somewhere in his mind' that he 'was out of town the day of the accident'. Peter believes that there is a 'strong message out there' that he 'should just get on with his life'. Peter says he finds this attitude 'trou-bling' because each 'person is different' and he believes that he 'might never get over it but eventually learn to live alongside it'.

We are writing to ask you to write a letter in support of Peter explaining (a) memories of your life with Peter, (b) what you shared, (c) who Mara was to you, (d) how you plan to support Peter while he grieves, (e) what Peter has given to you in your life, and (f) what you think your lives will be like together once he leaves the hospital.

Thank you for your help,
Peter, Stephen and the team

Personally, we found the reflections and readings with Peter, and the eight members of his community of concern who attended, extremely profound. Our letter-writing campaign meetings sometimes lasted two and three hours (we schedule them at day's end). Suffice to say, the texts written by the community of concern acted upon Peter's anticipation of hope, acceptance of who he was and his willingness to further live his life.

Four weeks after Peter left the hospital – on a forward-stepping path to be free of medication and concern – he and Mara's mother, Caitland, then entered into therapy with us to try to restore their marriage. They brought the letters. Together they anticipated the possibility that they could reconstruct their marriage. Hope is a wonderful potion.

REFERENCES

[1] Madigan, S. (2011) *Narrative Therapy – Theory and Practice*. Chicago, IL: APA Publications.
[2] Epston, D. and White, M. (1990) *Narrative Means to Therapeutic Ends*. New York: W. W. Norton.

SUGGESTED READING

Epston, D. (1988) *Collected Papers*. Adelaide: Dulwich Centre Publications. David Epston's *Collected Papers* represents the early writing and formational ideas of narrative therapy. The book is divided into 31 case studies and demonstrates Epston inventing new ways of post-structural practice across a wide range of persons and problems.

Madigan, S. (1999) 'Destabilizing chronic identities of depression and retirement', in Ian Parker (ed.), *Deconstructing Psychotherapy*. London: Sage. This work by Stephen Madigan deconstructs/critiques modern psychology theory and mental health practice and through a post-structural analysis reconstructs an alternative method when working with persons in therapy.

Madigan, S. (1992) 'The application of Michel Foucault's philosophy in the problem externalizing discourse of Michael White', *Journal of Family Therapy*, August. Viewed as the 'primer' article in showing how post-structural ideas of Michel Foucault are used in the practice of narrative therapy.

Nylund, D. (2000) *Treating Huckleberry Finn: A New Narrative Approach with Kids Diagnosed ADD/ADHD*. San Francisco: Jossey–Bass. David Nylund's book offers a fresh narrative therapy look at treating young persons diagnosed with attention deficit/hyperactivity disorder.

DISCUSSION ISSUES

1. How does the theory and practice approach to persons and problems differ in narrative therapy to all forms of therapy?
2. Narrative therapy resists the temptation of privatizing problems and pain in client's bodies. Discuss.
3. What do you feel the experience would be like to get an appreciative letter from your therapist outlining your abilities and skills – sent to you after the therapy session?
4. Do you feel the issues of race, gender, sexuality, class and ability are important to discuss in therapy sessions?

26

Neuro-Linguistic Programming

*Juliet Grayson and
Brigit Proctor*

Neuro–linguistic programming (NLP) is a systemic way of working. This means we see people as a system of interactions (for example, physical, mental, emotional and spiritual) and also see the system within a system within a system (for example, a child within a family, living in a village, living in England and so on).

NLP arose from studying the structure of an individual's everyday experience in detail, particularly focusing on people, on how people do things. From this NLP developed:

- a set of presuppositions (guiding principles and attitudes)
- a methodology for modelling (a detailed process to establish, with a particular skill, how they do what they do)
- a system of coding (a detailed description of the process)
- a series of models (ways of thinking that bring new perspectives or insights)
- a trail of techniques (processes that can be taught to other people, who wish to learn the skill that has been modelled).

An NLP therapist will encourage us to interact trustingly with our unconscious, and help us learn how to do that using movements, sensations, sounds, language and visualisations. The words we use will be taken seriously and literally. By paying close attention to language, and sharing an understanding of the deeper implications of using certain words, phrases and tenses, the therapist will help us to explore and experience different ways of thinking, and consider alternative meanings behind our hopes, behaviours and experiences. When coming for help we will probably have explored most of the conscious solutions (those we are aware of). The NLP process is designed to help us become more aware and use all the possibilities that are within us, including the unconscious ones, which have been out of our awareness, lying dormant and unknown.

DEVELOPMENT OF THE THERAPY

Richard Bandler and John Grinder, two Americans at the University of Santa Cruz in the early 1970s (Richard a student of mathematics, and John a professor of linguistics), became fascinated by the question 'What is the difference that makes the difference between everyday competence and excellence?' They decided to do an indepth study of Fritz Perls (the founder of Gestalt therapy), Virginia Satir (a founder of family therapy and systemic therapy) and Milton Erickson (founder of the American Society of Clinical Hypnosis). They observed what Perls, Satir and Erickson *actually said and did* when doing their work, as opposed to what they *said* they were doing. The modellers discovered that their conscious maps were very impoverished versions of their actual practice, and discovered a rich variety of extra unconscious (out-of-awareness) attitudes and skills. Bandler and Grinder also drew on and incorporated relevant skills, information and models from the fields of systems theory, anthropology, behavioural psychology and linguistics.

In Britain the governing body for NLP therapy is the Neuro-Linguistic Psychotherapy and Counselling Association (NLPtCA), which was established in 1992 and has its own code of ethics. NLPtCA is a member organisation of the United Kingdom Council for Psychotherapy (UKCP) in the Experiential Constructivists section.

THEORY AND BASIC CONCEPTS

NLP is curious about the rich complexity of people. The broad tools that each person uses to process the world (sight, sound, sensations, etc.) are the same, yet the way in which they use those tools is individual. It is an underpinning concept of NLP that the processes of generalisation, deletion and distortion will be common to all.

Generalisation, distortion and deletion

Humans need to selectively edit their experience of the world. Not to do so would be overwhelming. We all make generalisations. I have generalised that chairs are for sitting on.

We also delete large parts of our experience. No doubt as you read this you are not aware of the pressure of your feet on the floor (or were not until I brought it to your awareness). By the way, how aware are you of the sounds outside your window? Much of what is happening around us is selectively deleted.

The third process that happens is that we distort. For instance, we turn processes into completed events. Have you ever stereotyped a person on one short interaction or impression? Maybe later you realised that you had made an error of judgement. That is an example of distorting. Because we are continuously generalising, deleting and distorting, we each live in a 'model of the world', in NLP called your **map of**

the world, which will be an impoverished and distorted version of what is actually there. However, many people believe their maps to be *the* truth.

Modelling and coding

One of the skills NLP has crystallised is the ability to capture an individual's experience or skill, which is known as modelling. It involves exploring that which is conscious, *and* also the things outside their awareness (for example their beliefs, or physiology). Detailed information is captured, so that ultimately, the skill can be taught to someone else. This modelling has various applications. We can model 'excellent' abilities, for instance how people who had a strong phobia about spiders overcame it (apparently) spontaneously. This skill can then be taught on to other people who have a phobia and want to live free of that. We can also model 'stuck states' (for example, how a client sustains jealousy), and thereby gain greater awareness, understanding and choice about maintaining this state, so that they can move beyond it.

From modelling Perls, Satir and Erickson, a set of supportive and empowering beliefs about people emerged. These are known as presuppositions, and in NLP we act 'as if' these were true. As Robert Dilts, a co-developer of NLP said, 'An NLP technique used without a deep understanding and demonstration of the presuppositions is not actually NLP.'

The presuppositions

Basically there are two *key* presuppositions out of which others emerge, 'The map is not the territory' and 'Life and mind are systemic processes'.

'The map is not the territory'

This phrase, coined by Alfred Korzybski, the father of semantics, means that each person is responding to his or her *perception* of how things are in the world, not to the world itself. It follows that if we are all responding to our own perceptions of reality then *each person will have his or her own individual map of the world*. Gregory Bateson was an anthropologist, psychologist and biologist interested in systems and their interaction. He had a profound influence in NLP. He once wrote:

> The story is told of Picasso, that a stranger in a railway carriage accosted him with the challenge 'Why don't you paint things as they are?' Picasso demurred, saying that he did not quite understand what the other gentleman meant, and the stranger then produced from his wallet a photo of his wife. 'I mean', he said, 'like that. That's how she is.' Picasso coughed hesitantly and said, 'She is rather small, isn't she? And somewhat flat.' (p. 161)[1]

A photo is a representation of reality, but we equate it with reality.

NLP further assumes that *people already have (or potentially have) all of the resources they need to act more effectively, and that people make the best choices available to them* given the possibilities and the capabilities that they perceive available to them.

'Life and mind are systemic processes'

Each individual is a system, and our relationships with our families and societies form systems, creating an ecology of systems and subsystems, all of which interact with and mutually influence each other.

Seeing things in this systemic way, like a series of wheels and cogs that turn and are inextricably linked, brings an awareness of, and sensitivity to, the larger system. Since *it is not possible to isolate completely any part of the system from the rest of the system,* and people cannot *not* influence each other, any change in clients in therapy may also cause a shift in client's relationships – with their partner and other significant people.

People form feedback loops for each other, so that a person will be affected by the results that their actions have on other people.

Systems are 'self-organising' and naturally seek states of balance and stability.

NLP presupposes that *all behaviour has a positive intention* and there is a context in which every behaviour has value. For example, the positive purpose behind fear is often safety; and the positive purpose behind anger may be to maintain boundaries. So when exploring a problematic behaviour, we trust in and seek the positive intention.

Another guiding presupposition is that *there are no failures, only feedback.*

Human nature and health

In NLP we believe that living by these presuppositions will enhance people's lives. Bandler and Grinder say.

> In coming to understand how it is that some people continue to cause themselves pain and anguish, it has been important for us to realise that they are not bad, crazy or sick. They are, in fact, making the best choices from those of which they are aware, that is, the best choices available in their own particular models [maps of the world]. In other words, human beings' behaviour, no matter how bizarre it may first appear to be, makes sense when it is seen in the context of the choices generated by their model. The difficulty is not that they are making the wrong choice, but that they do not have enough choices – they don't have a richly focused image of the world. The most pervasive paradox of the human condition which we see is that the processes which allow us to survive, grow, change, and experience joy are the same processes which allow us to maintain an impoverished model of the world. (p. 14)[2]

So how does all this work in practice?

PRACTICE

The practice of NLP will vary according to the way individual practitioners choose to use their skills, tools and techniques, with each individual client. There is no set format for an NLP session. There will, however, be some broad goals that may generalise for all NLP practitioners, and some key points to which NLP practitioners will pay attention.

The goals of NLP

Building a relationship, rapport, and working alliance between the therapist and the client, with the therapist holding the NLP presuppositions and attitudes (of respect, curiosity, open–mindedness and possibility), is the key to creating a space where the client can change.

Initially a conscious contract will be agreed, with clear goals for the work. The therapist will seek an explicit and detailed understanding of how the client (and therapist) will recognise that those goals have been achieved, the 'evidence'. What will the client be feeling, what will they see, what will they be saying to themselves?

The therapist will be particularly careful to ascertain the level at which the client is wanting and able to work. An NLP therapist will work differently with an identity level issue – 'I'm not that kind of person', to an issue at the level of capability – 'I don't know *how* to …'.

The therapist will encourage the client to ask questions of themselves, to find a wider map of the world, so more choices become available. He/she will strengthen the client's awareness of their conscious/unconscious feedback loop, thus helping the client to become aware of the signals that their own mind/body system is sending to them, and help them be curious about what these signals may mean.

The therapist may wish to guide the client to explore and understand the deeper structure of the problem, for example the **secondary gains**, the benefits of maintaining the 'problem' state, and limiting beliefs that may have been formed. They will work to uncover deletions, generalisations and distortions of the problem so that a richer perception of the underlying issues and patterns can be obtained.

The relationship between the therapist and the client

One of the processes that Grinder and Bandler observed was the art of building deep rapport with the client, in order to enter into the client's world. Indeed, the way Milton Erickson entered the system has been described as so complete that he was in the 'weave of the total complex'. Robert Dilts, a leading NLP trainer, author and co–developer, wrote that:

The process of healing requires an intention [a goal], a relationship [rapport], and a ritual [technique]. While external techniques and tools may be used mechanically to ... aid the healing process, the source of healing is within the system of the individual. (p. 293)[3]

Non-verbal clues from the client provide feedback to the therapist

The therapists who the originators of NLP observed had an acute degree of sensitivity to tiny physiological changes, for example facial colour change, the size of the lips changing, tightness across the forehead, eye movements and breathing shifts. They used these non-verbal clues from the client as feedback, often without being consciously aware of what they were doing.

In NLP we place strong emphasis on reading tiny changes in body language. The therapist will use this as a guide in helping the client achieve their *desired state*. It becomes possible to explore and understand much of the unconscious internal communication, and how the client both manages and expresses what is happening for him/herself. Clients learn to know, trust and appreciate their own unique system.

NLP techniques

The therapist, having paid attention to how the experience of a particular client is coded, by noticing language patterns and physiological changes, can offer a myriad of specific techniques that enable him or her to experience the effects of conscious and unconscious patterns of behaviour, memories and goals. Much NLP work uses such experiential play, which can be engaging, often amusing, whilst 'moving' clients profoundly. In outline, a few of these are as follows.

Creating well-formed outcomes

Establishing goals that

- are achievable
- are stated in the positive ('I don't want to hold back in that meeting' may become 'I want to speak up')
- fit with the kind of person the client sees him or herself as being
- will have effects on the people around the client that the client is willing to tolerate
- have clear evidence that will let both the client and the therapist know when they have achieved the goal
- acknowledge the resources that are needed to achieve the goal

Anchoring techniques

These use the process of association to create a 'trigger' or an 'anchor' for a response. A naturally occurring experience of this is the smell of newly cut grass. When later we smell newly cut grass again, it acts as an anchor to elicit a state, taking us back to an earlier time when we smelt that before.

In therapy we may help clients learn how to re-experience, for instance, a delightful and creative occasion. By reliving this in the present, they explore and learn how they can 'trigger' this response for themselves, discovering how to re-access that 'creative' state appropriately and consciously whenever they wish, in the future.

First, second and third positions

This involves seeing a situation from three different perspectives. First position is standing in your own shoes, living the experience. Second position is becoming the other person, seeing the world as if through their eyes, taking on their 'map of the world', beliefs and physiology. Third position is taking that of an objective observer, as if you are standing on a balcony. In third you are able to see from a dispassionate perspective the two people over there who are having a discussion or dispute and you are not involved in the emotional reactions. By being able to get multiple perspectives on a situation, and also see yourself from someone else's point of view, this model can allow complex information to become available, often changing the way a situation is perceived and experienced.

Reframing

An event is given meaning according to the 'frame' within which it is set. When meaning changes, then a person's responses and behaviours also change. A client who complained of tiredness two weeks after a serious operation realised that this was in fact her body slowing her down to allow her to heal. This reframe allowed her to accept her condition and rest, thereby speeding her recovery. By changing the frame, we change the meaning.

Talking to parts

For many of us there is an internal dialogue which continues at a level that is barely conscious. This can be energy-consuming. Talking between different parts of ourselves is one of the techniques used to enable clients to become more aware, and allow these conversations to happen more usefully. An NLP therapist may have the client communicate directly with different parts of the body, or different aspects of the self.

These are examples of some of the powerful therapeutic techniques NLP uses. We would like to stress that such techniques need to be underwritten by a developed self-awareness and integrity, respect for other people and appreciation of diversity.

The process of change

Bandler and Grinder say:

> People who come to us in therapy typically have pain in their lives and experience little or no choice in matters which they consider important. All therapies are confronted with the problem of responding adequately to such people. Responding adequately in this context means to us assisting in changing the client's experience in some way which enriches it. Rarely do therapies accomplish this by changing the world. Their approach, then, is typically to change the client's experience of the world. (p. 156)[2]

People get stuck in habitual ways of looking at things, making it difficult to think creatively and flexibly. By **reframing** their own experience, working 'as if' the presuppositions are true, we discover that people 'seem' to heal in a natural self-organising manner. A behaviour that may have been seen as problematic, being depressed, may come to be seen as a useful, but ultimately ineffective form of self-protection.

WHICH CLIENTS BENEFIT MOST?

As NLP has such wide interpretation, and there is no prescriptive format to follow, it can be of value to a wide variety of clients.

Traditionally NLP has been thought of as a short-term, effective therapy. However, many practitioners also use it for deep and long-term work. The basic orientation of NLP is solution-focused, looking forward to changes people want, and to how they might achieve those. It therefore has an orientation towards the future.

NLP has realised the benefits of being able to be fully 'in' an experience (associate fully into a particular state), and also to be able to step back and see a problem as separate from oneself (disassociate). The ability to associate and disassociate appropriately is particularly useful, and NLP has some particularly valuable techniques using this skill in relation to exams, phobias and traumas.

CASE STUDY

The Client

Jenny is in her mid-forties. Her mother died two years ago, which she found very difficult to accept. She came to therapy to resolve issues around her mother. My intention here is to show one piece of work she did, and the subsequent impact.

The Therapy

(J.G.) I suggested that we use a model to elicit information. Sorting out where different pieces belong allows the client to step back and see the problem clearly delineated, and separate from herself. I asked if she would like to explore and experiment with this. She seemed enthusiastic. We used a model called the SCORE:

    S Symptom
    C Cause
    O Outcome
    R Resource
    E Effect

First we looked at the 'Symptom' space, and I said, 'Let's look at the situation now, how is it for you now – what's the problem?' She said, 'I'm not able to look at a photograph of Mum.' As she said this she moved her head and body back, her face reddened and her breathing quickened. She described how she literally could not look at a photograph of her mother, and so had no photos of her in her house. She could not visit her father because he had photographs of her on show.

I asked her gently what she wanted ('Outcome') and she said 'I want to be able to look at a photograph of my mother.' As she said this she breathed out a long sigh, and her hands became still and rested on her lap. I felt some resolution, that she had clarified her goal, and I supposed that she did too. I suggested exploring the 'Cause'.

'So what led to this situation arising, a situation where the idea of looking at a photo of your mother has seemed so challenging?' Jenny talked of the close relationship she had had with her mother, and how hard her death had been, how Jenny still could not believe it was true. Jenny's voice became quieter, her breathing more shallow still, and she clutched her hands tightly across her chest.

It seemed time to move on to the 'Effect'. A number of things influenced this decision. She had been in a tense and distressed state for a while. I was also aware of the time and the need to sustain the rhythm of the process. I began by pacing (carefully reflecting what she had said), then leading her on to look at the 'Effect'.

'So the situation has been about not wanting to look at a photograph of your mother [using my language to put the problem into the past tense, thus opening up another possibility] and you had a very close relationship with your mother, and she was always nearby. Let's leave those feelings behind for a moment, let's step out of all of that, and think instead of what you want. You want to be able to look at a photograph of your mother. Imagine now, that you can do this, and I know this may seem difficult right now, but just imagine being at a time in your life, in the future, when you can enjoy looking at a photograph of your mother, and it feels absolutely OK. What does that do for you? What will the effect of that be in your life?'

Jenny began talking. At first I could see she was still in a state of distress, a necessary stage of the process but one in which it is almost physically impossible to tap fresh resources. However, as she talked I noticed her face

(Continued)

(Continued)

began to light up and she gradually became more animated as she imagined herself and associated into the new possibility.

'Well, I guess that being able to look at the photograph of Mum would mean that I have accepted her death, and then I could begin to remember her, and some of the happy times we had.' Jenny began to make larger gestures as she spoke of this.

'So ... as you are able to remember the happy times with your mother, because you can look at her photo and feel OK, what does that bring you, or allow you to do?', I asked, in a tone of gentle curiosity, reflecting back not only her words, the varied tone and faster speed, but also her gestures, thus matching the way she had expressed herself.

'Well,' said Jenny, 'If I can bear to look at photos of my Mum then I'll be able to go to their house and visit Dad. At the moment he has to come round to me. I can't bear to go into his house and see pictures of her all over the place.'

At this point I felt it was time to move on. Jenny seemed to have a sense of the benefits, and I could see from her physiology, from the tone and speed of her voice, that she was in a very different state from earlier in the session. I asked what 'Resources' she might need. She told me that talking it through had helped, she had realised it was important not only to her, but also to her father. She felt that remembering this would help in any difficult moments. She also remarked that breathing more deeply changed how she felt, and she could use that. She also said she just needed more time and said, 'When I look at the photo it will mean that I have accepted that I'm never going to see my mother in the flesh again, that she really has gone. A part of me knows that, but there's part of me that still doesn't want to accept that. Whilst I don't look then I can feel her to be alive and just away for a while.' This demonstrated an acceptance of the positive intention of what she had perceived as problematic.

I encouraged her to trust that her own wisdom would let her know when it was time to look at the photo, and that she would know when, and how, she wanted to do that.

When we considered what the original 'Symptom' had been, Jenny realised that her experience of it had shifted. She no longer felt it to be such a problem. It wasn't that she would be able to look at a photo yet, but she no longer saw not looking as a problem. Now she saw it as a choice. She had already begun to organise her own healing in relation to this issue.

Jenny and I continued to work together for the next few months, working on issues mainly to do with Jenny's health, which was not good at this time. We did not discuss the photograph again until about three months later, when Jenny walked in and said, 'I've brought the photo of my mum; it's in this carrier bag. I may not look at it today. I haven't looked at it yet.'

I said, 'You let me know if you feel you want to look. I'll leave it up to you to decide when or whether you want to look.'

Twenty minutes later Jenny said, 'OK, let's look now', and we spent the rest of the session with her looking, crying and talking to her mother in the picture. It was a very beautiful experience for me, and I was delighted to have been privileged to share it with her.

In the earlier session a number of things had been achieved. She had begun to make clearer distinctions and discovered extra information. Realising that her physiology was linked to the state associated with each space, she had discovered the power of changing her breathing and noticed how that changed her state. She also began to trust the wisdom of her own self, and her ability to understand her own healing process.

REFERENCES

[1] Bateson, G. and Bateson, M. C. (1988) *Angels Fear: An Investigation into the Nature and Meaning of the Sacred.* London: Rider Books.

[2] Bandler, R. and Grinder, J. (1975) *The Structure of Magic: A Book about Language and Therapy.* Palo Alto, CA: Science and Behavior Books Inc.

[3] Dilts, R. B. (1995) *Strategies of Genius,* Vol. III: *Sigmund Freud, Leonardo da Vinci, Nikola Tesla.* Capitola, CA: Meta Publications.

SUGGESTED READING

Bandler, R. and Grinder, J. (1993) *Frogs into Princes.* Utah: Real People Press. Written by the originators of NLP, this book teaches you about the basic NLP techniques in an immediate and humorous way.

Hall, M. (2004) *The Sourcebook of Magic: A Comprehensive Guide to NLP Change Patterns,* 2nd edn. Carmarthen: Crown House Publishing. A handbook for therapists which is studded with frequent stories, interesting background and why/how the intervention works.

Jago, W. and McDermott, I. (2001) *Brief NLP.* London: Sage. A guide to the underpinning core concepts of NLP as used in a therapeutic practice. Includes case studies.

Lankton, S. (1993) *Practical Magic: A Translation of Basic NLP into Clinical Psychotherapy.* Capitola, CA: Meta Publications. A book for established therapists who wish to use NLP in their work.

DISCUSSION ISSUES

1. (a) Close your eyes, and for a moment take on the belief that 'the world is a truly dangerous place'. Step fully into believing that … take your time to build the internal feelings, and notice any sounds or pictures. After a few minutes open your eyes, look around and notice what you see.
   (b) Shake that off.
   (c) Now close your eyes, and take on the belief that 'the world is a friendly and completely safe place'. Spend time allowing that sensation to build. After a few minutes open your eyes, looking around you notice what you notice.

(d)   In small groups discuss the different experiences. Be aware that you just utilised two very different maps of the world. How fully were you able to engage in each one? What caught your attention when you opened your eyes?

2. (a)   Imagine a particular issue that you consider a problem.
    (b)   Now think of the wisest person you know. Step inside their skin, take on their beliefs and their physiology (posture, the way they hold their body, facial expression, gestures, etc.), *become the wise person*. Look at the problem from their perspective. What supportive insight would you, as a wise person, offer them about that problem, and what steps would you have them take in relation to moving the situation forward?
    (c)   Now become a very young child. Step inside his/her skin, and take on all of his/her beliefs. What supportive insight would you, the child, offer them about that problem, and what steps would you suggest he/she takes in relation to moving the situation forward?
    (d)   Discuss the experience, and the insight you have gained. What particularly surprised or delighted you in this exercise?

3. Think of something you have avoided doing (e.g. dancing in public, or writing a report). In small groups brainstorm what the positive intentions of this behaviour could be.

4. (a)   Work in twos. One of you think of a problem, and state it in one brief sentence: e.g. I lack confidence with my work colleagues.
    (b)   The coach re-states the problem using the past tense: e.g. So you have been having a lack of confidence with your work colleagues.
    (c)   Notice the impact of putting the problem into the past. Discuss.

27

Personal Construct Counselling and Psychotherapy

Fay Fransella and Stephen Palmer

INTRODUCTION

Personal construct counselling and psychotherapy is based on George Kelly's theory of personal constructs which attempts to explain, 'how the human process flows, how it strives in new directions as well as in old, and how it may dare for the first time to reach into the depths of newly perceived dimensions of human life' (p. 5).[1]

Personal construct psychotherapy and counselling do not fit easily into any one pre-existing category. The psychology of personal constructs that underpins them is *cognitive* in the sense that it deals with how people make sense of the world around them. It is *humanistic* in the sense that it deals with the total person and not just how we think or how we behave. But it is also behavioural in the sense that it gives a prominent and unusual place to our behaviour. In addition, it is more than any of these.

It is essentially an approach to helping those with psychological problems that focuses on how we experience the world as individual human beings. It does not see us as being the victims of our past history although we can trap ourselves if we come to see past events in that way. We impose our own individual meanings on everything and the work of the counsellor or psychotherapist is to try to look at the world through the client's eyes. Only in this way can they get some idea of why the client is having the problems for which they are seeking help.

DEVELOPMENT OF THE THERAPY

To fully understand a theory it is important to know something about the theorist. The psychology of personal constructs was described by George Kelly in 1955.[2] He

was born in 1900 and took his first degree in physics and mathematics. This was followed by another degree in education taken in Edinburgh, and then a higher degree
in sociology and finally a doctorate in philosophy on neurological and physiological
aspects of stuttering. With that background, it is not surprising that he suggested we
might see how useful it would be to take 'the scientist' as our model of the person.
This is coupled with his concern that we should be able to assess a person's construing, that is, get beyond the words (see Fransella[3] for more details of George Kelly).

When he started working on his theory in the 1930s, the approaches of Sigmund
Freud and other 'psychodynamic' theorists and the behaviourists were dominant.
Kelly saw his theory as being an alternative to both of these. He saw Freud as a genius
who had come up with some very creative ideas but whose followers had done him
a disservice. He had no time at all for the behaviourists. He thought they made the
person into a puppet that reacted only when a 'stimulus' prompted them into action.

Personal construct counselling and psychotherapy are the application of the basic
theory and methods of personal construct theory. While Kelly used psychotherapy as
the focus of his theory, he saw that as only an example of what people might do with
it. The theory is now used in very many settings including teaching, management,
nursing and medicine.

The main development since 1955 has been the creation and elaboration of
personal construct psychotherapeutic theories and practice for those with specific
problems. These include the type of disorder of thinking found in some of those
medically diagnosed as suffering from schizophrenia (summarized in *Inquiring Man*);[4]
stutter;[5] depression;[6] those who are traumatised and those who have been bereaved.[7]
Some have described how the personal construct approach can be used as an alternative to behavioural methods[8] and as a way of coming to understand the problems of
children.[9]

THEORY AND BASIC CONCEPTS

Underpinning all of Kelly's thinking is his explicit philosophy, which he called **constructive alternativism** – not as complicated as it sounds. It says there are always
alternative ways of looking at, construing, events. We are not stuck with what has
happened to us in the past. Reconstruing is always possible but is not always easy.

The nature of construing

To understand what construing means, we can take Kelly's idea of looking at ourselves
and others 'as if we are all theory makers', as if we are all scientists. Personal constructs
indicate ways in which we have noted similarities between some events that thereby
make them different from other events. We may construe some people as *intelligent*. By
doing that we are, at the same time, saying that there are others who are *stupid*. An essential

feature of personal construct theory is that all our personal constructs have two poles. You cannot know what *good* is without having some idea of what being *bad* means.

When making sense of someone, a person may go further and note that intelligent people are all kindly whereas stupid people are all indifferent. Now intelligence, kindliness, stupidity and indifference do not reside in the people we are construing but they reside in the eye of the construer. That person has a theory about others. Essentially what happens in practice is that every time she or he meets a person she construes as intelligent she behaves towards that person 'as if' they were intelligent and makes a prediction that they will behave toward her in a kindly way. Construing is essentially about *predicting*. Whenever we make a prediction of any sort, we look to see whether this prediction is more or less right or wrong. Kelly was doing here something that had never been done before in a psychological theory; he made our behaviour the **experiment** we carry out to test the prediction we have made from our mini-theory. In this way, we are always launching ourselves into the future. Our behaviour is thus totally linked in with our construing.

As well as being a personal scientist, Kelly suggested we might usefully look at ourselves and others as a total entity. That may seem strange at first sight as one might ask how it is possible not to be a whole person. But behaviourists, for instance, certainly in Kelly's day, saw us in terms of our behaviour; cognitive theorists focus on how we think; and Freud or those who subscribe to psychodynamic theories focus on our unconscious processes. Kelly argued forcibly that it is not possible to separate our behaviour from our thinking or from our feelings.

Construing goes on in every aspect of our being. Our feelings are linked to an awareness of our construing in action. If we construe something that is happening as likely to challenge some core aspect of our notion of our 'self', we will have the unpleasant feeling of being threatened. Construing definitely does not just go on in the head alone, nor is it divorced from our behaviour or our feelings.

As well as being bi-polar, and predictive, construing goes on at all **levels of awareness**, from the level of the 'gut reaction' to the high levels of cognitive awareness as you try to understand the psychology of personal constructs. We are, each one of us, seen as a total construing process.

As has been touched on several times, construing is personal. No two people see the world which they inhabit in precisely the same way. But, to the extent that we have developed in similar cultures, so we may construe events in similar ways and so are able to communicate. Personal construct theory highlights **reflexivity** in that the theory applies as much to the counsellor as it does to that of the client.

The nature of psychological disturbance

Kelly argued fiercely also against the use of concepts from medicine being applied to psychological problems. The psychology of personal constructs does not see clients who come for psychotherapy as being 'ill'. Kelly suggests that we might use the concept of 'functioning' instead. A person who is fully functioning is someone who gets their predictions about other people and events more or less right most of the time.

When things do not turn out quite as predicted, the fully functioning person may respond by saying 'OK, I got it wrong that time, I'll hope to do better next time.' If that person concludes that the invalidation is more serious than that, they may deal with it by looking at the event from another viewpoint they reconstrue.

A person who is not functioning so well may be incapable of dealing with much invalidation. He may resort to being *hostile*. Kelly gave personal construct definitions to some everyday words. Hostility is one of them. He wanted to be sure that all we experience could be accounted for within the same psychological theory. Not for him was there to be a theory of behaviour and another for emotion and another for learning and so forth. We are a totality. *Hostility* is used when we are aware, at some level, that our prediction is a failure but we cannot give up that way of construing because that would mean giving up some core aspect of how we see ourselves. So, 'intelligent people just must be kindly because my mother was intelligent and extremely kindly and this person is like my mother so she just *must* be kindly'. So he behaves in a way that forces the person to pay attention to him. There is nothing essentially 'bad' about such hostility. It is a way we protect ourselves against hard psychological times. Clients in psychotherapy will use hostility as a way of guarding themselves against the very success of the therapy if they see it as encouraging them to move psychologically too fast. But it can become a problem if an individual uses such a method too often, whether in therapy or in everyday life.

There are a number of ways in which an individual can be seen as acquiring a problem or 'symptom'. Remembering that all behaviour is seen as an experiment, a major way of acquiring a problem is to find yourself repeating the same experiment again and again in spite of persistent invalidating results. There is no reconstruing, no hostility. The person has ceased to be in charge of their own behaviour. The person has got psychologically stuck. They are, for some reason, unable to reconstrue. Such a person will find it possible to reconstrue only when they are able to understand why it is they have to keep conducting such experiments.

Another person may not have a problem with constant invalidation of their personal experiments, but rather find difficulty in making predictions at all. They are finding that the world is becoming an increasingly confusing place. In Kelly's sense, they are immersed in a sea of anxiety. Their way out is to anchor themselves to a 'symptom'. Perhaps they are feeling really bad and someone says 'You are depressed'; or they say 'I'm feeling bad because I am overweight.' They have found a reason for their otherwise chaotic experiences. Although not desired by the client, these symptoms are preferable to the anxiety. Many will find out that it is not the symptom that is the problem.

Other problems may be due to the use of personal construing that has been developed in early childhood, before the development of language. In one sense, this was Kelly's theory of 'unconscious' construing. Many people associate any discussion of 'the unconscious' with the ideas of Freud. And they would be right to do so. Freud gave the idea of human beings having an inner life public credibility and it has proved enormously useful. But George Kelly could not accept the idea that there were forces within us influencing our daily experiencing of the world. Kelly suggested the radical idea that there are no psychological forces within each one of us at all. He pointed out that in physics some concept of a physical force was necessary in order to explain why inanimate objects moved. A rock only moves if something hits it or gravity takes over; it does not move of its own accord. Freud brought the notion of physical energy into psychology and talks of 'psychic energy'. But Kelly asked the fundamental question, 'Why do I have to start with the construct of force or energy?' Inanimate objects are different from human beings in that human beings are alive. One of the defining characteristics of living matter is that it moves.

Therefore, for Kelly, you do not need to invoke the idea of a force to explain why living matter moves; it does it of its own accord. What has to be explained is why we do what we do in the way that we do it. Kelly calls the construing developed before the onset of language a 'pre-verbal construing'. No force or energy is involved. Pre-verbal construing comes into play when a situation arises in adult life that makes the construing relevant. For instance, a child falls into a pond in the garden, cannot swim, feels panic but is rescued before any damage is done. For a time that child fears all water until he learns to distinguish the sink, the bath and the toilet as different from the pond, a lake and the sea. With a thoughtful and caring teacher the child learns to swim. That does not mean the fear of water disappears but only that swimming with a caring adult is all right. The child grows into adulthood and stays away from large stretches of water. He meets a girl who loves sailing. Problem. He starts quarrelling with the girl. The student counsellor manages to help him discover where his fear of water comes from. He can now talk about it and relate it to the fact that he can now swim. The situation is totally different from the one that caused his fear. In Kelly's terms, he has 'updated' his construing. By putting verbal labels on his pre-verbal construing he can reconstrue. Much of the psychotherapeutic process is to do with understanding the client's pre-verbal construing.

Kelly relates pre-verbal construing to two other aspects of human experiencing. One is what some call 'acting out'. What can one do with pre-verbal construing except behave it? The other connection Kelly makes is with psychosomatic complaints. This is obviously a complex connection. He argues that we are a total construing system (also see **personal construct system**), and that one way of expressing our construing is through our bodily processes.

PRACTICE

The goals of personal construct counselling and psychotherapy

Taken at its simplest, a person has a problem because they have become psychologically 'stuck'. They are not happy with the way things are and yet cannot find any alternative ways of dealing with life. Personal construct therapy, as well as theory, says that we do have choice, but can only operate that choice if we feel we can explore alternatives. In ordinary circumstances, the choice we make in elaborating our notions of our selves and what we make of others is always towards that which we imagine will enable us to make increasing sense of our world. When we get psychologically stuck we are unable to make that choice. So, a major goal of therapy is to enable the client to 'get on the psychological move again'. Central to this is the idea that we are a form of motion. When we say we have a problem we say we are doing things we do not like.

Establishing the framework of the relationship

At the very start, the client needs to understand, in a very general way, what they may expect from a personal construct therapist. For instance, they will have to work hard, for the personal construct therapist has no specific answers to the problems the client has brought. The therapist only knows some ways in which the client may be helped to reconstrue themselves, the people and the events in their life. The relationship is spelled out as something like a partnership: both work hard to understand how the client construes his or her world. To help their struggle to understand their own construing of the world and particularly the areas related to the problem, the client needs to understand that they will be asked to carry out tasks between sessions. These tasks will be agreed between therapist and client and will often consist of trying out new or alternative behavioural experiments and so the client comes to see that their own behaviour affects how others see them.

At the start of this understanding process, the therapist/counsellor listens to, and believes, everything the client says. That *credulous listening* is an essential starting point because everything the client says is deemed to have meaning for the client, even if the therapist knows it to be untrue. For it may not be untrue to the client or it may be of value to know why the client feels the need to tell an untruth to the therapist. To be able to adopt the *credulous approach* the therapist must be able to suspend their own personal values. That is, the therapist has to be able to hear what the client is saying and not have it filtered through the therapist's personal ideas of what is right or wrong, good or bad. In personal construct therapy the therapist does not provide. The client will be helped to find their own solutions.

A typical session

In the sessions themselves there is no particular format, only some guiding principles. For instance, the therapist and counsellor will keep in mind that their own behaviour is a tool in providing validation for the client's behavioural experiments. For instance, a client may inexplicably start behaving in a way the therapist/counsellor interprets as 'rude'. Their response will be very important since it will be seen by the client as supporting or negating the client's own experiment. It cannot be said too often that, when talking about construing, we are not saying that the client 'thinks' about their own behavioural experiments in a conscious way.

Sessions will usually include a discussion of the previous week's homework and the designing of work to be carried out the following week. Unlike some therapies, the personal construct approach sees the major work being done between sessions rather than during the sessions.

Defining the problem

Before a personal construct psychotherapist can start to help the client reconstrue, the therapist has to formulate a theory about the nature of the client's problem. That formulation would be called 'the diagnosis' in a medical context. Kelly's formulation is in terms of personal construct theory using what he calls 'professional constructs'. It can be to do with the *process* of the client's construing or its *content*. Their construing may be too 'loose' for the client to pull their thoughts or feelings together sufficiently for them to have any meaningful perception of the world around them and so conduct behavioural experiments that have any clear-cut predictions. Alternatively, it may be seen as so 'tight' that any change at one level could cause a collapse of the entire system; just like taking away a card in the middle of a house of cards – the whole lot crumples. Change for clients with either of these process problems would be most likely to be seen by a personal construct psychotherapist rather than a counsellor. The personal construct practitioner makes a distinction here. A person who is having to change aspects of their whole construing system and not just the personal constructs themselves will require psychotherapy.

Problems with the *content* of construing can, of course, be almost anything. But some are as deep-rooted as the process problems and require psychotherapy rather than counselling. 'Pre-verbal' construing can cause us much trouble in adult life. For instance, if part of the diagnosis is that the client is continually behaving so that all attempts at forming close, long-term relationships fail because of some construing that evolved during early childhood, then the psychotherapist can expect to be with the client for many sessions. Only when these construings are given words to anchor them in present reality can the client construe them from their present perspective.

Part of the problem-formulation process involves making a best guess about why the client persists in being someone they are not happy with.

The change process

As we are seen as forms of motion, change is with us all the time. So what we are looking for here is a theory about how psychological change comes about. We are truly in the land of speculation because there is little hard evidence to show how we actually do change our views, 'our minds' or 'our selves'. Kelly's theoretical speculations focus on 'diagnosis'. For that, a personal construct counsellor uses the 'professional constructs' mentioned in the last section. If a client's construing is seen as being too loose for comfort, leading to much anxiety, then part of the change process will include helping that person to tighten it and so make better sense of their world. Basically, personal construct counselling and psychotherapy are based on the application of the whole of personal construct theory.

Major therapeutic strategies and techniques

Personal construct counselling and psychotherapy are heavy on theory and light on techniques. In fact, there no techniques that are a *must*. The counsellor or psychotherapist chooses that technique which they believe will bring about changes in construing toward which both client and therapist are working. Kelly puts it this way:

> Personal construct psychotherapy is a way of getting on with the human enterprise and it may embody and mobilize all of the techniques for doing this that man has yet devised. Certainly there is no one psychotherapeutic technique and certainly no one kind of inter-personal compatibility between psychotherapist and client. The techniques employed are the techniques for living and the task of the skilful psychotherapist is the proper orchestration of all these varieties of techniques. Hence one may find a personal construct psychotherapist employing a huge variety of procedures not helter-skelter, but always as part of a plan for helping himself and his client get on with the job of human exploration and checking out the appropriateness of the constructions they have devised for placing upon the world around them. (pp. 221–2)[10]

He created two techniques that might be used to come to a deeper understanding of how our client sees the world – the self-characterization and the **repertory grid** – and one for helping the client reconstrue – fixed role therapy.

The self characterization

Kelly is reported as having said that if he were to be remembered for only one thing, it would be his first principle: 'If you do not know what is wrong with a person, ask him, he may tell you' (p. 241).[2] This is how he saw the self–characterization. The person is asked to write a character sketch of him- or herself, in the third person, as if describing a character in a play. But this is written by someone who is very sympathetic to them and knows them better than anyone can ever know them. The person starts off with their own name, for example, I (F. F.) would start: 'Fay Fransella is ...'. There is no very detailed method of analysis, but it can reveal a great deal about someone if you become skilled at reading between the lines.

The repertory grid

This has become a technology in its own right and can be found in many forms. The original version was described by Kelly to 'get beyond the words'. A grid is basically a matrix made up of personal constructs and the 'elements' to be construed. Thus, if it is designed to look at interpersonal construing, the elements would most likely be people and relatives close to the client and the constructs would have been elicited from the client. The matrix can be analysed by several different statistical procedures. The pattern of relationships shows how an individual views important people and relationships.

Fixed role therapy

George Kelly was much influenced by the development of psychodrama by psychiatrist Jacob Moreno.[11] Kelly places considerable emphasis on role play and enactment as part of his psychotherapeutic and counselling approach. He elaborated this specifically into fixed role therapy. He did that to show how his theory might be put into practice rather than to spell out a specific technique. You take the client's self-characterization and write another that is similar to the original but different in certain respects. The client has to agree that the new sketch is someone he or she *could* be. Once agreed, the client adopts that role for a certain period of time. The aim is to show the client that one is not trapped forever in the same mode. We can all change; all re-create ourselves if we have the will. Writing the new sketch is not as easy as it sounds and Kelly spells out the procedure in some detail (pp. 239–68).[2]

WHICH CLIENTS BENEFIT MOST?

It is not possible to say which sort of people with which sort of problems may benefit most from the personal construct approach. It has been used with a wide range of problems. For example, it has been used with clients with schizophrenia,[4] clients with long-standing problems such as stuttering,[3] clients with problems of depression or anxiety or phobias. Some work has been done by Landfield,[12] who created the interpersonal transaction group method, and Neimeyer,[13] who described some clinical guidelines for carrying out such group therapy. It should be said that, in most cases, where there is perceived to be a limitation, it is usually the limitation of the therapist rather than the client.

CASE STUDY

The Client

My client, whom I (F. F.) will call Flora, gave me the impression of being reasonably poised and self-confident. There was also a friendliness and warmth about her that suggested she was used to dealing with people. Her hand was cool and dry as we shook hands, suggesting she was probably not too stressed by the situation.

Flora had made the appointment by telephone. She explained she was having trouble with her personal life and would just like to talk to someone about it. She had read the book that personal construct psychotherapist Peggy Dalton and I had written on personal construct counselling[14] and liked what she had read. She said she thought the personal construct approach was good because

(Continued)

(Continued)

it would not impose some outside ideas upon her and the issues she wanted to talk about. It would not explain her problems in terms of her complexes or unconscious urges. It seemed to her that the approach would look at how she saw her life and herself and that was it.

The Therapy

The methods and procedures used in personal construct counselling make no distinction between gathering information about the client and their problem and the counselling or psychotherapy process itself. In some sense, the process has already started for many clients from the time they start to contemplate talking to a professional about their problem.

As we started talking, the question I had in mind was the extent to which this dazzling picture before me was indeed a picture, a front, or an accurate expression of the person herself. In addition, I was wondering whether the fact that Peggy and I were women influenced her choice of counselling as well as the personal construct approach itself.

Flora began to show signs of nervousness as she began to talk. She explained that her problem was that whenever she thought she had found a man who attracted her and who seemed to be attracted by her, the relationship never ended in marriage. They would start to have rows and eventually split up in acrimony.

She described herself as moderately intelligent but under-achieving at school because she did not think she would ever make the top class. By being in a lower class she could usually guarantee coming near the top in examinations thus pleasing her parents. She had taken two A-level examinations, one in history and the other in economics. She now had what she described as a good job with a large travel agency and expected to rise to senior management level in a couple of years. She surprised me by saying that she was 39 years old.

She knew what to expect from personal construct counselling so we did not need to cover that. She agreed to my suggestion about a contract to meet for six sessions and then have a review to see where we had got to.

Before coming up with any formulation of the problem, it was necessary to get more information or data. It is by no means a requirement of personal construct counselling or psychotherapy to explore childhood experiences and parental attitudes, but it was clearly necessary here to explore earlier relationships, including ones with her parents. Flora had given the main theme of her problem relationships with men always ending in failure. Was that recent or long-term?

She described her father first. A nice man, kindly, not spontaneous in his demonstrations of love, but Flora clearly felt loved by him. However, she always felt that her father gave more of his attention to her brother, six years older than her and mentioned here for the first time. Her father was still alive and well and a successful accountant. Flora always felt welcomed by him when she visited home. I noted that she described the parental house as 'home' and not her own self-contained flat. Flora then went on to describe her brother, with whom she had a reasonably good, if somewhat distant, relationship. Her brother took up law and her father was demonstrably proud of this.

After a very long pause, she started to talk about her mother and slowly became more and more agitated. She loved her mother but never seemed able to please her. No, her mother did not reject her or say unkind things to her, she just never made her feel loved and wanted as a child nor now as an adult. She always felt that her mother would really have liked another boy instead of a girl. Flora was vehement that her mother was a good mother and a good person, it was just that she never held Flora in her arms and gave her uninhibited love.

To explore Flora's construing of the world in greater depth, or as Kelly says 'to get beyond the words', I asked her to write a self-characterization. At this stage, the second session, I decided that a repertory grid would not add to our insights greatly. Flora was very articulate and able to introspect with some ease and to talk about her non-verbal or emotional experiences as well. Her self-characterization was quite short:

> Flora is a reasonably intelligent and lively person. She takes a pride in her appearance and thinks it important to make the best of oneself both in her work and in her private life. She is quite ambitious and wants to do well in her job. She has quite a lot of friends, both men and women, but increasingly wants to have a relationship with a man that lasts. She does not mind whether this includes marriage or not. She does not understand why, when she has most of the characteristics men seem to go for, no one seems to want her. I think she is really a little afraid that, nearly 40, she may spend the rest of her life alone.

If we take the first and second sentences as a description of how she sees herself now, we have a picture of a perfectionist, at least as far as her appearance is concerned. Then taking the last sentence as a description of where she sees herself as going, we have the picture of a bleak and lonely future.

With these data, and at the end of the third session, it was possible to formulate the first idea of what the problem might be in personal construct terms. Why is it that Flora kept failing in her relationships with men? Whenever there is a behavioural theme, one looks to see whether the client is 'extorting validational evidence for a social construction that has, at some level of awareness, already shown itself to be a failure'. Perhaps she was being *hostile* in Kelly's sense and 'making' it happen. She might be acting so as to ensure her relationships always fail. Where there is *hostility*, look for the *guilt*. What core role would she be dislodged from, in her terms, if she were to have a successful relationship? My idea was that, in her view, she was 'a person no one can love' or 'a person who can never please someone however hard I try'.

If this formulation were at all accurate, then this would involve helping her work on some pre-verbal construing. If she construed her mother as someone who really wanted her to be someone other than she was at a relatively early age, then it would be quite a struggle for her to accept this as true but that she now, as an adult, need not be a prisoner of that past. She would have to be helped to free herself. It was hypothesized that her father had not been able to compensate Flora for her lack of her mother's love.

(Continued)

(Continued)

This is an example of one difference between the personal construct view of counselling and psychotherapy. Psychotherapy involves helping someone change some aspect of their core construing of themselves; counselling does not.

The plan was to use the remaining sessions of the contract to explore just how open to the idea of change Flora was. To what extent did she see herself as having 'good' characteristics? To what extent was she able to see these as 'good' even though her mother did not/would not agree?

It transpired that 'Flora at work' was successful. She gave many examples of how her work was clearly valued, how she used her initiative, how she had good working relationships with senior and junior managers and so forth. The very gentle exploration of how her personal relationships with men failed revealed a theme here also. Her belief that no one could really love her for herself led her to start accusing them of being unfaithful to her/or not loving her enough with the result that they did, indeed, leave her.

This confrontation with her own construing had a profound effect on her. She accepted it as 'true'. She also came to glimpse that she, herself, might be afraid of loving someone and risking not having it returned just like her relationship with her mother. Of course, knowing something is true does not mean that we can immediately change our behaviour. She had to disentangle it all from her construing of her mother. We agreed to extend the contract for another 10 sessions.

These sessions focused on 'time-binding' her relationship with her mother as well as invalidating her view that no man could ever love her in her adult life. Much use was made of role play and enactment. She and I would enact mother and daughter, past man-friend and she herself, and other types of relationships. She came to see how she had made herself a prisoner of her past and gradually came to construe herself as someone who had the capacity to love as well as be loved. In this sense, we moved from counselling to psychotherapy. In a very real sense, she became a different person.

REFERENCES

[1] Kelly, G. A. (1973) 'Fixed role therapy', in R. M. Jurjevich (ed.), *Direct Psychotherapy: 28 American Originals*. Coral Gables: University of Miami Press.

[2] Kelly, G. A. (1991) *The Psychology of Personal Constructs*, vols 1 and 2. London: Routledge. (Previously published 1955, New York: Norton.)

[3] Fransella, F. (1995) *George Kelly* (Key Figures in Counselling and Psychotherapy Series). London: Sage.

[4] Bannister, D. and Fransella, F. (1986) *Inquiring Man*, 3rd edn. London: Routledge.

[5] Fransella, F. (1977) *Personal Change and Reconstruction*. London: Academic Press.

[6] Rowe, D. (1978) *The Experience of Depression*. Chichester: John Wiley & Sons.

[7] Winter, D. A. and Viney, L. L. (eds) (2005) *Personal Construct Psychotherapy: Advances in Theory, Practice and Research*. Chichester: John Wiley & Sons.

[8] Winter, D. (1988) 'Constructions in social skills training', in F. Fransella and L. Thomas (eds), *Experimenting with Personal Construct Psychology*. London: Routledge.

[9] Ravenette, A. T. (1997) *Tom Ravenette: Selected Papers: Personal Construct Psychology and the Practice of an Educational Psychologist.* Farnborough: EPCA Publications.

[10] Kelly, G. A. (1969) 'The psychotherapeutic relationship', in B. Mäher (ed.), *Clinical Psychology and Personality: The Selected Papers of George Kelly.* New York: John Wiley.

[11] Hare, A. P. and Hare, J. R. (1996) *J. L. Moreno.* (Key Figures in Counselling and Psychotherapy Series). London: Sage.

[12] Landfield, A. W. (1979) 'Exploring socialization through the interpersonal transaction group', in P. Stringer and D. Bannister (eds), *Constructs of Sociality and Individuality.* London: Academic Press.

[13] Neimeyer, R. A. (1988) 'Clinical guidelines for conducting interpersonal transaction groups', *International Journal of Personal Construct Psychology, 1,* 181–90.

[14] Fransella, F. and Dalton, P. (1990) *Personal Construct Counselling in Action.* London: Sage.

SUGGESTED READING

Fransella, F. (ed.) (2005) *The Essential Practitioner's Handbook of Personal Construct Psychology.* Chichester: John Wiley & Sons. This edited book covers the theory and practice of personal constructs and its application to counselling and psychotherapy and other domains.

Fransella, F., Bell, R. and Bannister, D. (2003) *A Manual for Repertory Grid Technique,* 2nd edn. Chichester: John Wiley & Sons. This manual provides an overview of personal construct theory, which underpins repertory grid methods. It includes access to a website with downloadable grid analysis programs.

Fransella, F. and Dalton, P. (2000) *Personal Construct Counselling in Action,* 2nd edn. London: Sage. This is a practical account of working with personal construct theory in the counselling context.

Winter, D. A. and Viney, L. L. (eds) (2005) *Personal Construct Psychotherapy: Advances in Theory, Practice and Research.* Chichester: John Wiley & Sons. This edited book has 27 chapters covering a wide range of topics relevant for the practice of personal construct psychotherapy.

DISCUSSION ISSUES

1. If the philosophy states that no one person has direct access to 'the truth', who knows more about the problem, the client or the therapist?
2. Discuss whether personal construct counselling is eclectic or integrative.
3. What are the implications of seeing behaviour as being 'the experiment' for understanding a client's problem?
4. Discuss the differences between the psychoanalytic notion of 'the unconscious' and the personal construct notion of 'levels of awareness'.

This chapter is dedicated to Fay Adah Rachel Fransella, psychologist, 1 October 1925 – 14 January 2011.

28

Solution-Focused Therapy

Bill O'Connell

INTRODUCTION

Solution-focused therapy (SFT) is a form of brief therapy which builds upon clients' strengths by helping them to evoke and construct solutions to their problems. It focuses more on the future than the client's past. In a solution-focused approach the counsellor and client devote a greater proportion of time to solution–construction than to problem–exploration. Together they try to describe in concrete detail what the clients would like to see happening in their lives (in this chapter I am not distinguishing between therapy and counselling or therapist and counsellor.)

SFT (often referred to by practitioners as simply SF) fosters a sense of collaboration between the counsellor and the client, with the latter being viewed as competent and resourceful. It pays little attention to the 'roots or causes' of a client's problem. This stance could be compared with driving a car where it is useful to look in the rear mirror from time to time but it is advisable to spend most of your time looking through the front windscreen! Solution-focused counsellors believe in minimal intervention in the client's life. Their task is to support an impetus for change which the client will be able to sustain.

DEVELOPMENT OF THE THERAPY

The solution-focused approach originated in family therapy. The key founding figures were the family therapists Steve de Shazer, Kim Insoo Berg and colleagues at the Brief Family Therapy Centre in Milwaukee, as well as Bill O'Hanlon, a therapist in Nebraska. The members of the Brief Therapy Practice in London pioneered the method in the United Kingdom. Many professionals in fields such as teaching, management, health and community care have adapted the core SFT skills and interventions to their context and client group. It is now used in a wide range of settings, including schools, psychiatric hospitals, counselling services, voluntary organizations, therapeutic groups and probation and social work teams. It is used with a wide variety of clients — problem drinkers, offenders, survivors of abuse, employees suffering from stress, couples and families. The number of practitioners of SFT has grown to such an extent that there is now a national association (www.ukasfp.co.uk), which is developing codes of practice and accreditation schemes.

THEORY AND BASIC CONCEPTS

Solution-focused therapy belongs to the constructionist school of therapies, so-called because they subscribe to a constructionist theory of knowledge. Other approaches that share the same theoretical basis are personal construct therapy, neuro-linguistic programming and the brief problem-solving model developed at the Mental Research Institute in Palo Alto, California.

The **social constructionist** theory of knowledge that underpins SFT states that the meaning of language is known only through social interaction and negotiation. We have no direct access to objective truth, because our attempts to articulate meaning take place in a context that includes the person who makes the observation. The 'knower' actively participates in constructing what is observed. Constructionism claims that this inseparability of the known from the 'knower' destroys the myth of absolute truth. Instead it claims to offer a richer, more diverse way of looking at our world and thereby extends personal choice. It contends that no one person or school of thought possesses more of 'the truth' than another. The therapist does not have access to hidden truths denied to clients. In therapy, the two parties can explore an extensive repertoire of meanings in relation to the client's experiences, in order to reach an understanding that will help the client to deal with his or her 'problem'.

Therapy is a dialogue in which both parties negotiate the 'problem and the solution'. The problem does not have an objective, fixed meaning which the clients bring with them. Instead they tell and retell their story using language that reshapes the social reality by which they live. As Paul Watzlawick, a therapist and philosopher, said, 'reality is invented, not discovered'.[1] Language does not reflect reality, but creates it. In our scientific culture we tend to assume that there is a necessary connection between a problem and its solution. The solution should fit the problem. If, for example, a client has had a problem for a long time it is expected that it will be a lengthy process before a solution emerges. If the problem is complex, then it is thought that the solution must also be complex. SFT challenges these assumptions and instead of trying to make the solution fit the problem, aims to find a solution that fits the client. This shift in thinking alters the content and direction of the work. The focus instead is on the changes the client wants, rather than the causes of the problem. In the psychological realm, the search for causal connections is often tenuous and elusive. Is a person depressed because he has a genetic predisposition towards depression, and/or because his family life was disrupted by his parents' separation when he was 10, and/or he lacked the social skills and confidence to make close relationships, and/or he has low self-esteem, and/or he is long-term unemployed? What weight ought we to give to each explanation? How do we prove they are 'true'? How do we know when we have gone far or 'deep' enough? Where does the counsellor start to work on such a complicated agenda? Is such an approach dictating the need for long-term therapy? Most forms of therapy seek explanations for clients' problems. Of course it is no doubt true that for many people, understanding their problems is of great help. However, solution-focused counsellors do not believe that it is always necessary to identify origins of problems for lasting solutions to emerge. They aim to help the clients understand their solutions more than their problems! They regard problems not as symptoms of pathology, but as an integral part of human experience. In SFT the emphasis is on how our future shapes what we do at the moment. Being clear about our preferred future motivates and clarifies our approach to the present. An analogy would be a journey in which the driver or pilot plans a drive or flight according to the time he or she wants the car or plane to arrive at its destination. With that end in view, decisions are made about the course, speed, amount of fuel required and stopping-off places along the way. The end point determines the means. When clients' lives are blighted by a major problem it tends to obscure the future or even destroy any hope for a better future. Problems represent ways in which people have lost their bearings or failed to use the skills or resources required to travel to their chosen destination.

Clients and counsellors often assume that there is a necessary sequence of events that needs to take place before the client will be 'better', that X has to happen before Y. For example, the client must learn to express emotions before she will be able to resume a normal life. The SF therapist questions such preconditions and is often able to demonstrate to the client that change can and does take place prior to the client ventilating her feelings. It challenges clients' framing of their problems when their understanding of it makes change more difficult, or even impossible.

The SF approach proposes that certain types of conversation are more likely than others to motivate and support a client towards change. These empowering narratives stress the client's competence, skills and qualities. It may be helpful for the reader to contrast a problem-focused model with a solution-focused one.

How can I help you? versus How will you know that counselling has been helpful?

The introductory phrases used by the counsellor indicate how he sees the dynamics of the relationship. The first question stresses the expert role, the 'privileged position' of the counsellor. It puts the counsellor centre stage. The second targets outcomes and puts the client centre stage. It actively recruits the client as a partner in a joint enterprise. This shift in power is captured in a SF phrase, 'Don't be a sage on the stage, be a guide on the side!' Similar opening questions may be: 'What are your best hopes about this?' 'How long do you think it will take before things will get better?' 'How will you know that it has been worth your while coming here today?' 'How will other people know that things have changed with you?'

Could you tell me about the problem? versus What would you like to change?

The first invites an account of the problem, the second ensures that the counsellor stays close to the client's agenda. It creates a climate of expectancy and implies that the client has the power to change.

Is the problem a symptom of something deeper? versus What are you already doing that helps?

The first question sets the counsellor on a quest for the hidden meaning behind the 'presenting problem'. The second question assumes that the client has begun in some way to deal with the problem, and if she can be more aware of the constructive things she is doing it will be a strong and empowering starting-point.

Can you tell me more about the problem? versus Can we discover exceptions to the problem?

In problem-focused counselling the counsellor listens carefully to the client's story in order to formulate an understanding of what has gone wrong. The second question is more interested in times when things went right. In the former the counsellor is trying to understand the client and the problem, in the latter the counsellor is trying to help the client to understand their solutions.

Which defence mechanisms is the client adopting? versus What resources does the client have?

In the psychodynamic model the counsellor aims to become sensitive to the unconscious strategies the client is using to defend her threatened ego. The second question

TABLE 28.1   *A comparison between a problem-focused and a solution-focused approach*

Problem-focused	Solution-focused
How can I help you?	How will you know that counselling has been helpful?
Could you tell me about the problem?	What would you like to change?
Is the problem a symptom of something deeper?	What are you already doing that helps?
Can you tell me more about the problem?	Can we discover exceptions to the problem?
How is the client protecting himself?	What resources does the client have?
How many sessions do we need?	Have we achieved enough to end?

gives greater priority to the client becoming more aware of their values, achieve-ments, attitudes and hopes, which will contribute to their solutions.

How many sessions do we need? versus Have we achieved enough to end?

The first question may constitute the basis of a contract with the client, the length of which may be dictated by the client's availability or finances. The second, used tact-fully, follows the minimal intrusion principle in the belief that the effect of therapy continues long after the sessions have ended.

PRACTICE

The goals of the therapy are the goals the clients bring with them, providing they are ethical and legal. The counsellor's role is to help clients to begin to move or continue to move in the direction they want. The counsellor does this by helping:

- to identify and utilize to the full the strengths and competencies which the client brings with him
- to enable the client to recognize and build upon exceptions to the problem, that is, those times when the client is already doing (thinking, feeling) something that is reducing or eliminating the impact of the problem
- to help the client to focus in clear and specific terms on what he would consider to be solutions to the problem.

The counsellor acknowledges and validates whatever concerns and feelings the client presents, and seeks to develop a rapport, a cooperative 'joining', in which the counsellor offers the client a warm, positive, accepting relationship and the client feels understood and respected. This recognition of the importance of the therapeutic alliance as a vital factor in facilitating change is relatively new in SFT. In its earlier stages of development SF practitioners tended to play down the importance of an empathic relationship. They preferred to see their work as primarily asking questions (skeleton keys) that would unlock any client's problem situation. Following on from that development there seems now to be a greater acceptance of the importance of emotions in helping people to change. In the past SFT seemed to some to be only interested in behaviours, not the client's thinking or feelings.

In SFT the counsellor uses her expertise in guiding therapeutic conversations by adopting a learning position, 'a one-down position', in which clients give the coun-sellor a sense of how they experience and understand their world. The counsellor matches the language of the client, offers encouragement and genuine compliments and adapts her stance depending upon what the client finds helpful.

Unless the counsellor's working environment and protocols determine how many sessions a client is entitled to, SF workers tend not to contract for a fixed number of sessions. It is more likely to be the subject of negotiation between the client and the counsellor. It is surprising how often clients want fewer sessions than the counsellor wants to give them or thinks they need!

Focal issue

In SFT the focus of the work is the issue presented by the client. The closer the counsellor keeps to the client's agenda, the more likely is a successful outcome. It is not always possible to achieve this as clients are often confused, anxious, overwhelmed and unsure how counselling can help them. There are also contexts in which the organization sets the agenda, for example, in safeguarding children or working with offenders.

The issue to be addressed must be solvable, at least in the sense that it can be managed better. It needs to be within the client's power to make those changes. The successful outcome will need to bring more benefit to the client than the status quo.

Guiding principles

There are a number of SF principles that provide signposts for the conversational route map.

- If it ain't broke don't fix it, but you may need to maintain it.
  This principle helps to give a focus to the work and reminds the counsellor that there is a danger of pathologizing normal human concerns and challenges. It also highlights the idea that clients need to keep doing what is already working and that 'there is nothing wrong with them that what's right with them can't fix'.
- Small change big difference.
  The SF process is one of breaking down 'solutions' into small steps. Clients are usually willing to engage in do-able mini-solutions. Having experienced their ability to influence events often leads them to make further changes. A small change may be a 'breakthrough' experience for clients and alters the way they view themselves.
- If it's working, keep doing it.
  When people are submerged by problems they feel that nothing is working, nothing is going right. But the reality is that they are actually doing some constructive things which, at the very least, are preventing the situation from deteriorating. Part of the consciousness-raising in a SF conversation is helping people to realize that they are not at the starting line or at the bottom of the pit, but are actually on the road to recovery, on the path to find sustainable solutions. But they need to redirect their attention away from problems and focus more on solutions.
- If it's not working, stop doing it.
  Our culture tends to encourage people to 'try, try and try again' if they are not succeeding. But this is often a complete waste of time. They are simply repeating what they already know are failed solutions. It can take courage for people to give

up these 'comfort solutions' and create the space to find genuine and long-lasting solutions.
- Keep it simple but not simplistic.
  Some people so complicate their situations that a clear solution is virtually impossible. SF practitioners follow Occam's principle that 'it is vain to do with more what can be achieved with less.' It makes the fewest assumptions necessary to explain the client's situation.
- Solutions fit the person not the problem.
  With the counsellor leading from 'behind', the conversation explores what will uniquely work for this client. There is no room for formulaic solutions, the best solutions are customized and personalized and above all owned and developed by the client.

Interventions

The following interventions are SF 'skeleton keys', which will always be used by the counsellor. They do not necessarily follow a pre-determined sequence.

Pre-session change

On first contact with an SF counsellor or agency, a client will be asked to 'notice any changes which take place between now and you coming for your first session'. Typically, the counsellor will enquire about these changes early on in the first session. If the client is able to report positive pre-session change it gives the work a flying start and conveys an important message that the conversation is not just about the client pouring over their problems, but is more about recognizing that they have already begun in some way to create a better future. This experience accelerates the process of change and increases the likelihood of the counselling being brief. Positive pre-session change is empowering for the client because the changes have taken place independently of the counsellor and, therefore, the credit belongs solely to the client.

Problem-free talk

This takes place at the start of the first meeting. The counsellor invites the client to talk about what they enjoy doing when they have some free time. This is not just an ice-breaker or rapport-builder question, it actually aims to draw out from the client resources, strengths and qualities that could be transferable to solution–construction. It also helps to give the counsellor an idea of how to work with this person and may influence the type of language employed, the examples and images used. Another version of problem-free talk is to ask the client questions such as:

- Would you say you were the kind of person who likes to take time in making decisions?
- Likes to be guided and directed or happier to be doing it on your own?

- Welcomes a challenge?
- When you start something do you stick with it until you finish?

The answers to such questions help the counsellor to learn from the client how to best help them.

Exception seeking

The counsellor engages the client in seeking **exceptions** to the problem, that is, those occasions when the problem is not present, or is being managed better. This includes searching for transferable solutions from other areas of the client's life, or past solutions adopted in similar situations.

Competence seeking

The counsellor identifies and affirms the resources, strengths and qualities of the client which can be utilized in solving the problem. Coping mechanisms that the client has previously used are acknowledged and reinforced.

The miracle question

This is a key intervention typically used in a first session, but which may also reappear in subsequent sessions. It aims to identify existing solutions and resources and to clarify the client's goals in realistic terms. It is a future-oriented question that seeks to help the client to describe, as clearly and specifically as possible, what her life will be like, once the problem is solved or is being managed better. The question as devised by Steve de Shazer follows a standard formula:

> Imagine when you go to sleep tonight, a miracle happens and the problems we've been talking about disappear. As you were asleep, you did not know that a miracle had happened. When you wake up, what will be the first signs for you that a miracle has happened?[2]

This imaginary scenario gives the client permission to rise above negative, limited thinking and to describe a unique picture of their preferred future. The counsellor helps the client to develop their answers to the miracle question by active listening, prompting, empathizing and questioning. When done well, the miracle question is a powerful intervention that can move people on in ways that surprise them. People begin to realize quite quickly that they don't need a miracle for some of these things to happen, in fact some of them are happening already. The counsellor probes and develops the answers reflectively, giving clients time and space to experience what life could be like once their problems are overcome.

Scaling

The counsellor uses a scale of 0 to 10, with 10 representing the best it could be and 0 representing the worst it has been. The purpose of scaling is to help clients set small identifiable goals; measure progress and establish priorities for action. Scaling questions can also assess client motivation and confidence. Scaling is a practical tool that a client can use between sessions. The use of numbers is purely arbitrary; only the client knows what they really mean.

The message

At the end of each session the SF counsellor will compliment the client on her contribution to the session; highlight their achievements and check with the client what their next step is going to be. Occasionally the counsellor will give the client a between-session task, but not that often. If the counsellor has gained the impression that the client is not ready to make changes the client will be asked to 'notice between now and the next time we meet those things you would like to see continue in your life and come back and tell me about them'.

WHICH CLIENTS BENEFIT MOST?

A comprehensive and up-to-date list of all the studies on solution-focused therapy can be found on Alasdair McDonald's website (www.solutionsdoc.co.uk). The SF approach has had considerable success with clients identified as 'hard to reach' or 'challenging'. The plain, down-to-earth, pictorial language used in SF conversations is more likely to be accessible to people who have not benefited from traditional schooling. So far, studies have been unable to identify clearly any problem or client group which would definitely *not* benefit from the approach. Clearly it helps if a client is motivated and has some idea of what their preferred future could be. SF practitioners need to follow whatever assessment protocols are laid down in their agency.

CASE STUDY
The Client

The client was a white female in her forties, married, with three children. She had a well-paid 'white-collar' job in which she had to work long hours while juggling child care and responsibilities for an elderly mother. Her husband often worked away from home. Approximately two years prior to coming for counselling, she had felt 'on the verge of a nervous breakdown' and had to take time off work. She had returned to work after three months and had re-negotiated a less stressful role in the organization. However, she had again begun to experience similar stress-related symptoms and immediately prior to presenting for counselling had taken sick leave. She described herself as being anxious, indecisive and short-tempered at home, particularly with the children. Her memory and concentration were poor and she was not sleeping well.

The Therapy

During the first session the client talked at length about her problems at home and at work, although she said she had felt unsure about doing so. The counsellor validated the client's feelings and experiences, while listening for examples of coping strategies. He asked the miracle question and received an answer which included:

- sleeping better
- feeling mentally calmer
- being more supported by her husband
- playing with her children and not shouting at them
- being back at work and coping with the pressures, without being snappy and making mistakes.

The counsellor asked, 'On a scale of 0 to 10, 10 representing the morning after the miracle and 0 the worst you've ever been, where would you put yourself today?' The client answered that she was at 3. At the end of the session the counsellor invited the client to notice times when she managed to control her worry habit even a little and to remember what she did to achieve that. She was also asked to write down a list of things which she thought she could do in order to reduce her stress levels. The client appeared motivated and keen to use the time off work to 'sort herself out'.

When she returned for the second session the counsellor asked, 'What's better?' She described situations when she felt free from stress – gardening, going out with her friend to an evening class, reading, taking her children to the cinema. The feedback given by the counsellor congratulated her on what she had managed to do. In terms of utilizing her skills and experience, the counsellor noted that she had a lot of energy and was creative and caring in her approach to the problem. The counsellor reminded her that she had overcome this problem before and wondered whether she could remember anything that had worked the last time. She felt that her husband had been very supportive then and that she needed him to support her more at the moment.

During the third session the client reported that she was surprised (as was her husband) at how well she was doing.

Client: I've been able to stop thinking about going back to work without it wakening me up in the middle of the night.
Counsellor: How did you manage to do that?
Client: I think I've come to see that there's more to life than just working all the time. I've begun to stand back from it.

(Continued)

(Continued)

The client had begun to change her 'viewing' of her problem. The counsellor invited the client to continue doing what was working and to think through the implications of her new way of looking at her job.

At the fourth session the client reported that she found scaling helpful and used it each day to measure how she had dealt with particularly stressful situations. She felt calmer, more relaxed and had stopped 'flying at' her daughter. She was experimenting in taking small manageable steps towards controlling her anxiety.

She reported that she was at 6 on the scale. She was sleeping better and had come to realize that things would never be perfect. She would be happy to achieve a 7, not a 10. The counsellor affirmed the client's self-awareness and problem-solving strategies and reinforced her repertoire by expressing the view that, once acquired, these skills would not be lost, as long as they were consolidated by regular practice. The counsellor also suggested that skills used in the domestic arena were transferable to the work environment. This belief helped to increase the possibility that the counselling could be effective and brief.

> *Counsellor:* I've seen you make progress and there's every reason to think that you can maintain that. I think people can transfer these skills. I think it's important to realize it's basically the same stuff. It's just a different place or environment. You've got the tools there. You're doing the job already.

By the sixth session the client felt she was handling relationships at home much better, but felt anxious about the impending return to work. Despite her apprehension, she had developed a 'survival plan' for her first few weeks back. Her solutions included a determination to say no to extra work, a request for a meeting with her boss to get more resources and avoidance of any unnecessary travel. The feedback to the client complimented the client on her self-care skills and her courage in facing up to a stressful situation. The client wanted reassurance that the counselling could continue for a few more weeks until she felt more confident about work.

In the next session the client said that she felt that she had had a setback and that she was quite depressed about work again. She had visited her workplace but had felt quite overwhelmed and her colleagues had not been very friendly. The counsellor reassured her that 'practising new habits is often bumpy'. He also explored how she was managing to stop things getting worse. Her answer was the increased support at home. In the final two sessions the client revisited the miracle question and applied it to her work situation, for example, how colleagues would be treating her, the amount and kind of work she would be doing. She recognized that she had 'moved down a gear' and was more in control. She liked her 'new self. After nine sessions she felt that she had learnt sound strategies for handling her stress. She decided to end counselling.

REFERENCES

[1] Watzlawick, P. (1984) *The Invented Reality*. New York: W. W. Norton.
[2] de Shazer, S. (1988) *Clues: Investigating Solutions in Brief Therapy*. New York: W. W. Norton.

SUGGESTED READING

de Shazer, S. (1994) *Words Were Originally Magic*. New York: W. W. Norton. The most influential figure in SFT explains the theory behind the practice. Advisable to read a 'how to do it' book first.

O'Connell, B. (2012) *Solution-Focused Therapy*. London: Sage. This practical book clearly identifies and explains the key skills needed to practise solution-focused brief therapy.

O'Connell, B. and Palmer, S. (eds) (2003) *Handbook of Solution-Focused Therapy*. London: Sage. The *Handbook of Solution-Focused Therapy* highlights how SFT is applied in different settings.

O'Hanlon, B. and Weiner-Davis, M. (1989) *In Search of Solutions*. New York: W. W. Norton. Packed with practical ideas. The book that inspired me to find out more!

DISCUSSION ISSUES

1. What do you think about the idea that it is preferable to spend more time with clients exploring solutions rather than problems?
2. We tend to think of clients as having defined problems. What part do you think the counsellor plays in negotiating the definition and explanation for the 'problem'?
3. 'Counselling should be as brief as possible so that people can get on with their lives.' Discuss.
4. Explore the miracle question with a friend or partner in relation to your personal goals.

PART 6

Research and Professional Practice Issues

29

Diversity in Counselling and Psychotherapy

Roy Moodley and
Shafik Sunderani

INTRODUCTION

Multicultural counselling, recently called **diversity** counselling, and psychotherapy has grown tremendously since the 1960s, with a large body of published literature covering a wide range of issues relating to theory, practice and research. Although much of this literature arises in the USA, Britain has produced enough multicultural counselling scholarship to warrant the legitimacy of such an approach. Yet, the number of black and minority ethnic groups that use counselling and psychotherapy by comparison is relatively small. It seems that those from these groups who use counselling or psychological services tend to drop out of treatment prematurely at higher rates than non-minority clients, or have poor outcomes.[1] While the reasons are often much more complex and not the same across all cultural groups, clients from black and African heritage groups appear to be over-represented, misdiagnosed and over-medicated in mental health care.[2] According to Suman Fernando, black and minority ethnic clients are often over-diagnosed for psychological difficulties and mental health issues, particularly for schizophrenia, arguing that the over-representation and over-diagnosis is reflective of an institutionally racist society.

Beginning in the 1960s, multicultural counselling evolved to address the misconceptions, the gross generalizations and stereotypes of black and minority ethnic groups based on white, middle-class, heterosexual participants (the YAVIS effect – young, attractive, verbal, intelligent, single). Constructing treatment based on these misperceptions led to inappropriate assessments, misdiagnosis and misinformed psychotherapy practices.[3] With its socio-political approach, multicultural counselling began to critique conventional psychological and counselling approaches for being Eurocentric, individualistic and focused on psychopathology.[4] Several scholars also began questioning the relevance of the traditional approaches, such as psychodynamic, client-centered and others. For example, Pittu Laungani argued that client-centred therapy (CCT) was not appropriate and relevant for black and minority ethnic clients; suggesting that culture-centred therapy was best.[5] Clemmont Vontress, one of the founding fathers of multicultural counselling in the USA, confronted Carl Rogers with the question of the relevance of client-centred therapy for African American clients at a conference. Not satisfied with Rogers' answers, Clemmont wrote: 'Although in awe of Dr. Rogers, I was not entirely satisfied with his response ... that was the day I started a lifelong search for a supplement to the Rogerian theory of counselling',[6] and for the next 50 years Vontress went on to research cross-cultural and multicultural counselling.[7] Since his involvement there has been a huge growth in the development of multicultural counselling, especially in the period from the 1990s and increasing in the 2000s. More and more racialised minorities were in counselling and clinical psychology training, particularly in North America, with specific programmes in Multicultural Counselling and Psychotherapy. This resulted in several changes: the shift towards research and theories in cultural competency as the criteria for clinical efficacy;[8] the focus on racial identity theories;[9] and the inclusion of the **Group of Seven** identities (race, gender, sexual orientation, disability, class, religion and age) issues in counselling.[10] At the same time, the focus on the counsellor's and psychotherapist's awareness, knowledge and skills was a clear shift away from the client and his or her own culture and ethnicity, which was the preoccupation of multicultural counselling right up to this time. Interestingly, this was happening at the same time that Rogers was advocating for his client-centred approach. The focus on developing skills and competencies was not done in isolation but in tandem with the client's worldview and lived experience. According to Arthur and Stewart, 'counsellors must be assisted to move from a position that assumes a singular, monocultural reality, to that of adopting a worldview that is respectful of multiple belief systems'.[11] This has now become a reality for multicultural counselling as it has changed from a single focus on ethnicity, race and culture to one that now embraces the Group of Seven identities.

In this chapter we will explore the historical journey that multicultural counselling has undertaken, since the 1960s, to become a distinct approach and the 'fourth force' in psychology.[12] We also consider how multiculturalism has been limited by the 'strait-jacket' approach to clinical work in the current era of only focusing on race, culture and ethnicity; and that changing to *diversity* has been more inclusive of all aspects of difference in terms of gender, sexual orientation, religion and disability. Through a discourse of diversity, this counselling approach sets out a distinct social justice and ethical clinical project for the future. Finally, we offer two short case studies that illustrate the principles and practices of diversity counselling.

PUTTING CULTURE INTO COUNSELLING: INFUSION THROUGH THE DECADES

Since the 1960s there has been a growing awareness of issues of race, culture and ethnicity in counselling and psychotherapy. During this period, as mentioned earlier much has happened in terms of changing what was essentially an Eurocentric discipline and profession to one that has given rise to its own particular field of cross–cultural or multicultural counselling. As time went on a wide variety of nomen-clatures, such as trans–cultural, intercultural, multi–ethnic, were added to cross–cultural counselling.

Throughout the 1970s and 1980s counselling scholars were becoming increas-ingly aware of the relationship between racism and mental health; taking their lead from writers such as Frantz Fanon. They argued that previous psychological conceptions of black and minority ethnic groups were ethnocentric, misguided and erroneous. Racialised groups were regarded as inferior, child–like, sub–species of human who needed particular kinds of treatments. Through research and prac-tice multi–racial mental health professionals arrived at the conclusion that 'rac-ism was itself a mental illness striking at the nation's health'.[13] Many multicultural counselling scholars argued that neglecting ethno–racial and cultural factors would lead to a culturally insensitive and unethical practice in mental health care ser-vices. Counselling research and writings began to interrogate mainstream practices with respect to the widespread use and presence of culturally insensitive models, institutional racism and the absence of mental health practitioners from black and minority groups. By the end of the 1980s the theory, research and practice had reached a particular point, at least in the USA, that multicultural counselling began to be seen as a distinct discipline and a challenge.

A significant shift occurred in the 1990s, in the USA, when Paul Pedersen made his grand pronouncement of multicultural counselling as the 'fourth force' in psychology and counselling.[12] This gave impetus to the multicultural counselling movement, with scholars attempting to fine-tune the discipline and establish clear theoretical, con-ceptual and practice-based ideas. Some scholars suggest that a more accurate under-standing of how culture influences psychological practice is reflected by transposing the sequence of words from 'the person within the culture' perspective to a 'culture within the person' perspective.[14] This linguistic shift is intended to underscore the importance of how cultural meanings and symbols become internalised and subse-quently govern our knowledge base, beliefs, actions, feelings, thoughts, worldview and values, among other psychological variables. Towards this end, culture-centred counselling became a priority; placing the client's worldview at the centre of mental health, therapists incorporate their clients' heritage and values, and attempt to under-stand them through how they conceive of their own problems and preferred mode of intervention.

Cultural competency and racial identity theories began to evolve as frame-works to guide practice and research. To improve multicultural competence, specialised programmes and courses were created and offered to develop these skills to work with diverse clients. This gave rise to a broad framework of guide-lines for multicultural counsellors: (1) identifying the effects of racism on mental health; (2) acknowledging the ways oppression affect identity; (3) developing an awareness of how history, politics and institutions intersect to disadvantage certain groups of people more than others; (4) understanding how race, socio-economic status, and the acculturation process can have detrimental effects on mental health.[15] Counselling competencies specific to working in multicultural settings (**MCCs**) can include: (a) the use of alternative modes of thought and information processing style to communicate more effectively with a client; (b) acknowledging 'racial'/ethnic differences in the beginning phases of therapy; (c) utilising a multiplicity of verbal and non-verbal responses to clients; (d) integrating or referring clients to traditional cultural healers; and (e) meeting the needs of clients through flexibility and accommodation.[16] A criticism of the multicultural counselling competency models was the primary focus placed on *multiculturalism* domains (i.e. cultural, race and ethnic issues) with less attention granted to issues around *diversity* (gender, sexual orientations, race, class, disability, religion and age). A similar idea was voiced by Patterson,[17] who argued that the multicultural counselling competency model, while emphasizing knowledge, skills and techniques, has omitted any discussion around the therapeutic relationship which involves: respect, genuineness, empathic understanding, communication and structuring.

FROM MULTICULTURAL TO DIVERSITY COUNSELLING AND PSYCHOTHERAPY

The 'fourth force' idea has raised several questions regarding claims to the category of multicultural, and who is included and excluded from it. While this was happening, issues of equity and social justice in counselling and psychotherapy were taking centre stage in therapy, with many marginalized groups (such as LGBTQ, Movement for Disability and Therapists for Social Justice) making a claim for being part of multicultural counselling and psychotherapy. For some, the multicultural approach (now fast becoming the diversity approach) was inclusive of all disadvantaged and marginalised groups. For others, the broader and more inclusive definition of multicultural counselling poses the disadvantage of diffusing issues of 'racism' with other important issues such as 'homophobia', 'sexism' and 'classism' taking over, thereby ignoring the unique concerns and needs of ethnic and 'racialised' minorities. Janet Helms argues that adopting an inclusive stance whereby all salient social identities (e.g. age, sexual orientation, gender) fall under the purview of the multicultural counselling competency models obscures and dilutes the attention and focus away from concerns specific to 'racialised' minorities.[18] However, it is also clear that client's narratives are embedded in several discourses of identity (e.g. the Group of Seven identities) within one therapy session so that a competency model that addresses the intersectionality of all of these identities is critical for an ethical practice.

The 2000s were a period of increased growth of diversity counselling, particularly in North America, with particular focus on the Group of Seven identities and its place in diversity counselling and psychotherapy. Much research, theory and practice has evolved in relation to intersectionality of the Group of Seven identities; critical mixed race studies, Aboriginal and First Nation studies and eco-multiculturalism are being added to the competency framework.

INTERSECTING THE GROUP OF SEVEN IDENTITIES

The Group of Seven identities – race, gender, sexual orientation, class, disability, religion and age – offer therapists a framework to engage with discourses of differences in counselling work. While these variables are the key domains within which clients construct their sense of self, there is a myriad number of other aspects of difference that are at play in therapy, some more obvious than others. The Group of Seven identities act as both visible and the non-visible aspects of a client's identity in counselling. If therapists are not conscious of the Group of Seven identities in therapy, the efficacy of therapy becomes compromised due to the omission of critical aspects of an individual's unique identity and sense of self.

A core value for counsellors and psychotherapists to practise ethically and competently is to be aware that the 'Group of Seven' identities are fluid, and not fixed entities that demand particular ways of being with clients in therapy. The socio–cultural identities that constitute our sense of being as individual is subject to the forces of history, culture and geo–political environments a client experiences. Indeed, while the Group of Seven identities need to be validated and honoured, a therapist needs to be cognisant that some of the client's concerns could be rooted in the domains of diversity that are being validated and celebrated. Engaging with diversity clinically means that counsellors would need to be clinically skilful to be able to see the specific emotional and psychological concerns of the client and engage with the client's Group of Seven identities.

The clinical competency that is required is for therapists to be able to hear the client's psychological concerns with a narrative that is embedded in personal constructs of identity. Clients' stories are embedded in life experiences that are enacted and performed through the Group of Seven identities; or their recall (from memory) and retelling (to the therapist) process in counselling is shaped by gender, race, sexual orientation, class and so on. A narrow therapeutic lens will deny one identity over another. If a therapist focuses on one aspect of the story, for example, listening to a client singularly in terms of race, i.e. a 'black woman', as opposed to understanding the complexity of identity variables that go into the client's make–up, i.e. a black, lesbian, middle class, elderly, person. Moreover, these identities must be seen as fluid, shifting over time in accordance with contextual influences, such as socio–political realities, economic possibilities, developmental transitions, personality variables and cultural histories. At a most basic level, the therapist's own awareness and perceptions of him/herself as a complex, multidimensional being are critical in working across cultures.[19] Lack of attention to the intersectionality of diversity can lead to the dangers of unethical practice, such as stereotyping and 'pigeon holing' the client, making assumptions that the client's presenting issues are cultural in origin, and subsequently ignoring or minimizing the reason for which the client seeks counselling. With a diversity framework a counsellor is able to take into account all these diverse aspects of an individual's identity while at the same time keeping in mind the presenting issues, making connection between the presenting issues and the client's identities, their developmental background and their desire for health and wellness. Listening to the client's story through the intersection and convergences of the client's Group of

Seven identities is critical for a non-oppressive way of working. Since no one identity takes precedence over the others in an individual's inner world, the client will feel respected and valued within the clinical room.[20]

Indeed, through an inclusion of the Group of Seven identities, multicultural counselling has both challenged the traditional definitions of what constitutes multiculturalism, while at the same time offered an invitation to the dominant white community to be part of multiculturalism. Transgendered, mixed race and bisexual people, on the other hand, have contributed by their presence a need for research to question the binary and essentialist positions of gender, race and sexualities. Counselling and psychotherapy is now more open to a variety of interpretations of gender orientations, and sexualities, and their various representations, formulations and performances. What is needed now is more research in these areas to support both clinical and cultural competency model development.

CASE STUDY

The story of Kristina: intersectionality of culture, gender and religion

Kristina (pseudonym) is a 23-year-old university student of Italian descent who identifies as a lesbian and moderately Catholic. She has aspirations to become a social worker. Kristina lives with her family – mother, father and 28-year-old brother. Her parents immigrated with their families, and still hold on to traditional views concerning family. Her family believes that Kristina should not move out of the family home until she is married (heterosexual marriage). There is also an assumption that Kristina will have children. Kristina's grandparents frequently 'joke' that they will not die unless they see Kristina walk down the aisle. When Kristina came to counselling she was in her first same-sex relationship. Struggles in her relationship have brought her to counselling. Other presenting issues are academic difficulties and achievement, including completion anxiety, and family assumptions about her heterosexuality. (Although her immediate family knows about her relationship with her girlfriend, there is no discussion about it.)

Working within a diversity framework of the Group of Seven identities we could see that there are several identities that tend to overlap. Some appear to be central, such as sexual orientation and Italian family culture, and being a student; while others are peripheral, such as age, class, religion. Using sexual orientation as the entry point into the client's narrative would initially validate the client's presenting issues as well as offer an excellent place for the other identities to be introduced and discussed. While sexual orientation appears to be the chief presenting issue, it may be prudent for a counsellor to be aware that it may be a red herring. In other words, the central problem could be Kristina's academic difficulties and desires (fantasies) to achieve and succeed at a particular level in her university work. This anxiety and stress is the basis for a difficult personal relationship. It may be important for a counsellor to be aware not to focus on the lesbian relationship to the extent that it becomes a pathological site. Since the diversity framework allows for the examination of all the variables of the Group of Seven identities, sexual orientation is clearly an important domain within the client's story. While keeping in mind that the core problem may not be sexual orientation, it seems a good entry point to begin the process, by seeking to understand the issues that are concerning her relationship. For Kristina there is a disconnect between her sexual orientation and her family members' assumptions of her heterosexuality. Although Kristina's parents know about her girlfriend, the impact of not discussing and not acknowledging Kristina's homosexuality may lead to feelings of shame and disappointment for Kristina. Often what is not said and not recognized can be as hurtful as overt comments of disapproval, especially taking into consideration that Kristina cares deeply about what her family think of her. Engaging Kristina in sharing her ideas (fantasies) about what members of her family think, feel or understand, is critical to uncover her own anxieties and tensions concerning her lesbian identity.

Bringing in religion, another one of the Group of Seven identities, may be crucial at some stage so that it serves as a monitoring device to alert the therapist that the family may not be the source of conflict if Kristina is more connected to Catholicism than she makes out to be. Kristina's sexual orientation interlocks and intersects with her religious beliefs of being Catholic and her ethno-cultural identity (i.e. Italian descent). At a broader level, Kristina may have difficulty reconciling her religious beliefs with her lesbian sexual orientation. It might be helpful as a counsellor to aid Kristina to understand that there are different interpretations of the Bible and the scriptures. Another area to explore with the Kristina is to trace whether she had received messages growing up that homosexuality is a sin. It might be therapeutic to highlight for Kristina that there is no singular understanding of religion and that there are more progressive denominations of the Catholic faith that accept homosexuality. Discussing religion may give Kristina an opportunity to uncover her childhood ideas, notions and fantasies about religion and her own immersion into its doctrine. Moving the discussion between religion (Catholicism) and family issues (Italian culture) will offer Kristina an awareness of her experience from childhood and adolescence of ideas related to sexuality, gender, age, class and so on. When exploring immigrant experiences, class can become a central factor in the way life experiences are shaped and narrated in therapy. Asking Kristina to explain her understanding of her grandparent's statement 'we will not die unless we see you walk down the aisle' could yield disclosures that relate to class, and also culture, age and religion. The intersectionality of some of the Group of Seven identity variables appears to be a reality when a therapist keeps a focus on one identity but shifts the discourse between a few of the others identities. This process will also help uncover any fantasies and fears that Kristina may feel concerning her family not accepting her partner for reasons other than her being a lesbian. This aspect of the conversation may signal if the counsellor would need to explore with Kristina (in future sessions) her 'coming out process' to her family. Another aspect to explore with Kristina is her presenting issues that relate to her academic difficulties and specifically, completion anxiety. It might be useful to explore with Kristina as to whether her completion anxiety signifies becoming one step closer to the next stage of her life, which is marriage. Thus, it is understandable that Kristina has hesitations

(Continued)

(Continued)

about finishing her university programme, especially considering it is difficult for her to address her homosexuality identity within her family who have expectations of her to get married to a man.

Some questions for the counsellor (perhaps not with Kristina) are: What is the cumulative emotional impact of living in a family constellation that assumes you have a core heterosexual identity? What would it mean for you if extended family members were to discover that you are not heterosexual?

CONCLUSION

Over the decades multicultural counselling has grown in leaps and bounds, developing a canon of work that has made inroads into the theory, practice and research of counselling and psychotherapy. Besides having a discipline called multicultural counselling, its ideas and theories have altered and changed the ways in which mainstream therapy is understood and conducted. For example, Buddhist mindfulness meditation is now part of cognitive behavioural therapy. Multicultural counselling, with its many journals specifically dedicated to race, culture and ethnicity issues in therapy, can now stand in its own right as a distinct discipline. The theory has shifted in each decade: from a focus on culture integration to racial identity theories and cultural competency, and then more recently onto equity and social justice issues. Also, in the last decade the issue of diversity across cultures, sexualities, disabilities, classes, religions, ages, etc., came to question the singular focus of multicultural counselling and psychotherapy. Identity politics changed the landscape of multicultural counselling and psychotherapy, raised several controversies and engendered new ways of working clinically with the Group of Seven identities. The inclusion of women, LGBTQ individuals, people with disabilities, multiple religions, class and ages has opened up the space of healing in ways that not even the diehard multiculturalists had envisioned; for example, the inclusion of feminist principles to critique the sexists underpinnings of psychoanalysis and psychotherapy, and the post–colonial and critical race theorists critiquing psychology for its racist undertones. With the incorporation and applications of non–Western techniques, such as Buddhism, mindfulness and yoga, into counselling and psychotherapy, rather than neatly dividing it into culture or science; the process appears to be demonstrating clear evidence for therapeutic outcomes.

REFERENCES

[1] Cheung, F. and Snowden, L. (1990) 'Community mental health and ethnic minority populations', *Community Mental Health Journal, 26,* 277–91.
[2] Fernando, S. (1988) *Race and Culture in Psychiatry*. London: Croom Helm.

[3] Turner, C. and Kramer, B. (1995) 'Connections between racism and mental health', in C. V. Willie, P. P. Rieker, B. M. Kramer and B. S. Brown (eds), *Mental Health, Racism, and Sexism*. Pittsburgh: University of Pittsburgh Press. pp. 3–25.

[4] Moodley, R. (2011) *Outside the Sentence: Readings in Critical Multicultural Counselling and Psychotherapy*. Toronto: CDCP.

[5] Laungani, P. (1999) 'Client centred or culture centred counselling?', in S. Palmer and P. Laungani (eds), *Counselling in a Multicultural Society*. London: Sage.

[6] Vontress, C. E. (2010) 'Culture and counseling: a personal perspective', in R. Moodley and R. Walcott (eds), *Counseling Across and Beyond Cultures: Exploring the Work of Clemmont Vontress in Clinical Practice*. Toronto: Toronto University Press. p. 28.

[7] Moodley, R. and Walcott, R. (eds) (2010) *Counselling Across and Beyond Cultures: Exploring the Work of Clemmont E. Vontress in Clinical Practice*. Toronto: University of Toronto Press.

[8] Sue, D. W., Arredondo, P. and McDavis, R. (1992) 'Multicultural counseling competencies and standards: a call to the profession', *Journal of Counseling and Development*, 70, 477–86.

[9] Helms, J. (1990) *White Identity Development*. New York, NY: Greenwood Press.

[10] Moodley, R. and Lubin, D. (2008) 'Developing your career to working with diversity', in S. Palmer and R. Bor (eds), *The Practitioner's Handbook*. London: Sage.

[11] Arthur, N. and Stewart, J. (2001) 'Multicultural counselling in the new millennium: introduction to the special themed issue', *Canadian Journal of Counselling*, 35, 3–14.

[12] Pedersen, P. (ed.) (1991) 'Multiculturalism as a fourth force in counseling (special issue)', *Journal of Counseling and Development*, 70, 4–250.

[13] Turner, C. and Kramer, B. (1995) 'Connections between racism and mental health', in C. V. Willie, P. P. Rieker, B. M. Kramer and B. S. Brown (eds), *Mental Health, Racism, and Sexism*. Pittsburgh: University of Pittsburgh Press. pp. 3–25.

[14] Pedersen, P. and Ivey, A. (1993) *Culture Centred Counseling and Interviewing Skills: A Practical Guide*. Westport, CT: Praeger Publishers/Greenwood Publishing Group.

[15] Sodowsky, G., Lai, E. and Plake, B. (1991) 'Moderating effects of sociocultural variables on acculturation and attitudes of Hispanics and Asian Americans', *Journal of Counseling and Development*, 70, 194–204.

[16] Maxie, A. C., Arnold, D. H. and Stephenson, M. (2006) 'Do therapists address ethic and racial differences in cross-cultural psychotherapy?', *Psychotherapy: Theory, Research, Practice, Training*, 43, 85–98.

[17] Patterson, C. H. (2004) 'Do we need multicultural counseling competencies?', *Journal of Mental Health Counseling*, 26(1), 67–73.

[18] Helms, J. E. (1994) 'How multiculturalism obscures racial factors in the therapy process': comment on Ridley et al. (1994), Sodowsky et al. (1994), Ottavi et al. (1994) and Thompson et al. (1994), *Journal of Counseling Psychology*, 41, 162–5.

[19] Moodley, R. and Lubin, D. (2008) 'Developing your career to working with diversity', in S. Palmer and R. Bor (eds), *The Practitioner's Handbook*. London: Sage.

[20] Moodley, R. (2007) '(Re)placing multiculturalism in counselling and psychotherapy', *British Journal of Guidance and Counselling*, 35(1), 1–22.

SUGGESTED READING

Lago, C. (eds) (2011) *The Handbook of Transcultural Counselling and Psychotherapy*. Maidenhead: Open University Press. This edited book has chapters that explore a variety of topics related to counselling and psychotherapy in a diverse and multicultural context. It discusses the effects of different cultural heritages on both counsellors and clients alike. Topics such as identity development, ethnic/racial matching, interpretation in bi-cultural settings, racism and discrimination, and immigration are explored.

Moodley, R. and Palmer, S. (eds) (2006) *Race, Culture and Psychotherapy: Critical Perspectives in Multicultural Practice*. London: Routledge. This book provides a thorough critical examination of contemporary multiculturalism and its relationship to clinical work. Some of the issues raised in this book are: governing race in the transference; racism and counter-transference; intersectionality of the Group of Seven identities (race, gender, sexual orientation, class, disability, religion and age).

Palmer, S. (eds) (2002) *Multicultural Counselling: A Reader*. London: Sage. This book is one of the first multicultural counselling texts in the UK that covers both theory and practice. It outlines different approaches to counselling and psychotherapy in a multicultural context. The book examines topics such as race in clinical practice; dilemmas in dealing with race in the therapy room; therapy with intercultural couples; counselling foreign students; Buddhism and counselling, and many more.

Sue, D. W. and Sue, D. (2012) *Counseling the Culturally Diverse: Theory and Practice*, 6th edn. Hoboken, NJ: Wiley. This is an excellent introductory book written by two leading scholars in the field of multicultural counselling. It provides an overview of all the key concepts in working with ethnic minority and diverse populations. Topics include: developing multicultural counselling competence skills, micro-aggressions in counselling, systemic oppression and barriers to counselling minority clients.

DISCUSSION QUESTIONS

1. 'The therapist's own awareness and perceptions of him/herself as complex, multidimensional beings are critical in working across cultures.' Explore the ways in which you are a multidimensional being and how does that influence your own understanding of working with others from a similar or different social location.
2. Recall an experience in which someone who you crossed paths with had been biased, prejudiced or discriminatory towards you on the basis of one (or more) of the Group of Seven identity markers. What was that experience like for you? How did that experience re-shape your own outlook of others?
3. One of the core areas among the Multi-Cultural Competencies (MCC) is committing oneself towards an ongoing process of self-awareness. Reflect upon some of the biases, stereotypes and assumptions you may have once

believed in but you no longer have now. What were some of these beliefs? Was there a specific experience that could be described as a turning point that influenced a change in one or more of these beliefs you once held?

4. In this chapter, a vignette about a woman named Kristina was presented. Kristina was a woman of Italian descent who struggled with reconciling her lesbian identity with her religious one. She also felt social pressure from her family to get married to a man upon completion of her degree, which complicated matters for her since she identified as a lesbian. Try writing out a vignette and using yourself as the central character of this mini-case study. Outline some of the systemic barriers, cultural challenges and social pressures you have experienced in your life. Share and discuss your vignette with someone else in the class or with the larger classroom group, if you feel comfortable.

30

Professional Issues in Counselling and Psychotherapy

Carina Eriksen, Robert Bor and Margaret Oakes

INTRODUCTION

Therapists are often required to deal with a diverse range of professional issues that may not always be easy to manage. What knowledge and support network can, for example, facilitate safe practice when working with suicidal clients? What are the ethical issues that counsellors and psychotherapists may need to consider for ensuring good practice? How can therapists ensure that they continue to develop both on a professional and personal level? These are some of the topics to be covered in this chapter. The chapter starts with discussing contemporary styles of *supervision* before proceeding to give helpful tips on how to gain the most from supervision. It will then do a brief outline of *continual professional development* before moving on to talk about *ethical* and *legal issues* and *advertising*. Finally, the chapter gives an outline on how to best deal with *vulnerable and suicidal clients*.

SUPERVISION

The purpose of supervision

The aim of supervision is to ensure good practice, reflect on process to ensure goals are attained, protect the **client–therapist relationship**, enhance confidence and develop skills. Professional bodies that govern the practice of counsellors, psychologists and psychotherapists all require practising members to have regular supervision for their client work. These include the United Kingdom Council for Psychotherapy (UKCP),

British Association for Behavioural and Cognitive Psychotherapists (BABCP), British Association for Counselling and Psychotherapy (BACP), British Psychological Society (BPS) and Health and Care Professions Council (HCPC). It is essential to familiarise yourself with the specific supervision requirements held by the professional body you belong to. Certain bodies may require a therapist to be supervised by a professional who has experience within their own profession (trainee clinical psychologist must be supervised by a clinical psychologist etc).

Choosing a supervisor

Although it is recognised that therapists may not always be able to choose their own **supervisor**, especially those who are on placement or working for an organisation, it is important that the **supervisee** and the supervisor are able to establish a professional relationship. Therapists who are able to choose their supervisor may want to start by firstly considering what they would like to achieve from supervision:

- Is it important for my supervisor to specialise in a particular therapeutic orientation or would it be better to meet with a supervisor who is familiar with several therapeutic approaches?
- Am I looking for a supervisor with a specific professional background, work history or type of experience?
- How often and for how long should I meet with my supervisor?
- Are there any limitations on the days of the week or time of the day I am able to meet with a supervisor?
- What is the furthest I am prepared to travel for supervision?
- How much money can I afford to spend on supervision?

There are various ways to locate a supervisor. The first step may be to ask colleagues, previous supervisors, *placement co-ordinators* or other therapists for a recommendation. Most professional bodies offer a list of supervisors that are able and willing to supervise other therapists. It is worth researching this option. Attending conferences, workshops and seminars can also facilitate opportunities to build up a professional network and meet prospective supervisors.

Choosing between various approaches to supervision

There are several different forms of supervision, each of which offers its own benefits and limitations. The most common one is *individual supervision* where a therapist meets regularly with another practitioner, not necessarily a more senior or more experienced one, but one who has some training in supervision. One of the main limitations of individual supervision is the possibility of developing a relationship that limits the supervisee's ability to develop as a reflective practitioner. The supervisee and the trainee may, for example, find that their differing orientation styles, personalities or worldview may clash in their supervision sessions. Most mismatches in supervision can probably be solved by having a candid conversation about them. Some supervisees will feel anxious about raising interpersonal issues with their supervisor. If you find yourself in this situation, it may be helpful to remember that in having conversations like this with your supervisor you are developing skills that will be valuable in your clinical work.

Another form of supervision is *group supervision*, where several supervisees meet with their supervisor at the same time. The advantage of this form of supervision is that supervisees may have an opportunity to learn from each other as well as from their supervisor. It may also be easier for participants to address potential difficulties within the group dynamics by eliciting the perspectives of other group members. There may be differing abilities within the group which can often enrich discussions and generate new insight. However, if the difference in abilities, skill set, experience or theoretical orientation between participants is too large, some supervisees may find the supervision group to be limiting. It is also worth noting that some participants may find it more difficult to bring up personal issues that affect their client work in a group setting. In these situations, it may be advisable to schedule an individual chat with their supervisor.

Peer supervision can be an effective context for therapists to get together on a regular basis to discuss a particular aspect of their work. This can often, but not always, take the form of a special interest group where therapists have a similar *theoretical orientation* or preference for working with a specific disorder (e.g. trauma) or client group (e.g. children and adolescents). The power imbalance that can occur between a supervisee and a supervisor is eliminated in peer supervision. Group members often take it in turn to set agendas and discuss their client work. Typically, other members are then invited to respond to any queries raised.

Getting the most out of supervision

Just as supervision can take various forms, it can also be structured in various ways.[2] Whether through videoconferencing or face-to-face interaction, the supervisor and the therapist may want to make a plan at their first ever meeting as to how supervision will be structured. This may include the following:

- setting a regular time and place that suits both individuals
- discussion about each person's expectations about the supervision, including individual differences in theoretical orientation, personal characteristics, preparation for sessions, forms that need to be completed and so on
- addressing ways to overcome potential difficulties in supervision
- identifying developmental needs and goals for supervision
- considering which methods or technologies will best allow a supervisor to help the supervisee meet developmental needs/goals (video recordings, audio tapes, client case load discussions, self-rating measurement scales).

To get the most out of supervision, it is important to regularly reflect on your clinical work between supervision meetings. This will mean that you are well prepared for supervision and will help you to develop the habit of reflecting on your practice. This is not always easy to do when you are in a session with a client but it may be wise to use 10–15 minutes after a therapy session to think about your work. Below are some helpful tips to help prepare supervisees for supervision:

- Are there any risk management issues that I need to discuss with my supervisor? If so, perhaps put these at the top of the agenda for your next supervision session.
- What has been difficult in therapy since I last saw my supervisor? Are any of these themes reoccurring? If so, this may be a good opportunity to elicit the help of supervision to manage such difficulties.
- Are there any client cases that I want to talk about in supervision? If so, preparing a short summary of the individual client's progress, including an identification of the problem, brief formulation, therapeutic interventions to date and any potential difficulties, would be helpful for both you and your supervisor.
- Are there any specific skills that I need to develop/refine in order to deliver more effective therapy to clients. If so, can I identify what types of skills I need?
- How have I managed the therapeutic relationship since I last saw my supervisor? Is there anything or anyone in particular I find difficult?
- How am I managing my workload? Am I feeling stressed or tired? Am I up to date with administration work such as writing reports, liaising with other professionals that are involved with my clients etc.
- Do I need skill development that my supervisor can guide me with?

Continual professional development

Continual professional development (CPD) is defined by the Health and Care Professions Council as 'a range of learning activities through which health professionals maintain and develop throughout their career to ensure that they retain their capacity to practise safely, effectively and legally within their evolving scope of practice (www.hpc–uk.org/)'.

The benefits of CPD are that it can help professionals to improve their skills and techniques. It also encourages individuals to reflect on their own learning thereby helping to ensure best practice. There are also organisational gains, such as ensuring that staffs are capable and professional, which in turn helps to protect the public against malpractice.

Training that counts for CPD is varied but as a general guideline it includes any activity that allows a therapist to enhance their therapeutic skills. This includes attending workshops, courses, seminars and conferences either as a participant or as a presenter. Activities that promote self-reflection that can be seen to help therapeutic practice can also form a vital part of CPD. Other events include reading therapy books or articles as well as writing academic or practice-based material that is publishable. Practising members should contact their professional bodies for a full list of CPD requirements and appropriate CPD activities. Therapists may consider the following points when preparing for their CPD:

- Remember to keep a personal record of CPD.
- Plan ahead to ensure that you meet the annual CPD requirements.
- Set aside time to reflect on the value of CPD.

ETHICS

Good ethical practice can support and protect both the individual therapist and the profession of therapy. It can be argued that, without ethics and professional guidelines, counselling and psychotherapy would not be taken seriously by those who use them and clients could be at risk of unscrupulous or under-qualified practitioners. In an increasingly litigious society where clients are more inclined – and indeed are encouraged – to voice concerns about questionable therapy, it is reasonable to expect an increase in the number of ethical practice problems that are brought to the attention of the respective disciplinary committees of the registering bodies. This does not suggest that a complaint against a counsellor or therapist is necessarily valid. However, therapists and counsellors should at all times practise with this possibility in mind.

We should distinguish between good ethical practice and clinical practice. The latter is often addressed and covered in clinical practice guidelines, such as those issued by the National Institute for Health and Care Excellence (NICE). These guidelines stipulate which methods of intervention are regarded as most effective, by clinical assessment and trial, for certain conditions or problems. These can be distinguished from ethical guidelines, which relate to the therapeutic relationship and how therapy is offered and delivered. Ethical practice requires both compliance with the relevant guidelines in 'black and white' areas such as the prohibition on sexual relationships with current or former clients, and open and honest peer scrutiny of the way in which 'grey' areas are resolved. The latter is an important element of supervision, particularly, though not restricted to, one's time of training. Fundamentally, resolving ethical dilemmas in open and appropriate discussion with peers or supervisors is your greater assurance of ethical practice and protection against legal and disciplinary proceedings.

Some readers will note, however, that guidance can be at times vague and possibly subject to variance in interpretation. By way of contrast, some practice guidelines are absolute and leave no room for interpretation or subjectivity. The case of sexual relations between a client and therapist is, for example, a case of absolute prohibition. On the other hand, it is debatable as to whether a therapist who displays a photograph of her family on her mantelpiece is committing an ethical breach when working with a client who faces fertility problems. This example has been the subject of some debate among therapists and reflects the real-life dilemma of one practitioner. The fact that some dilemmas are not clear-cut or absolute demands self- and peer-reflection among the practitioner, as well as regular clinical supervision. All practitioners, whether psychologists, counsellors or psychotherapists, are required to have up-to-date knowledge of good, ethical practice and to be familiar with the respective ethical code of their registration body.

The main relevant professional registration bodies in the UK are currently the Health Professions Council of the United Kingdom for psychologists (www.hpc–uk. org/), the United Kingdom Council for Psychotherapy (www.psychotherapy.org. uk/), the British Association for Counselling and Psychotherapy for counsellors and psychotherapists (www.bacp.co.uk/), and the British Psychological Society (www/ bps.org.uk). There are links to ethical guidelines on each of the respective sites. In each, there are requirements that therapists must fulfil (for example, at the very minimum, to keep a clinical record of client attendances and a summary of the issues addressed in the session), as well as stipulations as to what must not be done in therapeutic relationships (for example, accepting any form of barter for payment, such as asking a client who is also a gardener to mow the therapist's lawn in exchange for therapy). Sometimes these are not clearly stated as such but can be gleaned from reading the stipulations and discussing their application with peers or a supervisor.

Therapists should at all times practise defensively and keep in mind that they can be held to account for any action or omission in the course of the care of their client. This does not mean that they have necessarily committed any wrong–doing, but that their practice may be subject to question or scrutiny. One framework for achieving this is to consider that the therapist is at all times accountable to:

a) the client
b) the conceptual framework or theoretical model in which they are practising
c) the organisation, context or setting in which they work and the respective practice guidelines for these
d) the professional practice guidelines and requirements for their professionals registration (e.g. HPC, UKCP, BACP)
e) ethical considerations, which may overlap with practice guidelines
f) the law of the country in which they are practising.

A useful rule of thumb to guide the practitioner is to anticipate what their own colleagues, a professional disciplinary committee of their registering body, or a lawyer or judge might challenge them over in relation to what actions the practitioner has taken, or why they did not take specific other actions.

There is also general acceptance that, from an ethical perspective, practitioners should at all times apply six general principles when they are working.[1] These are as follows:

1. respect for the client's autonomy (to be non-judgemental and to appreciate differing views, and especially those that may not be consistent with the therapist's self-belief)
2. fidelity (to recognise the issues pertaining to emotional and physical safety which exist in the client–therapist relationship)
3. justice (being fair to the client and ensuring that the therapist's services are available to as wide a range of people as possible)
4. beneficence (an undertaking to seek to benefit the client and to hold them in unconditional positive regard)
5. non-maleficence (ensuring that no harm comes to the client, or to others where such a threat exists)
6. self-interest (the therapist's reciprocal entitlement with regard to all the preceding).

Increasingly, when working within certain organisations, such as the NHS, therapists struggle with the limitation on the number of client sessions they are able to offer, and may find that this limitation may be at variance with the therapist's duty of care and preferred model or theoretical framework for practice. This is a matter that challenges even the most experienced therapists and may raise ethical concerns, especially where there is a duty of care toward the client. It is incumbent upon the therapist in such situations to argue the case with their supervisor and manager for extending the number of client sessions, where appropriate and where indicated.

INSURANCE

Professional indemnity insurance is surely a requirement for any counsellor or therapist who practises with clients, though there is no requirement to take out such a policy. Do not rely upon your employer, such as the NHS, to provide indemnity. Whilst insurance does not provide protection against illegal or immoral practices on the part of the professional, it can help to protect the therapist from unreasonable claims brought against them by a client or another practitioner, or party. It also provides indemnity in the event that something goes wrong in the care and treatment of a client. The client or relatives may seek damages from the professional, which can prove enormously costly. There are several companies that provide professional indemnity insurance for counsellors and therapists. Commonly used ones are Towergate (www.towergateprofessionalrisks.co.uk/) and Howden (www.howdengroup.com/en/business_insurance/retail_sectors/insurance_for_professional_associations); an online search will reveal details of others.

Avoiding being sued by a client or being subject to a professional malpractice claim being brought by a colleague is not a matter to be left to chance. The pages of professional therapy and counselling magazines describe malpractice suits involving therapists and counsellors and there are common threads that run through these. Every counsellor or therapist should regularly read these accounts and, by becoming acquainted with the most common issues, should be more likely to avoid them.

Below is a list of measures which, if every therapist adhered to, would significantly reduce their risk of being sued:

- Know your professional practice guidelines.
- Always practise within your areas and limits of competence; refer patients outside of these limits to other suitable colleagues and professionals.
- Discuss ethical issues in peer supervision to maintain currency in these complex matters.
- Do nothing illegal or immoral with clients.
- Ensure there is no ambiguity in your contract with a client, especially with regard to your payment and terms.
- Never be tempted to form a personal friendship or deeper relationship with a client or ex-client (inevitably such a relationship will go awry).

- Have regular supervision to discuss progress as well as any concerns you may have around client behaviour; it is better that you can demonstrate that you have discussed a challenging situation with colleagues should any claim arise than to ignore concerns.
- Regularly attend CPD.
- Keep good client records and ensure that they are complete and up to date.
- Always work within a known psychotherapeutic framework.
- Avoid making exceptions with clients (e.g. when and where you see them) if you have any reservations about these; invariably these tend to go wrong.
- Do not instruct clients or give direct advice unless this is absolutely warranted; clients can sue you if the advice proves to be incorrect.
- Always act when you have a fear for the safety of a client, a child or third party.
- Picture yourself answering to a judge or a disciplinary committee, explaining why you did what you did in therapy (and also why you chose not to take other actions); this mental process will keep you on track in therapy.
- Never criticise a fellow therapist with or to a client.

ADVERTISING

When qualified and registered with one of the relevant professional bodies, and when setting up in practice, most counsellors and therapists will seek to promote their service in order to attract clients and grow their practice. This is understandable and to be encouraged. Nonetheless, there are certain guidelines as to what can and cannot be included in advertisements. There is also evidence that certain approaches to promoting a practice may be more effective than others.

Counsellors and therapists should not make claims about their practice which are either false or contestable. Most acceptable promotional and advertising activity contains a description of the therapist's attainments. This may include their qualifications and professional title as well as the name of the registering body and the professional's registration or licence number. It is important, however, to desist from making any claims relating to such things as providing more effective or faster cures or treatments than another practitioner. Any such comparisons not only bring the profession into disrepute but will, in all likelihood, attract a sanction from one of the professional registering bodies.

Some practitioners feel that it is helpful to highlight that they undertake regular supervision. They may also draw positive attention to aspects of their practice, including access for disabled people, close proximity to public transport, ease of parking, and conceptual models within which they practise so that prospective clients may better understand what they might expect from the therapy. It should be borne in mind that many clients may not have an in-depth understanding of therapeutic approaches, and it is always helpful to give, in plain language, a short explanation as to the benefits of a particular approach or any specific attributes.

It is also desirable, if such is appropriate, to highlight professional practice times that may be especially attractive to prospective clients. This may include offering weekend appointments or evening appointments. Also, if the professional has more advanced qualifications and experience, the offer of seeing couples, children, or whole families may also form an attractive offer to prospective clients. As a small tip, avoid the liberal use of the first person 'I' in advertising. It detracts from professionalism and gives the impression of an ego-centric therapist!

A dilemma for many practitioners starting out may be where best to advertise their services or practice. Most of the professional registering bodies (with the exception of the HCPC) have a directory where prospective clients can find a therapist with specific expertise in the required area and/or who are located geographically close to them. Placing advertisements in magazines, online and with local related services such as GP practices or the offices of law firms may also yield some benefit in terms of client inflow. However, it is important to bear in mind that, where clients come of their own volition rather than through professional referral, the therapist may wish to have contact details of the client's GP in case the need arises to have contact with a professional who knows the client, in case of any threat of self-harm.

The most effective way of doing this is to undertake good, ethical and effective client work. Clients who have had a positive experience of counselling or therapy are the best form of advertising. However, if they have had a poor experience, this will be damaging to your reputation.

WORKING WITH VULNERABLE AND SUICIDAL CLIENTS

In the final part of this chapter, we will introduce you to the professional and ethical principles of working with vulnerable and **suicidal clients**. Our aim is to enable you to identify such clients, prepare to manage their safety, respond appropriately in critical situations and protect yourself.

Identifying vulnerable people

Any individual who is either less competent to make decisions about and consent to treatment or less able to care for and protect themselves than a reasonably competent adult should be considered vulnerable. Some vulnerable groups are easily identifiable: children, adults with some obvious disabilities, learning difficulties etc. What about the woman screaming at the receptionist? She might be difficult, angry or simply irritating. She might also have been forced to come by a partner, social worker or parent or be very frightened. In that case, you have a vulnerable client. The less obvious groups of vulnerable clients will include adults with mild-to-moderate mental health disorders, people who are being abused or bullied, and frightened clients. Some services and NHS trusts have vulnerable adult policies that specifically identify all adults referred to mental health services as vulnerable and have guidelines for working with them.

As a counsellor or therapist you also have a responsibility to respond appropriately if your client identifies other vulnerable people who might be at risk. For example, if you are working with a parent with mental health issues, you need to know if their children are safe. If your client is being or has been bullied or abused, are other people at risk? If you are in any doubt, consult your supervisor or line manager.

Before you start working with clients in any placement, job or private practice, take the time to identify the resources you will need for the groups of vulnerable clients you might encounter. Also discuss what level of risk you are expected to manage. Your supervisor or manager will probably have a contact list that might include:

- the local urgent care or crisis team
- your appointed child protection officer or point of contact
- local Community Mental Health Teams
- Accident and Emergency departments with psychiatric cover
- local specialist services.

This preparation is fundamental to working safely with vulnerable clients. As you continue, as long as you practise carefully within the ethical guidelines we described earlier in this chapter, stay within the limits of your competence and involve appropriate support services when necessary, you can work constructively with vulnerable clients. Again, use your supervisor to support you.

Identifying suicidal clients

Some clients will spontaneously tell you that they are thinking about suicide. Others find it more difficult to discuss but will often be relieved to be asked a direct question. Many services ask about suicidal ideation and self-harm as part of standard assessments. It is particularly important to check for suicidal ideation or self-harm when assessing and working with depressed, hopeless or psychotic clients. This should be repeated at regular intervals throughout therapy. Remember, for example, that a depressed client who starts to improve their activity levels may become able to put their affairs in order and act on their suicidal thoughts before their mood improves. Tragically, starting to get better may make suicide possible.

Asking about thoughts of suicide or self harm isn't something that many people do regularly before they begin to train in this area. We know that many trainees find it difficult or intrusive to ask or may be frightened of the answer. It is useful to prepare the words you will use and practice them. Here are some suggestions:

- When people have problems or difficulties like the ones you are describing, they sometimes find that they start to think about hurting or killing themselves. Have you thought about doing that?
- Have your difficulties ever meant that you wanted to hurt yourself or kill yourself?
- On a scale of 0 to 10, where 0 is you would definitely not do this and 10 is you will do it today, how likely are you to try to hurt or kill yourself?
- (If someone describes psychotic symptoms) Do the voices/people/images you described ever tell you to hurt or kill yourself?

If your client reacts in surprise, perhaps saying 'No, of course not!', you might want to explain that because you need to know that they are safe, you will probably ask again at intervals throughout your work together. If they say 'Yes', aim for an accepting and reassuring response and focus on gathering more information. You need to know:

- Do they have a plan and how detailed is that? How? When? Where? Do they need to do anything first (write letters, get the house sorted etc.)?
- What do they want to do (die or hurt themselves)? Can they explain why?
- When are they most likely to find themselves having or acting on suicidal thoughts? Ask them to describe an incident where they felt close to acting on these thoughts? What stopped them? Were they able to stop themselves?
- What protective factors are there? These might be family members that your client doesn't want to upset, children they want to see grow up, activities they used to enjoy, goals or anything that makes life worth living.

This discussion should give you a clearer idea of the risk that your client might hurt themselves. It may be safe to let them go home at the end of the session or you may need to arrange for additional or even immediate support. If you are at all unsure, consult your supervisor or another professional before your client leaves. If you need to leave the room, you may want to telephone for someone to stay with your client while you do this. If you are the only professional in the building, you should have a plan for accessing urgent support, such as the local urgent care team. If your client is at immediate risk of hurting themselves then you must arrange to hand them over to an appropriate service. When the risk is lower it may be sufficient to agree with the client to call their GP to book an emergency appointment on the day. At other times you may, with your supervisor's agreement, be able to continue working with them. In this case, the 'Safety Card' described below may be useful.

TABLE 30.1   *An illustration of the Safety Card*

Risk	What I might notice	What do I need to do
10	Struggling not to run into the road right now	Go to local A&E – Royal Infirmary on Main Street (Bus No. 6), ask Marjory to come with me and tell them I am thinking of killing myself
9	Thinking I want to kill myself	Call crisis team – 01234 567895
7–8	Feeling sad or hopeless most of the time, not moving from sofa, thinking what it would be like to be dead	Make an urgent appointment with GP 01234 987654 or counsellor 01234 789654. Tell James I am struggling
5–6	Feeling OK some of the time but snapping at James and kids and often very sad or angry	Use controlled breathing to calm down, tell James I'm not feeling great. Go for a walk. Make an appointment with GP 01234 987654 if it goes on for more than 3–4 days
3–4	Feeling mostly OK but sometimes sad. Too tired to play with kids	Call Marjory for a chat or talk to James after work. Plan something nice to do with the kids at the weekend

| 1–2 | Feeling generally OK, tending to watch TV rather than go out. Still enjoy playing with the kids after school | Make some more plans for doing something enjoyable or meeting friends |
| 0 | Feeling OK. Making plans for pleasurable activities, pottering in the house or garden or meeting friends | Keep doing this! Make sure that you have pleasurable activities planned |

The Safety Card

This simply provides a lower-risk client with a card they can carry with them to identify moments when they are becoming more likely to hurt themselves and quick access to the appropriate help. The idea is that they ask themselves to rate their risk from 0 to 10 regularly (where 0 is no risk and 10 is very likely to hurt themselves today) and act according to the card. Table 30.1 gives an example.

CONCLUSION

In this chapter we have outlined a range of professional issues you are likely to encounter as a counsellor or psychotherapist. Rather than provide a detailed answer to every possible ethical or professional dilemma, we described the basic principles that underpin the professional conduct of ethical therapists. We hope we have demonstrated that ethical and professional conduct requires regular reflection and study. As you will have come to understand, some dilemmas have obvious and specific answers. Many more will challenge your ability to practise ethically and professionally. In these cases, knowing your professional body's ethical code and having an open, honest and reflective relationship with your supervisor and line manager will be your most effective route to professional and ethical conduct. Finally, remember two things: first, very few ethical and professional dilemmas require an instant solution – if you and your client are safe, take the time to consult your supervisor or appropriate peers. Secondly, there are rarely perfect solutions to complex ethical dilemmas. If you have worked openly and reflectively with supervision and remained mindful of your clients' vulnerabilities and needs, it is likely that you will have acted in a way that would be judged as ethical by your peers.

REFERENCES

[1] Bond, T. (2011) 'Guidelines for professional practice', in R. Bor and M. Watts (eds), *The Trainee Handbook*. London: Sage. pp. 147–60.
[2] Creaner, M. (2013) *Getting the Best Out of Supervision in Counselling and Psychotherapy. A Guide for Supervisees*. London. Sage.

SUGGESTED READING

Bond, T. (2011) 'Guidelines for professional practice', in R. Bor and M. Watts (eds), *The Trainee Handbook*. London: Sage. pp 147–60.

Cann, D. (2011) 'Supervision: Making it work for you', in R. Bor and M. Watts (eds), *The Trainee Handbook*. London: Sage. pp. 161–78.

Cross, M. and Papadopoulos L. (2011) 'What do I do if ...? Questions commonly asked by trainees', in R. Bor and M. Watts (eds), *The Trainee Handbook*. London: Sage. pp. 223–40.

The Trainee Handbook provides psychologists, therapists, counsellors and psychotherapists with an effective way to progress and gain confidence in their personal and professional development. In this second edition, the authors have sought to highlight developments in teaching and learning as well as professional practice. The book is suitable for trainees as well as qualified professionals.

DISCUSSION ISSUES

1. Put together a CPD plan for the next year which complies with the requirements of your professional body.
2. Identify how you and your clients will benefit from CPD activities.
3. Design an appropriate marketing leaflet for setting up in private practice.
4. Potential ethical dilemmas for reflection:

   a) How do you respond to clients giving gifts?
   b) How do you respond to a client disclosing a crime or threat to others?
   c) How do you respond if the police demand confidential records?
   d) How do you respond to a parent of an adolescent client demanding to know if your client is having sex?

31

Research in Counselling and Psychotherapy

Terry Hanley and Laura Anne Winter

This chapter reflects on research in counselling and psychotherapy and provides an introduction to a number of issues professionals in these fields may encounter when engaging with research. To begin, we discuss the development of research looking at counselling and psychotherapy, and consider both what research is and why it is done in this area, and who this may be done for. We briefly introduce a number of core methodological approaches and reflect on potential ethical considerations as well as considering the question 'has research demonstrated the *effectiveness* of counselling and psychotherapy?'

DEVELOPMENT OF RESEARCH INTO COUNSELLING AND PSYCHOTHERAPY

Throughout the history of counselling and psychotherapy literature the importance of systematically reflecting upon the work that we do has had a presence. For instance, key proponents, such as Sigmund Freud, Aaron Beck and Carl Rogers, all engaged in research activities. Freud produced some of the most influential case studies that have ever been presented,[1] Beck has been involved in utilising experimental designs[2] and Rogers contributed substantially to the field of qualitative research in psychology.[3] These are all products of the time in which they were written but reflect the influence of the world of research upon the roots of the discipline.

In more recent years researching counselling and psychotherapy has gathered momentum and it is no longer just prominent theorists that undertake it. It has become a significant part of the curriculum for many, if not all, of the therapeutic professions. So, if we pause for a moment and ask 'What is research?', what do we come up with? One influential definition in the UK is that research is an 'original investigation undertaken in order to gain knowledge and understanding'.[4]

As is evident in these words, it is an incredibly broad activity. It might even be thought that the act of therapy in itself could be viewed as a research activity when using this definition. Although this is clearly true to some extent, we would argue that this is not the case when considering a more conventional definition. Here we would outline that an important distinction is that research aims to communicate its findings to a wider audience[5] and that this goal often separates it from more informal practice review activities. Thus in doing so, the activity moves from serving a relatively 'local' agenda (i.e. supporting a single client) to one that is much larger and contributes to a larger narrative (e.g. contributing to a pool of literature related to a particular issue). Engaging with this bigger picture brings with it different ethical responsibilities, which we will return to later in this chapter.

Despite the central place that research has had in the development of therapeutic theory, it is not often at the forefront of practitioners' minds when they enter into the profession. For many practitioners there is a reticence towards what it can achieve and questions about the relevance to the work that they undertake. One influential study of 4,000 therapists found that research was way down the pecking order when considering what influenced practice.[6] In contrast, activities such as previous experience with clients, practice supervision and personal therapy were rated much more highly. So why is this? The answer to this question is not clear cut, but there are clearly those who find research to be overly complicated, boring or just not relevant.[7]

Recognition of the need for trainees to become research-literate has received a great deal of attention, in part due to the political pressures upon therapeutic services.[8,9] In many instances, services no longer have a choice not to engage with research activities, such as asking therapists to utilise outcome measures, as commissioners now insist upon the collection of such information prior to handing over any money. Researching counselling and psychotherapy is therefore an activity that is gathering momentum, and it has become more integrated into core syllabi for counselling and psychotherapy courses. As a consequence, newly trained counsellors and psychotherapists are becoming increasingly familiar with the different discourses that surround the world of research and the implications of undertaking such work. In the following section we dip our toes into this water ourselves.

WHO IS RESEARCH FOR?

As we have already mentioned, research in counselling and psychotherapy has a long history and it is becoming an everyday occurrence in the work that therapists undertake. But two further questions spring to mind: 'Why do we do it?', and 'Who is it for?' Below we scratch the surface of these debates and identify four broad groups for which research is conducted and reported:

Clients

One group of people for whom research is conducted is the clients that we meet – the users of counselling and psychotherapy services. A significant portion of high-profile reported research looks at the question of 'What works for whom?' in counselling and psychotherapy. The aim of this type of research is to guide therapists in better supporting service users by offering the most appropriate form of therapy. Such an approach is often referred to as **evidence-based practice**. This approach works with the premise that in order to be used, a particular type of therapeutic practice should be proven to work with a particular type of client or presenting issue. There is, of course, a great logic to such an argument. However, we would urge some caution about wholeheartedly jumping into this approach because many therapeutic relationships do not follow such a regimented rulebook. We would therefore encourage therapists to be 'research informed' rather than directed by it.[10]

Therapists

Research is also conducted and reported for the therapist. There are two (overlapping) camps of therapists here we might speak of: those who conduct research and those who read or consume research. Corrie and Callahan interviewed a number of counselling psychologists, clinical psychologists, psychologists and counsellors, and found that they thought that having an awareness of research is a professional responsibility and a contributor to effective practice.[11] That is to say, therapists may conduct and/or read research to improve their own practice, and because they view it as a responsibility. West and Byrne[12] describe the view that reading research is an important aspect of continuing professional development, and is a way of therapists keeping abreast of developments in the area they work in. We can therefore see from this that research is conducted both for clients and therapists. If, as is indicted by the research by Corrie and Callahan, therapists think that knowledge of research is a contributor to effective practice, they are likely to feel more competent and able if they have this knowledge. McLeod[13] also considers another angle on why conducting research specifically is good for therapists: 'Research can be a self-renewing counterbalance to practice, justifying and supporting periods of creativity and reflection away from the demands of clients and waiting lists.'

Services

As we have already suggested, questions are often raised about what evidence there is for a specific intervention or treatment, with a view to considering the commissioning of particular services. From a counselling and psychotherapy perspective this potentially manifests as the question 'What evidence is there that a specific therapeutic approach works?' and behind this lies the idea of 'legitimacy'.[13] Specifically, research is done in counselling and psychotherapy to add weight to the argument that counselling and psychotherapy do in fact make a difference to people's lives and are therefore services worth commissioning. For instance, this might be useful when services are considering which type of professional to employ. Therefore, one reason why research is conducted and reported is to legitimise the pursuits of counselling and psychotherapy.

Society

On a broader level again, it might be said that research is done for the benefit of society. If we look at many of the sources that fund therapeutic services the intention is not solely to improve the wellbeing of the individuals. For instance, schools may provide funding for a school counselling service with the hope that it might improve their academic attainment record, or governments may decide to fund therapeutic services with a view of reducing the number of people claiming benefits due to being off work for substantial periods of time.[14] Thus, although therapy might often feel like an isolated personal endeavour, ultimately it is very difficult to truly escape the more systemic societal rationale that may lie behind such provision.

METHODS OF RESEARCH

There are a multitude of methods of researching counselling and psychotherapy. These can range from single case study approaches focusing upon a single piece of client work to surveys reflecting upon larger groups of people. Each of these methods serves a different purpose and in this section we briefly outline some of the key terms that you might come across.

Quantitative research

Hanley, Lennie and West[15] describe **quantitative research** as research that 'summarises concepts into categories that can be counted' (p. 75). In brief then, quantitative research involves the exploration of phenomena using mathematical or statistical methods. Common methods of data collection include surveys and questionnaires, and experiments. For example, if you want to find out how much people's wellbeing changes after therapy, you might get a sample of individuals to complete a quantitative measure of wellbeing at the beginning of therapy, and then again at the end, and compare the sets of scores. When you have got this quantitative data you might want to analyse it in different ways. Within quantitative research we consider two categories of analysis: *descriptive* and *inferential*.

Descriptive statistics are used to summarise or describe a set of scores. So for example, if you have asked 2,500 people to rate how helpful therapy was on a scale of 1–7, you are likely to want to be able to summarize that data rather than just present the 2,500 scores independently, because this is going to be challenging to understand and not necessarily very helpful. Instead you might want to work out the average rating, the range of ratings, or the most common score chosen.

Inferential statistics on the other hand are used to draw 'inferences' or conclusions from a set of data, which go beyond the actual scores you have. So if we take the 2,500 ratings of how helpful therapy was, you might want to draw some inferences about the type of person who is likely to rate therapy as being more helpful. You might, for example, think that people of a white British origin would find it more helpful than another group perhaps, in which case, you could use inferential statistics to see whether the data you have collected support this prediction or not.

Qualitative research

In contrast to quantitative research, which would attempt to summarise concepts into numbers, **qualitative research** is concerned with obtaining a more detailed picture of a particular phenomenon – '[T]he qualitative researcher aims to explore the worlds that individuals inhabit and make sense of the stories that individuals tell them'.[15] Common methods of data collection include individual interviews, collecting field notes on observations and focus groups. For example, if you were interested in people's experiences of therapy you might interview a number of people who have had counselling or psychotherapy recently and ask them about their experiences. These interviews might be quite open and the participant might be able to talk about whatever they want in that time in relation to your research topic, or you might have quite specific questions you want to ask them. Interviews can therefore be unstructured, semi-structured, or structured. Alternatively, you might collect qualitative data by getting a group of these people together at one time and getting them all to talk together about their experiences of therapy, which is known as a focus group.

Once you have collected this qualitative data, in the same way as if collecting quantitative data, you then are going to want to analyse it – but how? There are now lots of different methods of qualitative data analysis. These include approaches like thematic analysis, grounded theory, discourse analysis and interpretative phenomenological analysis (IPA). All of these approaches have different methods associated with them but, as with quantitative reporting, commonly research reports aim to digest a massive amount of information and provide the reader with a useful summary of it.

Ultimately each of these approaches plays an important part in the world of counselling and psychotherapy research and it is the research question of interest that should inform and guide the choice of methodology. For instance, if you are interested in finding out whether a particular approach of therapy appears to reduce levels of distress you are likely to utilise a questionnaire and adopt a quantitative approach. In contrast, if you are interested in the specific experiences that clients have whilst attending therapy you might want to interview them and adopt a qualitative approach. Increasingly, researchers are also seeing the value of doing both within research projects and this is referred to as mixed methods research.

Mixed methods research

Mixed methods research involves collecting, analysing and integrating both quantitative and qualitative approaches in a single study.[16] Mixed methods research can be done in a number of different ways. Typically these vary in terms of the timing of the quantitative and qualitative elements of the research, the level of integration between the two elements and the priority given to the different phases. For example, a piece of mixed methods research might involve an initial quantitative phase, followed by a second qualitative phase, or vice versa. A researcher might conduct a quantitative experiment and follow it up with some interviews with people who participated in the experiment. Alternatively, a researcher might explore through qualitative means how individuals describe a topic, and use the findings to develop a quantitative survey instrument which they may then distribute to a larger group of people. Both of these mixed methods designs would be called *sequential*, in that the phases of the research proceed after one another. Another option is to conduct *concurrent* mixed methods research, where qualitative and quantitative data are gathered at the same time. A researcher might decide to give either the qualitative element of the research or the quantitative element priority, or they might decide that they are both equally important in answering the research question.

HAS RESEARCH DEMONSTRATED THE EFFECTIVENESS OF COUNSELLING AND PSYCHOTHERAPY?

Probably the most common question asked of any therapeutic approach is 'Does it work?' One very influential answer came from Hans Eysenck, who was a widely known psychologist who is well-known for his work on personality and intelligence, but wrote about a range of topics and regularly sparked debate and controversy. In 1952 Eysenck claimed that there was very little evidence to suggest that attending therapy was any more effective than not attending it. This challenge acted as a substantial catalyst for a culture shift in therapeutic research, and numerous decades, and thousands of studies, later we can say with at least some confidence that for many people therapy does appear to be effective (see for instance Cooper[9] for a summary). However, the answer is not necessarily a straightforward 'yes' or 'no'. If we consider the four perspectives noted above (the client, therapist, service and society), each is likely to have a slightly different set of criteria by which they would judge the notion of effectiveness. For instance, a societal view might be primarily to see people get back to work whilst a client may want to feel less anxious when they leave the house. These do not have to be mutually exclusive, but capturing this information is likely to take a different form.

Within the therapeutic literature it has been observed that the focus of research has moved through several different phases. These have included considering whether therapy generally works, which approach is most effective, which approach is most cost effective and attempting to work out the most effective therapeutic ingredients. A relatively new focus also seems to be upon whether using research methods 'with', rather than 'on', clients might actually improve therapeutic outcomes itself. This shifting emphasis reflects some of the major questions that the counselling and psychotherapy communities have been confronted with throughout their history. Furthermore, just as there are numerous agendas at play when considering research, there are also numerous varieties of effectiveness study. Primarily, although not exclusively, many of the studies looking at the efficacy and effectiveness of therapy are quantitative in nature. These include popular designs such as the randomised controlled trial and pre- and post-therapy studies, which are introduced below.

The *randomised controlled trial* attempts to compare outcomes of a particular intervention between different randomly allocated groups of similar people (e.g. a group with high symptomatology of depression may be divided into two groups, one that receives CBT and one that does not). This is often viewed as the 'gold standard' of research and provides an indication of the *efficacy* of certain interventions when as many aspects as possible are controlled for. Such designs are often challenged for their lack of real world application, which leads to our second category.

Pre- and post-therapy studies: this approach is often applied within real world settings and simply takes a measure of a relevant concept (e.g. severity of the symptoms of anxiety or general wellbeing) at the beginning and the end of therapy. It is then possible to reflect upon the distance travelled during the period of therapy. This is incredibly common within therapeutic services as a means of monitoring the *effectiveness* of therapeutic work using what has come to be known as **practice-based evidence** (in contrast to the earlier mentioned evidence-based practice, which is more commonly associated with RCTs). This provides an important everyday reflection upon therapeutic practice but is open to challenge due to the limited control applied to the factors that might influence change (e.g. how do we know what the therapeutic intervention is?) and the omission of a comparison/control group, thus how can we feel assured that the change indicated would not have just happened without the therapeutic intervention?

Although there are those who are vehemently for and against these different approaches, we would argue that each of these designs can prove useful as long as the information is treated appropriately – it's not what you do, it's what you do with it that's important. Thus, we arrive at our final section of this chapter in which we consider the ethical issues associated with conducting counselling and psychotherapy research.

ETHICAL ISSUES

Over the past 100 hundred or so years psychological research has led to fascinating revelations about the ways that humans engage and interact with one another. Interesting phenomena have been explored and important messages have been conveyed by some incredibly provocative studies that have made a lasting impact upon the public consciousness. For instance, Stanley Milgram's work on obedience to authority figures[17] involved asking participants to administer 'electric shocks' to another individual whom participants believed to be also taking part in the study, and who, participants believed, had been randomly assigned to the role which involved receiving 'electric shocks' if they didn't answer questions correctly. Ethical issues in this research involved that participants were deceived on a number of levels, including that the 'electric shocks' were not real, and the person they believed to be their fellow participant was actually part of the research team. Furthermore, participants were placed under a great deal of stress in the experiment and taking part may have caused long-term psychological harm. This study is only one in a number of famously controversial psychological studies. Nevertheless, despite the impact of such work it is important to note that many of these studies would not be allowed to be repeated today (at least as research projects, television is another matter!). The rationale for prohibiting such work is that institutions have become much more sensitised to the ethical considerations related to research with human participants. Within a UK context, professional bodies often govern the work of counsellors and psychotherapists. For example, counsellors and psychotherapists might gravitate towards organisations such as the BACP, BABCP or the UKCP whilst those in the applied psychologies are likely to lean towards the BPS and HCPC. As is reflected earlier in this book, organisations such as these outline their own ethical codes of conduct from which people should consider their therapeutic work (most also have accompanying statements regarding research with human participants too). These vary in terminology but basically request practitioners to work respectfully, with integrity, and do no harm to participants involved. These codes of codes of ethics and practice should inform all aspects of the work we do, including research. Adopting an ethical stance to our research may seem relatively simple, but there are numerous pitfalls to such practice. Some of the core elements are noted below.

Ethical review

Research projects should always be scrutinised by some form of ethical review. This will vary from setting to setting, with organisations such as the National Health Service and universities having their own processes in place. They will commonly expect people to outline the rationale for the project, the design that is to be adopted and what will happen to any information associated to the project. For some this can be a daunting task, however it is useful to remember that therapists are often very sensitive to ethical nuances.

Informed consent

As therapeutic practitioners we value the notion of informed consent. Although we acknowledge that it is difficult for a client to fully give informed consent to a process that is often one of unknown discovery, we still work hard to provide a transparent insight into the processes in which we ask clients to become engaged. Within therapeutic research the issue is much the same. Einstein is cited as saying 'If we knew what it was we were doing, it wouldn't be research, would it?' Such sentiments reflect the similarity of the concept of informed consent in both activities. With this in mind, in a much similar way as with therapy, we therefore attempt to provide those involved in research with us with enough information to opt into the projects we undertake.

Right to withdraw

Linked to the concept of informed consent is also the issue of being able to withdraw from the study at any point in time prior to publication of any findings. This is relatively self explanatory but can feed into a complicated dynamic between the participant and the researcher if dual roles are involved. For instance, if a person is recruited via a therapist they may find it difficult to then say they do not want to be involved at a later stage. Information therefore needs to be provided outlining that withdrawing from the study will not have a negative impact upon their care.

Data protection and confidentiality

Researchers should be aware of legal issues that may impact upon their work. One such issue is that of data protection. The key piece of legislation here is the Data Protection Act 1998, which regulates the use of 'personal data'. This is defined as data that relate to a living individual and either: (i) identifies a specific individual; or (ii) may identify an individual when combined with other data that is in the possession of, or likely to be in the possession of, the person seeing the data.

Trustworthiness

'A source that itself is not trustworthy is not useful.' We return here to another quote attributed to Albert Einstein. The issue of trustworthiness of research is commonly discussed within qualitative research[18] but receives less explicit attention in quantitative work. However, as an ethical underpinning to the work of researchers it plays equally as important a role, and resonates firmly with the ethical codes of conduct noted above. Researchers should therefore be mindful of treating information provided by participants with due respect and provide transparent accounts of how they came to the conclusions that they arrived at.

SUMMARY

Within this chapter we have hoped to provide a brief introduction to a number of key issues that counsellors and psychotherapists may encounter when engaging with research. We have provided a historical perspective of such work and reflected upon how research can permeate so many levels of the counselling and psychotherapy profession, impacting upon clients, therapists, services and society. Following on from this we reflected upon how counselling and psychotherapy research has engaged with research to work towards demonstrating its effectiveness with a variety of different client groups. To end, we presented an introduction to some key ethical issues that people should be mindful of when undertaking research – good research is ethical research. We hope that we have provided a thought-provoking taster that might encourage you to read more around this important area of therapeutic work.

REFERENCES

[1] Freud, S. (1901/1990) 'The case of Dora', *Pelican Freud Library, Vol. 8: Case Histories 1*. Harmondsworth: Penguin.

[2] Beck, A., Ward, C. and Mendelson, M. (1961) 'An inventory for measuring depression', *Archives of General Psychiatry, 4*, 561–71.

[3] Rogers, C. (1985) 'Towards a more human science of the person', *Journal of Humanistic Psychology, 25(4)*, 7–24.

[4] Research Assessment Exercise (2005) *RAE 2008: Guidance on Submissions*. Bristol: HEFCE.

[5] McLeod, J. (2003) *Doing Counselling Research*, 2nd edn. London: Sage.

[6] Orlinsky, D. E., Botermans, J. and Rønnestad, M. H. (2001) 'Towards an empirically grounded model of psychotherapy training: four thousand therapists rate influences on their development', *Australian Psychologist, 36(2)*, 139–48.

[7] Morrow-Bradley, C. and Elliott, R. (1986) 'Utilization of psychotherapy research by practicing psychotherapists', *American Psychologist, 41*, 188–97.

[8] Wheeler, S. and Elliott, R. (2008) 'What do counsellors and psychotherapists need to know about research?', *Counselling and Psychotherapy Research, 8(2)*, 133–5.

[9] Cooper, M. (2009) *Essential Research Findings in Counselling and Psychotherapy*. London: Sage.

[10] Hanley, T., Cutts, L., Gordon, R. and Scott, A. (2013) 'A research informed approach to counselling psychology', in G. Davey (ed.), *Applied Psychology*. London: BPS Wiley Blackwell.

[11] Corrie, S. and Callahan, M. M. (2001) 'Therapists' beliefs about research and the scientist–practitioner model in an evidence-based health care climate: a qualitative study', *British Journal of Medical Psychology, 74*, 135–49.

[12] West, W. and Byrne, J. (2009) 'Some ethical concerns about counselling research', *Counselling Psychology Quarterly, 22(3)*, 309–18.

[13] McLeod, J. (2001) 'Developing a research tradition consistent with the practices and values of counselling and psychotherapy: why counselling and psychotherapy research is necessary', *Counselling and Psychotherapy Research, 1(1)*, 3–11.

[14] Layard, R. (2011) *Happiness. Lessons from a New Science*, 2nd edn. Harmondsworth: Penguin.

[15] Hanley, T., Lennie, C. and West, W. (2013) *Introducing Counselling and Psychotherapy Research*. London: Sage.

[16] Creswell, J. W. and Plano Clark, V. L. (2011) *Designing and Conducting Mixed Methods Research*, 2nd edn. London: Sage.

[17] Milgram, S. (1963) 'Behavioral study of obedience', *Journal of Abnormal and Social Psychology, 67(4)*, 371–8.

[18] Elliott, R., Fischer, C. T. and Rennie, D. L. (1999) Evolving guidelines for publication of qualitative research studies in psychology and related fields. *British Journal of Clinical Psychology, 38,* 215–29.

SUGGESTED READING

Cooper, M. (2009) *Essential Research Findings in Counselling and Psychotherapy.* London: Sage. This book provides an introduction to some of the important research findings in counselling and psychotherapy, including research that answers questions such as are some therapies more effective than others?

Hanley, T., Cutts, L., Gordon, R. and Scott, A. (2013) 'A research informed approach to counselling psychology', supplementary chapter to G. Davey (ed.), *Applied Psychology.* London: BPS Wiley Blackwell. This book chapter can only be accessed online and is not part of the print publication. It reflects on the ideas of evidence-based practice and practice-based evidence as discussed above, and outlines what a research-informed approach might look like in practice.

Hanley, T., Lennie, C. and West, W. (2013) *Introducing Counselling and Psychotherapy Research.* London: Sage. This textbook provides an overview of the place of research in the world of therapy, including information on what research is, issues to consider before starting research, a discussion of the various types of methodological approaches introduced in this chapter, and what to do with research when it is done.

McLeod, J. (2003) *Doing Counselling Research*, 2nd edn. London: Sage. This is a practical introduction to the research process, with details on how to review the literature, select methods, collect and analyse data, and evaluate your findings.

DISCUSSION ISSUES

1. What type of evidence would you look for if you were commissioning a service?
2. What ethical issues might you need to consider when planning a piece of research evaluating the effectiveness of a therapy service?
3. What are the relative merits and disadvantages of quantitative, qualitative, and mixed methods research? How might you decide between the different approaches?
4. What benefits do users of therapeutic services get from counselling and psychotherapy research? Are there any negative impacts you might see counselling and psychotherapy research having on current or potential users of therapeutic services?

Afterword

I hope this book has provided the reader with sufficient information to acquire a basic understanding of the theory and practice of each of the 26 approaches covered. Appendix 2 highlights some of the varied counselling and psychotherapeutic approaches that I initially considered before making the final selection to be included in this introductory text. Inevitably there was insufficient space to incorporate all of them!

In case readers wish to receive therapy or attend a suitable recognized counselling or psychotherapy course, in Appendix 1, I have provided a list of the main professional bodies that may be able to assist. If a reader is interested in making a career in this field of work, it is relatively important when progressing onto advanced training programmes to attend courses that may lead to a qualification recognized by one of these organizations. It is worth noting that in recent years, the advent of professional accreditation or recognition of practitioners has frequently led to employers asking applicants for therapeutic jobs to be accredited or recognized, and in some countries, licensed or on a state register.

If readers wish to give me feedback about this book my contact details are below. Please indicate in the subject title of the email the nature of your communication. Thank you.

Centre for Stress Management www.managingstress.com
International Academy for Professional Development www.iafpd.com
Email: stephen.palmer@iafpd.com

APPENDIX 1

Professional Bodies and Related Networks

Professional counselling and psychotherapy bodies provide a range of services and resources to the profession, their members and to the public. Most hold annual conferences and run workshops. They usually publish newsletters and journals, some of which are freely available. The internet has few borders so most professional bodies around the world are now easily accessed online. Below are listed a number of them that you may find useful.

American Counseling Association
www.counseling.org

Argentina Association of Counsellors (Psychological Consultants)
www.aacounselors.org.ar

Association for Humanistic Psychology (AHP)
www.ahpb.org.uk

Association for Rational Emotive Behaviour Therapy (AREBT)
www.arebt.eu

Association for the Development of the Person-Centered Approach
www.adpca.org

Australia and New Zealand Association of Psychotherapy
www.anzapweb.com

Australian Counselling Association (ACA)
www.theaca.net.au

Brazilian Association of Family Therapy
www.abratef.org.br

British Association for Behavioural and Cognitive Psychotherapies (BABCP)
www.babcp.com

British Association for Counselling and Psychotherapy (BACP)
www.bacp.co.uk

British Association for the Person-Centred Approach (BAPCA)
www.bapca.org.uk

British Psychoanalytic Council (BPC)
www.bpc.org.uk

British Psychological Society (BPS)
www.bps.org.uk

Canadian Counselling and Psychotherapy Association (CCPA)
www.ccpa-accp.ca

COSCA (Counselling and Psychotherapy in Scotland)
www.cosca.org.uk

European Association for Counselling (EAC)
www.eac.eu.com

European Association for Psychotherapy (EAP)
www.europsyche.org

Independent Practitioners' Network (IPN)
www.i-p-n.org

International Academy of Behavioral Medicine, Counseling and Psychotherapy
www.iabmcp.org

International Association for Counselling (IAC) (incorporating the International Round Table for the Advancement of Counselling – IRTAC)
www.iac-irtac.org

International Association for Educational and Vocational Guidance
www.iaevg.org

International Transactional Analysis Association (ITAA)
www.itaaworld.org

Irish Association for Counselling and Psychotherapy (IACP)
www.irish-counselling.ie

National Counselling Society (NCS)
www.nationalcounsellingsociety.org

National Hypnotherapy Society
www.nationalhypnotherapysociety.org

Network for the European Associations for Person Centered and Experiential Psychotherapy and Counselling
www.pce-europe.org

New Zealand Association of Counsellors (NZAC)
www.nzac.org.nz

Psychotherapy and Counselling Federation of Australia (PACFA)
www.pacfa.org.au

Singapore Association for Counselling (SAC)
www.sac-counsel.org.sg

Society for Dialectical Behaviour Therapy (SFDBT)
www.sfdbt.org

Society for the Exploration of Psychotherapy Integration (SEPI)
www.sepiweb.org

Southern African Association for Counselling and Development in Higher Education (SAACDHE)
www.saacdhe.org

UK Association for Humanistic Psychology Practitioners
www.ahpp.org

United Kingdom Association for Solution Focused Practice (UKASFP)
www.ukasfp.co.uk

United Kingdom Council for Psychotherapy (UKCP)
www.psychotherapy.org.uk

World Council for Psychotherapy (WCP)
www.worldpsyche.org

APPENDIX 2

Counselling and Psychotherapeutic Orientations

Colin Feltham and Stephen Palmer

This list is intended to give a brief overview to the current range and proliferation of psychotherapies. It must be acknowledged that no attempt has been made to ascertain just how current all these approaches are, although to the best of our knowledge they are all currently being practised. Some therapies listed here are merely variants of others (e.g. redecision therapy is a kind of transactional analysis) and might be better described as schools within a particular approach. On the other hand, we have not included, for example, creative novation therapy or other varieties of non–classical behaviour therapy, nor the different schools of Jungian or post-Jungian therapy. Family therapy (and its many variants), group and couple therapy, sex therapy, child psychotherapy, and so on, have all been omitted. We have not included the many forms of brief therapy, such as short-term anxiety-provoking psychotherapy, not to mention different approaches to crisis intervention. Not all humanistic therapies and complementary or alternative medicine approaches to psychological/emotional/holistic problems or concerns, have been included either. You may wish to add to the list any forms of therapy you find of interest to you.

Acceptance and commitment therapy	Bioenergetics
Adaptive psychotherapy	Biofeedback
Adlerian therapy (individual psychology)	Biosynthesis
Art therapy	Body psychotherapy
Attachment-based therapy	Brief dynamic interpersonal therapy
Behaviour therapy	Clinical theology
Biodynamic therapy	Cognitive analytic therapy

Cognitive behavioural therapy

Cognitive humanistic therapy

Cognitive-interpersonal therapy

Cognitive therapy

Communicative psychotherapy

Compassion focused therapy

Contextual modular therapy

Daseinanalyse

Dialectical behaviour therapy

Dialogical psychotherapy

Dramatherapy

Ecotherapy

Emotional freedom technique

Encounter

Existential therapy

Experiential psychotherapy

Eye movement desensitization and reprocessing

Feminist therapy

Focused expressive psychotherapy

Focusing

Gay affirmative therapy

Gestalt therapy

Hakomi therapy

Human givens therapy

Hypnotherapy

Implosive therapy

Inner child advocacy

Integrative psychotherapy

Intensive short-term dynamic psychotherapy

Interpersonal psychotherapy

Jungian analysis (analytical psychology)

Kleinian analysis

Lacanian analysis

Lifeskills counselling

Logotherapy

Mentalization-based therapy

Micropsychoanalysis

Mindfulness-based cognitive therapy

Morita therapy

Motivational interviewing

Multicultural counselling

Multimodal therapy

Narrative therapy

Narrative-constructivist therapy

Neuro-linguistic programming

Object relations therapy

Past lives therapy

Personal construct therapy

Pluralistic counselling and psychotherapy

Primal integration

Primal therapy

Process-oriented psychotherapy

Psychoanalysis

Psychoanalytic energy psychotherapy

Psychoanalytically oriented psychotherapy

Psychodrama

Psychosynthesis

Rational behaviour therapy

Rational emotive behaviour therapy

Reality therapy

Rebirthing

Redecision therapy

Re-evaluation counselling

Reichian therapy (Orgone therapy)

Reminiscence therapy

Rolfing

Single-session therapy

Social therapy

Solution-focused therapy

Stress inoculation training

Systemic therapy

Thought field therapy

Transactional analysis

Transpersonal therapy

Twelve steps therapy

Will therapy

APPENDIX 3

Issues for the Client to Consider in Counselling or Psychotherapy

1. Here is a list of topics or questions you may wish to raise when attending your first counselling or psychotherapy (assessment) session:

   a) Check that your therapist*[1] has relevant qualifications and experience in the field of counselling/psychotherapy.
   b) Ask about the type of approach the therapist uses, and how it relates to your problem.
   c) Ask if the therapist is in supervision (most professional bodies consider supervision to be mandatory; see endnote).
   d) Ask whether the therapist or the counselling agency is a member of a professional body and abides by a code of ethics. If possible obtain a copy of the code.
   e) Discuss your goals/expectations of therapy.
   f) Ask about the fees if any (if your income is low, check if the counsellor operates on a sliding scale) and discuss the frequency and estimated duration of therapy.
   g) Arrange regular review sessions with your counsellor to evaluate your progress.
   h) Do not enter into a long-term counselling contract unless you are satisfied that this is necessary and beneficial to you.

If you do not have a chance to discuss the above points during your first session, discuss them at the next possible opportunity.

General issues

1. Therapist self-disclosure can sometimes be therapeutically useful. However, if the sessions are dominated by the therapist discussing his/her own problems at length, raise this issue in the therapy session.
2. If at any time you feel discounted, undermined or manipulated within the session, discuss this with the therapist. It is easier to resolve issues as and when they arise.
3. Do not accept significant gifts from your therapist. This does not apply to relevant therapeutic material.

---

*We use the term 'therapist' to represent counsellor or psychotherapist in this guide.

4. Do not accept social invitations from your therapist – for example, dining in a restaurant or going for a drink. However, this does not apply to relevant therapeutic assignments such as being accompanied by your therapist into a situation to help you overcome a phobia.
5. If your therapist proposes a change in venue for the therapy sessions without good reason, do not agree. For example, from a centre to the therapist's own home.
6. Research has shown that it is not beneficial for clients to have sexual contact with their therapist. Professional bodies in the field of counselling and psychotherapy consider that it is unethical for counsellors or therapists to engage in sexual activity with current clients.
7. If you have any doubts about the therapy you are receiving, then discuss them with your therapist. If you are still uncertain, seek advice, perhaps from a friend, your doctor, your local Citizens Advice Bureau, the professional body your therapist belongs to or the counselling or therapy agency that may employ your therapist.
8. You have the right to terminate therapy whenever you choose.

Endnote: Counselling and psychotherapy supervision is a formal arrangement where therapists discuss their therapy practice in a confidential setting on a regular basis with one or more professional therapists.

© 2014, Palmer and Szymanska

Glossary

Actualizing tendency   is the fundamental capacity each person is born with and identifies the person-centred approach as a positive psychological and psychotherapeutic approach to change. *Person-centred*

Alliance   a term used variably to denote a component of the therapeutic relationship; a pan-theoretic framework for interpersonal change processes; or the whole therapeutic relationship (see **working alliance**). *Therapeutic relationship*

Alternative stories   also called counter-stories. Narrative therapists are interested in the unknown more than the accepted known. They will often act with purpose to undermine numerous so-called 'factual' and overwhelming thin conclusions of problem stories/orientations told by the people who come to see them in therapy. Narrative therapists are more interested in conversations that seek out alternative stories that are identified by the person in therapy as stories they would like to live their lives through. *Narrative*

Anchoring   the process of connecting an internal response with an external trigger so that the internal response can be activated at will. *Neuro-linguistic programming*

Angst   Anxiety experienced as an intense dread of life and doubt about oneself, typically felt in the face of rising energy when meeting (or avoiding) existential challenges. *Existential*

Anti-individualism   modern psychology is based in individualism, narrative therapy is based in anti-individualism. Contemporary philosophy is dominated by anti-individualism, which holds that a subject's thoughts, meaning and expression are a relational response to a discursive and a cultural context and not determined by what is a priori – inside her head. The fact that the utterances and thoughts of a person have a certain content and refer to certain things, states, or events in the world is determined not only by her brain state, but also by her relations to her linguistic community, dominant norms and her physical environment. *Narrative*

Archetype   universal and innate motifs/ideas that structure human perception of life experience. Transcending the personal, they come from the collective unconscious. They cannot be experienced directly but through their manifestations in dreams, myths, fairy-tales and legends and such universal experiences as birth, marriage, death and separation. By their very nature archetypal images are infinitely varied and exert a fascination and power. *Jungian*

Attachment theory   a theory that helps to explain how the relationship between parent and child emerges and influences later development. *Interpersonal*

Automatic thoughts   (also known as cognitions) and images reflect the client's 'internal dialogue', i.e. what they are saying to themselves. Negative automatic thoughts (NATs) are unhelpful in their content and contribute to the individual's moods, such as anxiety or depression. Underlying the client's automatic thoughts are their intermediate beliefs and core beliefs. *Cognitive behavioural*

Autonomy   that quality which is manifested by the release or recovery of three capacities – awareness, spontaneity and intimacy; any behaviour, thinking or feeling that is a response to here-and-now reality, rather than a response to script beliefs. *Transactional analysis*

Avoidance   a term that has a particular meaning in behaviour therapy, and refers to a person with anxiety evading the object or situation which they fear. It prevents exposure and needs to be challenged in therapy. It is a major difficulty in phobias and obsessive–compulsive disorders. *Behaviour*

Awareness   the process of identifying and owning our thoughts, feelings, bodily sensations and actions. *Gestalt*

BASIC I.D.   an acronym and aide-memoire for the seven key modalities: Behaviour, Affect, Sensation, Imagery, Cognition, Interpersonal, Drugs/biology. *Multimodal*

Behavioural analysis   a detailed description of a person's problem behaviour, including items that precede the unwanted behaviour and items that maintain it (through reinforcement). These 'items' may include thoughts, feelings, actions, body sensations and environmental circumstances. This analysis is used to finely tune the focus of therapy. *Behaviour*

Borderline personality disorder (BPD)   a personality disorder in the erratic/dramatic category, characterized by severe unstable emotional states. *Dialectical behaviour*

Bridging   a method that involves a therapist initially 'keying into' a client's preferred modality and then taking an indirect route via a second (and occasionally third) modality and then finally arriving at the avoided modality. *Multimodal*

Catharsis   the vigorous expression of feelings about experiences that had been previously unavailable to consciousness. This generally produces a purging or cleansing effect, which enables radical restructuring of consciousness to take place. *Primal integration*

Client–therapist relationship   the working alliance between the person who delivers therapy and the person who receives therapy *Professional issues*

Cognitive or **cognitive behavioural hypnotherapy (CBH)**   the use of clinical hypnosis in a manner integrated with cognitive behavioural theories of psychopathology, treatment strategies and theories of hypnosis itself. It is therefore potentially more than just 'hypnosis plus CBT'. Cognitive behavioural theories of hypnosis were developed decades before modern CBT, in the writings of influential researchers such as Ted Sarbin and T. X. Barber, and associates. *Hypnosis*

Collaboration   the process of working together to accomplish a shared objective, based on an attitude of mutual respect. *Pluralistic*

Compassion   commonly defined as 'a sensitivity to the suffering of self and others, with a deep commitment to try and alleviate this'. In compassion focused therapy (CFT) this definition holds two psychologies: (i) the ability to engage with, tolerate and move towards suffering (rather than avoid it), and (ii) the desire, motivation and wisdom to alleviate suffering and prevent if from returning. *Compassion focused*

Complex   the network of emotionally charged associations that builds up around significant experiences and people and affects subsequent encounters with people or situations perceived to be similar. At the centre of the complex is an **archetype**. *Jungian*

Complicated bereavement   an interpersonal therapy focal area when there is unresolved or delayed grief, which has been postponed and then experienced long after the loss has occurred. *Interpersonal*

Condition of worth   can be many different things and describes a block a person has to feeling positive about themselves. *Person-centred*

Conscious   mental contents that are known and can be called upon at will (see also **unconscious**). *Jungian*

Constructive alternativism   this philosophy underpins the whole of personal construct theory. It states that there are always alternative ways of construing events, even though they may be hard to find. That means no one need be the victim of their past, although we can make ourselves a victim if we come to construe it that way. *Personal construct*

Contamination   part of the content of the Child or Parent ego-states that the individual mistakes for Adult content. *Transactional analysis*

Contextual CBT   a new generation of cognitive behavioural therapies that seek to alter the psychological context, or perspective, in which people approach difficult or challenging internal experiences. *Acceptance and commitment*

Contract   an explicit bilateral commitment to a well-defined course of action; an Adult commitment to oneself and/or someone else to make a change. *Transactional analysis*

Core beliefs   deep-seated beliefs about ourselves, others and the world, such as 'I'm worthless', 'Others are untrustworthy' and 'The world is a threatening place'. They are usually developed in childhood and are often inflexible and rigid. They are below the **intermediate beliefs**. *Cognitive behavioural*

Core conditions   the name given to the therapeutic conditions required for a client to move towards less emotional distress. *Person-centred*

Counter-transference   thoughts, feelings aroused in a therapist by the client's material. *Freudian*

Counter-transference   the feelings and phantasies activated in the therapist/counsellor as a result of the client's transference phantasies. *Kleinian*

Creative adjustment   children deal with the normal socializing process by doing the best they can in the circumstances in which they find themselves. Adaptation in a hostile environment is a means of survival in childhood but can lead to problems in later life. *Gestalt*

Cultural resources   potentially therapeutic activities, experiences, objects, places, individuals and institutions that are available to an individual within his or her everyday social world. *Pluralistic*

DASIE model   DASIE stands for lifeskills counselling's five-stage model of counselling practice focused not just on managing current problems but on altering underlying problematic skills to prevent and manage future problems. *Lifeskills*

Dialectical   a philosophy based on the idea that any concept or argument contains polar opposites, each of which has some validity, and it is these opposing forces that come together to make the whole. *Dialectical behaviour*

Directive   counselling and psychotherapy may very broadly be divided into two approaches: directive and non-directive. Directive approaches assume that the therapist brings knowledge and skills about particular types of problems to the therapeutic encounter and, with these, directs the course of therapy with the client's collaboration. Nondirective approaches assume that the client has within him or her the key to the resolution of his or her problems and the therapist therefore leaves the client to determine the direction of therapy. *Behaviour*

Distress tolerance skills   a set of acceptance skills that can be used when the stressor is unavoidable and there is no immediate solution to the problem. These skills make it easier to bear the distress. *Dialectical behaviour*

Diversity   the term diversity is currently used in place of multiculturalism. It is regarded as a more inclusive term since it includes other disadvantaged groups such as women, homosexuals, people with disabilities, social class categories and different religions. It is also a term that does not carry a single ideological philosophy of the subject (e.g. race, gender, etc.), but constructs the self as an integration of multiple identities. *Diversity*

Eclecticism   in counselling, eclecticism refers to the combining of techniques and/ or approaches from different schools of therapy. Multimodal therapy is an example of an eclectic approach.

Ego–state   a consistent pattern of feeling and experience directly related to a corresponding consistent pattern of behaviour. *Transactional analysis*

Emotion regulation skills   a set of change skills helping to either reduce the client's vulnerability to labile emotions, or to down–regulate problematic emotions to a more manageable level. In some circumstances emotions need to be up–regulated if an appropriate emotion is not present, for example if the client is in a dissociative or numbed state. *Dialectical behaviour*

Emotional compass   instrument for understanding the way in which each emotion expresses a value and a meaning in life. *Existential*

Emotional responsibility   clients must accept emotional responsibility, i.e. your beliefs largely determine your emotional reactions to events. *Rational emotive behaviour*

Empathic affirmation   validating the client's perspective. *Therapeutic relationship*

Empathic evocation   using evocative, probing yet tentative language to enliven the client's experience. *Therapeutic relationship*

Empathic explorations   therapist attempts to identify and voice key underpinning themes. *Therapeutic relationship*

Empathic understanding   the therapist communicating understanding of the client's experience. *Therapeutic relationship*

Empathy   is one of the six core conditions and is the capacity for a person to understand another person's experience as if it were their own. *Person-centred*

Encouragement   the emphasis on the positive in a person by the therapist. Clients are helped to appreciate the good things they have to offer. They learn to acknowledge that they have value as people. *Adlerian*

Engagement   the capacity for a person to immerse themselves in life and to reach out to projects and purposes that lead to productive action, which will in turn create meaning. *Existential*

Evidence-based practice   the use of current best evidence in making decisions in clinical practice. *Research*

Exceptions   occasions when the problem unexpectedly does not happen at all or only happens in a diluted form. *Solution-focused*

Experimentation   in personal construct theory our behaviour is the experiment we conduct to test out our construing predictions about each event that confronts us. Our subsequent behavioural experiment will be directly related to whether our last prediction proved right or wrong. Seeing behaviour as an experiment rather than as an end in itself is one of the unique features of personal construct theory. *Personal construct*

Exposure or exposure therapy   terms used in behaviour therapy. A person is encouraged to remain with the object, such as a spider, or situation, such as open spaces, which they fear. Initially, their anxiety increases, but will gradually lessen over time. This reduction in anxiety will become established if the exposure is regularly practised. The reduction of fear, in this way, is known as extinction (see also **avoidance**). *Behaviour*

Externalizing   Narrative therapy uses a method of externalizing problems to bring forth possible re-descriptions and the chance for clients to reposition themselves with the problem. The identity of the described problem is viewed as separate from the identities of the person. Those problems that are considered to be inherent as well as those relatively fixed qualities that are attributed to persons and to relationships, are rendered less fixed and less restricting. Externalizing of the problem enables persons to separate from the dominant stories that have been shaping their lives and relationships. Externalizing is by no means a requirement of narrative therapy and represents one option within a range of narrative practices. *Narrative*

Family constellation   the pattern of positions that the children take in their family when they are young. The children unconsciously choose through trial and error what sort of children they will be and take up their own unique positions like stars in a constellation. *Adlerian*

First, second and third positions   different perspectives for looking at the same issue. First is seeing the issue through our own eyes, second involves stepping into someone else's shoes and seeing the issue from their point of view, and third involves stepping right outside the whole situation to be able to gain an objective view of the whole situation. *Neuro-linguistic programming*

Flooding   this is a form of exposure to the worst-feared situation for a prolonged period of time, continuing until anxiety reduces. This may take place in reality or in imagination. Great care and professional guidance are recommended. *Behaviour*

Fourfold world   the four dimensions of human existence at which we live our lives: physical, social, personal and spiritual. *Existential*

Goal-setting   in goal-setting the acronym SMART helps clients focus on what they want to achieve. SMART refers to goals that are Specific, Measurable, Achievable, Relevant and Time-bound. *Cognitive behavioural*

Group of Seven   the term used to include the seven major domains of identity; for example, race, gender, sexual orientation, class, disability, religion and age. It is often a zooming-in of the term **diversity**, so that specific issues related to each major disadvantaged identity group can be focused on within a wider foundation of multiple identities and intersectionality. *Diversity*

Hamilton Depression Scale   a clinician administered measure to ascertain the severity of depressive symptoms. *Interpersonal*

Homework assignments   are considered integral to cognitive and cognitive behavioural therapy. They can take the form of bibliotherapy, that is reading self-help books, or the practice of cognitive or behavioural techniques outside the therapy sessions on a regular basis in order to help clients overcome their problems quickly and effectively. *Cognitive behavioural*

Hypnosis   the state of mind of someone who has been hypnotized. Researchers traditionally disagree as to whether it is a special neurological or psychological state, or simply an unusual way of using ordinary cognitive processes, such as concentration, imagination and expectation. Sometimes also the process of hypnotizing. We speak of 'self-hypnosis', when it is self-induced, or 'hetero-hypnosis', when a hypnotist induces someone else. The word 'hypnotism' is not normally used for the state but only the study of hypnosis or the process of inducing it. *Hypnosis*

Hypnotherapy   the use of hypnosis as the main strategy for psychological therapy, or psychotherapy. Can be viewed as a highly technically eclectic form of therapy, which draws on strategies and procedure from many other approaches. *Hypnosis*

Ideal compassionate other   using creative imagery to develop an image (human or non-human), which personifies certain qualities such as caring-commitment, strength and wisdom. Once developed and practised, our ideal compassion other is then used as 'another mind' to help us deal with our distress, and help us to think through ways of alleviating our distress. *Compassion-focused*

Ideal compassionate self   the cultivation of certain qualities of mind (motivation, thinking, emotion, behaviour) and body (voice tone, body posture) through various imaginal, empathy and acting techniques that lead to a sense of an 'ideal compassionate self'. This version of oneself is then used to engage with suffering and threat-based emotions and memories. *Compassion-focused*

Identity   the experience of being authentically oneself. *Psychosynthesis*

Ideo–motor reflex   the original theory of hypnotic suggestion, developed by Carpenter and subsequently Braid, and adopted by Bernheim and other Victorian hypnotists. The theory basically holds that many ordinary psychological phenomena involve the natural tendency for our bodies and minds to react in a reflex-like manner to things we imagine, especially when these are accompanied by focused attention and expectation of the response occurring. Ideo–motor responses are responses in the voluntary (or 'skeletal') muscles, which control movement. Braid preferred the broader term 'ideo–dynamic', which he used to denote 'the power of the mind over the body' more generally, e.g., including salivation or increases in blood pressure, and other physiological responses. Braid wanted to replace the problematic term 'hypnotism', with its connotations of sleep or unconsciousness, with the technical term 'mono–ideo–dynamics', meaning the use of focused attention on a single expectant idea or image, suggested to the subject, in order to bring about automatic reactions in the mind and body. *Hypnosis*

Implosion   a form of prolonged flooding carried out in imagination, usually with a great deal of anxiety. *Cognitive behavioural*

Individuation   the process that goes on throughout life, but is particularly important in the second half, of becoming more fully and consciously oneself, facing both strengths and limitations. Paradoxically it involves recognizing both one's uniqueness and ordinariness. *Jungian*

Inner world   our inner world is our own personal (three-dimensional and dynamic, changing) 'map' or construct which is made up of all the phantasies we have about ourselves and others, and which we use to understand the external world. The inner world is influenced by what happens in the external world, and vice versa. For example, we may relate to our partner as if he or she were the partner 'in our head', or in our internal world, rather than in the actual one. The partner in our internal world may be very similar to the one in the external world or may have important differences. *Kleinian*

Intermediate beliefs   consist of underlying assumptions that are normally articulated as 'if … then' or 'unless … then' statements (e.g. if I make a mistake then I'll be a failure). Intermediate beliefs include rules (e.g. I must not make mistakes). *Cognitive behavioural*

Internalization   the process by which formative relational experience becomes part of the mental structures of the developing self. It describes how the 'inter-psychological becomes intra-psychological'. Following Vygotsky this is understood to transform these structures resulting in a self that is different and culturally diverse, depending on formative relational and social experience. *Cognitive analytic*

Interpersonal sensitivity/deficits   an interpersonal therapy focal area when the client has a history of inadequate or unsupportive interpersonal relationships, which cause difficulties with developing and maintaining current relationships. *Interpersonal*

Interpersonal and social rhythms therapy (IPSRT)   a therapy for individuals with bipolar disorder that combines a focus on interpersonal relationships with techniques designed to regulate timing of daily routines. *Interpersonal*

Interpretation   putting the unconscious processes into words. *Freudian*

Introjection   the 'swallowing whole' of the attitudes, values, beliefs and opinions of significant people in our lives. This process shapes the development of our attitudes to self, others and the world (our intrapsychic process). *Gestalt*

Irrational beliefs   are illogical, unrealistic and unhelpful and lead to unhealthy negative emotions. *Rational emotive behaviour*

Levels of awareness   personal construing can take place at different levels of awareness ranging from the clearly conscious level to the level of construing that we all evolve before we have acquired language. *Personal construct*

Life-script   a preconscious life-plan made in childhood, reinforced by the parents, 'justified' by subsequent events, and culminating in a chosen alternative. *Transactional analysis*

Lifeskills   sequences of choices affirming or negating psychological life that people make in specific skills areas. *Lifeskills*

Lifestyle   Adler's term for the unique and consistent pattern of behaviour in people consisting of their short and long-term goals, their beliefs and feelings. People form their lifestyles in childhood. *Adlerian*

Map of the world   as humans we can never know reality, in the sense that we have to experience reality through our senses, and our senses are limited. A bee looking at this page would perceive it very differently because the way a bee perceives things is very different from the way a human perceives things. Our individual perception of how the world is, and what is important, forms our own unique 'map of the world'. *Neuro-linguistic programming*

MCC (Multicultural Counselling Competencies)   MCCs are skills and knowledge that are required by a counsellor or psychologist to undertake therapy in a culturally effective way. Specifically, MCCs comprise a set of guidelines that are suggested by the major counselling and psychology associations for ethical practice with diverse and multicultural clients. When other disadvantaged groups (e.g. women, gay, etc.) are included then we refer to this as Diversity Counselling Competencies. *Diversity*

Metacommunication   an act of creating a space within the on-going flow of communication, to enable each participant to give an account of their reactions to, and understanding of, what has taken (or could take) place. *Pluralistic*

Mindfulness   the skill of bringing one's attention into the current moment in a deliberate way, with full awareness. The skill of unhooking from judgements and interpretations to see the current moment as it is. *Dialectical behaviour*

Miracle question   an imaginative question that enables clients to get behind problems to describe what their preferred future would be. *Solution-focused*

Mixed methods research   research that employs and integrates both quantitative and qualitative methods of data collection and analysis. *Research*

Modality profile   this consists of an analysis of a client's identified problems divided into the seven **BASIC I.D.** modalities with the specific interventions written adjacent to the problems. *Multimodal*

Modelling   young children are often observed to imitate adults' behaviour, such as feeding themselves with a spoon. Not only children model the behaviour of others. In behaviour therapy, specific behaviours are demonstrated to the client who then models them. For example, an unassertive client may observe a therapist acting assertively by saying no to a request and be encouraged to replicate this behaviour. *Behaviour*

Multicultural counselling   the philosophy of multiculturalism underpins the definition of multicultural counselling. Traditionally, multicultural counselling was understood as therapy with individuals or groups who are black and ethnic minority. In recent years multicultural counselling has become more inclusive of other diverse or marginalized groups, such as race, gender, disability, sexual orientation, age, religion. *Diversity*

Multimodal Life History Inventory   a 15-page questionnaire used in multimodal therapy to assist in assessing the BASIC I.D. modalities, history-taking and client expectations of therapy. *Multimodal*

Narcissism   taking the image of the self as the object of love; preventing the client from seeing others as they are. *Freudian*

'Not your fault'   a key understanding that emerges from psychoeducation is how so much of our sense of self, and experience of distress, is due to the interaction between problematic glitches in our evolved minds, genes and the social circumstances of our lives. A recognition of 'not your fault' can lead to a reduction in personalization and shame, increase a sense of common humanity and a willingness to take responsibility and learn what we can do to deal with our difficulties. *Compassion-focused*

Organismic self-regulation   the human organism is in constant interaction with the environment. In this process a person will be able to receive what is nourishing and reject what is toxic, thereby completing Gestalts. In an ideal world there would be no unfinished business (incomplete Gestalts). *Gestalt*

Paradox   the philosophical principle that allows us to grasp the polarities, contradictions, conflicts and dilemmas of life, in the realization that both ends of the spectrum are necessary to fully make sense of something. *Existential*

Personal construct system this is the sum total of personal constructs we have created to make sense of (interpret, construe) events in our world as they take place and, in so doing, we are able to make predictions about their outcomes. *Personal construct*

Phantasies mental constructions we use to make sense of our experiences. They involve people and things phantasized as inside us or outside us, doing things to each other and ourselves. They are dynamic and constantly changing. They influence our understanding of the world around us as well as being influenced by it. *Kleinian*

Pluralism the idea that there is no single truth, and that the human condition consists of on-going dialogue between contrasting and incommensurable perspectives, beliefs and values. *Pluralistic*

Power/knowledge one of the most important features of narrative therapy is that mechanisms of power produce different types of knowledge which collate information on people's activities and existence. The knowledge gathered in this way further reinforces exercises of power. The DSM and the use of client files are examples of these techniques as a form of social control. Foucault's work cautions that what we may take to be knowledge, may instead be nothing more than powerful concepts perpetuated by authorities and those concepts may change our understanding of our selves and our world. *Narrative*

Practice-based evidence research conducted in 'real life' settings, where real-life practice is investigated. *Research*

Private logic the unconscious beliefs and ideas that people have about themselves and the world and how they will move through life. *Adlerian*

Professional indemnity insurance an insurance for therapists to cover law suits or any other legal issues arising in the work setting. *Professional issues*

Projection process of throwing an image onto a person or thing in the present that really belongs to the past. *Freudian*

Projective identification a phantasy whereby someone gets rid of into another person an emotional state they cannot bear in themselves. In reality, many subtle means are used to bring this phantasy to life. It is the most primitive means of communication between parent and infant or therapist and client. It may be used as a form of unconscious attack. *Kleinian*

Psychodynamic refers to the constantly changing aspect of the way we relate to others and ourselves; perceiving ourselves and others differently from moment to moment, according to our unconscious phantasies. *Kleinian*

Psychological flexibility people's ability to fully contact the present moment and pursue their meaningful life directions even when experiencing difficult or challenging internal experiences. *Acceptance and commitment*

Psychopathology   originally a psychiatric term referring to mental sickness or to an underlying personality problem, often classified into disorders such as depression, agoraphobia, post-traumatic stress disorder, borderline personality disorder, etc. Many counsellors dispute the reality behind or helpfulness of such labelling.

Psychospiritual   a psychological term used to denote that there are always two levels of experience, the first psychological and the second more essential or 'spiritual'. *Psychosynthesis*

Qualitative research   research that explores in depth an experience or phenomenon, commonly using interviews or focus groups as methods of data collection and analytic techniques that aim to summarize or categorize data into themes. *Research*

Quantitative research   research that involves the exploration of phenomena using mathematical or statistical methods. *Research*

Rational beliefs   are logical, realistic and helpful and lead to healthy negative emotions. *Rational emotive behaviour*

Re-authoring conversations   re-authoring conversations re-invigorates people's efforts to understand what it is that is happening in their lives, what it is that has happened, how it has happened, and what it all means. In this way these conversations encourage a dramatic re-engagement with life and with history, and provide options for people to more fully inhabit their lives and their relationships. Questions are introduced that encourage people to generate new proposals for action, accounts of the circumstances likely to be favourable to these proposals for action, and predictions about the outcome of these proposals. *Narrative*

Reciprocal role (RR)   a CAT-specific term referring to a relational position between self and other. An internalized (formative) reciprocal role is understood to comprise both poles of that subjective experience (i.e. childhood-derived and parent/culture-derived). A reciprocal role comprises an implicit (often unconscious) relational memory (which may be traumatic) and also the emotions, cognitions (including cultural values and beliefs) and even body language associated with it. It may be associated with a clear dialogical 'voice'. *Cognitive analytic*

Reciprocal role procedure (RRP)   CAT-specific term referring to an aim-directed coping or 'responsive' pattern of thoughts and behaviours arising out of the experience of formative reciprocal role(s). RRPs are usually long-standing, often unconscious and highly resistant to change. They may be highly maladaptive, symptomatic and self-reinforcing (as in 'vicious circles'). RRPs may be enacted in both 'external' interpersonal situations and also in 'internal' self-management. *Cognitive analytic*

Redecision   replacement of a self-limiting early decision by a new decision that takes account of the individual's full adult resources. *Transactional analysis*

Reflexivity   personal construct theory is reflexive in that the theory applies as much to the construing of the counsellor as it does to that of the client. *Personal construct*

Reformulation   the collaborative creation early in therapy of an agreed description of presenting problems and their apparent origins, particularly in terms of formative relational and social experiences. Both a written narrative reformulation (in the form of a letter) and a sequential diagrammatic reformulation (SDR or 'map') will be constructed. Both attempt to describe in a non-judgemental manner the patterns of difficulties with which the client presents and their background origins along with ultimately possible ways of moving forward (aims or exits). These would serve as 'route maps' for therapy and also as a means of making sense of and repairing possible problematic interactions between client and therapist. *Cognitive analytic*

Reframing   offering an alternative meaning for similar constituent parts like a jig-saw which can be made into two different pictures. Examples of reframing would be 'thinking about things differently', 'taking another point of view', or 'taking other factors into consideration'. *Neuro-linguistic programming*

Regression   going back in time to an earlier part of one's life. This means actually re-experiencing and reliving early life, not just remembering it. It is important to realize here that early experiences are registered in the cells and muscles of the body, not only in the brain. There is little benefit in regression in psychotherapy unless it is also accompanied by recession, that is, the move inward into the depths of one's own inner world. *Primal integration*

Re-membering conversations   re-membering conversations are not about passive recollection, but about purposive engagements with the significant figures of one's history, and with the identities of one's present life who are significant or potentially significant. These figures and identities do not have to be directly known in order to be identified as significant to a person's life. *Narrative*

Re-storying   the therapeutic notion of re-storying creates the possibility that change is always possible. Therefore, any totalized description of a person's past, present or future can be reconfigured, recollected and re-remembered differently. *Narrative*

Relational frame theory   modern theory of language and cognition that underpins ACT. *Acceptance and commitment*

Repertory grid   a technique for creating mathematical relationships between the personal constructs of an individual. George Kelly described it as a way of 'getting beyond the words'. There are now many versions and many statistical and non-statistical ways of making sense of the data. *Personal construct*

Response prevention   clients often avoid further exposure to particular anxiety-provoking objects, situations or thoughts, collectively known as cues, by carrying out rituals that lessen the anxiety. In response prevention, the client is encouraged not to carry out the ritual that is usually triggered by the cue, so that continued exposure is allowed to take place. *Behaviour*

Restatement   in skills terms, taking a client's problem and breaking it down into hypotheses about the component thinking skills and action skills deficits that maintain the problem and require addressing during and after counselling. *Lifeskills*

Role dispute   an interpersonal therapy focal area when the client and at least one other person are have differing expectations of their relationship. *Interpersonal*

Role transition   an interpersonal therapy focal area when a client has difficulty coping with life changes that require the development of new roles. *Interpersonal*

Ruptures   common phenomena in therapy ranging from minor tensions to major disagreements between client and therapist characterized by a lack of collaboration on tasks and goals, or strain in the bond between therapist and client. *Therapeutic relationship*

Safety behaviours   a person may not avoid an activity or situation. However, they may take precautions in order to reduce their anxiety about facing them. *Cognitive behavioural*

Secondary gain   where a problem carries a benefit at another level, e.g. smoking may help someone relax. An unconscious secondary gain may override the conscious desire to change. *Neuro-linguistic programming*

Self-acceptance   the recognition that you have worth just because you exist, imperfections and all. *Rational emotive behaviour*

Self-acceptance   is a positive experience for any individual and enables a freeing up of various tensions that may have been causing distress. *Person-centred*

Self-concept   is how a person believes they are and may involve beliefs about how they are seen and experienced by others. *Person-centred*

Self-control training   is aimed at helping the client with problem behaviour to change their behaviour by initially becoming more aware of the events that immediately precede it. Self-monitoring, such as keeping a daily record, is often used by the client. Eventually the client will be able to identify specific cues and exert self-control when these occur. *Behaviour*

Self-esteem   your worth is usually dependent on achievement and approval. *Rational emotive behaviour*

Self-realization   is the life process by which individuals find meaning and purpose and by which they realize their potential and self. *Psychosynthesis*

Self-responsibility accounting for one's own needs and taking the relevant action to meet them. This should not be equated with self-sufficiency since it includes the capacity to receive from others. *Gestalt*

Sick role helping the client initially within therapy to acknowledge that they are ill and can accept support from others. *Interpersonal*

Skills language consistently using the concept of skills to describe and analyse people's behaviour. Conceptualizing and conversing about client's problems in terms of lifeskills strengths and deficits. *Lifeskills*

Social constructionism a theory of knowledge which states that the meaning of language is known only through social interaction and negotiation. *Solution-focused*

Social interest the feeling of belonging as an equal and the willingness to cooperate and make a contribution to society. *Adlerian*

SMART goals see **goal-setting** *Cognitive behavioural*

Strengths the sources of courage, skills, knowledge and capability that have sustained a person through the course of his or her life. *Pluralistic*

Subpersonalities are different parts of the individual with unique feelings, thoughts, behaviours and characteristics, each having its own voice and needs. *Psychosynthesis*

Suggestion in the field of hypnotism, 'suggestion' or 'hypnotic suggestion' + specifically refers to the use of related forms of suggestion. These take many forms. However, traditional hypnotism employs mainly direct verbal suggestions, which are actually best understood as implicit invitations for the subject to imagine the things being described by the hypnotist, rather than commands to their unconscious mind. *Hypnosis*

Suicidal client a person who is at risk of taking his or her own life. *Professional issues*

Supervisee a therapist who meets with another therapist to discuss his or her client workload and work issues *Professional issues*

Supervisor a therapist who supports another therapist with his or her work *Professional issues*

Symbol/symbolic the best possible way of describing or expressing something relatively unknown. Symbolic thinking is non-linear, complementary to conscious logical and concrete thought, and functions through metaphor, images, etc., which are pregnant with meaning if sometimes enigmatic, e.g. in dreams. *Jungian*

Take–away sheets are used in lifeskills counselling during sessions for taking down learnings from the whiteboard. In addition they are used for recording mutually agreed homework assignments. *Lifeskills*

Task responsibility clients must accept task responsibility, i.e. you are in charge of carrying out your goal–related tasks to overcome your emotional disturbance. *Rational emotive behaviour*

Technical eclecticism a therapeutic approach that applies techniques taken from many different psychological theories and systems, without necessarily being concerned with the validity of the theoretical principles that underpin the different approaches from which it takes its techniques. *Multimodal*

Teleological purposeful and goal-directed. Adlerians consider that all behaviour has a purpose and to understand behaviour the goal has to be identified. *Adlerian*

Theoretical orientation (also known as approach, model, school, brand name) usually refers to any kind of clearly espoused therapeutic identity, such as Freudian, Jungian, TA, Gestalt, cognitive, eclectic, etc., but may also refer broadly to humanistic, psychoanalytic, etc. BAC require accredited courses to have an acceptable core theoretical model.

Thinking errors (also known as 'cognitive distortions') are logical errors based on faulty information processing. These include jumping to conclusions, personalization and all–or–nothing thinking. *Cognitive behavioural*

Thinking skills are the mental processes through which people can create and influence how they think: for example, perceiving, explaining cause, predicting and visualizing. *Lifeskills*

Tracking when tracking, the 'firing order' of the different modalities is noted for a specific problem. Once assessed, the client is instructed to match the firing order of the modalities with a corresponding sequence of modality interventions. *Multimodal*

Transference thoughts, feelings, images transferred from the client's past and replayed in the therapy. *Freudian*

Transference the way we relate to others is based on phantasies that were created as a result of our experiences of people (usually family members) in our past. We interpret every action of the therapist through our phantasies, which derive ultimately from our experiences (real and imaginary and coloured by our emotions, our desires, our wishes) in relation to our parents. Transference refers to this process. As the therapy activates and changes different phantasies about our parents, so the way we perceive a therapist will change (see also **counter-transference**). *Kleinian*

Transpersonal   going beyond the pre-personal and the personal into the realm of mystical experiences. There are a number of different levels of mystical experience, such as the Centaur, the Psychic, the Subtle, the Causal and the Nondual, which have been well explained and described by Ken Wilber. *Primal integration*

Transpersonal   the realm of human experience which is beyond the personal, everyday and existential awareness. *Psychosynthesis*

Trauma   is the infliction of pain on an organism. Frank Lake has distinguished between four levels of trauma. Each level of trauma produces different effects. The first level may be quite stimulating, and benefit the organism. The second level is harder to overcome, but can be handled effectively and healthily in most cases. The third level produces neurotic defences such as repression, dissociation and splitting. The fourth level is quite unendurable, and produces a turning against the self and a wish to die. *Primal integration*

Unconscious   is used by psychodynamic counsellors to indicate all those processes of mind which occur outside of consciousness. The assumption that there is an unconscious with its own methods of processing information was imputed by Freud from the reports of his patients describing dreams or from observations of slips of the tongue or from disturbances of affect that were associated with the return of material that Freud proposed had been repressed as a result of trauma. While there is no difficulty in assuming that much of our processing occurs outside of awareness there are great philosophical problems that results from leaping from this to assume that there is a subdivision of mind with its own distinctive methods of processing that in some way knows what to repress. *Freudian*

Unfinished business   an unmet need does not go away but remains active and demands completion. An accumulation of unmet needs may seriously impair functioning in the present. *Gestalt*

Working alliance   reflects the quality of the negotiated and purposive partnership of client and therapist collaboratively and actively participating in working towards the client's change goals. *Therapeutic relationship*

Working through   is the process of testing phantasies against reality, which has to be repeated again and again until we have changed our phantasies to bring them closer into line with reality. *Kleinian*

Index

Figures and Tables are indicated by page numbers in bold print. The letters *bib* after a page number refer to bibliographical information in 'Suggested Reading' sections.